THE

HISTORICAL GEOGRAPHY

OF

ASIA MINOR.

BY

PROFESSOR W. M. RAMSAY.

THE

HISTORICAL GEOGRAPHY

OF

ASIA MINOR.

BY

W. M. RAMSAY

AMSTERDAM
ADOLF M. HAKKERT - PUBLISHER
1962

Unchanged reprint of W. M. Ramsay, The Historical Geography of Asia Minor. Royal Geographical Society, Supplementary Papers, Volume IV. London John Murray, 1890.
Made with the permission of Dr. M. P. Ramsay, and the Royal Geographical Society, London.

CONTENTS.

—◆◆—

DEDICATION.

———+———

THE Rector and Fellows of Exeter College, Oxford, will, it is hoped, find in the following pages a justification of the indulgence and generosity which they have extended to the writer, and which have at once impelled him and made it possible for him to devote to the present work the needful years of study.

The writer also hopes that the research fellowships, instituted by the enlightened liberality of the college, while held by more distinguished successors, may perhaps be judged hereafter to be not ignobly inaugurated by the first holder with this book.

PROLEGOMENA.

The following work requires some prefatory notice, to explain the delay in its appearance, to apologise for its shortcomings, and to indicate those friends to whose encouragement and help it owes so much.

The Royal Geographical Society, which had liberally helped the Asia Minor Exploration Fund, required from me a contribution; and from the effort to make the lecture worthy of the audience this book has grown.

In May 1886 the first sketch of it was read before the Society. The difficulty of the subject, and the distraction caused by other work both as a Professor (first in Oxford and afterwards in Aberdeen), and as a traveller (I left London for Smyrna the day after reading the paper, and spent considerable part of the summer of 1886, 1887, and 1888 in Asia Minor), delayed the completion and publication of the sketch. In the beginning of April, 1888, I brought the complete MS. with me to London to hand over to the printer.* I discovered, thirty-six hours after starting from Aberdeen, that the manuscript was no longer in the bag where I had placed it, and which had been for most of the time close to my hand, and I have never found the slightest clue to the time or manner of its loss (I have no other reason to suspect myself of somnambulism). At that time the manuscript was about as long as Part I. of the present work. I have found it impossible to rewrite the paper in its original form. All notes for it had been destroyed, and when, after months spent partly in travel and partly in despair, I began to rewrite it, the task proved impossible. The literary form, which it had been my ambition to give to my treatment of the subject, could not be recovered; not merely had I no time and no heart to go through the work of writing and rewriting, but also I had lost in residence at home the inspiration that formerly arose from intimate familiarity with and love of the country and the scenery. I have therefore worked into Part I. everything that I could recollect of the lost paper; and I have added in Part II. my collection of material for the history and antiquities of the country, so far as it has any bearing on geography and seems to be new.

* It was practically complete in February 1886, when I read considerable extracts from it before the Aberdeen branch of the Royal Scottish Geographical Society.

The organisers of the Asia Minor Exploration Fund and the contributors to it, private individuals and corporations like the Royal Geographical Society, the Society for the Promotion of Hellenic Studies in England, and the Ottoman Railway Company through their manager, Mr. E. Purser, have been the real authors of this work. The reward they wish for lies in the scientific results, and in estimating these, there must be reckoned not merely the present writer's works (whether those already published or that history which, if circumstances are propitious, may hereafter be completed), but also the works of those who have been trained in the first instance through the expeditions made in connection with the Fund, chief among whom I may reckon Professor J. R. S. Sterrett and Mr. D. G. Hogarth. The brilliant explorations of Prof. Sterrett were inaugurated by four months' preliminary training with our Exploration Fund; and I have his own authority for stating that he would never have thought of Asia Minor exploration, but for the invitation to join in our expedition of 1883. The credit and honour of his admirable work are not diminished by giving a share to the English Fund: indeed, according to the principle laid down by Shelley * his own share of the glory is only increased by giving away a little of it.

I am specially bound to express my gratitude both to the College and to the Fund,† for the confidence and generosity which they have shown in making so little restriction on me, in leaving so much to my own discretion, and in making me practically complete master of my own time and work during all the period of my connection with them.

To mention in detail those to whom I am indebted for help, and information in the preparation of this work would require a separate chapter. I have utilised everybody I knew in every way possible, and to such an extent that I cannot now even thank them, but mention one or two names as specimens. Ἐκ Διὸς ἀρχώμεσθα: the Camden Professor of History, Mr. Pelham, has done so much for the Fund that every one will recognise the propriety of mentioning him before any other.

In one case only I have not availed myself of the best help that I could get, viz., on p. 173. After I had already written my own theory as to the pragmateutes, Mr. Pelham pointed out to me that actor was the proper equivalent. But it seemed to me more fair in this case, as Ben Jonson says, " to put weaker and no doubt less pleasing of mine own than to defraud so happy a genius of his right by my loathed usurpation," and to give Mr. Pelham's view in the Addenda under his own name. The change needed in my text is little more than the substitution of actor for negotiator in two or three cases; all inferences

* Epipsychidion, 174 ff.

† Directed by a committee consisting of the Provost of Oriel College, the late Mr. Ferguson, and Mr. H. F. Pelham from the first: in more recent years also of Sir C. W. Wilson and Mr. Douglas W. Freshfield, with Mr. G. A. Macmillan as Honorary Secretary.

follow equally, whichever servile title is used. But in general I have used the best I could find; Prof. Th. Mommsen has often generously interrupted his own work to answer my questions; Mr. Bywater was often a present help; and many friends in Smyrna and other parts of Asia Minor have given me invaluable help in numberless ways which I gratefully remember.

While the opportunity of carrying out the work up to the present has been given me by the Travelling Archæological Studentship, instituted by the late Professor M. Bernard, by the Research Fellowship to which Exeter College elected me, and by the Exploration Fund,* the training and the incentive are due to Colonel Sir C. W. Wilson, Consul-General in Anatolia from 1878 to 1882, in whose company and by whose invitation I made two long journeys in the country in 1881 and 1882. To him and his subordinate officers, especially Colonel Chermside, Major Bennet, and the late Colonel Stewart, who was killed on his way back from Khartum, I am indebted for help in numberless ways.†

The coins at the British Museum, described to me especially by Mr. Head, or seen by me, have often helped me over a gap: would that the wonderful collection of M. Waddington were public property, whether in a descriptive work or in any other way! Without the constant help of the "Historia Numorum," many trains of reasoning in the present work would not have suggested themselves; and a slight taste of M. Waddington's collection in 1882 enables me to realise how much this book loses for want of better knowledge of it.

Throughout the work I have been helped in various ways by my wife, and numerous slight typographical errors were detected by her in finally reading the proofs.‡

Finally, I am specially indebted to Mr. Hogarth for volunteering to go over the proofs and to make the Index of 'Authors Quoted,' for many salutary criticisms and useful suggestions, and most of all, for that intelligent sympathy which is able to find human life and history in earth and atmosphere, and which is unfortunately so much less common now-a-days in our own country than it was among our older scholars and is still among foreign scholars. The narrowness which would limit the study of antiquity to fireside perusal of a few great authors, is so easy and seductive an error, that few are conscious of its narrowness.

---

* It is in justice necessary to add that, quite apart from these sources, and apart also from our own time and work, my wife and myself have been much the largest contributors to the expense of our explorations in Asia Minor.

† I owe to Colonel Chermside the explanation of the term passus, viz. that passus does not mean a "a pace," but a complete motion of the body involving two paces. A different and far-fetched explanation of the word is given in Zft. f. Latein. Lexicographie, 1889, p. 567.

‡ She also compiled the index to Part I., after I had started for Turkey, with even too great minuteness and patience. It is therefore more complete than the index to Part II., see p. 12.

Of the references made to ancient authors in the course of the present work, 95 per cent. have been found in my own perusal of the original documents, undertaken for the purpose and still far from complete. The great majority of them have already been used by some one or other of the modern authorities, though no single modern writer has made any tolerable collection of the references; but in a number of cases I have added the decisive passage, which completes the chain of evidence. Even those references which have been already used by modern geographers have not been taken at second hand, nor even merely verified in the original authorities. My scheme has been (after several experiences of the difficulties caused by accepting wrong conjectures of modern writers) to make an absolutely fresh work founded on the ancient authorities alone, in which the geographical situation, the natural surroundings and the commercial advantages of each city, should be set forth in an account of its history. That scheme is interrupted by the present work, in which topography gets the lion's share in Part II., while some general reflexions on the effect exercised by natural situation and surroundings on the history of the population compose Part I.; but though the greater scheme is interrupted for the present, yet my belief is, that the vigorous criticism which I should like to arouse, and the stimulus and precision which I hope may be given to further exploration of the country, may really facilitate the completion of the larger work. Had circumstances permitted, my desire was to complete that undertaking myself; but the current of events, which at one time, by no choice of my own, prescribed this work for me and drifted me into a position of unique advantage for it, is now making it more and more difficult for me to continue. There has, therefore, been always present in my mind, while writing Part II., the intention to make it useful for the successors who may carry out the larger undertaking.* What they can find elsewhere I do not try to give them.

In order to keep down the size of the book, I have in numberless cases restricted myself to an obscure hint or a dogmatic statement, where I might have spent pages in clothing the bare fact with life, and expressing it in its relations to human history. This rigorous self-denial was necessary if Part II. was to appear before the public at present. The ordinary reader will find it a mere mass of dry dust and lifeless details, but he may be sure that human life is latent in every detail, and that, whether or no the present writer possesses the art of expressing that life, it can be so set forth in a larger picture as to possess the deep interest of real history.

From the arrangement and compression thus imposed on the writer,

---

* I cannot resist the temptation to say that an unusual number of the necessary qualities are united in Mr. Hogarth, whose co-operation in the exploration of the country has been my greatest help in recent years.

arises much that may be found puzzling in the order of exposition and in the proportion of the parts. It may almost seem as if the space devoted to each name were inversely proportionate to its historical importance; and it is almost strictly true that the attention given to any place is in proportion to the difficulty and obscurity of the subject. It would have been easy to write a hundred pages about Ephesos, Celaenae, or Smyrna: it was difficult to avoid writing a score about these and many other great names. The civilising power of the "Mother of Sipylos," in early time, culminating in the Smyrna of the Roman period with its "Golden Street" extending from her temple right across the city to the temple of Jupiter, exercises an extraordinary fascination on all that have come under her influence, and all that is wanting to make the fascination universal on educated minds is the literary art; the artist, however, is still to be discovered. In this book, on the contrary, even the attempt has been precluded by the *lex operis;* and if the reader wishes to find what I have to say about the great cities, he must use the index to Part II., collect the disiecta membra from it and from the ordinary authorities, and breathe the life into the fragments by his own historical genius.

Similarly if the reconstruction of the ancient map and the topographical discussions which are given in this work, hit the truth, much light must be thrown on the history of the long warfare between the Saracens or the Turks on the one hand, and the early or later Byzantine rulers on the other hand. The numerous discussions on special points in these campaigns will show how much use has been made of this hitherto almost untouched source of topographical information; but, however delightful a task it would be to write the story of the long struggle waged by Mohammedanism for the possession of Asia Minor, that is not the subject of the present work, and the references to it must be picked out by those who will from the mass of details.

After some preliminary studies published in my earlier papers, I was in 1883–4 driven to the opinion that the only hope of progress in the geography of Asia Minor lay in the discovery of new authorities; and I resolved to read over the Byzantine authors, the Acta Conciliorum, and the Acta Sanctorum, as well as the ordinary authorities, for the purpose. I know that there is still a great deal more to be learned from these documents; but the reader may be assured that 95 per cent. of my quotations were copied out as I came on them in my reading, and that most of them have been re-read several times in the original authorities while the proofs have been going through the press. As to the remaining 5 per cent,, they had escaped me while making my original collections, and my attention has been directed to them by seeing them quoted by modern authorities; but in such cases I have always gone to the original source, studied each passage in its context, and copied it out as I read it.*   One or two exceptions, where I had not access to the original authority, are mentioned as such and quoted on the authority of the writer from whom I take them. While making my own independent study of the country, I carefully avoided using any modern works, except of course the indispensable foundation laid by Prof. H. Kiepert in his maps; but my intention has been, after finishing my own first sketch, to peruse afresh all that has been said by modern authorities with a view to comparison, and to give every one the credit for everything that he had said rightly. Absolute want of time, unless the completion of this work was to be delayed for a whole year, has prevented me from doing this as fully as I intended; and I take this opportunity of apologising to any writer whose thoughts I have appropriated either unconsciously through ignorance of his priority or carelessly through forgetfulness of my debt to him. Every instance of the kind is regretted deeply by me and is directly contrary to the plan and intention of my work, which I once hoped would contain an outline of the history of discovery in Asia Minor. In the introduction to Part II. I have spoken more fully about my debt to modern writers.

It will be found that I have referred more frequently to the errors of modern authorities than to their excellencies. This is greatly due to the above-mentioned failure to complete the plan of the work; and every one who takes into consideration that more faults are pointed out in Prof. H. Kiepert's works than in those of any other modern scholar, and who at the same time is able to appreciate Kiepert's absolute devotion to truth, his marvellously wide knowledge, and the liberality with which that knowledge is placed at the service of students, as well as my own conviction that it is almost an impertinence in me to praise him, every one who does this will understand that my corrections are really a homage to the authority and the value of the writers criticised : I should rarely criticise them were it not necessary to prevent their deservedly high authority from giving wide currency to their occasional faults. If I succeed in rousing any one to make a minute and sharp criticism of this book, I shall be grateful for the salutary medicine he may administer, provided he teaches me better.

I can truly say that it gives me far greater pleasure to confirm an identification proposed by previous geographers than to correct one that seems to me mistaken. The contemplation of human error impresses one with the vanity of human effort, and the sense that one's own turn to be corrected must soon come. Moreover the correcting of a previous error has often involved pages of extra argument, which I would gladly have spared myself and my readers.

---

* Circumstances prevented me from making a final revision of the references, but I hope to do this before the book appears, and add a list of errata.

Among the acknowledgment of previous work made in the beginning of Part II., I observe that too little has been said of the École Française d'Athènes. Besides the statement made on p. 101, that its journal, the 'Bulletin de Correspondance,' has done more than any other to aid the student of Asia Minor, I feel bound to add that the first young travellers in the interior of Asia Minor were members of the École Française. MM. Duchesne and Collignon in 1876, set the example of plunging boldly into the heart of what was then an unknown land. They had little in the way of proper equipment, and had everything to learn about the method of travel in Mohammedan lands. Accordingly they have suffered the fate of most originators in research. Their work has been superseded by other more elaborate and better equipped investigations, which in their turn must suffer the same fate at the hand of subsequent workers in the same field. But no account of exploration in Asia Minor will ever be complete without an honourable mention of their names.

In the Epilogue to Vol. V. of his great work, 'Histoire de l'Art dans l'Antiquité," p. 899, Monsieur G. Perrot says "ce sera un travail pour les bibliographes de l'avenir, que de réunir les titres de tous les articles où M. Ramsay a éparpillé, dans je ne sais combien des recueils différents, les précieux renseignements qu'il a recueillis. Que de peine il leur aurait épargnée en écrivant un livre!"

I can answer only by the question, "who would publish the book?" In the present instance my best thanks are due to the Royal Geographical Society, through whose liberality this book is able to appear. The text has been altered and cut about during the printing in a way that has at once greatly shortened the time of its composition, and increased the expense of its printing. In many cases, where my reasoning depends on the balancing of many different arguments drawn from widely separate sources, the task has been much facilitated by having the whole of my previous work always before me in a printed yet only provisional form. The correcting and revising of the proofs took in many places more time and work than the first composition. I give as a single example the following. In August 1889, ten complete and undivided days' work was devoted to about fourteen pages of print, which during that time grew into nearly twenty pages.

During great part of the period since the printing began, it has been in my power to correct freely what was in print; and while I have fully availed myself of this power, I have been much encouraged by finding that, although I was continually discovering new matter and new arguments, and have often been able to cut out the word "perhaps" from my pages, and to substitute comparative certainty for probability, I have rarely been obliged after expressing in this book an opinion about the situation of any city, to alter that opinion, even when it was formed on grounds that were in my first draught expressly said to give a mere probability. Yet so closely does the whole of Part II. hang together, that the addition of a sentence or the specification of another site in the later parts of the work has frequently necessitated a score or more of slight modifications throughout the proofs. My views have changed greatly while writing, but the change has been almost wholly in the way of steady growth. Minor changes have been innumerable; some specimens are given at the end of this preface.

On the other hand I have now found it necessary to alter in this general and more mature study a number of opinions stated in my earlier papers, founded on a narrower view of single districts. Few changes (though many additions) are needed as yet in my " Antiquities of Southern Phrygia and the Border Lands," 1887–8, or in my " Cities and Bishoprics of Phrygia, Part II.," 1887.* More are required in " Cities and Bishoprics, Part I.," 1884,† and still more in earlier papers. But I can still point to the following identifications, made in consequence of the experience of 1881 and 1882, and printed years ago, as justifying confidence in my maturer opinions of 1890: the very names show how obscure and difficult were the problems that were solved in many of these cases—Brouzos, Hieropolis and Otrous and Stektprion approximately, Akroenos, Augustopolis, Aquae Sarvenae, i.e. Basilika Therma (the widely divergent opinions since expressed by Kiepert and Hirschfeld prove how difficult it is to attain certainty about them), Anaboura, Metropolis with Rhotrini or Rhocreni Fontes, Amblada with various small Pisidian villages, Larissa and Aigai in Aeolis, Neonteichos, Temnos, Sasima, Nazianzos.

The chronology of the various parts of the book is of some consequence to those who may use it, inasmuch as the arrangement of topics, which has a rather haphazard appearance, is to a great extent the order of discovery, tempered by consideration of the convenience of printing (a consideration which is, I fear, not so apparent as to be recognizable without an express statement).

Part I., Chapters I.–III., and Part II., Chapters L to S and part of T, were written in the autumn of 1888, after returning from Asia Minor, and were printed in the early months of 1889. The work was interrupted by the Aberdeen University Session, during which I find that no work involving the comparison of many authorities is possible.‡

* A complete change is made as regards Temenothyrai, Germa and Eudokias of Galatia.

† Keretapa, Sanaos, Soa, Tiberiopolis, and the arrangement of part of the comparative table, are the chief changes.

‡ There is no inconsistency between this statement and the fact that my " Study of Phrygian Art, I.," "Laodiceia and Sinethandos," "Syro-Cappadocian Monuments in Asia Minor," "Inscriptions Inédites d'Asie Mineure," and four papers on "Early Christian Monuments in Phrygia" were written during the winter. Such papers, involving little research at the moment, but merely stating results of previous study, can be written piecemeal, being taken up in occasional hours of leisure.

Part II was almost finished, the proofs corrected, and the whole set up in pages during the five months, May to September, 1889. I had hoped to finish the work during that time; but two papers for the 'Journal of Hellenic Studies' took up too much time, and at the end of September the task was still incomplete. October to December, 1889, were entirely taken up, partly with college duties, partly with an engagement rashly entered into with Dr. Westcott to give a lecture in Cambridge on October 18; during these months Mr. Hogarth and Mrs. Ramsay helped me by reading the proofs. In the next three months, the brief Christmas vacation and occasional hours of leisure in the intervals of college work sufficed only to finish Part II., pp. 407–451,* to write the Addenda, to prepare the maps and to revise the whole. Part I., Chapters IV.–VIII., together with this preface, were written in April and May, 1890 : owing to a change of plan in the printing, it became necessary either to alter the entire paging of Part II. with the index of authors and all the references, or to fill up exactly pages 1–88. As the least of two evils the latter course was preferred.†

Besides the time indicated in the preceding paragraph, I have been collecting material with the view to a " Local History of Asia Minor " since 1883, and most of this material has been equally applicable to the present work in accordance with my principle of giving everything I can say about all but the great places, except what has been already correctly said in the ordinary authorities.

In stating my opinions I have tried to steer between two dangers, on the one hand merely leaving a choice between alternatives to the reader, on the other hand stating my own opinion too absolutely, as if there were no difficulty in the choice. It is easier for one who knows the country to make the choice, and I have put as clearly as possible the opinion to which I incline in each case. Of the two dangers it is preferred to incur the charge of dogmatism and confidence rather than of helplessness. My principle has been to carry out each train of reasoning to its extreme consequences and present a definite result : it is a real step to have a distinct theory to test by subsequent discovery, even where the proofs are confessedly incomplete.

A series of indexes are required to make such a work as this thoroughly useful; and I am conscious that the two which are given are not sufficient. But to make a sufficiently minute set of indexes would have added seriously to the expense and would have postponed the publication for another year : a new expedition to Asia Minor in 1890 will take up my whole time till the beginning of college duties. The index of authors will show where most remains undone by the

---

* Hence the very summary way in which the last provinces, Pamphylia, Caria, Lycia, are treated : pp. 452–460 were added in May, and a footnote, p. 454, in September.

† Miscalculation of my MS. produced some inequalities in the execution; and a concluding chapter has been omitted.

present writer, that may yield further information.   The proper names for the Index, as far as regards Part II.,* were all marked by myself, the transcription and arrangement being performed by the index-maker of the R.G.S.   I have intended to insert in this index all names and words that were most likely to be useful in helping the student of history or geography; but modern Turkish names are usually omitted.

In regard to the spelling of ancient names of places, my original intention was, to transliterate the Greek form in all cases except a few names like Iconium, which are household words; but when the proofs came to hand, it was obvious that this principle had not been carried out completely.   It then seemed preferable to leave the variety of forms than to weary the printer by correcting every *c* to *k* and every *us* to *os*, or vice versa.   In some cases the variation is intentional: Cilicia denotes the country, Kilikia the *strategia*.†

I cannot better conclude this preliminary statement than by quoting the opening words of the preface to M. de Mas Latrie's ' Trésor de Chronologie.'   " Je ne présente pas sans quelque appréhension ce livre au public studieux et au public savant.   Non pas que j'ai épargné ni le temps ni les soins pour le rendre digne d'un bon accueil;· mais, modifié dans sa composition première, ralenti dans son exécution par suite de circonstances indépendantes de ma volonté, il peut, au premier abord, sembler un œuvre où manque l'ordre et la cohérence."

Since Part II. was in type certain additions have come to my know-ledge, the chief of which, in April and May, 1890, are here appended.

P. 104 (A 3) and 430.   M. de Mas Latrie, ' Trésor de Chronol.' p. 1799, would identify Pyrgi or Birgui as one of the names of Tralleis, comparing Schebab Eddin, 339, 369; Ibn Batoutah II. 295–310.   In that case Ducas, p. 83, must be guilty of writing Tmolos for Messogis, when he describes the position of Pyrgion.   The Seljuk principality of Aidin was also called Birgui; but as that principality extended from Smyrna to Tralleis and included the Kaystros valley, it might naturally have had a fortress with the family mausoleum of the chiefs in the Kaystros valley at Pyrgi, where Tchineit was taken and buried.

P. 109 (A 15).   Herakleia ad Sipylum is fixed by the boundary-stone, published in my 'Contributions to the History of Southern Aeolis' (Journ. Hell. Stud., 1881).   The name disappears in the Byzantine time, and either it was merged in Archangelos, or else the testimony of Aelius Dionysius, quoted by Eustathius ad Hom. Iliad. B (I take the reference

* As regards Part I., see p. 5, *note*.

† Much variation is due to the attempt to reproduce faithfully the Byzantine spelling, which often gives a clue to local pronunciation.

from Wesseling's note on Steph. Byz., s.v.) Ἡράκλεια ἡ καὶ Μαγνησία, must be accepted literally, and it must be concluded from this statement compared with the inscription above mentioned that Magnesia bore the name Herakleia during at least the third century B.C. But precisely during that century we have the great inscription, C. I. G., 3137, containing the treaty between Smyrna and Magnesia, concluded about 244 B.C. Perhaps the truth is, that the territory along the north and west of Sipylos was divided between Magnesia and Herakleia, and the load-stone found there was called indifferently Μάγνης and Ἡρακλεώτης λίθος, giving rise to the mistaken belief that Magnesia and Herakleia were names of the same place.

P. 116 (A 37). Titanus is the name given by Pliny, V. 32, to a city and a river on the Aeolic coast. There can be no doubt that the river which he means is the Titnaios, known from coins of Aigai. The coins with legend ΤΙΣΝΑΙΟΣ and ΤΙΣΝΑΙΟΝ are referred by Imhoof-Blumer, Monn. Gr., p. 275, to a city Tisna, which is the place meant by Pliny under the name Titanus; the original form must have been Titna, whence comes the river name Titnaios. Schuchhardt takes this view, and understands, like his predecessors, MM. Pottier and Reinach, that the Pythikos of Agathias is the same river as the Titnaios. He places Tisna at Uzun-Hassanli, one hour up the river from Myrina: see Bohn, Altert. von Aegae, p. 61.

I may mention an extraordinary omission in Dr. Schuchhardt's argument as to the site of Aigai. He has apparently not looked into Hierocles with Wesseling's admirable notes, reprinted in the Bonn edition, and hence has not noticed the quotation from Galen, Αἰγαῖς καὶ Περπερίνῃ, τῇ μὲν ὁμόρῳ Μυρίνῃ, τῇ δὲ Περγάμῳ (see p. 117). MM. Lechat and Radet also omit it when discussing the evidence about Aigai in Bull. Corr. Hell., 1887; and I did so myself in 1881. At that time the reason, though not the excuse, for my omission lay in my isolation from books, and my consequent ignorance of the Byzantine authorities. The subsequent writers on the subject, some reaching the wrong and some the right conclusion, give also an incomplete list of authorities. They may be presumed to have made an independent collection of the materials; yet, though I have for more than six years been urging that the Byzantine lists must be the foundation of all topographical study in Asia Minor, they have not looked into Hierocles or Wesseling's indispensable commentary on the Synekdemos while studying Aigai.*

P. 121 (A 2). Mr. Head, in his 'Hist. Num.,' s.v., interprets a coin of Sardis with the legend ΔΙΟΣ ΓΟΝΑΙ as referring to the worship of a supposed Zeus Gonaios. The legend is complete, and is interpreted by the type as Διὸς γοναί, the circumstances connected with the birth and rearing of Zeus.

* The passage is quoted by MM. Pottier and Reinach, 'Myrina,' p. 20.

In the Talmud the morning meal, taken about six o'clock, is called "the Meal of the Lydians" (Neubauer, 'Géographie de Talmud, p. 316). The Lydian traffic in sandals and in eunuchs is also alluded to (l.c.).

P. 139 (C 44). Hieropolis of the Glaukos valley is probably meant on the coins of Synnada, showing Apollo standing and Zeus sitting, with the legend

ΣΥΝΝΑΔΕΩΝ·ΙΕΡ[ΑΠΟΛΕΙ]ΤΩΝ·ΟΜΟΝΟΙΑ

See Imhoof-Blumer, Monn. Gr., p. 413. Zeus Pandemos represents Synnada, as is often the case on coins. Apollo often appears on the coins of the Hieropolitan valley. Probably O should be restored in place of A in the name on this coin. Mionnet gives a coin with a similar legend, where O is used, but the word OMONOIA is omitted. I have in 'Trois Villes Phrygiennes,' p. 506, interpreted the coin as referring to Hieropolis beside Sandykli.

P. 139 (C 46). The people of Synnada placed on their coins the head of ΑΚΑΜΑΣ (see Drexler in 'Numism. Zft.,' 1889, p. 177); and Stephanus mentions that Akamas after the Trojan war wandered into Phrygia and founded Synnada. This legend was evidently adopted in the city; and probably Stephanus derives it from Metrophanes of Eukarpia, who wrote a work in two books on Phrygia, from which Stephanus quotes the story of the bunch of Eukarpian grapes which was so large as to break a waggon.

Synnada boasts on its coins to be a city of Dorians and Ionians. These Greek colonists perhaps looked to the hero Akamas as their oikist: such myths tended to be developed in the process of hellenisation of Phrygia. The native Phrygian part of the population looked to Thynnaros as their hero and ancestor. Dokimion was a Macedonian military colony (see pp. 125, 126).

P. 143 (C 76), compare 164 (D 29). The baths of Phrygia and its wines are mentioned in the Talmud as having separated the Ten Tribes from their brethren (Neubauer, 'Géogr. de Talmud,' p. 315).

(P. 144 (C 78). Kakkabas or Kakkabokome seems to involve the word Kakkabe, the name of the citadel of Carthage, which is connected by Ad. Sonny in Philologus, 1889, p. 559, with the Phœnician stem âqab, in the sense of "hill." He remarks that the Phœnician letter ain is represented in the Septuagint sometimes by the spiritus lenis, sometimes by the spiritus asper, sometimes by kappa, and sometimes by rho. Hence he explains the initial kappa in Κακκάβη. A similar phenomenon occurs in Katenneis or Etenneis (see p. 418). On Phœnician names in Phrygia, see Sonny, l.c.; he connects Κύβελα (which Hesychius explains by ὄρη) with Hebrew Gebel, and thence explains Κυβέλη as Μήτηρ 'Ορείη, from which 'Ρείη is a shortened form (Crusius, Beitr. z. griech. Mythol., p. 26, n. 4): the connection will probably not find general approval.

P. 173 (E 22), 438 and 449. Mr. Pelham also quotes Corp. Gloss.

Latin., II. 14, Actor πραγματευτής, and II. 177, Saltarius ὀρεοφύλαξ; and he points out to me in corroboration of the large imperial estate which I have proved at Tyana that in Justinian's Nov. XXX. (ed. Zachariæ von Lingenthal, I. p. 163) more than half the territory of Cappadocia is said to be imperial property. Prof. Sayce also refers me, in corroboration of my description of the horse-breeding on this estate, to Proc. Soc. Bibl. Arch., 1881, Nov., p. 14, where Mr. Pinches published a tablet from Kouyunjik mentioning horses imported into Assyria from Dana.

P. 176 (E 23). I must retract the opinion that there was at Lagbe an imperial estate. I now accept the interpretation of μισθωτής proposed by the Austrian editors, as more probable in itself; moreover Lagbe struck coins and therefore cannot have been an estate. The other points, however, I still maintain, both the restoration I have proposed for the fragmentary inscription published in such varying forms by the Austrian editors and by Mr. A. H. Smith, and the opinion that Lagbe must have been in the conventus of Kibyra and in the province of Asia. The phrase ὁ κατὰ τόπον μισθωτής may be compared with τοῦ κατὰ τόπον τηρητοῦ τοῦ ἔργου in an inscription of Hierapolis (Le Bas, 1680), which seems to denote the officer charged with the duty of looking after the proper condition of the graves along the sacra via.

P. 183 (F 25). From a comparison of the list of bishops given by Le Quien with the principles stated on p. 427, and with the account given of Basilinopolis, we may reach the probable conclusion that Linoe, Gordoserba, and Mela or Modrene, were formed into bishoprics by Justinian; that previously, although Nikaia had been an autokephalos bishopric of great dignity owing to the wide extent of territory over which its influence extended, yet no bishoprics were subject to it, and it had in vain attempted to establish its claim over the bishopric of Basilinopolis in A.D. 451, and that Justinian recognised the growing importance of the territory, which lay south of Nikaia and politically was included in its territory, by founding Justinianopolis-Mela on his military road, and also by giving the status of cities and bishoprics to Linoe and Gordoserba. The elevation of Tataion, Noumerika, Daphnusia and Maximianai to be bishoprics belongs to a later period, probably that of Basil in the ninth century. The earliest known bishop of Mela dates 553, of Gordoserba 680, of Linoe 692, of the others 869 (see Le Quien).

P. 191 and elsewhere. For 65 B.C., the date assigned by Marquardt for the institution of the province Bithynia-Pontus by Pompey, the date 64 B.C. is substituted by Niese (Hermes, XIII., p. 39, and Rhein. Mus., XXXVIII., 1883, p. 577).

P. 203 (G 11). In a note added by Kiepert to Humann and

Puchstein's 'Reisen in Kleinasien,' p. 18, Melangeia is identified with Karadja Sheher, besides Dorylaion: he follows Hammer-Purgstall, who says that Karadja Hisar, Greek Melangeia, was besieged by Ertogrul in 1240, and captured by Osman in 1288. My discussion has probably established that this identification is erroneous. If any further reason is needed, it may be found in the fact that the valley of the Tembris (Porsuk Su, in Humann Pursak) had been long in the undisturbed possession of the Turks, and that they were in the thirteenth century fighting for the lands near the Bithynian coast.

P. 205 (G 15). In Humann and Puchstein, 'Reisen in Kleinasien,' p. 11, Dr. Humann remarks that Ine Göl, "Needle Lake," or Inek Göl, "Cattle Lake," is the proper form of the name, and not Aine Göl, "Mirror Lake," as it is usually given. I have also observed that the village four hours east-south-east from Philadelphia (Ala Sheher) is properly named Ine Göl (or Inek Göl, which would be pronounced in almost the same way) not Aine Göl.

P. 219 (G 23) and p. 444. The same explanation of the name Gaizatorix has already been given by M. Belley, Mém. de l'Acad. des Inscript., as quoted in C.I.G., 4039. Another Galatian name involving the same word is Gaizatodiastos, which occurs in that inscription.

P. 225 (H 8). In Humann and Puchstein's 'Reisen in Kleinasien,' Gordion is identified with Tchakmak on the Sangarios a little south from Yürme. Humann rightly remarks on the want of clear evidence to connect Germa with the site of Yürme, but Kiepert in a note still supposes that the name is a modern form of Germa, and that the name strictly belongs to the hot springs. I have visited these springs: no ancient city was situated at them, but they in all probability belonged to the territory of the city situated at Yürme.

P. 226 (H 9). Gratianopolis cannot be interpreted as an error for ἡ Κρατιανῶν πόλις: Philadelphus was bishop of Gratianopolis and Epiphanius of Krateia at Concil. Ephes., A.D. 431.

P. 251 (K 18). In his 'Reisen in Kleinasien,' p. 47, Humann gives the distances—

Angora to Tchakal Keui	.	. 27 kilom.
Angora to Binam	.	. 33 „
Binam to Tcheshnir Keupreu *	.	53 „

Sir C. Wilson estimated the horse-road (which would be shorter) as 19 miles to Binam and 31 thence to the bridge. The probability even

---

* Humann does not give the name from personal observation; but mentions that old travellers call it Tchasnegir-Köprü. I have noted it as Tcheshnir, where g has disappeared between vowels according to the common change in modern pronunciation; cp. Deirmen, "mill," for Degirman. He gives the bridge as 735 metres above sea level; the village on the east bank as 758 metres.

suggests itself that Sarmalius of the Itinerary is Malos : the distance, as given by the Itinerary suits exactly. In that case, Bolegasgus would be an intermediate station on the road to Ankyra (see pp. 257, 259).

P. 277 (N 9). In glancing hastily by the aid of the index at Humann and Puchstein's notes on Marash and their report of Kiepert's latest view on Germanicia, I find no reason to alter any word that I have said. The frontier that I have assigned to Kommagene is confirmed by the latest discoveries and maps. The words of Theodoret, who on such a point is a first-rate authority, that Germanicia was ἐν μεθορίῳ τῆς Κιλίκων καὶ Σύρων [καὶ *] Καππαδοκῶν in the province of Euphratesia, are a complete justification of the at least approximate accuracy of the position which I assign, and a complete disproof of Kiepert's view. The same inference may be drawn from Theodoret's expression, Haeret. Fab., IV., 2, Γερμανικείας τῆς τῷ Ταύρῳ γειτονούσης πόλεως. The frontier assigned on my map requires only a slight modification, which does no violence to the evidence, inasmuch as the boundaries lie among uninhabited mountains, to make Marash close to the meeting of the three provinces.

P. 280 (N 16) and p. 287. The variant a Cotena cannot be accepted, for the name Lacotena occurs in Ammianus, XX., 11, a Cappadocia ipse per Melitenam, minoris Armeniae oppidum, et Lacotena, et Samosata, transmisso Euphrate, Edessam venit. (I owe the reference to Surita, quoted in Wesseling's edition of the Itineraries as XXI., 11).

P. 295. It is very doubtful whether Suenda, in Cappadocia, which was captured by Antiochus (Front., Strat., III., 2, 9) can be identified with Soanda. The MSS. vary greatly in the reading.

P. 304. In Humann and Puchstein's, 'Reisen,' p. 402, an inscription of Diarbekir (Amida), given by Sterrett, ' Wolfe Expedition,' No. 631, is repeated from a fresh copy :

μνημ[ῖον] Δεον (?)
Μαρωνίου ἀσκ-
οπ(οιοῦ) ἀπὸ Καμπ(ῶν) [in Kappadokien]. †

This reference to Kampai is purely conjectural, and cannot rank as an argument against my view that in Kambe the b stands for ou.

P. 312 (note). Tarkundwerras must be a local pronunciation at Isaura of the name Tarkondarios, which was a surname of Kastor, king of the Tektosages from about 62 to 45. Prof. Sayce has read the name of Tarkhundara(is) [last symbol doubtful], king of Arzapa, on a tablet from Tel-el-Amarna (Proc. Soc. Bibl. Arch., 1889, June, p. 336). The name Rondberras at Corycos confirms my reading Tarkundberras.

P. 317. That the theme of Koloneia was originally part of the

* This word does not occur in the text of the Cambridge edition, Hist. Eccles., II., 25. I owe this and the following reference to Wesseling ad Itin.

† Sterrett reads μνημῖ[ο]ν more correctly, and KAMT which is probably less correct.

Armeniac Theme is also implied by the fact that Kamacha was in the Armeniac Theme (Theophan. 469, 444, 377).

P. 346 (Q 30). Strabo, p. 587, mentions, as an example of a river with twenty-seven fords, one that flows from Tyana to Soloi-Pompeiopolis. The river meant is the one that runs beside the road from Faustinopolis to Podandos. But it is an error to say that it flows to Soloi: it really joins the Saros. The error, however, is not Strabo's, for Meineke considers the passage to be a gloss.

P. 370 (T 26). The name Bidana or Bidane seems correct, being defended by Bizana* of Armenia (Procop., de Aedif., III. 5). Bidana-Leontopolis must probably be the modern town Siristat or Tris Maden, about 13 miles west of Isaura. This situation would explain why Leontopolis and Isauropolis were under the same bishop. Moreover Leontopolis was clearly a city of importance in later Byzantine time, and it is a general rule† that the important cities of that time correspond to Turkish cities. This identification of Leontopolis as Siristat explains everything known to us, and may be looked on as pretty certain. Siristat is the seat of government of Boz Kyr Kaimmakamlik. Prof. Sterrett in his ' Wolfe Expedition,' p. 98, is too severe on Hamilton, when he says that the latter was " misled into giving the place the name of Tris Maden:" Hamilton was no doubt true to the fact of his time, though the " maden" and the name are now disused. The distance of Bidana from Isauropolis seems too small, but stadia may be used in the sense of miles (see pp. 190, 258). I should look for Nea Isaura here rather than where Sterrett places it. There are inscriptions at Siristat.

P. 412. The ethnic Μαηνός or Ἰμαηνός, and the local name Maion or Imaion corresponding to it, are related to the name Maes (on which see M. Th. Reinach's excellent paper in ' Rev. des Ét. Grecq.,' 1889, p. 270) as Tataion or Tottaion to Tatas or Tottes, and the other instances quoted on p. 439.

P. 420 (W 14). The interpretation of Eudocias and Jovia as epithets of Termessos makes intelligible the following signature at the Council of Chalcedon, Zenodotus Telmessi et Eniadis civitatis Ioniae. This is obviously corrupted from Termessi civitatis et Eudociadis et Iobiae. Zenodotus of Telmessos in Lycia is frequently mentioned at this council; but no bishop of Termessos occurs in the lists to warrant the supposition that two successive entries had been mixed up. Most probably Zenodotus of Telmessos and Zenodotus of Termessos were both present (Mansi, VI. 575, VII. 433). At the Council of 325, Heuresios of Termessos was present; in 431, Timotheus of Termessos and Eudokias; in 448, Sabinianus of Termessos, Eudokias and Iobia; in

---

* Compare Nazianzos or Nadiandos, Podandos and Bozanti; see p. 348.

† Not a universal rule; see p. p. 454.

692, Constantine of Eudokias; in 787, Callistus of Eudokias. This list shows the epithet gradually establishing itself and displacing Termessos, according to the theory advanced in my A.S.P. The two bishops of 458, Auxentius and Innocentius, are the sole difficulty in the way of this theory, and I have conjectured that one of the two names is a corruption or marginal correction, which crept in between "Termessi" and "Eudociadis," and thus caused the single bishop to become double.

P. 423. The mountain CAΛBAKOC is mentioned on coins of Apollonia: Drexler in Num. Zft., 1889, p. 122.

P. 423. Olymos, a place near Mylasa, is mentioned in a series of inscriptions, Le Bas, 323 to 338, Athen. Mittheil., 1889, p. 367.

P. 426. Strabo often mentions the Solymoi; but the words of Herodotus, I., 173, οἱ δὲ Μιλύαι τότε Σόλυμοι ἐκαλέοντο tends to show that they were even then an extinct people, whom Strabo afterwards identified with some existing people; such is the suggestion of Sittl, Berlin. Phil. Wochenschr., 1888, p. 338. He also quotes Cicero's words (Verr., IV., 10, 21) Lycii, Graeci homines, to prove that the græcising process had progressed very far in Lycia early in the first century B.C.

P. 110 (A 20). On the coins of Ephesos-Theologos and Magnesia-Manglasia see Mr. Grueber's description of the find at Ephesos in Numism. Chron., 1872, p. 120 ff. M. de Mas Latrie, 'Trésor de Chronol.,' p. 1799, quotes from Schlumberger, 'Num. Orient.,' p. 483, on the coins of Magnesia, but omits those of Ephesos.

P. 115 (A 33). The Homereion at Smyrna is mentioned in an inscription, Mous. Smyrn., IV., p. 176, no. τξ.

P. 125 (B 16). M. Waddington assures me that no coins of the Mosteni known to him give the title Macedones: considering his unique knowledge, this may be taken as final, and the coins in question may be rejected as misread.

P. 135 (C 7, 8). Ducange on Zonaras (vol. VI., p. 187, ed. Dindorf) quotes the miracle at Khonai. The published versions (Bonnet, 1890) are late and topographically absurd, but must be founded on an original of good character, full of local colour.

P. 136 (C 23). Peltai was a Macedonian colony.

P. 136 (C 24). Eumeneia, as a seat of the worship of Isis, is quoted by Drexler, in Num. Zft., 1889, p. 167. An additional proof is furnished by the inscription, which may belong either to Peltai or to Eumeneia, C.I.G., 3886, more correctly in Bull. Corr. Hell., 1885. None of the editors have observed that καὶ Εἴσει[δος] must be read in line 6, if M. Paris has rightly copied the inscription. I have three times searched in vain for this inscription, about the locality of which Hamilton and Paris give very different accounts. Eumeneia boasts on its coins to be a city of Achaeans; the title was assumed by the Pergamenian colonists in opposition to the Macedonians of Peltai.

P. 138 (C 35). Another Alia, a mere katoikia, has been proved by M. S. Reinach to have been situated at or near Kirgol, between Tiberiopolis and Aizanoi : it is mentioned in an inscription found there, which will soon be published.

P. 172. Prof. G. Hirschfeld has recognised in the modern name Baradis the ancient Aporidos Kome of Livy.

P. 178. Hogarth, in Journ. Hell. Stud., 1890, gives several examples of the common Lycaonian name Sousou.

P. 187 and p. 352. The line of beacons is also given by Zonaras, II., p. 162, ed. Par. His enumeration agrees with Cedrenus, except in the names Mimas and Kyrizos. Ducange quotes in his notes on Zonaras also the forms Aigiklos and Augilos as variants in Scylitzes and Theoph. Contin. He mentions that the hill of Saint Auxentios was about 10 miles from Chalcedon, and was the same as Oxeia (see p. 189, F 65). Saint Auxentius, who lived under Marcianus and Leo, built a monastery there. Ducange quotes the Menaea, June 1, 3, 13, and January 19. Theophanes, p. 436, says that this hill was near Damatry (see pp. 218, 312 ;. and Ducange, Constant. Christ., IV., p. 177).

P. 190 (F 76). The passage of Constantine Porphyrogenitus, de Thém., p. 25, where Προυσιάς almost certainly denotes Prousa ad Olympum, may serve to elucidate two passages in Pliny's Epist. ad Tra., 58 and 81, where also Prousias is used in a similar way. Mr. Hardy in his edition, takes a different view, making Prousias an adjective.

P. 242. The road Ancyra 24 Crentius 32 Legna 24 Carus (Garus v.l.) Vicus 30 Krateia 24 Claudiopolis has been accidentally omitted in the text. Crentius, a suspicious form, seems to be the modern Girindos, where I have placed Manegordus.

P. 295. The description of Ozizala as abounding in gardens, streams, and groves, should in the parched country of Cappadocia, make it easy to prove its precise situation (see Greg. Naz., Ep. 26). I have not travelled along the left bank of the Halys above the situation where I place Parnassos, but to judge from the appearance of the district as seen from the road on the right bank, it corresponds to the above description better than any other part of Cappadocia that I have seen. When Ozizala is once placed, the situation of Parnassos and Nyssa would be still more narrowly defined.

P. 324 (P 6) and p. 448. M. Duchesne follows the lead of the Bollandists (so also does Muralt) in saying that Euchaita was renamed Theodoropolis in A.D. 972, in honour of the great victory gained by John Tzimisces over the Turks. Cedrenus, II., p. 411, says that the emperor rebuilt the church in which the body of Saint Theodorus lay, and changed the name of the place from Eukhaneia to Theodoropolis. The authors whom I am arguing against assume that, because the biographies of Theodorus say that he was buried at Eukhaita, and Cedrenus says that the emperor rebuilt the church where Theodorus's body lay, therefore the city which is meant by Cedrenus is Eukhaita. They take Eukhaneia and Eukhaita to be the same place (M. Duchesne does not even notice the difference of name) ; but on the following page Cedrenus speaks of Theophilus, archbishop of Eukhaita, distinguishing it as a neuter plural from Eukhaneia as a feminine singular. Did Cedrenus make a mistake, and distinguish as two different names two forms of the same name, or do the Bollandists and MM. Muralt and Duchesne wrongly identify two different places as a single place ? They certainly only follow Zonaras, II., p. 214, ed. Par., who gives Eukhania and Eukhaita as equivalent forms of the same name. This can hardly be correct. Notitiæ II. and X. mention Eukhania and Eukhaita as separate metropoleis ; and Gelzer shows, " Jahrb. f. protest. Theol.,' 1886, p. 540–2, that Eukhaita became a metropolis between 386 and 911 (see Addenda, p. 448), and Eukhania between 1035 and 1054. I therefore refuse to accept Zonaras's evidence as to the identity of the names, and believe that he was misled by the resemblance between them. Because Saint Theodore helped the Byzantine army against the Russians, a church would naturally be erected to him near the battle-field, and not in Helenopontus. The singular analogy of the names, and the coincidence that both Eukhania and Eukhaita were associated with Theodore, betrayed Zonaras into his error. Thus the last shred of evidence, on which M. Duchesne relied for the theory that the name Theodoropolis belonged peculiarly and specially to Eukhaita, has now disappeared. Eukhaita might be styled the ' city of Theodore,' but so equally might any city in which a church was dedicated to him. This long disproof of M. Duchesne's interpretation of the inscription of Safaramboli (see p. 320) may seem unnecessary, as the case is so clear ; but my experience in the case of Koloe, Themissonion, Eriza, &c., shows me how I may go on for years reiterating in vain the disproof of errors, suggested without any evidence and accepted implicitly by the world. The nature of Theodorus the Soldier, as a saint worshipped in Pontus and Paphlagonia, about whom there grew up purely legendary accounts without a trace of historical truth or verisimilitude, has been thoroughly illustrated in our discussion.

P. 364 (T 7). I had thought that the exact site of Olba might be at the remarkable ruins seen by Mr. Hogarth when travelling from Maghra to Seleukeia in 1887. About three hours before reaching Seleukeia he saw these ruins at no very great distance to the east, but divided from him by a ravine. He was assured by various informants at Maghra that Mr. Sterrett had visited these ruins, and therefore did not go to them, as his companion was ill, and they were hurrying to the coast for a steamer. But in the utter uncertainty as to the mapping of this district and even of Said Pasha's new road from Seleukeia to Maghra (see p. 361), nothing but a loose approximation to the site is possible.

This identification was arrived at in the early winter of 1888–9, and was printed in the appeal issued by the Asia Minor Exploration Fund in December, 1889, for funds to carry out a new expedition into the eastern part of Asia Minor. The programme of the route proposed was there printed, part of which was to examine this site, perhaps that of Olba.

More recently I heard from Mr. Bent that he has found Olba south of Maghra at a site some miles north-east of the one seen by Mr. Hogarth, which also has been examined by Mr. Bent. The name Oura, which is still attached to the site of Olba, shows that I was right in maintaining that Ourba (i.e. Ourwa, for beta denotes the sound of w, cp. footnote on p. 312) was the native form of the name, and Olba a grecism to suggest a connection with ὄλβος.* With Ourba compare Ouerbe in Pisidia (Pamphylia Secunda). Mr. Bent's discoveries confirm the general course of my arguments, and will add greatly to the further development of them. †

* Seleuceia also was originally named Olbia, and may have been in the country of Olba.

† I add a note after visiting Olba, Mr. Bent's discovery. It is rightly placed in my map : but the map attached to Mr. Bent's paper in Proceed. R. G. S., Aug. 1890, is far from accurate. Uzunja Burdj should be placed much further south, about lat. 36° 37' ; Oura should really be east by north from it, instead of south. Maghra should be much further south. Euren Keui, which we did not visit, is more nearly correct. We estimate the height of Uzunja Burdj 2000 feet lower than Mr. Bent. In the 'Athenæum,' July 19, p. 105, Mr. Bent discards Kastabala of Cappadocia entirely, and infers from Strabo that Tyana and Kybistra were in Cilicia near Kastabala. I adhere to all that I have written : my opinions were in print months before Mr. Bent travelled, and I consider them confirmed entirely by his brilliant discoveries.

HISTORICAL GEOGRAPHY OF ASIA MINOR.

PART I.
GENERAL PRINCIPLES.

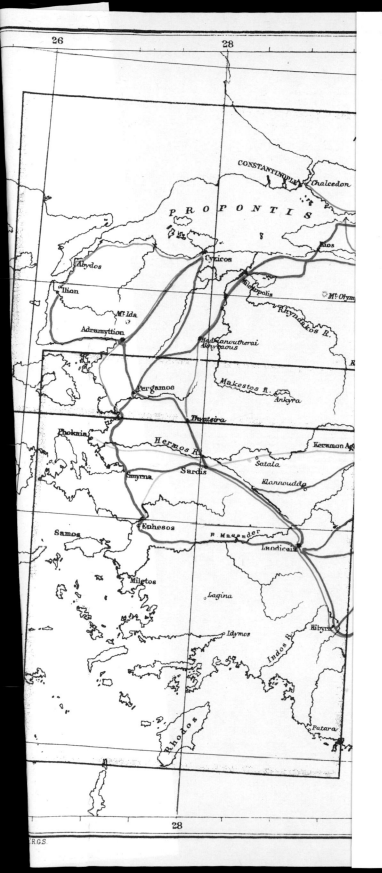

HISTORICAL GEOGRAPHY OF ASIA MINOR.

PART I. GENERAL PRINCIPLES.

I. HELLENISM AND ORIENTALISM

PLANTED like a bridge between Asia and Europe, the peninsula of Asia Minor has been from the beginning of history a battlefield between the East and the West. Across this bridge the religion, art, and civilisation of the East found their way into Greece; and the civilisation of Greece, under the guidance of Alexander the Macedonian, passed back again across the same bridge to conquer the East and revolutionise Asia as far as the heart of India. Persians, Arabs, Mongols, Turks, have all followed the same route in the many attempts that Asia has made to subdue the West.

The very character of the country has marked it out as a battle-ground between the Oriental and the European spirit. The great mass of Asia Minor consists of a plateau, 3000 to 5000 feet above sea-level, around which there is a fringe of low-lying coast-land. The plateau is like a continuation of Central Asia, vast, immobile, monotonous. The western coasts on the Aegean sea are full of variety, with a very broken coast-line and long arms of the sea alternating with pro-minent capes.

In the scenery also, the plateau presents an equally strong contrast to the western coast. The plateau from the Anti-Taurus westwards con-sists chiefly of great gently undulating plains. The scenery, as a rule, is monotonous and subdued; even the mountains of Phrygia seem not to have the spirit of freedom about them. The tone everywhere is melan-choly, but not devoid of a certain charm, which, after a time, takes an even stronger hold of the mind than the bright and varied scenery of the Greek world. Strong contrasts of climate between the long severe winter and the short but hot summer, a fertile soil dependent entirely on the chances of an uncertain rainfall, impressed on the mind of the inhabitants the insignificance of man and his dependence on the power of nature. The tone can be traced throughout the legends and the religion of the plateau. The legends are always sad—Lityerses slain by the sickles of the reapers in the field,* Marsyas flayed by the god Apollo, Hylas drowned in the fountain—all end in death during the prime of life and the pride of art.   But the scenery of the Ægean coast-lands is as bright and varied as that of Greece itself.   There is not a trace of monotony or melancholy in the constant alternation of sea and promontory, of sharp rugged mountains and deep fertile valleys.   The sense of life and vigour is wonderfully quickened in the clear atmosphere and the bright light, where cape after cape stretches far out to the west as if trying to bridge over the " estranging sea " to the islands, and where the water of the inlets, offering an easier road than the land itself, provokes the navigating instinct.   The thought of death is never present where the incitements to life and action are so great.

Thus the plateau is in every way characterised as a border-land between East and West, and a battlefield between the Oriental and the European spirit.   The idea of this great struggle was a formative principle which moulded the gradual development of the Iliad, and gave the tone to Herodotus's epic history.   We can trace its main features from that time onwards.   Greece and Persia were the representative antagonists for two centuries.   Then the conquests of Alexander, organised and consolidated later by the genius of Rome, made the European spirit apparently victorious for many centuries.

But the conquest was not real.   Romans governed Asia Minor because, with their marvellous governing talent, they knew how to adapt their administration to the people of the plateau.   It is true that the great cities put on a western appearance, and took Latin or Greek names : Latin and Greek were the languages of government, of the educated classes, and of polite society.   Only this superficial aspect is attested in literature and in ordinary history, and when I began to travel the thought had never occurred to me that there was any other.   The conviction has gradually forced itself on me that the real state of the country was very different.   Greek was not the popular language of the plateau even in the third century after Christ: the mass of the people spoke Lycaonian, and Galatian, and Phrygian, although those who wrote books wrote Greek, and those who governed spoke Latin.   The people continued to believe in their own religion: their gods were identified by educated persons with the gods of Greece and Rome, and called by Greek names; but they had none of the Greek or Roman character, they were Asiatic deities.   Christianity conquered the land, and succeeded in doing what Greece and Rome had never done: it imposed its language on the people.   But the Christianity of Phrygia was never like the Christianity of Europe: sects of enthusiasts who

---

* The tale is commonly given in the form that Lityerses slew all strangers and hid their bodies in the sheaves, and that he was himself slain by Herakles and lamented by the reapers in the Lityerses Song: but he must ultimately be an impersonation of the life of nature cut down in the harvest, and celebrated in harvest songs.

perpetuated the old type in the new religion always flourished there, and the orthodox writers frequently inveigh against the numerous Anatolian heresies. It is a suggestive fact that the old names of many cities which had been replaced by Greek or Latin names often survived and returned into use. There was a city of Isauria named Diocaesareia : it is often mentioned in the first seven centuries after Christ. In the later Byzantine writers Prakana, a name unknown in earlier writers, is regularly used ; but the identity of Diocaesareia and Prakana would be unknown, where it not for a casual phrase in the proceedings of a Christian Council (Concil. Nicaen. II.) of the eighth century, which shows that at that time the popular name Prakana was forcing itself into the official registers alongside of the official name Diocaesareia.

The foundation of Constantinople was a sign that the West had not really conquered Asia Minor. The immense power of governmental organisation which Roman genius constructed maintained itself for many centuries. But the Oriental character grew stronger century by century in the Byzantine government ; one dynasty overturned another dynasty, and each was less "Western" than the preceding one. Phrygians, Isaurians, Cappadocians, and Armenians, ruled under the style of Roman Emperors, till at length a purely Oriental dynasty of Osmanlis eliminated even the superficial forms of the West. The change was not in all respects so great as we are apt to suppose. The language and the religion and the government of Anatolia reached at last the Oriental goal to which the genius of the land tended. There is no more interesting process in history than this which was completed by the conquest of Constantinople in 1453.

At the present day, after the East has ruled for centuries undisturbed in Anatolia, the old struggle has recommenced. The Greek element is gradually supplanting the Oriental on the Aegean coast. That strength and vitality which the Greek race seems to possess under every government except its own,* is gradually placing the coast valleys in its hands. The Oriental element does not retreat, it is not driven back by open war: it dies out on the coast by a slow yet sure decay. But the interior is still wholly Oriental, and if the same peaceful development continues I believe that the Turks, as soldiers, and the Greeks, as traders, will, united, make a happier country than either race could by itself. English railways are gradually pushing their way into the country from Smyrna, which is the metropolis of the western element ; and western commerce is trying to reorganise the lines of trade. The same trade routes across Asia Minor now lead to Marseilles and to Liverpool, which once led to Rome, and the railways are reopening the roads of ancient times. There are two competing routes. One follows the line of the

* I must confess that the development of Greece during the last few years is disproving the innuendo in this sentence, which was written four years ago.

great Eastern highway of Græco-Roman time: it passes through Ephesos, the Græco-Roman capital, which has now lost its harbour and sunk into complete decay; and from Ephesos onwards it follows, and must continue to follow step by step, the Roman road. The other is opening up the old line of the "Royal Road": its engineers have surveyed both the original route and the modified course that it followed in the Roman period, and the prophecy is not a dangerous one that the latter will finally be adopted.

These movements of armies and peoples and civilisations have taken place along a few lines of road, some of which have been more important at one time, some at another. To trace in outline the history of these roads, to show how they are marked out by nature, and how the variation in their comparative importance, produced by historical reasons, has reacted on the distribution of the chief centres of population, is the subject of this essay.

The road-system of Anatolia is at present in a transition state. Since steam navigation was introduced the great land-routes, starting from Constantinople and leading to the various provinces of the empire, have fallen into disuse and disrepair. Previously the necessities of government required the maintenance in tolerable repair of roads and a postal service. This Turkish road-system was practically the same as the Byzantine system, which was gradually introduced after the foundation of Constantinople as the capital of the eastern world. That event soon produced a total revolution in the road-system, which previously had been arranged for commercial and military purposes with a view to easy communication with Rome. We must therefore go back to an older road-system, of which Rome was the centre. According to that system all roads led to Rome: all the products of the provinces of Asia Minor, from the huge monolithic columns of Phrygian marble to the red Cappadocian earth (μίλτος) for making pencils, were carried to the harbour of Ephesos, and thence shipped to the West; from Rome came all the governors and officials, and to Rome they returned; along the same roads all alike travelled, merchants, officials, tourists, every one who was attracted towards the great centre of life. The same road-system, on the whole, existed under the Greek kings, except that it was unorganised and only inchoate. The only road whose existence is expressly attested under the Greek kings, and whose course is described, coincides with the great Roman highway from Caesareia to Ephesos. But before the conquest of Alexander we find a different set of roads, whose course testifies to a wholly different system of communication, and opens a glimpse into another period in the history of the country.

II. The "Royal Road."

Herodotus describes the great road of the Persian period from Ephesos by the Cilician Gates to Susa. It was called the "Royal Road," because the service of the Great King passed along it; and it was, therefore, the direct path of communication for all government business. This road crossed the Halys by a bridge, which Herodotus had heard of, probably from the narrative of merchants at Sinope, among whom a bridge over such a great river as the Halys was certainly considered a wonderful work of engineering. Now the centre of Asia Minor is occupied by a great salt lake and a salt desert, and there are really only two routes across the plateau from east to west, one south and the other north of the desert. If the "Royal Road" had passed south of the desert, it could not have crossed the Halys; it must, therefore, have taken the northern route.

The southern route is the great highway of the Graeco-Roman period. The history of Asia Minor for six or seven centuries depends mainly on it. It is a far shorter way from Ephesos to the Cilician Gates than the northern route, which involves an immense détour. It is also by far the easier. It follows the one easy path that nature has made between the Aegean coast and the high grounds of the plateau, while the northern route has a very difficult path for a hundred miles in the western part of its course. What was the reason why the Persian road preferred the difficult and circuitous to the direct and easy route? The only reason can be, that the Persians simply kept up a road which had developed in an older period, when the situation of the governing centre made it the natural road. It is an accepted fact that in several other cases roads of the Persian Empire were used by the Assyrian kings long before the Persian time, and, in particular, that the eastern part of the "Royal Road," from Cilicia to Susa, is much older than the beginning of the Persian power.

A similar phenomenon presents itself in the eastern part of Asia Minor. At the present time the harbour for Cappadocia is either Samsun on the north coast, or Mersina on the south. In the time of Strabo, the harbour on the north coast was the same, and he describes the great trade-route from Central Asia by Komana Pontica to Amisos (Samsun), which obviously coincides with the modern route, Sivas-Tokat-Samsun (See below, p. 262.) But if we go back to an older time, we find that not Amisos, but Sinope, was the harbour on the north for the products of Cappadocia and Central Asia. In the time of Strabo, Sinope was a city whose greatness lay in the past. Its situation, as the natural harbour of a coast district, and one of the three chief seats of the tunny fishery, gave it a certain importance, and even at the present day Sinub, as it is still called, is a harbour where the Turkish steamers call. But this is not sufficient to account for its great importance in older history. It could not have been such a centre of historical legend as it is, except as the port of the eastern trade. Curtius has recognised the secret of the early greatness of Sinope* as lying in the fact that it was the terminus of a caravan-route along which the products of the East were brought to the Greek cities. To Sinope converged the routes from the Euphrates, by Mazaka (Cæsareia in later times) and from the Cilician Gates by Tyana. But before the first century B.C. Sinope had lost this advantage. The trade of the East was borne, chiefly to Ephesos by the great Græco-Roman highway from the Euphrates and Caesareia-Mazaka, partly also to Amisos by Sebasteia, Komana, and Laodiceia.

One trace of this early importance of Sinope as the harbour of the Cappadocian trade is preserved by Strabo (p. 540). The red earth ($\mu i\lambda\tau o\varsigma$) which was found in Cappadocia was much used in Greece and Italy. During the last centuries B.C. it was carried along the great eastern highway of Græco-Roman time to Ephesos, and there shipped to the West; but before that commercial route had been organised, the red earth had found its way to Greece by Sinope, and was known to the Greeks only as Sinopic Earth.

Now the natural road, the easiest and shortest, from Cappodocia in general to the Black Sea, goes to Amisos. Sinope is cut off from the interior by broad and lofty mountains, most difficult to traverse.† We have here a second case, where the earlier road prefers the longer and more difficult route to the shorter and easier, and the reason must be the same: the road must have come into existence at a time when the centre of power made it the natural one.

These two roads, from Ephesos to the Cilician Gates over the Halys, and from Central Cappadocia to Sinope, meet in the parts of Galatia east of the Halys. Precisely in this quarter lie the most remarkable remains of early Anatolian history.

At Boghaz Keui are situated the ruins of by far the most extensive ancient city in Asia Minor. Its wall, whose remains show that it was of great thickness and height, embraces a circuit of four or five miles.‡ The remains of a palace (or possibly temple) in it are unique in Asia Minor for size and style. The rock-sculptures beside it show it to have been an important religious centre. Here we have the only city in Asia Minor which is marked by its remains as a ruling city of the Oriental type, unaffected by, and earlier than, Greek influence. Its situation explains all the difficulties presented by the early roads. It communicated naturally with Sinope, and the road from it to Ephesos crosses

---

* Griech. Gesch., ed. 5, vol. I. p. 408.

† I have never crossed this road, but, according to Sir C. Wilson, its difficulty was described by Col. (then Lieutenant) Kitchener in the very strongest terms.

‡ I speak from eyesight only; but Dr. Humann, who has surveyed the whole site, tells me that the estimate is not exaggerated.

the Halys. We are thus led back to an early state of Asia Minor, when a great capital at Boghaz Keui communicated on the one hand with the East through the Cilician Gates, on the other hand with Ephesos. The road from the Gates to the capital passed through Cappadocia, and the products of Cappadocia were carried along it, and then on to Sinope. The name Pteria, which its discoverer Texier saw to be right, has been accepted by every traveller. History has recorded only one fact about it. When Crœsus made war against the Persian conqueror of the Median Empire, he marched on Pteria.* He crossed the Halys by a bridge, obviously the bridge on the Royal Road, along which therefore his march was directed from Sardis to Pteria. A bridge implies a road, and in this passage we have a clear proof that the "Royal Road" was already in use before the Persians had entered Asia Minor.

Other considerations show that this road is older than the Persian period. Herodotus represents it as known to Aristagoras, and therefore, existing during the sixth century, B.C., and the Persians had had no time to organise a great road like this before 500; they only used the previously existing road. Moreover, the Lydian kings seem to have paid some attention to their roads, and perhaps even to have measured them, as we may gather from Herodotus's account of the roads in the Lycus valley, and of the boundary pillar erected by Crœsus at Kydrara.†

The exact route which this "Royal Road" followed between Pteria and Sardis cannot be determined with certainty, but in all probability it went by Pessinus and the city of unknown name which lies above the Tomb of Midas. Sculptures, similar to those of Pteria, are found at intervals along this route. The style of art is similar, and they are generally accompanied by hieroglyphics of the same type. Whereas the cities on the southern route, the great Græco-Roman highway, bear names which belong to the Greek or the early Imperial period: Cæsareia, Archelais, Laodiceia Combusta, Philomelion, Julia, Lysias, Apameia, Laodiceia ad Lycum, Antiocheia, Nysa;‡ the names of the cities on the northern route are of an older stamp: Tavium, Ankyra, Gordion, Pessinus, Orkistos, Akmonia, Satala, Sardeis.§ Yet some of these cities were, at one time, great religious and commercial

---

* Herod. I. 76. He declares his own opinion that Crœsus crossed by the bridge, but mentions the common Greek story that Thales had enabled the army to cross by dividing the river. Herodotus, who had heard at Sinope of the Halys bridge, saw that Crœsus must have crossed by it, but the fact is inferred, and not taken from written authority, nor even from popular tradition.

† Herod. VII. 30.—ἔνθα στήλη καταπεπηγυῖα, σταθεῖσα δὲ ὑπὸ Κροίσου, καταμηνύει διὰ γραμμάτων τοὺς οὔρους.

‡ Several, perhaps all, of these cities had an earlier existence and name, but the refoundation under a new name was generally on a new site, chosen for commercial convenience.

§ Trajanopolis is the only exception: Ankyra was called also Sebaste, but the name never acquired popular currency. Trajanopolis is balanced by Hadrianopolis on the southern road.

centres,* and they could not have become so unless they were on an important track of communication; moreover, they were greater in the earlier period, as is shown by their place in legend, while in the Roman period they are either ordinary provincial cities like Pessinus, or mere villages like Gordion.

Greek historical legend always localises the old Phrygian kings, not in southern Phrygia on the later route, but in the broad Sangarios valley traversed by this older route.

The following are the points where I think that traces of this old road exist. Between Ephesos and Sardis it crossed the pass of Kara Bel, in which are the two monuments of Syro-Cappadocian art, one of which has long been known as the "Sesostris." Near Sardis it probably joined another road of this earlier period, coming from Phokaia and Kyme by the north side of Mount Sipylos, past the famous "Niobe," another monument of Syro-Cappadocian art, really a cult-statue of the Great Goddess Meter Kybele.† From Sardis its first stage cannot be doubtful; it went nearly due east, not far from the course of the Mæander, passing through Satala,‡ the seat of a cultus of a goddess Artemis-Anaitis-Leto, which appears to have been the chief religion of the *Katakekaumene*. I think that there is a large tumulus about the place where it probably issued from the mountains on to the plain of Ushak (Temenothyrai and Grimenothyrai).§ It must have passed through Keramon Agora (Islam Keui), for there is no other possible road. A little south-west of Islam Keui, close to the natural line of the road, is a large tumulus. It must then have ascended the Hamam Su, and climbed the slope of the ridge in which that river rises. On the highest point of this ridge, close to the line of the road, is another large tumulus. At this point alternative routes are open: the road might either turn to the south-east through Prymnessos and Amorion to Pessinus, or keep on towards the north-east. The road probably followed the latter route, traversed hilly country and issued on to the plain of Altyntash at *Besh Karish Eyuk*, "Five Span Mound," a village which derives its name from the large tumulus beside it. It

* Gordium haud magnum quidem oppidum, sed plus quam mediterraneum celebre et frequens emporium.—Liv. 38, 18. Πεσσίνους ἐμπόριον τῶν ταύτῃ μέγιστον· οἱ δ᾽ ἱερεῖς τὸ παλαιὸν μὲν δυνάσται τινὲς ἦσαν.—Strab., p. 567.

† Herodotus's statement — δύο τύποι ἐν πέτρῃσι ἐγκεκολαμμένοι τούτου τοῦ ἀνδρὸς (i.e. Sesostris) τῇ τε ἐκ τῆς Ἐφεσίης ἐς Φώκαιαν ἔρχονται, καὶ τῇ ἐκ Σαρδίων ἐς Σμύρνην, —which is, strictly understood, utterly incorrect, is perhaps a confused account founded in a report or description of these two monuments, one on the road Phocaea to Sardis, the other on the road Ephesos to Sardis. (See Chapter IV., p. 60.)

‡ The name Satala also occurs in Armenia; it retains its name as Sandal near Koula. —Cf. 'Journ. Hell. Stud.' 1887, p. 519. From Satala there are two alternatives, through Kadoi and Bel Ova, or through Trajanopolis and Keramon Agora; they meet at Five Span Mound (Besh Karish Eyuk).

§ I speak from recollection of my first journey in May 1881. It is not mentioned in my notes.

crosses the plain nearly due east, and enters the hills again beside Bey
Keui. In the pass by which it enters the hills is a large tumulus, out
of which I have dug a block of stone, of a trachytic species, on which is
an inscription in Syro-Cappadocian hieroglyphics. It then crossed the
hills to Bakshish, Yapuldak, and the city over the Tomb of Midas,
where there is at least one monument of Syro-Cappadocian art. It then
went nearly due east to Orkistos, crossed the Sangarios to Pessinus,
traversed the hills to Gordion,* and then, passing the Sangarios a
second time, ascended the Hamam Su to its source beside the Syro-
Cappadocian monuments of Giaour Kalesi. Up to this point the possible
routes are so few, that when we assume that Pessinus and the Midas
city were on the road, its course is nearly certain. Natural conditions
leave no choice. But east of Giaour Kalessi it is very difficult to
determine the exact path, partly because the country is so little
known, partly because there are more alternatives open. It probably
passed actually through Ankyra, which appears to have been an important city before the Gauls entered the country.

Such a road as this implies a considerable amount of regular intercourse and a fairly settled and peaceful state of the country, and
may be considered to prove that there was, long before the Persian
conquest, a well-developed civilisation along the north side of the plateau
of Asia Minor, that there was regular and frequent communication from
Sardis to the countries beyond the Halys, and that peaceful and settled
government maintained and encouraged this communication by a well-
constructed road with at least one bridge. It is a striking fact that
sufficient civilisation and engineering skill to build a bridge over a deep
and rapid river like the Halys already prevailed in the highlands of
Asia Minor before the middle of the sixth century B.C. It may very
safely be affirmed that after the Persian conquest the skill to make such
a bridge did not exist until we come down to the time of the Romans.
We may gather from the language of Herodotus that this bridge
was famous as a wonder among the Greeks of Sinope, none of whom
had ever seen it, but who knew it by report. All the other great
rivers on the Royal Road are crossed by boats; the Halys alone has a
bridge.

Whether there was a regularly consolidated empire in Asia with a
capital at Pteria, or whether this state of peace and commercial intercourse was due to a homogeneous civilisation and religion over the
country, must remain doubtful. But the evidence seems clear that such
a homogeneous religion and social organisation did exist over the whole
country, characterised by the worship of a Mother-Goddess, Kybele or
Leto. In this connection I shall refer to one point which has some
geographical bearing. The sacredness of the pig as a purificatory sacri-

* On the site of Gordion at the village Yürme, see p. 225. Germa is usually
placed, in defiance of epigraphic evidence, at Yürme; but Humann, who has seen the
place, agrees with me in doubting the identification (see p. 16).

fice is a remarkable feature in the religion of Greece. It is not a feature which is original to the Hellenic tribes, as is proved by various arguments—(1) The pig as a purificatory sacrifice is not found in those religions which seem to be most purely Hellenic, whereas it is found in those which on other grounds are generally believed to be borrowed. (2) The ritual of purification for murder, which involved the sacrifice of a pig, was identical in Greece and in Lydia, as Herodotus mentions * : Lydia certainly did not learn religion from Greece, but Greece probably did from Lydia (Pausan. VI., 22, 1).

East of the Halys we find that the Semitic horror of the pig prevails; this is not the case west of the Halys. At Komana Pontica the presence of a pig, even in the city, much more in the sacred precinct, was forbidden.† But in Lycia we see a pig under the seat of the deified dead on the Harpy Tomb. In Lydia the pig was a purificatory sacrifice. I bought a small image of a pig in Egyptian porcelain, which I believe to have been found in a tumulus at the Bin Tepe near Sardis; and the late Mr. James Whittall, of Smyrna, possessed a small archaic terra-cotta pig, which he believed to have been found there also. In Phrygia the custom of sacrificing the pig is proved to have existed by the curious story which Strabo (p. 576) tells of Cleon, the Phrygian robber-chief, who was raised by Augustus to the high-priesthood of Komana Pontica, and who shocked the priests there by sacrificing pigs: it is clear that he was simply carrying out his national habit of sacrifice. The Semitic horror of this animal which prevailed east of the Halys was probably due to the conquest of that part of Asia Minor by the Assyrians, who never actually penetrated west of the Halys. The detestation of the pig is natural to the hotter countries of the south, where its flesh is an unhealthy and hardly eatable food. A northern nation does not naturally share this horror.

The boundary between the pig-eaters and the pig-haters was not exactly at the Halys. In Pessinus, according to Pausanias, VII., 17, 10, the rule of abstinence from the flesh of the pig existed, and this abstinence may be taken to imply general horror of the animal, and the belief that it caused impurity to every thing and person that touched it. But the influence of the eastern religion on the west may have spread the Semitic idea beyond the actual bounds of Semitic rule; and history shows a continuous process of religious influence from east to west.

Whatever be its origin, the difference between western Asia Minor and Greece on the one hand, and eastern Asia Minor, beginning from Pessinus on the other hand, is most striking. In the west the pig is used in the holiest ceremonies; its image accompanies the dead to their graves to purify them, and the living wash with their own hands (in Greece at least) the pig which is to be their sacrifice. In the east the

---

* Herod. I. 35.—ἔστι δὲ παραπλησίη ἡ κάθαρσις τοῖσι Λυδοῖσι καὶ τοῖσι Ἕλλησι.
† Strab., p. 575.

very presence of a pig in the holy city is a profanation and an impurity. My theory of explanation is that the religion which prevailed throughout Asia Minor in early time was the religion of a northern race which had no horror of the pig, and that Semitic influence subsequently introduced that horror into the eastern parts of the country.

I have unhesitatingly assumed the truth of the identification of Boghaz Keui with Pteria; but this is not universally accepted,* and it may therefore be advisable to discuss the evidence. In the first place the ruins at Boghaz Keui are those of the greatest city of Asia Minor in early times, and are on such a scale as to leave no doubt in the mind of any trained observer that they must belong to the metropolis of a great empire. In the next place the description of the roads which has just been given, proves that the capital of a great empire in early time must have been situated somewhere in the country where Boghaz Keui is situated. In the third place, when we are informed that Crœsus declared war against the Medes and marched on Pteria, the natural inference is that Pteria was the Anatolian metropolis of the Median empire: this of course is an assumption, but no one who makes that assumption and has seen Boghaz Keui can doubt the identification. The only other hypothesis that is open, is that Pteria was not the metropolis, but merely a fortress of the Median empire. In that case Pteria loses all interest for us, and we must be content to be ignorant of the name of the metropolis. But, in the fourth place, Pteria was probably situated on a road that led from Sinope direct south across the peninsula to the Cilician coast, and Boghaz Keui is situated on that road. If the former assertion can be proved, then the identity of Pteria and Boghaz Keui may be regarded as proved, so far as proof can be expected in ancient topography without actual epigraphic evidence discovered on the spot. The proof of this statement, that Pteria was situated on a road from Sinope to Cilicia, lies in Herodotus, I. 76. Herodotus considers that the north coast is a line extending east and west, and that Pteria was situated on a line at right angles to this,† extending from Sinope southwards. This line was, as I believe, the road from Sinope by Boghaz Keui and Tyana to the Cilician Gates. It is obvious that Herodotus had no knowledge of the interior of the country except what he gathered from the report of traders at Sinope, who told him about the road to the south, about Pteria, and about the Halys bridge (I. 75).

We naturally ask about the date of this ancient empire. I think it is possible to indicate approximately the time of its downfall in western

* All travellers who have seen the place, I think, accept the identification; but I have added this paragraph on account of the scepticism of a foreign friend, whose opinion is of value in all matters connected with Asia Minor. I am now glad to see that the identification of Pteria is also accepted by Humann-Puchstein, "Reisen in Kleinasien."

† ἡ Πτερίη, κατὰ Σινώπην . . . μάλιστά κη κειμένη.

Asia Minor.   In the wide plains of the Sangarios it gave place to another race, the Phrygians, whose half-mythical, half-historical kings are familiar in history.   Our Greek authorities unanimously assert that the Phrygians are a European race, some of whom found their way across the Hellespont into Asia, while others continued to exist under the name Briges in Macedonia.   I have found myself gradually forced by archæological evidence to the same conclusion.   I believe that the Phrygians penetrated across the Troad; that the Troy whose power and whose downfall supply a slight historical basis for the Iliad was probably their earliest foundation in Asia; that they were originally a people of the coast, and that they were forced up into the interior by later migrations of barbarous Thracian tribes into Asia Minor.   The Greek chronologists mention that in early times the Phrygian ships ruled the Aegean Sea (911–900), and the time when they were forced up into the Sangarios valley may be approximately fixed in the earlier half of the ninth century before Christ.   The statement in Iliad, III. 185, that Priam of Troy had assisted the Phrygians in their wars against the Amazons on the banks of the Sangarios, probably contains a reminiscence of the actual wars between the people of Pteria and the Phrygians.

About 900 B.C., therefore, the ancient empire, whose capital was Ptéria, began to decay.   On the west it gave place to the Phrygians; on the east and south-east the peoples of Syria and Assyria pressed on it. Pteria, however, long continued to be the great city of Cappadocia and the seat of foreign governors : changes and the growth of new cities are slow in an Oriental empire, but at last Pteria did give place to cities on the direct routes of later times.

The hypothesis which identifies the people of Pteria with the Hittites of north Syria has found numerous adherents; but it appears to me to require considerable modification before it can be accepted. That hypothesis, in the form in which it is usually put, necessitates a capital far to the south in Syria, and leaves the old road and the situation of Pteria quite unintelligible.   Pteria must at one time have been the capital of an empire, for it lies so far out of the direct lines of communication with the capitals of Assyrian or Persian power that its origin under these later empires is impossible.   But the close relationship, I might almost say the identity, of art and hieroglyphic writing which prevails between the early monuments of Asia Minor and the Hittite monuments of northern Syria seems to me a fact which must be the starting-point of all hypotheses.   This close relationship has to be explained in some way or other, but the analogy of Seljuk* Turkish art, which is

---

* The Seljuk monuments, almost unknown to Europeans, are the most beautiful ruins in Asia Minor.   They abound in the cities from Konia eastward.   Strictly, as Sir C. Wilson writes, the style of art in the Seljuk remains is Persian; the Seljuks of Roum or Asia Minor shared in the art of the Seljuk Grand Sultan's court, where Arabic was the language.

purely Arabic in style and language, shows that identity of art does not necessarily prove identity of race. The Hittite monuments in Syria are clearly more developed in style and later in date than those of Asia Minor, with the exception of the rock-sculpture at Ibriz, which is later in character.

An important road probably existed, connecting Pteria with Assyria by the Anti-Taurus region, traversing Taurus by the important pass between Al-Bostan and Marash (or in ancient times between Arabissos and Germaniceia). It probably passed through Komana and Mazaka. Professor Kiepert* long ago observed the difficulty of understanding why the " Royal Road " should cross the Halys instead of taking the shorter southern route. His explanation, that the " Royal Road " went north in order to join the trade-route from the Euphrates to Sinope, is, however, not sufficient. He gives no explanation of the equally difficult fact that Sinope was the old harbour for the Asiatic trade. But he has seen that the explanation of the Persian road lies in the existence of an older line of road, and I have merely carried this principle a little further.

III. Beginning of the Trade-Route.

When Asia Minor was only a province of an empire whose governing centre was in Mesopotamia or Persia, the natural road from the Ægean coast to the capital was the southern route, and this road gradually came into use during the Persian period. The earliest direct proof of the existence of this trade-route is the quotation given by Strabo (p. 623) from Artemidorus (about B.C. 100). But the foundation of such cities as Laodiceia (twice), Apameia, and Antiocheia, shows that the route was important as early as the third century before Christ. These cities were founded as centres of Greek influence, and their situations were selected on the most important line of communication. It is an interesting and suggestive detail that the gate of Laodiceia *ad Lycum*, through which this road issued, was called the " Syrian Gate." The custom of naming city-gates according to the chief object of the road which issued through them is well known.† The importance of the route as early as 301 B.C. is proved by the campaign which ended in the battle of Ipsos. Seleucus coming from Cappadocia, and Lysimachus coming from Heracleia, succeeded in effecting a junction, and the decisive battle was fought at Ipsos. Now Ipsos, the later Julia, is a city on the direct line of the road, while Synnada is only a little way to the north of the road, and indeed it was a frequent custom to take Synnada on the line of road by a slight détour. The events show the critical importance of this part of the road, and therefore imply the existence of the whole road. It is probable that the design of Antigonus was to

* 'Berl. Monatsber.' 1857, p. 126 f.
† Magnesian Gate at Ephesos, Ephesian Gate at Smyrna, &c.

prevent the junction of his enemies' forces by intercepting Seleucus during his march from the east; but the allied kings eluded him either by concentrating along the northern route in the north of Phrygia, and then advancing towards Synnada to give him battle, or by concentrating along the southern route about Ipsos before Antigonus expected them.

Even during the fifth century we can trace the southern route. When Alcibiades was on his way, in 404 B.C., to the court of Artaxerxes, he was assassinated at Melissa, a village on the road between Synnada and Metropolis, where Hadrian afterwards erected a statue to his memory (Athen, p. 574).* He was therefore travelling along the southern route towards the Persian court, and the incident proves that the southern route was already in use for communication with the east as early as the latter part of the fifth century. It may be traced more doubtfully at an even earlier period. In the spring of B.C. 480, Xerxes, after his army had mustered in Cappadocia at Kritala, crossed the Halys, according to Herodotus, VII. 26, and therefore took the northern route, but instead of attempting the difficult passage of the mountains by Satala, he crossed Phrygia from north to south, and came along the easy southern route by Celænæ and Colossæ. Such a circuitous march seems so improbable as to suggest that Herodotus mentions the Halys in this case only because he knew that the Halys separated Cappadocia from Phrygia,† and therefore concluded that Xerxes must have crossed it on his march from Cappadocia across Phrygia. The question may be asked whether such an error is in accordance with Herodotus's knowledge of the geography of Asia Minor.

---

* Melissa was probably situated at Baljik Hisar, two hours south of Synnada, where there are ancient remains with what the natives called a *kale* on the summit of a little hill, round which the road winds upward. *Bal* in Turkish means *honey*, and *jik* is the diminutive termination, hence there may be a connection between the ancient name Melissa and the modern name. I know no other point on the road where Melissa could possibly be placed, and have little hesitation in placing it here, although the following epigram on a stele built into a foundation by the roadside near the village might at first sight seem inconsistent :—

> Ἀρχιερεὺς Ἀσίης Δημήτριος οὗτος ἐκεῖνος,
> ὃν πάντω(ν) φωναί φασι πολυστέφανον,
> Θυνναρίδαι δ'ἔστησαν ἐν εἰκόνι δόγματι κοινῷ
> βουλῆς καὶ δήμου κλεινὸν ἄγαλμα πάτρης.

The Thynnaridai are the people of Synnada, as descendants of Thynnaros, a local hero mentioned on coins of the city, as Drexler has observed in ‘Numism. Zft.’ 1889, p. 177. But Melissa must certainly have been a village of the territory of some city, probably of Synnada, for it was not a self-governing city; and its inhabitants would therefore be Synnadeis or Thynnaridai. Drexler describes the coin in question as follows: obv., bearded head to right, ΘΥΝΝΑΡΟϹ; rev., Isis standing to left, in r. sistrum, in l. situla. Perhaps Thynnaros was a hero of native Phrygian legend, while Akamas, who appears on coins and who is mentioned by Stephanus as founder of the city, was a hero of the Dorian and Ionian colonists, who were settled in the city when the Greek foundation was made. See p. 14.

† Compare I. 72.

With one exception, all references which he makes to the geography of the plateau are vague notices which he has gained either from the traders of Sinope or from those of Miletos. From the former he learned that the breadth of Asia Minor in the narrowest place, i.e. from Tarsos through the Cilician Gates direct north, was five days' journey for an active man (I. 72), and that Pteria was over against Sinope, i.e. it lay on a road which led direct south from Sinope. He also heard from them the description of the great bridge over the Halys, and of the precautions and guards upon it.

From the latter he heard of the road up the Mæander valley to Colossæ and Celænæ, and of the natural wonders of both places. The existence of communication and trade between Miletos and Phrygia is attested as early as the sixth century by Hipponax, who mentions the bad Greek spoken by the Phrygian traders at Miletos; * and the only possible road from Miletos to Phrygia goes up the Mæander to Celænæ-Apameia.

The only passage in which Herodotus gives any thoroughly trustworthy information about the roads of Central Anatolia is the description of the " Royal Road," which has generally been recognised as founded on an official document. He certainly believed that the Halys separated Phrygia and Cappadocia (I. 72), and it is therefore not out of keeping with his method or with the amount of knowledge which he shows of the interior that he should have made the error which has been suggested above.

If we could assume that Herodotus had no express evidence that the march of Xerxes crossed the Halys, and that the statement is merely due to the vague geographical ideas of his time, we should have in the march of Xerxes from Cappadocia viâ Celænæ, a distinct proof that the advantages of the southern route had become known as early as 481 B.C. Such evidence, which explains away a direct statement, is not of course in itself trustworthy, and it will be proved in a subsequent paragraph that Herodotus is right. But we are not dependent on this passage alone for evidence. An early monument of the Cappadocian art and hieroglyphics exist on the direct line of the road from Celænæ to the Cilician Gates, viz. at Tyriaion, which seems at one time to have been a great city, though it was in later years overshadowed by Laodiceia Combusta and Philomelion. This monument, taken in conjunction with the traces of a city, now almost wholly buried, is a proof that a certain amount of intercourse existed along the line of this road at an early time.

The view then, which is most probable, is that the southern route

---

* Καὶ τοὺς σολοίκους, ἢν λάβωσι, περνᾶσιν

Φρύγας μὲν ἐς Μίλητον ἀλφιτεύσοντας.—' Hipponax,' frag. 36 (30).

The story of Tottes and Onnes, the Phrygians who introduced their ἱερὰ to Assessos, also vouches for this intercourse.

from the Cilician Gates direct to the west through Lykaonia and southern Phrygia was gradually developed at a later period than the northern route from Pteria to Sardis. In the case of the northern route, a doubt has been expressed above * whether it was formed to connect two chief centres of a single great empire, or grew up owing to commercial intercourse, accompanying the spread of a homogeneous civilisation and religion from the monarchy in the north-east, of which Pteria was the capital. But in the case of the southern route no such doubt can exist; it was certainly formed by the gradual penetration of commerce and intercourse, pushing on the one hand west from the Cilician Gates, on the other hand east from the Mæander and the Lycus valley. In the first place it was in process of formation at a period so recent that there can be no question of the existence of an empire in Asia Minor. In the second place its character and the obvious preference of ease to straightness in several sections, mark it as a caravan route. It is only in highly developed commerce that rapidity of transmission becomes really important; the caravans and the muleteers of more primitive trade jog along the traditional route that is most advantageous to their animals, without any wish to gain a few hours by any bold path. Moreover, we can perhaps trace certain tentative routes from the side, both of the east and of the west, which proved unsuitable and were disused in favour of the route that is described by Strabo, p. 623. These tentatives will be described in the following paragraphs; but first the contrast in all these respects between the northern and the southern routes suggests itself. The existence of the northern route has been traced back to a period earlier than the Assyrian domination in Cappadocia, and probably earlier than 900 B.C. So far as we can trace its character it prefers the direct path to the easy one, and aims at rapidity of communication; it has not the character of a trade and caravan route, but of a military and administrative road. So far therefore as the evidence from this side goes, it tells in favour of the hypothesis already suggested by Orientalists, that there was at one period an empire embracing some considerable part of Asia Minor, and that this empire was already in process of decay before 900 B.C. But whereas some Orientalists place the governing centre of that empire in Northern Syria, the evidence that has been stated above necessitates its position at Pteria, and makes the Syrian parts of the empire mere dependencies, which apparently acquired independence and strength at a later period, when Pteria lost its imperial character. Hence the monuments of Northern Syria belong to a later period than those of Pteria, and hence they show a certain difference of type, which I have described as Assyrian, in contrast to the Egyptian character of Pterian art. This difference of character has misled Prof. G. Hirsch-

---

* See p. 31.

feld * to deny all connection between the two groups of monuments. The differences which he has pointed out certainly exist, and have been acknowledged more or less distinctly by almost all observers; but his denial of all community of character is as great an error on the one side as the denial of any difference of character and period would be on the other. There is every probability that Cilicia shared in this later development of Syro-Cappadocian art, and that from Cilicia that art, with the accompanying civilisation and religion, spread through the Cilician Gates towards the west. As they spread westwards, the path of commerce was opened up, and thus the great trade route between the Aegean coast and the east gradually came into use. Whether all the monuments that mark the early stages of the trade route are to be attributed to this later period, or whether any belong to the older Pterian imperial period, is uncertain. Tyana or Dana † must probably have been important in both periods, but especially so in the later period: the same may have been the case with other places. The hieroglyphic inscriptions of Tyana and of Tyriaion belong to the later period, as does also the rock monument of Ibriz beside Kybistra-Herakleia. But the clay tablets with cuneiform inscriptions, which probably come from Tyana,‡ though I bought them at Caesareia-Mazaka (Kaisari), are considered by Orientalists to be comparatively early; and the monument of Fassiller (Dalisandos) appears to me to show more analogy with Pterian art than with that of a later period,§ though such an inference from a single monument of a peculiar and unusual type is naturally very uncertain.

As communication pushed westwards from the Cilician Gates, it first attempted the path along the northern skirts of Mount Taurus, by Kybistra-Herakleia, Dalisandos, and perhaps Parlais.‖ There the Pisidian mountains barred its further progress to the west. It turned northwards up the east shore of Lake Karalis, and also began to seek a direct path on a more northerly line through Iconium and Vasada. This stage is marked by the monument of Iflatun Bunar (Plato's Spring ¶).

* I state frankly and bluntly my own opinion. The gradual progress of discovery will show which view is right. In the meantime the method which is most likely to assist progress is that each person should state clearly his own opinion, and carry it out to its logical conclus⸍ ns, acknowledging that, as yet, certainty is not attainable, owing to the scantiness of evidence. † See p. 449.

‡ See pp. 449 and 346-8. In 1890 we could find no evidence that these tablets have been found at Tyana: perhaps they originate from Komana or even Mazaka itself.

§ See my paper on "Syro-Cappadocian Monuments in Asia Minor," in 'Athen. Mittheil.,' 1889.

‖ See p. 390, ff. The remarkable types on coins of Parlais suggest that remains of a pre-Roman religious centre ought to be discovered there.

¶ The curious name dates from the Seljuk period, and is a proof of the interest in Greek philosophy (through Arabic translations probably) that characterised the Seljuk court at Konia. Another Iflatun Bunar exists on the palace hill at Konia. Popular pronunciation uses also the forms Elfatun and Elflatun Bunar.

Finally the long inscription at Köli-tolu, near Tyriaion,* marks the line which was ultimately adopted through Laodiceia Combusta and Thymbrion-Hadrianopolis.

On the west similar tentative routes may be traced, as the line of rade between Miletos and Celaenae, which was in existence in the time of Hipponax, six centuries before Christ, pushed towards the inner country. At first a connection with the " Royal Road " was probably established through Hieropolis (near Sandykli) and the northern Metropolis of Phrygia (at Ayaz Inn). This connection has left no monument; but is rendered probable by the tumuli on the route and by the existence of an old religious centre at Hieropolis: round this centre are gathered reminiscences of the old Phrygian heroes and religion, Mygdon,† Otreus (the Phrygian form of Atreus), and Aeneas.‡

A better connection was established through the southern Metropolis, Synnada, and Dokimion as early as the fourth century; this is to be inferred from the foundation of a Macedonian colony at Dokimion, bearing the name of Dokimos, who in B.C. 302 surrendered Synnada to Lysimachus, and from the foundation of Synnada itself. Such colonies were always founded as military stations and centres of Greek civilisation and government on important roads. Now the only roads that can come into account as determining the situation of Dokimion are the route from Celaenae to Dorylaion and Bithynia, and that from Celaenae towards Galatia or rather north-eastern Phrygia, i.e. the connection with the " Royal Road." But, of these two routes, the former would naturally take the far shorter and easier path by the northern Metropolis and Hieropolis, which was already in existence; and moreover it is highly improbable that the Bithynian connection was important at that time; whereas the connection with Pessinus and Ankyra was certainly important. The foundation of a Greek colony at Dokimion, compared with the foundation of Synnada,§ probably about the same time, marks the importance of the route Apameia-Synnada-Dokimion-Pessinus in the period 350–300, and may therefore be taken as a proof both that the connection between east and west was

---

* " Syro-Cappadocian Monuments " in ' Athen. Mittheil.,' 1889.

† Pausanias, X. 27, 1. On the whole subject see my " Trois Villes Phrygiennes," in ' Bull. Corr. Hell.,' 1882; and below, p. 139.

‡ I see no reason, with Imhoof-Blumer, ' Monn. Gr.,' p. 412 (see also Head, ' Hist. Num.,' 567, 569), to doubt that Aeneas is meant on the coins of the two cities, Otrous and Stektorion, three miles distant from each other, which are described by Mionnet and himself. I hope that the analogies quoted in my " Trois Villes Phryg.," and the explanation of the name Brouzos for Broughios = Φρούγιος (see CB, § xviii.) establish this. The legends have taken a Greek form, as was always the case in Lydia and Phrygia, as Greek literature became known, but the names of the heroes are rooted in the district.

§ Smaller native settlements of older date on or near the site are of course not excluded by the term " foundation."

seeking the best route by way of Celaenae-Apameia, and that it had not so early as 300 B.C. settled down to the one route that was finally adopted. When, however, Synnada was founded, no long time could elapse before the route by Lysias, Philomelion, and Tyriaion established itself in preference to any other.

The answer to the doubt expressed on the preceding page about the description that is given by Herodotus of the route of Xerxes is now obvious. Herodotus is quite right; and the very difficulty of reconciling his account with the character of the country and the routes known in subsequent centuries, adds additional evidence to corroborate the history of the roads as here stated. According to the account of Herodotus, VII. 26, Xerxes, after mustering his army in Cappadocia at Kritala, which may probably be placed in the plain of Tyana (pp. 346-8), crossed the Halys and traversed Phrygia, i.e., marched along the " Royal Road." He reached Celaenae, and must therefore have taken one or other of the routes just described, passing either by Synnada or by Hieropolis. Circuitous as the march seems, the record is clear, and when other considerations have led us to the view that such a road was at the time in use, it seems imperatively necessary to accept the authority of Herodotus. Nearly eighty years later Alcibiades, when proceeding to the Persian court, also took the route through Melissa and Synnada.

I must here refer for a moment to a great expedition which is connected with this road—the Anabasis of Cyrus and Xenophon in 401 B.C. Cyrus started from Sardis, passed by the spot where Laodiceia was afterwards founded, and advanced to Apameia-Celænæ. Here he turned off the road and made a wide détour to the north. This strange détour has always been a puzzle. Perhaps the explanation is that if he advanced straight to the east, he feared lest the object of his march might become evident to the Greeks, and he was as yet very doubtful whether he could trust them. He therefore turned right away back towards the north-west, and after a long circuit, ventured to lead the army eastwards; when his object became apparent, he found great difficulty in inducing the Greek mercenaries to accompany him.*

Hamilton first determined with general accuracy the line of Cyrus' march; his only serious error is in the position of Keramon Agora. From Celænæ Cyrus marched down the Mæander to Peltæ (see p. 136); he then turned straight north to Keramon Agora, beside the modern Islam Keui. This is an exceedingly important point on the modern road system, lying at the entrance of the valley which divides two lofty and impassable ranges of mountains. Roads to the north, north-east, and east all pass through the same valley, that of the little river Hamam Su. Keramon Agora, the Potters' Market, is never mentioned except in this one passage of Xenophon; it did not rank as

* Xenophon mentions that they only began to suspect the object of the march after they reached Tarsos.

an independent city, it was only a great market, lying in the open plain and incapable of defence, a commercial not a military centre, included in the territory of the great neighbouring fortress Akmonia, which is only a few miles distant. From this point the march of Cyrus coincided for a short distance up the Hamam Su with the route which has been described above as the " Royal Road," but soon he diverged along the great open valley of Phrygia Paroreios to Tyriaion. In this part Hamilton has correctly described his march, except that Thymbrion appears to be the older name of Hadrianopolis on the Karmeios, he river which flows by Doghan Hisar and Arkut Khan. See CB, LI.

Between Tyriaion and the Gates Cyrus marched through Iconium and Dana. His march diverged near the site of Laodiceia Combusta from the later trade-route, and took a more southerly path. From Iconium he went to Dana or Tyana, the important city at the northern entrance to the chief pass through the Cilician Gates, on the line of the " Royal Road."

The line of this march certainly gives no reason to think that the trade-route was yet established. But it is not safe to draw any inference from it, except that, on the supposition that the regular road to the Persian capital still went either by Synnada and Pteria or else by Satala and Pteria, Cyrus's route was excellently calculated to prevent the army from suspecting his design till they reached the Cilician Gates; whereas if the trade-route were in regular and common use, it would be more difficult to understand how the army was so long kept in ignorance of his design. The route agrees perfectly with the view stated above, but could hardly be used as an argument for it.

The objection may here be urged that the " Royal Route " from Sardis to Susa, so far as the evidence now stated goes, must have passed through Apameia, Melissa, and Synnada, not through Satala and Keramon Agora, as I have described it. My reply is that, in the first place, the inference with regard to the primitive importance of Pteria as the metropolis of an empire remains untouched, for it becomes still more difficult than before to understand how a road from Celaenae-Apameia to the Cilician Gates should cross the Halys: the only reason for such an extraordinary détour would lie in the previous existence of a regular road to the metropolis Pteria. The objection therefore only strengthens my main purpose. In the second place the only reason for the road from Ephesos to Susa passing through Sardis * would be to take the way through Satala. Thirdly the distances given by Herodotus are :—

Sardis to the Halys, 94½ parasangs,

Halys to Cilician Gates, 104 parasangs.

These distances are utterly irreconcilable with a route through Celaenae to the Halys, which would be much longer than that from the Halys to

* Herodotus, V. 56, expressly says that the Road began from Ephesos and passed through Sardis; but the way from Ephesos to Celaenae is by the Maeander valley.

the Gates; but the shortest route from Sardis to the Halys through Satala, is a little shorter than that from the Halys through Pteria to the Gates,* and reckoning the parasang at 2½ miles, the measurements are approximately correct. Finally the reasons already advanced seem sufficient to prove the existence of communication and higher civilisation along the north side of the plateau, i.e., along the line we have assigned to the "Royal Road."

The history therefore of the roads of Asia Minor before the Roman period is the slow and gradual substitution of a natural and easy system for a difficult system, which was established originally to suit the convenience of administration during a special condition of the country.

The great trade-route was in regular and exclusive use at least as early as the first century before Christ (Strabo, pp. 540 and 663). The earliest indication of its rising importance is the battle of Ipsos in 301; but the foundation of Dokimion and Synnada show that about that time the older route was still in more common use. It must be remembered that Synnada, though near the trade-route, was not actually situated on it, but was on a northern road which diverges from the trade-route at Metropolis or at Dinia-Chelidonia. It was sufficiently near the trade-route to retain its importance after that route became the great artery of communication across the country. See pp. 139, 142, 171.

IV. THE EASTERN TRADE-ROUTE.

In the preceding chapter it has been shown that this road came into use between 300 and 100 B.C. We have now to trace its development, so far as the scanty indications permit.

Under the Persian empire the main purpose of the "Royal Road" was administrative: that road was maintained with a postal service and regular stations and khans, for the service of the Great King. During the two centuries that followed the conquest of Alexander the Great, the set of intercourse varied at different periods according to the seat of the dominant power for the time being. No dynasty gained complete mastery of the entire peninsula, and the transference of power from one centre to another took place so frequently that no uniform and single system of communication had time to grow up. While the Seleucid kings exercised dominant authority over great part of Asia Minor, the direct southern route from the Cilician Gates to the Aegean coast must have been much used. It is marked by such foundations as Laodiceia, Apameia, Antiocheia, Nysa, Seleuceia, whose names show the intention that they should be seats of Seleucid power. These foundations belong

---

* I should hardly expect the difference to be so great as stated by Herodotus, the distances seem nearly equal. Probably the road passed by Mazaka, where it joined the route from Pteria to Kommagene.

chiefly to the line of the great Eastern highway,* and to the country south of it towards Taurus, implying a supplementary route leading eastwards through Seleuceia of Pisidia and Antioch of Pisidia. The Macedonian colonies of Asia Minor may also be assigned as a general rule to the Seleucid rule, though some of them, e.g., Dokimion, are probably earlier. Of the Greek colonies that belong to the century after Alexander, few lie north of the great highway except Synnada and Dokimion (both pre-Seleucid), and Peltai and Blaundos which imply a supplementary route from Thyatira and Sardis to Apameia.† But the names of Tralleis-Seleuceia-Antiocheia, Nysa, Antiocheia on the Mæander, Laodiceia ad Lycum, Apameia, Laodiceia Combusta, sufficiently attest the importance of the great highway, which is only confirmed by the supplementary routes.

When Pergamenian power took the place of Seleucid, the roads leading to Pergamos were the most important. But on the whole the set of intercourse is much on the same lines, though in opposite directions, under Seleucid and under Pergamenian rule. Pergamos had no direct line of communication with the upper plateau, and the chief road from the east to Pergamos comes by way of Apameia, Laodiceia on the Lycus, Philadelpheia, and Thyatira. During the wars of the Attalid and Seleucid dynasties, this road was of central importance, and rival foundations, on or near it, can be traced in opposition to each other. As Pergamenian foundations I may mention Apollonia, Apollonis, Philadelpheia, Attaleia, Eumeneia, Dionysopolis, and probably Lysias and Philomelion ; while after the power of Pergamos was established, several Seleucid foundations lost their Seleucid name, which perhaps marks a remodelling of their constitution by the Attalid kings.‡

The kingdoms of Bithynia and Pontus created a certain divergent tendency towards other centres during the Greek period; but this was never so important, and we cannot prove that there was any great amount of communication along any road leading from the upper plateau to a Bithynian or Pontic centre at this time. On the whole the kingdom of Bithynia remained isolated from the general development of Asia Minor, and concentrated on its internal improvement by such great foundations as Nikomedia, Apameia, and the various cities named Prousias. In Pontus, the foundation of Laodiceia on the route

---

* Even Seleuceia occurs on the line of this highway, as being the temporary name of Tralleis, soon disused in favour of Antiocheia, which also proved only temporary.

† On the Seleucid Macedonian Colonies, see an admirable paper by Schuchhardt, in 'Athen. Mittheil.' 1888, p. 1.

‡ The Pergamenian foundations are often planted over against Seleucid colonies, e.g., Apollonia answers to Nakrasa, Attaleia to Thyatira, Dionysopolis to Blaundos, Eumeneia to Peltai, Apollonia of Pisidia to Seleuceia; while Apollonis was perhaps actually planted on the site of Doidye, and Tralleis-Seleuceia-Antiocheia resumed its pre-Seleucid name.

to the harbour of Amisos, belongs to this period. Finally the wars between the two kingdoms, and afterwards the wars between the Romans, who used Bithynia as their base, and Mithradates, king of Pontus, gave temporary importance to the chief route that connects Pontus and Bithynia, viz., the road that leads from Nikomedeia and Nikaia by Boli (Claudiopolis), Keredi (Krateia), Tash Keupreu (Pompeiopolis), the valley of the Amnias, and Vezir Keupreu, to Amaseia. This route, however, was forced into temporary consequence during an exceptional state of the peninsula, and had no importance except where Pontus and Bithynia are concerned. Except in the Mithradatic wars, we hear little of it; and it almost eludes our notice, except through the important foundations of Bithynion-Claudiopolis, Krateia-Flaviopolis, Pompeiopolis, and perhaps Hadrianopolis, until the later Byzantine period.*

That system of routes, lying east and west, which had been growing during the previous two or three centuries, was on the whole developed without essential alteration during the Roman rule. In the Roman period the main object was to connect the provinces with Rome, and therefore the set of communication still lay along lines stretching east and west. The southern route between Ephesos and Cappadocia still continued to be the great eastern highway, though a line corresponding to the old "Royal Road," yet not exactly coinciding with it, rose to importance as connecting Galatia and Northern Phrygia with the Aegean Sea at Smyrna, and with the seat of Government at Ephesos. We are therefore justified in saying that the Græco-Roman road-system had on the whole a uniform character during the last three centuries before Christ, and the first three centuries after Christ. The Roman government completed a system which began to grow up before any Roman set foot in Asia Minor. I shall therefore describe the system in its completed form, and we may safely say that the Roman roads were as a rule already coming into use under the Greek kings. For example, the road from Laranda across Taurus down the Kalykadnos was probably in use when Seleucia † was founded at the mouth of the river. Again, the important decree found near Eriza ‡ may be taken as a

---

* It is quite a mistake, due to following the Peutinger Table, to say, as e.g., Mr. Hardy in his excellent edition of 'Pliny's Letters to Trajan' does, that the main road from Nikomedeia to Amaseia passed through Gangra; such a road did exist, but never had the importance of the other.

† Seleuceia was formerly called Olbia (Stephanus s.v.); i.e. Olbia was an earlier city, situated a few miles north of Seleuceia on the road to Olba. Its remains are distinct, and it was evidently depopulated to make the new city.

‡ See MM. Holleaux and Paris, in 'Bull. Cor. Hell.,' 1885, p. 324; 1889, p. 523. The editors, with a perverseness that is almost inconceivable to one who knows the country, the distance, and the lofty intervening mountain pass, all of which can be seen by a glance at any map, suppose the inscription to have been carried from Laodiceia to Dodurga (which they call Durdurkar). MM. Cousin and Diehl on the other hand suppose it to have been carried from Kara Eyuk Bazar, which they identify, in apparent

proof that the road from Laodiceia to Kibyra, Isinda, and the Pamphylian coast, was already becoming important before 200 B.C.; and the same inference may be drawn from the account of the raid of the Roman general Gneius Manlius Vulso as far as Termessos in 189 B.C.

In the Græco-Roman road system we are not dependent on a few chance references in ancient writers. We have two documents which profess to give an account of the roads, the Peutinger Table and the Antonine Itinerary, besides several useful works by which to check them. But the documents are so incomplete and so full of blunders that the student frequently is obliged to give them up in despair, and to resign himself to the hope that some fortunate discovery in the country may clear up the insoluble difficulties and contradictions of the documents.[*] Systematic exploration will in time show the exact course of every Roman road. Actual remains of the roadway indeed are very rarely found, and it is probable that the roads of the Anatolian province were never constructed with the same elaborate foundations as the great roads of Italy. If we may judge from the scarcity of the remains, even bridges were very scarce. The only traces of Roman roads in the country that I have seen are: (1) numerous milestones, (2) a few remains of bridges, (3) a pavement near Gorbeous, which is much broader as well as better than the pavement of the early Turkish roads, and is therefore probably part of the Roman road Ankyra-Parnassos,[†] (4) rock-cuttings or levels in the hills between Synnada and Apameia. The natural features of the country are of course of the greatest importance, but all published maps are so inadequate and inaccurate that it is rarely safe to affirm anything about the course of a road unless it has actually been traversed by some competent observer with a view to studying the road-system.[‡]

Asia Minor was, in general, a peaceful country, and the roads were on the whole determined mainly by commercial considerations, with the view of easy transit to Italy. But there are several exceptions to this rule. In Eastern Cappadocia and Lesser Armenia the roads were planned with a view to the defence of the frontier. Melitene was the great military station; the roads led to Melitene, and the distances engraved on the milestones were measured to Melitene. Along the southern edge

---

ignorance or defiance of Waddington, Kiepert, and myself, with Eriza (see 'Bull. Corr. Hell.,' 1889, p. 339.) The inscription probably belongs to Ishkian Bazar (Eriza: see pp. 101, 135, 136).

* The above sentence was printed before Part II. of this work was written. In the following Chapter VI., I have given a statement of the principles which I have been driven to in using the Peutinger Table, Ptolemy and the other authorities. These principles are much more sceptical than those of modern geographers.

† The remains are like those described by Von Diest ('Von Pergamon zum Pontus,' p. 57) as discovered by Prince Carolath near Mudurlu, "sorgfältiges Quaderpflaster in einer Breite von 12 Schritt."

‡ Great progress is made in Kiepert's maps published since the above was written.

also of the plateau another series of roads was constructed for the defence of the plains against the unruly mountaineers of Isauria and Pisidia. These roads were planned in the time of Augustus, who built a series of Roman colonies and fortresses along the skirts of Taurus, and connected them all with the central colony, Antioch of Pisidia. This system of roads may be safely assumed as a necessary part of Augustus's scheme for the defence of the empire: a Roman colony and fortress necessarily implies the existence of a military road. But actual evidence is almost entirely wanting. Neither of the documents which treat of the Anatolian roads mentions this series of roads, and no writer refers to them. Absolutely the only piece of external evidence known to me is a milestone, which I found two years ago on the site of a hitherto unknown colony: it gives the date, 6 B.C., the name of the Emperor Augustus, the name of his lieutenant-governor, and a number which can only be explained as the distance from the military centre, Antioch of Pisida. The stone, therefore, proves the existence of a road made to connect this colony with Antioch in the very year that Augustus founded his Pisidian colonies, and a similar road may be safely assumed in the case of the other colonies. The reason why this series of roads has remained so obscure is that the Pisidian mountaineers were conquered and incorporated in the empire within the next century, and that the Isaurians also ceased to be a terror. The colonies, therefore, soon lost their military value, the system of military roads sank into decay, and the roads of the district were merged in the general Anatolian system.

The usual aim of the Anatolian roads was to connect the provinces with Rome. In general, therefore, their course was guided by convenience, and they followed the natural lines. In a few cases, however, historical reasons caused a violation of this rule. I shall mention one example. About the year 129 B.C. the Proconsul Manius Aquilius laid down the roads throughout the province which the Romans named Asia. The salt lake Ascania, now called Buldur Lake, formed the boundary between Asia and Pisidia, and at that time Pisidia was an independent country. The road which Manius Aquilius constructed was, therefore, forced to keep the Asian side of the lake; and the milestones prove that the road kept to this course for quite four hundred years. But the Pisidian side of the lake is the natural course for the road; on this side is the great city of modern time, in a wide open fertile plain. Yet the Roman road on the Asian shores maintained for a long time the importance of the town on that side, although there is merely a narrow strip of ground between the mountains and the lake. Many years before Manius Aquilius constructed his road, the Roman general Manlius led his army along the natural path by the Pisidian shore of the Lake; but for five centuries the influence of a Roman road defied the course of nature, and kept the chief city on the barren northern shore.

Before discussing the Roman roads which crossed the plateau, a few preliminary remarks are necessary. The sum of distances, stage by stage, along a road as given in the Itineraries is greater than the total distance as given by a milestone from end to end of the road. This I have proved in one special case, Ephesos-Apameia-Takina,* and frequent examples will be met with below. It arises from the fact that cities were, in many cases, a little apart from the necessary line of the direct road. Besides this there are, of course, frequent corruptions of numbers, as well as of names on the roads.

The proper understanding of the Peutinger Table is much impeded by its superficial appearance. It has been made in the Byzantine period by a person who was accustomed to the Byzantine systems of roads radiating from Constantinople across Asia Minor, and who tried to represent the roads on this idea, yet it is ultimately founded on a map of the Roman empire and the Roman roads. Hence we find that the roads radiate from Constantinople and are fairly complete so long as we follow the tracks from Constantinople. For example, we have a complete road from the Asiatic shore of the Bosphorus along the Black Sea coast, and another viâ Nicomedia to Gangra and Amasia; another goes by sea to Prainetos and Nicæa, and thence direct to Ankyra, Tavium, &c.; another by sea to Pylae and thence to Prusias, Pergamon, &c. But no road which leads across country from the Aegean coast is represented with any approach to completeness: the roads in this direction are given in fragments with frequent gaps.

The same remark applies to the Antonine Itinerary: the compiler is interested chiefly in the roads to Constantinople, and represents with that prepossession the roads of the Roman period, even adding some Byzantine roads. The evidence of milestones, where it exists, is, therefore, our only sure and certain guide, beyond the few roads which are certified by Strabo.

One of the most fruitful causes of difficulty and error is the assumption, tacitly made in almost every case, that the roads given in the Itineraries are direct roads between the two extreme points. In a number of cases the road goes along two sides of a triangle. Prof. Kiepert has argued that this is so in one case ("Gegenbemerkungen zu Prof. G. Hirschfeld," 'Berl. Sitzungsber.,' 1884, pp. 52 ff.); and though I do not agree with his view in interpretation of the particular case, yet the general principle is most important. When we consider how badly the ancient maps represented the face of the country, it is quite natural that in many cases a road which was really circuitous should have been represented as fairly direct, and a direct road as circuitous.

Some examples occur of a remarkable error. A station is intruded from another road between two adjoining stations, which are

* See ASP, A, ix.

quite correctly given.   The following certain cases may be given as specimens:—

Comana Ptanadaris Cocusos.   Anton. Itin.

Arabissos Ptanadaris Cocusos.   Anton. Itin.

Cæsareia Sinispora Arasaxa.   Peut. Tab.

but it occurs to a greater degree than has been suspected even in the Antonine Itinerary, which is the best authority we have.   In the eastern parts of Asia Minor the Peutinger Table carries this transference of stations to an extraordinary degree.

One certain case occurs in the Peutinger Table, where the stations are put in the reverse order, viz. between Ancyra and Archelais.

It may be of use to give one typical example of the way in which an important road is represented in our authorities.   The backbone of the Roman road system is the great road from Ephesus to the east.   It is given in a fragmentary way in the Peutinger Table, but not as a direct continuous road.   I give a list of the stations, bracketing those which are not mentioned in the Table.   Several stations mentioned in the Table are given on other roads : these I write in Greek character.

Έφεσος, Magnesia, Τράλλεις, [Nysa], [Mastaura], Antiocheia, Caroura, [Attoudda], Laodiceia, [Colossæ], [Sanaos], Apameia, [Metropolis],* Euphorbium, [Lysias], Julia, Philomelion, [Tyriaion], Laodiceia Katakekaumene, Σάυατρα, [Koropassos], Ἀρχελαίς, [Soandos], [Sakasena], Cæsareia, Arasaxa, [Erpa, Coduzabala, Ptanadaris, Arabissos], Ἄργα, Μελιτήνη.

At important points this road was joined by cross roads from north and south.   Such roads came down the Marsyas from Alabanda and western Caria and Lycia, down the Harpasos from Tabæ, down the Morsynos from Aphrodisias and Heracleia ad Salbacum and Apollonia and Sebastopolis.   But the first really important knot was at Laodiceia. Here roads from all sides crossed.   From the south came the road from the Pamphylian towns Attaleia, Perga, &c., by Isinda, Lagoe or Lagbe, Kibyra, Themissonion.   From the north came a road Brouzos-Eumeneia-Peltæ-Lounda, another Sardis-Philadelpheia-Tripolis-Hierapolis, and perhaps another from Dionysopolis, Mossyna, and the Hyrgaleis.

Apameia was the next knot.   Here came in a road from the valley of Baris and Seleuceia Sidera, joined by another from the district of Lake Ascania, a road Antiocheia-Apollonia-Apameia, a road Amorion-Dokimion-Prymnessos-Synnada-Metropolis-Apameia, another Dorylaion-Nakoleia-Meros-Konne-Kidyessos-Brouzos-Hieropolis-Eukarpia-Apameia, and another from Seiblia and Eumeneia.

At Laodiceia Katakekaumene roads came in from Iconium on the south, and from Dorylaion-Amorion on the north.

---

* Two routes exist here : one Metropolis-Synnada-Julia, the other Metropolis-Euphorbium-Julia.   The Table confuses the two, and gives Apameia-Euphorbium-Synnada Julia.

At Archelais Colonia roads from Tyana-Sasima-Nazianzos, from Tavium-Mokissos, from Ankyra-Parnassos, and from Pessinus-Pitnisos-Perta came in.

At Cæsareia roads from Sebasteia, from Pontus, from Tavium, and from Cilicia, converged.

Each of these knots represents a centre of provincial life and government, and it is worthy of note that they are all refounded and renamed either by the Greek kings or by the early emperors. They formed seats of Græco-Roman civilisation, which spread thence through the country round. The history of great part of Asia Minor for many centuries depends on this road. I will here quote one slight example, viz. the arrangement of the Roman provincial administration during the first century B.C. From 80 to 50 B.C. the Upper Mæander valley and the whole of southern and eastern Phrygia were disjoined from the province of Asia, to which they belonged before and after that time, and placed under the jurisdiction of the Governor of Cilicia. This arrangement, which is at first sight so unintelligible, was due to the fact that the Governor of Cilicia in proceeding to or from his province avoided the sea voyage along the south coast of Asia Minor, on account of the pirates, who were masters of the sea. The governors were forced to land at Ephesus, and go by land along the eastern highway to Cilicia. On their march it was easy for them to hold the assizes and arrange the affairs of the districts which they traversed. But after Pompey destroyed the pirates and reopened the sea, the pax Romana was restored, and the governors of Cilicia soon began to prefer the voyage to the long and fatiguing land journey.

In the Peutinger Table the line of this road is frequently broken. There is no connection between Magnesia and Ephesos: Tralleis is transposed to another road; the connection between Laodiceia and Apameia is made through the intervention of a different road; from Apameia the road turns sharp back to Synnada, and then again equally sharply back to Julia and Philomelion. The alternative routes by Synnada and by Euphorbium are united in one road; between Laodiceia Katakekaumene and Savatra, a station, Kaballa, is interpolated from a different road; there is no connection between Savatra and Archelais, but Laodiceia-Savatra-Pyrgos-Iconium is given as a straight road; there is no connection between Archelais and Cæsareia-Mazaka. If this most important of the roads is so disfigured and cut up in the Table that it has been recognised only from the description quoted by Strabo (p. 663) from Artemidorus, we may expect to find similar errors elsewhere.

The description of the roads is necessarily founded in many cases, where the evidence of milestones and other traces of the actual roadway fails, on the identification of the cities which were situated on them. In the case of Phrygia and western Pisidia, I have already elsewhere discussed the whole of the cities and given a complete scheme of the ancient topography. In these provinces, then, the roads are entirely fixed, and I need do little more than refer to my previous papers.* But in the case of Galatia, Pontus, Lycaonia, eastern Pisidia, and Cappadocia, the ancient topography is quite unsettled. Only about one in six of the ancient cities have been correctly placed on the map. I have therefore inserted a discussion in the briefest possible form of these provinces, which makes an outline of the Roman topography of the half of Asia Minor. For the sake of convenience I recapitulate a small number of separate identifications in these provinces which I have published in scattered papers, chiefly in foreign journals.

V. THE ROMAN ROADS IN ASIA MINOR.

The "discussion in the briefest possible form," mentioned in the preceding paragraph, has grown in the lapse of a year into the 370 pages of the second part of this book. I have however left the paragraph unaltered to show the original intention of the work, and the way in which it has grown upon my hands. The authorities on the Roman road-system are so defective and so inaccurate,† that a minute examination of the topography was required to justify the results which are given in the accompanying map. This grew to such a size that it had to be relegated to a separate part of the work.

While Part I. carries, as I hope, its own justification in a way that is obvious, I perhaps owe the reader an explanation of the length and complicacy of Part II., in which (as my friend the Camden Professor of Ancient History, to whom most of the credit or the blame for this book must be given, remarks, with a certain heightening of the effect), nearly 400 pages are spent in discussing a set of names, none of which anybody has ever heard of before.

Topography is the foundation of history. No one who has familiarised himself with Attic history in books and has afterwards ascended Pentelicus and seen that history spread forth before him in the valleys and mountains and sea that have moulded it, will ever disbelieve in the value of topography as an aid to history. What idea of Attic history could be got, if we were uncertain whether Athens was situated in the plain of the Kephissos or a few miles further east beyond Hymettus! I had often wondered why the plain of Marathon was so long connected with Chalcis and separated from Attica. The wonder ceased when from Pentelicus I saw it connected with Chalcis by the quiet landlocked sea that tempted navigation, and separated from Attica by the rugged and difficult mountains. Yet few that study Greek history, and play the part of examiner or examinee in it, realise what we owe to the greatest of modern topographers, Leake. Who, that goes through the usual course of highest honours in ancient history and

* The papers whose results I assume are " The Cities and Bishoprics of Phrygia," in 'Journal of Hellenic Studies,' part I. 1883, II. 1887 ; "Antiquities of Southern Phrygia and the Border Lands," in 'American Journal of Archæology,' Part I. 1887, II.–IV. 1888.

† On this point see Chapter VI.

literature ever hears the fame of Leake, or knows that he has done more to make a real understanding of Greek life possible than any other Englishman of this century? We all know Curtius' 'History of Greece:' how many of us know a finer and greater work, Curtius' 'Peloponnesos'? Some of us are even so narrow as to imagine that the reading of some modern books, supplemented by a little study of Thucydides, Herodotus and Xenophon (a few reach Polybius—how very few go deeper!), will enable us to understand ancient history. If we want to understand the ancients, and especially the Greeks, we must breathe the same air that they did, and saturate ourselves with the same scenery and the same nature that wrought upon them. For this end correct topography is a necessary, though a humble, servant.

The justification of Part II. then is that if we are ever to understand the history of Asia Minor, we must know the places in which that history was transacted. The scholar, already steeped in Homer, who will spend months in the Troad and Aeolis, and who will learn to know the land until at last he understands it and sympathises with it,—that scholar will place the Homeric question on a new plane. But while an uncertainty of ten or a hundred* miles exists as to the situation of any place, we cannot even set about mastering its history.

In Part II. brevity has been my aim, and repetition of anything that has been sufficiently well said in ordinary books has been avoided. Hence I have, as a rule, less to say on the more important cities, each of which needs a monograph to itself;† whereas to some names that are not even mentioned by ordinary geographers, I have devoted several pages. I mention one typical example. Eukhaita, a Pontic archbishopric, was not, so far as I was then aware, mentioned by any modern geographer before I wrote a paragragh, printed on p. 318, in which I stated in twenty lines the evidence, and placed the city at Tchorum. The evidence appeared to me clear, and I did not wish to spend time in explaining its precise force. While the first proof was in my hands, a number of the *Bulletin de Correspondance Hellénique*, containing a paper on the subject by M. Doublet and the Abbé Duchesne, reached me. Here the latter quoted almost the whole evidence that I had used, and yet, in order to support a possible but unnecessary and forced interpretation of an inscription, came to the conclusion that Eukhaita was situated at Safaramboli, 100 miles further west. The same evidence, therefore, which seemed to me to point conclusively to a site east of the Halys and probably to Tchorum,‡ appeared to such a

* This is literally true; see Saravene, Eukhaita, &c.

† These would compose great part of that local history of the country, which is the second stage in the work I had once marked out for myself.

‡ The description of the modern town, with its mosques and its fanaticism, by Humann and Puchstein, furnishes an incidental confirmation. The permanence of religious feeling under new forms is one of the most striking features in the history of the country ; and Eukhaita was certainly distinguished as a centre of religious enthusiasm.

high authority as the Abbé Duchesne, to be consistent with a situation west of the Halys, 100 miles from Tchorum. I felt compelled, in courtesy to the upholders of the other view, to examine the evidence fully and show its bearing. This necessitated an addition of four pages. After this was printed, I observed in the 'Acta Sanctorum' two quotations made by the editors from unpublished sources, which, with a slight correction of the text, took the whole matter out of the range of controversy. Had I known them sooner, my readers would have been spared four pages; but if they escaped such a master of hagio-logical literature as M. Duchesne, I may find pardon for not sooner observing them. Thus was produced the apparently disproportionate space that I have devoted to Eukhaita, and in the case of many other cities the few lines which I have occupied in a brief statement of the evidence, sometimes by mere reference to the original authorities, might be expanded to several pages, if I tried to show its precise import and strength.

The order of exposition must appear so disorderly that a word of explanation is needed. The order is that of discovery: each point as it was settled formed a support for further advance. In numerous cases the arguments in favour of particular views seemed to myself at the time I first stated them to be weak, and yet in the gradual progress of my own knowledge these views were confirmed, partly by the fitting in of other parts of the puzzle, and partly by the discovery of striking analogies; the discussion of Pinara, Sidyma, Rhodiapolis, &c., in Lycia, gives an example of such a subsequently discovered analogy.

The Roman road-system will be best understood from the accom-panying maps. Mere description of the general principles would not be intelligible without keeping the eye on the map; but the study of the map will be facilitated by a statement of the plan on which the roads were laid out. But in the first place I must make a general explanation in regard to all the maps, that in drawing them and indicating the boundaries of provinces or the precise situation of towns, it has often been necessary to assume an appearance of certainty which I do not really feel. In these cases the text will show what evidence exists, and in the map the lines must be understood as mere approximations. If the towns or boundaries are indicated at all, they must be indicated in some definite position. The text of Part II. must therefore be constantly used as an auxiliary to the maps.

The plan of the Græco-Roman road-system may be briefly described as consisting of

1. The great trade-route and the supplementary roads that connect side-lying districts with it. This set of roads can be gathered from the map and from the description already given in chapter IV. One illustration of the manner in which trade followed this route may be given. The marble of Dokimion was conveyed to the sea, not by the

apparently much more direct route by Keramon Agora (Islam Keui) and Philadelpheia, but by Synnada and the great trade-route. This may be inferred from the name Synnadic, which is usually given to this marble. Dokimion was a self-governing municipality, and the marble would not have been known to the world as Synnadic, unless it had in some way come into connection with Synnada.* In fact this marble, when exported, never actually passed through Dokimion, which is about two or three miles from the quarries. It was carried direct to Synnada, where in all probability was situated the chief office of administration, to which the orders for marble were sent; and thence passed along the trade-route. It is moreover very doubtful whether the road between Klannoudda and Philadelpheia was ever made passable for monolithic columns; though there can be no doubt in the mind of one who has seen the bold engineering by which the road is carried over the mountains between Synnada and Metropolis that the Romans were quite able to make the road to Philadelpheia passable even for the largest columns.†

2. A road connecting northern Phrygia and Galatia with Sardis and the Aegean coast at Smyrna. The Peutinger Table preserves in an unusually complete and accurate form ‡ the part of this road which led from Dorylaion and Kotiaion by Apia, Hierokharax, Akmonia, Aloudda, Klannoudda, and Philadelpheia. Besides this I incline to the belief that another branch came from Pessinus by Orkistos and joined the former road at Hierokharax (see pp. 168, 230). But I can find no evidence that the important modern trade-route from Afiom Kara Hisar (Akroenos, near Prymnessos) by Hierokharax to Philadelpheia was in use during the Roman period, for the trade of Prymnessos and Dokimion must have gone by way of Synnada and Apameia. This set of roads fulfilled the functions of the "Royal Road," though they do not exactly coincide with it. The map shows the great importance of the pass in which lies Hierokharax. The valley of the little stream Hamam Su, which is probably to be identified with the ancient Senaros,§ is the only

* See my paper "Inscriptions Inédites de Marbres Phrygiens," in 'Mélanges d'Arch. et d'Hist,' 1882.

† The route Philadelpheia-Klannoudda-Akmonia is not nearly so difficult as that which, according to my view, was followed by the "Royal Road;" but it was not, I think, brought into use till the period of the Diadochi. It must be remembered that the way from Synnada to Metropolis was not strictly part of the trade-route, which went from Metropolis to Kinnaborion and Lysias, and that Manlius did not cross the mountains that bound the Synnada valley on the south (see p. 170).

‡ The only omission is the insignificant Hierokharax; the chief fault is Cocleo for Cotleo, i.e. Cotiaion; see p. 168.

§ The name Senaros occurs on coins of Sebaste, see Head, Hist. Num., s.v. It may indicate perhaps the fine fountains, now called Bunar Bashi, near Sebaste, or more probably the neighbouring river Banaz Tchai. The Hamam Su is more naturally reckoned the main stream; but the name Banaz Tchai is now applied to another branch coming from the village Banaz, north-west of Islam Keui.

route of communication from a great part of western Phrygia towards the north-east and east; for the path by Akmonia and Dioklea or Dokela towards the Hieropolitan valley can penetrate further to the east only by a footpath across very rugged mountains. At the entrance to the pass up the Hamam Su lay Keramon Agora, in the territory subject to Akmonia.

3. The military roads guarding the eastern frontier towards the Euphrates. These have as their centre Melitene, where was the standing camp (stativa) of Legio XII. Fulminata; and they are partly mixed up with the eastern part of the great trade-route through Erpa and Melitene to the crossing of the Euphrates at Tomisa. The military roads consist of a road from Satala, the station of Legio XV. Apollinaris, along the right bank of the Euphrates through Arauraci or Arauraka (see p. 275) and Daskousa, the station of Ala II. Ulpia Auriana,* to Melitene, and thence, still along the Euphrates, to Samosata in the province Syria. From Melitene a road ran along the northern side of Taurus by Arabissos, an important military centre at the entrance to the main pass over Taurus (pp. 276–280, 311), to Kokussos. From Kokussos a road ran north to Komana, Ariarathia and Sebasteia, and thence east along the Halys, through Nikopolis and Colonia to Satala. This completes the outer circle of roads, in addition to which there were also direct roads from Arabissos to Sebasteia, from Melitene to Sebasteia, and from Karsaga to Nikopolis. Two passes across Taurus into Kommagene were traversed by the roads from Melitene through Perre to Samosata, and from Arabissos to Germaniceia: the last must have been in all ages, and is still, a very important road. The pass from Kokussos to Germaniceia, which is still very little used though not exceedingly difficult, cannot be proved to have been in use until the ninth century (p. 276). The Anti-Taurus passes are more numerous than those across Taurus. Reckoning from south to north, Major Bennet has told me that the following passes lead across the Anti-Taurus† mountains, counting from south to north; but probably only two were traversed by Roman roads.

1. Gez Bel, approached from Keuseli.
2. Dede Bel, ,, ,, Seuagen.
3. Geuk Bel, ,, ,, ,,
4. Kuru Bel, ,, ,, ,,
5. Kuru Tchai, traversed by the great trade-route.
6. Kabak Tepe, not important.
7. Yedi Oluk, traversed by the military road to Ariarathia.

---

* See C. I. L., III., Supplem., No. 6743; where Mommsen refers to Arrian ἔκταξ., p. 80, 6, and Notit. Dignit. Orient., 38, 22; Pliny, V. 24, 84, VI. 9, 27; Orosius, I. 2, 23.

† The mountains on the west side of the Saros in the upper part of its course especially bear this name. But the Bimboa Dagh on the east side may also be called Anti-Taurus.

Some of these military roads are described in Part II., pp. 270–280. The rest are indicated in the map of eastern Cappadocia and Armenia Minor; where it has been necessary to select the probable line of several roads, and the probable situation for several towns. The following hypotheses are adopted, in addition to the remarks made in Part II. The broken road which is given in the Peutinger Table as :—

Nikopolis 21 Ole Oberda 15 Caleorsissa 24,

which Kiepert connects with Analibla (Analiba), is corrected in accordance with Ptolemy to Nikopolis-Seleoberroia-Kaltiorissa, and connected with Karsaga. It is also assumed that the indirect road (Anton. Itin., p. 215),

Nikopolis 24 Olotoedariza 24 Carsat 24 Arauracos 24 Suissa 26 Satala,

has been corrupted through the analogy of the direct road Nikopolis 24 Olotoedariza 26 Dracontes 24 Haza 26 Satala. The indirect road falls at Carsat (Karsaga) into the frontier road along the Euphrates, and is really identical with the road of the Peutinger Table when properly interpreted. The name Klotoidariza or Olotoidariza has been substituted for the two stations of the Peutinger Table, Kaltiorissa and Seleoberroia (corrupted to Caleorsissa and Ole Oberda). The situation of Klotoidariza or Olotoidariza suggests a connection with Basgoidariza, which is mentioned by Strabo, p. 555, together with Hydara and Sinoria, as one of the forts built by Mithridates in the country towards Armenia (by which he seems to mean Ptolemy's Pontus Polemoniacus, for Saunaria in that district must be Strabo's Sinoria). Basgoidariza in Polemoniacus was therefore probably not far from Klotoidariza in Armenia Minor. The form of the latter name is very doubtful. The initial guttural is given in some of the authorities; but Olotoidariza * has the support of most of the MSS., and is defended and confirmed by Procopius, de Aedif., iii. 4, p. 253, who mentions in this very district Lytararizon. If the Bonn edition made any attempt to comply with the conditions of a scholarly work, we perhaps should find that variants existed which justified such a restoration as Lytadarizon or Alytada-rizon.† The ending -ίζων became usual in Byzantine time in certain Armenian names, and is doubtless equivalent to the earlier rendering -ίζα   The name Kitharizon (see p. 325) probably shows that δαρίζων and θαρίζων were equivalent terminations.

In the Byzantine, but not in the Roman period, we find allusions to

---

* The variants Clotoedariza, Clotedariza, occur in p. 207; but amid ten variants in p. 183, none have the initial consonant and many have the ending -lariza instead of -dariza. In p. 215 the variants are fewer, but none have the initial consonant.

† In the form Klotoidariza probably the K arises from the confusion with Kaltiorissa. In the name as given by Procopius the loss of an initial vowel would be quite in accordance with analogy, and therefore the balance of probability is in favour of the forms Olotoidariza, Alytalarizon, Lytalarizon, where L has taken the place of original D. In Procopius the L has been modified in its turn to R.

a route Sebasteia-Tephrike-Kamacha. This route is implied in a passage of Michael Attaliota (see below, p. 267), while the connection as far as Tephrike (Divrigi) is implied in all the campaigns against the Paulicians, whose chief stronghold was Tephrike, for the campaigns against them are conducted along the route by Basilika Therma, Sibora, Agrane, and Sebasteia. This road is not proved to have existed in Roman times. The identification of Kamacha with Theodosiopolis is justified by the comparative table given on p. 282 and by the remarks on p. 447. There were several cities named Theodosiopolis in the eastern parts of the Byzantine empire : this one is perhaps mentioned by Procopius, de Aedif., iii. 4, p. 253, and another occurs in the same work, p. 255, and in Bell. Pers., p. 82, where it is said to be 42 stadia south of a mountain in which rise both the Euphrates and theTigris.

Koloneia or Kolonia was evidently the chief fortress in the northern district of the frontier in the later wars, and the central city of the Theme Koloneia. The great fortresses of the Byzantine period were as a rule situated on lofty precipitous rocks, and Procopius, de Aedif., iii. 4, p. 253, mentions that Koloneia occupied such a position (ἐν ἀκρωνυχίᾳ λόφου κατακρήμνου). Cities which, like Koloneia, are of great importance in later Byzantine time retain as a rule this importance under Turkish rule. In this district the important city of Shaban Kara Hisar complies with all these conditions; and its military importance is such that it must be a leading fortress in the Byzantine wars. I have therefore, p. 267, identified it with Koloneia. The Armenians still call this city Nikopoli; Kiepert has rightly seen that this is a mistake, but he has not explained the origin of the error, which certainly must lie in the gradual desertion of Nikopolis and the union of the two bishoprics, Koloneia and Nikopolis: in the combined title Nikopolis must have held the first place, and the second must have fallen into disuse.

4. The military roads laid out about 6 B.C. or earlier for the defence of the province Galatia and the coercion of the mountain tribes of Pisidia and Isauria. The military centre was Antioch of Pisidia. The stations, all Roman colonies, are enumerated on p. 398. The military necessity for these roads soon disappeared as the mountaineers were incorporated in the empire; and the road system cannot be understood until more early milestones are discovered. The little that is known is mentioned on pp. 358, 391, 398-9. In the supplement to Vol. III. of the 'Corpus Inscriptionum Latinarum,' No. 6974, I have stated the opinion that the distance CXXII from Antiocheia to Colonia Comama was measured by Apollonia and the ancient city beside Elyes or Elles on Lake Askania (perhaps Okoklia). This view is unsatisfactory, as implying that a military road of the Province Galatia ran through a part of the Province Asia; but I am still unable to see any other way in which the measurement can be explained. Milestones of the second or third century found in this country cannot be taken as sure

evidence of Augustus's roads; they belong to the time when the military roads were merged in the general system of the country and perhaps modified.

5. The tendency of commerce during the Græco-Roman period was chiefly along the routes from east to west. But besides this there were seaports on the Black Sea and the Mediterranean, which were employed in a less degree for the purpose of direct trade with the west. Tarsos was the port for Cilicia, Seleuceia for Cilicia Tracheia (which in later Roman and Byzantine time was called Isauria), Side and Attaleia for Pamphylia, Telmessos, &c. for Lycia ; and on the north Cyzicos, Amisos, and several other harbours, still retained considerable importance. To each of these points roads converged, and they were points of departure for a coasting traffic, great part of which ultimately found its way to Rome. It would be a useful study to collect the references to this coasting trade,* and try to determine its character and importance. But a serious work on the trade of the Roman empire is still a desideratum; and the foundation for a history of trade in Asia Minor must rest on a "Local History" of the country, which ought to complete the present work. It is not probable that Attaleia was used as a shipping port for any produce except that of the coast-land of Pamphylia, or Seleuceia except for the Kalykadnos and other valleys that lead down to the Isaurian sea. The mountain‧wall of Taurus prevented all heavy traffic from crossing the short lines between the plateau and the southern sea, and turned it along the road that led to the Aegean. The same remark (*mutatis mutandis*) applies to Sinope; and even Tarsos was probably not used as a port for any country except the Cilician plain, for Strabo, p. 540, seems to make it clear that the Cappadocian trade went to Ephesos by land. The easiest path from Cappodocia to Tarsos was through the Cilician Gates, and it is said that the rocky walls which form the Gates approached so close that, until Ibrahim Pasha blasted a road for his artillery, a loaded camel could just pass between them. Similarly it may be doubted whether Amisos was a harbour for more than the trade of the Pontic plains and the trade-route from Armenia by way of Sebasteia and Komana Pontica.

This coasting trade lies apart from my proper subject, which is completed when I have enumerated the points round the coast where lines of road converge. I have as yet hardly touched on the western harbours to which the roads that cross Asia Minor from east to west conveyed the produce of the country. In the early Greek period Miletos appears, so far as the evidence goes, to have been the seaport for the trade with Celaenae and the Upper Maeander. The evidence lies partly in the early coinage as indicating commercial importance, partly in Hipponax's reference to the Phrygians, who came down to

---

* For example, in the legend of Aberkios (Act. Sanct., Oct. 21), the saint went to Attaleia and thence took ship to Rome.

Miletos. Ephesos, however, was really a more convenient harbour than Miletos for a considerable part of the Maeander valley; though the commercial energy (in other words, the thoroughly Greek character) of Miletos seems to have given it much greater importance as a trading centre in the earlier period; whereas in Ephesos the Greek spirit had not so complete mastery as in Miletos.* But the energy of Miletos disappeared under the Persian rule, and the natural suitability of Ephesos as the nearest harbour for a road coming down the Maeander valley made it the terminus of the great trade-route. The harbour also of Miletos was silted up, and it is now miles distant from the sea. Ephesos retained its commercial importance throughout the Roman Period; but its harbour also has now long ceased to exist, the town is absolutely deserted,† and the whole trade along the ancient eastern highway now passes across the quay of Smyrna. Before the Ottoman Railway was opened, connecting Smyrna with the Maeander valley, the harbour of Scalanova took the place of Ephesos, and maintained a feeble competition with Smyrna for the trade of the Maeander valley : but with the advantage of railway communication Smyrna is beyond competition.

The railways that radiate from Smyrna have taken the place of the old roads. One of them goes by the Hermos valley to Philadelpheia, and corresponds therefore to the " Royal Road." The other connects Smyrna with Ephesos, the Maeander valley, and Apameia-Celaenae: it corresponds to the eastern trade-route. The latter, which was first built, cut out Scalanova and gave Smyrna the entire command of the trade of the Maeander valley. To take one example, the liquorice root of the Maeander valley, in which a great trade has sprung up during the last forty years, was formerly shipped from Scalanova : now it all goes to Smyrna.

One phase in the recent history of the great trade-route furnishes an interesting commentary on the period when the road from Pergamos by Philadelpheia to Laodiceia and the east was the great route. After the Hermos Valley Railway was completed to Philadelpheia, it was easier to carry the eastern trade from the Lykos valley across the short mountain pass to Philadelpheia, than down the Maeander valley to the terminus of the other railway at Tralleis (now Aidin). The trade was thus for a time diverted through special circumstances away from the natural line, and did not return to it till the Aidin railway was carried on to the Lykos valley.

* These two phrases "the Greek spirit," and " the commercial energy," are merely two different ways of expressing the same idea. One of them cannot be taken as a reason for the other. To give a reason for the difference between Miletos and Ephesos is difficult; it does not lie in some phrase such as that the Greek element was stronger in Miletos, the native element in Ephesos. The Greek spirit is not the property of some single tribe; it is imparted by the air, the sea, and the mountain barriers to that varying amalgam of many different tribes and stocks which constituted the Greek peoples.

† Ayasaluk, the modern village, is about a mile from the nearest part of Ephesos.

A similar competition seems at an early time to have been maintained between Phokaia, Smyrna, and Ephesos, for the trade with the Hermos valley and the inner country along the "Royal Road." Herodotus, v. 54, names Ephesos as the sea-end of that road; but the probable explanation of his problematic language in ii. 106 (compared with v. 54), is that he is stating in a confused and inaccurate way an account that he had not fully understood of the three roads, Sardis-Phokaia, Sardis-Smyrna, and Sardis-Ephesos. A few words on this famous passage and on the value of Herodotus's testimony with regard to Asia Minor may not be out of place here. The text is, εἰσι δὲ καὶ περὶ Ἰωνίην δύο τύποι ἐν πέτρῃσι ἐγκεκολαμμένοι τούτου τοῦ ἀνδρὸς τῇ τε ἐκ τῆς Ἐφεσίης ἐς Φώκαιαν ἔρχονται, καὶ τῇ ἐκ Σαρδίων ἐς Σμύρνην.

After reading various attempts to explain Herodotus's road from Ephesos to Phokaia, I feel only more strongly that, as I have already said in 'Journal of Hellenic Studies,' 1881, p. 53, either his account is bad or his text corrupt. The very idea of defining a road as leading from Ephesos to Phokaia is as absurd as it would be to say that a monument was on the railway that leads from Scarborough to Lincoln. Moreover the natural way from Ephesos to Phokaia would be through Smyrna, and no one could possibly understand from Herodotus's words a road through the pass of Kara Bel, which involves a journey of quite double the distance. To say that Herodotus's words, ἐκ τῆς Ἐφεσίης, mean a road that led not from Ephesos itself, but from some part of the territory of Ephesos which communicated with Phokaia by a different road, does not help us: in the first place it is geographically false, in the second place it is, in my opinion, contrary to the habits and thought and expression of the Greek time. My view is still that, as there is no reason to believe that any serious fault exists in the text, Herodotus's words can be understood only by hypothetically restoring the account which he heard. This was to the effect that three great roads led to Sardis from the coast, one from Phokaia, one from the Ephesian territory, and one in the middle from Smyrna. Two of these roads were marked by monuments erected by the Egyptian conqueror Sesostris. Herodotus represents these monuments as of the same type; but I incline to think that in this also he is inaccurate. One of the monuments must be the so-called "Sesostris" in Kara Bel pass; the other must be the "Niobe." On this view the passage of Herodotus becomes a very simple and also a most natural one.

With regard to Herodotus's accounts of Asia Minor, the opinion is irresistibly borne in on every one that knows the country,* that in every case where he speaks about scenery or phenomena of the interior he speaks from hearsay, and not from personal knowledge. There is

---

* E.g., Prof. G. Hirschfeld, in his account of Apameia-Celaenae, says that Herodotus "spricht offenbar nicht als Augenzeuge."

not a sentence in his work that gives the slightest ground for thinking he had ever gone into Asia Minor more than a few miles from the coast. He was a Greek above all in his love for the sea and his hatred of the inner country. Where he could go in a ship, *e.g.*, up the Nile or to Sinope, he was glad to go; but I feel that except as a slave or a prisoner or an ambassador, he never would have gone to Babylon.* In regard to the inner parts of Asia Minor, even points so near the coast as Apameia, Kolossai, Kara Bel, and Magnesia ad Sipylum with its "Niobe," his language shows that he had not seen them. No one who is intimately acquainted with a place can mistake a hearsay account for the account of an eye-witness; the mistakes of an eye-witness are of one kind (with which I have become familiar as made both by myself and by others), the mistakes made in reporting in one's own words an account heard from an eye-witness are of quite a different kind. Close and minute study of what Herodotus says about Asia Minor, pondered over for years and looked at from many points of view, produces in me the belief (1) that he was not an eye-witness, (2) that he did not carefully reproduce verbatim the accounts which he heard, but rewrote them, probably in many cases from memory. The scenery and character of the coast-lands which he knew personally were so familiar to him that he did not think of describing them; it was the strange and the novel things that he had heard about and not seen which he describes most carefully: in the case of Egypt it is precisely those things which struck him as unlike his ordinary experience that he brings most prominently into his work.

In speaking of the pass of Kara Bel, the high authority of Prof. G. Hirschfeld is likely to give wide currency to a strange error that he makes in his "Felsenreliefs in Kleinasien und das Volk der Hittiter," p. 10.† He says that the name Kara Bel means 'Black Stone,' and denotes the "Sesostris" monument. The name means "Black Pass," ‡ and denotes the mountain pass in which the monument is situated.

At first the geographical situation of Smyrna must have given it a decided advantage in the competition for the trade of the Hermos valley, but it developed such a strong Greek spirit, and it was so dangerously close to the Lydian capital, that it was destroyed as a rival to Sardis by the rising military power of Lydia. So long as the pass from the little valley of Smyrna across the ridge by Kavakli Dere to the east was in the hands of a Greek state, that state was a perpetual menace to the Lydians of the Hermos valley, which it commands by means of the

---

* In regard to this point I have no knowledge to justify any opinion as to whether or not he actually saw Babylon: every reader is as able to form an opinion as I am, and I shall not insult him by expressing mine.

† 'Abhandl. Berl. Akad.,' 1887.

‡ Kara means 'Black,' or rather 'Terrible:' the term is often applied in a moral sense to dangerous or powerful or impressive looking objects or persons. Bel means literally "neck," and is regularly applied to high open passes.

strong fortress that overhangs the pass * in the same way that Sardis itself does. Hence arose the long conflict between Smyrna and Sardis, which is sung by Mimnermos, and which ended in the downfall of Smyrna and its obliteration from the number of ancient cities.†

When Smyrna was destroyed, the trade of the Hermos valley was probably monopolised by Phokaia, and after the spirit and power of Phokaia were broken by the Persians, Ephesos succeeded to its place. The period when Phokaia commanded this trade is marked by its rich coinage, about 600–560: the coinage of Ephesos begins to be important at a later date. The question then suggests itself whether the prosperity of Smyrna was not accompanied also by coinage. It is usually assumed that the destruction of Smyrna took place before it began to coin money. But it was destroyed by Alyattes, who in the beginning of his reign had on his hands a six years' doubtful war against the powerful Miletos, and afterwards a war against Media ; the probability is that he did not succeed in breaking the power of Smyrna till after the conclusion of the Median War in 585. We should certainly expect that a great Greek commercial state in the sixth century would coin money : and I should attribute to Smyrna some of the early electrum or gold coins usually classed to Sardis. The lion type is equally suitable to both cities.

VI. The Value of the Peutinger Table, Ptolemy, and the Itineraries as Geographical Authorities.

I cannot pretend to discuss this difficult subject thoroughly ; but in as much as I have been led to assign far less value to these authorities in comparison with Strabo and the Byzantine lists than modern geographers usually do, I am bound to offer a few remarks in defence and explanation of my opinion.

The ordinary method of using the Peutinger Table is carried to its logical conclusion (and to a *reductio ad absurdum*) by Dr. Konrad Miller in his work, 'Die Weltkarte des Castorius, genannt die Peutingersche Tafel,' which is dated in the year 1888, though amid many acute and useful observations there are some opinions in it which might suggest a date in the seventeenth century. To judge from his whole tone (*e.g.* pp. 79–80, 121) Dr. Miller thinks that the Table is a document of very high authority, that many of the faults charged against it by modern writers are proofs merely of their ignorance, that the progress of research is justifying and will continue more and more to justify

---

* I have described this fortress and its military importance in the 'Journal of Hellenic Studies,' 1880, in a paper on "Newly Discovered Sites near Smyrna."

† It must not be thought that Smyrna ceased to exist: it was organised on the native Anatolian village system, not as a Greek πόλις, but it is mentioned by Pindar in the fifth century, and in an inscription of the beginning of the fourth century. Grote and Curtius saw this, and the inscription has confirmed their opinion.

the accuracy of the Table, and that one must be very careful of one's ground before accusing either the copyist of a fault in the copy or the original author of ignorance in any detail : the obvious inferences are that the Table must be our fundamental authority, that the presumption is in favour of all its statements, and that these ought to be accepted where they cannot be proved to be wrong.   Every one of these inferences I consider to be absolutely false and diametrically contrary to the true principles. I suppose that the most recent geographers would consider Dr. Miller rather to over-estimate the authority of the Table; but they would probably consider my view to be as great an error in the opposite direction, and in practice they really assume his conclusions in numerous cases where, because two known and fixed cities occur as the termini of a road in the Table, they place the intermediate names of the Table at corresponding intervals along the road in their map. My rule is that this must never be done unless independent evidence is brought forward to justify the position assigned to these intermediate stations.   I would go even further and maintain that the agreement of Ptolemy and the Peutinger Table is far from a strong argument, and needs external corroboration. I consider that the principle which is here being criticised is one of the chief reasons that have retarded the progress of topography in Asia Minor.   The foundation of topographical study (given knowledge of the country) must lie in fixing from epigraphic evidence as many points as possible, and thereafter working from the Byzantine lists, comparing them with Strabo and the campaigns that took place in the country. The Table and Ptolemy may be used as corroborative evidence or to supply gaps, but where they are at variance with the above authorities, their value is naught.

The absolute contradiction between Dr. Miller's results and mine may be gathered from the fact that in collecting on pp. 118–120 the material which may be used for the elucidation and criticism of the Table, he does not even allude to those authorities which in my opinion are fundamental.*

The proof of the principles which I have laid down is to be found in the second part of this book, in which may be found numerous examples of roads that are utterly misrepresented in the Table : the Itineraries are better authorities than the Table, but Part II., Chapter N, which discusses the roads in eastern Cappadocia, a district where the Antonine Itinerary and the Peutinger Table are unusually minute and detailed, will show how utterly impossible it is to recover from these authorities any approximately accurate picture of the road system.   In

---

* His nearest approach to a recognition of the Byzantine lists is in the words ' die Bischofssitze des 4. Jahrhunderts (s. Gams, Series Episcoporum u. a.).' He makes no reference to the campaigns fought in the country, except in mentioning ' Procops Schriften ' and ' Ammianus Marcellinus.'

general, we find in the Table that sometimes the right names are mentioned in the wrong order, frequently an entirely false set of names is placed on a road, and sometimes true and false names are put side by side among the stations. Frequently an important Roman route is represented in mere fragments, or appears as a set of disjointed zigzags across the map, while fragments of two or three roads are united into a single straight line.* In addition to the details given in Part II., I add here a few examples of the character of these documents : these will at the same time prove that, while every statement made in the last two sentences would be accepted by the best recent geographers, and have in fact actually been made by them in express terms, these geographers have not been consistent in accepting the logical conclusion that the Table must not be followed without external confirmation, but have on the contrary followed it in many cases where it is either demonstrably false or at least absolutely unsupported by any independent authority.

1. The principle that even striking agreement between the Peutinger Table and Ptolemy does not justify confidence in the road which they describe is admirably exemplified in the case of the route from Tavium to Caesareia-Mazaka. The Table gives this in great detail, and Prof. G. Hirschfeld has pointed out in his paper on Tavium† that Ptolemy gives nearly the same series of stations in almost a direct line. Hirschfeld was misled by this agreement to accept the route as accurate, and to found on it a series of startling topographical novelties, e.g., that Tavium was at Iskelib west of the Halys, and that no part of Galatia reached beyond the Halys to the east. The route is entirely untrustworthy, and the inferences drawn from it are wrong. See pp. 243, 258, 267.

2. The description given in the Peutinger Table of the road from Nikomedeia to Pompeiopolis and Amaseia, the most important route in the north of Asia Minor, may be taken as a fair specimen both of that document and of the confidence that modern geographers place in it. The Table describes this road thus :—

> Nicomedia XVII XXIIII Lateas XVIII Demetriu XIII Dusepro Solympum XXX unnamed town XX river Sangarios. Manoris XXXII Potomia. Cepora XV Antoniopolis XXVIIII Anadynata XXXVI Gangaris XXX Otresa XXV Virasia XVI Amasia.

The distance from Nicomedia to the Sangarios according to this route is 122 miles; in reality it is about 15 or 18 miles. Something, therefore, must be wrong, and some correction is needed. The cure adopted by Mannert, Forbiger, &c., and even, I regret to see, by Kiepert in his

---

* 'Weite Ausladungen erscheinen als direkte Wege,' Hirschfeld, 'Ueber unsere geogr. Kenntnis der alten griech. Welt,' p. 63, in 'Geogr. Jahrbuch,' XII., 1888. Kiepert has put the same truth excellently in the 'Sitzungsber. Berlin. Akad.,' 1884, p. 52.

† 'Sitzungsber. Berlin Akad.,' 1883, p. 1243.

latest map, is to move all the names to the other side of the Sangarios. Then we have Plateae, Demetrium, Dusae figuring as towns of Bithynia, and a mount Olympos is invented to account for the epithet attached to Dusae. Now, in the first place, whether this arrangement is right or wrong, it cannot claim to have in its favour the authority of the Peutinger Table. It is a mere theory to get rid of an obvious corruption in the Table. I shall not waste time by showing in detail how absurd it is, but shall merely state a new theory, and if any one is bold enough hereafter to follow the current theory, I shall be ready to discuss it with him. One or more other roads in the country have been misplaced through bad drawing and mixed up with the real road, of which the only certain remains are Antoniopolis and Pompeiopolis, placed in an empty space above the road.

Antoniopolis, i.e. Antinoopolis, is an epithet of Claudiopolis as birthplace of Antinoos (of which fact its coins boast). If a critic objects that this name is nowhere else applied to the city, I appeal to the frequent variety of names applied to Anatolian cities. The common name of this city on coins is Bithynion-Hadriana, but the invariable name in Byzantine times is Claudiopolis. I do not venture on any conjecture as to other names on this road, except that we might try to find the name of Tarsia, which was certainly the station beside the Sangarios on the east, concealed under one of the names. At one time I thought that it might be hid under Lateas; but this conjecture, as I now perceive, is most improbable. I think it more probable that Lateas, Demetriu and Dusepro Solympum all belong to a road leading from Prousa to Nikaia or Nikomedeia. Lateas then would be a corruption of Platanea, which is mentioned by Pachymeres (ii. p. 413; quoted G 17, p. 207) as situated in the district through which the road from Prousa by Nikaia to Nikomedeia would pass, and which is given as Platana by the Geographus Anon. Ravennensis, p. 109.*

Dusepro Solympum ought to have given the clue to one of the roads that are here mixed. Some modern critic, unheeded, has remarked the obvious fact that this is an error for Prusa pros Olympum. It is true that Prusa pros Olympum occurs also on another road, but similarly Lamasco (i.e. Lampsakos) and Amasia, each occur twice in different parts of the Table. Most of the other names are hopelessly corrupt; and I utterly refuse to accept such towns as Manoris, Potomia, &c., until they are confirmed by another authority than our copy of the Table.†

Kastamon, the modern Kastamouni, was situated on this road, between Pompeiopolis and Claudiopolis. It was evidently an important city in later Byzantine times, but is never mentioned in Roman or early

---

* His order is Atravion (i.e. Tatavion), Agrilion, Platana: the last name has been correctly explained by previous writers as a corruption of Laganeia, like Λατάνεια in Ptolemy. V., 1, 14.

† Potomia is perhaps Potamia, which was in the district; see p. 246.

F

Byzantine documents. It must have lain in the territory of some bishopric, or more correctly it became in later time the centre of population of a district which had a different centre in earlier time, and which therefore appears in the Notitiæ under a different name. I have on p. 323 shown the probability that Dadybra-Kastamon was the bishopric in question.

Hadrianopolis probably lay on the same road, further west than Dadybra and Sora.

3. Let me give one other out of many examples. Kiepert, in his latest map, indicates a road from Komana Cappadociae to Melitene, along a route which seems to me quite inadmissible, and which is, as I believe, in part quite impracticable. On this road he places the following towns * on the authority of the Peutinger Table :—

> Komana 24 Asarinum 24 Castabala 20 Pagrum 30 Archelaopolis 30 Singa 14 Arega 12 Nocotessus 24 Lagalassus 18 Sama 13 Melitene.

Of these there can be no doubt that Castabala is either the Cappadoco-Lycaonian or the Cilician city, falsely transferred to this place; Arcilapopoli (as the Peutinger Table gives it) is either Archelais Colonia, or else Archæopolis of Lazica,† wrongly placed; Singa is the Kommagenian town; Arega is Arca, still called Arga, while the others are quite unknown. Of all the towns given on this route only Arca or Arega belongs to the road from Komana to Melitene, and it appears in a corrupt form.

4. Besides the examples given above of the Cappadocian roads, the Antonine Itinerary is demonstrably wrong in other places, e.g., in the road Dorylaion-Ankyra, in making the route Nikomedeia-Nikaia-Ankyra a direct route, and in the road from the Cilician Gates to Baiae. It gives this road as follows :—

> Podando 27 Nampsucrone 21 Aegeas 24 Catabolo 16 Bais.‡

The order ought to be either

> Podandos, Mopsoukrene, Tarsos, Aigai, Baiae ;

or else (as in the Jerusalem Itinerary),

> Podandos, Mopsoukrene, Tarsos, Adana, Mopsouestia, Kastabala, Baiae.

These two routes have been mixed up, and the confusion was facilitated by the similarity of the names Mopsoukrene, Mopsouestia. If the position that I have assigned to Kastabala on the Pyramos (p. 342) is right, the second route as far as Kastabala is the main road to Kommagene, and at that point turns south through Epiphaneia to Baiae.‡

---

* He puts a mark of interrogation after each, for the route is too obviously absurd.

† Procopius, ' Bel. Goth.,' IV., 527.

‡ This theory, which boldly attributes to the Table an error of a kind common in it, has since been proved to be correct by Mr. Bent.

I do not of course maintain that everything in the Peutinger Table that is uncorroborated is wrong : some of it may yet turn out to be right, or a corruption of what is right, as e.g., in the Bithynian example given above, Plataneai appears on the wrong road corrupted to Lateas (accusative). But it is at present a mistaken and dangerous method to follow the Table as guide ; it must be used only as a support for better authorities. I also expressly refrain from concluding that because the Table is so very untrustworthy in central and eastern Asia Minor, it is equally untrustworthy in all other countries. For example, it is much freer from error in the western, and especially the south-western parts of the country.

The Itineraries are much less corrupted than the Table, and though errors abound in them, yet many of these can be easily explained as due to bad mapping. Both the Peutinger Table and the Antonine Itinerary probably depend ultimately on a map, as is usually believed, " die officielle Reichskarte." * In regard to these two documents the problem is : first, how far do they rightly represent the ultimate authority ? secondly, what degree of accuracy did that ultimate authority attain ? In answer to the second question, Kiepert † has pointed out in very strong terms that we must not suppose that the official map had the accuracy of a modern map. In answer to the first question we must point in the first place to a number of corruptions, some apparently hopeless, others explicable only by uncertain conjectures. To take a few examples from the less corrupt authority, the Antonine presents such names as Zoana, p. 181, Mogaro and Dorano, p. 205, and various other absolutely unknown names, which are, probably, in most cases corrupt ; while Scanatus, p. 206, is conjecturally explained (see p. 295) as Scandis, Eumeis and Gundusa, p. 182, as Kamisa and as Godasa of Ptolemy, Sacoena as Siccasena, Ochras as [D]ogra, Adapera as Lassora or Laskoria, Fiarasi as Siara (the Si being a correction of Fi). By similar conjecture I should explain the P in Ptandaris and Puspena ‡ as derived from a preposition which was attached to the name (according to a custom of which various examples remain in the Peutinger Table) ; it is doubtful whether the Greek ἐπί or ἀπό, or the Latin ab was used.§ Even if all the corruptions of single names could be eliminated, there remains the further difficulty that many names have been transferred from the proper road to an adjoining one.

I owe to Dr. Miller's information (' Weltkarte des Castorius,' p. 119) the reference to a fragment of an itinerary through Cappadocia, which bears so pointedly on the subject of this chapter that I add it here. In

---

* Kiepert in ' Berlin. Sitzungsber.,' 1884, p. 52 ; cp. p. 51.

† Kiepert, l.c., p. 51.

‡ Parthey and Pinder prefer the still more serious corruption Euspoena, p. 177, but Puspena has MS. authority. The name conceals Ptolemy's Ispa in the adjectival form, which is so commonly used in Cappadocia.

§ Compare Pisinda in Ptolemy for ἐπὶ ᾿Ισινδα.

the year 1847 Mercklin published an inscription copied by himself and by Prof. Mommsen in Rome.* I add the transcript here—

 III Id(us) Mopsu-Cre[ne]
 Pr(idie) Id[us), Panhormo
 Id(ibus) Oct(obribus), ad Aq(uas) Calida(s)
 XVII K(alendas) Nov(embres) [T]ynnam
 XVI K(alendas) Tyana
 XV K(alendas) Nov(embres) Anda[balim]
 XIII K(alendas) Nov(embres) . . . .

We see from this fragment that Tynna, which is mentioned only by Ptolemy,† must be near Faustinopolis-Halala. In the Table Aquae Calidae is put in an unconnected way near this road, and Leake rightly conjectured that it must belong to it. The hot springs are still well known. I saw them in 1882, but no ancient remains exist; and nothing in the surroundings would lead one to expect the splendid picture given of them in the Table. The springs lie a little west of the direct road to Tyana, and perhaps Caena was a village on the road at a point near the springs. The name Panhormos is otherwise unknown; it doubtless indicates a great khan for travellers, probably beside the present Bozanti Khan. It should be observed that the proper names appear in this fragment in oblique cases, just as in the Table and Itineraries: Panhormo,-Tynnam.

The problem in regard to Ptolemy is far more complicated, because he certainly used several authorities, and tried with various degrees of success to combine them. For example: the list of cities in Phrygia Magna, v., 2, § 22–26, must be founded on a different authority from the cities of Mysia, § 14. The former extends Phrygia so far west as to include Ankyra, Synaos, and Blaundos, while the latter includes Aloudda, Trajanopolis, and Prepenissos in Mysia. Both these views were entertained by different authorities, on account of the proverbial uncertainty of the boundary between Mysia and Phrygia; but Ptolemy uses sometimes one, sometimes the other, without perceiving the contradiction in which he is thus involved (see p. 145).

He learned from one authority that Paphlagonia was governed by the legatus pro praetore of Galatia; from another authority he learned the full extent of Paphlagonia. He then placed this large Paphlagonia in the province Galatia, though considerable part of it really belonged to the province Bithynia-Pontus.

The character of his account of the Strategiai is fully discussed in Part II., chapters O, Q, and S, which enumerate his long series of mis-

---

* "Beim Besuch des grösseren Campana'schen Columbariums in einer Vigne an der rechten Seite der Via Sebastiana." He adds: "Sollte hier vielleicht zum erstenmal ein zur Reichsvermessung des Augustus gehöriges Actenstück ans Licht getreten sein?" See C. I. L., VI., 5076.

† The statement on p. 311 must be corrected.

takes about the eleventh Strategia, which existed for a short time in the first century before and after Christ. He attributes the cities of this Strategia, sometimes to Cilicia, sometimes to Strategia Antiochiane, sometimes to Lykaonia (Khasbia for Kastabala), sometimes to Cappadocia (Kyzistra in Strategia Kilikia), sometimes to Armenia Minor (Kybistra, Claudiopolis, Dalisandos in Strategia Kataonia).

In the Strategia Laviniane or Laviansene, which Ptolemy places to the south instead of to the north of Melitene, he mentions the towns Kaparkelis, Sabagena, Kizara. Of these Kaparkelis is (see p. 302) identified with Capareas of the Antonine Itinerary, p. 194 (in northern Syria), which may be corrected by means of an inscription, C. I. L., III. Supplem., No. 6814, to Caparceae. Sabagena is difficult to separate from Sobagena of Strategia Sargarausene, or from Sebagena of Strategia Kilikia. Kizara seems to come from a different direction, viz., from the north-west. Strabo, p. 560, mentions Ikizari as a fort in the eastern part of Phazemonitis, a district which apparently forms part of Ptolemy's Pontus Galaticus. It is impossible not to conjecture that Ptolemy's Kizara and Strabo's Ikizari are the same place, wrongly placed by Ptolemy through trusting to a bad map. According to the true situation, Laviniane is not so far distant from Phazemonitis as Ptolemy's assignment would make it. The identification of Kizara with Ikizari, is of course uncertain: the names seem identical, but there may have been two places bearing the same name. Prof. Kiepert's identification of Sibora and Ibora was tempting, but has been proved incorrect (see p. 265, 326): the names, however, have in the latter case only a superficial resemblance, for the Greek forms are Σίβορα and Ἴβωρα.

I do not venture on the difficult question as to the particular authorities used by Ptolemy in the different sections of his account of Asia Minor; though there is no doubt that his work loses most of its value until the exact authority on which each of his statements rests has been determined. It is shown on p. 372 that his Strategia Antiochiane bears a name which must have been given to it in 37 A.D., when it was ruled by Antiochus IV. and Iotape; and that its extent as indicated by Ptolemy was not true after 41, when it was greatly curtailed. The simplest, though not the only possible, explanation is that his authority on the Strategiai wrote about 37–8 A.D.

In Pontus Galaticus and Polemoniacus, Ptolemy's authority seems to have been so accurate as to suggest a Roman official list. By a comparison of his account of these districts with Strabo's unusually detailed description, it will in all probability be easy after actual exploration of the district, to recover the ancient topography almost perfectly. Comparing Ptolemy's account of these Pontic districts with his description of Cappadocia, we see how entirely he depended on his authority: where he had some single good authority to trust to, he is useful; but where he tried to combine different authorities, he falls into the grossest blunders.

In some cases his authority was the same as that of the Peutinger Table and the Antonine Itinerary, viz., the official map of the empire exposed in the Porticus Octaviae, or a copy of it. In the eastern parts of Asia Minor this is proved by the tables on the opposite page, which show how many names unknown from any other sources, are common to Ptolemy, the Peutinger Table, and the Antonine Itinerary.

Various other errors in Ptolemy probably spring from his use of the same authority. In a number of cases, e.g. Kaparkelis, Kiakis, Leandis, Karnalis, Tanadaris, Tirallis, Ladoineris, Sinis, he seems to mistake Latin ablatives plural of second declension * for nominatives. Such errors suggest the forms Parnasso, Mogaro, Dorano, Sebastopoli, &c., of the Antonine Itinerary, and Pesinunte, Tavio, Corveunte, &c., of the Peutinger Table.†

The error made in the name Fiara (for Siara) in the Antonine Itinerary has been explained above (also see p. 308) : this error existed in Ptolemy's authority, and from his false idea about the position of Sargarausene, which he puts in the place of Saravene, he places Φίαρα in it.

In other cases Ptolemy is misled by the letter F substituted for E in his Latin authority (which we must probably understand to be the Roman map). Just as Φουβάγηνα in Galatia is clearly derived from the town Euagina, corrupted in a Latin document to Fuagina, so when Φουσιπάρα and Εὐσιμάρα occur side by side in Melitene, the conjecture at once suggests itself that both names indicate the same place, but that the former was taken from a Latin authority where Eusipara was mistaken as Fusipara.

Kyzistra is given as a city of Strategia Kilikia. The name occurs elsewhere only in Concil. Nicaen., A.D. 325 ; where a bishop of Kyzistra is mentioned. It is therefore only a fault for the bishopric Kybistra, misplaced by Ptolemy like so many other names in his lists of the Strategiai.

The repetition by Ptolemy of places like Olba (as Olbasa), Kybistra, Kormasa or Korbasa, &c., in different districts is paralleled by the Peutinger Table with its repetition of Prousa, Lampsakos, Amasia, &c.

Finally, I give a list of some very obvious corrections in the text of Ptolemy, some of which have been made by previous writers, some by myself.

1 § 13 Ταταούιον for Παταούιον.

1 § 14 Λαγάνεια for Λατάνεια.

---

* Sinis from a masculine form, compare [Pi]sonos of the Itinerary : Kiakis, &c., from neuter forms : Kaparkelis from a feminine form which appears as accusative in the Itinerary, p. 194.

† Accusative forms also occur in both the Itinerary (Capareas, Arauracos, &c.), and in the Table (Stabiu = εἰς Τάβιον, Aquas Aravenas, &c.).

1. CITIES IN ARMENIA MINOR.

Ptolemy.	Peutinger T.	Anton. Itin.	Other Authorities.
Satala	Satala	Satala	Satala (often)
Domana	Domana	Domana	
Tapoura	Patara		
Nikopolis	Nicopoli (ablative)	Nicopolis	Nikopolis (often)
Chorsabia	Eregarsina	Carsagis, Carsat	
Charax (l. Rarax.)		Arauracos	᾽Αραύρακα (Const., &c.)
Dagona (l. Dragona)	Draconis	Dracontes	
Seleoberroia	Ole Oberda		
Kaltiorissa	Caleorsissa		
Analibla	Analiba	Analiba	Analibla (Act. Conc.)
Pisingara, Pinsigara			
Godasa		Gundusa, Gondosa	
Eudoixata			
Karape			
Masora, Kasara			
Oromandos, Oromandros			
Ispa	Hispa	Euspena, Puspena	
Phouphena			
Arane	Arangas (accus.)	Aranis (ablative)	
Phouphatena			
Mardara		Malandara	
Ouarsapa, Ouaisapa			
Orsa, Orsara			

2. CITIES ALONG THE EUPHRATES.
(a) *In Armenia.*

Sinibra		Sinervas (accus.)	
Aziris			
Ladana (v. l. Dalanda)			Still called Derende; not on Euphrates
Sismara *			
Zimara	Zimara	Zimara	Pliny, V. 83
Daskousa	Dascusa	Dascusa	Pliny, V. 84

(b) *In Melitene.*

Dagousa †	Saba ?	Sabous ?	
Sinis Kolonia		Pisonos (ἐπὶ Σίνους ?)	
Melitene	Melentenes	Melitene	Often mentioned; not on Euphrates

(c) *In Laviniane or Laviansene.*

Korne	Corne		
Meteita	Metita		
Klaudias	Glaudia		Claudiopolis Cappadociae, Pliny, V. 85

(d) *In [S]aravene.*

Juliopolis			
Barzalo	Barsalium		

* Dittography of the following?
† Dittography of Daskousa? or is it corrupted from the name that appears in the Antonine Itinerary as Sabous, and in the Peutinger Table as Saba.

2 § 14 Δάγουτα, which has often been doubted, is defended by the Δαγοτθηνοί of Constantine Porphyrogenitus.

2 § 15 Γριμενοθυρῖται for Τριμενοθ., as M. Waddington rightly perceived.

2 § 16 Αἰγαιαί for Αἴγαρα (cp. Λυσήναρα of Hierocles, and 2 § 24).

2 § 18 Ἀττούδδα has been by some suggested for Ἰτώανα.

2 § 20 Ἐριζηνοί has been proposed with obvious correctness for Ἐρίζηλοι.

2 § 21 Δάλδεις for Δαδαλεῖς, see p. 131.

2 § 23 Κερκωπία has been corrupted from Ἀπία through the influence of the following Εὐκαρπία.

2 § 24 Μελίταια should be restored for Μελίταρα, compare § 16.

2 § 25 Βροῦζος for Δροῦζος.

Βλαῦνδος for Βλέανδρος.

Σίβλιον, Σιβλία, or Σειβλία is the more correct form, not Σίλβιον.

2 § 26 Σαναός for Σανίς.

Τάγηνα or Τάκινα for Γάζηνα.

2 § 27 Transpose Φυλακήνσιοι and Λυκάονες:* the alteration arose from the latter being placed beside Λυκίαν. Φυλακήνσιοι is a Greek rendering of a Latin original Phylacenses.

Μακ. Καδοηνοί (as in Pliny) for Μοκκαδηνοί.

Κιδυησσεῖς for Κυδισσεῖς.

Μοξεανοί is more correct than Μοξιανοί.

Ἱεροπολῖται was the native name, Ἱεραπολῖται the form used by Grecising writers.

4 § 3 Ζαλήκου for Ζαλίσκου.

4 § 4 It is unnecessary to alter Διδύμου to Δινδύμου: the forms are equivalent, see Athen. Mittheil., 1888, p. 237.

4 § 5 Γερμανικόπολις for Γερμανόπολις.

4 § 7 Τολιστοβώγιοι for Τολιβωστοί.

Τολιστοχώρα for Τολαστάχορα.

4 § 9 Φουβάγηνα is a Greek rendering of a Latin original Fuagina, an error for Euagina, see p. 261.

4 § 10 Προσειλημμενῖται (inhabitants of the χώρα προσειλημμένη) for Προσερλιμενῖται.

Τυριάϊον for Τετράδιον.

4 § 12 Ὀρονδικὸν for Ὀρονδικοί: the tribe was called Ὀρονδεῖς.

5 § 3 Σύεδρα for Σύσδρα.

5 § 6 Περμινοδέων δῆμος for Μενεδήμιον.

Οὐερβιανόπολις for Οὐρανόπολις.

Ἴσινδα for Πίσινδα (i.e. ἐπὶ Ἴσινδα).

5 § 7 Πρόσταννα is more correct than Πρόσταμα.

5 § 8 Κόμαμα Κολ. for Κόμμακον.

6 § 3 Φαναροίαν for Φαναγορίαν.

* ASP., B 4.

Cappadocia, Lykaonia, and Cilicia have all been discussed sufficiently in Part II., and I need not recapitulate the suggestions made there.

These views about the authorities under discussion were arrived at during the composition of Part II., being forced upon me by the discovery of successive errors in them. The example of Tynna given in this chapter, shows that a statement unsupported at present may afterwards be confirmed by new evidence. But the numerous errors that are proved show that we cannot safely accept any statement until we can confirm it by some independent evidence, direct or indirect.

This long discussion is perhaps not too long for the necessities of the case. For example, I have in regard to Cappadocia and its Strategiai discarded entirely the authority of Ptolemy, which has been hitherto accepted implicitly, even by Prof. Kiepert, and have, in dependence on a few sentences of Strabo, placed some Strategiai as much as 100 miles from the situation assigned to them by Ptolemy's minutely detailed map, and followed by all modern geographers. This proceeding may seem too bold; but we must follow either Ptolemy or Strabo, whose evidence is in irreconcilable contradiction. My general impression with regard to Strabo's account of Asia Minor is, as stated on p. 96, that as a rule "his brief descriptions are marvellously accurate, and, to the eye-witness, marvellously lucid." Individual cases of vagueness, and even slight inaccuracy can be pointed out, but they are exceedingly rare.* In some cases his description of the scenery of the eastern part of the plateau is so good as to depend either on his own observation, or to be reported with closest precision from the account of an eye-witness. † The western part of the plateau, including Phrygia, on the other hand, he has evidently not seen. Now his own distinct evidence is given (see pp. 535, 536) that he had travelled in Cappadocia: he had been in Komana of Cappadocia and had seen the wonderful gorge where the Pyramos breaks through Taurus. A native of Amaseia could not see these two places without seeing a good deal more of the country; and must indeed have been travelling for the purpose of observation. ‡

Finally, with regard to Hierocles, whose authority I place so high, I have discussed the subject both on pp. 92–95, and at numerous places throughout Part II. The many cases in which his order has been

---

* I have shown in 'Cities and Bishoprics,' Part II. § XLIII., that the puzzling arrangement of the cities of Phrygia in four groups becomes accurate when the single slight change of EYMENEIAN to AKMONEIAN is made.

† Von Diest ('Von Perg. z. Pontus,' p. 15) says that a passage in p. 625 shows actual experience of the road from Pergamos to the east. On the other hand he shows that Strabo gives an inaccurate account of the Aeolic coast.

‡ Niese shows that Strabo does not profess to have seen any places away from the sea in Asia Minor except Komana, the Pyramos, Hierapolis in the Lycus valley, and Nysa in the Maeander Valley : see his 'Beiträge zur Biographie Strabos' in Hermes, XIII., 1878, p. 42, where he shows that Strabo lived from about 63 B.C. to 19 A.D., and that he wrote his geographical work in Rome, for a Roman public, about 18–19 A.D.

confirmed by new discoveries, have given me great confidence in him, though of course it is necessary to look as much as possible for corroborative evidence. I have tried to show that, (1) his chief authority is a list of bishoprics, which he modifies into a list of cities; (2) this list must have been arranged in an approximately geographical order, partly according to roads, partly according to districts; (3) Hierocles modified it and even added to it in Bithynia and still more in Hellespontus; (4) there is great corruption and transposition in the lists of Lydia and Hellespontus.

VII. The Byzantine Roads.

A change in the road-system began in A.D. 292. Diocletian made Nikomedeia the capital of the east, and the roads that connected it with the provinces acquired increased importance. This tendency was confirmed when Constantinople was founded in 330; for precisely the same set of roads lead to Nikomedeia and to Constantinople. The centre of attraction was now no longer Rome, but Constantinople, and the roads which served only for the Roman traffic rapidly sank into mere cross-country paths.

At first the old Roman roads were utilised as far as possible, and both the Peutinger Table and the Antonine Itinerary show us these roads adapted to the new requirements. But a steady and progressive change was produced over the whole of Asia Minor. Previously prosperity had been greatest in the southern half of the plateau. But during the two centuries that elapsed between Constantine and Justinian, the northern half of the plateau grew steadily in importance as being nearer Constantinople and in easier communication with it; and many new centres of population were formed, which gradually acquired the rank of cities and bishoprics.* Steadily also the system of communication altered, as it was gradually found that new routes served travellers better than the Roman roads. By the time of Justinian the change was complete, and it is clear that in his reorganisation of the administration he recognised the new system and put an end to the old.

No document has been preserved that attempts to give us a complete account of the Byzantine roads. We are reduced to piecing together scattered hints in the historians, and interpreting them in accordance with the natural features of the country. We are aided by the fact that on the whole the Byzantine system continued in use throughout the Turkish domination; but the best result attainable with regard to the two centuries of change is a few isolated pictures of separate points. We know that Apameia had been one of the chief centres of Græco-

---

* This principle is stated C. B., § lxvii., and is proved in many details in Part II.

Roman civilisation and commerce, and also cf the rising power of Christianity. But its prosperity depended on its situation at a knot on the great eastern trade-route. That route lost all importance under the Byzantine rule; and Apameia sank into a third or fourth-rate town.

Various other examples of a similar kind are given in Part II.,* only one of which I shall refer to here. A fortunate chance has preserved to us a petition addressed to the emperor Theodosius about 380-90 A.D., intreating him to build a bridge over the Halys for the sake of preserving a constant connexion between Caesareia-Mazaka and the provinces of Galatia and Pontus. I have interpreted this document (p. 255 ff.) as marking the transition from the old Roman road between Ankyra and Caesareia, which did not cross the Halys, to the modern road, which crosses the Halys twice. I have shown how Parnassos on the old road lost consequence, whereas Mokissos on the new road rose to importance, was constituted by Justinian the capital of Cappadocia Secunda,† and is still one of the chief cities of Anatolia. Probably the document which has preserved to us this interesting episode is not unique, and more careful investigation of the records of the period will reveal others.

The completion of the Byzantine road system dates from Justinian. The most important part of the system was the Military Road forking east of the Halys to Caesareia and to Sebasteia. The character of this road has not, so far as I know, been observed hitherto by any historian, and I have therefore in Chapter G discussed it in detail from the first stage onwards. Much of the Byzantine military history in the east depends on the recognition of this great road. At intervals there were standing camps in convenient places near it, and as the emperor passed along towards the seat of war, he was joined by the contingents of troops from the different provinces which had concentrated at these camps. A march in spring from Constantinople along the military road, a summer campaign on the eastern frontier, a return march to the capital along the same road at the approach of winter, and a few months in Constantinople before the next campaign began—such was the life year after year of many of the vigorous emperors. The line of their march, where nothing is expressly mentioned, may as a rule be assumed

---

* See pp. 205, 216, 220, 223, &c. I must maintain that the road from Tavium by Korniaspa to Sebasteia is a Byzantine interpolation in the Antonine Itinerary. It is entirely out of keeping with the Roman system, and is strikingly illustrated by the Byzantine records.

† I have, for convenience sake, always spoken in Part II. of Mokissos as metropolis of Cappadocia Tertia. But it must be remembered that politically there were only two provinces of Cappadocia, of which Caesareia and Mokissos were the respective metropoleis from the time of Justinian onwards, while Tyana, which had been metropolis of Cappadocia Secunda from the time when Valens divided Cappadocia into two, retained its ecclesiastical rank and its authority over a few bishoprics.

to be the military road: and in many cases this is of great importance for the understanding of the operations described. I shall here quote only one example, viz., the march of Romanus Diogenes in 1068, from Helenopolis to the east. After crossing the Halys, he avoided the road to Caesareia.* It is only the fact of the road forking beyond the Halys to Caesareia that gives any point to the statement that the emperor did not touch Caesareia, a city that lay quite sixty miles from the nearest point of his march, and a hundred miles from the crossing of the Halys. He then encamped at Krya Pege, for some days; and the beauty, the plentiful water, the trees and the grass of this place are described in glowing terms. This is obviously the camp called Bathys Rhyax, by Constantine Porphyrogenitus, I., p. 444, and Genesius, pp. 123, 124. He then proceeded to Sebasteia, where again he took the left road to Koloneia, not the right to Tephrike (see pp. 57, 267).

I have ascribed to Justinian the formation of this road and the institution of the whole system of *aplekta* connected with it. The fact is nowhere recorded, and I depend for proof of the statement entirely on inference from a number of slight details, which are collected in ch. G. They prove that the great importance of the road is as old as Justinian; and if so, there is little doubt that he also arranged its military connection, for its importance lies mainly in its military character: it is not the shortest route, but it is the best route for an army.

The general map shows the chief lines of road, radiating from Constantinople, whose existence in the Byzantine period can be proved. Some of these we hear of first in the latest warfare under the Nicæan empire or the Palæologi, when the theatre of operations was narrowed down to the west of Asia Minor, But the previous existence and importance of many of them cannot be doubted (see pp. 129, 130).

A study of the chief references to these roads and of the operations that took place along them would form the proper completion of this subject: the incidental references that occur in Part II. are quite insufficient to show its importance. Such a study would probably show that several other lines of road, used in the Turkish time, but not indicated on my map, are referred to by the Byzantine historians in passages that have escaped me. But such a study would expand into a discussion of the Byzantine campaigns in Asia Minor, which is too great a task to enter on at present: it forms the third part of the programme of work on the history and antiquities of Asia Minor which I had once sketched out for myself.

During certain conditions of warfare other roads besides the great military road, and even occasionally others in addition to those that radiate from Constantinople, assumed a temporary importance in Byzantine history. On p. 197 ff. I have described all the routes that led from Constantinople to the east, and have given some examples of

* τὴν Καισάρειαν παρελθών, Scyl., p. 691; τῇ Καισαρέων μὴ προσμίξας, Attal., p. 146.

marches which took place along them. The long frontier wars against the Saracens tested every route; for the light-armed marauders, crossing from Cilicia for a run in the Christian lands, took sometimes one pass, sometimes another. The two leading routes during these wars are through the same passes that have been important at all periods, that from Germanicia to Arabissos, and the Cilician Gates (Loulon, see p. 350). But almost every important mountain pass in the whole of Asia Minor has its great battle, and some of them their score of conflicts (see pp. 368, 381, 382). I add one example.

The campaign of 860 is described very vaguely. The only express statement as to the situation of the great defeat of the Saracens is that of Genesius, that it was 500 miles from Amisos, which is of course so absurd as to suggest a doubt about the text. But when we compare the accounts,* we find (1) that the battle took place near the confines of the Armoniac and Paphlagonian Themes, (2) on the west side of the Halys, (3) on the road that leads south from Sinope, (4) on a river that flows from north to south, (5) near the Halys, for a very few fugitives escaped across the Halys into the Kharsian Theme, (6) among the hills in a glen, where the Saracens were surrounded. There are only two localities which can suit this description, one where the road from Sinope descends to Boiabad and the Halys, the other further south, where it again descends towards Andrapa and the Halys. The fact that the crossing of the Halys led into the Kharsian Theme decides in favour of the latter. Historians differ greatly about the names: probably Lalakaon was the district, Poson or Porson the place, and Gyris the river.† But Genesius and the Continuator call the district Abysianon or Amysianon, Porson the place, Lalakaon the river, and Gyris the meadow on the river by the Saracen camp. Amysianon is perhaps connected with Amnesia (see N 12, p. 278). Amysianon was on a road leading probably from Paphlagonia to Kommagene (see p. 354), and Amnesia was on a road from Arabissos to Constantinople, perhaps by Eukhaita. Accurate exploration might probably determine the very spot where the battle was fought.

With the Turkish invasion in the latter part of the eleventh century, a new period of military history begins. Civil history and commercial intercourse have from this time onward hardly any existence, owing partly to the misery of the situation and partly to the degrading and enfeebling influence of the Byzantine rule,‡ in which the Roman

---

* Georg. Mon., 825; Symeon Mag., 666; Theoph. Cont., 181; Leo Gram., 238; Cedr. II., 164; Genes., 96; Zonar. II., 159, ed. Par.

† Ducange on Zonar. quotes Epist. 167 of Photius, addressed Θεοδότῳ Σπαθαρο-κανδιδάτῳ κατὰ τοὺς Λαλάκωνας.

‡ This had gradually destroyed the spirit of the different communities, discouraged the free flow of trade between the provinces, and produced an oriental stagnation, in which each district got on as best it could on its own resources. Exceptions can be

character had almost wholly given place to an Oriental despotism. Great part of the plateau passed into the hands of the Turks, whose power extended over Lykaonia, Cappadocia, and considerable part of Phrygia and Galatia. Dorylaion was the north-western limit of their authority; but Kotiaion they did not hold. From Dorylaion they advanced along the road to Constantinople, and even seized Nikaia. On the south-west they held for a time Sozopolis, Apameia (then a mere village), and Laodiceia. It would appear that their right to these territories was recognised in the disgraceful agreement concluded with the Turks about 1076 A.D., when their help was bought by the surrender of a great territory.

The Seljuk Turkish capital was at Iconium, and the four chief roads that led to it became the chief scene of warfare from this time onwards until the rise of the Osmanli Turks. Two of these roads were the same as roads of the earlier period, viz., those which led by Dorylaion and by Kotiaion. We also begin now to hear of a third, which coincided 'for some distance with the road to Kotiaion through Bilejik and Basilika, and then diverged to Dorylaion (see pp. 208, 236, 445). . The fourth road was one which is first heard of at the end of the eleventh century, though we then find that it must have been of some military consequence from a much earlier time; it was the central road of the Theme Khoma.

The first three of these roads form a connected group. The great road to Dorylaion was the most direct, but fell earliest into Turkish hands. The road through Kotiaion was important because that city did not fall under the power of the Seljuks till 1182.* It was apparently in Byzantine hands in 1156, but the limit of their power, when Manuel Comnenus marched towards it from Isauria. In 1116 also it was certainly in Byzantine hands, and probably in 1113.

The campaign of 1116 furnishes an excellent proof of the use of the road by Kotiaion and Dorylaion. Alexius Comnenus then advanced with a large army through Dorylaion to Philomelion. Here by one of his pious frauds he ascertained that the will of heaven forbade him to advance to Iconium. He therefore retired towards Constantinople, and was then hard pressed by hordes of Turkish light troops, who had offered little opposition to his advance. After two days of continuous fighting the army reached a point between Polybotos and Ipsos, where they diverged from the road by which they had advanced, and turned towards Ampoun. There were only two roads open to them. One led

---

proved, but such was the general condition of the later Byzantine empire, and herein lay its weakness.

* Dorylaion was not maintained as a fortress by the Seljuk Turks, who never showed any organising ability; it sank into ruins, and the fertile valley was occupied by nomadic bands until 1175, when Manuel refortified it.

by Polybotos, and then across difficult country where the Turkish skirmishers would have had a great advantage; and by this road it would be many days before they reached Byzantine territory. The other went along the valley towards the village now called Ambanaz,* a few miles north of Akroenos. The latter road, usually known as the route to Kotiaion, was preferred; and on the following day, when the army was between Augustopolis and Akroenos, a truce was concluded. This may be taken as a fair indication that Akroenos and the country between it and Kotiaion were still in Byzantine hands.

In 1145 Manuel Comnenus advanced along the Kotiaion route almost up to Iconium, and retired by Khoma.

Again, in 1175 Manuel resolved to make a great effort to break the Turkish strength. As a preliminary he rebuilt two deserted fortresses, Dorylaion and Soublaion. In 1176 he chose the latter route to deliver his great blow at the Seljuks. He advanced from the Rhyndakos (obviously by Akhyraous Thyateira) to Khonai, and thence to Khoma. This campaign, therefore, was conducted along the fourth of those roads which we have mentioned as of pre-eminent importance in the Turkish wars.† Soublaion was situated at the site now called Khoma, retaining the name which was coming into use among the historians of the twelfth century. The change of name is of course a common phenomenon in Asia Minor. It is probable that the name of the Theme Khoma was applied to the central fortress of the Theme. Anna Comnena mentions the Khomatenoi several times, and it is clear from her language, II. pp. 325–7, that the frontier defence against the Seljuks was divided between the Themes of Khoma and Cappadocia.‡ But why the name Khoma was given to the Theme, whether the troops were first called Khomatenoi from some reason unknown to us, and the country where they were stationed got the name Khoma from them; § or whether the local application is the earlier, and the troops were called after the country in which they were stationed, it seems now impossible to discover.‖

The central road of the Theme connected the two great fortresses, Khonai and Khoma. Two routes are possible for it. One, which was actually traversed by Barbarossa, went up the Lykos, along the salt

* Obviously the same name as Ampoun in Anna Comnena. On the whole subject see my paper in 'Athen. Mittheil.,' 1882, p. 140.

† On Manuel's defeat, see p. 136 and my "Notes and Inscriptions, IX.," in 'Amer. Journ. Arch.,' vol. ii.

‡ On the changes of the Theme Cappadocia, see pp. 216, 250, 316.

§ See p. 316.

‖ I have in ASP, in a final appended note, suggested the possibility that Khoma, which is known also between Konia and Bey Sheher (where we find Yokari Khoma and Ashagha Khoma), may be actually the Turkish name of the town, adopted like many others by the Byzantine writers; but this is not probable. The name has not a Turkish appearance, and there is no time for a Turkish name to have gained currency between the appearance of the Turks and the use of the name by Anna.

lake Anava, and then struck across by Bolatli direct to Khoma. I think, however, that the other route by Denizler (different from Denizli) and Harir Boghaz, was the Byzantine road (see ASP). In either case the line is a strange one, diverging as it does from the Roman trade route; but the evidence seems conclusive. Khoma lies on the shortest road between the Hermos valley or the upper Mæander valley and the east in general. That line is indeed not an easy one, but to light active troops such as rode in the Arab forays into Asia Minor, it presents no serious difficulty, while its directness recommended it to them. Probably the same state of things also existed when the Sassanians were ravaging the whole country up to the Bosphorus and the Aegean during the earlier centuries. Two possibilities suggest themselves as to the period when Khoma was made an important fortress, viz., either the reign of Justinian or the time of the Iconoclast emperors. Many reasons induce us to prefer the former. One is that the pair of fortresses, Khoma and Khonai, were apparently on the same scheme; and I cannot think that Khonai was founded so late as the Iconoclast period. The very name Khonai supplanted that of Kolossai between 692 and 787, and that can hardly have taken place immediately after the foundation of the fortress of Khonai. Another lies in the bishopric Justinianopolis or Oikokome. I understand Οἰκο-κώμη as a grecised term for the Vicus marked in the Peutinger Table between Eumeneia and Apameia. Justinianopolis would then be the fortress above it united under one bishop with the settlement in the open plain.* Moreover, I am unable to discover any signs of the foundation of fortresses or cities by the Iconoclasts. The whole system of organisation and defence had been so admirably planned by Justinian, that nothing remained for later emperors to do except to maintain or restore what he had built.

Justinian then built the fortress of Khoma or Soublaion (Siblia) beside the pass leading towards the Aegean coast. Nicetas Choniata distinguishes that fortress from another actually in the pass, called Myriokephalon,† which was a ruin in the time of Manuel Comnenus.

During the period 1076–1119 the line of the Roman trade-route between Laodiceia and Apameia appears to have been entirely in the hands of the Turks. In 1119 John Comnenus advanced by Philadelphia to Laodiceia and captured it: and in 1120 he advanced further and captured Sozopolis, which remained in Byzantine hands till 1182. But even after 1120 it appears that the line of the trade-route through Apameia was deserted and unsafe, owing to the bands of Turkish nomads who infested it. In 1146 Manuel Comnenus was attacked and wounded beside his own camp by a troop of these Turks, when he was encamped near Soublaion, and had incautiously gone out towards Apameia to hunt.

The history of the reigns of the three Comneni, Alexius, John and

* See p. 136, C. 25.   † On the name, see p. 220.

Manuel, suggests that during that entire period the road through Apameia was not used by the Byzantine armies; and the phrase used at a later date by Tagenon in describing the march of Barbarossa past the salt lake Anava, "loca desertissima Turcorum" (see p. 130), suggests the reason. The route by the Harir Boghaz was employed, and I have placed Charax and Graos Gala on it.

Apart from the temporary changes caused by such circumstances as the Seljuk empire with its capital at Iconium, there has been little alteration in the road system of Anatolia as it was fixed by Justinian until our own time. But the roads are now in a transition stage. When all Turkish government business had to be carried across Asia Minor to the eastern and southern parts of the empire, the important routes had to be maintained in decent condition; and a postal service, with relays of horses, was kept up along them. When Leake was sent in haste from Constantinople to Egypt in 1800, he rode across Asia Minor by Dorylaion and Iconium to Anemourion, and there took boat to Cyprus. At present a traveller or a government messenger to Cyprus would take the steamer. The difference in this case is typical of a vast number of similar changes, which have curtailed the number of roads along which a horse-post is kept up.

Another cause of change lies in the growth of Smyrna, which has become the commercial capital of Turkey. Railways from Smyrna have crept up the country into Lydia and Phrygia. One follows the general line of the old "Royal Road," until it has reached the foot of the plateau and is confronted with that step of 2000 feet, which is required to place it on the plateau. The other keeps closely to the line of the great trade route, and has already reached Apameia. The expansion of commerce between Asia Minor and the west has made these railways, in spite of many difficulties interposed by government. One ground for the action of the government concerns us. These railways would make Smyrna the central city of Asia Minor, but the government wishes that Constantinople should continue to be the governing centre; and that wish has led to the projected railway from Constantinople to Ankyra (Angora), which as a commercial enterprise has no prospect of being remunerative for a long time.

Within my own knowledge of Asia Minor, great activity in road-making has been shown by the Turks. In some cases the new roads are a blessing to the country; but I have also seen broad new roads, whose path across the country was conspicuous by their greener and more luxuriant crop of grass, and I have seen numerous roads made in unconnected fragments, or in a more advanced state with everything ready except the bridges. In the great majority of cases one quarter of the expenditure would be sufficient to improve the existing roads in their worse parts. But the new scheme of renovation is usually on too grand a scale. An entirely new route is laid out, great expense is incurred, and

then the road is left unfinished; or, worst fate of all, the broad new
road, with small stones scattered over the smooth level surface, is not so
pleasant for pack-horses as the old narrow well-trodden path; and
traffic deliberately prefers the old road, leaving the new road to grow a
magnificent crop of grass. Part of the reason why the roads are in
many cases so fragmentary lies in the fact that they are built by the
labour of the villagers : each adult is bound to give his labour for a few
days in the year; and when his time is done the conclusion of his work
must be postponed till the next year. This plan is the only one possible
in the country, and it demands from the inhabitants their fair contribution to the common good in the way that presses most lightly on them;
but it needs more skill in the proper application of the labour than is
generally shown. But in other cases the reason for the failure of the
new road lies in mismanagement or in fraud. I have seen a ruined
fragment of a new bridge over the Halys, composed of a mere shell of
masonry filled in with earth : this bridge was once completed, and must
have looked very well during the summer months, till the first high
water swept great part of it away.

This deficiency in the Turkish road-system is likely to have important political consequences. Anatolia is essentially a Mohammedan
country, but Armenia is a Christian country, where the inhabitants tend
surely to union with Russia. The consummation of that union is only
a matter of time, and probably of no long time. The Russian railways
have reached the frontier: there are no Turkish railways, existing or
even projected, near the frontier, and few roads even that are in decent
repair. Nor is there any likelihood that Armenia proper would content
Russia. The Halys, the greatest river of Asia Minor,* has often been a
river of boundary. The province on the east of the river, one of the
finest in the Turkish empire, contains a number of Armenians; and it
is not improbable that the next step made by Russia will carry her to
the banks of the Halys.

VIII. Change of Site.

The variation in the site of cities at different periods of history is a
point which is frequently touched in the present work. One of the
thoughts which oftenest occur to the traveller in Asia Minor is to ask
why modern towns so rarely occupy exactly the site of ancient cities.

In some cases the change was made from purely accidental reasons.
Prof. J. R. S. Sterrett† mentions that during the Egyptian war " a
large number of Turkish troops were quartered for an indefinite period
on the people of old Malatia, which stood on the site of Melitene. This

---

* It is the longest, though it drains an area decidedly smaller than the Sangarios.
† 'Epigraphical Journey,' p. 300.

was more than the long-suffering inhabitants could bear; so they abandoned their old houses to the soldiers, and built a new city among the gardens seven or eight miles south-west of Melitene." The story has a look of popular mythology about it, and Prof. Sterrett does not state on what authority he has received it; but, if true, it would be an excellent example of a kind of change which can be properly treated only in a 'Local History' of Asia Minor. There is an infinite variety in the history of the various districts; but a few general considerations may be here brought together.

The ancient site is sometimes absolutely deserted. At other times it is succeeded by a mere village, while the modern town which is the heir to the importance of the ancient city is situated at a considerable distance. In the Lykos valley, Denizli, several miles from Laodiceia, may be taken as both geographically and in respect of importance the representative of the now deserted Laodiceia; for the tiny villages in the plain which are nearer the ancient site, are chifliks, and do not correspond to the ancient city. But Tripolis is represented geographically by Yeni Keui, in name by the pass called Derebol, and in importance by Bulladan; Attoudda is represented geographically by Haz Keui, but in importance by Serai Keui *; and Hierapolis is represented geographically by Pambuk Kalesi, but in importance by Denizli.† In the following pages when I speak of a modern town as the representative of an ancient city, I mean that it has succeeded it as the chief centre of population and the seat of government; but I do not imply that it actually occupies the ancient site, or that it is the nearest inhabited place to the ancient site. The rule is general that each modern centre is the representative of some ancient city, and conversely that almost every ancient city has a modern representative.

Roads which were important in one period of the history of Anatolia, often lost all importance in another period. In such cases it frequently happened that along with the road, a city on it lost importance, and its influence was transferred to a new centre. Apameia (see p. 75) was great in the Roman period, insignificant in the Byzantine time; and quite recently it has taken a new start in life, as the mere possibility of a railway reaching it became evident. Other examples in abundance are to be found in Part II. The fact that almost all the cities on the line of the " Royal Road " bear old Phrygian names, while almost all those on the great trade-route bear names that mark them as refounded by Greek kings or Roman emperors, needs no comment.

Apart from changes in the road-system, however, we observe that

---

* A market, which used to be held almost on the site of Attoudda, has been transferred within living memory to Serai Keui.

† Yeni Keui is about a mile from the site of Tripolis, which is quite deserted; Bulladan is about six miles distant. Pambuk Kalesi lies close below the actual site of Hierapolis.

certain character in regard to situation, access, and local surroundings can be traced in the cities of each period.*

The chief characteristics that are observed in the sites of ancient cities in Asia Minor are (1) military strength, (2) ease of access and commercial advantages in general, (3) convenience of water-supply.

Military strength seems to have been the determining consideration in the earlier time. Sites were in many cases selected on hills whose sides either were naturally precipitous or could readily be scarped. Thus great strength was attained without much positive fortification. In some cases a slight parapet at the top of a perpendicular wall of rock 50 to 100 feet in height was all the artificial work needed. The description which I have given of the early Phrygian cities in my "Study of Phrygian Art"† sufficiently illustrates this subject. Similar fortifications were all that were needed in Blaundos, Akmonia, Palæo-Sebaste, Lounda, Celaenae, &c. The people must have lived in the open plain except during attack by an enemy, when they retired into the fortified town. Too little is known of this old period to justify us in saying much about it; but that a certain amount of commerce and a certain regard to commercial convenience existed even then is shown by the very name as well as by the situation of Keramon Agora on the "Royal Road." So also Pessinus, on the same road, can hardly have been a strong fortress; its chief defence was religious veneration.

The sacred cities of this early period often grew up around some place, where the divine power was most strikingly manifested, e.g. by hot medicinal springs, a hole with mephitic exhalations, or any other natural phenomenon. A sacred village, *Hiera Kome*, grew up near or round the sanctuary, and depended on the divine power alone for protection.‡ Such was the temple of Artemis at Ephesos, which stood apart from and often in opposition to the Greek city. A city of the native character often grew out of this sacred village, and the name Hieropolis was often attached to it. Wherever native feeling is strong, the form of this name is Hieropolis, "City of the Hieron;" but where Greek feeling and education spreads, the Greek form Hierapolis, "the Sacred City," is introduced. The difference of form, though apparently so slight, really corresponds to a remarkable difference between the native and the Greek spirit. According to the former the Hieron, according to the latter the Polis, is the leading idea. Types of these

---

* Professor G. Hirschfeld in his essay on ' Typologie griechischer Ansiedelungen im Alterthum,' should be read in connection with these remarks; see " Aufsätze Ernst Curtius gewidmet." Hirschfeld has many excellent remarks on the same subject in his ' Reiseberichte.'

† ' Journ. Hell. Stud.' 1888 and 1889.

‡ On this subject see the description of the village named Atyokhorion near Dionysopolis in my " Artemis-Leto and Apollo-Lairbenos " in ' Journ. Hell. Stud.," 1889.

priestly foundations are to be found at Hieropolis in the Glaukos valley, Soa among the Prepenisseis,* Aizanoi † in Phrygia, Komana in Cappadocia, &c.

But apart from these hieratic centres and a few markets like Keramon Agora, safety and military strength determined the sites of the earliest cities. Water-supply often constituted a serious difficulty in them. Water was sometimes stored in large cisterns to provide for the contingency of a siege. In Amaseia a passage was cut through the rock down to a plentiful supply of water. Each individual city has its own method of supply.

The foundations of the Greek kings were of a different character. Military strength was still a prominent factor in determining the sites chosen during the century that followed the death of Alexander; but it was not the sole dominant consideration, and it was sought more by artificial fortification. Ease of access and commercial convenience were also aimed at. These cities were intended to be centres of civilisation and of a foreign domination in the country; and they must therefore be in easy communication with each other and with other countries. The site of Celaenae was now deserted, and Apameia was founded near it on a site of the new character. Synnada, Seleuceia Sidera, Laodiceia ad Lycum, Antiocheia in Pisidia, Antiocheia ad Maeandrum, and many others, belong to the same type. They are situated on rising grounds at the edge of open plains. They are thus easy of access, yet their walls, placed on the edge of the low hills that constitute the sites, rise high over the plain and make them very strong fortresses, so long as the fortifications are kept in thorough repair.

The size of these cities was determined by the hills on which they stood. Synnada, one of the oldest, must have been a tiny city; and indeed Strabo expressly remarks on its small size. The water-supply would have to be studied separately in each case. In Laodiceia ad Lycum it could be well seen a few years ago. The line of the underground conduit which brought the water from the abundant sources that flow through every street of the modern Denizli could be followed for several miles from Laodiceia: I did not attempt to trace it up to the source. In the northern part of the city it rose in the large earthenware pipe that brought it to a height sufficient to dominate the whole city: there it communicated with a number of smaller pipes. In this way the pressure was diminished to the amount needed for distribution, and the supply could be easily cut off from any of the smaller pipes.

---

* I have shown, p. 144, that the form Bennisoa has no existence except in the misinterpretation of an inscription; Soa, "the Grave" (i.e., of Atys), shows that the character of this religious centre was similar to that of Atyokhorion near Dionysopolis. See also my "Study of Phrygian Art," part ii., in 'Journ. Hell. Stud.,' 1889.

† Aizanoi with its priestly dynasts, who looked to Euphorbus as first of their number and probably as their ancestor (such priests being generally hereditary), seems to be proved by the quotation from Hermogenes, ap. Steph. Byz., s.v.

This interesting building was in process of destruction when I visited Laodiceia in the spring of 1883.

In the peaceful period which began with the ascendency of the Pergamenian kings after B.C. 190, and continued under the Roman rule, the population tended to concentrate in open defenceless situations on the plains, where the conditions of life were more pleasant than in the strong but uncomfortable cities of the early period. The foundations of the earlier Diadochi indeed, being on low hills close to or even in the middle of open plains, maintained their existence. But where the ancient custom of living partly in the open plain, with a city in a lofty situation as a military refuge, had continued, open defenceless cities grew during the Pergamenian and Roman periods. In many cases, e.g. at Lounda and at Sebaste, the older situation was abandoned owing to the gradual concentration of the population in more pleasant homes : the name continued as before, but the locality changed.

The new cities founded by the Pergamenian kings were placed in situations of a similar character. Eumeneia, Dionysopolis, Philadelphia stand on very gentle slopes under the shadow of hills on which no fortifications existed. Apollonia of Pisidia stood in a quite defenceless situation in an open plain. This character may be used, in concurrence with other considerations, to prove that such cities as Lysias and Philomelion were Pergamenian foundations. Dorylaion and Metropolis (in the Tchul Ova) also occupied during the Roman period similar situations ; but the latter at least was of the same character as Lounda and Sebaste, having been originally situated on a high hill in the neighbourhood.* The Roman Dorylaion was situated at Shahr Eyuk, a little to the north of Eski Sheher in the plain. After it had sunk into desolation Manuel rebuilt it at Karadja Sheher (see p. 212–3). Von Diest affirms that there are traces of early work beneath the mediæval ruins at Karadja Sheher, and I should readily admit that the ancient Dorylaion was moved to the open plain and afterwards back to the defensible, but waterless old site.†

In Lykaonia the situations of such cities as Laodiceia Combusta and Barata (Bin Bir Kilise) struck me as characteristic of that country. They lie in theatre-shaped recesses in the outer skirts of the mountains. From whatever reason it may be, no cities have left such an impression of charm on my mind, and yet I fear that their situation in their bald and bare gently sloping recesses would be found most disappointing by the tourist in search of striking effects. In several other Lykaonian

---

* The site of Metropolis can be traced in the centre of the plain between Tatarli and Haidarli (see p. 142). I was told that there were traces of fortification on a hill which I did not visit.

† On Kiepert's opinion, see p. 15. Von Diest describes Eski Sheher as feverish: his experience was bad, but on his own showing it cannot be blamed on the place. My account, given p. 212, was derived from the people. Koula and Eski Sheher have been more lauded to me than any other towns in Anatolia.

cities, e.g., Iconium and still more Kybistra, the luxuriance of the well-watered orchards is doubly pleasing by contrast with the bare and waterless plains that stretch in front for a hundred miles.*

In the period of trouble, when the defences of Asia Minor had to be considered,—against the Sassanians, the Arabs, and the Turks—when foreign armies ravaged every valley and advanced to the Bosphorous, sites of great natural strength again came to be of surpassing importance. Such marauding inroads as were practised especially by the Arabs, required for purposes of defence fortresses impregnable against a sudden attack ; but a lengthened siege was not a danger to be dreaded. Fortresses perched on the summit of precipitous rocks then became common, and some of them became the centres of great cities. Such are Afiom Kara Hisar and Sivri Hisar. At Kara Hisar, only three miles from the Roman city Prymnessos, a single mass of volcanic rock rises out of the plain erect like a column to the height of 900 feet : it can be ascended only by a zigzag series of stairs cut in the rock. The fortress is first heard of at the beginning of the eighth century. In 740 the famous Seid Batal Ghazi was defeated and slain before it; and from that time onwards it is mentioned not rarely under the names Akroenos and Nikopolis. On the site of Prymnessos there is now a village Seulun, while Kara Hisar is one of the greatest cities of Anatolia.

Sivri Hisar, the Pointed Castle, lies about ten or twelve miles north-west of the Roman city Pessinus : a fortress on the lofty volcanic rock with its two sharp points was impregnable in ancient warfare except to starvation. It was fortified by Justinian, and called Justinianopolis. Pessinus is now a mere village, while Sivri Hisar is a great city, as cities are in Anatolia.

Numerous other fortresses, mentioned in Part II., belong to this class. They were founded generally in the time when a reorganisation of the government and attention to the defences of Asia Minor gave the Byzantine empire new life. They were suited to the warfare of the period, for they were impregnable against a mere foray ; but they could never have been provisioned with food and water against a long siege. The cities which have grown up under their shadow are situated in the open plain, and, as a rule, are quite defenceless.

The foundations and changes of cities, which we have hitherto discussed, spring from vigour and growing or recuperative power ; but there are other changes of a later kind which are symptoms of decay and of waning civilisation. In the case of many towns and villages in modern time, it seems to be purely the neighbourhood of the water-supply that determines the situation. The Roman and even the Byzantine engineers did not hesitate to bring water from a considerable

* The ruinous state of modern Konia partly hides its beautiful surroundings from the hasty traveller; a drive or walk to Meram is the shortest way to learn what might be the case everywhere in the neighbourhood.

distance to supply their cities.   It is indeed true that to this day
necessity has maintained some skill in this one branch of engineering
(so far as my experience goes, among the Greek Christians only): the
modern aqueducts are constructed with considerable skill in underground channels which wind round the slope of hills to secure a slow,
continuous descent from the source to the public fountain or Tcheshme.
But even where such aqueducts have recently existed, they have often
been allowed, like all things in Turkey, to go to ruin.   Moreover, the
ancient engineers were far less dependent on the nearness of their
sources than the modern.   In many cases a modern town has grown up
at some point where abundant water is at hand, while the Roman or
Byzantine city a few miles distant has sunk into decay.   Examples of
this class are Tyana, formerly supplied by a large aqueduct, now a mere
village a few miles distant from the towns of Bor and Nigde,* and
Laodiceia, now supplanted by Denizli.   In general the probability is
that some such convenience is the reason for any change of site that has
occurred in the last few centuries.

In the later Byzantine period an instructive example which bears on
this point occurs.   Tralleis had gradually descended from the high
plateau, where the Roman city commanded one of the grandest inland
views I have ever seen, down the slope towards the lower valley of the
Mæander.   As the valley was made unsafe by Turkish incursions, the
city became entirely deserted.   Andronicus Palæologus about 1306
made an attempt to restore the city on the Roman site above; but the
inhabitants found the water-supply deficient, and were soon forced to
desert Andronicopolis or Palæologopolis, as the new city was called
during its brief existence.   The water-supply, which was sufficient for
a rich and large city in the Roman time, and which even at present is
conducted in a channel nearly on the level of the ancient city, would
have been quite enough for Andronicopolis, if engineering skill to use
it had been possessed by the founders.

* Tyana is still a considerable village, as good springs rise close to it   The ancient
aqueduct came from Eski Gumush, about 12 miles N.E., and was carried in a subter-
ranean channel for great part of its course.   The arches which extend for a mile near
the city are pre-Roman, and probably pre-Persian.   The modern village is as large as
the natural water-supply permits : the ancient city could not have existed without an
artificial supply.

PART II.

A SKETCH OF THE HISTORICAL GEOGRAPHY OF THE VARIOUS PROVINCES.

INTRODUCTION.

IN the following pages the attempt is made to indicate the principles on which the topography of Asia Minor must be studied, and to give a sketch of the subject as a whole. In addition to this I give a number of details about special points which have been collected in the course of my readings, and which have become too numerous to hold together in my mind, amid the distractions of other work, without the printer's aid. I have not tried to make them complete, or to give what may be found in ordinary sources of information. Every fact * has been gathered from the original sources, and represents the impression which the context has made on my mind : I cannot, of course, feel sure that the impression has always been correct, but from the first page to the last this sketch springs from a fresh collection and an independent valuation of the material.

A comparison of the lists of cities in each province whose existence at various periods can be traced forms the basis of this study, and a brief criticism of the chief authorities is necessary as an introduction.

First may be mentioned the Notitiæ Episcopatuum. The most important Notitiæ published by Parthey and Pinder are VII., VIII., IX., I., III., X., XIII. All the unpublished Notitiæ that I have seen are mere variations of some of these. A complete Notitia consists of two parts, a list of metropolitans and archbishops, and a list of the bishops subordinate to each metropolitan : the first of these two parts is wanting in IX., III., XIII., and the second is contained only in the seven Notitiæ above mentioned. VII. is a mere fragment. It will appear on examination that the lists were very carelessly kept, and were not altered to suit the actual changes that took place. When an ordinary bishopric was raised to the dignity of an archbishopric, it was often left in its old place in the list and entered a second time as an archbishopric. Sometimes an entire group of bishoprics disappears from some or all of the Notitiæ, e.g. the Akmonia group and the Khonai group in Phrygia, or the Kormasa-Komama group in Pamphylia Secunda.

* A very few exceptions have been carefully noticed. They are quotations from books inaccessible to me in Aberdeen, which I have found cited in modern books during the summer of 1889.

Among these seven Notitiæ, III., X., XIII. form a class by themselves, which I frequently mention as "the later Notitiæ." VII., VIII., IX. form another class, not so distinct and well marked, which I often refer to as "the earlier Notitiæ." I. stands in an intermediate position, but is on the whole much closer to the earlier class, and may almost be included in it and contrasted with the later class.

Within the latest group of Notitiæ, X. and XIII. are much closer to each other than to III., and are also later than it. Among the earlier Notitiæ there are much more serious variations, so that in many provinces the class has to be subdivided. The chronological order in this group is VII., VIII. and IX., I.* The two intermediate Notitiæ agree sometimes with VII. and sometimes with I. VII. approaches Hierocles more closely than any other Notitia does: the mutilation of this document is bitterly to be regretted, and has deprived us probably of much valuable information. An early Notitia is one of the chief desiderata in the history of Asia Minor, and may yet be found in manuscript.

The correction of the first part of a Notitia, viz. the list of Metropolitans and Archbishoprics, was naturally much more carefully performed than the correction of the second part. Hence the date which can be ascertained for the first part of each list cannot be assumed for the second part. The facts of the second part had often ceased before that date to exist. The second part of Notitiæ III., X., XIII. differs greatly in many provinces from that of VII., VIII., IX. and I., and on the whole belongs to a later date, presenting some remarkable analogies to the Councils of 859 and 869. The first part of VII., VIII., IX., I. is liker the older Councils and even Hierocles. Still the difference between the two classes does not simply lie in the fact that the later class gives the result of certain changes made in the older class. There are peculiarities in the later class which distinctly belong to an early period and to the arrangements of Justinian. I think that Notitiæ III., X., XIII. go back to a different register from VII., VIII., IX., I. Perhaps the former were taken from a register kept by the ecclesiastical authorities in Constantinople, and the latter from a register kept by the civil authorities in the palace.† The first part in the Notitiæ,

* Parthey and Pinder, on the other hand, maintain that they have arranged the Notitiæ in chronological order: I. the oldest, and XIII. the latest (*Praef.*, p. vi). In Lycia, III. agrees with I., not with X., XIII.

† Compare especially I. and IX. The ecclesiastical register was the only one accessible to the writer of Notitia XIII. later than 1621, A.D., but the facts in that Notitia obviously belong to an epoch centuries earlier. Ecclesiastical registers of various kinds were kept. For example, at Conc. Mopsuest., A.D. 549, we read: Recitentur sacra diptycha, quae declarant sanctae memoriae connumerationem sacerdotum istius Mopsuestenae civitatis, usque ad hunc sacerdotem qui in praesenti tertiadecima indictione defunctus est. Et recitati sunt et habent sic: "Pro requiescentibus episcopis, Protogene, Zosimo, Olympio, Cyrillo, Thoma, Bassiano, Joanne, Auxentio, Palatino, Jacobo, Zosimo, Theodoro, Symeone." Ex alio diptycho: "Pro requiescentibus episcopis" [same list follows]. Et ex aliis diptychis: "Pro requiescentibus episcopis"

being more carefully corrected than the second part, approximates closely in the two classes.

As to date the following facts may serve as typical. (1) Amastris became an archbishopric* about A.D. 800. VIII., IX. give it as a bishopric under Gangra, but VIII. also gives it as an archbishopric (VII. is mutilated, but does not give it as an archbishopric). It is clear therefore that VIII., IX. give a state of the Church later than 800, but are not properly corrected. I., which is dated 883, gives Amastris as an archbishopric, not as a bishopric. III., X., XIII. do the same.

(2) Nakoleia became an archbishopric between 787 and 862. Notitiæ VII., VIII., IX., I. give it only as a bishopric under Synnada. Notitia X. gives it as an archbishopric.

(3) Khonai became an archbishopric in 858. Notitiæ VIII., IX., I. do not mention it; and omit along with it a group of bishoprics lying close to it. This is due to the fact that this group must have been attached to Khonai, and that the list of Phrygian bishoprics had been corrected, but the new group had not been entered in its proper place. III., X., XIII. give Khonai as an archbishopric, but assign to it no subordinate bishoprics.

(4) Akmonia must have been at some unknown time metropolis of a group of bishoprics. This group is entirely omitted in VIII., IX., I.; whereas III., X., XIII. give them in their due place under Laodiceia. The latter arrangement was in force in 787.

(5) Five north-western bishoprics of Phrygia Pacatiana were separated from Laodiceia at some date before 787; according to my conjecture this arrangement was made by Justinian. Here III., X., XIII. agree with Concil. Nicaen. II. in placing this group under Hierapolis, while VIII., IX., I. assign them to Laodiceia.

(6) Amorion became an archbishopric before 787, and a metropolis of a group of bishoprics at some time in the ninth century. Notitiæ VIII., IX. give it as a bishopric subject to Pessinus, yet VIII. also mentions it

---

[same list follows, but ends with "Jacobo," omitting the last three]. (Mansi, vol. ix., p. 278.) But we learn that the lists had been altered, Theodorus, the heretical bishop who along with Diodorus of Tarsos originated the Nestorian heresy, being ejected, and Saint Cyrillus of Alexandria being named in his place. This had taken place before the memory of the oldest persons, but all knew the facts. Again: Theodorus episcopus fuit in mea civitate [Tyana] temporibus Gregorii sanctae memoriae. Praedicatur enim in sacris diptychis ita: "Pro Eupsychio, Anthemio, Aetherio, Deodato, Calliopio, Longino, Theodoro." (Speech of Euphrantes of Tyana in Council of Constantinople, 553, A.D. Mansi, ix., 258.)

* Saint George of Paphlagonia, son of Theodosius and Megetho of Kromna (quod propinquum est Amastridi urbi), was a hermit in Mount Agrioserica, and afterwards a monk in the monastery of Bonyssa. He was consecrated bishop of Amastris by the patriarch Tarasius, 784–806, and obtained from the emperor (Constantine (?), who died 790), that Amastris should be no longer subject to Gangra, but should be auto- kephalos ('Act. Sanct.,' Feb. 21, p. 268 ff.).

among the archbishoprics. I. gives it as metropolis of a group of bishoprics; so do III., X., XIII.

The principle that the formula ὁ Στρατονικείας ἤτοι Καλάμου, and many similar entries, indicates two cities included under one bishop, is often quoted in the following pages, generally as "Hirschfeld's canon." Hirschfeld was the first, so far as I know, to give any convincing example of it, but does not lay it down in general terms nor give it such wide application as I do.* I consider that wherever two centres of common life, towns or villages, were included under the care of one bishop, this formula might be used; in many cases one of these towns was a new growth which gradually replaced the old centre (as Hirschfeld has rightly remarked), but there were, as I think, also many cases in which the two centres both existed simultaneously, without being sufficiently important to have two separate bishops. The Notitiæ unfortunately very rarely give a second title to a bishopric, but there were probably very many such. For example, Πίναρα καὶ Δίδυμα occurs only at Conc. Seleuc., 359 A.D. Such omission of half the title accounts for the disappearance of many old names in Byzantine lists. These lists are really complete statements of the ecclesiastical organisation of the whole country, and (except for unintentional faults) every village and town in the whole land is included under some one of the bishoprics mentioned.

The lists of bishops present at the different councils are of the highest value, and would be by far the most important authority accessible to us, were they more complete. Unfortunately numbers of bishops were often absent, and it is very rare that a metropolitan signs on behalf of his absent suffragans and names them. Moreover, we often have only an incomplete list even of the bishops who were present. The most valuable lists are those which give the signatures of the bishops as they were added to the records. As a curiosity among these I may cite from Conc. Constant., A.D. 449: "Elias, episcopus Hadrianopolis Asiae,† definiens subscripsi per Romanum episcopum Myrorum, eo quod nesciam literas" (Mansi, VI., p. 929).

It is as yet impossible to state positively the sources and the method of composition of Hierocles' Synekdemos. In the first place the doubt may be raised whether we have more than an index or epitome of the contents of Hierocles' "Travelling Companion": the name certainly implies naturally more than a mere list of names, but on the other hand some of the omissions are hardly possible if a description of each province and of its cities had ever formed part of the work.

* Reisebericht, in 'Berl. Monatsber.,' 1879, p. 315: "Den erwünschten Aufschluss über Aghras geben zwei der Notizien, wo ein Bischof Σελευκείας ἤτοι 'Αγρῶν genannt wird; also Agrae war auch der alte Name dieses einst zu Seleukeia gehörenden Ortes, der allmälich den verfallenden Hauptort überflügelt und schon im Djihan-numa s. 699 als ein blühender Ort erwähnt wird."

† Asiae is an interpolation, not given in the Greek version.

In the second place the question has been raised whether the list is taken from an ecclesiastical list of the bishoprics, or a civil list of the administrative districts. The answer to this question has usually been given prematurely without an attempt to determine the relation of the civil to the ecclesiastical lists. I may here state my opinion briefly.

(1) There was in general a practical identity between the ecclesiastical and the civil lists. The policy of the civil administration was to keep them the same as far as possible : but the Church often resisted, and refused to alter its organisation to suit political changes. In older time the Church had to submit : even Basil was unable to preserve his authority over the bishops of Cappadocia Secunda, when that province was separated from Prima. About 408 Pope Innocent, writing to Alexander, bishop of Antioch, laid down the principle that the Church should maintain : " sciscitaris utrum divisis imperiali iudicio provinciis, ut duo metropoles fiant, sic duo metropolitani episcopi debeant nominari : non vere visum est ad mobilitatem mundanarum Dei ecclesiam commutari " (Mansi, Act. Conc., III., p. 1055). But, even in the twelfth century, the archbishops of Ankyra and Herakleia tried vainly to preserve their authority over Basileion-Juliopolis and Madytos, after these cities had been made metropoleis (see under Basileion Galatiae).

The principle that every city should be also a bishopric was expressly enacted, with two exceptions, by an imperial law, probably of Zeno, 474–91 ; " unaquaeque civitas proprium episcopum habeto. . . . . . Excipitur autem Tomensium Scythiae civitas, illius enim episcopus reliquarum etiam civitatum curam gerit ; * tum etiam Leontopolis Isauriae subest episcopo Isauropolitano " (Cod. Just., I., 3, 36). Some other differences of detail, however, existed, owing to the fact that some divisions were kept up by the Church and ignored by the state.

(2) In the province Scythia Hierocles follows the civil list, and gives Tomis with the other towns.

(3) He omits Leontopolis, following the ecclesiastical lists, in which only Isauropolis was given.

(4) Eukhaita was a city of Helenopontus, and would certainly be mentioned in a civil list : † but being an archbishopric it would be omitted in ecclesiastical lists. Hierocles, following the latter, omits it.

(5) Pamphylia was ecclesiastically divided into two districts not later than the first half of the fifth century ; one district being subject to Side and one to Perga. This division seems never to have been made in the civil administration. Hierocles apparently follows the civil list, giving Pamphylia undivided ; but examining his names we find that he

---

* Sozomen says of Scythia (H. E. 6, 21), τοῦτο δὲ τὸ ἔθνος πολλὰς μὲν ἔχει καὶ πόλεις καὶ κώμας καὶ φρούρια, μητρόπολις δέ ἐστι Τόμις, . . . εἴσετι καὶ νῦν ἔθος παλαιὸν ἐνθάδε κρατεῖ, τοῦ παντὸς ἔθνους ἕνα τὰς ἐκκλησίας ἐπισκοπεῖν.

† For example, it is given in the list of cities of Helenopontus by Justinian, Novel. XXVIII.

has really used the ecclesiastical lists, and gives first the names in Pergensis, then those in Sidensis.

(6) Kotiaion occupied a peculiar position in Phrygia Salutaris, being a great heretical centre. It was an archbishopric, and though perhaps mentioned as a bishopric under Synnada in Notitiæ VIII., IX.,* this if true must have been only a temporary degradation. Hierocles omits Kotiaion, whereas if he had used a civil list, this, the largest and richest city of the province, could not have been omitted.

(7) Bithynia was divided ecclesiastically, not civilly, between Nicomediensis and Nicæensis, and Chalcedon was an archbishopric. Hierocles, like the civil list, gives the whole set of cities without any division.

(8) There are many other cases besides Leontopolis and Isauropolis, in which two neighbouring cities were united in one bishopric. Hierocles sometimes follows the civil list in giving these places as separate cities,† and sometimes he gives only one of them,‡ as if he followed an ecclesiastical list in which (as was often done) one of the names was omitted.

I need not give any other examples here; several will be found in the following pages. But the preceding are enough to· establish the following conclusion as probable. Several of the facts are inconsistent with the use by Hierocles of a civil list, while, of those which suggest the use of a civil list, none imperatively demand it: e.g., even though Tomis was the only bishopric of Scythia, ecclesiastical lists might give the names of the cities in the province. § All the facts that I have observed suggest that Hierocles used an ecclesiastical list of the period, and that he did not simply reproduce it, but made use of it along with some other evidence. This other evidence did not include a civil list of administrative divisions or cities, and it is difficult to say whether it included more than the general knowledge possessed by an educated man, except in Hellespontus, with which he shows such intimate acquaintance as to suggest that he was an inhabitant of the province. Bithynia, which was so near Constantinople, is also treated by him in a more independent way, though without giving more than the names of the bishoprics. But in more distant provinces he makes errors which are explicable only through his slavish and unintelligent use of ecclesiastical lists, omitting names which his authority omits, and misunderstanding names in their ecclesiastical form.‖

* VIII. Κομιτίου, IX. Κυτιμίου. As Komition is unknown, we must probably understand Kotimion as an error for Kotiaion.

† Limnai and Dabinai, Nikopolis and Palaiapolis, &c.

‡ Palaiapolis without Alieros, &c.

§ The Notitiæ, especially some MSS. in Paris, often give some statistics beyond the actual lists of bishoprics.

‖ E.g. ὁ Τιμβριάδων (ἐπίσκοπος), Θεμισόνιος, and genitives like Σαταλέων, Ἡρακλείας Ὀγμοῦ, Ἡρακλείας Σαλβακόνος, and the many instances of δήμου, while he wrongly infers from ὁ Κερασέων a name Κήρασε, from ὁ Βριανῶν Βρίανα, from ὁ [Ἀ]τεανῶν Τιάναι.

It is very difficult to determine the origin of the numbers given in the heading of each province in the list of Hierocles. They are probably not genuine, but are added by some ignorant person, who often counted as two a city with a name consisting of two words. They, however, seem to be older than certain corruptions of the text. The following numbers are wrong.

(1) Asia has 42 cities. The number $\mu\gamma'$ is got by counting either Magnesia Maiandria or Adramyttion quae antea Lyrnesus as two cities.

(2) Hellespontus has 34 cities, even taking Ξίος Τράδος and ᾽Αδριανοῦ Θῆραι ῾Ηραι as each a single city. The number λ' is older than the corruption which transferred from Lydia to Hellespontus at least three cities: these are—

Βλαῦνδος which appears as Βλάδος
Κάλανδα   „   „   „ Σκέλεντα (i.e. [εἰ]ς Κάλαντα)
Στρατονίκαια „   „   „ Ξίος Τράδος (i.e. εἰς [σ] Τράδον[ίκεαν].

(3) Phrygia Pacatiana has 38 cities. The number λθ is got by counting Τημένου Θύραι as two.

(4) Lydia has 22 cities. The number κγ' is got by counting ᾽Απόλλωνος Ἱερόν as two: if the view stated in (2) is correct, κγ' must be a later alteration.

(5) Pamphylia has at most 44 cities, even taking Jovia as a distinct city from Termessos, Myodia from Choria Milyadica, Maximianopolis from Ktema Maximianopolis, and Demousia from Demou Sabaion. In reality I think only 40 cities existed in it. The number μζ' is got by counting as two cities Χωρία Μιλυαδικά, Θερμεσσὸς καὶ Εὐδοκία, Πανέμου Τεῖχος, Κτῆμα Μαξιμιανουπόλεως.

(6) Lycia has 32 cities. The number λδ' is got by counting double Μύρα Μητρόπολις and Κώμη Μάσταυρα · the number is therefore older than the corruption Κομιστάραος.

(7) Insulae has 18 cities. The origin of the number κ' is not clear, for Πορο-σελήνη and ᾽Αστυ-πάλαια could hardly be counted double.

(8) Caria has 27 cities. The number λ is got by counting double ῾Ηρακλείας ᾽Ογμοῦ, ῾Ηρακλείας Σαλβακόνος and Μητρόπολις ᾽Αφροδισίας, and is therefore older than the gloss [κο]Κτημα-λικαί,* which has crept from the margin into the list.

Ptolemy is a writer whose value depends greatly on his authority, and who has used and combined in unintelligent and self-contradictory style several different authorities. He has used to a certain extent an authority whose value as to the apportionment of the cities between the different Roman provinces was very high, possibly an official authority of some kind. But he has tried to subdivide the provinces according to

---

* I.e. Κτῆμα Φυλικαῖον. On this imperial estate see below, C 11, and ASP, B 4, where some correction of my arguments is needed.

the old historical countries, and has made various errors in doing so.[*]
His paragraphs describing the districts and demoi of Phrygia, Lydia,
and Mysia are borrowed from one authority, and his lists of the cities
from at least one different and contradictory authority. In Cappadocia he has used in part an authority who described the country as it
was divided into eleven strategiai, the eleventh consisting chiefly of
Lykaonian and Cilician territory. This division had long ceased to
exist, and Ptolemy combines it in the most blundering way with inconsistent authorities. Hence he gives Olba of Cilicia Tracheia twice,[†]
both in Cilicia Tracheia, district Ketis, and in Strategia Antiochiane of
Cappadocia. The former assignation was true in his own time; the
latter was true in the time of king Archelaos, and partially true under
Antiochus IV., who was king of the eleventh strategia in 37–8; the
name Antiochiane must be derived from this brief dominion, and seems
to give a date for Ptolemy's authority on the strategiai. Hence also we
have such absurdities as Lykaonia under Cappadocia, but Derbe and
Laranda under Antiochiane of Cappadocia, and Isauria under Galatia.
Almost every statement in Ptolemy can be traced as true at some
period, yet as combined they often make a tissue of contradictions.

While Ptolemy is so difficult to use and so liable to mislead unless
the greatest caution is used, Strabo can hardly be praised too highly.
His authority is naturally higher, perhaps, in Asia Minor, than in any
other country. His brief descriptions are marvellously accurate, and, to
the eye-witness, marvellously lucid. I hardly ever venture to attribute even the fault of vagueness to him.

The Peutinger Table is descended from an original of the fourth
century. It gives us a rather distorted and inaccurate picture of an
original, in which the roads of Asia Minor were represented as radiating
from Constantinople as capital. But although it thus gives the roads of
the new, post-Roman, period, yet the original was made before the old
Roman road system had been entirely superseded by the Constantino-
politan system of roads. The lines of road are indicated as fairly
straight, radiating from Constantinople; but roads crossing from east to
west, though really great and direct routes of the Roman period, are
made up of extraordinary zigzags, and are frequently interrupted.

My obligations to modern writers are too numerous to mention.
Kiepert's maps, both the published maps and others in manuscript of
large districts of Asia Minor, have been of course my chief aid. His
generous and genial letters and talk have done much to help me. I
should also like to say how much I have learned in the way of method
from Waddington's occasional topographical fragments — models of
reasoning alike in boldness and in sobriety—and from some of the

* He separates Lycia-Pamphylia into its two parts, and puts Sagalassos and Trebendai
in Lycia.

† In both cases Ὄλβα should be read in place of Ὄλβασα.

general principles enunciated by G. Hirschfeld. The germ or the first clear statement of almost every principle with regard to the relation of cities to their natural surroundings and the preference accorded in different periods to different sites for cities, are to be found in Hirschfeld's writings : on the other hand, I am frequently obliged to differ from his opinions as to the placing of cities, and sometimes, *e.g.* in Tavium and Metropolis, he appears to me to draw the wrong conclusion from the facts before him. Sterrett's two volumes are a rich mine of unused information, gathered with great skill and care. His inscriptions give the situation of Adada and Pappa (though he himself draws in both cases the opposite inference), also Heracleia, Anaboura and Sebastopolis (already known),* Tymandos, Lystra, and Hadrianopolis, beside many villages, Astra, Artanada, Plinna, Sobagena, Sarromaena, Gorgorome, and Sedasos. He has also deduced from the modern survival the ancient names of Lalassis, Lauzados, Minassos and from general considerations the sites of Derbe, Tavium, Sirica, and Timbrias. But his remarks about the situation of Aarassos, Nora, Neronopolis [*sic*], Domitianopolis [*sic*], Delendis [*sic*], Maragos as a survival of Sarromaëna, Papporondeis, and Savatra (many of which have been quoted as conclusive and are, owing to the great merits of his work, likely to become accepted identifications), show defective acquaintance with the literature of the subject, and fall back from the modern standard of topographical reasoning to the primitive guesswork of sixty years ago.†

The brilliant character of his discoveries makes it necessary to protest in the interests of science against the easy acceptance of his mistakes.

At one time I hoped to ascribe to its originator the identification of each ancient site, but time has failed. It may perhaps be possible to add in the indices a rough list of the cities placed by a few of the more important of modern writers. It has become inevitable in a work which is really an investigation to refer more to the mistakes than to the merits of such writers as Le Quien : his frequent errors have passed into literature, and his lists of bishops are quoted by writers on ecclesiastical history without apparently any attempt to verify his statements. I have quoted a few of the mistakes which I have observed as a warning that he needs verification. It is a matter of great regret to me to mention only the faults in such a splendid work as his, and to find that I have so rarely alluded to his merits, which far surpass those of most later writers.

It has always been a pleasure to record the cases where Leake's guesses are correct. His work, however, is that of a student in his

---

* Anaboura, the discovery of which is ascribed to him by Kaibel in Hermes, was placed from an inscription by me in 'Athenische Mittheilungen,' 1883 ; Heracleia by Waddington, on general grounds, and by Paris and Holleaux from an inscription. Sebastopolis was placed by Schönborn from an inscription.

† I also do not accept his Isaura Nóva, which has been generally applauded, but it is a not unnatural inference from his inscription ; his Tekmorion as a town also seems to me a mistake.

study, not of an eyewitness,* and though he has made many admirable guesses, his wonderful topographical eye and instinct had not a fair opportunity in his book on Asia Minor. A word must suffice for the admirable commentaries of Wesseling, for the accuracy and care of Hamilton, and for Schönborn, to whom insufficient equipment denied a fair chance of work. Ritter's 'Kleinasien,' an indispensable work, suffers from bad arrangement: perhaps it was want of knowledge of the country that often made him unable to distinguish between important and unimportant facts. I have not been able to determine whether Mannert or Forbiger is the worse authority : Forbiger, as more detailed, has more opportunities to err, and uses them.

The whole subject of Anatolian topography is at present in such a state that it cannot be discussed without a number of combinations which have only more or less probability. These combinations may be proved or disproved in two different ways. Either direct external evidence may be discovered to show the name of the sites in question, or indirect evidence may be found agreeing or disagreeing with the scheme which is proposed for the district as a whole. My experience is that an identification seldom stands the test of several years' careful study without some indication turning up to confirm or disprove it. For example, no direct evidence has been discovered to disprove the hypothesis which I suggested in 1883, that Tiberiopolis was near Altyntash, but that hypothesis is now so completely out of court that I have not even referred to it as antiquated in discussing the district. The backward state of civilisation and city-organisation around Altyntash, as disclosed by the inscriptions, is quite inconsistent with a city like Tiberiopolis, which coined money from Trajan onwards, and must have been made a city of the Græco-Roman type under Tiberius.

It will be convenient to put together here a few references which show how far the native languages were retained in Asia Minor, and how badly the Greek language was pronounced even where it was used. The result of this was that local names were exposed to great alterations when native names were turned into Greek, or when Greek words were pronounced by natives. In the former case, the native names were especially liable to modification through the etymologising tendency, which tried to get forms with a meaning in Greek. In Vit. Auxentii ('Act. Sanct.,' Feb. 14, p. 780), which dates perhaps about 500, we read, "ille, qui nos de hoc instruxit, erat quidem lingua barbarus, ut qui esset ortus ex Mysia." As to Cappadocia, Philostratus (Vit. Soph., II., 13) says,—παχείᾳ τῇ γλώττῃ καὶ ὡς Καππαδόκαις ξύνηθες, ξυγκρούων μὲν τὰ ξύμφωνα τῶν στοιχείων, συστέλλων δὲ τὰ μηκυνόμενα καὶ μηκύνων τὰ βραχέα. As to Cilicia, Thalelaeus, an anchoret near Gabala in Syria, spoke naturally in Greek : "ille enim, Graeca lingua usus, erat enim Cilix genere "

---

* He made only one hurried run in winter across country from Constantinople to Selefke, and touched at a few points on the west coast.

('Act. Sanct.,' Feb. 27, p. 681). It is implied that, if Thalelaeus had been a Syrian, he would probably not have spoken Greek. As to Lykaonia, " the speech of the Lycaonians " was the ordinary language in the time of Saint Paul, whereas in Lydia Strabo (p. 631) mentions that the Lydian language had entirely disappeared in his time, but was still spoken in Kibyra alongside of Greek, Pisidian, and the language of the Solymoi. In Phrygia and Pisidia I have several times shown * from the evidence of inscriptions, that the rustic population knew little or no Greek: on the borders of Phrygia and Lykaonia this was the case as late as the fourth century. But there was a general belief that the native language was vulgar, and that all persons of education ought to use Greek: even Greek names were substituted for Phrygian, αἰσχρὸν γὰρ ὄνομα Φρυγιακὸν γυναῖκ᾽ ἔχειν (Machon, ap. Athen., p. 578). The bad Greek of the Syrians is described about 450–60 A.D. in terms similar to the Cappadocian Greek, ὅσα κατὰ τὴν τῶν Σύρων διάλεκτον καὶ τὴν προσοῦσαν αὐτοῖς δασύτητα ἐδόκει πρὸς τὴν συνήθη διηλλάχθαι φωνήν, τουτέστι τοῦ Η στοιχείου εἰς τοῦ [read τὸ] Ε μεταβολήν, ἢ τοῦ Ω εἰς τὸ Ο, ἢ τὸ ἀνάπαλιν, ἢ τοιαῦτά τινα βραχέα ('Vit. Hypatii,' Act. Sanct., June 17, p. 308).

In discussing the topography of the least known parts of Asia Minor, my aim is to be as brief as is consistent with clearness. Often I might spend two or three times more space in giving the reasons which justify the position assigned, by showing that other positions which might at a first glance seem equally suitable are, on a careful examination, found to be impossible. It has happened in the case of Derbe and of other places mentioned in the following pages, that a situation, suggested by one of the ancient references taken alone, has been preferred by me for years, until at last I found that it led to impossible conclusions about other places. It is, however, inconvenient to discuss every place in this elaborate way, and, while I do it in one or two cases, in general I simply state the positive reasons, and must ask a critic to examine whether any change of position which suggests itself to him as plausible would not be inconsistent with the situation of some better known town. It must, however, be stated plainly at the outset that in many cases the evidence is not sufficient to give certainty. I have in these cases tried to state it without prejudice at its fair value. In these cases, experience of my own gradual progress in the past makes me recognise the great probability that I shall have to correct my present scheme in various details; but I have confidence that the main outlines are correctly drawn in these pages. This essay, however, ought to be supplemented by an annual survey of the progress of discovery, such as Prof. Hirschfeld makes occasionally in a wider and briefer way for ancient geography in general. Such a résumé, which I hope to make annually, is, however, possible only as supplement to a single general survey.

* "The Graeco-Roman Civilisation in Pisidia," in 'Journ. Hell. Stud.,' 1883; " Artemis-Leto and Apollo-Lairbenos," ib., 1889 ; " Phrygian Inscriptions of the Roman Period," in 'Zeitschr. f. vergl. Sprachf.,' 1887.

The time seems to have come when some such general survey as I here attempt ou͟ t to be made. To those who regard the history of the past as a right and profitable study, I need not defend myself for trying to lay the foundations on which alone a study of the history of Asia Minor can be built up: every page of history furnishes example that false topography would distort our view of the facts narrated. That the topography of Asia Minor is at present in a most unsatisfactory state can readily be proved by a few examples from the recent map iu which Prof. H. Kiepert has embodied the results of modern investigation. To praise Kiepert is unnecessary: his work is accepted as the sum of present knowledge. Yet he places *strategia Saravene* quite 100 miles away from the position which I shall try to prove it ought to have: this, of course, vitiates all his ideas of the topography of Cappadocia. Except a few old-standing identifications, there is hardly a single place in the whole of Cappadocia which he places anywhere near the situation that I consider right. Justinianopolis-Mokissos, one of the greatest Byzantine cities, does not appear on his map, and its place is usurped by Aquæ Sarvenæ, which ought to be 20 hours to the north-east.

In defiance of two clear statements of Strabo that the river Karmalas flowed through Cilicia, he makes it a tributary of the Euphrates. It is instructive, as an example of almost wilful error, to read the remarks devoted to this river by modern writers. The Karmalas and the Melas (the latter a tributary of the Halys) are made by Mannert tributaries of the Euphrates, and Strabo is all wrong about both of them. Forbiger identifies the Karmalas and the Melas, and sees a proof of Strabo's ignorance in his remarks about them. Finally, alluding to my brief correction of the modern errors (published in the 'Revue Archéologique'), Prof. G. Hirschfeld gently rebukes my fault—"ist es dieser Karmalas von dem Ramsay sagt er gehe nicht in den Euphrat, ... oder liegt da auf irgend einer Seite ein Missverständniss vor?" The only misunderstanding is that Prof. Hirschfeld, like most people, looks on the Zamanti Su (i.e., the true Karmalas) as a mere tributary of the Saruz or Seihun (Saros), whereas both in length of course and (so far as I have seen) in volume of water the Zamanti Su is the chief river, and the Saros is its tributary. The maps misled Prof. Hirschfeld; I spoke from personal knowledge. Prof. Kiepert is almost the only scholar who does not condemn an eye-witness that differs from his maps.

When two important points on a road are identified, e.g. Ankyra and Archelais, it might seem to be an easy matter to place the intermediate stations at suitable distances on the map between them. Prof. Kiepert's map in eastern Asia Minor often confines itself to this, taking as correct numerous errors of the Itineraries.* But, even where the Itineraries are approximately correct, he sometimes makes roads follow a route which

* For example, the town which ought to be called Ozizala appears on his map as Ozalla, and a number of roads are given, in which sometimes all and sometimes several of the stations are falsely inserted there by mistakes in the Peutinger table.

is incorrect and in defiance of natural features, and thus the position which he gives to the intermediate points is far from the true situation : take, for example, the roads from Ankyra to Archelais, from Ankyra to Cæsareia, and from Amaseia to Neocæsareia, and compare the situations of the towns on them with the following elucidation.

In a word, either my work is a mistake, or the map of a great part of Asia Minor must be revolutionised.

The lesson which is frequently enforced to the student of topography is the need of caution in accepting identifications founded on resemblance between the modern and the ancient name.   Such resemblance is often quite illusory, yet identifications founded on it possess the most enduring vitality; some of them have been my enemies for years, and I have exposed them time after time, only to find them repeated afresh in almost every new writer.   Several of them, fortunately, have been rejected by Prof. Kiepert in his new map, and there is some hope that they may now gradually pass into oblivion : among them are the identification of Koloe with the modern Koula, and of Themissonion with the present Tefenni.   The latter, however, has been a striking example of the vitality of error.   Started by some one who pointed out that the two names had some likeness,* it has maintained itself in spite, first of all, of M. Waddington's proof that Themissonion could not possibly be near Tefenni, and that it must be in the valley of Kara Eyuk, and afterwards of my proof, referred to or repeated in French, English, and American journals, to the same effect in a more detailed way, showing that it was at Kara Eyuk Bazar, and finally in spite of Prof. Kiepert's new map ; and its effects are seen in the latest number of the ' Bulletin de Correspondance Hellénique,'† where MM. Cousin and Diehl labour to show, on the evidence of an inscription found miles away to the south, that Eriza was at Kara Eyuk Bazar.   Prof. Kiepert, however, repeats the equally absurd suggestion that Ilouza was at Ilyas or Elyes; the resemblance is here a little greater, but Ilyas means " Elias," and has nothing to do with Ilouza, which is frequently called Elouza and is apparently the same as Aloudda.‡

Even when a correct identification has been made by a skilful or happy conjecture, it often fails to find acceptance.   For example, Leake correctly identified Lystra, but nobody accepted his opinion till Prof. Sterrett discovered the proof that he was right.   Leake also correctly stated that Manlius marched along the lake of Buldur, but even in his latest map Kiepert follows Hirschfeld's view that he marched along the

* The likeness is not really so great even as that between Macedon and Monmouth; there is a T in both in English, but not in Greek.

† This journal, more valuable than any other to the student of Asia Minor, has during recent years sometimes treated very insufficiently the topography of the country. See Aigai, Eukhaita, Kyon, Lystra, Isba, &c.

‡ D and Z are often equivalent in Asia Minor names, e. g. Nazianzos and Nadiandos.

Kestel Lake. Uncertainty remains so long as no definite evidence is given to support an identification. In many cases no epigraphic evidence remains or can be hoped for; and then all that can be done is to examine the evidence, not for a single town, but for all the towns of the district, and thus to form a complete scheme. In many cases it is found that the evidence about a town is so vague as to suit several different positions equally well; but a systematic investigation will show that other names have to be given to some of these positions, and that only one remains open to the town in question.

The references in the following pages have been gathered in the course of years: many of them were copied out at the time when I first found them, and in a number of cases I have not the opportunity of verifying the references, but must trust to my manuscript notes. The references to Byzantine historians are to the pages of the Bonn edition, except in Theophanes (de Boor), Zosimus (Mendelssohn), and Zonaras. The references to the 'Acta Conciliorum' have been gathered at different times from three different editions.*

In some cases it may perhaps appear that the changes which I assume in the Byzantine rendering of old names are too violent. Some of these are due to corruption of the text, but the majority are the real spoken names, and the variations from the literary form are of great interest. But I think that any one who goes over the Byzantine documents will find many cases which are beyond doubt, and yet which are quite as violent as any that I now propose. In 1883 I showed that Konioupolis of Hierocles had no connection with Konni, but is a corruption of Dionysoupolis; and probably no one doubts this. Such errors as these occur often, even in Hierocles, and his lists are far more correct than the ecclesiastical lists. I take one example of subsequent confirmation. In 1883 ὁ Ἰκρίων was misunderstood by me. In 1887 I saw that it was an error of the scribe for Ἰβρίων, and denoted the city Bria.† Looking over the MSS. in the Bodleian Library in 1888, I found this conjecture confirmed (see Bria).

In the following pages great use has been made of the Byzantine authorities, the lists in the 'Acta Conciliorum,'‡ in the 'Notitiæ Episcopatuum,' and in 'Hierocles,' the local references (which are sometimes useful in default of other evidence §) lurking in the 'Acta Sancto-

* I often refer to my 'Cities and Bishoprics of Phrygia' as CB (see 'Journal of Hellenic Studies,' 1883 and 1887), to my 'Antiquities of Southern Phrygia and the Border Lands' as ASP (see 'American Journal of Archæology,' 1887 and 1888). I formerly hoped to include here everything of any value in all other old papers of mine, but economy of space has made this impossible.

† See the tables of Pacatiana, CB, parts I. and II.

‡ I might quote as examples of the information to be gained from a signature, the identification of Ptolemy's Talbonda with the bishopric Tymandos, and the specification of the Phrygian Pentapolis.

§ The decisive information, e.g., about Satala Lydiæ and Sozopolis Pisidiæ comes from this source.

rum,' and, above all, the description of campaigns in the historians. The comparison of the accounts given of the same campaign by different writers (except where one copies from the other) frequently makes the situation quite plain : some detail occurring in one writer makes all the others quite clear. Frequently, also, the study of the strategy in one campaign has given the clue to explain another campaign which took place centuries earlier or later. These references have been entirely collected from the original authorities in the course of my own reading.[*] It might have saved me much time if I had known sooner of Muralt's 'Essai de Chronographie Byzantine;'[†] but I should also have lost much, for if I had known that work I should perhaps never have gone through the originals myself, and should have missed a number of useful references which are not given by him, as being useless for his purposes. But still much evidence remains, for I never spend a few hours over a Byzantine historian without discovering passages that had either eluded my observation or baffled my understanding.

The space devoted to the different cities is not proportionate to their historical importance, but only to the new topographical material that I have collected. In some cases I have practically nothing to add to the information published already. It is unnecessary to discuss once more cities whose situation is universally accepted ; and even where a situation, not universally accepted, seems to me to have been satisfactorily proved by any writer, I content myself with the reference.

In giving an account of the roads, I have generally added a statement of distances. Some of these are very rough approximations, and perhaps should have been omitted altogether ; but as in some cases, where I knew the country well, I have confidence that my estimates are near the truth, I have thought it more likely to be useful if I gave similar estimates in other cases also. The native system of reckoning by hours is wonderfully accurate. You cannot be sure, if you ask a single native, that his estimate is the commonly accepted one ; but if you get several together, and they discuss the matter, their final opinion is almost invariably a very good estimate of the distance. I reckon three miles to the native hour ; but for my own hours of actual riding I allow three and a half English miles.

For the sake of completeness, it has appeared more useful to violate a principle on which I have usually acted, and to write a sketch of districts which I have never seen. It was otherwise impossible to give

[*] In a few cases I have borrowed and acknowledged quotations which I have not, in Aberdeen, the means of verifying.

[†] I met the book first in the Library of the American School of Athens in 1888. It has been of the greatest use to me, and, in order to facilitate the work of other students, I have inserted the dates according to Muralt (which often are decidedly arbitrary), so that reference to him is always easy. But I owe to him, as yet, only one useful reference that had escaped me—Const. Porph., de adm. imp., c. 50. The use which I have made of this passage will show its extreme importance.

that account of the roads which is the chief object of the whole paper. Moreover, it is now, with the additional light thrown on Hierocles by the thorough examination of Phrygia and the border lands, possible to give a sketch of other provinces, which should fix their bounds and be useful both to scholars and to travellers, without aiming at that minuteness which can be ventured on in the districts which I have examined personally. It is possible, e. g., to prove that Hadrianoutherai or Olba or Adrasos is to be sought in a particular neighbourhood, and leave to future discoverers the pleasure of discovering the exact situation of each.

In examining the Roman road-system in detail, I have divided it into districts. In some districts I first describe the main lines of road, and then, inasmuch as during that description I have often to assume the exact situation of cities which occur on the roads, I add a sketch of the ancient topography of the district. But in most of the provinces it is easier to take the cities first, and the roads after. The description and the sketch depend each on the other to such an extent that either might, with almost equal propriety, be placed first; but, on the whole, the order of exposition which I have adopted seemed better. The order of exposition is often rather awkward : this is partly due to a change and enlargement of plan after half of the essay was in type. The index will, I hope, help the reader to collect all the references to any city.

A. —Cities and Bishoprics of Byzantine Asia.

1. Asia, in the restricted Byzantine sense, is too wide and too little known to me, so that I cannot venture to discuss minutely the sites of all the cities. But it is easy to divide Hierocles' list into geographical groups.

He begins with the metropolis Ephesos, and then takes a city on the coast to the south—Anea. This brings him to the lower part of the Mæander valley. The Mæander seems to have divided Byzantine Asia from Caria, and in older times Lydia from Caria.

2. He enumerates the cities of the Mæander valley from west to east—Priene, Magnesia, Tralleis, Nyssa, Brioulla, Mastaura. Mastaura retains its name as Mastavro, near Nazli, and Brioula as Billara, near Horsunlu (see ASP, c. 2); strictly, Mastaura should come before Brioulla in the order. Strabo (p. 650) has it correctly, Βρίουλα, Μάσταυρα, Ἀχάρακα.

3. He crosses to the Kaystros valley. Anineta is unknown, but the following ten are for the most part certainly in that valley. Hypaipa was probably at or near Odemish. Arkadiopolis is apparently a temporary name of the ancient Teira, modern Thira. Dios Hieron was perhaps even lower down the valley than these two cities, and nearer Ephesos, for it appears from the first onwards as Διοσιρῖται in the

Notitia I.	Notitiae III., X., XIII.
esos	1 Ephesos
a	21 Anea
nê	22 Proïne
nêsia Mae.	4 Magnesia
eis	3 Tralleis
a	15 Nyssa
ula	11 Byrioulla
taura	9 Mastaura
iata	19 Aninata
epa	2 Apatos
dioupolis	{ 23 Arkadioupolis } { 36 Thyraioi }
Hieron	25 Dios Hieron
aza	26 Augaza
ê	10 Kaloê
..	..
ioupolis	35 Palaioup.
tta	18 Bereta
liopolis	14 Aurelioupolis
Aule	24 Nea Aule
hônê	28 Kolophôn
opolis	17 Metropolis
los	29 Lebedos
	30 Teos
yrna	II. 1 Smyrna
menai	II. 4 Clazomenai
rai	31 Erythrai
êsia	II. 3 Magn. Anêliou
..	II. 6 Archangelos
..	II. 7 Petra
a	II. 2 Phokaia
nê	13 Myrrhina
	34 Kymê
mos	{ 37 Khlyaroi } { 20 Pergamoi }
	5 Elea
nnê	12 Pittamnê
	27 ὁ Σιών
osioupolis or } e }	{ 33 Theodosioupolis } { or Peperineus }
ytion	6 Atramytion
droi	32 Attandros
ra	8 Gargara
	7 Assos
a Kome	16 Mascha Kome
..	..
..	II. 7 Sosandra

Magnesia and Basil of Magnesia
as archbishopric and as bishopric.

To face page 104.

ASIA.

			Notitia VII, VIII, IX.	
	ΕΦΕΣΟΥ Ι.		1 Ephesus	
	ΝΕΑΠΟΛΙΤΩΝ · ΑΥΡ ·		23 Anea	
	ΠΡΙΗΝΗΣ		24 Proele	
	ΜΑΓΝΗΤΩΝ		4 Magnesia Mae.	
	ΤΡΑΛΛΕΩΝ		3 Tralleis	
	ΝΥΣΑΕΩΝ		16 Nysa	
	ΒΡΙΟΥΛΕΙΤΩΝ		11 Bryoulla	
	ΜΑΖΑΤΑΜΒΕΙΤΩΝ		9 Mastaura	
	ΑΝΙΝΗΤΩΝ		41 Aninta	
	ΥΠΑΙΠΗΝΩΝ		2 Hypepa	
	ΚΑΥΣΤΡΙΑΝΩΝ			
	ΔΙΟΣΙΕΡΙΤΩΝ			
	ΚΑΥΣΤΡΙΑΝΩΝ			
	ΚΙΛΒΙΑΝΩΝ · ΤΩΝ · ΑΝΩ		10 Koloe	
	ΚΙΛΒΙΑΝΩΝ · ΝΙΚΑΕΩΝ		38 Palaiopolis	
	ΚΙΛΒΙΑΝΩΝ · ΚΕΛΙΤΩΝ		19 Bareta	
	ΑΥΡΗΛΙΟ · ΤΜΩ ·		15 Antrinoupolis	
			20 Nea Aule	
	ΚΟΛΟΦΩΝΙΩΝ		30 Kolophon	
	ΜΗΤΡΟΠΟΛΕΙΤΩΝ		18 Metropolis	
	ΛΕΒΕΔΙΩΝ		31 Lebedos	
	ΤΗΙΩΝ		32 Teos	
	ΖΜΥΡΝΑΙΩΝ		11 Smyrna	
	ΚΛΑΖΟΜΕΝΙΩΝ		34 Klazomenai	
	ΕΡΥΘΡΑΙΩΝ		33 Erythrai	
	ΜΑΓΝΗΤΩΝ · ΣΙΠΥΛΟΥ		20 Magnesia Meios	
	ΑΙΤΑΙΕΩΝ · ΑΙΓΑΕΩΝ			
	ΤΗΜΝΕΙΤΩΝ			
	ΦΩΚΑΕΩΝ · ΦΩΚΑΕΩΝ		35 Phokaia	
	ΜΥΡΙΝΑΙΩΝ		12 Myrina	
	ΚΥΜΑΙΩΝ		13 Kyme	
	ΠΕΡΓΑΜΗΝΩΝ		22 Pergamos	
	ΕΛΑΙΤΩΝ		5 Elaia	
	ΠΙΤΑΝΑΙΩΝ		13 Pitane	
	ΑΤΤΑΕΙΤΩΝ		14 Atea	
	ΠΕΡΠΕΡΗΝΙΩΝ		25 Theodosioupolis	
	ΑΔΡΑΜΥΡΗΝΩΝ		6 Adramytion	
	ΑΝΤΑΝΔΡΙΩΝ		27 Antandros	
	ΓΑΡΓΑΡΕΩΝ		7 Gargara	
	ΑΞΕΙΩΝ			
	ΝΑΥ.			

lists of the Delian Confederacy, to which only cities near the coast belong. It may be beside Kos Bunar, where some remarkable archaic monuments exist.* Euaza seems to be the same as Augaza in the 'Notitiæ'; its site is unknown. Kolose is usually called Koloe or Kaloe in the 'Notitiæ' and Councils; it is still named Keles. Algiza seems to be the same place as Argiza; I shall discuss it more fully below. Nikopolis is certainly the Nikaia of coins, one of the cities of the Kilbianoi. The inhabitants of the middle Kaystros valley were called Kaystrianoi, and of the upper valley Kilbianoi. Palaiapolis is still called Baliamboli, which is only the modern pronunciation of παλαιὰν πόλιν. Baretta is unknown.

All these cities appear in the 'Notitiæ Episcopatuum' except Nikopolis and Algiza. In addition, the Thyraioi are mentioned in Not. iii.; this appears to be a false entry, as Thira is already mentioned under the name Arcadiopolis. The double entry arises from the carelessness with which the registers were kept. The official name had disappeared from common use, and the popular name Thyrea or Thýraia was added at the end.

4. Next, Hierocles gives the cities between the Kaystros and Hermos valleys. We have Auliou Kome, and Nea Aule, which is proved by the inscription published as No. κα' in the Smyrna Mouseion, vol. i., p. 120,† to have been not very far from Philadelpheia, probably in a glen of Mount Tmolos. Kolophon, Metropolis, Lebedos, Teos, Smyrna, Klazomenai, and Erythrai (mis-spelt Satrote), all belong to this group.

5. The following belong to the lower Hermos valley, Magnesia, Aigai (called Apae)‡, and Temnos; the middle Hermos valley belongs to Byzantine Lydia. Ducas calls the river Hermon.§

The whole of groups 4 and 5 appear in the Notitiæ except Aigai, Temnos, and Auliou Kome.

6. On the coast between Hermos and Kaikos are Phokaia, Myrina, and Kyme (called Myke); strictly Kyme should come before Myrina.

7. The Kaikos valley embraces Pergamos, Elaia, Pitana, Tianai or Tiarai, and probably Theodosiopolis or Peperine. I regard Tianai as the correct form, not Tiarai, and see in it an inference of Hierocles from the ecclesiastical form ὁ Τιανῶν (ἐπίσκοπος), which is probably derived from Attea, known to be a town of Mysia, and in this district. ὁ Τιανῶν is probably the same bishop who is commonly mentioned in Councils and Notitiæ as ὁ Σιών. ||

* Described by M. Weber in Μουσεῖον Σμυρν., vol. iv.

† Read Διὶ Κορυφαίῳ Δία Σαουάζιον Νεαυλείτην : the stone is at Philadelpheia.

‡ 'Απάη, a mistake in the MSS. for 'Αγάη, which Hierocles gets from some ecclesiastical list, similar to those of the later Conc. Nicaen. ii.

§ Σάρδεις Νύμφαιον μέχρι τοῦ ῞Ερμωνος ποταμοῦ. Ducas, p. 83.

|| The form ὁ 'Ασαίων in ' Concil. Chalced.' seems to connect the others: 'Ασδιων seems to be for 'Ασαιέων (= 'Ασαιαίων), and this for 'Αταιέων or 'Αταέων from ῎Αταια, ορ. Κοτιαέων, Δορυλαέων, 'Ακκιλαέων.

8. Along the north coast are Adramyttion, Antandros, Gargara (called Gadara), and Assos.

The whole of groups 6, 7, and 8, are mentioned in the 'Notitiæ.'

9. The Notitiæ, while omitting Nikopolis, Algiza, Auliou Kome, Aigai, and Temnos, add to this list Mascha Kome and Aureliopolis. Not. iii., x., xiii., also add Khliara, which is mentioned by Anna and other late writers as situated a little east of Pergamos. Of these omitted cities, Argiza, Auliou Kome, Aigai, and Temnos are mentioned at Concil. Chalced. A.D. 451,* and were, therefore, bishoprics in the time of Hierocles.

10. Hierocles is confirmed as to Auliou Kome by the lists of the Council of Chalcedon. In a list appended to Actio XV. the name appears as Thomas Auliocomenus et Valentiniapolitanus, proving that Valentiniana or Valentinianopolis was either a title given to Auliou Kome in the fourth and fifth centuries, or more probably the name of a neighbouring small town united with it in one bishopric. Now we have seen that, according to the order of Hierocles, Auliou Kome lies between the Hermos and Kaystros valleys, and probably, like Nea Aule, in a glen of Mount Tmolos.† In this situation there was a town which struck coins under Hadrian and M. Aurelius Cæsar with the legend ΤΜΩΛΕΙΤΩΝ, and with such types as ΤΜΩΛΟΟ. It was afterwards named Aureliopolis, but the identity of the two places is proved by a coin shown me by Mr. Lawson of Smyrna, who rightly inferred the identity from the legend ΑΥΡΗΛΙΟ · ΤΜΩ. The probability that Auliou Kome is an error for Au[re]liou Kome is thus suggested. Now we have seen that Auliou Kome, or Au[re]liou Kome was a bishopric, and yet it is omitted in the Notitiæ Episcopatuum; but the latter all give Aureliopolis, which Hierocles has not, even although it was so important as to strike coins already under Commodus. Now the principle is accepted throughout this study that a city which coins money under the Roman Empire, and can be traced as a bishopric in the Notitiæ, ought to be mentioned by Hierocles, and where it fails, we have the alternative either that it appears under some other name, or that it is omitted only through some error. In this case the probability is that Aureliopolis of mount Tmolos is the same as Au[re]liou Kome, also of mount Tmolos.‡

11. NIKOPOLIS ought perhaps to be considered only as a fault of

* The relation of Hierocles to the lists of Chalcedon is often very close. The agreement in respect of these four names is noteworthy, and, besides this, Kyme is given as Myke in both authorities, and both also agree in the form Euaza as distinguished from Augaza of the Notitiæ.

† Tmolos was a remarkably fertile range, as is proved by the following quotations:— Πεφύτευται ἐς κορυφὴν ἄκραν, ὥσπερ ὁ ἐν Λυδίᾳ Τμῶλος, Philostr., Vit. Apoll., ii. p. 26 (49); Γεώδη ὄρη καὶ παραπλήσια τῷ Λυδῶν Τμώλῳ, Philostr., Vit. Apoll., vi. p. 123 (239). It is famed for its vines, Ovid, Met., 6, 15 vineta Timoli; Virg. Georg., 2, 97.

‡ Being on the frontier of Byzantine Asia and Lydia, it seems to have been inserted in the lists of both provinces; compare Hadriani. Valentinianopolis is then a name of Perikome, see Lydia. M. Earinos, in Mous. Smyrn. II., gives a totally different theory about Aureliopolis.

separation : the entry in Hierocles ought to be a single city Nikopolis (or Nikaia) Palaiapolis. Palaiapolis and Kolose are neighbouring cities which seem to have struck coins under the name Kilbianoi in the Roman period. The list of the Council of Chalcedon has Algiza Palaiapolis, while Hierocles has Algiza Nikopolis Palaiapolis.* Nikaia or Nikopolis was one of the cities of the Kilbianoi, and, therefore, must probably have been, as Hierocles gives it, between Kolose and Palaiapolis, if it be not identical with the latter. There is therefore only a choice of two alternatives : either Nikopolis Palaiapolis is one city, or they are two neighbouring cities, making one bishopric.

12. ARGIZA, or ALGIZA, is mentioned with both spellings at Chalcedon and always appears among the bishoprics of Asia. Now Argiza has been recently discovered by Dr. Fabricius in the province of Hellespontus, and Hierocles gives it in that province. Algiza is also mentioned at Concil. Nicæn. II., A.D. 787, and there also it always appears among the cities of Asia. The order of signature at the latter Council is closely according to provinces, and at Chalcedon it approximates to that arrangement. Two possibilities are therefore open. There may have been two cities, one Argiza in Hellespontus, known only from an inscription and from Hierocles; the other, Algiza, or Argiza, in Asia, known only from Hierocles and from two Councils. The other possibility is that, through some old connection or some unexplained reason, Argiza of Hellespontus was in the earlier ecclesiastical system subject to the metropolitan of Asia, and Hierocles, being much influenced by the ecclesiastical lists in that province, inserted Algiza among the cities of the Kaystros valley,† while in Hellespontus, where he is quite independent of the ecclesiastical lists, he gives it as Argiza. The second alternative seems more probable.

13. The discrepancies between Hierocles and the Notitiæ are now reduced to this, that the latter omit Aigai and Temnos, and give Mascha Kome, which Hierocles has not. I shall proceed in the next paragraphs to show that Aigai and Temnos were separated from Ephesos and placed under the metropolis Smyrna. As to Mascha Kome, I can only suggest that it was raised to the rank of a bishopric later than A.D. 530. I cannot accept M. Earinos's view about it; his identifications of Palaiapolis and Stratonikaia are excellent (Mous. Smyrn. II.).

14. SMYRNA was raised to the rank of a metropolis, probably later than Hierocles, but certainly before the date of the Notitiæ. The order of signatures at the Councils shows that it was not a metropolis in 451 A.D., but it was so certainly in 692, and probably even in 536. The

---

* I assume here the close relationship of Hierocles' list of Asia with that of the *Concil. Chalcedon.*

† At Chalcedon it is put next to Palaiapolis; Hierocles separates them only by Nikopolis. In 787, at Conc. Nic. II., the names often go in groups closely approximating to groups in Hierocles. An Algiza also occurs in the Tekmorian inscriptions.

probability is that it was raised to the rank of a metropolis by Justinian (A.D. 527–63). Notitiæ iii., x., give a list of the bishoprics which were placed under it. They are as follows:—

Notitia III.	Notitia X.
τῷ Σμύρνης ’Ασίας.	τῇ Σμύρνῃ τῆς ’Ασίας.
α′ ὁ Φωκαίας.	1 ὁ Φωκαίας.
β′ ὁ Μαγνησίας τοῦ ’Ανηλίου.	2 ὁ Μαγνησίας. 3 ὁ ’Ανηλίου.
γ′ ὁ Κλαζομενῶν.	4 ὁ Κλαζομενδῶν.
δ′ ὁ Σωσάνδρου.	7 ὁ Σωσάνδρων.
ε′ ὁ ’Αρχαγγέλου.	5 ὁ τοῦ ’Αρχαγγέλου.
ϛ′ ὁ τῆς Πέτρας.	6 ὁ τῆς Πέτρας.

These six * bishoprics form a distinct local group, readily accessible from their metropolis Smyrna. Phokaia, Klazomenai, and Magnesia ad Sipylum,† are well known, and were bishoprics previously under Ephesos. Sosandros was probably Nymphaion, the modern Nymphio (Turkish *Nif*). John Ducas died at Nymphaion, and was buried ἐν τῇ μονῇ τῶν Σωσάνδρων, ἣν αὐτὸς ἐδείματο, in the great church of the Virgin of Sosandra, at Magnesia, which he had built himself. Now, the bishopric Sosandra or ·Sosandros cannot be Magnesia itself, for that is a separate bishopric, but it must be some place conveniently near Magnesia, so that the same Virgin might be worshipped at both places. It must also be naturally connected with Smyrna, so as to be subject to that metropolis. Now, if Nymphaion were a bishopric at all, it must almost necessarily be subject to Smyrna; and its importance, arising from its position as chief city of a fertile little valley, and attested by the frequent references in later history, shows that it must have been a bishopric. It appears, therefore, in the ecclesiastical lists, not by its heathen name, but by a Christian title. ‡

15. ARCHANGELOS. The bishopric of the Archangel (Michael) also bears a Christian title, derived from its chief church, which has replaced the Pagan name. The following passage seems to prove that it was identical with or close to Temnos:—In A.D. 1413, Mahomet came by Pergamos and Kyme into the plain of Menemen, and thence to Nymphaion. There are only two ways to advance from Menemen plain to Nymphaion; one along the coast and through the valley of Smyrna, the other round the north side of Sipylos. Mahomet could not take the former road, for Smyrna was in the hands of his enemy Tchineït, and

* Nilus Doxapatrius says that there were five bishoprics under Smyrna, but does not name them. Probably 5 is a mistake for 6 in his text.

† On Magnesia and its water-supply, see Georg. Pachym., ii. p. 440.

‡ A city receiving the name of its principal church is very common in Byzantine times. Nymphaion is mentioned by Georg. Pachym., i. p. 125, ii. p. 220; Niceph. Greg., ii. pp. 44 and 50, also 137, 190; Ducas, 83, 104, 193· Anna Comn., ii. 252.

only after capturing Nymphaion was he able to march against Smyrna. He therefore must have taken the other road, past Temnos and Magnesia. The Turkish name of the fortress of Archangelos was Kayajik.* The rock on which Temnos was situated, high and difficult, was a very strong fortress by nature, commanding the narrow pass between the lower and middle valleys of the Hermos: it is, moreover, only a small rock, " Kayajik," in comparison with the surrounding mountains. The only other possibility is that Archangelos-Kayajik was Neonteichos or Menemen, and in either case Archangelos would replace the older Temnos. In modern time Menemen has entirely taken the place of Temnos, which is deserted.

16. The plain of Menemen is mentioned in another passage, when Musulman marched from Lopadion by Pergamos and Menemen to Smyrna and Ephesos.† The bishopric of Temnos or Archangelos must have included the entire territory along the lower Hermos from the sea to the borders of the Magnesian territory at the entrance to the Boghaz. There would be included in it the following old Greek towns:—Larissa, Melanpagos, Leukai, Neonteichos, and Herakleia ad Sipylum, besides the town of Menemen, which seems to have risen to importance in later Byzantine time. I have placed these cities in my 'Contributions to the History of Southern Aeolis,' Part II., ‡ where I omitted to mention that Herakleia ad Sipylum coined money under the later emperors. This bishopric then included the whole territory bounded by Smyrna, Magnesia, Aigai, Kyme, Phokaia, and the Gulf of Smyrna.

17. PETRA is unknown to me, but as Aigai and Temnos naturally go together, and as the former was conveniently situated so as to be in connection with Smyrna, I conjecture that Petra took the place of Aigai.

18. Notitiæ i., vii., viii., ix. do not give any bishoprics as subject to Smyrna. It is also clear that at Concil. Nicæn. II., in 787, Smyrna had not yet subjected to it Phokaia, Magnesia, Aigai, and Temnos. It is not therefore clear why these Notitiæ should omit Aigai and Temnos, though it is easy to see why these two cities are omitted in Notitiæ iii., x.

19. I may add here a few notes on some of the cities in this list, on points which are either disputed or unnoticed.

EPHESOS was famous for the great church of St. John Theologos, built on the hill beside the modern railway station, Ayasaluk. This church and the castle on the hill § gradually became the centre of a town, while

---

* εἰς τὸν τοῦ Μαινομένου κάμπον· ἦν δὲ ἐκεῖ φρούριον ὀχυρὸν τὸ τοῦ ᾿Αρχαγγέλου λεγόμενον, οἱ Τοῦρκοι δὲ Καγιατζὴκ μετωνόμασαν, Ducas, p. 103.

† From Lopadion εἰς Πέργαμον (κἀκεῖθεν) ἐν τῷ κάμπῳ τοῦ Μαινομένου, ἀπὸ δὲ τοῦ κάμπου ἐν Σμύρνῃ, Ducas, p. 85. I have conjecturally inserted two words, which are absolutely necessary to the sense.

‡ 'Journal of Hellenic Studies,' 1881.

§ On the church see Procopius de Aedif., V.; Theophan., p. 469, κατελθὼν εἰς ῎Εφεσον καὶ εἰς τὸν Θεολόγον. The Paulicians penetrated into the Thrakesian Theme as far as

Ephesos decayed and is now deserted.   Thus the plain reverted to its original state; for before the Greek city was built, the sanctuary of Artemis, which is near the hill, was the centre to which the whole valley looked.   The name Ayio Theológo has become Ayo-thológo, and finally Ayosoluk, or Ayasaluk.   Mr. Wood has been misled by the last syllable of the modern name, and understands it as Ἅγιος Λούκας, and even Prof. G. Hirschfeld has followed him in this error.*   But the latter name could only become Ayo-luk or Aïluk: moreover, no connection of St. Luke with Ephesos is known, for the so-called "Tomb of St. Luke" is, as M. Weber has proved, and as Prof. G. Hirschfeld recognised even from Mr. Wood's description, a Greek *polyandrion*.   The name Theologos is known to have been used both in Byzantine writers, conformably to the habit of naming towns according to the chief church in them, and also in early Turkish times, for coins of an early Turkish chief are known with the Latin legend, "*Moneta que fit in Theologo*." †   At or beside one of the theatres in Ephesos was a shrine of Heracles Apotropaios.‡   The plain beside Ephesos was called Τζουκανιστῆριν (Theoph., p. 439).   The mountain on the north side was, as has been generally recognised, Gallesion or Galesion: there was a monastery in the mountain.§   M. Weber has published a useful study of Ephesos, with the only good map of the city and surroundings.

The smaller detached hill to the north within Ephesos, which was named Pion in Roman time, was apparently called by a different name afterwards: the Cave of the Seven Sleepers in the hill, which is still shown, and which has always been a place of annual pilgrimage,∥ is said in 'Act. Sanct.' (July 27, p. 395), to be in Mount Chaos or Celeos, Caelius, Ochlon or Χείλαιον.   Pyrgion was a village at some little distance from Ephesos, on the skirts of Mount Tmolos.   (Ducas, p. 83.)

The following quotations refer to an ἔξοδος of the goddess, who was carried through the city and back to her temple (such a progress of the goddess through her city is well known at Komana Pontica and elsewhere).   I think that they have not been used by the writers who have discussed the cultus of Artemis at Ephesos; παρ' Ἐφεσίοις ἑορτὴ, Καταγώγιον ὑπ' αὐτῶν καλουμένη· κατὰ γοῦν ταύτην ῥόπαλά τε ἀναιρούμενοι,

St. John Theologos, and stabled their horses in the church, Genes., p. 121. On the castle τῷ κατ' Ἔφεσον φρουρίῳ, Georg. Pachym., ii. 220.

* Note on his paper on "The March of Manlius" in Gratulationsschrift der Königsb. Univ. f. d. Arch. Inst. in Rom, 1879.

† Compare the similar coins of Magnesia, *moneta que fit in Manglasia*.

‡ τὸ θέατρον, οὗ τὸ τοῦ Ἀποτροπαίου ἵδρυται, ... ἔστι δὲ Ἡρακλῆς, Philostr., Vit. Apoll., iv. p. 68 (130–1).

§ Niceph. Greg. iv. p. 107, compare note in ii. p. 1172. Joseph, head of the monastery, is mentioned by Georg. Pach., i. p. 291.   On the extent of Gallesion, cp. Ducas, 87 and 194.

∥ In recent years, under the influence of Mr. Wood's researches, this pilgrimage and festival are extended to the so-called "Tomb of Saint Luke," but previously Saint Luke had no share.

καὶ εἴδωλα διὰ χειρὸς ἔχοντες, καί τινα περιτιθέντες ἑαυτοῖς προσωπεῖα, τῆς τε πόλεως ἀναίδην τὰ ἐπισημότερα μέρη περιιόντες καί τινα τούτοις ἐπᾴδοντες, ἀνδράσι τε καὶ γυναιξὶ λῃστρικῶς ἐπιόντες, πολὺν αὐτῶν εἰργάζοντο φόνον, ταύτῃ τὸν οἰκεῖον ἡγούμενοι δαίμονα τιμᾶν. Metaphr., Vit. Timoth., i. p. 769.

In nefanda festivitate eorum quam vocabant Catagogiorum, quæ est secundum Asianos quidem mensis quarti die tricesima, secundum autem Romanos mensis Januarii vicesima secunda die, regnante in Romanorum civitate prædicto Nerva, procurante autem Asiam Peregrino. Vit. Timoth., AA. SS., Jan. 24, p. 566.

20. MESAULION was six hours' march from Ephesos, on the road to Smyrna. There was a bridge over the Kaystros towards Mount Galesion,* which was crossed between Mesaulion and Ephesos.

21. Ducas (p. 87) mentions, under the name αἱ Κλεισοῦραι αἱ πρὸς Μαίανδρον, the pass leading from Ephesos to Magnesia, now traversed by the railway.

22. ANEA, or Anaia, is mentioned only in Byzantine times; it was a harbour (G. Pach., ii. p. 420). It did not coin money. It was certainly in the παραλία Ἐφεσία (Strabo, p. 639). It was perhaps at Scalanova (Turkish Kush Adasi), which has taken the place of the harbour of Ephesos, now silted up. It is perhaps to be identified with one or other of the following two harbours, which were in the same coast.

23. PYGELA, or Phygela, an ancient city with a shrine of Artemis Mounychia, founded by Agamemnon, disappears almost entirely during the Byzantine period. The only late reference to it that I have found is in Michael Attaliota (p. 224), who tells that Phokas was about to sail from Pygela to Crete, and that, when all was ready, he enquired the name of the harbour. Hearing the name Phygela, he disliked the omen (arising from the resemblance to ἔφυγον), and asked what was the name of a promontory which was visible at a considerable distance; when he learned that the name was Hagia, he ordered all the force to disembark, march by land to Hagia, and re-embark there. Hagia appears to be the promontory of Scalanova (Turkish Kush Adasi), and Pygela must be a harbour at some distance. Strabo (p. 639) mentions on the coast the Panionion, then Neapolis,† then Pygela, then the harbour Panormos, and finally Ephesos.

24. On the coast, at the mouth of the Mæander, there was a place named 'The Gardens' (Κῆποι, Cedren., ii. 198). It is also mentioned in Theophan. Contin., p. 204, as in the Thrakesian Theme,‡ and, p. 236, as on the coast beside the Mæander. Genesius, p. 103–5, also alludes to it. Another Κᾶποι was in the Carian island Pserimos, Paton in Bull. Corr. Hell., 1888, p. 282.

* ἀπὸ τῆς γεφύρας τῆς πρὸς Γαλήσιον ὄρος κειμένης, Ducas, p. 87.

† Neapolis coined money under the Roman empire, sometimes with the title ΑΥΡ ηλία.

‡ It was therefore north of the Mæander. The Kibyrrhaiot Theme began at the southern bank of the Mæander.

25. On this coast there was also a place Melanoudion, and near it a castle which, according to Pachymeres, was formerly called Didymion; but his words imply perhaps that he had no express authority for the identification, but inferred it from the name "Castle of the Two Hills."* We may, however, be sure that unless it had been in this neighbourhood towards Miletos, Pachymeres would not have made the identification. Another Melanoudion is mentioned as a quarter of the city of Mitylene (Ducas, p. 346).

26. MAMALOS, a seaport in Caria, is perhaps a variant of Marmara (Ducas, p. 82).

27. TRALLEIS. Numerous names are said to have also been given to this city, some apparently mere epithets, such as Antheia, Erymna, &c. Others depend on a mere confusion, such as Larissa, the foundation for which lies in the title Larasios, which is usually given to Zeus at Tralleis. The epithet is sometimes corrupted to Larissaios, and thus suggests the old name Larissa, but inscriptions and coins give the true form. Strabo derives the epithet, which he gives as Larisaios, from a village Larisa in the mountains above Tralleis (p. 440, cp. 649); the true spelling must be Larasa.

The name Tralleis, mentioned twice by Xenophon, is an interesting proof of the connection with Europe, due, as I believe, to a set of warrior tribes who crossed the Hellespont and settled as a ruling caste among the subject population in Mysia, Lydia, Phrygia, Caria, and Lycia. The name also occurs as that of a city on the Lydo-Phrygian frontier.

The name Tralleis was applied to a body of mercenaries τοῖς βασιλεῦσιν, and is explained as a Thracian word meaning warriors. Fick considers that this is a mistake, and that the word really is Sclavonic, on the ground that the old Thracian language could not have survived till Byzantine times; but this objection has no force, for the term might have continued in use even after the Thracian language was disused. Moreover, I believe that the native languages of Asia Minor, and perhaps also of Thrace, continued in use much longer than is generally supposed. All doubt, however, is removed by the recently discovered inscription,† dating under Eumenes I. (263–41), which shows that the Pergamenian kings divided their army into horse, foot, and τράλεις. The latter were no doubt Thracian mercenaries in the Pergamenian service. The βασιλεῖς are not, as Fick understood, Byzantine emperors, but Pergamenian kings.

Tralleis, from its position, was the most powerful fortress in the

---

* Φρούριον πρὸς τὸ Μελανούδιον τῶν δύο βουνῶν, ... ὃ πάλαι οἶμαι τὸ Μιλησίων Διδύμιον ἐφημίζετο, ii. p. 211: οἶμαι would not imply hesitation or even inference in an Attic writer, but I think it does in Pachymeres. The temple of Didymean Apollo must be the place referred to.

† Jahrb. der kgl. Preuss. Kunstsamml., ix., 1887, p. 82, quoted by Schuchhardt, *Athen. Mittheil.*, 1888, p. 1 ff.; Fick, *Ehemal. Sprachenheit*, p. 420; and Hesych. Τράλλεις· οὕτως ἐκαλοῦντο μισθοφόροι Θρᾷκες τοῖς βασιλεῦσιν, οἱ τὰς φονικὰς χρείας πληροῦντες.

Mæander valley, and therefore was a stronghold, first of the Seleucid kings, as is inferred from the names Seleuceia and Antiocheia, which for a time supplanted that of Tralleis, and after 190 B.C. of the Pergamenian rule, as is shown by the great numbers of cistophori coined there.

Beside the village of Larasa was a sanctuary of Meter Isodrome, obviously a form of Meter Leto, who was worshipped all along Mount Messogis.*

In the reign of Andronicus Palæologus, the cities of the Mæander valley had entirely ceased to exist, and those to the north. nearer the centre of the empire, were terribly wasted (τὰ κατὰ Μαίανδρον καὶ Καρίαν καὶ ᾿Αντιόχειαν ἤδη καὶ τετελευτήκει, τὰ δὲ τούτων καὶ ἔτι ἐνδοτέρω δεινῶς ἐξησθένει, καὶ ἡλίσκοντο μὲν τὰ κατὰ Κάϋστρον καὶ Πριήνην, ἡλίσκοντο δ᾿ ἤδη καὶ τὰ κατὰ Μίλητον, καὶ Μαγεδὼν καὶ τὰ πρόσχωρα . . . ἐξηφανίζοντο). Andronicus rebuilt Tralleis, and intended that it should, under the name Andronicopolis or Palæologopolis, perpetuate his glory. But no provision was made for a water supply, and the inhabitants suffered much in consequence, till after a year or two the Turks under Mentesh captured the city.—Georg. Pachym., i. p. 468–72.

Akharaka lay between Tralleis and Nyssa; it was the seat of a singularly important and interesting cultus of certain gods, named in the hellenising fashion of the Roman period Plouton and Kora. Hot springs in the neighbourhood are mentioned by Athenæus (ii. p. 43A) in a passage where the reading must be amended τὸν ᾿Αχαρακακωμήτην ποταμόν. C. I. G. 3923 refers to the worship at Akharaka, and is wrongly referred by MM. Waddington (Le Bas, 1663c) and Perrot (Rev. Arch., 1876, p. 283) to Mastaura. I have distinguished between the inscriptions of Nyssa and Mastaura in Bulletin de Correspondance Hellénique, 1883, p. 270.

Nyssa, with its tribes Sebaste Athenais, Octavia Apollonis, Germanis Seleukis, Antiochis (less certain), and Kaisarios, is recorded to have been a foundation of the Seleucidæ, and the names point to this period.† A prominent citizen of the second century is in inscriptions sometimes called Alkibiades and sometimes Alkipales; the variants are certain and strange.‡

28. BRIOULA is often said to have been situated at the modern Vourla; but the sole evidence is the resemblance of name, and the order of Hierocles is confirmed by Strabo, who expressly gives it in the Mæander valley east of Mastaura, and by Pliny who gives it in the conventus of Ephesos (v. 111). ΗΛΙΟC and ΜΗΤΗΡ . ΘΕΩΝ occur on its coins.

Vourla is mentioned by Ducas (p. 175), τὰ Βρύελα § καὶ αἱ ᾿Ερυθραὶ

* Strab., p. 440, cp. A S P, A ii.
† Bull. Corr. Hell., 1883, p. 270.
‡ Bull. Corr. Hell., l.c.; C. I. E., 2747–8; Le Bas, 1652 f.; Sterrett, Epigraphical Journey, 3.
§ Pronounced Vryela.

Κλαζομεναί τε : in this form it certainly resembles very closely the ancient Brioula, and the latter name perhaps occurred twice. Vourla is near the ancient Klazomenai, on the opposite side of the peninsula from Erythrai.

29. Dios Hieron is placed by Kiepert on the coast between Notion and Lebedos.* This is impossible, for it violates the order of Hierocles, and, moreover, the river Kaystros is named on its coins. It is sometimes called Christopolis in Byzantine lists; the name was changed to avoid speaking of Jupiter, as Aphrodisias was changed to Stauropolis. It can hardly have been farther away from the coast than Kos Bunar, and the ancient remains in that neighbourhood point to some early city.† The lists of the Delian confederacy have the name Διοσιρῖται; coins have ΔΙΟΣΙΕΡΕΙΤΩΝ.

30. The Kilbian, Kelbian, or Kerbian plain was the upper part of the Kaystros valley, with the cities of Kolose and Nikaia. Coins of the Kilbianoi are numerous ; they are of three classes, Kilbianoi of Nikaia, Kilbianoi of Kea or Keaia, and Upper Kilbianoi. The third class perhaps corresponds to the city of Koloe.‡ The second is represented by one coin only, and is rather doubtful; the reading is ΚΕΑΙΤΩΝ or ΚΕΛΙΤΩΝ.

The Kilbian plain was in the Thrakesian Theme.§ A path from it over Tmolos to Sardis is mentioned by Theophanes (p. 417); Di Boor, in his index, understands that this passage refers to a city Kelbianon, but the word which is understood is πεδίον.

31. Teira perhaps means " the town," as in Thya-teira, the town of Γhya, compare Thyessos and Thyassos.‖

After the name Arcadiopolis was disused, it is frequently mentioned in the later writers, as Θύρεα and Θύραια, Ducas, pp. 97, 175, 196. Georgius Pachymeres mentions (ii. 588) that Sasan removed many of the inhabitants of Ephesos to Thyraia, after pillaging the church of St. John, in 1308.

The river Kaystros is now called the Little Mæander. This name may perhaps be traced in use as early as Anna Comnena. The entire coast from Smyrna to Attaleia was exposed to the ravages of the Turks. Alexius sent Philokales with an army. He rebuilt Adramyttion, which had been entirely destroyed. He learned on enquiry that the Turks

* His authority is Stephanus, πόλις μεταξὺ Λεβέδου καὶ Κολοφῶνος. The other evidence proves that this is an error.

† On these remains see Weber in Mous. Smyrn. IV.

‡ The name Kolose has hitherto been accepted on the evidence of an inscription (Smyrn. Mous. No. ζ'), but the most recent copy reads Κολοηνῶν, Mitth. Ath. 1889, p. 98; and the form Kolose must for the present be discarded. The Byzantine authorities have Koloe or Kaloe.

§ Cinnam. p. 39; cp. Anna Comnena, ii. 252, 268.

‖ This suggestion, which has been in my mind for years, can now be quoted from M. S. Reinach's paper to the French Institute, which will soon be published. The first statement, and therefore the discovery, must be credited to him.

were in force at Lampe, and sent a detachment against them, which defeated them, and behaved with horrible cruelty. The detachment returned to Philokales, who stationed himself at Philadelpheia. Hassan, governor of Cappadocia, now came against him with a large army, passed beside Philadelpheia, and taking no notice of Philokales, whom he considered too weak to be dangerous, he divided his army into three parts; one was sent into the Kilbian plain, one to Nymphaion and Smyrna, and one to Pergamos and Khliara. Philokales then defeated the first two divisions singly, but the third escaped him by a hasty retreat. Anna mentions that the fugitives of the second division were overwhelmed in the Mæander (ποταμὸς δὲ οὗτος περὶ Φρυγίαν, σκολιώτατος ποταμῶν ἁπάντων). The passage is unintelligible except on the supposition that this statement refers to the fugitives of the first division, and has been through Anna's error referred to the second division. The river would in that case be the Little Mæander, now the Cutchuk Menderez, the Cayster.

33. SMYRNA. It is customary to identify the famous river Meles with the stream that flows under Caravan Bridge on the eastern skirts of the modern Smyrna. A study of the references shows that this is a mistaken view. This stream rises in the plain of Kolophon, near Sevdi Keui, and is little more than a torrent, dry during the greater part of the year, but swollen in the rainy season. It may be granted that it was most probably richer in water in ancient times, owing to greater abundance of trees and rain; but there can be little doubt that the whole of its water must have been diverted above Smyrna to supply the city. On the other hand, the Meles is described in great detail by Aristides, Philostratus, and Himerius.* It flowed with an equal volume of water in winter and summer, quiet and gentle, and never swollen. It has not a long course, but rises close to where it flows into the sea after a curved course. It rises in a grove of the Muses beside Smyrna. Aristides bathed in it and found its waters warm and pleasant in the depth of winter. Such points, and many others that I might quote, prove that it is the stream rising in the springs now called "Diana's Bath," whose waters never vary, and have their temperature the same in winter as in summer.

34. Between Klazomenai and Smyrna there were hot springs. Philostratos calls them the springs of Agamemnon; they were 40 stadia from Smyrna.† Aristides mentions them as one of his resorts during his illness.

* τῷ Μέλητι παρεχομένῳ τὰς πηγὰς οὐ πόρρω τῶν ἐκβολῶν. Philostr., Imag. 8. ἐκεῖ ἐκβάλλων ὅθεν ἄρχεται, id. ib. ὅτι μὴ λάβρους τὰς πηγὰς ἐκδίδωσι, id. ib. τί οὖν αἱ Μοῦσαι δεῦρο· τί δὲ ἐπὶ ταῖς πηγαῖς τοῦ Μέλητος (then he explains the natural connection of the Muses with Ionia and with the Meles), id. ib. τὸ νέμος τῆς Σμύρνης ἐν ᾧ ὁ Μέλης. Philostr., Vit. Apoll., vii., § 8,

† Strab. p. 645, cp. πηγαὶ θερμαὶ ἐν 'Ιωνίᾳ, ἃς ἔτι καὶ νῦν 'Αγαμεμνονείους καλοῦσιν οἱ Σμύρναν οἰκοῦντες· ἀπέχουσι δὲ οἶμαι τετταράκοντα στάδια τοῦ ἄστεος, καὶ ἀνῆπτό ποτε αὐτοῖς αἰχμάλωτα κράνη Μύσια, Philostr., Heroic. ii., p. 160.

35. Villages in the valley of Smyrna, or in the neighbourhood, are (1) Karina; a woman *ex vico Carina* in prison at Smyrna, *v.* Acta Pionii in Act. Sanct., Feb. 1, p. 44. It seems impossible to understand here the town on the Mysian coast, north of Atarneus, mentioned by Herodotus, 7, 42, and Pliny, H. N., 5, 30.

(2) Phlebia (perhaps Flavia) may be the baths of Agamemnon. The Emperor Theodore Lascaris II. left Nymphaion in the spring, and after passing some days ἐν τοῖς Φλεβίοις, went to Klyzomene (i.e. Klazomenai); at this place the Emperors were accustomed to pass a good part of the spring after leaving Nymphaion, as the place offered a fine open grass-covered plain, watered with abundant sources (κατάρρυτος δὲ τυγχάνει καὶ ὕδασιν), and with numerous villages and cities close at hand.*

(3) Periklystra is now called Bunar Bashi; it was a summer residence of John Vatatzes, and Nymphaion was his winter residence. When he was sick at Nymphaion he went to Smyrna to pray to the Christ of Smyrna. The prayers which he addressed to the deity of Smyrna brought him no relief. He stayed at Periklystra in a tent.†

(4) Zeleia and (5) Sykai are mentioned in an inscription published in Le Bas-Waddington, 1534.

36. MAGNESIA became, in later Byzantine time, one of the greatest cities of Western Anatolia. In early Christian time it boasted a martyr Charalampius, whose story, laid in the time of Severus, is devoid of local colour and historical verisimilitude (Act. Sanct., Feb. 10). Its Turkish coins, with the legend " moneta que fit in Manglasia," are known.

37. AIGAI.‡   The territory of Aigai must have been very wide.   It extended from Myrina and Kyme on the west to Apollonis and Magnesia on the east; it was bounded on the north by the territory of Pergamos, and on the south by that of Temnos.   In the ' Bulletin de Correspondance Hellénique,' 1887, MM. Lechat and Radet have been led into error through not distinguishing between the town and the territory.   They have discovered a sepulchral inscription at a village Mafullar Keui, on the eastern frontier of Aigai and Apollonis, which mentions that copies are deposited in the archives of Aigai (as the city of which the deceased ranked as citizens, though they lived in a village) and of Pergamos (as the seat of the conventus).   On the evidence of this text they seek to move Aigai from Nemrud Kalesi, and to fix it at a village Sari Tcham, some distance to the east of Mafullar.   They lay stress on the vague statements of Strabo that Magnesia was not distant (οὐκ ἄπωθεν) from Temnos and Aigai, and of Suidas that Aigai was near Magnesia and Smyrna; but they place no value on the more numerous authorities

* Georg. Acropol., p. 187.

† Acropol., p. 91, cp. 110, ὅπως τῷ ἐκεῖσε προσκυνήσῃ Χριστῷ and τόπος δέ ἐστιν οὗτος ἐγγύς που τῆς Σμύρνης διὰ τὸ πολλοῖς τοῖς ὕδασι περικλύζεσθαι οντω πως κατονομαζόμενος.

‡ Aigaiai is the most correct form.

who expressly connect Aigai with the Aeolic cities of the coast, and
they do not even quote the most valuable testimony about Aigai, viz.
the statement of Galen * that Aigai bordered on Myrina and Perperine
on Pergamos. I lay no stress, after this testimony, on Stephanus (Αἰγαὶ
ἐν Μυρρίνῃ), nor on Wesseling's excellent and certain emendation of
Suidas, πλησίον Μαγνησίας καὶ Μυρίνης. The light-heartedness with
which recent writers discuss the topography of Asia Minor is rapidly
becoming one of the greatest evils that research in Asia Minor has
to contend with.† Every one thinks that he can take a few references from his predecessor and contradict him, and in so doing
frequently wastes pages of his useless dissertation and pages of the
necessary confutation. While the proof that Aigai was situated at
Nemrud Kalesi is not yet quite complete, the proof that it is either
there or in that neighbourhood is complete.

38. PERPERINE is fixed on the coast on the borders of Pergamos, by
the passage of Galen quoted under Aigai, and other references.
Schuchhardt has specified the exact situation at Bergas. It is generally called Theodosiopolis in the ecclesiastical lists. A very large
number of places were named after Theodosius during the fifth and sixth
centuries, and many others bear the names of members of his family. ‡

39. KHLIARA. Its approximate situation is shown by a wonderful
march of the Turkish chief Tchineit. Leaving Lopadion in the first
watch of the night with a few followers, Tchineit rode all night over
hill and plain, till in the morning he reached the Lydian frontier
about Khliara and Thyateira (ἐν τοῖς μέρεσι τοῖς πρὸς τὰ Χλιερὰ καὶ
Θυάτειρα); at the third hour he crossed the Hermos, and reached
Smyrna about nightfall. § In this hurried ride he certainly took the
shortest road, and at the point where he entered Lydia Khliara and
Thyateira were the nearest cities. The account is obviously exaggerated,
for the distance from Lopadion to the Hermos could not be traversed
between evening and next day at the third hour. The distance between
the Hermos and Smyrna is about ten hours of the modern reckoning,
and to this Tchineit requires the time between the third hour and
sunset, about nine hours. The distance from Lopadion to the Hermos
must be quite forty hours. Still the route is trustworthy, though the
time is not correct, unless we suppose that a whole day is to be added.
We may feel confident that his route was either by Balikesri, Soma,
and Kirk Agatch, or by Boghaditch and Gelembe; but in either case

* περὶ εὐχυμίας, p. 358, ed. Basil: I quote from Wesseling.
† S. Reinach and Schuchhardt have already taken the correct side against
MM. Lechat and Radet (see Addenda).
‡ One of these, which does not occur in any list, is Arcadiopolis of Caria: ἔκτισε δὲ
καὶ ἑτέραν πόλιν ἐπ' ὀνόματι τοῦ υἱοῦ αὐτοῦ, τὸ πρὶν Βεργούλιον λεγομένη. Cedren. i. 568.
In Hierocles Bargylia seems to be concealed under either Marcianopolis or Anastasiopolis
The Notitiæ give it under its original name.
§ Ducas, p. 174.

the expression "Khliara and Thyatira" suggests that Kirk Agatch is Khliara, for Ak Hisar and Kirk Agatch form a natural pair to define the frontier.

Another passage fixes Khliara still more certainly. In A.D. 1306 Roger marched up the Kaikos valley to Germe, and thence by Khliara to Philadelpheia.* There is no doubt he went by the direct road, as Philadelpheia was in extreme danger; his road would then lead through Kirk Agatch and Ak Hisar, i.e. Khliara and Thyateira.

The situation of Khliara beside Nakrasa might suggest rather that it belonged to Lydia, but there was much uncertainty about the dependence of the cities in this neighbourhood.   Ducas (p. 174) mentions that it was on the Lydian frontier.   A town still further east, Kalanta or Kalanda, is assigned to Asia in Concil. Trull., A.D. 692,† while Hierocles gives it to Hellespontus as Skelenta (i. e. εἰς Κάλαντα), and the Notitiæ include it under one bishop with Stratonicea in Lydia.   It is probably the modern Seledik.

40. Assos takes its modern name Behram from a Byzantine officer Machram, whose history is told by George Pachymeres, ii. p. 438. Ducas mentions Μαχράμιον as the name of Assos (p. 332).

41. GARGARA, a few miles east of Assos, has been discussed in an admirable paper by Mr. J. T. Clarke (Amer. Journ. Arch., 1888).

42. The conventus of Ephesos includes—

*Metiopolis.‡	Magnesia ad Mæandrum.
Notion.	Tralleis (*Cæsarienses).
Kolophon.	Nyssa.
*Dios Hieron.	*Mastaura.
*Hypaipa.	*Brioula.
*Kaystriani (with their cities).	*[Mysomacedones].
*Kilbiani (with their cities).	Neapolis.
Teira.	Priene.

The name Mysomacedones is certainly false, for no city on the north side of Mount Tmolos is included in the conventus of Ephesos; the true reading is doubtless some city of the Kaystros valley or of the Mæander valley, where there was a Macedonian colony.

43. Smyrna was the seat of a conventus; Pliny mentions that most of the cities of Aeolis belonged to it, and also Magnesia and the Hyrcani. We may attempt to complete the list—

---

* κἀντεῦθεν Χλιαρὰ διελθὼν καὶ τἄλλα τὴν ἐπὶ Φιλαδελφείας ἔσπευδεν ἐσχάτως κινδυνεύουσαν. Aulax is the only other place named before he reached Philadelpheia, and its exact distance is not given, Georg. Pach., ii., 426 ff. Anna, ii., pp. 252, 265, 280. Nicetas Chon., p. 194, puts Khliara in Asia.

† Unless Le Quien is right in altering Καλαντῶν to Κολοηνῶν.

‡ Names mentioned by Pliny in his list of the conventus are asterised. On the interpretation of Cæsarienses as Tralleis, see under LYDIA.

Leuke.	Magnetes a Sipylo.
Phokaia.	Macedones Hyrcani.
Kyme.	Klazomenai.
Myrina Sebastopolis (?).	Erythrai.
Larissa.	Lebedos.
Neonteichos.	Teos.
Temnos.	Nymphaion.

It is possible that Kolophon should be added to the list, but not Aigai. This list shows that the country from about Myrina to Teos and inland all round the skirts of Sipylos was attached to Smyrna. No city that belongs to another conventus can be placed within these limits, hence, for example, M. Fontrier and M. Foucart * err in restoring an inscription with the name of the Mostenoi and placing that people on the south side of the Hermos about Hadjilar.

44. The conventus of Pergamos includes (names mentioned by Pliny are asterised):

Elaia.	*Perpereni.
Aigai.	*Tiareni.
*Mosteni (Mossyni in Pliny).	*Hierolophienses [Hierocæsarienses?].
*Mygdones.	*Hermokapelia.
*Bregmeni.	*Attaleia.
*Hierocometæ.	*Ateenses (Pateenses, Panteenses).
*Apollonis.	Pitana.
*Thyatira.	Nakrasa.
Akrasos.	Stratonikaia-Hadrianopolis.

Tiareni, Mygdones, and Bregmeni are false names. Ateenses are the people of Ataia, which should be placed where Kiepert erroneously has Attaleia.† Hierokometai are the inhabitants of some village beside an important temple called Hiera Kome, a common title.

45. The conventus of Adramyttion includes:

*Apollonia ad Rhyndacum.	*Macedones Asculacæ.
*Erezii (read Argizii).	*Polichnæi.
*Miletopolis.	*Pionitæ.
*Poemaneni.	*Hellespontii.
*Cilices Mandacadeni.	Cyzicos.
*Abretteni.	

Cyzicos was according to Marquardt a conventus for the district along the Hellespont and the Troad; it is so important a city that we can hardly suppose it was dependent on the unimportant Adramyttion. But Pliny takes no notice of it, and gives the Hellespontii under Adramyttion. Miletopolis and Poimanenon would naturally be expected

* Bull. Corr. Hell., 1887, p. 90 ff.
† I think this is better than to take the variant Pateenses and correct it to Pitanenses.

to be under the conventus of Cyzicos if there was one; but Pliny places them under Adramyttion. Marquardt's quotation from Aristides may prove either that the conventus of Adramyttion was subdivided after Pliny's time, or that the meetings of this conventus were sometimes held at Cyzicos. Similarly, Kibyra, which was originally far more important than Laodiceia, was in the same conventus with it, and the courts were usually held at Laodiceia.

46. The conventus of Sardis includes the following (names mentioned by Pliny being asterised):

*Philadelpheia.   *Maionia.
*Tripolis-Antoniopolis.   Satala.
*Apollonos Hieron.   Saittai.
*Mesotimolos.   Silandos.
Tmoleitai.   Bagis.
Blaundos.   Tabala.
Sala.   Daldis (?).
Tralla.   *Kadoeni Macedones.
Temenothyrai-Flaviopolis.   Loreni (Gordeni ?).
Grimenothyrai-Trajanopolis.
Ankyra.   Synaos.

B. CITIES AND BISHOPRICS OF LYDIA.

1. The lists of the province Lydia are a puzzle as yet unsolved. The remarkable discoveries of M. Fontrier, of Smyrna, supplemented by MM. Radet and Lechat,* have only rendered the character and order of the lists more puzzling than before.

The order of the first five bishoprics suggests a connection between Hierocles and the ecclesiastical lists, but the former omits Sala, Hyrcanis, Blaundos, Daldis, and Stratonikaia, which the latter give; and Julianopolis in Hierocles perhaps is the name of Silandos of the Notitiæ. The connection between Hierocles and the ecclesiastical lists, then, is not nearly so close, if it does exist, as in Asia. On the other hand, the numerous omissions in Hierocles cannot be explained by his having used a list of the cities of Lydia compiled for purposes of government. I long entertained the view, suggested I think somewhere by M. Waddington, that Hierocles used as his authority the government lists of cities in each province, but I have found myself obliged to renounce this view. It is impossible to suppose that any government list would omit five cities, all striking coins under the empire, and all bishoprics both in the fifth century and in later times. I had also entertained the idea that Sala Daldis and Blaundos,† being on the eastern frontier, might

---

* M. Fontrier's work, published first in the Smyrna Μουσεῖον, is more generally accessible in M. Foucart's account, published in 'Bulletin de Correspondance Hellénique,' 1887.

† Daldis being Theodosia and Blaundos Pulcherianopolis.

	Concil. Nicaen. II., 787.
	Σαρδέων
	Φιλαδελφείας
	Τριπόλεως
	Θυατείρων
	Σετῶν
ma	Αὐρηλιουπόλεως, Περικόμματος
	Γόρδου
	Τράλων, Στάλλης
	Σάλων
	Σιλάνδου
	Μαιονίας
	...
	Ὑρκανίδος
ə	..
	{Ἀκρασοῦ Λίπρων
	..
	Ἀτταλείας
	..
	Τρακούλων
	..
	..
	Ἱεροκαισαρείας
	Δάλδης
dos	Στρατονικείας (Καλάντων Ἀσίας, 692)
	Κερασέων
	..
	Ταβάλων
	Ἑρμοκαπήλου
	..
	..

is, Daldis, Attalia.

To face page 120.

have been included by the civil lists in Phrygia Pacatiana, and therefore been omitted by Hierocles from Lydia, and that Stratonikaia, which is near the northern frontier, actually was mentioned by Hierocles (following the government distribution), in Hellespontus, under the corruption Ξίος Τράδος. But even setting aside the uncertainty of this identification, I have found myself forced, by closer study of the frontier line, to the view that all these cities were included in the province Lydia.* The only possible view seems to be that the list of Hierocles has been mutilated and dislocated, so that it has reached us both imperfect and out of order. We should then be able to understand why it violates the geographical order so much, while in general his lists follow it so closely.

2. SARDIS is an old Lydian word meaning year, as Joannes Lydus says (p. 39). Its coins mention Zeus Lydios, and Men Askenos, who is obviously the same as the common Phrygian Askaenos.

3. PHILADELPHEIA was certainly founded by Attalus Philadelphus. Joannes Lydus (p. 45) says it was founded by Egyptians, but this statement is probably due to an erroneous connection with Ptolemy Philadelphus. It was called a "Little Athens" on account of its festivals and temples. Its hot springs are mentioned,† and are still much used. It was a great and warlike city in the later Byzantine time, when it was a frontier fortress against the Turks.‡

Its coins sometimes read ΦΛΑΒΙ ΦΙΛΑΔΕΛΦΕΩΝ, showing that for some time it bore the epithet Flavia or Flaviopolis in honour of the Flavian emperors. The coins also mention an alliance with the unknown people Ὀρεστεινοί.

4. TRIPOLIS also bore the name Antoniopolis, as Pliny mentions. It mentions on its coins the goddess Leto, the games Letoia Pythia, and the river Mæander.

5. THYATEIRA was originally called Pelopeia and Semiramis. It was peopled with a Macedonian military colony by the Seleucid kings in the third century. Its coins and inscriptions mention Artemis Boreitene and Apollo Tyrimnaios.

These first four cities lie on the important road described under Asia, and it might be a mere coincidence that both Hierocles and the Notitiæ place them first; but these lists also agree in putting Saittai fifth, which must be due to imitation.

6. SAITTAI retains its name as Sidas (i. e. Saittas) Kale. It names

* Even assuming that this view is correct, we should still have to explain why Sala, &c., are omitted from the Phrygian list. The only explanation would be that Hierocles was there under the influence of the ecclesiastical lists, and hence omitted Sala, &c., in both cases. See below, § 41.

† Joan. Lyd., pp. 75, 349, where he also speaks of the hot springs of Laodiceia and Hierapolis.

‡ Ἐπὶ τὴν Φιλαδέλφου ἀφίκετο· μεγίστη δὲ αὕτη πόλις καὶ πολυάνθρωπος καὶ ὁπλίζεσθαι δεδυνημένους οἰκήτορας ἔχουσα καὶ μάλιστα τοξείαν ἀσκοῦντας. Georg. Acropol., p. 111.

the rivers Hyllos and Hermos on its coins. Near it was a fortress Magidion, which became important in the later Byzantine time, and should be readily found (v. Georg. Acropol., p. 30). It mentions (Men) Aziottenos on its coins.

7. AURELIOPOLIS and PERIKOME * have been placed in Mount Tmolos (see ASIA).

8. JULIA GORDOS is still called Gördiz. It has alliance coins with Kadoi.

9. TRALLEIS and Sala I conjecture to be a pair of cities on the southern frontier of Lydia, adjoining Phrygia. The coins of Sala mark it as under the influence of the Laodicean coinage, and moreover Ptolemy places it in Phrygia, near Tripolis and Laodiceia, which he assigns to Lydia. I therefore place Sala at Alamsalam, 10 or 12 miles N.W. from Bulladan, and Tralleis (or as some lists give it, Tralla) at the site discovered by Hamilton east of Göne. On the name Tralleis, see ASIA.

10. SALA. The omission of Sala by Hierocles is difficult to account for: perhaps it is a mere error of the scribe, due to the number of similar names in the list, Tralla, Attalia, Satala. We cannot look for it under the temporary title Julianopolis, for that name denotes Silandos. On coins it bears the epithet Domitianopolis, and it mentions the ΗΡΩΣ ΑΝΤΙΝΟΟΣ.

Sala is omitted by Le Quien, but the following bishops of Sala are recorded (1) Noumenius Helenopolis Lydiae, Conc. Ephes., 431 A.D. Le Quien invents a bishopric Helenopolis of Lydia; but Helenopolis is only a bad rendering of τῆς Σαληνῶν πόλεως. (2) Anatolius Sellenorum, A.D. 458, is attributed by Le Quien to Silandos; but Silandi or Silandensium is a violent alteration: read Salenorum. (3) Michael Salorum is attributed by Le Quien to Satala.

It is not improbable that Sala and Tralleis were included in one bishopric: none of the signatures are inconsistent with this hypothesis.

11. SILANDOS is understood to have retained its name as Selendi. The identification cannot be called certain, for the name Selendi occurs elsewhere, as e.g. in the Hermos valley at Hierocæsareia, and in the Kaikos valley, east of Kirk Agatch. Moreover, Silandos names the Hermos on its coins, while Selendi is on a different stream, a tributary of the Hermos, at a point far from the main river.† It is apparently disguised in Hierocles as Julianopolis. Still the territory of Selendi must have extended to the Phrygian frontier on the east and

* Often written Perikope: Perikomma, as the lists of Conc. Nic. II. give it, is perhaps the correct form.

† Saittai, on the Hyllos, names both Hyllos and Hermos on its coins; but it is a little nearer the Hermos than Selendi is, and its territory must have extended to the Hermos on the south, while Tabala perhaps separates Selendi from the Hermos. Yet Selendi-Silandos must be pronounced a very tempting identification, like Seledik-Kalanda in the Kaikos valley.

north-east towards Kadoi, and, therefore, would touch the upper Hermos.

This second group, 6 to 11, is given by Hierocles almost in the reverse order of the Notitiæ, except that Gordos is omitted and added at the end of the list as an afterthought. In the rest of the list no resemblance whatever can be detected.

12. MAIONIA retains its name as Menye, as Hamilton observed. Opsikion is the modern Koula: the latter is quoted as the Turkish name by Georgius Pachymeres (ii. 435), and the former is mentioned by Georgius Acropolita (p. 30). Zeus Olympios is mentioned on coins of Maionia.

13. It will be convenient to add a word here about the modern Koula. There is now at Koula an inscription erected by Κολοηνῶν ἡ κατοικία. The resemblance of this name Koloe to the modern Koula led Wagener, who first saw and published the inscription, to say that Koula is the modern form of Koloe. Tsakyroglos, in publishing the inscription independently, drew the same inference: he was aware * that the owners of the stone say they brought it from a place far away to the north, but the coincidence of names seemed too remarkable, and he disbelieved their evidence. The coincidence of names, however, is quite accidental; the name Koula is a good Turkish name, which was used even by the Byzantine writer Pachymeres. It is the name, meaning "fortress," which they applied to the strong fortress called by earlier Byzantine writers Opsikion. There is, therefore, no reason to doubt the evidence of the owners of the stone, whom I have questioned on the subject. It was found in the district of Kara Tash, on the southern side of the mountains (probably part of the ancient Temnos) which separate Synaos (Simav) from the Katakekaumene, eight hours north of Koula. Kara Tash produces madder root in great abundance, and Koula, which is one of the chief centres of the carpet manufacture, formerly carried on a great trade with the district where the root was found. In recent time bad but cheap European dyes are used in place of the fine but troublesome native colours, and the people of Koula have little or no intercourse with Kara Tash, while the district of Kara Tash is ruined.† In the time when the trade in-madder-root was brisk, one of the Koula Greeks brought back this stone with him. The name Koloe, therefore, belongs not to Koula but to some village in the Kara Tash district. Such is the evidence, and we must follow it, instead of turning aside into the fanciful path of etymological similarity.

14. APOLLONOS HIERON struck imperial coins with the legend ΑΠΟΛΛΩΝΙΕΡΕΙΤΩΝ. The only clue to its situation, besides the fact that it was in the conventus of Sardis, lies in its being in later

---

* I conversed with him on my first visit to Koula.

† The people of Kara Tash, in one of whose villages I stayed a night in 1884, enquired of me what the reason was why their madder was no longer wanted.

Byzantine lists included in the same bishopric with Aetos, which, therefore, may be understood to be a fortress that rose to importance in the Turkish wars. Now Aetos is mentioned on the march of the Germans under Frederick, in A.D. 1190, from Philadelpheia to Laodiceia.* It is, therefore, very probable that Apollonos Hieron is at the upper end of the plain of Philadelpheia, and Aetos a fort commanding the pass across the mountains to the Lykos valley.

15. The HYRCANI and MOSTENI were two neighbouring peoples in the middle Hermos valley. The general indications are quite sufficient to place them between Magnesia, Sardis, and Thyateira; but the discoveries of M. Fontrier of Smyrna have given additional epigraphic evidence to localise them along the Hermos on the east side of the Magnesian territory. They were neighbouring peoples, if any stress can be laid on the phrase of Tacitus, *Ann.*, 2, 47. This part of the Hermos valley was called the Hyrcanian plain, from the colonists settled there by the Persian kings. One of the Hyrcanian villages was called $\Delta a\rho\epsilon\iota o\nu\kappa\dot\omega\mu\eta$,† and the plain was called sometimes the Hyrcanian plain, sometimes $K\dot\upsilon\rho o\upsilon$ $\Pi\epsilon\delta\dot\iota o\nu$ (Strab., pp. 627, 629). This explanation assumes that Cyrus's colonists were *anastatai*, according to a frequent custom of the oriental sovereigns.

16. The Mosteni were in the conventus of Pergamos, and are therefore to be sought on the north side of the Hyrcani, who were in the conventus of Smyrna. There is little room for doubt about them: the reference of Tacitus shows that they were neighbours of the Hyrcani, and they must therefore be placed between them and Apollonis, perhaps at Sari Tcham. They sometimes bear on coins the title KAICAPEΩN and ΛΥΔΩΝ. The epithet Cæsareia, which is thus proved to have belonged to the city, might perhaps suggest that the Cæsareia which Pliny gives in the conventus of Ephesos might be the city of the Mosteni. This, however, seems to be impossible, for Pliny's Cæsareia is more probably Tralleis, and it can hardly be allowed that any part of the Hermos valley belonged to the conventus of Ephesos; moreover Pliny distinctly includes the Mossyni in the conventus of Pergamos, and this name, Mossyni, when compared with that of some coins, MOΣΣINΩN, seems to denote certainly the Mosteni. This evidence seems stronger than the restoration M[osteni] given by M. Fontrier in an inscription of Tchoban Isa,‡ and followed by M. Foucart and Dr. Schuchhardt. Moreover, even admitting the restoration, it cannot be reckoned a certain proof that the Mosteni were south of the Hermos.

Schuchhardt, in his excellent paper,§ supposes that there was a

---

* Nicet. Chon., p. 539. Another Aetos in Thrace, Nic. Bry., p. 149.

† Wrongly referred to Magnesia by M. Foucart, Bull. Corr. Hell., 1885, p. 398; 1887, p. 79.

‡ Tchoban Isa, i. e. Shepherd Jesus, a curious but not uncommon Turkish name.

§ Athenische Mittheilungen, 1888, p. 1.

colony of Macedonian veterans among the Mosteni. The inference from Tacitus's words indeed is not quite convincing, and there is no other evidence. M. Foucart speaks of "plusieurs monnaies portant la légende Μοστηνῶν Μακεδόνων," but he should not on this point have accepted the evidence of a traveller who got a hasty glance at certain coins : no coins with such a legend are known. The contrast drawn by Schuchhardt himself between the coins of the Mosteni and the Hyrcani suggests that the former had more of the native Anatolian character, while the latter were more Greek in character. The words of Tacitus, " quique Mosteni aut Macedones Hyrcani vocantur," (Ann. ii. 47), may very well be explained as " the peoples who bear the name of Mosteni or of Macedonian Hyrcani." *

The Hyrcanian plain, then, is that through which the Hermos flows, between the territory of Sardis on the east and of Magnesia on the west. The Hyrcani inhabited both sides of the Hermos, and the Mosteni adjoined them on the north-western frontier.

Asynkritos, bishop of Hyrcania, martyred on April 8th, perhaps belonged to this city, and not to the country Hyrcania.

17. DAREIOUKOME, ORMOITA, and TYANOLLA, were three villages of the Hyrcani on the south side of the Hermos, known only from the inscriptions discovered by M. Fontrier of Smyrna. They are referred to Magnesia by M. Foucart, who has republished them in the Bulletin de Corresp. Hell., 1885, pp. 394 ff. (cp. Bulletin, 1887, p. 79, note). But the evidence of locality is conclusive that they do not belong to Magnesia, and this is confirmed by the fact that they mention a stephanephoros : this magistracy is often found on Hyrcanian, but never on Magnesian coins. The only doubt that can exist is about Ormoita. The inscription of Ormoita is in honour of Tib. Claudius Kleitianos : now the family of Kleitianos seems to be Magnesian, for a strategos of that name is mentioned on Magnesian coins of Alexander Severus, i.e. not later than 235, and another, Aurelius, is mentioned as twice Strategos under Philip, 245–50. The older Kleitianos also probably was a Magnesian; he was a man of high standing through the province, and was honoured by the Hyrcanian Ormoiteni for certain special services.

18, 19. AKRASOS was in the Kaikos valley, and mentions the ΚΑΙΚΟΣ on its coins. Its precise situation is unknown, but it was probably on the upper part of the river, for an Acrasiote was buried at Yenije Keui, eight miles north-east of Thyateira (Bull. Corr. Hell., 1887, p. 176). The two cities, Akrasos with coins ΑΚΡΑΣΙΩΤΩΝ, and NAKRASA with coins ΝΑΚΡΑΣΕΩΝ or ΝΑΚΡΑΣΕΙΤΩΝ, in the same valley, are confusing, and it is often difficult to tell which of the two is meant by the corrupt

---

* The unusual form of expression is due only to Tacitus's love of variety in a long list of names. Schuchhardt, in his remarks, appears not to have remembered that Tacitus is giving a list of twelve cities, and that two separate cities are summed up by him in this clause, as is well known from other authorities who give the list.

forms of the ecclesiastical lists.* The following forms can be distinguished:

Hierocles Notitiæ	Ἀκρασός. Ἀκρασοῦ, Ἀκαρασοῦ. or Ἀκρασσοῦ,	Κήρασε (read Κερασέ[ων]) Κερασέων, Καιρασέων.

It is remarkable that one of the cities always appears in the ethnic, the other only in the city name : this is perhaps for the sake of distinction, and the form in Hierocles seems to show that this peculiarity of the ecclesiastical lists was preserved by him.† The first syllable of Nakrasa always disappears without a trace. The name Akrasos occurs in Phrygia as a plain on the lower Tembris, Κρασσοῦ πεδίον or Κρασός. Nakrasa is marked by an inscription at Bakir on the road Thyatira-Nakrasa-Germe-Pergamos, which shows that, like Thyateira and other cities, it received a Macedonian colony in Seleucid time.

Lipara and Akrasos are included in one bishopric by Notitiæ X., XIII., but at Conc. Nic. II., Basil of Lipara, Constantine of Akrasos, and Michael of Keraseis, were all present. Lipara was therefore a separate city from Akrasos, and at some period they were united under one bishop.

20. APOLLONIS was long known to have been near Palamut, but M. Fontrier was the first to place the site above doubt. Strabo says it was 300 stadia alike from Sardis and from Pergamos, referring to a direct road between these two cities by Apollonis. Schuchhardt has, in an excellent paper, shown that it was probably originally named Doidya, that it was made a colony of Macedonian soldiers by the Seleucids about 270-50 B.C., and refounded as Apollonis by Attalos II. soon after 159 B.C.

21. Apollonis is to be distinguished from APOLLONIA, a city of the Kaikos valley on the left as one goes from Pergamos to the east (Strab., ·p. 625). This Apollonia is not mentioned elsewhere. Probably it was a Pergamenian refoundation, and the name Apollonia‡ was replaced after a time by the original name. It lay high, probably on the hills on the north of the Kaikos (μετεώροις ἐπικειμένη τόποις).

22. MASDYENOI. A people called Μασδυηνοί are mentioned as included in the population of the Pergamenian kingdom without having full rights of citizenship. The citizenship was given to them, along with the Macedonians, Mysians, &c., after the death of Attalus III.§ They ∥

* I do not mean that these forms are mere corruptions of scribes. In a great many cases they are real indications of popular pronunciations, though gross clerical errors also exist among them.

† Compare Σαταλέων in the list of Lydian cities, gen. of the ethnic from Σάταλα.

‡ Apollonia is a Pergamenian city name in Pisidia.

§ Inscription (inv. 295) published by Fränkel in Jahrb. der kgl. Preuss. Kunstsamml., ix. (1887), p. 84. I take the reference from Schuchhardt, Athen. Mittheil., 1888, p. 14

∥ See ADDENDA.

are probably Paphlagonian mercenaries. The name **Masdya** may be with Doidya; compare Mastaura, Mastusia (a hill near Smyrna).

23, 24. TRAKOULA and GANDEIA. The later Notitiæ mention a bishopric of two towns, Gandeia or Gaudeia and Trakoula. A bishop of Trakoula was present at Conc. Nicæn. II. in 787. No other reference to these places is known to me. Trakoula seems to have retained its name as Trakhala, a village and mountain near Soma. Soma is near the site of Germe, a small town which probably struck no coins,* and is never mentioned in the ecclesiastical lists. Apparently it was subordinate to Trakoula in later Byzantine time, and Gandeia or Gaudeia was somewhere near. Germe, however, seems to be mentioned under the name Karme by Anna Comnena (see Bithynia).

25. ATTALEIA was originally named Agroeira or Alloeira (v. Steph.) It was refounded by one of the Pergamenian Attali. The site, first approximately determined by M. Radet, has been more accurately specified by Dr. Schuchhardt at Seljikli near Gördük Kalesi, a few miles north of Thyateira (Athen. Mittheil., 1888, p. 13).

26. BLAUNDOS mentions the river Hippourios on its coins. The site at Suleimanli was proved by Hamilton. The people are called Mlaundeis on early coins, and Phlaudeis in some of the Notitiæ. There can be no doubt that the name is really the same as that of the Mysian Blados,† and the Pisidian Amblada or Amlada. The native form, involving the syllable Mlad- or Blad-, was adapted to Greek pronunciation by various devices, giving such forms as Amilanda, Ampelada, Amplada, Amlada, Amblada, Blandos, Blaudos, Blados, Blaundos, Phlaudos.

27. KLANNOUDDA is known only from some very rare coins of the second or first century before Christ, and from the Peutinger Table, which places it 35 miles from Philadelphia on the road to Akmonia. There is every probability that we should read 40, and that the site was beside Ine, where there are several inscriptions. The reason why the name does not appear in Byzantine lists is either that the place took a new name, or that it was included under another bishopric; the former alternative seems impossible, and the probability is that the town passed under the influence of the neighbouring Blaundos, and hence lost the right to strike coins under the empire.

28. MESOTIMOLOS, has usually been wrongly identified with Tmolos, the identification being aided by the fact that the Byzantine lists apparently omit the latter, concealing it under the name Aureliopolis. A clue to the position of Mesotimolos is given by several Notitiæ,‡ which give it as included in the same bishopric with Blaundos, though

---

* The coins ΓΕΡΜΗΝΩΝ all perhaps belong to the city near the lake of Apollonia.

† This Mysian Blados, however, is perhaps an error, and Blados is really the Lydian **Blaundos**, see below, § 41.

‡ No confidence can be placed in such hellenised names; this name seems more plausible, but has no more real character, than Thyateira for Θυγάτειρα, because Seleucus heard there of his daughter's death (Steph.).

most omit ἤτοι, and turn a single bishopric into two. The corruption, Φοῖβος ἐπίσκοπος Πολυχαλάνδου τῆς Λυδίας, at Conc. Seleuc., 359 A.D., perhaps hides the double name. A situation on the east Lydian frontier near Takmak is probable, to suit the connection with Blaundos.

The name Μεσοτίμωλος, which is possibly the correct form, has been probably hellenised in order to suggest a meaning. The name of mount Tmolos occurs also as Timolos (Ovid, ' Met.', 6, 13), and Mesotimolos was understood as " in the middle of mount Tmolos."* But the connection with Blaundos is fatal to this view. Probably the correct name is Mysotimolos, distinguishing it from the western city Tmolos, as the Mysian Timolos. It is possible that the original name was Tomaros, and that it struck rare coins with the legend TOMAPHNΩN, one of which names a river Kissos. Tomaros may have been changed to Tumolos or Timolos, or perhaps Tomaros and Timolos are equivalent forms : when the name was pronounced Timolos, the desire for distinction produced the name Μυσοτίμωλος.

The name Tomaros may be compared with that of the mountain beside Dodona, which has the forms Tmaros, Tomaros, and Tomouros.

Mesotimolos then is probably the name of the city whose ruins lie near the road from Takmak to Ushak, about four hours from the former on the north side of the road ; and the river beside them is the Kissos. Tmolites ille vicanus (Cicero, pro Flacco, § 3) was a native of Tmolos, not of Mesotimolos ; Eckhel wrongly quotes it as Timolites.

29. HIEROCÆSAREIA has been placed by M. Fontrier beside the villages Beiova and Sasova, about seven or eight miles S.E. of Thyateira. The cultus of Artemis Persica, mentioned on coins, was said to have been founded here by Cyrus. The same goddess was worshipped at Hypaipa. Pausanias (V. 27) mentions some curious details about the Magian priest of the goddess, her spontaneously flaming altar, and the religious invocations in a strange language (cp. Tac., Ann. iii., 72).

Le Quien most unjustifiably alters Rufinus Areopolis, A.D. 458, to Cossinius Hierocaesareae. Rufinus was bishop of Aureliopolis.

30. THYESSOS struck a few coins, and is mentioned by Stephanus as a city of Lydia. It may perhaps be the older name of Hierocæsareia, as the coins seem to be of an early date. The name Hierocæsareia cannot be older than Augustus, and cannot be proved before the earthquake of A.D. 21. The oldest coins of Hierocæsareia are of Nero.

31. DALDIS: nothing is known as to the situation of this city. I formerly thought that it might lie east of Julia Gordos on the Phrygian frontier, and be included by Hierocles in Phrygia, under the name of Theodosia,† but I was obliged to dismiss the latter supposition, for Theodosia is mentioned in Phrygia at the council of Constant. 448, ‡

---

* See last note, p. 125.

† At the same time I fancied that Blaundos was by Hierocles given to Phrygia under the name Pulcherianopolis ; this idea also I have reluctantly given up.

‡ Also Thomas Theodosiopolis Phrygiae Pacatianae in 451 (Labbe, p. 333)

while Paul bishop of Daldis signed the Epistola ad Leonem Imperatorem from the province of Lydia, in 458. It is, however, possible that this situation is correct, for it is favoured by Ptolemy, who puts Kadoi, Saittai, and Dadaleis in a group on the east of Lydia. Dadaleis is a corrupt name, and the easiest correction is Daldis, which then might be placed about Demirdji Keni. The correction, however, is uncertain, for Σαδαλεῖς or Σαταλεῖς is perhaps the correct reading (see SATALA).

32. STRATONICEA-HADRIANOPOLIS mentions the Kaikos on its coins. It has been fixed near Seledik by M. Radet. All the ecclesiastical lists, including Conc. Chalced. 451, and Epistola ad Leon. Imp. 458, place it in Lydia. The later Notitiæ unite it in the same bishopric with Kalanda or Kalamos. The position of Kalanda and of Stratonicea, when compared with Akrasos and Attaleia, certainly suggests that they were in Lydia, which probably included the whole upper Kaikos valley, and not in Hellespontus; so that the identifications of Ξίος Τράδος in Hellespontus as a corruption of εἰς Στρατον[ίκαιαν], and of Σκέλεντα, in Hellespontus, as εἰς Κάλανδα, if correct, cannot be taken as proof that these cities were ever reckoned part of Hellespontus, but must be considered as the result of a serious dislocation of the text (see § 41).

33. KALAMOS. This form of the name is more usual, though the Kalanda of some MSS. of the Notitiæ is probably a real variety, not a clerical error; the latter form is perhaps retained in the modern Seledik. The references of Georgius Acropolita are quite explicit. He speaks on pp. 30 and 194 from the point of view of one looking along a road from the Kaystros and Hermos valley towards Constantinople. Kalamos is on the road south of Akhyraous, and is the northern limit of the Theme Neokastron, which belonged to Theodore Lascaris, while Akhyraous and the Kiminian mountains belonged to the Latin emperor. The operations of the Greek emperors were conducted chiefly along the road by Akhyraous towards Poimanenon and towards Miletopolis. Kalamos is mentioned on the march of Frederick in the year 1190 under the form Kalomon; Muralt wrongly identifies it with Sardis.

March 22–28. Frederick crosses the Hellespont at Gallipoli.

April 2. After three days' difficult road and one day along a grassy valley, the Crusaders cross the river Diga † (probably the Granikos).

April 3. Cross river Anelonica (Angelokomites, Anna II. 280) with difficulty.

April 7. Reach the great paved road, Constantinople to Tragonium and Iconium (at a point between Miletopolis and Akhyraous); desert country in front.

April 9. Enter the valley of Ascaratana, i.e. Akhyraous.

* Bull. Corr, Hell., 1887, p. 108.
† Muralt takes this for the Hermos. After completing the statement in the text, I observe on Kiepert's map that Frederick took the same road as Alexander the Great.

April 14.   Kalomon,* this castle is found deserted ; advance to
             Thyateira.

April 21.   Philadelpheia : two days spent here ; battle with the
             Greeks. Aetos : this point is omitted by Muralt (Nic.
             Chon., 539). Tripolis the Less : Hierapolis : battle
             with the Greeks.

April 27.   Laodiceia : hospitable reception by the Greeks.

May   1.   Through loca desertissima, past lacus salinarum (Anava),
             reach place ubi fluvius Mandra (Maeander ?) oritur.†
             Battle.

May   2.   Sozopolis.

May   3.   Ginglarion (Chateau Cingulaire). Traverse the pass
             where Manuel had been defeated.

May   9.   Beside civitas Sirma.

May 18–26.   Iconium.

May   30.   Laranda. For the details see LYCAONIA.

June 10.   Seleuceia of Isauria ; Frederick is drowned.

June 14.   Curca.

June 21.   Antioch.

Kalanta is mentioned in 692 as a bishopric of Asia, not of Lydia :
this is perhaps a mere error.

34. Neokastron. The Theme Neokastron is clearly identical with
the Hermos and the upper Kaikos valleys, as is shown by the enumeration of the Greek possessions under Theodore Lascaris, Neokastron,
Kelbianon (the Kaystros valley), Khliara and Pergamos (the lower
Kaikos valley), and the fortresses lying to the side Magidion and Opsikion
(Saittai and Koula).‡ Neokastron begins from (i.e. has its northern
frontier at) Kalamos. Pachymeres (II. 210, 220) confirms this situation.
The origin of the name is mentioned by Nicetas Choniata (p. 194–5) :
the fortresses restored by Manuel Comnenus in the twelfth century,
viz., Khliara, Pergamos, and Adramyttion, were styled as a group
Neokastra. Another Neokastron, which is mentioned by late writers, is
identical with Yeni Kale at the mouth of the Hellespont.§

  * So Muralt : Tagenon calls it Caloniora.

  † Muralt, following Nicetas, makes the Crusaders reach Philomelion on May 1.
Obviously either Philomelion or Sozopolis is an error. It seems somewhat improbable that Frederick would march by Philomelion, and it is impossible that after
his delay and battle at Philadelpheia and his battle at Hierapolis, he could reach
Philomelion on May 1. Moreover, Muralt quotes on April 29, "ubi fluvius Mandra
oritur," which obviously refers to the sources of the Mæander. Philomelion may be a
false rendering of some place between Apameia-Celaenæ and Apollonia-Sozopolis, on the
direct road to Iconium. I have not access to all the authorities, and must reserve
opinion.

  ‡ τὰ πλαγίως ἐγκείμενα Μαγίδιά τε καὶ ᾿Οψίκια : the enumeration is made from the
point of view of one looking to Constantinople, and the two fortresses then lie off to the
side (Georg. Acropol., pp. 30, 195, cp. 14).

  § Its position is clearly defined in ᾿Ιέρακος Χρονικόν, Sathas, Bibl. Gr. Med. Aev.,

35. METEORON is unknown to me except in the passage of Georgius Acropolita just quoted (p. 194); it must have been in the Hermos valley, and may possibly be the purely Byzantine fortress Gurduk Kalesi, a few miles north of Thyateira, near the site of Attaleia.

36. SATALA still retains its name as Sandal, about an hour to the north-west of Koula, near the Hermos. The only passage which gives any clue to its situation is in "Acta Sanctorum," May 27, p. 683. Therapon, after having been tortured in the neighbourhood of Ankyra and Synaos, where there was a river Asteles, was conducted to the Thrakesian Theme along the course of the Hermos. He passed through the bishopric of Satala, where he was put to death. It is not easy to be sure of the exact sense, for the writer of the abridgment, which is published, did not understand it very well; but apparently Satala was near the Hermos on the road from Synaos to the Thrakesian Theme, which is true of Sandal.*

The form Σαταλέων in Hierocles is obviously derived from a list of bishops.

The chief sanctuary of the Katakekaumene was situated at Satala; it was dedicated to a goddess and a god, in whom we may recognise the usual Anatolian pair of σύνβωμοι θεοί, the Mother and the Son. The goddess is generally called Artemis-Anaeitis, the former being the Greek name that seemed to suit best her character, the latter being a Persian term derived perhaps from the colonists settled in the Hermos valley by Cyrus; but besides these, the name Leto is also applied to her, and is perhaps a more genuinely native name. The god is called by many names, Men or Sabazios, with a variety of additional epithets, of which Aziottenos or Axiottenos is perhaps the most remarkable and widespread, as it occurs on coins of Saittai and on an inscription of Bagis, as well as at Satala.

It is remarkable that Satala, the religious centre of the Katakekaumene, struck no coins: it probably continued to be a mere village attached to the temple, and was not the seat of a real municipal organisation. It is possible that Satala is mentioned by Ptolemy under the form Δαδαλεῖς, corrupted from Σαδαλεῖς:† but probably the correction Δαλδεῖς is to be preferred.

37. TABALA still retains its name as Davala, on the north bank of the Hermos, which is mentioned on its coins.

38. BAGIS has been placed by Keppel's inscriptions near Sirghe on the Hermos. It takes the epithet Cæsareia on coins. The site of the

p. 555–70. It was built by Mehemet to afford an alternative crossing of the Hellespont to that of Kallioupolis, and at the western end. It is now called Yeni Kale, or Neokastro, and occupies the place of the ancient Sigeion. Besides this, Alexiopolis or Neokastron was a fort beside Philippopolis, built by Alexius Comnenus.

* Act. Sanct., May 27, vol. vi. p. 680. Satala, Maionia, and Opsikion (Koula), were in the Opsikian Theme.

† I find Daedalorum for Satalorum in Conc. Chalced.

city is said to be on the north bank, but Sirghe is on the south side of the river. It mentions the Hermos on its coins.*

39. DECAPOLIS was a term sometimes applied to the Katakekaumene.† We have therefore to look for ten cities in it. The following six are certain: Satala, Maionia, Tabala, Bagis, Silandos, Saittai. Of the remainder three are probably Daldis, Philadelpheia, and Apollonos Hieron; and if Mesotimolos has been rightly placed, it would fall within the natural bounds of the Katakekaumene and make the tenth. Gordos also might suggest itself.

40. HERMOKAPELEIA was in the conventus of Pergamos. The name might suggest a situation on the Hermos, but it is probable that a city on the Hermos would belong to the conventus of Sardis. Perhaps it is to be placed at Mermere, where there are considerable remains, to which M. Fontrier wrongly gave the name Attaleia.

The tale related by Nicolas of Damascus about Thyessos (Dindorf, 'Hist. Gr. Min.' I., p. 30) may be a legend to explain the name Hermokapeleia: the words occur in it, Θυεσσός . . . . . ὁ κάπηλος . . . . . ἀγορὰν πλησίον αὐτοῦ καὶ Ἑρμαῖον εἵσατο. It is probable that this is merely an explanation of the two city names Thyessos and Hermokapeleia. We might almost gather that they were names for the same place, but the existence of coins of both cities would rather prove that they were separate but neighbouring places. No inference can be drawn from the tale as to the situation of the cities; for though according to the story Kerses ought to be fleeing from Sardis to Kyme when he meets Thyessos, such foundation legends are always careless of consistency. As we have conjecturally placed the cities,‡ they make the genesis of the legend quite natural.

41. Hierocles' list of Lydian cities defies all geographical order, while it omits many names which are contained in all lists, older, contemporary, and younger. The opinion which seems to me most probable is that the MSS. have suffered some serious corruption, which has disturbed the order and caused the loss of several names. The list of Hellespontine cities contains several names, indubitably corrupt, which have a striking resemblance to some of the names in Lydia. The theory which I advance is that the archetype became mutilated in Lydia, that several names written in the margin were afterwards inserted by an error of the copyist in Hellespontus on the preceding page, and that the order of the Lydian list was disturbed. The number

* Le Quien infers from the signature Chrysaphius Balcenus (Δάγης) at Conc. Ephes., A.D. 431, that there was a bishopric Balcea, called Balicia by Pliny, H. N., V. 30; but Chrysaphius (or Chrysanthus) is a bishop of Bagis: read Bagenus and Βάγης.

† For the name, see Metaphrastes, Acta Pionii, in Acta Sanct., Febr. 1, p. 43; Vos Decapolim, Lydiæ regionem, igne combustam videtis.

‡ It may be worth remarking that this paragraph is inserted as an afterthought, when the rest of the argument about the two cities was already in type.

of Hellespontine towns was given in the archetype as 30, and this
number was reproduced by the copyists, though the addition of these
Lydian names made the list much longer. The number in Lydia is
however given according to the shorter list.

(1.) Σκέλεντα and Ξίος Τράδος of Hellespont have for many years
seemed to me to be errors for [εἰ]ς Κάλαντα and εἰς (σ)Τραδον[ίκαιαν], but
I long made the mistake of thinking that Hierocles placed them inten-
tionally in Hellespont. This I now see to be impossible : Hierocles
was certainly aware that the whole upper Kaikos valley belonged to
Lydia. The difficulty disappears when we consider that he gave them
in Lydia, and that they have been accidentally transferred to Hellespontus. Another argument against my older theory may suggest itself:
Kalanta occurs only in the latest Notitiæ, included in the same bishopric
as Stratonikaia. But I shall show that Hierocles had an exceptionally
good knowledge of Hellespontus, probably arising from personal
acquaintance : this knowledge extended also to the Kaikos valley.
Moreover Kalanta occurs in 692 as a bishopric, and may have been
originally a separate bishopric from Stratonikaia, though afterwards
united with it ; as, *e.g.*, Lipara and Akrasos were separate bishoprics in
787, but are united in the late Notitiæ.

(2.) Βλάδος of Hellespontus was long ago recognised by M. Waddington as transferred by mistake from Lydia.* He has subsequently
abandoned the idea (on Le Bas, No. 1011). It is now held by him and
by authorities generally that there was a city Blados in Mysia, which
has retained its name as Bolat. No explanation is offered as to why
this place is omitted from all Notitiæ : its situation distinctly marks it
out as a bishopric. I cannot admit that Bolat is the modern form of
Blados : the resemblance may be accidental, for Bolatli is a Turkish
village near the N.E. end of the lake of Anava. I consider Bolat as a
Turkish name, and place there the bishopric Neocaesareia or Ariste.

One other reference is traced to this supposed Mysian Blados ; it is
in Strabo (p. 567), who speaks of Blaudos as a πόλις Φρυγιακή near
Ankyra. I shall show under HELLESPONTOS that the name Phrygia
cannot possibly be extended so far as to include Bolat. There is therefore no alternative except to understand that Strabo is making a loose
and vague reference to Blaundos on the Lydo-Phrygian frontier, and
that his vague expression near Ankyra is intended only to indicate the
position of Blaudos on the west frontier of Phrygia. I admit that
Strabo rarely uses such a vague expression as this, but the other theory
necessitates an even greater degree of vagueness, for Strabo places
Blaudos† on the Lydian frontier of Phrygia, which is strictly true of
Blaundos, but implies an extraordinary vagueness if said of Bolat.

M. Waddington supports his later view by the argument that
Hierocles mentions Blaundos under the form Lounda, but places it in

---

* 'Voyage Numismatique,' p. 64.　　　　† πρὸς Λυδίαν περὶ Βλαῦδον.

Phrygia. Lounda, however, is now known to be a distinct Phrygian city and bishopric: it is mentioned also in Notitiæ III., X., XIII., which give Blaundos in Lydia.*

(3.) Σάγαρα was suggested by M. Waddington to be a misformation of Σάταλα, transferred from Lydia. It is true that γ is frequently written for τ in the ecclesiastical lists, as Ἀτγουδα, Ἀτγάλεια Ἀτγαίων,† Ἀτγανασός. But Σαταλέων occurs in Hierocles' Lydian list, and the theory therefore does not suit well; a confusion between Sala and Satala must be invoked to help it.

In spite of this undeniable difficulty the theory may be in the main true, and it certainly eliminates several serious difficulties. It still leaves unexplained the omission of Daldis and Hyrkanis, and perhaps also of Lipara, Gaudia or Gandia, and Trakoula in Lydia, and the existence of such seeming corruptions in Hellespontus as Reketa, Kerge; but the former may have disappeared entirely when the archetype was injured, and the latter may be villages of Hellespontus, as Artemea certainly is.

I may add here a list of the Lydian bishops, who appear at the Council of Nikaia, 325 A.D. :—

	Artemidorus Sardiensis	Sardis Lydiæ
	Soron Thyatirensis	Thyatira Lydiæ
Thomasiou	Ethymasius Philadelphiae	Philadelpheia Lydiæ
Barensis	Polliou Peperensis	Perperene Asiæ
	Agogius Tripolitanus	Tripolis Lydiæ
	Florentius Anticyrrae	Ankyra Phrygiae
	Marcus Standitanus	Blandos or Blaundos Lydiæ
	Antiochus Aureliopolitanus	Aureliopolis Lydiæ

C. Cities and Bishoprics of Phrygia.

1. Laodiceia, with the χῶροι, Eleinokaprios and Kilarazos, Lakerios, Panasios, Karia, and Tantalos (which perhaps are also χῶροι),‡ the rivers Kapros, Eleinos, Lykos, Asopos, and Kadmos, mounts Salbakos and Kadmos, the Syrian Gates, and the title Trimitaria, see ASP, A, i. In that place I pointed out that Hyelion and Leimmokheir are two villages on the Mæander beside the bridge, which under the Roman Empire was not very far from Antioch, and which is represented on coins of that city. Harmala was perhaps lower down the Mæander valley, and Louma and Pentakheir are certainly much lower down. Possibly, Pentakheir is beside Mount Latmos, now called Besh Parmak, "Five Fingers." It has since occurred to me that the name Tantalos, which

---

* ὁ Βλαδέων or ὁ Φλανδέων.   † Ἀτγάιων = Ἀττέων = [Σ]Ἀττ[αλ]έων, Not. VIII.
‡ On the term χῶρος, compare Le Bas-Waddington, No. 1745.

occurs on the march from Kolossai towards Antioch, is perhaps retained in the modern form Dandalo Tchai, applied to the river Morsynos.

2. HIERAPOLIS, CB, ii.; ASP, A, ii.

3. MOSSYNA, CB, iii.; ASP, A, iii. It is the mountainous country between Hierapolis, the Mæander, and Dionysopolis. The modern villages Geuzlar, Ak Devrent, Sazak, and Geveze all belong to it. In CB, ix., this territory was divided between two bishoprics, Mossyna and Metellopolis; but the latter has now been identified with Motella, on the other bank of the Mæander. Thiounta (ASP, A, xii.), a demos of Mossyna, had quarries of a stone commonly used for making sarcophagi. The stone was used at Hierapolis, where it was called Thiountene; this reading, rightly defended by M.|Waddington (Le Bas, 1683), was altered by Franz, C.I.G., 3915, to Δοκιμηνή. Strabo mentions that it was a variegated kind of marble. It was also exported to other districts, where it was known as Hierapolitan,* just as Dokimian marble was known to all the world as Synnadic.

4. ATTOUDDA (ASP, A, iv.) was situated at Haz Keui, a mile or two west of Serai Keui.

5. KAROURA (ASP, A, iv.) was on the south bank of the Mæander, about eight miles west of Serai Keui, in the territory of Attoudda. MENOS KOME, with the temple of Men Karou, was between Karoura and Attoudda. The hot springs of Karoura and Menos Kome are mentioned by Athenæus (ii. p. 43; see below, No. 31).

6. TRAPEZOPOLIS, near Assar and Kadi Keui (ASP, A, v.).

7. KOLOSSAI, a defenceless city in the level plain, sank into decay in the Byzantine wars. Its site is now absolutely deserted, ASP, A, vi.

8. KHONAI, on a steep, precipitous hill, three miles south of Kolossai, took its place about A.D. 692–787. It was an important military station; doubtless there was a Turma Khonai, probably of the Thrakesian Theme,

9. KERETAPA-DIOCÆSAREIA, at Kayadibi, on the lake Aulindenos (ASP, A, vii., correcting CB, xv.)

10. THEMISSONION, at Kara Eyuk Bazar, with the river Kazanes,† a tributary of the Indos, rising in Mount Kadmos. The god Lykabas Sozon is mentioned on its coins.

11. PHYLAKAION or PYLAKAION,‡ on the road Kibyra—Phylakaion—

---

* Compare Constant. Porphyrog., de Cerim., p. 644, and Strabo, p. 374, where we must read τῆς Καρυστίας καὶ τῆς Δοκιμαίου καὶ τῆς Ἱεραπολιτικῆς, for Συνναδικῆς is a mere gloss on Δοκιμαίου, and has crept into the text from the margin.

† Even on Kiepert's new map this river is called Casus. M. Waddington long ago showed what the true name is (Mél. Numism., i. p. 110).

‡ I presume that no one will defend Koktemalikai as a genuine uncorrupted name. While I still believe in the identification of Phylakaion, I must withdraw the suggestion that pilycon is a corruption of Pylakaion. I must admit that various examples of Greek names (and perhaps also of corruptions due to Greek letters) occur in the Table. But the Anon. Ravenn. mentions Filaction, and this proves that Phylakaion was mentioned in the original of the Peutinger Table. Laodicea epi lyco may have caused the Pylakaeon, coming as second name after it, to drop out.

Eriza—Themissonion—Laodiceia, seems to have been an imperial estate mentioned by Hierocles as χωρία πατριμόνια with the dittography Koktemalikai, i.e. Κτῆμα [Πυ]λικαι[έων]. ASP, B, 4.

12. ERIZA, at Ishkian Bazar, ASP, B, 5.

13. TAKINA, at Yarashli, ASP, A, ix.

14. SANAOS or ANAVA, ASP, A, x., correcting CB, XV.

15. MOTELLA, the Byzantine Metellopolis, retains its name as Medele, on the north side of the Mæander, opposite Dionysopolis. It is probably the Pulcherianopolis of Hierocles, which would imply that it attained the rank of a city under Pulcheria (414–453 A.D.). CB, ix.; ASP, A, xi.

16. ATYOKHORION, the ancient village at the temple of Apollo Lairbenos, on the south bank of the Mæander, in the territory of Dionysopolis. ASP, A, xii., J. H. S., 1887, p. 380; 1889, p. 221.

17. DIONYSOPOLIS, beside Orta Keui. CB, iv.; ASP, A, xii.

18. SALOUDA; 19, MELOKOME; 20, KAGYEITA; are demoi of Dionysopolis or perhaps of Mossyna. ASP, A, xii., J. H. S., 1889, 230.

21. HYRGALEIS, on the Mæander, between Bekirli and Demirji Keui. CP, vii.; and (with a slight correction) ASP, A, xiii.

22. LOUNDA, in the angle of the Mæander, near Mahmud Ghazi. CB, xi., where inscription No. 16 ought to end κόψας καὶ [νομ]ίσματ[α], and should probably be attributed to Peltai. ASP, A, xiv.

23. PELTAI, between Kara Agatchlar (pronounced Karayashilar) and Yaka Keui. CB, xii.

24. EUMENEIA, at the sources of the Kloudros, between the Glaukos and the Mæander, on the site of the modern Ishekli. The known tribes of Eumeneia are Herais, Athenais, Hadrianis, Argeias. CB, xiii.

25. SIBLIA, or SOUBLAION, at the modern Homa, which retains the Byzantine (or Turco-Byzantine) name. The plain in front is the plain of Lampe, in which is the village Vicus (called *ad vicum* in the Peutinger Table) or Oikokome. The name JUSTINIANOPOLIS appears to have been given to Soublaion in the sixth century. The Douz Bel, east of Homa, was an important Byzantine Kleisoura, commanded by the fortress Myriokephalon; and the Turrije Boghaz, leading down to the east from Douz Bel, is the Τζυβριτζή of Nicetas Choniata. ASP, A, xviii.; CB, xiv.

26. ATTANASSOS is the modern Aidan, CB, x., ASP, A, xvi. Eski Aidan is on the eastern, not as I have stated on the western, bank of the Glaukos; * it lies on the eastern side of Yeni Aidan.

27. KHARAX and GRAOS GALA were on the road between the fortresses of Khonai and Soublaion. Kharax cannot be connected with Alexandrou Kharax, mentioned by Stephanus, near Kelainai-Apameia.

28. OKOKLIA, known only from coins, may perhaps be the city situated near Elles, or Elyes, on Lake Askania (lake of Buldur). In Byzantine time it probably took the name VALENTIA, given in Phrygia by

* I spoke only from information, but have since visited Aidan.

Hierocles, but afterwards apparently attached to the division of Pamphylia, which was separated from the rest, and which in my list (ASP, D) is distinguished as Tertia.

Okoklia then must be included in the conventus of Kibyra or Laodiceia (CB, xxviii.), taking the place doubtfully assigned to Adada. It is also necessary to add Lagbe to this conventus, and therefore to include it within the Roman province of Asia. An inscription (ASP, D, 14) provides that a penalty for violating a tomb at Lagbe is to be paid to the " City of the Kibyratai." This implies either that Lagbe was subject to Kibyra, or that it was in the conventus of Kibyra ; * as it was an independent city, coining money, the latter alternative must be accepted. To this conventus it is probably necessary to add also the two *demoi*, Thiounteis, and Kagyetteis ; and perhaps there were several other small *demoi* near Lagbe, such as Sinda, which were included in the conventus. The imperial estates of the Ormeleis, Tymbrianasa, and Alaston, and the town at Gebren, all of which seem sometimes to have used the Asian era, 85 B.C., should also go with Lagbe. In this way we may reach Pliny's total, xxii. or xxv. (the reading varies).

In the conventus of Apameia it is necessary to substitute Motella for Blaundos ; the latter must have been under Sardis.

29. PEPOUZA, probably at Yannik Euren, on the road from Eumeneia to Stektorion, Otrous, and Hieropolis ; CB, xvii. There were two towns named Pepouza : Πέπουζαν πόλιν τινὰ ἔρημον ἀνάμεσον Γαλατίας καὶ Καππαδοκίας καὶ Φρυγίας· ἔστι δὲ καὶ ἄλλη Πέπουζα (tract. de hæresibus, ap. Coteler., Eccles. Gr. Mon., II, p. 293).

30. BRIA, i. e. " the town." Macedonius, bishop of Bria,† was present at the Council held 553 A.D. Bria is mentioned under the form Ἴκρια in Notitiæ i., viii., ix., where κ is an example of a very common clerical error for β : this conjecture, in accordance with which I modified in the table attached to CB, part II. the table of part I., is proved to be correct by the Bodleian MS. Baroc. 185, fol. 16, which reads Ἰυρία. The prothetic iota is common before the two initial consonants. CB, xviii.

31. SEBASTE, about Seljükler, Sivasli, and Bunar Bashi ; CB, xix. PALAEO-SEBASTE: the old site at Payam Alan, for want of any better name, has been thus labelled. It seems of too little importance to have been a separate bishopric. In my CB, part II., § xx., I advanced the conjecture that the place which bore the name of the god Men ‡ might be Palæo-Sebaste : but this view is impossible. Athenæus (II. p. 43) speaks of the hot springs beside Menos Kome, and this Menos Kome must be the same place that Strabo says was called after Men. The hieron of Men in the place called by his name is undoubtedly the famous

* This principle, which might, I think, be safely assumed, has been carefully discussed by Prof. G. Hirschfeld and Dr. Treuber.

† There is frequently in the lists a confusion between him and Macedonius of Brouzos, who was also present.

‡ τὸ τοῦ Μῆνος [ἱερὸν] ἐν τῷ ὁμωνύμῳ τόπῳ, Strab., p. 557.

temple of Men Karou beside Attoudda. The village attached to the temple was called Menos Kome; compare above, 16, Atyokhorion. Hiera Kome is a generic name for such villages.

32. ALOUDDA or ELOUZA. The identity of these two names seems to me certain, and the subjection to Sebaste under the Romans seems probable. In that case it would have reached the rank of a πόλις in the early Byzantine time. Site at or near Hadjim (or Hadjimler). Aloudda is placed there by a consideration of the road Akmonia — Aloudda — Klannoudda — Philadelpheia, and the order of Hierocles requires a situation in this neighbourhood for Elouza.

33. AKMONIA, at Ahat Keui. CB, pts. I. and II. § xxii.; Amer. Journ. Arch. 1885.

34. KERAMON AGORA, at Islam Keui, CB, xxii. bis. A large tumulus, about an hour south-west from Islam Keui, may some day yield results to its excavators. This identification seems to me as certain as any one of the kind can be; it explains the route of Cyrus and makes it reasonable, and it suits the distances. Hamilton's identification with Ushak, still followed by Kiepert in his latest map, seems absolutely without reason. It is quite out of keeping with the distances, and it attributes a march to the army of Cyrus over a country which no army would attempt except under dire necessity, first across a low mountain ridge, then over the enormous cañon of the Banaz Tchai. Cyrus was not anxious to discourage his army by long unpleasant and unnecessary marches at the outset.

35. ALIA. Its situation near Kirka seems probable, but the proximity of Kirka and Hadjimler prevent any confidence in the exact position until a more thorough exploration has been made. The general situation seems well established, if the order of Hierocles is as true to geography as usual.* It is beside Akmonia and Hierokharax, but it is not in the district subject to Akmonia. A situation north-west of Akmonia and south-west of Hierokharax would be still more in accordance with Hierocles, if such a site could be found. Possibly an ancient town may have existed on the Banaz Su, towards its source, north-west of Islam Keui. The thought has also occurred to me that the site at Islam Keui may have been, under the Romans, an independent town, and not a village subject to Akmonia; and in that case it might be Alia. But a town at Islam Keui could only be one of the bishoprics attached to Akmonia, viz. Hierokharax, Diokleia, Aristion, and Kidyessos.

On the whole, therefore, Alia, though uncertain, may best be placed at Kirka, unless some site be discovered further north than Kirka, but west or north-west of Islam Keui, on the south-eastern skirts of Murad Dagh (Mount Dindymos). A situation beyond the vast mass of Dindymos is quite out of keeping with the order of Hierocles.

* It must of course be admitted that isolated exceptions occur, but there seems no reason to suspect one here.

36. HIEROKHARAX, disfigured as Ioukharatax in Hierocles, and as Oraka in the Notitiæ, was one of the cities of the Moxeanoi. It was probably at Otourak,* on the road from Akmonia to the north and the east in general. Moxeanoi is the form in Ptolemy and an inscription ; Mozeanoi on coins.

37. DOKELA or DIOKLEA, one of the cities of the Moxeanoi, was situated at Doghla, on the road from Akmonia to the Pentapolis of Phrygia.

38. ARISTION is unknown except as occurring in the Byzantine lists: it is to be sought in the western Sitchanli Ova.

39. KIDYESSOS, at Geukche Eyuk, in the eastern Sitchanli Ova. The name is frequently corrupted in the ancient authorities, e. g. Κυδισσεῖς in Ptolemy, and the false form is regularly quoted by modern writers, e. g. Meyer 'Carier' and Pauli 'Altgriechische Inschrift aus Lemnos' (CB, xxvii.). Kidyessos is related to Kadoi, as Selgessos to Selge (see Sagalassos).

40. PENTAPOLIS was the name of the valley of Sandykli, with its five cities: (41) OTROUS (Tchor Hisar), (42) BROUZOS (Kara Sandykli), (43) STEKTORION (Emir Hisar), (44) HIEROPOLIS (Kotch Hisar), and (45) EUKARPIA. In his recent map Prof. Kiepert places Eukarpia twelve miles north of its real position, probably a slip.†

46. SYNNADA was detected by M. Perrot, from inscriptions copied at Tchifut Cassaba by M. Choisy. CB, xxxv. Theodosius, bishop of Synnada, 408, in 'Act. Sanct.,' Jan. 13, p. 477c.

47. DOKIMION, at Istcha Kara Hissar (CB, xxxvi.).

48. PRYMNESSOS, at Seulun, two miles S.S.E. from Afiom Kara Hissar (CB, xxxvii.). The third milestone (A PRYMNESSO III Γ) is still beside its original position at a bridge to the north-east.

49. KONE or KONNA, at Beuyeuk Tchorgia, five or six miles north of Afiom Kara Hissar, was united with Metropolis under one bishop; the latter was probably at Ayaz Inn.

50. AMBASON is given by Stephanus as equivalent to Metropolis. It was probably the Byzantine Ampoun and the modern Ambanaz, a little to the east of Beuyeuk Tchorgia (CB, xl.).

51. AKROENOS, now Afiom Kara Hissar, took away the importance of Prymnessos. The form implies a stem, akru, as Kadoenos implies kadu (in Kadys) and Otroenos implies Otru (in Otreus). Akroenos was perhaps called Nikopolis on account of the great victory over the Arabs under Seidi Ghazi in 740 A.D. (CB, xli., xlii.). Notitiæ iii., x., xiii., have probably omitted the word ἤτοι between Prymnessos and Akroenos, as is done by most Notitiæ in the case of Mesotimolos and Blaundos.

52. PAROREIOS Phrygia, was the country between Sultan Dagh and

* Otourak, "leisure," from otour, to sit.

† The name Pentapolis is known only from the signature to Conc. Constant., A.D. 553, Paulus episcopus Stectorii civitatis, Pentapoliticae regionis, Phrygiae Salutaris Provinciae.

Emir Dagh, including the large lakes, and the cities Polybotos, Julia-Ipsos, Philomelion, Thymbrion-Hadrianopolis, and Tyriaion. Its north-western limit was Holmoi, now Tchai; its south-eastern limit was Tyriaion. The ancient names of the lakes are unknown, except that in the twelfth century Ak Sheher Göl was called the Lake of the Forty Martyrs (Anna Comnena, ii. p. 329). Forty-two martyrs, captured in Amorion and slain at Samara on the Euphrates on refusing to become Mohammedans, are worshipped by the Greeks on March 6th, Act. Sanct., p. 457. M. Perrot in Rev. Arch. 1876, I., p. 190 ff, wrongly infers from Strab. p. 576, that Synnada was in Paroreios : on the meaning of that passage and the necessary alteration 'Ακμόνειαν, see CB, xliii.

53. JULIA, the Roman correspondent to the place called in more ancient and in Byzantine times Ipsos, was in all probability near Sakli. It seems to be near the KAYSTROU PEDION of Xenophon. See Addenda.

54. POLYBOTOS retains its name as Bolowodun.

55. PHILOMELION, Ak Sheher, was pointed out by Hamilton, who also correctly placed

56. TYRIAION at Ilghin.

57. THYMBRION seems to have been refounded as Hadrianopolis. It was a little way south of Philomelion, on the direct road to Ikonion viâ Kaballa. Thymbrion was the great city of earlier time, until Philomelion (probably a foundation of the Diadochi, perhaps of the Perga-menians) took its place. The fountain of Midas, five miles north of Philomelion, is, according to Xenophon, apparently included in the territory of Thymbrion. In his recent map, Prof. Kiepert still identifies Thymbrion with Philomelion, in defiance of Pliny, who mentions the Tymbriani as one of the peoples in the same conventus as Philomelion. Philomelion was in all probability a foundation of the Seleucid or Pergamenian kings, and, in the time of Xenophon, Thymbrion was the nearest city on the march past the Fountain of Midas.

58. DIPOTAMON is several times mentioned without any precise indi-cation of locality ; it was an imperial estate, and bore also the name MESANAKTA.* Mesanakta was on the road by which Romanus Diogenes marched from Constantinople to Syria in A.D. 1032. On his previous expedition he marched by way of Philomelion, and in all probability the same reasons which made that road convenient in 1030 acted also in 1032.† Moreover, the operations of the year 977 seem to make it prac-tically certain that Dipotamon-Mesanakta was on a road leading by way of Kotiaion to the east, and there can be hardly any doubt that this road must be by way of Philomelion (see Cedrenus, ii. 424).

We are not left to probability, however, for Anna Comnena mentions (ii. 329) that a place named Mesanakta was situated on the road between

---

* χωρίον δὲ βασιλικὸν τὸ Διπόταμον, ὃ Μεσάνακτα κατονομάζουσιν οἱ ἐγχώριοι, Cedren, ii., 424. Cp. Leo Diac., p. 120.

† Cedren., ii., 491, 499.

Polybotos and Philomelion, beside the Lake of the Forty Martyrs (Ak Sheher Göl). The imperial estate no doubt included the splendidly fertile land at the north-west end of the lake, where the beautiful " fountain of Midas " flows into it. This stream is perhaps the Διὸς Ποταμός, from which the name Dipotamon is derived : On the estate see E, 22.

Haase has reached a very different conclusion. He places Dipotamon-Mesanakta at the junction of the Tembris, either with the Bathys or with the Sangarios.* The error arises from his taking into account only Cedrenus, ii. 424, and Leo Diaconus, 120, without observing the other references. His suggestion that the Bathys is identical with the Bathyrrhyax is shown to be impossible by the discussion given in Section G of the latter stream, which proves it to be near Yeni Khan, west-north-west of Sivas.

59. ANTIGOUS. After Dipotamon has been fixed, it becomes possible to place on the map some other names which Leo Diaconus mentions in connection with it (p. 120-2). In A.D. 971 Skleros advanced from Constantinople against the rebel Bardas Phokas. He halted at Dorylaion till the troops of the surrounding themata concentrated there,† and in the meantime communicated with Phokas, vainly urging him to submit. He then advanced to Dipotamon, and again halted, sending emissaries to corrupt the adherents of Phokas. It is clearly implied that Phokas was encamped not very far away, at a place called Bardaëtta; and as his followers gradually deserted him he fled to the castle of the Tyrannoi, called Antigous.‡ Cedrenus, with whom Zonaras agrees, tells the circumstances differently, saying that Phokas was encamped all the time at Cæsareia of Cappadocia, until he fled to Tyropoion. But Leo is clearly a better authority. He relates that Phokas escaped from Amaseia, where he was living in banishment, to Cæsareia, where he stayed some time collecting an army. It is implied that he then advanced towards the west, and the circumstances are very similar to those of A.D. 667, when Sapor advanced from Cappadocia to Hadrian-opolis (see HEXAPOLIS below). Phokas also advanced into Phrygia Paroreios, obviously by the great Roman highway leading from Cæsareia to Philomelion, Synnada, and Ephesos, and encamped at Bardaëtta,§ a little to the south-east of Dipotamon. Cedrenus and Zonaras omit the forward march of Phokas, and even Leo only implies it without expressly describing it. He then fled to Tyrannoi or Tyropoion. Right on the line of his flight towards the east lies Tyriaion, and it seems impossible to doubt that τὸ τῶν Τυράννων φρούριον stands for τὸ τῶν Τυραηνῶν φρούριον, and that Τυρόποιον is an alteration of Τυριάϊον, due to the

* See art. Phrygia in Ersch & Grüber.

† I expand the brief references of Leo and Cedrenus, p. 387, in accordance with the account given below of Dorylaion.

‡ Τὸ τῶν Τυράννων κάστρον, ὃ 'Αντιγοὺς κέκληται, Leo Diac., p. 122.

§ The name is modified by the popular etymologist to give the sense, " the defeat of Bardas." Is Baretta the true name ?

etymologising tendency. Standing by the hieroglyphic inscription a mile or more north of Köli-tolu, I saw a high steep hill, beneath which Ilghin lay out of sight. On this hill there may have been a Byzantine castle. A rocky hill was also pointed out to me from the inscription, apparently about an hour or two distant,* which was said to be a fortified Kale.

60. HEXAPOLIS. A district in Asia Minor of this name is occasionally mentioned.† The Arabs ravaged it in 667. Sapor, the Strategos of the Armeniac Theme, rebelled against the Emperor Constantine in 688, and, as we may infer, marched westwards. He occupied Hadrianopolis, and was there thrown from his horse and killed. Phadalas was sent by the Khalif Moawiya to help Sapor, and when he reached the Hexapolis he learned of the death of Sapor. He halted until he could send for further reinforcements, and when they arrived he advanced to Chalcedon, and as he retired he captured Amorion. This account seems to imply that Hadrianopolis was in the Hexapolis. Now the Armeniac Theme at this time embraced the whole of Cappadocia, and a very natural road for Sapor to advance towards Constantinople was through Phrygia Paroreios and Hadrianopolis. It seems impossible to understand in this passage any other of the cities named Hadrianopolis. In that case the Hexapolis must be equivalent to Paroreios, and the six cities may be Julia-Ipsos, Philomelion, Hadrianopolis, Tyriaion, Sinethandos, and Laodikeia; these six, lying on or near a great route, might be classed together for some government purposes, and thus form a Hexapolis.

61. LYKAONES, in the Cutchuk Sitchanli Ova (CB, lxxxv.), are called in inscriptions Λυκάονες πρὸς ἔνδον.

62. AUROKRA or Aulokra, with the famous fountain called Rocreni (i.e. Aurocreni) Fontes by Livy,‡ and Aulokrene by the Greeks generally, is the name of the Dombai Ova (CB, lxxxvi.).

63. METROPOLIS, in the Tchul Ova, three miles west of Tatarli (CB, lxxxvii.).

64. KINNABORION, probably at Geneli, in the south-western corner of Karamyk Ova (CB, lx.).

65. OINIA, still called Oinan, in a valley which was probably called Euphorbium (CB, lxi., lxii.).

66. KHELIDONIA, mentioned by Strabo (p. 663), between Metropolis and Holmoi (Tchai), must have been the DINIÆ which Livy mentions between Metropolis and Synnada. It is to be looked for below Karadilli, at the south-western extremity of the Oinan Ova (see below).

---

* The inscription is about two miles from Köli-tolu, a yaila of Khadyn Khan. From the stone I read the hill over Ilghin 275°, Köli-tolu 139°, Khadyn Khan 116°, and the Kale 320°. See my paper in ' Athen. Mittheilungen,' 1889.

† Theophan., p. 348, 350.

‡ Rhotrinos in the text of Livy (xxxviii., 15), is an error for Rhocrinos; but the common correction Obrimæ is absurd and utterly unjustifiable.

67. Sibidounda, not mentioned by Hierocles, but perhaps to be included under his *demos Amadassos*,* which may also be the true form corrupted by Ptolemy as Gammaousa or Gamboua. Perhaps it is to be sought between Augustopolis, Polybotos, Holmoi (Tchai), and Lysias. Sibidounda is to the Isaurian name Sbida as Attoudda is to Attaia, and as Aloudda to Alia (CB, lxiii., lxiv.).

68. Lysias, probably a Pergamenian foundation, about Bazar Agatch and Karadja Euren (CB, lxv.)

69. Augustopolis, at Surmene (Athen. Mittheil., 1882).

70, 71. Kleros Oreines and Kleros Politikes formed between them a great imperial estate, the latter being the territory of Augustopolis, and the former probably in the hilly country to the north. They seem to have been used, among other purposes, for breeding horses, " quos Phrygiæ matres sacris præsepibus edunt." †

72. Trokonda was a village, mentioned in an inscription found at a bridge three miles north of Prymnessos, and four miles west of Augustopolis.‡ It may possibly be the old name of Augustopolis.

73. Anaboura, is the station between Mandri Fontes and Beudos on the march of Manlius. It is to be sought a little way south-east of Surmene, or possibly even at Kara Arslan. The latter, however, seems too near Beudos. Anaboura was also a city of the Phrygo-Pisidian frontier, now called Enevre, six miles west of Kara Agatch.

74. Mandri Fontes, altered by the editors of Livy (xxxviii., 15) to Alandri Fontes, are the fountains that flow away towards Polybotos, a few miles north of the village of Mandra, and a few miles east of Seidilar. Rev. des Ét. Grecq., 1889.

75. Beudos Vetus (as opposed to the new city of Synnada, five miles distant, which was probably a foundation of the earliest Diadochi), at the village Aghizi Kara. Boudeia, and Phyteia are perhaps other forms of the name. Hierocles gives it corruptly as Debalakia. Mirus was bishop of Beudos in 451 A.D.

76. Leontos Kome is mentioned in Athenæus as a village of Phrygia, with hot springs, the water of which was harsh and impregnated with nitre.§ The reference possibly may be to the hot springs about 14 miles E.S.E. from Afiom Kara Hissar, between Tchobanlar and Yeni Keui, or to the series of hot springs about three hours north-west of Afiom Kara Hissar. It is possible that the same place is referred to by Leo Diaconus (p. 122) as Ὠηλέοντα, or in the rustic speech Γωλέοντα: Leon Phokas fled thither, A.D. 920, from Chrysopolis on the Bosphorus. Cedrenus says that he first came to the fortress Ateous, and when refused

---

* The name is not quite certain. Hierocles has Ἀλαμασοῦ, which is probably a transposition, with the additional fault of Λ in place-of Δ.

† See E., 22.

‡ Mr. Hogarth reads Ἀντίωνος in this inscription. I have omitted the name in publishing it. See CB, lv.

§ τραχύτερα καὶ νιτρωδέστερα, Athen., ii., 43 A.

admittance there he went to Γοηλέοντος. Symeon Magister gives the names Aetous and Γοηλέοντι (dative).* Aetoi is said by him to be a city, Goeleon an open field or country village. Leo Grammaticus agrees, but has Ateous and Γοηλέοντι. Georgius Monachus mentions only τὸ κάστρον 'Ατεοῦς. None of these references give any clue to the situation.

77. MEROS, at Kumbet (CB, lxvi.). The order of Hierocles is clear.

78. NAKOLEIA, at Seidi Ghazi, as J. R. Steuart and Dr. Mordtmann saw and proved (CB, lxvii). Villages in its territory were SEREA, VEK-ROKOME, SANTABARIS, KAKKABAS, and perhaps RYMA (CB, lxviii.–lxxiii.).

79. SANGIA, 150 stadia from Pessinus, at the sources of the Sangarios. This distance, as given by Strabo, is a decided understatement. It was near Tchifteler; and PAZON, where a Novatian Synod was held, seems to have been in the same neighbourhood.

80. MEZEA, a village near Dorylaion (CB, lxxix. See below, p. 212). The Bathys joined the Tembris, Tembrogius, or Thybris, at Dorylaion, v. Nic. Chon., p. 89, Cinnam., p. 81, 191.

81. AKKILAION is placed on the road between Midaion and Germa Colonia (see Galatia).

82. KRASSOS, the plain of the Tembris below Midaion, and probably also below Akkilaion, for Akkilaion was in the province of Asia,† while Κράσσου (πεδίον) seems to be placed by Galen outside of the bounds of Asia (CB, part I., App. I., where it is unnecessary to correct Κράσσος for Κράσσου: πεδίον is understood).

83. KOTIAION is still called Kutaya. The name is given on coins with the spelling KOTIAEΩN, but probably the form Κοτυάϊον, which often occurs, is more strictly accurate. It is the city of Kotys, as Midaion of Midas, Tataion of Tatas, Dorylaion of Dorylas, Akkilaion of Akkilas. It was the seat of a marked type of Christianity from the second century onwards.‡

84. PRAIPENISSEIS are a people on the upper Tembris or Tembrogius, about Altyntash. The chief town or village of the district was called Soa, and the inhabitants Soenoi. The name Bennisoa has hitherto been given as a variant or rather a fuller form of Soa, but this is a mistake arising from misunderstanding of the following inscription, a dedication to the god of the district, Benneus or Zeus Bennios; ὑπὲρ τῆς Αὐτοκράτορος Νερούα Τραιανοῦ, etc., νείκης Διὶ Βεννίῳ Μηνοφάνης Τειμο[λά]ου τὸν βωμὸν ἀνέστησεν Βεννεῖ Σοηνῶν. The inscription is badly engraved, and is the work of an unpractised engraver and an uneducated composer.§ The last two words must not be joined into a single word; they are added in a final line, apart from and unnecessary to the rest of the inscription,

---

* Cedren., ii., 293; Symeon, p. 730 (Bonn Ed.); Leo. Gramm., p. 302; Georg. Mon., p. 889 (Bonn).

† Its rare coins belong to Asia, rather than to Galatia.

‡ See my papers in the *Expositor*, 1888 and 1889 and Addenda.

§ The letters are rude, and TEIMOAΛ ΟΥ, with a gap between Λ and O, is clear.

possibly even by a different hand. They are simply intended to bring into special prominence the god to whom the dedication is made, Benneus of the Soenoi. The forms Benneus and Zeus Bennios are both used in other inscriptions, though not side by side as here. The construction is awkward, but such explanatory additions are not a rare feature in the rude patois which was called Greek by the Phrygians, while the addition of a genitive Βεννεισοηνῶν, according to the current interpretation, is both equally awkward and absolutely contrary to analogy. More-over, the name Soenoi occurs in another inscription of the same village, and we are bound to accept its authority, when it is confirmed by the natural and simple explanation of the former inscription. Soa is apparently identical with the Carian soua, ' grave,' see Stephanus, s.v. Σουάγελα.

The names Tottoia, Abeikta, Trikomia, Zingot, Iskome, and Isgerea, also Skordapia (corrupt?), Spore (corrupt?), Gaiou Kome (corrupt?), Tribanta (uncertain), are found in this district at different periods ; they denote apparently for the most part separate villages (CB, xc.–xcvii.).

85. EPIKTETOS. In order to understand Ptolemy's description of this part of Phrygia, we must bear in mind that he uses more than one authority. One of his authorities made Phrygia extend on the north only as far as the Kidyesseis and the Makedones Kadoenoi. The authority whom he uses probably considered that along this frontier line Phrygia was bounded by Mysia. Hence the Praipenisseis, who are north of the Kidyesseis, are assigned by Ptolemy to Mysia. But when Ptolemy gives a list of the cities of Phrygia, he follows a different authority, who reckoned this entire district as far west as Synaos and Ankyra to Phrygia. This uncertainty as to the limits of Mysia and Phrygia was a proverb among the Greeks, as Strabo mentions. Ptolemy makes the Kadoenoi and Kidyesseis border not on Mysia but on Bithynia. So also Strabo, p. 795, makes the Mysians (called Olympenoi and Helles-pontii) intervene between Bithynia, with its capital Nikaia, and Phrygia. In other places also Strabo assigns a considerable territory along the north frontier of Phrygia to Mysia. At other times he assigns both Mysia and Epiktetos Phrygia to the district about Olympos between Bithynia and Great Phrygia. Epiktetos contains the six cities, Midaion, Dorylaion, Kotiaion, Nakoleia, Aizanoi, Kadoi, though Strabo adds that Kadoi is by some reckoned as part of Mysia (p. 571, 576). But when (p. 567), he extends the name Phrygia to include Blaudos near Ankyra, which must be the Blados of Hierocles, it is impossible to think, as most authorities do, that he extended the name Phrygia to include the modern Bolat (see p. 133). Bolat is in Strabo's Mysia Abrettene.

The solution of these apparent contradictions lies in the sense of the word Epiktetos, which perhaps was given by the Pergamenian govern-ment * to a territory, considerable part of which had previously been

* The coins of Epiktetos are Pergamenian in type.

reckoned Mysian. Hence there is a tendency to vary and confuse between Phrygia Epiktetos and Mysia. Not merely Ankyra and Synaos, which Strabo reckons as Mysia Abbaitis, but also Kadoi (where an inscription of the Abbaeitai occurs, Le Bas, No. 1001), Praipenissos (reckoned by Ptolemy in Mysia), and, therefore, necessarily also Aizanoi, were at one time and by some writers reckoned as part of Mysia. Hence it is quite natural that Xenophon should call Keramon Agora (Islam Keui) ἐσχάτη πρὸς τῇ Μυσίᾳ χώρᾳ.

The name Phrygia was given to the country ruled by a conquering tribe of Phryges, crossing from the Macedonian side of Thrace by the Hellespont. At a later time new troops of European barbarians, the Mysoi, penetrated into Asia, pressed the Phryges farther inland, and partially occupied their country. In this way the extraordinary interlacing of the two names becomes intelligible. The situation of the parts called Mysia, which, according to Strabo, separated Hellespontine Phrygia from Great Phrygia and Epiktetos, and on one side adjoined the Kaikos and the Pergamenian territory as far west as Teuthrania, while it extended through Abbaïtis and Abrettene to the Mysian Olympos (p. 571, 576), can only be explained if we suppose the Mysoi to have crossed into Asia at a point much farther west than the Phrygians did, probably following the route which afterwards Alexander and Barbarossa both took.

86. APPIA, on the Roman road between Akmonia and Kotiaion, is well known since the journey of Le Bas. It is still called Abia, OB, xcviii. Coins have the spelling Ἀππιανῶν, but the true name is probably Apia, like the Ἀπία γαῖα of the Peloponnesus: the name is connected with the stem apa or akwa, " water." Le Quien omits Paul, bishop of Appia, 325 : the Acta have Apameensis for Apianensis, and Le Quien reads Acmoniensis.

87. EUDOKIAS is a name which, like Pulcherianopolis, Valentia, and Theodosia, points to the fourth and fifth centuries. At one time I was disposed to see in it a temporary name of Kotiaion, but as all authorities assign Kotiaion to the province of Salutaris, I have been obliged to give up this view, and to regard Eudokias, according to the order of Hierocles, as occupying the north frontier of Pacatiana, between Apia and Aizanoi. There is a tract of unexplored country in this neighbourhood, on the north skirts of Murad Dagh, reported to contain many villages. Eudokias, however, is probably the imperial estate, on which see E., 22.

The next five bishoprics were an ecclesiastical district, and were, therefore, according to the principle which is observed in many cases, a local district also. Four of them, Aizanoi, Kadoi, Ankyra, and Synaos, are well known, and the fifth, Tiberiopolis, must be placed adjoining them.

88. AZANOI or AIZANOI. The site at Tchavdir Hisar, with its extensive and interesting ruins, is well known. Stephanus mentions * that

* On the authority of Hermogenes.

Euphorbus was the first priestly dynast of the temple, and was appointed because he taught the proper method of sacrifice. The story may be taken as proof of the former existence of priestly dynasts, at Aizanoi, such as are well known at Olba, Pessinus, Comana, &c.; where the priest ruled as interpreter of the will of the god. Euphorbus prescribed the sacrifice of the hedgehog and the fox (ἔξιν and οὐανοῦν), and hence comes the name of the city, which ought strictly to be Ἐξουάνουν. Were it not for this form, I should be disposed to connect Azanoi with Phrygian ἀζένα, accus., "beard." The Zeus of Aizanoi is doubtless of the same character as the Zeus Benneus of the Praipenisseis, and as the Zeus Bronton of Dorylaion and Nakoleia. The two latter are identified in a dedication found in the district of Nakoleia Διὶ Βροντῶντι καὶ Βεννεῖ. This Zeus was apparently the god of the European tribe, which, according to my view, overran Phrygia about 900 B.C., or possibly even earlier, and which adopted the religion of Cybele and much of the civilisation and social customs of the older race, among whom it settled as a conquering caste. I regard Benneus as connected with the Thraco-Illyrian Benna, a car, and as denoting the thundering god, who drives in his car across the heavens. In the more civilized states of Nakoleia and Dorylaion, the Greek term Bronton was substituted for the native name Benneus.

89. TIBERIOPOLIS, about Amed, Assarlar, or Egri Göz. There was here a cultus of the ὁμοβώμιοι Θεοὶ Σεβαστοί, either Augustus and Livia, or more probably Tiberius and Livia, the imperial mother and son taking the place of the divine mother and son, who were often worshipped in Asia Minor as Leto and Lairbenos. The district around it was called Abrettene, as M. Waddington has shown in his admirable discussion (Le Bas-Waddington, No. 1011).

90, 91. ANKYRA and SYNAOS were proved by Hamilton to have been situated at Kilisse Keui and Simav. They were joined in one bishopric in later Byzantine time. Ankyra sometimes bore the epithet Sidera or Ferrea, apparently to distinguish it from the Galatian Ankyra.* The river Makestos rises in the lake of Simav, and the district around was called Abbaeitis.

92. KADOI. The accusative form has remained till the present day in the form Ghediz. The ethnic Καδοηνός shows that Kadoi is derived from the name Καδύς, a Lydo-Phrygian hero.† The proper form, therefore, is ΚάδοϜοι or Κάδοι, ΚαδόϜους or Καδούς. Hence comes the personal name Καδουᾶς, i.e. ΚαδοϜᾶς, found on the southern Phryo-Pisidian frontier. Kadoi was a Macedonian colony (Pliny).

93. THEODOSIA is placed by the order of Hierocles at Shap Khane : no other evidence exists.‡ I have assumed that Theodosia and Eudokias

---

* M. Waddington (l.c.) says "quant à l'épithète de Ferrea qu'il [Le Bas] lui donne, je ne sais où il l'a rencontrée." It occurs in the lists of the Nicene Council.

† ΚαδοϜηνός, ᾽ΟτροϜηνός, imply an original stem Καδυ, ᾽Οτρυ.

‡ Domninus Theodosiopolis Phrygiæ Pacatianæ in 536 (Labbe, p. 74); cp. p. 128.

disappear in the interval between Hierocles and the earliest Notitia. This may be justified by the example of Dabinai in Pisidia, which does not occur later than Hierocles, and of Kinnaborion in Phrygia and of Atenia in Pisidia, which appear in Hierocles and the earliest class of Notitiæ, but disappear in the latest Notitiæ. In such cases the town did not, as I think, disappear entirely, but was only merged in the same bishopric with some neighbouring place.

94. TEMENOTHYRAI. The situation of this city is a difficult problem, as two sources of evidence, each apparently precise, seem to conflict with each other.

In the first place Temenothyrai bears also the name Flaviopolis on its coins, and Arundel heard of an inscription of Flaviopolis at Ushak, and an inscription of a native of Temenothyrai, found at Ushak, is published in Le Bas-Waddington, No. 727. Now the site of Grimenothyrai-Trajanopolis was about six miles east of Ushak, and it is natural to suppose that the two names designate a pair of cities of the valley of Ushak, one on the east side and the other on the west. I have found coins of Temenothyrai offered for sale in great numbers at Ushak.

In the second place, however, Pausanias mentions that Temenothyrai was a small city of Upper Lydia, where there was a tumulus containing the corpse of Hyllos, son of Ge, "from whom the river took its name." It seems a natural inference from this that the river flowing past Temenothyrai was the Hyllos. Now the Hyllos is known from coins to be the tributary of the Hermos flowing past Saittai. This river, whose course I have traced from its source, is incorrectly given in Kiepert's maps. It rises in the lofty mountains immediately south of Synaos (Simav), and has a course similar to that of the Demirdji Tchai. This range of mountains runs apparently continuously along the south side of the Makestos valley, and there can be little doubt that the western part of the range at least was called Τῆμνος. The name Τημενο-θύραι was clearly understood to mean "the passes of Mount Temnos," * and the case then might seem made out that Temenothyrai lies on the upper waters of the river Hyllos, on the southern slopes of Mount Temnos. The situation suits Pausanias's expression, "a city of Upper Lydia." It must be acknowledged that we should expect Temnos to be the division between Lydia and Phrygia, and all places on the south of the mountains to be Lydia. The only difficulty, then, would arise from the fact that all Byzantine lists place Temenothyrai in Phrygia; and this difficulty cannot be considered insurmountable.

The second view seemed to me the more probable when writing CB, § cvii., and Prof. H. Kiepert has since followed it in his recent map of Asia Minor. He has, however, made the error of placing Temeno-

* I have however no doubt that M. S. Reinach's explanation of θύραι as altered by popular etymology from teira, "village" (compare Thyateira, Teira, and perhaps Hadrianoutherai), is quite right.

thyrai, not on the river which flows by Saittai, but on the Demirdji Tchai. Owing to the small scale of the map, the site of Saittai seems to be half-way between the two rivers, but really it is not in the valley of the Demirdji Tchai, but near the course of the next river on the east. I then imagined that Arundel's authority could not be trusted in regard to this inscription, which he gives only in cursive text, remarking that Flaviopolis is known as a bishopric. As this remark is wrong, being based apparently on a confusion with Trajanopolis, I thought that the inscription could not be accepted as evidence. But Monsieur S. Reinach has since convinced me that I was unjust to Arundel. He has found two inscriptions of Ushak, copied in the early part of the century by a French traveller, which mention Temenothyrai.*

The first view then must be accepted, and the words of Pausanias may then be perhaps understood as not implying that "the river" in question flowed past Temenothyrai, but merely as referring to the Lydian river at no great distance, which flowed into the Hermos. Pausanias seems to speak not as an eye-witness. But perhaps a better interpretation is to suppose that there were two rivers Hyllos, one at Saittai, and one at Temenothyrai, the latter flowing towards the Mæander. The story seems much more natural if Hyllos be a local personage; and if the name Hyllos were not actually preserved in the local nomenclature, it is hard to see why the hero Temenos, who is mentioned on the coins of the city, should not have been made the proprietor of the bones. I should then look for Temenothyrai a little to the west of Ushak, on the higher ground separating the basins of the Hermos and the Mæander. The "throne" mentioned by Pausanias, as wrought in a projecting rocky spur of a hill at Temenothyrai may perhaps yet be discovered.† The neighbourhood of Kure and Yeni Keui, or possibly Ushak itself, may be given as the site of Temenothyrai.

95. Trajanopolis was refounded and renamed in A.D. 119, about the end of September, by permission of the Emperor Hadrian.‡ Trajanopolis was a city of the people called Grimenothyritai, as Ptolemy § mentions. Coins of the Grimenothyritai are found under the earlier emperors, but none are later than Hadrian. It would appear, then, that a city was founded in their territory and named Trajanopolis, by special leave of Hadrian, in honour of his deceased imperial father. It was apparently named in emulation of Temenothyrai-Flaviopolis. The name

* The copies are very fragmentary, but I could see no reason to doubt his restoration of the full name, Temenothyrai Flaviopolis.

† Θρόνος ἀνδρός ἐστιν ἐνειργασμένος ὅρους λιθώδει προβολῇ, Paus. i., 35, 7.

‡ The inscription mentioning the date was copied first by Hamilton, and is published in a more complete form in my CB, cviii. It is at Tcharik Keui. The inscription is older than, and cannot be connected with, Hadrian's journey in Asia Minor, and does not therefore justify Duerr in quoting it as evidence in his "Reisen des Kaisers Hadrian."

§ The text has Τριμενοθυρῖται; the correction is made by M. Waddington, on Le Bas, 727.

Grimenothyrai disappears henceforth from use, so far as coins and the Byzantine lists are concerned; but the name Flaviopolis was soon disused, and Temenothyrai remained current. The order of Hierocles places them together, and so also do Notitiæ iii., x., xii. The actual site of Trajanopolis was at Giaour Euren, near Orta Keui, which is about six miles east of Ushak.

96. PULCHERIANOPOLIS is probably the name under which Motella was first raised to the rank of a πόλις, CB, cix. The name seems to be a false form. Πουλχεριούπολις and Πουλχεριανή are both correct forms, but ·Πουλχεριανούπολις confuses the two.

97. LYKOKRANITAI were a division of infantry stationed at some place in Phrygia in the time of Justinian (Theophan., p. 178). It is possible that they derived their name from the fort where they were stationed; but more probably the name belonged to them as a regiment, perhaps derived from the type of helmet that they wore. See Addenda.

98. MANTALOS was mentioned as a city of Phrygia by Alexander Polyhistor, quoted by Stephanus. The name occurs in two inscriptions, one copied by Mordtmann,* and both copied by me in a deserted cemetery on the road between Arab Euren and Kaimaz (Troknades). In it are two small broken columns, apparently of Synnadic marble, very like others which I saw at Kaimaz. Each of these columns has two inscriptions on opposite sides at the same height. On one side is Ἁγία Θέκλα in Byzantine letters, not earlier than the fifth century: on the other side is

(1) ΑΔΙΑΜ   (2) ΔΙΑΜ
   ΟΛ   ΟΛΑ

It is remarkable that both these inscriptions are written from right to left, whereas the name of the saint is written in the ordinary direction. The difference in the form of the letters might suggest a later date for the name of the saint than for the word Mandalo, but the exact correspondence of the two inscriptions can hardly be accidental. " Mandalo " may be connected with the city Mantalos.

99. The divisions of Phrygia vary much at different times. In earlier time we have Phrygia Magna in the interior and Phrygia Hellespontia on the south of the Hellespont and Propontis. To these was added Phrygia Epiktetos, probably in the Pergamenian time, a district intervening between Phrygia Magna and Bithynia, and in part assigned by many writers to Mysia. Phrygia Paroreios was the great high-lying valley between Emir Dagh and Sultan Dagh, extending from Polybotos to Tyriaion. The name Phrygia extended apparently to a point south of Apollonia and Antiocheia Colonia (usually called Antiocheia of Pisidia), but north of Konane, Neapolis, and Anaboura.

* Mordtmann in 'Sitzungsber. d. Bayer. Akad.,' 1862, p. 14. He speaks of the enigmatic inscription as written boustrophedon; this is a mistake, as his own transcript shows. He saw the one which I give as (2).

In the earlier Byzantine period we hear little or nothing of Phrygia Hellespontia. Part of Paroreios, besides Apollonia, the southern Metropolis, Apameia Kibotos, Tymandos, and Antiocheia were assigned to Pisidia. All the rest of Phrygia was divided into two provinces, which were at first called Prima and Secunda, towards A.D. 400 Magna and Parva, and beginning from about A.D. 360 Pacatiana and Salutaris. The last pair of names became universal during the fifth century, and all other titles disappeared. At what exact time the division into two provinces was accomplished is still a matter of doubt. On the whole the probability seems to me to be that it was made, not by Diocletian, but soon after him by Constantine.* The border towns in Salutaris were Kotiaion, Praipenisseis, Akroënos, Lykaones, Brouzos, Stektorion, Eukarpia, Aurokra; and in Pacatiana Aizanoi, Eudokias, Kidyessos, Dioklea, Pepouza, Soublaion-Justinianopolis.† Some trace remains of a division into smaller districts, perhaps for governmental purposes: Pentapolis included the five cities of the upper Glaukos valley.

At the division into Themes, Phrygia was divided between the Anatolic and the Opsikian. The latter included Midaion, Dorylaion, Kotiaion, and marched with the former at Meros. Drawing a line from this point so as to include the fortress of Opsikion (Koula), we may safely say that Ankyra, Synaos, Theodosia, Kadoi, Aizanoi, Tiberiopolis, Eudokias, Apia, and perhaps Praipenisseis were included in Opsikion, and that Dindymos (Murad Dagh) was the boundary towards the Anatolic Theme. The rest of Phrygia, together with Lykaonia and part of Pisidia, formed the vast Anatolic Theme. It may however be doubted whether the Lykos valley, with the strong fortress Khonai, which was probably a Turma, was not included in the Thrakesian Theme, though Constantine says nothing about it. In a scheme of defence the Lykos valley goes naturally with the Thrakesian Theme. The name Hexapolis, denoting apparently the cities of Phrygia Paroreios,

---

* Malalas says that Constantine made the province Salutaris Phrygia (xiii., p. 323); but he uses the name that was customary in his own time. How far Malalas, a very poor authority, can be trusted on such a point is uncertain, but nothing is known that conflicts with his statement. Mommsen and Czwalina are inclined to discredit his statement and to attribute the division to Diocletian; Kuhn, Jullien, and Duchesne are inclined to accept a date later than Diocletian. The two Phrygias are, according to Duchesne, separated in preamble to Concil. Sardic., A.D. 347, but even this inference cannot be justified. The list is Mysia, Asia, Caria, Bithynia, Hellespont, Phrygia, Phrygia altera, Pisidia, Cappadocia, Pontus Euxinus, Cilicia, Pamphylia, Lydia, Cyclades, Galatia (Mansi, ii., 715-6); this list is obviously a later and unhistorical fiction, for Mysia, Pontus Euxinus, and Cyclades were never Byzantine provinces. The epistle of the same council gives a much more trustworthy list: Cilicia, Isauria, Cappadocia, Galatia, Pontus, Bithynia, Paphlagonia, Caria, Phrygia, Pisidia, Insulae Cycladum, Lydia, Asia, Hellespontus (ib., 731).

† In 'Const. Porph. de Them.,' p. 14, read, or at least understand, ἀπὸ τοῦ 'Ακροΐνοῦ καὶ μέχρι τοῦ 'Αμωρίου καλεῖται Φρυγία Σαλουταρία. Either the text has been corrupted or Constantine has misrepresented his authority.

HELLESPONTUS.

Roman Coins.	Hierocles.	Notitiae.	Concil. Chalc., A.D. 451.	Ep. ad Leon., A.D. 458.	Concil. Nicaen. II., A.D. 787.
Kyzikos	Κύζικος	I. 1 Κυζίκου	Diogenes Cyzici	Euoptius Cyzici	Nicolaus Cyzici
Proconnesos	(Προικόνησος	III. Προικοννησοῦ	Acacius Proeconnesi		Nicetas Proeconnesi
	(ἡ Ἐζορία				
Priapos	Βαρίς	II. 5 Σασαβδρεως	Eutychianus Bareae	Dominus Varenus	Theodotus Paleon
Parion	Πάριον	Παρίου	Thalassius Parvi	Thalassius Parii	Joannes Lampsaci
Lampsakos	Ἀδράμακος	7 Λαμψάκου	Daniel Lampsacensis	Armonius Lampsaci	Theodorus Abydi
Abydos	Ἄβυδος	8 Ἀβύδου	Hermias Abydensis	Hermias Abydi	Strategius Dardanes
Dardanos	Ἀδράανον	9 Δαρδάνου	Petrus Dardanensis	Petrus Dardani	Nicetas Ilii
Ilion	Ἴλιον	10 Ἡλίου	Theusebius Ilii	Theosebius Ilii	
Alexandria Troas	Τρωάς	11 Τρωάδος	Pionius Troadensis	Pionius Troadis	{Leontius Troados / Leo}
(Skamandria, Greek)	Σκάμανδρος				
	Πολίχνα				
Poimanenos	Ποιμάνεντος	3 Πημαηνοῦ	Stephanus Pymanena	Joannes Poemaneus	{Leontius Poemaninon / Leo}
	Ἀρτεμέα				
	Ῥέκετα				
	Βλάδος				
	Σκέλεντα				
Miletopolis	Μόλις	13 Μελιτουπόλεως	Gemellus Melitopolis	Sotominus Mileti	Michael Melitopoleos
Hiera Germe	Γέρμαι	2 Γέρμης	Timotheus Germae	Timotheus Ceramensis	Theodorus Germes
	Ἄπταος				
	Κέργη				
	Σέχαρα				
Hadrianotherai	Ἀδριανοῦ Θῆραι	6 Ἀδριανοῦ Θηρῶν	Patricius Adrianopolitanus	Patricius Adrianotheres	Basilius Hadriani
Pionia	Πιονία	12 Πιωνίας	Eulalius Pionensis	Sabbas Pioniae	
	Κονιοσίνη				
	Ἀργιζα				
	Ἔλος Τράδος				
	Μανδάκαδα				
	Ἐργαστήριον				
	Μάνδραι				
	Ἵπποι				
	Ὄκη	4 Ὄκης	Alexander Ocae	Alexander Occae	Simeon Oces
Scepsis	Σίδηρον	14 Ἁγίου Κορνήλου	Philostorgius Scepsii		
Hadrianoi	Σκέψις [Σκήψις]	15 Ἀδρανέιας	David Adrianensis	David Andrianae	Sisinnius Adraniae

Notitiae VIII, IX, give Adraneia as 13; X, XIII, alone give Saint Cornelius; III, by error inserts 3 Daphnusia.

is found during this period (in the eighth century). During this period the Church retained the old division and names, Pacatiana and Salutaris.

In late Byzantine historians the names Great and Little Phrygia reappear in a new sense. Great Phrygia is defined by Ducas * as the territory from Assos to the Hellespont: it is apparently much the same as the modern vilayet Karasi, and was ruled by a Turkish chief of that name. This name obviously arises from a dim recollection of Phrygia Hellespontia, and is purely literary with no real political existence. In contrast to it the two provinces Pacatiana and Salutaris are summed up as "Entire Phrygia," or "Upper Phrygia" (Nicet. Chon., p. 68; Cedren. ii., p. 69) as distinguished from "Lower Phrygia" or Karasi (Ducas, p. 72). Ducas still uses the two names Pacatiana and Salutaris as divisions of Upper Phrygia, and mentions (p. 77) that the latter was called by the Turks Kara Hisar (Καρασάρ), which approximates in a very rough way to the truth.

D. Cities and Bishoprics of Hellespontus.

1. The province of Hellespontus is entirely unknown to me. Except on a short excursion from the Dardanelles to Assos, I have never been in the country. The Byzantine lists differ so much from each other, and Hierocles is so corrupt,† that the topography of this province is more difficult than that of any other in Asia Minor.

Hierocles gives many places which the Notitiæ omit. Many of these are small towns, or even villages, which perhaps never had the rank of cities or bishoprics. But it is certainly difficult to see why Argiza, Blados, and Skepsis are omitted by the Notitiæ. Skepsis is, however, included under the title Saint Cornelius by Notitiæ X., XIII., and its omission in the others is perhaps only a slip.

2. A comparison of the Notitiæ with the lists of the Councils shows that the bishoprics are almost the same at all times in Hellespontus, and that Hierocles does not found his list on them. His list in general keeps close to the geographical order,‡ and is probably either founded on intimate knowledge of the country or on a government list of town-

* Φρυγία πᾶσα παρὰ τοῦ Καρμιάν, ἐτέρα Φρυγία Μεγάλη ἀρχομένη ἀπὸ ᾿Ασσοῦ πόλεως ἄχρι καὶ ῾Ελλησπόντου παρὰ τοῦ Καρασῆ, p. 13. The words Φρυγία Μεγάλη, Φρυγία Καππατιανή on the same page have been often utterly misunderstood, as if Μεγάλη was Salutaris; but the passage really means that the Byzantine power extended over Hellespontine Phrygia (Μεγάλη) and Pacatiana, but not over Salutaris.

† Hierocles has dittography in Βαρίς [ΠΗ] Πάριον, ᾿Αδριανοῦ Θῆραι ΗΡΑΙ, omission in Μ{ιλητόπ}ολις, and utter corruption in Ξίος Τράδος, Κέργη (perhaps = Κεβρήνη), ᾿Ρέκετα, Κονιοσίνη (Pliny, Conisium?), &c.

‡ Exceptions generally depend on doubtful identifications, such as Wesseling's Sideron with Sigeion, Mandrai with Neandreia, Kerge with Kebrene, Rheketa with Rhoiteion, and Artemea with Atarnea, all of which, therefore, are probably to be rejected.

ships. But of all the places which he mentions and which did not become bishoprics, only one struck any coins, viz., Skamandros ; and its coins are older than B.C. 300, so that it had passed out of existence, or at least ceased to be of any importance, about that time. On the other hand, all the bishoprics also struck coins, except Baris (which took the place of Priapos, a city coining money) and Oka. Hellespontus, therefore, gives no reason to believe in any exceptions to the rule that city and bishopric are equivalent terms. All the places which he gives in addition to the "Cities and Bishoprics" seem to be unimportant little places, with the exception of Blados and Argiza. The former however is probably a city of Lydia, which has been transferred to Hellespontos by a corruption of some scribe.* Argiza is a puzzle which has already been discussed under ALGIZA Asiae. If Hierocles's authority for Hellespontus was a government list, it cannot have been a list of πόλεις, for he gives many places that never were πόλεις (to judge from the evidence accessible to us). In all probability he knew the country intimately, and spoke from his own knowledge more fully than in other provinces, where he confines himself rigidly to the "Cities and Bishoprics."

3. Hierocles begins with Cyzicos, and then, after giving the island Proconnesus, goes along the Hellespont and down the west coast to Troas, and then up the Scamander. Baris was probably on the Granikos, and ruled the district along the coast as far as Cyzicos.† This district probably contained the town Aulonia, which is mentioned by Georgius Acropolita (p. 13) between Baris and Poimanenon. Aulonia may have derived its name from the Aulon of the Aisepos, which seems to have been a noteable feature of the country (Strab., p. 603). Baris then must have replaced (probably in a different situation) the older Priapos, which struck a few coins from about 100 B.C. down to Gordian ; and Aulonia must have been near it, for Acropolita mentions them as a pair, and Nicetas, p. 121, actually identifies them, a mistake which probably arises from there being a bishop Βάρεως ἤτοι Αὐλωνίας.‡ Polichna is mentioned by Strabo (pp. 603, 607), as in the glen of the Aisepos near old Skepsis : it was on the north-eastern slopes of Ida, near the sources of the Scamander.

4. Hierocles then returns eastward, keeping a little inland. Polichna is to be found on the left bank of the Aisepos, perhaps about the middle of its course. Artemea is not, with Wesseling, to be altered to Atarnea, which was in Byzantine Asia. Artemea is obviously a village with a hieron of Artemis, and this consideration leaves us no hesitation in identifying it with the hot springs on the lower Aisepos. There was

---

* The subject is discussed under Lydia, § 41.

† Ἐξορία is probably an epithet of Προικόνησος ; see ADDENDA.

‡ πόλις κατὰ τὴν τῶν Αἰγαιοπελαγιτῶν χώραν, Βάρη καὶ Αὐλωνία παρωνύμως ὠνομασμένη, Nic. Chon., 121 ; τῇ κατὰ Ἑλλήσποντον Αὐλωνίᾳ, ib., 711, in distinction from Aulonia near Dyrrachium. On Baris, see § 13.

there an Artemis Thermaia, to whom Aristides composed hymns (vol. i., p. 503, ed. Dind.).

Rheketa is quite unknown and probably corrupt, and then we have Germe * and Miletopolis on the eastern frontier.† Hierocles next gives the towns to Hadrianoutherai, all of which are unknown. The following towns are on the southern frontier:—Pionia was apparently south or south-west of Skepsis, to judge from Strabo (p. 610), who mentions it along with Andeira and Gargaris. The latter is in Byzantine Asia, and the former is otherwise unknown.‡ Argiza was recently discovered by Dr. Fabricius; it is mentioned by Pliny as Erezii, and by the Peutinger Table as Argesis. Ergasteria was 440 stadia from Pergamos on the road to Cyzicos, and was therefore on the upper waters of the Tarsios. Skepsis was on the upper waters of the Aisepos (Strab., p. 603). Mr. J. T. Clarke places it at Kurshunlu Tepe on the upper waters of the Scamander: the situation does not seem quite to accord with Strabo,§ but it is better for the present to follow the opinion of a scholar who is now throwing so much light on the antiquities of the Troad, and who knows the country better than any other. Perhaps he means that new Skepsis was at Kurshunlu Tepe, and that old Skepsis, in a higher position 60 stadia distant, was about the common source of the Scamander and Aisepos.

Mr. J. T. Clarke remarks acutely that Andeira and Pionia, as enumerated by Strabo, are on a road from Skepsis to the coast. Hierocles does not give them in this order, for there is every probability that his Sideron refers to the iron-mines beside Andeira (Strab., p. 610); Pionia, however, he places after Hadrianoutherai. Perhaps Argiza, Mandakada and Ergasterion are to be sought on the Aisepos or the Tarsios.

Sagara is never mentioned elsewhere, but may be a correct name, related to the name of the river Sagaris as a place name to a personal name. Compare Ariassos and Aryassis, Kidramos and Kidramouas, Kadoi and Kadouas, &c. But see Lydia, § 41.

5. HADRIANOUTHERAI was founded by Hadrian after a lucky bear-hunt. Its situation is given by the writer in Smith's Dictionary as on the road between Ergasteria and Miletopolis, but this seems only to be a mistake founded on the road Pergamos-Hadrianoutherai-Miletopolis in

* Germe, or Hiera Germe, has been generally recognised as situated near Kirmasli Kassaba, where the Byzantine Aorata seems to have been (G., 20). The Germian hills mentioned by Anna II., p. 314, are not connected with this Germe, as Forbiger fancies, but are on the east side of Olympos.

† Omitting Blados and Skelenta, on which see Lydia, § 41.

‡ Mr. J. T. Clarke places Pionia on the north bank of the Satnioeis, in the rich plain of Aivajik, and Andeira in an undetermined situation between it and Skepsis (Am. Journ. Arch., 1888, p. 317). Andeira was in Hellespontine Phrygia, as we may infer from Pliny, who gives it as one of the cities of Phrygia.

§ τοῦ δ' αὐλῶνος τοῦ περὶ τὸν Αἴσηπον ἐν ἀριστερᾷ τῆς ῥύσεως αὐτοῦ πρῶτόν ἐστι Πολίχνα τειχῆρες χωρίον, εἶθ' ἡ Παλαίσκηψις—— ἐν δεξιᾷ δὲ τοῦ Αἰσήπου μεταξὺ Πολίχνας τε καὶ Παλαισκήψεως ἡ Νέα Κώμη καὶ 'Αργυρία (Demetrius of Skepsis ap. Strab., p. 603.)

the Peutinger Table. The distances in the Table are unfortunately utterly untrustworthy. The best clue to the position of the city is to be found in the Byzantine documents. In tne later Notitiæ we find the name Akhyraous given as alternative to Hadrianoutherai.

6. AKHYRAOUS, then, is either the Byzantine name of Hadrianoutherai, or else a neighbouring fortress which took its place.* Akhyraous was situated on the great route to Miletopolis and Constantinople from the Hermos and Kaikos valleys : this route passes through Balikesri,† and the evident importance of Akhyraous in the late Byzantine times leaves little doubt that it is to be placed there. Hadrianoutherai was on the road from Pergamos to Miletopolis : this road and the other meet about Balikesri, and Hadrianoutherai is to be sought somewhere in that neighbourhood.

The importance of Akhyraous in later time, as shown by the references in historians, explains its elevation to the rank of a metropolis. This is attested only by Notitia XI., and by two unpublished Notitiæ in the MSS. of the Bibliothèque Nationale in Paris,‡ in all of which it is last in order. It, therefore, must have been elevated at a very late date in the twelfth or thirteenth century.

7. MILATAI. Cedrenus (I., p. 437) has the phrase Ἀδριανοῦ Θήρας ἐν τοῖς μιτάτοις.§ This strange expression probably conceals the name of the people or district in which the city was found. If it was the dative of an ethnic in -της, the ending -ταις would be readily altered to suit the article τοῖς. Now Aristides, in a story whose scene seems to be laid at Pergamos, speaks of a Μειλάτης ἐξ ἀκροπόλεως.‖ The god had told him to take a goose's egg. He sent out for one, but the messengers could find none in the whole market; at last, partly by chance, partly by information received, they went to a certain Milatian who lived on the acropolis. The Milatian replied that he had an egg, but was keeping it to be used for a cure as the god had ordered him. If this Milatian was a native of Aristides' own district, the story is full of the trivial coincidences which Aristides loved. Now, it seems probable that the whole district from Hadrianoutherai down the Makestos to Miletopolis and to the lake Miletopolitis was called Mila, or at least was inhabited by a people called Milatai. Miletopolis, then, was the city of the Milatai, and its name was hellenised to suggest a colony from Miletos. The lake, which is some distance from Miletopolis, would more readily get its name if the people who dwelt on its southern and eastern

---

* Probably the latter is the correct view, according to Prof. G. Hirschfeld's canon.

† I think the true form of this name is Balyk Hisar—"town of the castle"; it has been distorted through the desire to get the form corresponding to Παλαιὰ Καισάρεια.

‡ 1356, fol. 288 ff.; 960, fol. 89.

§ The text may have been changed to give the sense "one of the Metata," on which see Gothofredus ad Cod. Theodos., vol. ii., p. 258, and Nov. Theodos., xxxii.

‖ I should conjecture that τις has been lost after -της.

shores were called Milatai. These facts show that in Cedrenus we should read ἐν τοῖς Μιλάταις.

8. A careful examination of some misunderstood passages in Aristides gives precision to this situation. Aristides' native place was two days' journey from the hot springs of the Aisepos (p. 502). The road lay through Poimanenon, which was 160 stadia distant : it is implied that this 160 stadia was a very long day's journey. It was 440 stadia (55 miles) from Cyzicos, 320, *i.e.* 40 miles, from the lake Miletopolitis or Aphnitis, and (as is clear from the route to Poimanenon) about 100 from certain hot springs which were on the road (p. 537). It was two or three days' journey from Pergamos (pp. 539–41, ed. Dind.)—the exact distance is not given—but after two short days' journey, he had to hurry over 300 stadia on the third day : according to his other journeys we may reckon 120 stadia for each of the first two days, and the total distance is 540 stadia, about 68 miles. The details of this last journey show that there was a plain about 400 stadia, and a temple of Apollo 300 stadia, from Pergamos. It is obvious that these measurements point with practical certainty to the neighbourhood of Hadrianoutherai. All doubt on this point is removed by p. 458, which shows that he could set out from his house to go to Pergamos towards evening, and be uncertain whether or not it would be possible to reach Hadrianoutherai the same night. His house, then, was some miles north of Hadrianoutherai, and the distance of the latter from Pergamos must be about 55 to 58 miles.

This result does not agree with the statements of Philostratus and Suidas, who say that Aristides was born at Hadrianoi. But Hadrianoi was quite 110 miles from Pergamos, 65 from Cyzicos, and 65 from Poimanenon, and it cannot possibly be reconciled with the statements of Aristides. Probably the error arises from the shorter name being substituted for the longer by an error of Philostratus or some other authority.*

9. POIMANENON was one of the strongest fortresses in this district (Anna, II., p. 281). There was there a famous church of St. Michael.†
Its situation, 280 stadia (35 miles) south of Cyzicos, on the river Tarsios, and 160 stadia from Aristides' estate, has been already proved (see HADRIANOUTHERAI). These distances do not suit Maniyas, which is the site commonly assigned, if we may judge from the published maps. Maniyas is not on the road from Pergamos to Cyzicos. In Kiepert's wall-map of Asia Minor in ancient time, he gives Poimanenon on the proper road. No modern names, however, are given, and it is not quite clear

---

* It is however possible that his birthplace should be distinguished from this hereditary estate which he possessed (see Addenda).

† ὁ ναὸς τοῦ 'Αρχιστρατήγου τῶν ἄνω δυναμέων (Acropol., p. 37). On the military importance of Poimanenon, cp. the inscription of Novum Ilium (Schliemann, ' Ilios,' p. 709), quoted by Lolling, ' Athen. Mitth.,' 1884. p. 30.

whether he would now represent the situation of Maniyas differently; but as he has entirely altered the course assigned to the Tarsios, and as Texier mentions that Maniyas is on the road in question, probably his new position for Poimanenon depends on better information as to the site of Maniyas. In the 'Athenische Mittheilungen,' 1884, p. 35, Lolling publishes an inscription found at Gönen on the Aisepos, which seems to contain the name [ΠΟΙ]Μ[ΑΝ]ΗΝΩ[Ν]; he is in doubt as to the site, but this inscription would only prove that the territory of Poimanenon extended to Gönen.

Poimanenon was 160 stadia, *i.e.* 20 miles, from Aristides' estate north of Hadrianoutherai. On the way, 100 stadia from the estate, there were hot springs, which should easily be discovered. Those marked in Kiepert's new ancient map seem to be too far from Poimanenon. There were also hot springs on the Aisepos, two days' journey from Aristides' estate, and the way to them lay through Poimanenon. They are marked on Kiepert's new map, but I do not know whether he has |actual information about them or only inserts them from Aristides.

M. Waddington and Dr. Lolling* prefer the form Ποίμανος for the town. This, however, is a mistake, arising from a wrong conception of the origin of the name. It is true that Ποιμανηνοί are the people, and that the legend on coins is the genitive of the name of the people. But in this, as in many cases, the people are older and the town is later. There were Poimanenoi long before there was a χωρίον Ποιμανηνόν to serve as a central city. In this way there was not a city Poimanos, giving name to the people Poimanenoi, but only a people Poimanenoi, some of whom lived in the Poimanenian town.† The hero Poimes is probably a mere eponymous invention.

10. LENTIANA was a district, a range of mountains or a hilly country, and a town in the neighbourhood of Poimanenon. The two are frequently named together.‡ In 1223 the Emperor John Vatatzes, after the battle of Poimanenon, captured Poimanenon, Lentiana, Kharioros, and Berbeniakon (Acropol., p. 38). Comparing a passage of Anna (II., 280) we find that Lentiana lay between Cyzicos and Poimanenon, and from Acropolita (p. 31) we see that Lentiana, the town, was close to Poimanenon, so that Kharioros and Berbeniakon are further north. Another passage (Acrop., p. 13) mentions the Frankish territory in Mysia, apparently counting from west to east, Baris and Aulonia and Poimanenon and the Lentiana up to Lopadion.

* Le Bas-Waddington, No. 1761; Lolling, 'Athen. Mittheil.,' 1884, p. 29.

† The same principle must be applied in many other cases, especially in Cappadocia, where we find Μελιτηνή and numerous other adjectival forms. But in Phrygia Bria is to be restored in place of Briana, both on account of the sense (Βρία = town) and on account of the entry in some lists ὁ 'Ιβρίων. This Bria was doubtless "the town" which a people of name unknown to us looked to as their centre (CB., Part I., § xx.).

‡ τῶν 'Ρωμαϊκῶι. αστέων Λεντιανῶι καὶ Ποιμανηνοῦ (Acropol., p. 31).

11. KATOIRAIKIA was a place close to Lentiana, which is mentioned only by Anna Comnena (II. 310).

12. KIMINAS was a mountain adjoining Akhyraous,* mentioned not rarely by late writers. Its situation is implied to be north or west from Akhyraous in the description which Georg. Acropolita (p. 30) gives of the territory belonging respectively to the Franks and to Theodore Lascaris. The latter possessed the country from the Kaikos valley southwards, and from Lopadion eastwards. The Franks had the north-west corner of Mysia, including the whole of Kiminas and even Akhyraous: Akhyraous was the extreme limit of their territory.† This mountain is often mentioned as an abode of monks and hermits.‡

13. BARIS, near the mouth of the river Barenos (which is apparently the Granicus), is probably the scene of the great defeat inflicted by the Arabs on the Thrakesian troops, A.D. 774. Theophanes (p. 456) gives the scene of the battle as Darenos, and a neighbouring place as Banes. It is usual to understand Banes as the lake of Nikomedeia, which was called by later writers Baanes, and so Zonaras takes it. But probably the reading in both cases should be corrected and we should then have ἐν τόπῳ λεγομένῳ Βαρηνῷ, and ἐκράτησε τὴν Βαρήν (i.e. Βαρίν). The circumstances show that this situation is required, while a situation on the lake of Nikomedeia is impossible. Harun advanced as far as the Bosphorus at Chrysopolis: he, therefore, was west of the lake. He detached Bourniche towards Asia, and this detachment defeated the Thrakesian general (who had probably advanced so as to be ready to act in defence of Constantinople). The battle took place near the boundaries of the Opsikian and Thrakesian Themes, but in the former, on the western side of Baris; but fresh troops from Constantinople seized Baris and intercepted the retreat of the Arabs. Baris probably commanded the passage of the river. Moreover Anastasius has Barim.

14. MILETOPOLIS is commonly placed at Mualitch, between the Makestos and the Rhyndakos, at their junction; but it is, in that case, hard to see, in the present state of the maps, why the lake to the west should be called Miletopolitis. We should rather expect the city close to the lake.§ Still, it is certain that Miletopolis and Lopadion were not far from each other, as they were in later Byzantine time united in one bishopric. This is stated in an unpublished Notitia Episcopatuum, in a MS. of the Bibliothèque Nationale, Paris, No. 1356, fol. 287-8. This

---

* τὸ ὄρος τὸ ἐγγὺς τῆς Ἀχυράους τυγχάνον (Georg. Acropol., 30).

† τὰ μὲν τοῦ Κιμινᾶ πάντα μετὰ καὶ αὐτῆς τῆς Ἀχυράους (id., ib).

‡ Act. S. Athanasii Conf., July 5, p. 247: "est vero mons hic Kyminas in Asia, altus et prope impervius; in quo erat monasterium cui praerat Michael cognomine Malinus." τοῖς ἐν ὄρεσι μοναχοῖς, τῷ τε Ὀλύμπῳ καὶ τῷ Κομινᾷ καὶ τῇ Χρυσῇ κατονομαζομένῃ Πέτρᾳ καὶ τοῦ Βαραχαίου ὄρει (Theophan. Cont., p. 419): ἐκ τοῦ περιωνύμου ὄρους Ὀλύμπου Ἄθω τε καὶ τῆς Ἴδης ἄλλα μὴν καὶ τοῦ κατὰ Κυμινᾶν συμπληρώματος (Genes., p. 82).

§ See, however, § 7. The name of the lake is more natural, if the Milatai lived on its southern and eastern shores.

MS. contains a list of the same class as Parthey's X., and agreeing with it down to the thirtieth Archbishopric, ἡ Γοτθία · ἡ Κόδρος. In the next place it originally added λα'. τὸ Λοπάδιον; but this is erased, and a note in red added at the foot of the page, τὸ Λοπάδιον ὕστερον γέγονε · συνήφθη δὲ αὐτῷ καὶ ἡ Μελιτούπολις ἐπισκοπὴ οὖσα πρότερον τοῦ Κυζίκου.* At the end of the list of Archbishoprics another addition to X. occurs, The last entry is μ'. τὸ Διδυμότειχον · εἶτα γέγονε μητρόπολις τὸ Λοπάδιον, συναφθὲν τῇ Μελιτουπόλει. This note is in black ink, written continuously with the rest of the Notitia.

As to the date of this event, it is later than the elevation of Kybistra-Herakleia to the rank of an archbishopric about A.D. 1059–64. It is also later than Nilus Doxapatrius, whose list, written 1142–3, gives Herakleia Kybistra, but not Lopadion, among the Archbishoprics. It is older than the changes introduced by Andronicus (1283–1328).

Philetus was bishop of Miletopolis in the latter part of the third century, when Parthenius was born. Parthenius was consecrated bishop of Lampsakos between 312 and 330 by Ascholius (or Achillius), bishop of Cyzicos. Eustathius was bishop of Parion when Parthenius died (Act. Sanct., Feb. 7, p. 40).

15. LOPADION, which still retains its name as Ulubad, is very frequently mentioned in the later Byzantine wars. Lopadion was an important point, as there was there a bridge over the Rhyndakos. This bridge was built later than 258, when the Scythians, who had plundered Nikomedeia, Nikaia, Kios, Apameia, and Prousa, found it impossible to cross the Rhyndakos, which was swoln with rain.† But in A.D. 1405 Musulman marched from Prousa, crossed the bridge at Lopadion and came to Pergamos, obviously by way of Akhyraous-Hadrianoutherai.‡ When this bridge was broken, it took a three days' journey over very difficult country to march round the south side of the lake and thus reach the west bank of the river, which could be crossed above the lake, but not below it (Ducas, p. 168).

16. ADRANEIA. The occurrence of Adraneia in Hellespontus in Notitiæ VIII. and IX. is a remarkable fact. They also give Hadriani in Bithynia Prima; and the question arises whether this is an error of double entry such as occasionally occurs in the Notitiæ, or whether there are really two distinct cities, Hadriani and Adraneia. In the first place, the name Hadriani often appears as Ἀδρανοῦς in the Notitiæ, while Adraneia appears in 458 as Andriane, so that there can be no doubt that the two names are the same. In the next place, Hadriani was actually on the frontier of the two provinces, and in the Roman

* It then continues, like X., λα'. ἡ Σουγδαῖα. λβ'. τὰ Ἡρακλέους. λγ'. αἱ Φοῦλλαι. A note in red is added (top of fol. 288 rᵒ), ἠνώθησαν ὕστερον ἡ Σουγδαία καὶ αἱ Φοῦλλαι, καὶ γέγονε μητρόπολις.

† Zosimus, I., 35, 2, p. 34.

‡ Ducas, p. 85. That he crossed a bridge is to be inferred from p. 168, which tells of the bridge being cut by Murad.

period it belonged to the province of Asia, while in the Byzantine period it seems to have been attached to Bithynia. The case, then, seems to be one of mere double entry; but then the question arises why only two of the Notitiæ place it in Hellespontus. The Council lists at the first glance seem to show that we must, after all, change our opinion, and admit that Adraneia, which is given as a bishopric of Hellespontus in Epist. Synodi Cyzicenæ, Conc. Chalced., and Conc. Nic. II., is not Hadriani of Bithynia transferred to the wrong province, for Nicephorus of Hadriani is regularly mentioned at Conc. Nic. II. among the Bithynian bishops, in addition to Basilius of Hadrianoutherai and Sisinnius of Adraneia in Hellespontus, and Nicetas* of Hadrianopolis in Honorias. The case is not so clear at Chalcedon, owing to the small number of bishops present from Bithynia,† but at least there can be no doubt that in both 451 and 458 a bishop David of Adrania or Andriana was subject to the Metropolitan of Cyzicos. It is, therefore, quite open to maintain, so far as the evidence of 451 and 458 is concerned, that Hadriani still was reckoned by the ecclesiastical system of the fifth century in its old Roman connection with the West, and not in the Byzantine connection with Bithynia and the East. This view accordingly might be unhesitatingly adopted were it not for the evidence of the Second Nicene Council. The probability is that some unknown fact, such as a quarrel between the Metropolitans of Nikomedeia and Cyzicos, underlies the double entry at that Council; each Metropolitan, insisting that Hadriani or Adrania belonged to his province, may have consecrated a bishop for the city. One Metropolitan would insist on the fact that Hadriani had always been in the civil administration of Bithynia,‡ the other would urge its old ecclesiastical connection with Cyzicos, and perhaps quote the evidence of the Council of Chalcedon. Notitiæ VIII., IX. seem to be under the influence of the older system; they are of the earliest class of Notitiæ, and then the only difficulty remaining is to explain why VII., the earliest of all, and usually very closely akin to VIII., IX., does not give Adraneia.

17. SKEPSIS took the name of Saint Cornelius the Centurion, who settled at Skepsis and converted the population and Demetrius the Prefect (Act. Sanct., Feb. 2). His grave was discovered in the beginning of the fifth century, when Silvanus was bishop of Troas.§ Apparently

* Nectarius or Nicetas; readings vary, but Nicetas is usual.

† At Chalcedon, Theophilus of Hadrianopolis in Honorias was represented by a presbyter, Pelagius; but neither Hadrianoi nor any other of the cities of Bithynia, except Nikomedeia, Nikaia, Kios, Apameia, and Chalcedon, were represented. Patricius of Hadrianopolis is really of Hadrianoutherai, as is proved by some of the lists and by the signatures of 458.

‡ Before this time it is true that the Themes had come into existence. Similar quarrels of an older date took place between Nikomedeia and Nikaia about Basilinopolis, and between Caesareia and Tyana about Doara, and of a later date as to whether Juliopolis-Basileion was subject to Ankyra or directly to Constantinople.

§ Silvanus was consecrated by Saint Atticus, who died 425 A.D.

it was at this time that the church which gave name to the city was dedicated. Another church was erected to Demetrius. On the death of Silvanus, Athanasius (who was bishop of Skepsis at the Council of Ephesos, A.D. 431) succeeded him at Troas, and Philostorgius was made bishop of Skepsis. It would appear, therefore, that the bishopric of Troas was a more desirable dignity than that of Skepsis.

18. ARTAKE was a town near Cyzicos, with a church of the Virgin (Theophan., p. 299). Procopius (B. Pers., p. 135) makes it a suburb of Cyzicos (προαστεῖον). Mount Dindymos overhung Cyzicos (Zos., II., 31, p. 97).

19. ARTÁNAS, a river of Bithynia, must be distinguished from Lake Artynias or Apolloniatis (v. Addenda).

20. SIGRIANE. The hilly country between Cyzicos and the mouth of the Rhyndakos was called Sigriane. In some places the hills reached down to the water's edge. There was in it a monastery, founded by Theophanes at a place named Agros, twelve miles from Hieria * (Theophan., II., pp. 7, 19, 26). The Μεγάλος Ποταμός mentioned as the eastern boundary is probably the Rhyndakos. The harbour frequently mentioned under the name of Pegai was on the eastern side of the Sigriane, for John Vatatzes traversed that district on his march from Lampsakos to Pegai (Georg. Acrop., p. 73). The Latins, marching from Kenkhreai and Lampsakos to Pegai, reduced on the way the fort Keramides, near Cyzicos.† This last passage might alone be taken to imply that Sigrene or Sigriane was close to Lampsakos on the east, but the other passages seem to show that it was further away from Lampsakos.

21. KENKHREAI was a fortress near the river Scamander.‡ The passage just quoted from Georgius Acropolita (pp. 50-1) might suggest that it was close to the sea, for the Latins are said to have marched along the coast while the Greeks kept on the high ground above them; and thus the Latins only succeeded in traversing the not great distance from Lampsakos to Kenkhreai. But, as I do not know the country, I follow the authority of Mr. J. T. Clarke, who identifies it as Kiz Kalesi, a Byzantine ruin a little to the north of Chigri.§

22. Monasteries in the Troad are mentioned not unfrequently. In 974 the patriarch Basil was banished to τὸ κατὰ Σκάμανδρον φροντιστήριον, which he had built himself (Leo Diac., p. 163). A monastery named Pelekete, apparently near the Hellespont, is referred to in Act. Sanct., March 28, p. 732 (cp. Jan. 12). A country place, named Celæus or Κήλλιος, apparently near Lampsakos, is mentioned Act. Sanct., Feb. 7, p. 40. There was a monastery there of which the head, Leo præses Celleorum, was at the second Nicene Council (Act. IV.).

---

* This Hieria is different from the harbour in Bithynia, opposite Constantinople.
† περί που τοὺς βουνοὺς διακειμενον τῆς Κυζίκου (Georg. Acrop., pp. 50-1).
‡ ἐν ταῖς κατὰ Σκάμανδρον Κεγχρεαῖς ἀπανθρώπῳ τινὶ φρουρίῳ (Georg. Pach., I., 485. II., 443).   § 'Amer. Jour. Arch.,' 1886, p. 140.

23. Ptelaia is mentioned as a place on the Hellespont in Acta S. Parthenii (Feb. 7, p. 41). He visited all the fishing emporia from Lampsakos as far as Abydos to stop the failure of the tunny fishery, and then he sat ἐν τῷ κατὰ Πτελαίας (vv. ll., Πτελέας, Πτελάρας) ἐμπορίῳ.

24. The river Rhyndakos changed its name, like almost all the others in this part of Asia Minor, before the time of Anna Comnena, who calls it Lampes,* as the Granikos became Barenos, and the Aisepos Angelokomites (see below, G § 17).

25. Metopa or Mesopa was a fort near the lake of Apollonia (Act. Sanct., Feb. 4, p. 543).

26. An inscription copied by Prof. Kiepert in the valley of the Granikos (Le Bas-Waddington, No. 1745) gives the name of six villages or χῶροι: viz. Mottianoi, Baisteanoi, Trinoixeitai, Ageanoi, Ilbeitenoi, Hykhantenoi.

27. Ἄπταος of Hierocles is possibly an error for Palaios or Palaia : a place of this name is mentioned by Strabo (p. 614) 130 stadia from Andeira. Paleos at the Second Nicene Council means Parion.

There are apparently three other places bearing this name in Asia Minor. Two of these are bishoprics mentioned in the Notitiæ, but not in Hierocles. One of them is in Galatia, the other in Lycia; and both have the alternative name Justinianopolis. The former has the forms Palia, Spaleia (i.e. s-Paleia), and Spania: the latter appears always in the genitive plural of the ethnic Παλιωτῶν, Παλλιωτῶν, Πολιοτῶν, Πολιωτῶν. Mordtmann, in his excellent paper 'Gordium, Pessinus, und Sivri Hissar' † remarked that Palia of Galatia was probably one of the forts founded by Justinian to defend the empire, and might therefore be safely identified with the powerful fortress of Sivri Hissar, which is now the chief city of the district. The third is a fortress named Palia or Paleai in Isauria. The only reference to it which I have observed is in Ammianus, XIV. 2, 13 : " Robbers, coming from the neighbourhood of Laranda, locum petivere Paleas nomine, vergentem in mare, valido muro firmatum, ubi conduntur nunc usque commeatus distribui militibus omne latus Isauriae defendentibus adsueti." I do not believe that the name Paleai or Palia is connected with the Greek adjective παλαιός: it is more likely to be a native word, resembling the Greek in sound. Three of the places named Palia appear to have been fortresses: and hence the set of names in Teichos and Charax suggest themselves for comparison Abonoteichos, Gordiouteichos, Panemouteichos, Neon Teichos, Hierocharax, Charax Alexandri, Charax.

28. The Acta S. Philetaeri (Act. Sanct., May 19, p. 316) contain some curious particulars about a journey from Nikaia towards Prokonessos. The Saint was conducted by the soldiers, after crossing the Rhyndakos, past Seroukome, to a village beside the river Koasta, and

---

* Anna, vol. I., p. 315, τὸν Λάμπην · ποταμὸς οὗτος περὶ Λοπάδιον.

† Munch. Gel. Anz., 1862.

not very far from a place named Kastallis. From Kastallis they did not take the direct road towards Cyzicos, but went through a village Kleodous and a place (or river?) Stribos to Poketos or Kopetos, where there was a sacred grove of cypresses (τὰ δένδρα τὰ ἀπὸ ἀνατολῆς ἐστῶτα τῶν κυπαρίσσων μέγιστα ὄντα ἐξέκοψαν, διὰ τὸ μάλιστα τοὺς Ἕλληνας ἐν ἐκείναις ταῖς κυπαρίσσοις τὰς πλεῖον θυσίας ἐπιτελεῖν). These Acta date from a much later time, and are of suspicious character, but may contain topographical fact. The reference to the sacred trees is interesting: the oldest religious document of the Troad, the Hymn to Aphrodite, and this the latest reference to the old religion, alike mention holy trees. From Poketos the guards went on to Cyzicos.

29. Beside the hot springs of Artemaia on the Aisepos, and those between Hadrianoutherai and Poimanenon, there were also hot springs at Daskylon, and at Larissa in the Troad, not far from Alexandria Troas. The list of Therma given by Athenæus II., p. 43, may here be quoted in full, as it is often referred to in these pages:—τά τ᾽ ἐν τῇ Τρωικῇ Λαρίσσῃ, καὶ περὶ Μαγνησίαν, ... ἐν δὲ Προύσῃ τῇ πρὸς τὸν Μύσιον Ὄλυμπον τὰ βασιλικὰ καλούμενα · τὰ δ᾽ ἐν Ἀσίᾳ περὶ Τράλλεις καὶ τὸν [Ἀ]χαρα[κα]κωμήτην ποταμὸν, ἔτι δὲ Νῦσαν πόλιν, οὕτως ἐστὶ λιπαρά ὡς μὴ δεῖσθαι τοὺς ἐναπολουμένους ἐλαίου. τοιαῦτα καὶ τὰ ἐν Δασκύλου Κώμῃ· τὰ δ᾽ ἐν Καρούροις κατάξηρα καὶ σφόδρα θερμά · τὰ δὲ περὶ Μηνὸς Κώμην, ἥ ἐστι Φρυγίας, τραχύτερά ἐστι καὶ λιτρωδέστερα, ὡς καὶ [τὰ] ἐν τῇ καλουμένῃ Λέοντος Κώμῃ τῆς Φρυγίας · τὰ δὲ περὶ Δορύλαιον καὶ πινόμενά ἐστι ἥδιστα.

30. Saint Philotheos was born in the village Myrmex in the Opsikian Theme (Act. Sanct., Sept. 15). It is probable that Marpessos, Marmessos, Mermessos, Myrmex and Myrmissos are forms of the same name : most of these forms are recognised by Forbiger as varying names of a place east of Lampsakos, birthplace of a Sibyl.

E. Roman Roads in the Province Asia.

1. The roads of this province are too well defined to require any special treatment. I have discussed some of them in my Contributions to the History of Southern Æolis, part I. The road from Ephesos to Magnesia, Tralleis, Antiocheia, Laodiceia, and Apameia, built by Manius Aquilius about 130 B.C., was continued by him along the southern frontier of the province through Ilyas or Elyes (perhaps Okoklia) as far as Takina, as is shown by a milestone there with the distance 223 g. In all probability Manius built the entire circle of roads Apameia-Takina-Kibyra, and Laodiceia - Themissonion - Kibyra. The exact distance in Roman miles from Ephesos to Tralleis is known from a milestone to be 32, and I have calculated the distances to Laodiceia as 107, and to Apameia as 173. The road is so extraordinarily distorted in the Peutinger Table that nothing can be learned from it.

2. The road from Ephesos to Smyrna and Cyzicos is given in the Peutinger Table as :—

Ephesus—Metropolis—Smyrna xxxiii Cyme viiii Marinna (*i.e.* Myrina) xii Ela[ea] xvi Pergamo xxxv Argesis xxx Phemenio (*i.e.* Poimanenon)—Cyzico.*

The following distances on this road can be determined in Roman miles. Ephesos to Smyrna must have been 45 miles : though Strabo gives it as only 320 stadia. I estimated the number formerly as 44 from the map, and am now able to appeal to the following passage.

Tchineit started from Amorion, crossed Phrygia Salutaris, came down to Laodiceia, and thence passed by Sardis to Nymphaion. Here he turned to the right, and, crossing by the ravine, descended on Triakonta, which is still known as Trianda. He crossed on the same day the mountains extending towards Galesion and the sea (τὰ πρὸς Γαλήσιον ὄρος κείμενα πρὸς θάλατταν ὄρη) and reached Hypsele in the first watch of night.† In the account given by Ducas (p. 194) of this hurried march, it is obvious that there is only one error : Laodiceia has been substituted for Philadelpheia. To one who knows the country, none of the way which Tchineit traversed is doubtful. On the other hand, it would be an enormous détour to go by Laodiceia, and from Laodiceia it would again be an enormous détour to go by Sardis. The name Τριάκοντα is important : it obviously means the thirtieth mile from Ephesos. Names of that kind are very common, as may be seen in the index to Parthey and Pinder's edition of the Itineraries under " Vigesimum," " Tricensimum." The railway has a station, Trianda, but not actually at the village ; the distance of this station from Ephesos is 23¼ English miles, say 25 Roman ; the modern village seems to be quite 3 Roman miles to the north of the station. The total is still only 28 miles ; but the ancient village may have been situated a little more towards Smyrna, and been slightly moved towards the south, though the name remains. Allowing for the change, it still appears necessary to measure 15 or 16 miles on to Smyrna, so that the total distance ‡ is 45 or 46.

The road from Smyrna to Ephesos still leaves Smyrna by a gate on the south-west, and passes on the west side of Pagos : this was also the line of the ancient road, and with the best measurements I can make the distance must be given as 45 miles.

Strabo gives 200 stadia from Metropolis to Smyrna, 120 from Metropolis to Ephesos. The latter number is clearly wrong, as the distance is fully 20 English miles ; if we take it as 160, we have the whole distance Smyrna to Ephesos 360 stadia or 45 miles.

A milestone (Le Bas, No. 6), stated to have been found at Burnabat,

---

* Phemenio, Pergamos, Argesis, are all ablatives.

† Hypsele, near the ancient Lebedos, is still called Ipsili Hisar.

‡ Owing to the great détour on the railway, the distance, 26¾, measured from the Smyrna station to Trianda, is of no use for estimating the Roman road.

but really, as I have been informed by M. Weber, found beside the sea where it approaches nearest to Burnabat, bears a number M., which may indicate any number from 41 to 49. The point where it was found must be quite 3 miles from the "Ephesian Gates" of Smyrna, so that M[H] or M[Θ] is the probable reading. The distances between Smyrna and Pergamos seem to be accurate, so far as I can judge. The distance to Elaea from Ephesos, then, is 99 miles, and it is hard to see how the reading Π H, 88, can appear on the milestone above mentioned. M. S. Reinach informed me that the stone is so large that the idea of its having been transported cannot be entertained.* There is, therefore, no apparent solution except that the number was carelessly inscribed, and that the true reading is 98, which is exactly correct, as the stone is a little south of Elaea.

3. At Pergamos the road forked, one branch to Adramyttion and the Troad, one to Cyzicos, and one to Miletopolis. A milestone found near Dikeli, on the former road, has the number PΛΑ, cxxxi. As we have seen, the distances Ephesos to Pergamos are correct on the Table, and the total distance is 115: the milestone gives a number a little greater than we should expect, and therefore proves that our estimate of the distance to Pergamos is not exaggerated.

The numbers given in the Table between Pergamos and Lampsakos are so utterly discrepant from those in the Antonine Itinerary that nothing is to be gained from a comparison except by one who knows the country far better than I do.†

4. Two roads led from Pergamos across country to the Sea of Marmora, one to Cyzicos, the other to Miletopolis. They are given in the Table as—

      (1) Pergamo xxxv Argesis xxx Phemenio—Cyzico.
      (2) Pergamo viii Hadreanuteba xxxiii Milepoli.

Galen mentions that Ergasteria was 440 stadia (say 55 miles) from Pergamos on the road to Cyzicos. It must be placed in an intermediate position between Poimanenon and Argesis of the Table. Poimanenon was 280 stadia from Cyzicos, which gives the distance omitted in the Table as xxxv. The sum of distances point to point is then 100 M. P. : and the distance in an air-line on Kiepert's recent map is about 95 English miles. We should expect therefore a larger total of Roman miles, for the proportion to air distance in the best known cases is decidedly greater. Perhaps restore

      Pergamos 35 Argesis 20 Ergasteria 20 Poimanenos 35 Cyzicos :
      total 110. Sée Addenda.

---

* The doubt which I formerly expressed as to the reading is now set at rest, and M. Fontrier's copy is justified.

† Mr. J. T. Clarke's restoration ('American Journal of Archæology,' 1888, p. 296) is "Adramyttion xvi Antandros xxi Gargara viiii Assos xv Sminthion." The distance of the Itinerary from Pergamos to Adramyttion, xxxi, should probably be increased by x. The Table gives two roads, one direct, and one along the coast. On the latter, Attalia should be changed to Attaia, as M. Radet has correctly observed.

Neither of the distances on the other road is correct: possibly it should be—

Pergamos LIII Hadrianoutherai XXXXIII Miletopolis,
but the total distance must be rather greater.

The position of the towns on these roads is discussed under HELLES-PONTUS.

5. The direct road from Miletopolis, or rather from Lopadion, which was the more important point in later time, to Thyatira and the Hermos valley, is frequently mentioned in Byzantine writers, but is not given in the older authorities. It passed by Akhyraous. References to it are made under Stratonicea Lydiae and Akhyraous Hellesponti, also F 10.

6. The road Pergamos by Germe, Nakrasa, and Sardis, to Laodiceia on the Lykos, is given both in the Antonine Itinerary and the Peutinger Table, and is historically a very important route. As the two authorities agree almost perfectly, they may be accepted as fairly correct—

Pergamos XXV Germe XXXIII Thyateira XXXVI Sardis XXVIII Philadelpheia XXXIII Tripolis XII Hierapolis VI Laodiceia,*
Only one of these numbers is certainly wrong. From Germe to Thyateira should be XXIII, not XXXIII.

The Table also gives a direct road from Thyateira to Philadelpheia with the distance XXV. This road is a mere error arising from bad drawing. The road *viâ* Sardis is really direct.

7. The distance given by Strabo, 300 stadia or 37½ miles, between Apollonis and Pergamos, is measured along a direct hill-road. He gives the same distance between Sardis and Apollonia, which is correct.

8. The direct road from Ephesos to Sardis passed through Hypaipa (beside Odemish) at the southern end of the pass over Tmolos. Between Hypaipa and Ephesos the Table gives a place Anagome, which is clearly a corrupt form, perhaps concealing a name ending in κώμη.† If, as the Table implies, Anagome was a village at the fork of the roads to Metropolis and to Hypaipa, it would be near Kos Bunar, 9 miles from Ephesos, and XXXIIII from Hypaipa. The numbers on the Table would have to be transposed; the XX between Sardis and Hypaipa appears to be correct.

9. The road Smyrna-Temnos-Magnesia, forking there to Thyateira and Sardis is very badly given in the Table, Temnos being transferred to another road, and Magnesia being omitted. The distances approximately are—

Smyrna 25 Temnos 18 Magnesia (25 Thyateira or) 36 Sardis.

10. The direct road from Smyrna to Sardis, passing near Nymphaion, is omitted on the Table, but a number of milestones on it are

* The Table omits XXVIII after Sardis, and has a dislocation after Hierapolis; it has also XXXIIII before Tripolis.
† In Greek the name was perhaps of the form ·····ανὴ κώμη.

preserved (Le Bas-Wadd., 6–9 ; C. I. G., 3179, 3180). The distance is about 54 miles.

11. No record is preserved of a Roman road from Sardis by Maionia and Satala to Temenothyrai, Trajanopolis, and Akmonia, perhaps also forking at Satala to Kadoi and Aizanoi. The pass between Satala and Temenothyrai is very difficult, but in 1881 Sir C. Wilson and I observed remains of two Roman bridges over the Hermos in it. One lies above the modern path when it first reaches the Hermos after leaving Koula ; it is a mere ruin. The other much further on is still in use, and the repairs do not wholly hide the Roman work.

12. The roads in Phrygia are all determined by the fixing of the cities which they connected. Dorylaion was the most important road centre in the north. The road from the Bosphorus and Propontis to Kotiaion (see BITHYNIA) is not known to have been used in early time, and all communication with the north probably passed through Dorylaion and thence radiated south, south-west, and south-east.

13. The Peutinger Table gives a road, which may be completed thus—

> Dorylaion xxxv Kotiaion xxx* Appia xvi Hiérokharax xII
> Akmonia xv Aloudda xx Klannoudda (near Blaundos) xxxx
> Philadelphia.†

The eleventh milestone north of Akmonia, and several between Apia and Kotiaion are known and published (C. I. L., III., Supplem., No. 7170 and CB., § xcvIII.).

A milestone near Altyntash and other evidence stated below under ORKISTOS make it probable that the road Akmonia—Hierokharax—Soa—Meros—Pessinus was constructed in Roman time.

14. The Table gives a road which may be restored thus—

> Dorylaion xxvi Nakoleia xvIII Meros xII Metropolis vi Kone
> xI Kidyessos xII Brouzos Iv Hieropolis vII Eukarpia xv
> Aurokra vIII Apameia.

The Table omits the completion from Eukarpia by Aurokra to Apameia, but this must necessarily be restored. In place of this part of the line, the Table, owing to bad drawing,‡ carries on the route straight to Eumeneia and Apameia. But the road Eukarpia—Apameia really diverges from the other at either Brouzos or Hieropolis, and thence goes

---

* Called Cocleo in the Table.

† Akmonia is about five miles off the direct road, which passes through Keramon Agora (Islam Keui). Blaundos is about six miles south of Klannoudda. Perhaps Alia should come between Akmonia and Aloudda. There is no evidence that a road Kotiaion—Aizanoi—Synaos—Ankyra—Makestos-valley—Stratonikaia—Pergamos, or a road Kotiaion—Aizanoi—Kadoi—Satala—Maionia—Sardis, was in use. But the existence of two ancient bridges (see § 11) makes it probable that the road Akmonia—Trajanopolis—Temenothyrai—Satala—Maionia—Sardis was constructed.

‡ Or, as Prof. G. Hirschfeld puts it, " weite Ausladungen erscheinen als direkte Wege," n. 411, 412.

to Eumeneia, Peltai, Lounda, and Laodiceia. Of this road the Table gives the line only as far as Eumeneia, and then adds the name of Peltai (under the corruption Pella). The existence of the complete road is proved both by the name Peltai, and by the following milestone, copied by Hogarth and myself at Baljik Hisar, about its original position between Eumeneia and Peltai:—

ΑΓΑΘΗ τύχη
ΑΥΤΟΚΡΑΤΟΡΙ
καιϹΑΡΙ Γ ΜΕϹϹΙѠ
κυΙΝΤѠ ΤΡαι
ΑΝѠ ΔΕΚΙѠ ΚΑΙ
ΕΡΕΝΝΙΑ ἐΤΡΟΥϹ
ΚΙΛλη ϹΕΒΑϹΤΗ

M^I Δ

This milestone was probably erected in 249 A.D., and later there were added in smaller letters, irregularly engraved round the number, the names of the two Cæsars, [K]υίντῳ 'Ερεννί[ῳ] Δεκ[ί]ῳ καὶ 'Ε[τρ]ούσκ[ῳ ?] Κυίντῳ, neither completely nor accurately given.

The connection, Eumeneia XII ad Vicum XIIII Apameia, given in the Table is clearly only part of a road giving a route from Apameia to Philadelpheia and the Hermos valley, but no other evidence exists to prove it.

15. The Table gives a third road—

> Dorileo—Fl. Sagar—Docymeo XXXII Synnada Asynnade Vforbio
> mil. XXXVII. Euforbio. Ab Euforbio. Ab amea Mil. XXXVI
> Apamea Ciboton.

This road is a false one, due to incorrect drawing of the lines, one of the commonest sources of error in our copy of the Table. This road should go to Pessinus, and not to Dorylaion. The position of the river Sangarios shows this, and a consideration of the possible routes led me long ago to this conclusion (CB., § XXXVI.).

Prof. G. Hirschfeld, in his 'Report on our Geographical Knowledge of the Ancient Greek World,' advances a different opinion as to this and the preceding road. He considers that the road Synnada-Dokimion-Dorylaion coincides in more than half of its length with the road Eucarpia-Nakoleia-Dorylaion. He therefore apparently holds that the road Dokimion-Dorylaion turned westwards to Metropolis or north-west to Meros, and thus coincided with it through Nakoleia to Dorylaion.* The point is one which cannot be determined; I cannot prove that there was not a Roman road from Dokimion to Metropolis or to Meros. I can only say that I for a time held the view that this road joined the other

---

* Unless this road joined the other a good way south of Meros, it could not coincide with it for more than half its length.

at Meros,* and was, after careful examination, obliged to give up this opinion: as to a road Dokimion-Metropolis-Meros-Nakoleia, I hardly think that Prof. Hirschfeld can have thought of it. Moreover, the simplest and easiest way of bringing the names and lines in the Table into harmony with each other and with the facts is to suppose that the line Dokimion-Sangarios-Pessinus had been drawn awry, so as to touch the line Dorylaion-Pessinus, &c., at the wrong place. Then two names which should fall between *flumen Sangarios* and *Dokimion*, viz. Amorion and Abrostola, got out of their right position: they continued to hold their place near Pessinus, but as the line Pessinus-Dokimion had ceased to exist, they got into the line Pessinus-Archelais.

16. The route from Dokimion to the coast is commercially almost the most important in Asia Minor. The road along which the enormous monolithic columns of Dokimian marble were transported as early as the time of Strabo must have been well-constructed and carefully kept. Its course is now quite certain. It passed through Synnada, where the central office for managing the quarries was situated, and which gave its name to the marble. Between Dokimion and Synnada was Prymnessos, a little west of the direct and easy path, but yet necessarily included in the XXXII miles placed by the Table between Dokimion and Synnada.† The road went straight south from Synnada to Metropolis by a route vià Baljik Hisar, crossing a lofty ridge by a finely engineered path, the cuttings and curves of which can still be observed.‡

The approximate distances are: Synnada to Metropolis XVIII miles, Metropolis to Apameia XXIV.

This road was, as I believe, constructed by the Romans. Before their time the case was probably the same as at the present day: there was a horse-road over the mountains, and a waggon-road round the détour by Uzun Bunar. Manlius, who was accompanied by an army heavily laden with plunder, must have taken the waggon-road, and Diniae, through which he passed, must be sought on it. Alcibiades, on the other hand, was more likely to travel by the direct horse-road, and MELISSA, where he was killed, was on the road between Synnada and Metropolis,§ and may be sought at Baljik Hisar, where there are said to be remains on a hill round which the road winds.

* At an earlier time I had fancied that the road Dokimion—Dorylaion joined the other at Nakoleia. This opinion also I had to abandon, or rather it is a bad way of saying that the road Dokimion—Pessinus intersected at Bayat the road Dorylaion— Nakoleia—Polybotos—Julia—Philomelion—Ikonion, so important in later time.

† The actual distance is about xxv miles at most, but if Prymnessos and the détour be counted in, we have 15 + 17. M. Choisy took seven hours to the journey from Afiom Kara Hisar to Synnada, and estimates the distances from 25 to 30 kilom. (15 to 18 miles): I took five hours ten minutes to the journey, and estimated the distance at 17 to 18 miles. Prymnessos is about two miles nearer Synnada.

‡ I wrongly believed formerly (CB., LXI.) that the road made a long détour to the east to avoid this lofty ridge. Until I crossed it, I thought that the monolithic columns could not have been carried over it.   § Athenæus, XIII. p. 574, F.

17. Strabo describes, after Artemidorus, the great caravan-route from Ephesos to Apameia to the east. Between Metropolis and the borders of Paroreios Phrygia at Holmoi it did not take the route by Synnada, which the Roman governors preferred. Now the natural path is by Oinan and Geneli. This path is singularly easy and is throughout practicable for carriages at the present day. Artemidorus probably wrote before the direct road Metropolis to Synnada was made: but even after that road was built it is hardly conceivable that merchandise should be carried round Lysias—Synnada—Metropolis, when there is a far shorter and more level road Lysias—Geneli—Oinia —Metropolis. Even without any artificial causeway, this natural path is perfectly easy for vehicles. Khelidonion then is to be sought about either Geneli or Oinia. The route by which Manlius marched co-incides with this road until it enters the Oinan Ova, and then turns off to the north. Dinia, through which Manlius passed, seems to be the second part of Khelidonia (for the difference of vowel is paralleled by the two forms Siblia and Soublaion), and therefore Dinia—Kheli-donia must be in the south-western end of the Oinan Ova.

19. The line Dorylaion 26 Nakoleia 12 Santabaris 9 Kakka-bokome 18 Etsya 15 Polybotos—Julia—Philomelion—Hadrianopolis—Kaballa—Ikonion became important after Constantinople was made the capital, but it is very doubtful whether it existed in the Roman period. It may, however, have been represented on the Table, which gives the routes radiating from Constantinople, for part of it, viz., the direct road Philomelion—Kaballa—Ikonion was given on the original from which our copy is taken, and this part has no importance except as the completion of the shortest line from Constantinople to Ikonion.

The observation, which Prof. Hirschfeld made, that circuitous routes are often given on the Table as direct (and, I will add, direct routes as circuitous) is a valuable one, and many examples of it occur in this paper. But a zigzag route on the Table serves as a proof that the complete roads, of which parts are given in the zigzag, already existed.

20. The route Smyrna — Sardis—Philadelphia —- Akmonia—Hiero-kharax—Aristion—Kidyessos—Prymnessos has been one of the important trade-routes in modern time, but apparently it was not constructed in Roman time. The trade of Dokimion and Prymnessos passed to the coast by Synnada and Apameia.

21. The Boundaries of Roman Asia are traced with approximate correctness by M. Waddington in Chap. II. of his 'Fastes des Provinces Asiatiques,' p. 25. His words are: " Commençant par le nord, le cours du Rhyndacus servait d'abord de limite (Plin., H. N., V., 142) jusque un peu au-delà de la ville d'Hadriani, qui appartenait à l'Asie et non à la Bithynie; la frontière se dirigeait ensuite à l'est, passant au nord de Dorylaeum [atteignait probablement le Sangarius],* puis redescendait

* Omit the words in brackets, which are due to the bad representation of the Sangarios in old maps.

au midi, en passant à l'est de Midaeum,* d'Amorium et de Philo-melium,† qui était la ville la plus orientale de la province." The rest of his description can be given more accurately. The boundary passed south of Hadrianopolis, and there turned north-west along the Sultan Dagh, leaving Neapolis and Antioch out, till it reached the long ridge which separates the valleys of Karamük, Oinan, and Tchul, from the country that drains into the great lakes Hawiran and Egerdir, which, as Hirschfeld has suggested, were probably known as Limnai. The boundary ran along this ridge till it came to the valley of Dombai (Aurokra), when it turned south to include the valley in Asia. One of the boundaries is still preserved in this part. The road from Apameia to Apollonia, after passing close over Aurokreni Fontes, reaches a small village Tchapali, and ascends a long steep slope. At the top of this slope there is a large pillar, square in plan, with base and capital of very slightly ornamental type: the pillar is now lying flat on the ground, but originally stood on a low circular basement, which still remains in a fragmentary state. On one side of the pillar is the following inscription ‡:—

	ΥΠΕΡΤΗϹΑΥΤΟΚΡΑ	ὑπὲρ τῆς αὐτοκρά-
	ΤΟΡΟϹΚΑΙϹΑΡΟϹΘΕ	τορος καίσαρος, θε-
	ΟΥΤΡΑΙΑΝΟΥΠΑΡΘΙ	οῦ Τραιανοῦ Παρθι-
	ΟΥΝ ΟΥΑΥΙ	κοῦ υἱοῦ, θε]οῦ Ν[ερ]ούα υἱ-
5	ΟΥΤΡΑΙΑΝΟΥΑΔΡΙ	ων]οῦ, Τραιανοῦ Ἀδρι[α-
	ΑϹΤΟΥΑΡΧΙΕΡΕ	νοῦ σεβ]αστοῦ, ἀρχιερέ-
	ΜΕΓΙϹΤΟΥΔΗΜΑΡ	ως] μεγίστου, δημαρ-
	ΟΥϹΙΑϹΤΟΙΟ	χικῆς ἐξ]ουσίας τὸ ιθ΄,
	ΥΠΑΤΟΥΤΟΓΠΑΤΡΟϹΠΑΤ	ὑπάτου τὸ γ΄, πατρὸς πατ-
10	ΟϹ ΙΑϹΚΑΙΑΙωΝ	ρίδ]ος, [σωτηρ]ίας καὶ αἰων-
	ϹΑΥΤΟΥΤΕΚΑΙ	ίου διαμονῆ]ς αὐτοῦ τε καὶ
	ΠΑΝΤΟϹΟΙΚΟΥ	τοῦ σύμ]παντος οἴκου
	ΟΥΗΒΟΥΛΗΚΑΙΟ	αὐτ]οῦ, ἡ βουλὴ καὶ ὁ
	ΔΗΜΟϹΟΑΠΟΛΛωΝΙΑ	δῆμος ὁ Ἀπολλωνια-
15	ΛΥΚΙωΝΚΑΙΘΡΑ	τῶν], Λυκίων καὶ Θρᾳ
	ωΝωΝΘΕΟΙϹ	κῶν κολ]ώνων, Θεοῖς
	ΝΟΡΙΟΙϹ	Ε]νορίοις

This dedication is dated in A.D. 135.

From this point the boundary ran to the village of Baradis, where the following boundary-stone was copied by me in 1882:—

FINIS

CAESARIS N

This stone probably indicates the boundary of an imperial estate, which included the rich valley of Ketchi Borlu and Kilij, and which was

* For Midaeum read Akkilaion, and add "de Troknades, d'Orkistos" before "d'Amorium."

† For Philomelium read Thymbrion-Hadrianopolis.

‡ I saw it first in 1882, when travelling with Sir Charles Wilson. It was in such a position that it could not be read. In 1888 I returned to the place, and after five hours' work, got the stone turned and the inscription copied.

included among the Phrygian estates directed perhaps by the Procurator Phrygiae. South and east of this boundary the territory belongs to Galatia, in which the city Konane was included.

The lake of Buldur (Askania) was probably the boundary, and near its south-western end at the village of Deuer, we find another boundary (which I copied in 1884), τὰ μὲν ἐν δεξιᾷ εἶναι Σαγαλασσέων, τὰ δὲ ἐν ἀριστερᾷ κώμης Τυμβριανασσοῦ Νέρωνος Κλαυδίου Καίσαρος. This imperial estate immediately adjoined the territory of Takina, which belonged to Phrygian Asia. It is therefore probable that it, like the other estates* Alastos and Ormeleis, was included among the Phrygian estates. The boundary, therefore, must have passed between Lysinia and Tymbrian-assos, and between Olbasa and the Ormeleis. We can then understand why a mile-stone at Hedje gives the distance from Kibyra. The whole line of this road† from Kibyra to Apameia by Ormeleis, Alastos, and Tymbrianassos, was in the province of Asia. The division between Asia and Galatia (after 74 A.D. between Asia and Lycia-Pamphylia) lay along the centre of a valley, a remarkable line.‡

After passing Olbasa the boundary turned south, probably along the upper waters of the Lysis, and included Lagbe in Asia. It then turned west, passing through the lake Karalitis, until it touched the river Indos, down whose course it went to the sea. See Addenda.

The boundaries of the Byzantine provinces have been given in the discussion of the cities in each province.

22. It will be useful here to recapitulate the imperial properties whose existence in the Roman province of Asia has been established on certain or probable grounds. First may be mentioned the great estates, probably continuous with each other, of the Ormeleis (afterwards called Maximianopolis), including Alastos, and Tymbrianasa.§

The inscriptions of this district are dated as a rule according to an ἐπίτροπος, πραγματευταί, and μισθωταί, i.e. a procurator Augusti, negotia-tores, and conductores.‖ The population of such an estate had a peculiar standing in Roman law, and the inscriptions show that the Ormeleis also had a peculiar organisation. Their magistrate or official is called

---

* See § 22 and Addenda to A, 42.

† This corrects some details in ASP.

‡ It is paralleled by some of the later divisions: Byzantine Caria and Lydia are separated by the Maeander, and take each half of the valley; Byzantine Lydia and Phrygia also are separated by the Maeander, Tripolis, which is in full view of Hierapolis, being part of Lydia. So on the south the Lysis may have been the line separating the two provinces.

§ In ASP., D 22-5, I described the general character of these estates. Franz on C. I. G., No. 4366 w, and MM. Duchesne and Collignon in 'Bull. Corr. Hell.,' 1878, misunderstand the character of the inscriptions, and speak of the pragmateutes as a sort of Archon Eponymos. The help of Mr. Pelham has enabled me to add greatly to the number of points which prove that the inscriptions were erected by the coloni of three imperial estates.

‖ The rendering actores would be more accurate for πραγματευταί; see Addenda.

προ ίγων, perhaps a translation of praepositus.*   A Proagon occurs also in two inscriptions of Pisidia, now widely separated, but perhaps originating from Bindeos (Sterrett, II. 89 and III. 465): see § 26.

The little information that we gather from the Ormelian inscriptions relates to their contributions for the benefit of the community; and usually the inscription begins with a vow for the health of the emperor: compare " pro salute imp. Caes. etc.: coloni saltus Massipiani aedificia vetustate conlapsa s(ua) p(ecunia) r(estituerunt), item arcus duos a(ere) s(uo) f(ecerunt) " (C. I. L. VIII. 587).† Similar constructions at the expense of coloni are often alluded to: " pro salute imp. Gordiani, etc.: murus constitutus a colonis eius castelli Cellensis" (Wilm. 756); "porticum ex pecunia saltuariorum " (C. I. L. IX. 3386). The frequently recurring phrase ἐτίμησε τὸν ὄχλον is perhaps equivalent to "contributed for the benefit of the community." Ἐτίμησε τὸν ὄχλον ἄριστον καὶ ἀττικὰς τό, " contributed a breakfast and 380 Attic drachmae," occurs.‡ The community is called ὄχλος: this seems to be a translation of *populus plebeius*, which was the proper term for the inhabitants of an estate (*saltus*: cp. Frontinus, ed. Lachm., p. 53; Fustel des Coulanges, ' Recherches sur quelques Problèmes d'Histoire,' p. 27).

There was in the provinces a procurator or rationalis, who administered the estates and revenues of the emperor. He was the official who exercised all real power, even that of life and death, in an imperial estate, and hence the Ormeleis date their inscriptions by his name. He let out the imperial properties in the province to conductores; and there were apparently three lots of property, let to three conductores, in the country of the Ormeleis.

The proper marking of the bounds of an imperial property was of course a duty of the procurator, and he was also bound to prevent discrderly persons from entering the estate (Dig. I. 19, 3). Among the Ormeleis the duty of protecting the boundaries and acting as guards was discharged by different corps called παραφυλακῖται: οἱ ἐν Ἀλάστῳ παραφυλακῖται were the corps who guarded Alastos, one of the three properties. We also hear of individuals called ὀροφύλακες. These correspond to the "saltuarii qui finium custodiendorum causa" (Dig. XXXIII. 7, 12), who were under the orders of the procurator.

About the three conductores we can gather very little from the inscriptions that are preserved. The conductor was close to the coloni, and his power must have been almost greater than that of the distant procurator, so long as he paid his rent and kept on good terms with the

---

* Unless προάγων, or προαγών, be President of the Games, which are a feature of Pisidian life and coins; but " Praepositus vect. ferr." (O. Hirschf., ' Röm. Verwalt.-Gesch.,' p. 86): for 'praepositus pagi': see C. Theod. xii. 1, 49, xii. 6, 8, ' praepositura horreorum et pagorum': Voigt, Drei Epigr. Constitutionen, p. 182.

† " r(efecerunt) " and " a s(olo) " (Henzen, 5313).

‡ Wrongly transcribed ἄριστον καὶ ἀ[νε]ικαστό[τατον] by Mr. Sterrett, ' Epigr. Journey,' No. 52, l. 9.

latter. Hence at Lagbe, fines for violation of the tomb were sometimes made payable to the local conductor (τῷ κατὰ τόπον μισθωτῇ), so as to ensure his aid in the prosecution of any violator. One of the conductores of the property at Alastos, M. Calpurnius Epineikos, was a freedman *a cubiculo* of a Roman named M. Calpurnius Longus. The latter may perhaps have been procurator, or was at least closely connected with the district, for we find a dedication to Dionysos by one of his dispensatores or stewards,* with the inscription ['Αρ]τέμων M. Καλπουρ[νί]ου Λόγου δοῦλος οἰκονόμος,] in the same neighbourhood.†

The conductores, as being permanent residents, were naturally also brought into relations with the Horophylakes; and probably issued orders to them in the absence of the procurator. This may perhaps be gathered from a fragmentary inscription, which I copied in 1884 in a deserted cemetery below Hassan Pasha:—

ΕΤΟΥCΛCΕΠΙΜΙCΘΩ	ἔτους λσ΄ · ἐπὶ μισθω-
ΤΟΥΛΥΡΤΡΟ≋ΟΝΔΟΥΝ	τοῦ Αὐρ. Τρο[κ]όνδου N
ΑΥΡΤΡΟΚΟ	Αὐρ. Τροκό-
ΙCΚΟΥΛΝΕ	νδου . . . . . ίσκου 'Ανε-
ΤΟΥΜΙCΘΩΤΟΥΓΕ	. . . . τοῦ μισθωτοῦ (ὑ)πὲ-
ΟΦΥΛΛΚΩΝΑΝΕCΤΗ	ρ ὁρ]οφυλ[ά]κων ἀνέστ[η-
ΕΙΚΑΙΑ	σεν].

The date is probably according to the Cibyratic era, and corresponds to A.D. 255.

Negotiatores (πραγματευταί),‡ as defined by Labeo (Dig. 32, 65), are slaves "qui praepositi essent negotii exercendi causa veluti qui ad emendum locandum conducendum praepositi essent." These pragmateutai were perhaps imperial slaves under the orders of the procurator, who were stationed on the estates to look after the imperial interests. The dispensator mentioned below (§ 27) was probably an official of a similar kind, an imperial slave. It is not possible that they were " middle-men," corn-dealers who bought up the grain from the conductores.§ The fact that there were special negotiatores, apparently the same in number as the conductores, points conclusively to the former view. Mere traders in corn would hardly be selected to date an inscription by: for this purpose some definite official position is required. The names of the negotiatores also are suitable for slaves, Abascantus, [A]nthinus, Marcellion, Aeithales, whereas the Proagontes are free-born with a pater, and the misthotai are libertini (Claudius Abascantus) or ingenui. In one inscription (Sterrett, No. 46) there are three negotiatores and three conductores, apparently one for each estate.

* Sterrett, 'Epigr. Journ.', Nos. 78, 79.

† An imperial slave, dispensator, at Tembrion-Eudokias, § 27.

‡ Perhaps analogous to the probatores or vectores connected with mines and quarries (see O. Hirschfeld, 'Röm. Verwaltungs-Gesch.,' i. pp. 80, 83). But on the proper sense of πραγματευταί εee Mr. Pelham's note in Addenda.

§ Like negotiatores in the saltus of Apulia and Calabria (see Cassiod.Var., ii. 26, &c.)

A boundary-stone of the estate Tymbrianasa has been published (ASP., D 22–5): as it is erected by the legatus and the procurator of Galatia, it might seem that the estate was at that time part of Galatia. But when almost the whole of Pisidia was taken from Galatia and annexed to Lycia-Pamphylia, apparently in the year 74, it would appear that Tymbrianasa was joined with the other Phrygian estates and put in the province Asia. The river Lysis was in all probability the boundary between Asia and Pamphylia. The three great estates seem to have included all the country on the left bank of the Lysis, and the dates on their inscriptions appear to be as a rule reckoned from either the Asian era, September 85 B.C., or the Kibyratic era 25 A.D. A road passed through them from Kibyra to the east, and the distances along it were reckoned from Kibyra. Crossing to the right bank of the river we find the Pisido-Pamphylian cities of Olbasa, Lysinia, and probably Palaiapolis; and in the last a double reckoning,* by the Kibyratic era and by the formation of Pamphylia-Lycia in A.D. 74. The former was used as being familiar in the district, and the latter as being the provincial date.

One peculiarity may be remarked about many of these Phrygian estates: they received during the fourth or fifth century an imperial name and a bishop. This was the case with Maximianopolis, Eudokia, Augustopolis,† Theodosioupolis, and perhaps Valentia, Theodosia, and Pulcherianopolis. We should gladly know whether this indicated that some new organisation with greater freedom and more rights was granted to these estates at this time. That privileges were sometimes granted to the inhabitants of an imperial estate is shown by C. I. L. VIII. No. 8280, 'Ephem. Epigr.' II. p. 273, which records the bestowal of the *ius nundinarum*. On each estate there was at least one village, and a head man (*magister vici*) is often mentioned, who seems to correspond to the proagon in these Phrygo-Pisidian estates. The proagon has a Greek name, and seems to be a native Pisidian.

23. At Lagbe (Alifachreddin, or Alifaradin, Yaila) there must have been another imperial estate. This results from the following inscription, already twice published, but not correctly restored ‡—ἔτους εἰσ´· Αὐρ. Κε[. . . . . gap of uncertain dimensions] κατεσ[κεύασεν τὸ μνημεῖον ἑαυτῷ] καὶ τῇ [γυναικὶ Αὐρ. . . . ., ἑτέρῳ δὲ οὐ]δενὶ ἐξὸν ἔσται ἐπισ-[ενέγκαι πτῶμα, ἐπεὶ ἔνοχος ἔ]σται ὁ ἐπι[χει]ρή[σας] τῷ ἔργῳ το[ύτῳ τυμ-βωρυχίᾳ κὲ δώσει τῷ μ]ὲν ἱερω[τ]άτῳ ταμείῳ (δηνάρια) βϕ´, τῇ δὲ Κιβυρατῶν πόλει (δηνάρια) αϕ´, καὶ τῷ [κ]ατ[ὰ τόπ]ον μισθωτῇ [τ]οῦ χωρίου (δηνάρια)

* ASP., D 16 : I have there reckoned the second era as 73, but 74 is equally possible : the dates are 102 and 150. The latter gives A.D. 175–6, and if the Kibyratic era began in the autumn, July 74 is probably the Pamphylian era.

† The name, though not found in Hierocles, is older than Conc. Seleuc., A.D. 359, when Φιλίκαδος Αὐγουστάδων Φρυγίας Ἐπαρχίας is mentioned.

‡ A. H. Smith, in ' Journ. Hell. Stud.,' 1887, p. 253, and Petersen and von Luschan, ' Reisen in Lykien,' &c., p. 168.

φ' · εἰ δέ τι βουλεύσ[ω, ταῦ]τα ἔτι ζῶν ἐπιγράψω. The restoration of the latter part is given by an inscription, side by side with the above, which the Austrian travellers omitted. It is engraved in faint and worn letters. I have published it in ASP., D 14; but the end must be read τῷ κατὰ τόπον μισθω[τῇ (δηνάρια φ')].

These references to a local μισθωτής have already been explained. Dr. Petersen, who restores τῷ κατὰ νόμον μισθωτῇ, misunderstands (as I think) the passage, considering that the land was hired from the local community. The fines are payable to the Roman treasury, to the city of Kibyra as chief of the conventus or as possessing some rights over Lagbe, and to the imperial conductor, who represented to the rustic mind the majesty of the emperor. He, having something to gain from protecting the tomb, might be expected to prosecute any one who violated it. Khorion or Kome is regularly applied to an imperial estate as distinguished from a city. It is remarkable that a coin ΛΑΓΒΗΝΩΝ should exist.

The date 215 must be reckoned from the Kibyratic era, and is equivalent to A.D. 240. Dr. Petersen reckons from the creation of the province Lycia in A.D. 54; but it is an error to place Lagbe in Lycia. The reference to Kibyra shows that it was in the conventus of Kibyra * and in the province of Asia.

24. Phylakaion or Χωρία Πατριμονιά[λια], between Eriza, Kibyra, and Themissonion: ASP., B 4.

25. It must be left doubtful for the present whether the Valentia of Hierocles and of Concil. Nicæn. II. was an imperial estate.

26. The estate called Bindeos: the form of the name is always ὁ Βίνδεος (Βίνδαιος) or τὸ Βίνδεον (with χῶρος or χωρίον understood). It seems to be the Theudosioupolis of early Byzantine time,† and to have been made a bishopric by Theodosius, probably the second emperor of that name. The two inscriptions, found at Sparta and at Bayat, and published by Prof. Sterrett,‡ which mention both an ἐρ(γεπιστάτης) [compare ἐργεπιστάτης τοῦ λατομίου, O. Hirschfeld, 'Röm. Verwaltungs-Gesch.' p. 83], and a προάγων, may have been brought from Bindaios. A boundary-stone of this estate has been mentioned above.

27. Between Apia, the Praipenisseis, and Kotiaion, we find a district called by Hierocles Eudokias. In it are two inscriptions which seem to prove that it was an imperial estate. One of these (C. I. L. Supplem. No. 7002) is the epitaph of Dionysius, Augusti dispensator. He was evidently a slave of the emperor, stationed in this district for some fiscal purpose, as described above. His friend Aelius Trophimus may

---

* See above, Aigai Asiae.

† Hierocles has Eudoxioupolis, perhaps only an error for Theudosioupolis.

‡ 'Epigraphic Journey,' No. 89; 'Wolfe Exped.,' No. 465. In both the beginning (as Mr. Hogarth detected) should be Θε]οῦ συνέσ(γου) καὶ Χριστ(οῦ) καὶ Ἁγίου Πν(εύματος).

have been a freedman. The other inscription (C. I. L. III. Supplem. No. 7004) is, I believe, one of the boundary-stones of this estate. The explanation which formerly occurred to me, and which was printed in 'Ephem. Epigraph.' V. n. 1452, that the stone marked a boundary between Apia and Aizanoi does not now satisfy me. We desire some reason why an imperial procurator should take the duty of marking the boundary, and this can I think only be explained by the supposition of imperial estate. The river Tembris, Tembrogius, or Thybris (Porsuk Su) flowed through or along this estate, which therefore may safely be identified with the imperial estate called Tembre or Tembrion (Const. Porph. vol. I. p. 488) in the Opsikian Theme, whence fishermen were taken to accompany the Emperor on a march. Stephanus gives the name as Tembrion, Tymbrion, or Tembrieion.

28. The imperial estate of Dipotamon, whose existence has been proved in the Byzantine period, can perhaps be traced as early as the third century by the following inscription, found at Kara Agha, one hour north-west of Doghan Hisar, near the site of Hadrianopolis. It is an epitaph on a tomb dedicated by parents to Σουσου υἱῷ ὀροφύλακι ἰσφαγέντι ὑπὸ λῃστῶν.* Sousou was a saltuarius on this estate. I know no other examples of Horophylakes except here and on the other great imperial estate of the Ormeleis. The situation of Kara Agha shows either that the inscription has been carried, or that Sousou was employed on an estate at some little distance from his parents' home, or most probably that the estate was a very large one, reaching to the south of Ak Sheher Lake and Philomelion.

29. A large estate in two divisions, Kleros Oreines and Kleros Poli-tikes, i.e. Praedium Rusticum † and Praedium Urbanum, has been traced in the country between Prymnessos and Dokimion (CB., §§ LIII., LIV.). It appears in most of the Byzantine lists as Augustopolis, but is named Kleroi at the Council of A.D. 869. The passages which prove that Augustopolis was an imperial property are in 'Vita Eutych.,' 'Act. Sanct.,' April 6, pp. 550–1: ὡρμᾶτο μὲν ἐκ τῆς τῶν Φρυγῶν χώρας, τόπου δὲ ὑπῆρχεν ἤτοι χωρίου, Θείου Κώμης, οὕτω προσαγορευομένου Θείας κώμης .... τίς οὖν ἡ ἀναθρεψαμένη καὶ τὸν μέγαν Εὐτύχιον ἴδωμεν· Αὐγουστόπολις οὕτω καλουμένη. A conductor of this estate, or at least of the praedium rusticum, is mentioned in an inscription quoted in CB., § LXVI. The head man among the coloni of the estate is there called κώμαρχος.

30. Theodosia, whose existence is inferred at Shap Khane in CB., § CVI., was perhaps an imperial estate. This may possibly be gathered from the name and from the alum-mines and works, which have caused the modern name, "House of Alum." Mines were usually imperial property.

---

* Sterrett, 'Epigraphic Journey,' No. 156, where the prothetic iota of ἰσφαγέντι, is misrepresented. Read also Δούδα Σούσου for Δουδᾶς Οὔσου.

† Unless it be " fundus saltuensis."

P   O

tetopolis

Nicra Germ

Mako

M. T

HELLESPONTUS
AND
BITHYNIA

31. Pulcherianopolis or Motella was perhaps an estate. Except the name, no other evidence is known; but nothing inconsistent with the hypothesis is known. Claudius Clemens, whose slave Rouphion is mentioned in an inscription,* was perhaps a Roman connected with the estate.

F. Cities and Bishoprics of Bithynia.

While it does not lie in my purpose to discuss carefully the topography of Bithynia, a country which I have never seen, it is necessary to study closely the line of one of the roads, and as a preliminary to this I must give a sketch of the general topography of Bithynia and a more detailed study of the country along the line of the road.

The ecclesiastical lists are given in the accompanying Table.

1. CHALCEDON. Hierocles begins, not with the actual metropolis of the province, but with Chalcedon. This city was, in the ecclesiastical organisation, not subject to Nikomedeia, but an independent metropolis.

2. NIKOMEDEIA, which still retains its name as Isnimid or Ismid † (εἰς Νικομήδειαν), was a foundation on the site of Astakos or Olbia. It was one of the greatest cities in Asia Minor under the Roman Empire.‡ Diocletian made it one of the capitals of the Roman World. In the tenth century it was the chief city of the Optimate Theme.

Hierocles then goes along the south coast of the Gulf of Astakos or Nikomedeia, reaching

3. PRAINETOS or Prietos, given as Prinetos in his text, whose situation is discussed more fully below. It was the third city in the Optimate Theme.

4. HELENOPOLIS, second city in the Optimate Theme, is discussed more fully below.

5. NIKAIA comes next in his list. It retains its name as Isnik (εἰς Νικαιαν). It was not subject in the ecclesiastical arrangement to Nikomedeia, but was an independent metropolis. § Its original name was Helikore or Ankore (Notitia III. and Stephanus).

6. BASILEINOPOLIS is to be looked for between Nikaia and Kios, probably at the western end of Lake Ascania. The contest between the bishops of Nikaia and Nikomedeia at Concil. Chalced. (451 A.D.) as to which was metropolitan of Basilinopolis, was finally settled in favour of the latter. This suits a position towards the western end of the lake, while the arguments adduced in favour of Nikaia show that Basilinopolis was not far from it. It is named after Basilina, mother of the emperor

---

* Artemis-Leto, &c., § 14, in 'Journ. Hell. Stud.,' 1889.

† In early Turkish the form is Isnigimid.

‡ τίς οὐκ οἶδε τὴν Νικομήδους, ὅπως μὲν θέσεώς τε καὶ μεγέθους ὅπως δὲ λαμπρότητος καὶ ὡρῶν ἔχει, καὶ ὡς τῶν Βιθυνῶν πάσης πόλεων μητρόπολίς ἐστιν αὕτη (AA. SS. April 27, add. p. LX., vit. Anthimi, episcop. Nicomed.)

§ Bithynia Secunda is not a civil, but an ecclesiastical, province.

Julian, and was raised to the rank of a city by Julian about 365 (Conc. Chalced., Actio xiii.): cp. No. 68.*

7. KIOS, at the head of the Gulf of Myrlea or Kios, was called also Prousias ad Mare. It is an independent metropolis in the ecclesiastical lists.

8. APAMEIA, surnamed Myrlea, was on the same gulf, and is usually placed beside the modern Mudania. It is an independent metropolis in the ecclesiastical lists.

9. PROUSA still retains its name as Broussa. It is distinguished as Prousa ad Olympum from Prousias ad Mare, i.e. Kios, and from Prousias ad Hypium in Honorias.

Hot springs beside Prousa, sometimes called Pythia, were famous in antiquity: see 'Act. S. Menodorae,' Sept. 10; Tillemont, 'Mém. p. servir,' &c. v., art. 62; Theophan., pp. 186, 471; Nicet. Chon., p. 701; Procop., 'Aedif.,' p. 315. In Act. S. Patricii, April 28, p. 576, 'Julius proconsul, cum, ingressus Thermas, sacra Asclepio et Saluti peregisset.'

The famous monastery of Medikion, near Prousa, was founded by Nicephorus, who died A.D. 810, and was succeeded by Nicetas, 'Act. Sanct.,' May 4, p. 500.

10. KAISAREIA strikes numerous coins as Cæsareia Germanica. The coins seem to show that it was a seaport and near Mount Olympos,† but these conditions are hardly consistent with each other. Dio Chrysostom places it beside Prousa, which agrees with the coins reading ΟΛΥΜΠΟΣ. Pliny calls it Helgas-Germanicopolis. Helgas is perhaps the old native name. If we could accept M. Imhoof-Blumer's opinion that the coin reading ΟΛΥΜΠΟC should be attributed to Germanicia in Kommagene (Monn. Gr., p. 439), some of the difficulties about the situation of Cæsareia would be eliminated. The coins, together with Chrysostom, seem to represent it as the port of Prousa, i.e. Mudania, where Apameia is usually placed. A passage in 'Act. Sanct.,' May 9, p. 362, seems to confirm this situation; it mentions that Codratus and others, under Decius, were taken by the Proconsul Perinius from Nikomedeia to Nikaia, then to Apameia, then to Cæsareia, then to Apollonia, and thence to Rhundaca et Hermopolim (apparently the river Rhyndakos and Miletopolis): this seems to describe the great road from Nikaia to Miletopolis ‡ (E. § 5), and suggests that Apameia was nearer Kios; and Strabo also says that Apameia and Kios were near each other. But the importance of Apameia corresponds to that of Mudania, and probably

* It is also possible that Basilinopolis gets its name from the estate which was bequeathed by Basilina to the church, and which Chrysostom was accused of having sold for his own benefit (*Act. Sanct.*, Sept. 14, p. 543). The reference in Conc. Chalced. is not inconsistent with this. I have not the opportunity of consulting the other passages quoted by Valesius in his notes to Ammianus, xxv. 3, as bearing on the point.

† Head, 'Hist. Num.,' p. 438 and p. 653.

‡ This was the important road from Lydia to Kios and Constantinople, as well as to Nikaia and the east.

Cæsareia is to be sought on the coast between Apameia and Dasky-lion.

11. APOLLONIA is fixed by the lake called Apolloniatis or Artynia. The town is still called Abulliont. It is called Theotokia at the Councils of 680 and 692.

12. DASKYLION lay between the two larger lakes Apolloniatis and Miletopolitis and the sea, on a small lake called Daskylitis (Strabo, 575).

13. NEOCAESAREIA appears only in the Byzantine lists. The order of Hierocles and the Notitiæ show that it is to be looked for about Bolat. The only other places that could suggest themselves are Kirmasli Kassaba (but Germe was probably situated there) and the neighbourhood of Egri Göz and Amed (but Tiberiopolis Phrygiae seems to have been there). Bolat remains without a name, after Hellespontus and Phrygia are completely mapped, and, as its situation and importance mark it as a bishopric, it must have belonged either to Bithynia or to Lydia. The north-eastern border of Lydia is not quite certain, but the province can hardly have extended to include Bolat, which therefore must belong to Bithynia and be the site of Neocaesareia. From about 787 onwards Neocaesareia was replaced by Ariste or Eriste; it is therefore omitted from Notitia I. On the other hand, Notitiæ III., X., XIII., which are founded on a different register, forget entirely that Eriste is the old Neocaesareia; and III. even confuses the latter with the metropolis Neocaesareia, which belongs to Pontus. They simply repeat the old register and add Eriste or Ariste at the end. If Balikesri is the true name of the modern town near Hadrianoutherai, we might imagine that Παλαιὰ Καισάρεια was opposed to Neocaesareia; but the name is doubtful (see D 6).

14. HADRIANI still retains the name Edrenos, which denotes a governmental district.

15. REGIO TATAIOS, also called Tottaion and Tatavion,* was a district immediately to the east of the Sangarios adjoining the territory of Nikaia and Nikomedeia.

16. REGIO DORIS was another district in the eastern part of Bithynia. There can be no doubt that it became a bishopric along with Regio Tataios, but appears only under another name. If it was south of Tataios, it would be under Nikaia, and is probably to be identified with Numerica. Now, if it were north of Tataios, it would be connected naturally with Nikomedeia, and could hardly have been a regio under Nikaia, as is expressly mentioned; therefore its southern position is established, and its probable appearance as the bishopric Numerica. Doris Regio, then, lay probably between Regio Tottaion and the Galatian frontier. In this part we find in older authorities the name Dableis. The two names are apparently two attempts to render in Greek a native name, in which there was a sound, probably like English V or W, that

* In Ptolemy Παταούιον, an error for Ταταούιον: see Addenda.

could not readily be pronounced or written by Greeks. This sound may have been rendered sometimes by B, sometimes by O or OY.* This view, probable in itself from the mere sound of the names, is proved by a passage in Cod. Theodos., XII., 1, 119, where we read of the curiales Claudiopolis, Prusiadis, ac Totai et Voridis † oppidorum sive mansionum per Bithyniam. We must here read Tottaei et Doridis, and we see that they are the two mansiones on the road to Ankyra, mentioned in the Itineraries, Tataion or Tottaion and Dableis. As there were curiales resident in them, they must have been places of some importance, which is natural considering their position on a great road. In ' Acta Conc. Chalcéd.' (Actio xiii.) we read: Ταττάϊος καὶ Δωρὶς ῥεγεῶνές εἰσιν ὑπὸ τὴν Νίκαιαν, and they seem at this time (451), not to have had bishops, though we must suppose that they still had curiales.‡ Hierocles mentions them as Regiones. The later Notitiæ gave Taïon, i.e. Tataion, as a bishopric, and, though Doris òr Dablis is not mentioned, it must be meant either by Noumerika or by Maximianai; but the earliest Notitiæ VIII. and IX. (VII. is mutilated) omit these three bishoprics. Taking into consideration what is said about regio Tarsia, No. 78, we see that the three regiones east of the Sangarios were elevated to the rank of bishoprics along with Daphnousia at a comparatively late period: to judge from the order in the list, Tarsia is Maximianai, and Doris is Numerika, but certainty as to the correspondence is impossible. The incompleteness of Hierocles's list is obvious. He got Regio Doris and Regio Tataion perhaps from the ' Act. Conc. Chalced.,' but omits Regio Tarsia, which was not mentioned there. He gives the bishoprics, and supplements the list where he can from any other source of information; but he had not a government list.

17, 18, 19. GALLOS, LOPHOI, and KADOSIA were probably three places near each other on the road between Prousa and Nikaia, on the upper waters of the river Gallos.§ They are subject to Nikomedeia, but do not appear in Hierocles.

20. DAPHNOUSIA was an island in the Euxine, on the Bithynian coast. It became a bishopric, but is not given in Hierocles. It was one of the group of bishoprics instituted at a late time. Notitiæ I., III., X., XIII. mention it, and III. also gives it in Hellespontus. It was 1000 stadia from Constantinople (Nic. Greg. iv., 85; cp. Pachym. ii., 138;

---

* Compare the Pamphylian Lagbe, Lagoe, and the ethnic Λαγγηνῶν in Byzantine lists.

† Gothofredus understands that Kios-Prusias is meant, and says that Voris may perhaps be the Βορύζα, πόλις Ποντιακή, of Stephanus. I think that Prousias ad Hypium is meant when Prousias is named simply by a later writer.

‡ It is remarkable that in the same passage the institution of curiales (πραγματευ-όμενοι) at Basilinopolis should be mentioned as equivalent to raising it to the rank of a πόλις.

§ The Gallos, which Leake placed rightly, is put by Kiepert on the wrong side of the Sangarios (see Modrene).

Acropol, 192). S. Sabas, bishop of Daphnousia, is mentioned in 'Act. Sanct.,' May 2, p. 282. Ptolemy has Thynias quae et Daphnousia; Pliny, H. N., v., 32, Thallusa quae et Daphnusa (see 86).

21. ERISTE or ARISTE is beside Neokaisareia, and is included in the same bishopric with it at Conc. Nicaen. II., where Leo Eristes or Aristes is also called Λέων Νεοκαισαρείας ἤτοι ᾿Αρίστης, Leo Neocaesareae Thraciae aut Aristes. It is added at the end of the list in Notitiæ III., X., XIII., as distinct from Neocaesareia; this is perhaps a mere error, arising from Neocaesareia having lost importance, and its identity with Ariste having been forgotten: I. omits Neocaesareia and gives Eriste.

22. The country in the south-eastern part of Bithynia was made into a series of bishoprics subject to Nikaia. It consisted originally in all probability of a vast territory belonging to Nikaia, and of two districts (*regiones*) which are said to have been to a certain extent subject to it, Tataion and Doris. The bishoprics of this district are—

23. MODRENE, which, like the following,

24. MELA, will be fully discussed in the following Chapter G.

25. LINOE, 26. GORDOSERBA, are in all probability to be placed on the two important roads leading from Nikaia to Kotiaion and to Dorylaion. One is probably Sugut, and one Bilejik or Inn Öngu. The district Gordos, in which Gordoserba is situated, lies along the Sangarios (see below, Modrene and Mela), and perhaps Gordoserba is Sugut.

27. The whole territory of Byzantine Bithynia beyond the Sangarios was divided into three regiones, which at a later time became bishoprics (see 16).

The district which lies along the roads from Chalcedon to Nikomedeia and to Nikaia is so important for my purpose, that I must discuss it accurately.

I take first the road from Chalcedon to Nikomedeia, already well discussed by others, and comparatively free from difficulty, though opinions are even here far from unanimous.

28. PANTICHION is still called Pandik, 4½ hours from Scutari.

29. NASSES is half-way between Chalcedon and Pandik. The form is doubtful.

30. PONTAMUS is between Pandik and the following.

31. LIBYSSA is to be sought at some point near Malsum, but probably a little nearer Nikomedeia: it is famous for the tomb of Hannibal, but is never mentioned in Byzantine times.

32–38. BRUNGA has, by Wesseling, been taken as perhaps an erroneous form for Bryas.* But BRYAS was a harbour on the Bithynian coast, where Yezid lay when besieging Constantinople in A.D. 717. His ships occupied the harbours (34) SATYROS and Bryas, and extended as

* The error would come through a Greek text, Βρύαντα being written Βρύαργα. Theophanes, p. 397 has accus. Βρύαν; Cedrenus, I., p. 789, Βρύαντα.

far as (35) KARTALIMEN, which is perhaps the modern Kartal, marked by
Kiepert close to Pandik.   Theophilus built a palace at Bryas in A.D. 836
in the Saracen style, using for it the stones from the monastery of
Satyros, the name of which was derived from the pagan worship of a
satyr practised there (Theophan. Contin., p. 28).   From the nearness of
Bryas and Satyros, the palace is called Satyros by Constantine Porphyrogenitus (vol. I., p. 497), who mentions four palaces on the Bithynian
coast not very far from Constantinople, as at Satyros, at (36) POLEATIKOS;
at (37) ROPHENIANAI,* and at (38) HIEREIA.   The second is unknown to
me, the third was in a famous suburb of Chalcedon, and the fourth was
a frequent landing-place at the shortest crossing from Constantinople.
It must be confessed that these references seem to place Bryas and
Satyros, at the furthest, about the narrow entrance to the gulf, and not
where "Brunga" was situated on the gulf near Nikomedeia.   The
same opinion results from Nicephorus Patr., p. 61, who says that

39. KALOS AGROS was a harbour on the Bithynian coast near 'Ακταὶ
Σατύρου, while Niketiata was between Kalos Agros and Dorkon.   Now
Niketiata can be placed with some accuracy, it was beside Dakibyza
(Ghevse), but on the side towards Chalcedon, on the sea-coast.   The
identity of Brunga and the harbour Bryas cannot therefore be accepted.

40. DAKIBYZA has been identified with Ghevse by Leake, and there
can be no doubt of the identity of the two names [Da]kibyza and Ghevse.
Moreover Procopius mentions that Justinian destroyed the road between
Chalcedon and Dakibyza, and compelled all the travellers [to Nikaia, in
place of taking the land-road to Dakibyza and there crossing the
narrow ferry Aigialoi to Kibotos,] to sail direct from Constantinople to
Helenopolis [beside Kibotos].†

41. NIKETIATA. The fort of Dakibyza is often mentioned by the later
Byzantine writers on the road between Nikomedeia and Chalcedon.
George Acropolita (p. 64) distinguishes it from the fortress Niketiata,
which was a little further west, while (42) KHARAX was a little to the
east of Dakibyza.   But Pachymeres speaks several times of τῷ πρὸς
θάλασσαν τῶν Νικητιάτων τῆς Δακιβύζης φρουρίῳ, as if there were a pair of
fortresses both called Niketiata, the eastern of which was distinguished
as Dakibyza.‡

43. DORKON. The famous monastery of Niketiata, founded by Saint
Sergius, who was born at Niketias, a place beside Amastris in Paphlagonia, is thus described in a Greek synaxarion quoted in Acta Sanctorum

* τὸ ἐν Ῥουφινιαναῖς πολίχνιον δυσμαχώτατον ὂν καὶ στόμα τῆς μεγαλοπόλεως κείμενον.
'Attal.,' p. 268 : cp. Sozom., 8, 17.

† Hist. Arc., § 30.   I have enclosed in brackets my explanatory additions to the
words of Procopius. Compare Socr., 'H. E.' 4, 13; Soz., 6, 14.

‡ This explanation, given in the 'Observat. Pachymer. Petri Possini,' p. 646, seems
correct. He gives the accent Νικητιάτων, which can hardly be correct (though it occurs
also in Pachymeres, vol. I., 192, 198, 307, II., 103), as the singular is Νικητιάτης of first
declension. But the form Νικητίατον may perhaps be used also.

(June 28, p. 385), μονὴν τῆς Θεοτόκου τὴν οὕτως ἐπονομασαμένην * τὴν Νικητιάτου τὴν ἐν τῷ κόλπῳ τῆς Νικομηδείας μεταξὺ τῶν δύο ἐμπορίων Καλοῦ Ἀγροῦ καὶ Δόρκωνος.

The harbour of Kalos Agros† is mentioned as on the Bithynian coast, not very far from the promontory Satyros or Ἀκταὶ Σατύρου, by Nicephorus Patriarcha (p. 61), which confirms the above account of the Synaxarion, yet Finlay says this is a mistake, and that Kalos Agros is Buyuk Dere on the Bosphorus, referring to Ducange ('Constant. Christ.,' 177) and Gyllius ('de Bosp. Thrac.' II., ch. 18, p. 301). Nicephorus, however, expressly declares that Kalos Agros was not on the Bosphorus, and if Ducange is right, there must be two harbours called Kalos Agros, one on the Bosphorus, and one on the Bithynian coast near Ghevse. The Synaxarion is not strictly correct in saying that Niketiata was on the gulf of Nikomedeia ; it is really outside the entrance to the gulf on the Bithynian coast.

44. PHILOKRENE. 45. RITZION. 46. PELEKANON. Several other places in this neighbourhood are mentioned by Cantacuzenus (vol. I., p. 360); Philokrene, Niketiata, Dakibyza, and Ritzion were the places to which the Byzantine army retired from Pelekanon, where a battle had taken place with the Turks, who had been besieging Nikaia, and who had advanced to meet the relieving Byzantine army. Ritzion is also mentioned by Cinnamus (p. 194) as on the Asiatic coast, not far from Chalcedon. Philokrene was perhaps the nearest to Chalcedon, for the whole army finally concentrated there and marched back to Skoutari. Pelekanon has perhaps the same name as the Phrygian or Pisidian Piliganon. Beside Pelekanon was a place Mesampela, with a shrine of S. George (Anna, II., 75).

47. GALAKRENE, which is also mentioned as a monastery in this quarter of Bithynia, may be connected with Philokrene. Nicolas the patriarch (elected 895) was disgraced by Leo for opposing his fourth marriage : per Boucoleontem ductum, lintrique impositum, in Hieriam traiecerunt, e qua pedes ad Galacrenos usque (monasterium a se conditum) pervenit, 'Act. Sanct.,' May, vol. III., 510.

48. ERIBOLOS. On the road from Nikomedeia to Nikaia, the first station is Eribolos, called by Ptolemy Eriboia : both names are grecised forms, adapted to give a meaning in Greek. Eribolos, as Xiphilin says,‡ was a harbour opposite Nikomedeia, i.e. on the south side of the Gulf of Astakos. The distance from Nikomedeia is probably ten, not twelve, miles.

49. AER. A passage of Anna Comnena (vol. II., pp. 312–3) mentions a place Aer, on the south coast of the gulf of Astakos. It lay near the east end of the gulf, for the Empress sailed from Aer to Constantinople,

---

* ἐπωνομασμένην is an obvious correction.

† v. Gyll. ad Dionys. Byz., fr. 44; Müller, 'Geogr. Gr. Min.,' II., p. 54.

‡ Ἐριβώλου τοῦ ἐπινείου τοῦ καταντικρὺ τῆς τῶν Νικομηδέων πόλεως ὄντος.

but on the way was detained for a time at Helenopolis by contrary winds. It was also apparently near the road to Nikaia, and is by these considerations placed beside Eriboia or Eribolos. It is possibly a shortened form of the same native name, which is grecised in these two forms.

50. But travellers to Nikaia would make a great détour. in going by Nikomedeia : the direct road does not touch Nikomedia. Now, during the Byzantine period, by far the most important road that led from Constantinople into Asia, passed through Nikaia to Dorylaion, and there forked in several directions. ·The direct path to Nikaia therefore acquired immense importance, and is very frequently referred to, while we rarely hear of the stations near Nikomedeia.

The land road to Nikaia coincided for some distance with the road to Nikomedeia. Travellers crossed the Bosphorus by one of the ferries, most commonly taking the ferry which went to DAMALIS. They then went through Pantichion and Dakibiza to Aigialoi, where they crossed the narrow entrance of the gulf of Astakos to Kibotos, and continued their journey by land to Nikaia.

51, 52. The ferry from AIGIALOI to KIBOTOS is described by Anna Comnena (vol. II., p. 279). There might otherwise be a temptation to identify Kibotos with Kibyza, the shortened form of Dakibyza and the modern Ghevse. But it is clearly necessary to place Kibotos on the south side of the ferry, near the narrowest part of the entrance to the gulf of Astakos. This ferry is still in use, and is described by Leake, who has not observed the ancient names, and errs in placing Libyssa where he should put Aigialoi. Ducange (*notae* in Alex., p. 683), following the reading of the *editio princeps*, gives the name as Aigylloi, and identifies it with Aigilos, but the latter is the second point from Argeos in the line of beacon-fires from Loulon to Constantinople, and must be in the north of Phrygia.

53. In place of the land-road and the ferry it was often found more convenient to sail from Constantinople direct to the south side of the gulf of Astakos, and Procopius sneers at Justinian (Hist. Arc., 30) for encouraging this method, and allowing the road between Chalcedon and Dakibyza to fall into decay. In the fourth century Prainetos was the usual port to land at, and it is the only one mentioned in the Peutinger Table. But Constantine founded a new city, Helenopolis, at a place called previously Drepana, which became the usual harbour for landing at throughout the Byzantine period. Justinian, who encouraged this method of making the journey, beautified Helenopolis by many fine buildings, as Procopius relates (de Ædif., v. 2). The emperors seem to have had some private landing-places at some imperial estates in this neighbourhood, for in A.D. 1068 Romanus Diogenes observed a bad omen

---

* Leake calls the north end of the ferry Malsum. Kiepert does not give the name. It is 2½ hours south of Pandik. It is often mentioned as Civitot in the Latin histories of the Crusades.

in the fact that, when he did not land at Neakomos, but at Helenopolis,* the vulgar pronunciation of the name was Eleinopolis. Attaliota reports the matter with some difference, and apparently more correctly. Romanus did not land at Pylai, where there was a royal palace, nor at Neon Kome, another imperial estate, but at Helenopolis.†

54. NEA KOME is probably the true name of the village on the imperial estate, called Neon Kome, or Neakomos, in the passages just quoted.

55. PYLAI ‡ was a coast town of Bithynia, west of the gulf of Astakos, probably near the promontory Poseidion, to judge from the Peutinger Table. Manuel Comnenus (A.D. 1146), settled there the Christian population whom he carried off from Philomelion ; but Cinnamus is quite wrong, when he says (p. 63) that Manuel gave the place the name Pylai. The name is at least as old as the fourth century : it occurs in the Peutinger Table. It is mentioned in 1068 by Attaliota § as an imperial estate, and evidently Manuel in 1146 gave the estate to the refugees. This passage of Attaliota also proves that Pylai was between Poseidion and Helenopolis. Pylai, Prainetos, and Nikomedeia, maritime towns (Attal., p. 268).

Constantine Porphyrogenitus mentions that Pylai was the usual place for the emperors to land when they were going to the East, and describes all the ceremonies of their reception (de Cerimon. vol. I., p. 474, and p. 493).

56. A hill called Mokilos, or Moukilos, above Pylai, was one of the line of beacons between Loulon and Constantinople. It must be Samanli Dagh. Then Kyrizos may be Katerli Dagh, and Olympos perhaps some point on the south-eastern skirts of Keshish Dagh rather than the main summit.

57. Helenopolis was founded in the year 318 at Drepana by Constantine, and named after his mother Helena. It was built in honour of Lucianus the martyr.‖ It continued, according to Procopius, to be a mere village, till Justinian gave it a water-supply by building an aqueduct,

---

* οὐκ ἐν Νεακώμου οὐδὲ ἐν ὑπατίας χωρίοις τισὶ βασιλικοῖς προσωρμίσατο ἀλλ᾽ ἐν Ἐλενουπόλει (Scylitz., p. 689).

† οὐθ γὰρ ἐν ταῖς Πύλαις καὶ τοῖς βασιλείοις δόμοις . . . ., οὐδ᾽ ἐν Νέων Κώμῃ, χωρίῳ τινὶ χωρητικῷ βασιλικῆς δορυφορίας ἢ ὑπατείας, ἀλλ᾽ εἰς Ἐλενόπολιν (p. 144). The Bonn text prints πύλαις for Πύλαις.

‡ Pegai, a port on the Hellespont near its eastern end, must be distinguished from Pylai. Both are frequently mentioned : ᾽Απὸ Κυζίκου εἰς Πηγὰς πόλιν τὴν κατὰ τὸν Ἑλλήσποντον ἐλθών (Cantacuz. I., 339). Cedren., II., 310, mentions the Church of the Virgin at another Pege, close to Constantinople.

§ See the passages of Attaliota (p. 144) and Scylitzes (p. 689) quoted and compared above

‖ Δρεπανὰν τὸν ἐν Νικομηδείᾳ ἐπικτίσας εἰς τιμὴν Λουκιανοῦ τοῦ ἐκεῖσε μαρτυρήσαντος (Cedren., I., p. 517, cp. Theophan., p. 28, where Di Boor accents Δρεπάναν, but quotes the variants Δρεπανὰν and Δρεπαναν). Act. Sanct. Jan. 7, p. 362, gives a very interesting account of the foundation and population.

and constructed baths and public buildings. According to Procopius, who actually says that Helena was a native of the place, Justinian's motive was to do honour to the founder of the empire; but the discussion of the Byzantine military road will show that this city was only part of his general scheme in making that great road. Malalas, p. 323, says that its original name was Suga.

Helenopolis was near the river Drakon, and Leake has shown that the Drakon was the river of the Forty Fords (Kirk Getchid). Helenopolis therefore was near the narrowest part of the entrance to the gulf of Astakos.

58. PRAINETOS, said by Stephanus to have been founded by the Phœnicians, is not mentioned till the Byzantine period, when it shared in the development of the country between Chalcedon and Nikaia. It was on the south side of the gulf of Astakos, and east of Helenopolis, as is proved by the Table and Hierocles.* It lay on the march of Nicephorus Botoniates from Nikaia to Constantinople in 1078,† but he may have diverged a little from the direct road to ensure its adherence to his cause. It is also mentioned on the route by which Taticius retreated from Nikaia towards Constantinople in A.D. 1085 (Anna, I., 305; see No. 73). The Peutinger Table also gives it on the coast xxviii miles from Nikaia, which agrees very well with the situation assigned. If it were west of Helenopolis, it would be more than xxviii miles from Nikaia. Its position on the Peutinger Table shows that it was one of the ports to which travellers from Constantinople to Nikaia were in the habit of going by sea. The native name was perhaps Prietos or Prinetos. ‡

It will be best here to discuss the situation of some other places beside or on the road to the important city of Nikomedeia.

59. SEMANA is mentioned as a village not far from Nikomedeia (Act. Sanct. April 27, p. 484, vit. S. Anthimi).

60. Sabandja Dagh, east of Nikomedeia, on the south side of the lake Sabandja, and overhanging the road to Ankyra, which passes between the mountains and the lake, has long been recognised as the Byzantine Sophon (τὸν λεγόμενον Σόφωνα τὸ ὄρος (Attal., p. 189 ; Scylitz., p. 710).

61, 62. SOREOI, and LIMNAI, were two neighbouring places on the south coast of the gulf of Astakos. They are mentioned only in the Acta S. Autonomi, Sept. 12, χωρίῳ τινὶ ᾧ τοὔνομα μὲν Σωρεοί, κεῖται δὲ ἐν δεξιᾷ τῷ εἰσπλέοντι τὸν τῆς Νικομηδείας κόλπον, and again κἀκεῖθεν ἐν Λίμναις γίνεται, χωρίον δὲ τοῦτο Σωρεοῖς πλησιάζον.

---

* Πρένετος, ἐμπόριον καταντικρὺ τῆς Νικομηδείας κείμενον (Socr., 'Hist. Eccles.,' VI., 14). Νικομήδεια, Πρίνετος, Ἑλενόπολις (Hierocles).

† Compare Scylitzes, p. 734, with Niceph. Bryen., p. 124, and Attal., 267.

‡ πρὸς Πρίετον, ἥτις Πραίνετος παρὰ τῶν ἐγχωρίων ἐπωνόμασται (Theophan. Contin., p. 464). The above is probably the intention, though the words mean the converse ; Πρίετον should probably be corrected to Πρίνετον. The passage goes on to mention that the place was named after some πάτριος Θεός of the Bithynians. Stephanus calls it Pronektos near Drepane (i.e. Helenopolis). The Table has Pronectos or Pronetios.

63. S. Hypatius, of the monastery Rufiniana or Drys, three miles east of Chalcedon, went to visit the brothers in the interior of Bithynia, on the river Rhibas :* it happened to be the time of the annual feast of Artemis, called ὁ Κάλαθος, at which time it was not right to undertake any long journey for fifty days (' AA. SS.,' June 17th, p. 343). The festival Kalathos may be accepted as a true part of the religion of Artemis. See Curtius in ' Arch. Ztg., 1853, p. 150, and other passages quoted in my Graeco-Roman Civilisation in Pisidia, ' Journ. Hell. Stud.,' 1883.

64. BAANES, the lake now called Sabandja Göl, is often alluded to by Byzantine writers.

65. OXIA, a mountain about ten miles from Chalcedon, ' Act. Sanct.,' Feb. 14, p. 772.

66. SIOPA, another hill between Oxia and Rouphenianai, ib.

67. HEMERUM, emporium Chalcedonis, ib.

68. ATROA, mentioned by Theophanes (p. 466) is perhaps the same place as Strabo's Otroia. The situation on lake Askania, which Strabo assigns to Otroia, would suit Atroa very well. Leo Diaconus (p. 177) speaks of τὴν τῷ Ὀλύμπῳ παρακειμένην τῆς Ἀτρώας πεδιάδα, which is quite consistent with this situation : it lay on the march of John Tzimiskes in 975 from the Cilician Gates to Constantinople along the military road. John Tzimiskes diverged a little from the road to enjoy the hospitality of one of his officers in a private estate at Atroa, near lake Askania (compare DRIZION). Otryai, which is mentioned by Plutarch (Vit. Lucull., 8), should probably be read Ὀτρόιαι,† and identified with Otroia or Atroa. The identity of the Greek Atreus with the Phrygian Otreus, was accepted even by G. Curtius, and is confirmed by the identity of the derivatives Ὀτροία and Ἀτρῴα,‡ which have replaced older forms ὈτροFία and ἈτροFία. Compare the personal names Attalos and Ottalos, and the Bithynian village called indifferently Tataion and Tottaion. I have described the cultus of Aeneas and Ascanius, which can be traced both at Otroia in Bithynia and at Otrous in Phrygia, in "Trois Villes Phrygiennes " (Bull. Corr. Hell,, 1882). It is probable that Otroia may be in the same district as Basilinopolis.

69. KABAIA, a fortress beside the Sangarios (φρούριον πρὸς τῷ Σαγγάρει κείμενον ποταμῷ, Pachym., i., 419), may have been one of the forts near Pithekas (G. 8).

70. SYMBOLUS SURIUS is mentioned in Vita S. Platonis (Act. Sanct., Feb. 21, p. 267) in the parts towards Olympos, locus Symbolus appellabatur Surius.

71. HYAKINTHOS ; a monastery of this name, mentioned by Acropolita, p. 20, was probably at or near Nikaia.

* Not. Bolland.; Rhibas qui et Rhebas et Rhoesus.
† υ for οι is a common spelling in later inscriptions and manuscripts.
‡ Ἀτρῴας should be read in Leo Diac. 177 on the authority of Theophanes, 466.

72. POUZANES, a castle in the Opsikian Theme, where Artavasdes took refuge in 743 (Theophan., p. 420). It was probably south of Nikomedeia and Nikaia.

73. BASILEIA was a place twelve miles* north of Nikaia. Taticius, commanding the Byzantine army, which was operating against the Turks of Nikaia, resolved to retreat to Constantinople by way of Nikomedeia. The Turks followed him, and overtook him at Prainetos (A.D. 1085), but were repulsed. This seems to imply that Prainetos was on the road from Nikaia to Nikomedeia, a little south of Eribolos; but Anna has probably merely made a slip, and means the road through Bithynia, as she says on the following page.† Nikomedeia was at this time in the possession of the Turks, and Anna immediately proceeds to describe the operations undertaken to recover it. The road in question is Nikaia-Basileia-Prainetos.

74. KISSAION, a place near Modrene, according to a very doubtful statement of Anastasius, ' Chron.,' p. 272, 7; compare De Boor's note on ' Theophan.,' ii., p. 638.

75. KOUBOUKLEIA, a fortress near Mount Olympos (φρουρίῳ τινὶ κατὰ τὴν Μυσίαν τὴν ἐν τῷ Ὀλύμπῳ, Pachym., ii., 580), sent for aid to Lopadion when attacked, and must therefore have been on the west side of Olympos.

76. DAGOUTA is placed by Ptolemy in Greater Mysia; and perhaps Forbiger is not far wrong when he says that it was situated at Sögut, though he has evidently no other reason than the accidental similarity in the names.‡ Ptolemy in the group of towns Dagouta, Praipenissos, Alydda, is probably following some authority who used Mysia in the wide sense already defined (see C, 85), though he absurdly adds Pergamos to the group. I know no other reference to this place till Constantine Porph., de Them., p. 25, who places in the interior of Bithynia a people Dagotthenoi, connecting them with the Mysian Olympos and with Prousa.§ He, however, conceives that the Dagotthenoi live between Olympos and the sea, towards Prousa. This situation is not consistent with Ptolemy, who has, however, very hazy ideas about Dagouta, and cannot rank so high as an authority in this case. The bishopric Gallos-Kadosia-Lophoi was perhaps the country of the Dagotthenoi.

77. AGRILLON or AGRILION is unknown except in the Peutinger Table, and in Ptolemy. It was 24 miles from Nikaia on the road to Dorylaion, from which the distance was 35 miles. It may be Aigialos (see F, 51). The name Aigialos (Aigyllos in Ducange, notæ in Alexiad., p. 683) is

---

* Anna says stadia; Niceph. Br., 160, says over 40 stadia: cp. pp. 251, 258.

† Vol. i., p. 306. Perhaps Νικομήδους is a false reading on 305.

‡ Sögut, a very common Turkish name of places, means " willow."

§ He uses Προυσιάδς for Prousa. He distinguishes the country of the Dagotthenoi from that of the Mysians, south of Olympos. In late writers Prousias should probably not be taken for Kios (Prousias ad Mare).

obviously a native name grecised so as to have a meaning in Greek, and it may have been misplaced in the Peutinger Table on the road Chalcedon-Nikaia-Dorylaion.

78. REGIO TARSIA was a district on the east* bank of the Sangarios immediately adjoining the regio Tataios on the north, and therefore opposite and near to Nikomedeia.† It was in the Optimate Theme, and formed part of the Nicaean empire of Theodore Lascaris (Acropol., p. 173). It was on the road between Herakleia Pontica and Nikomedeia (Nicet. Chon., p. 319). The chief village centre of the regio is to be looked for on the important road which led from Nikomedeia to Krateia and Paphlagonia in general. It was in later time probably raised to the rank of a bishopric along with Daphnousia, Tataion, and Doris, and was named Maximianai (see No. 16).

79. KHELAI or KHELE was a promontory 180 stadia west of the mouth of the Sangarios, and a score of stadia east of the island Thynias. It is mentioned also by Anna Comnena, vol. ii., p. 26, and is described by Pachymeres, i., 419, 475.

80. KALPE, a little west of Thynias, is mentioned under the name Karpe (or Karpis) in Martyrium S. Agathonici (Act. Sanct., Aug. 22); κατέλαβε Βιθυνίαν εἰς ἐμπόριον λεγόμενον Κάρπιν (perhaps read Κάρπην).

81. The Roman province, Bithynia, was instituted on the death of the last king, Nikomedes III.,‡ who bequeathed his sovereignty to the Romans. To it Pontus was added by Pompey, who in 65 B.C. annexed the western part of the kingdom of Mithradates but left the eastern parts to native dynasts. The Roman part of Mithradates's kingdom was divided by Pompey into eleven cities (πολιτεῖαι). Marquardt considers that the eastern boundary of the Roman district was the Halys, and that the frontier was frequently altered so as to include at some periods even Amisos; but this view presses too closely the passage of Strabo to which he refers (p. 544). According to this passage, Paphlagonia extends along the coast from the Halys to Herakleia, and in the interior reaches even east of the Halys. Of inner Paphlagonia Mithradates ruled over the nearest part (τὴν ἐγγυτάτω), while the rest was ruled by dynasts. As to the bounds of Bithynia-Pontus, the evidence is not sufficient to show the exact frontier line, but the following facts are known. As much of Paphlagonia as belonged to Mithradates was made into the Roman Province Pontus by Pompey (μέχρι δεῦρο τοῖς Ῥωμαίοις ἡ

---

* S. Eleutherius, cubicularius of Maximian, was beheaded at his estate on the east bank of the Sangarios in Bithynia, in the district Tarsia, Act. Sanct., Aug. 4, p. 321–5.

† τὴν ἄγχουρον Νικομηδεῦσι Ταρσίαν, Nicet. Chon., p. 553. Eustratius e Tarsia (sic indigitata regio est Optimatum ordini subjecta), vico Bitziano, Act. Sanct., Jan. 9, p. 598 (transl. from Greek Menaia).

‡ Marquardt, following Waddington on Le Bas, No. 409, gives the date as 74 B.C., and makes the Bithynian era identical with the Pontic, 297 B.C.; Mommsen in ‘Zft. f. Numism.,’ 1884, p. 158, fixes the era used during the Roman period as 281 B.C. See Addenda.

Ποντικὴ ἐπαρχία ἀφώρισται):* the rest of Paphlagonia continued as before to be ruled by dynasts even after the final defeat of Mithradates. Strabo then goes on to describe the country ruled by Mithradates, and called Pontus [by the Romans], while he postpones till p. 561–62 the description of the interior of Paphlagonia, which was not ruled by Mithradates [and was not called the Roman Pontus]. He then describes Amastris and Sinope, and crosses the Halys to Amisos. He mentions that part of the country, Gazelonitis, between the Halys and Amisos, was under the power of that city, and part was given by Pompey to Deiotaros, tetrarch of the Galatian Tolistobogii. If we compare with this the passage on p. 541, where he says that of the whole kingdom of Mithradates, including Pontus and a portion of Paphlagonia, Pompey gave the parts towards Armenia to the dynasts who had helped him, while the rest he divided into eleven politeiai and added to the Roman province Bithynia, we can hardly doubt that Amisos was included among the eleven politeiai. This is confirmed by the fact that two governors of Bithynia-Pontus, C. Papirius Carbo, 61–59 B.C., and C. Caecilius Cornutus, 56 B.C., are named on its coins.

Inner Paphlagonia was ruled by kings till 7 B.C., when it was incorporated in the province Galatia. Of several kingdoms into which it was at times divided, the chief seems to have been the eastern, with Gangra as capital, ruled by a great-grandson of the elder Deiotarus, viz,, Deiotarus, son of Kastor. If so, Andrapa (Neoclaudiopolis) was also probably given to Deiotarus, because it goes naturally with Gangra, and because Gangra and Andrapa were in the same year, 7 B.C., taken into the Roman province Galatia, and date their coins from that event as era. Amaseia uses the same era: it had also been ruled by a series of kings,† and it was absorbed in Galatia in 7 B.C.

82. The lot of Pompeiopolis is doubtful. Strabo, taken literally, implies that it was not included in the Roman province by Pompey, for he describes it, not in the parts of Paphlagonia which had belonged to Paphlagonia and were taken as a Roman province (p. 544), but in that part of Paphlagonia which he postponed to a later occasion (p. 562), and which was ruled by native dynasts. But it seems impossible that this city, on the direct and essential route from Pontus to Bithynia, should have failed to be part of Mithradates's empire; and, if it was not in the Roman province, there would remain to the province none of the interior of Paphlagonia but only the coast-land. Perhaps it is for the sake of avoiding the natural inference from his arrangement that Strabo

---

* It is doubtful whether μέχρι δεῦρο means "up to the Halys," or "as far as the Mithradatic part of Paphalognia extended." Marquardt unhesitatingly takes the former view ; I incline to the latter. Strab., p. 544.

† ἐδόθη δὲ καὶ ἡ Ἀμάσεια βασιλεῦσι, νῦν δ᾽ ἐπαρχία ἐστί, Strab., p. 561. Marquardt, p. 359, gives a different account of these cities; but cp. Strab., pp. 541, 544, 562. Still Marquardt's view that Gangra and Andrapa were given to Pylaimenes's family may be true.

calls the districts about Pompeiopolis ἡ ἐκτὸς Ἅλυος χώρα τῆς Ποντικῆς ἐπαρχίας,* a very peculiar phrase, whose exact sense is not clear. If it were ἡ ἐντὸς κ. τ. λ., we might understand in the natural way, " the district of the (Roman) province Pontus that lay west of the Halys," as distinguished from a part that lay to the east. But ἐκτὸς Ἅλυος implies that Strabo is speaking from the Pontic point of view, and in that case he can hardly be speaking of the Roman province, but of Mithradatic Pontus.

All doubt about Pompeiopolis would be at an end if Prof. G. Hirschfeld's † interpretation of the Pompeiopolitan era as 64 B.C. could be accepted. But the inscriptions which he gives do not contain any internal evidence to support this view, and he seems not to have observed that another inscription (C. I. G., 4164) is dated by a different era, which must fall between 17 B.C. and 2 A.D.‡ If Borghesi, V. 429, is right in making the era 7 B.C., then we should have to admit that Pompeiopolis, like Gangra, Andrapa, and Amaseia, was added to Galatia in that year, which would rather favour the view that, like them, it had been hitherto governed by dynasts and had not formed part of the province Bithynia-Pontus. Another piece of evidence is quoted under ' C. I. G.,' 4157, where an unpublished inscription is said to speak of a Ποντάρχης at Pompeiopolis as at Sinope and Amastris; the date is unknown, but is most probably later than B.C. 7. The presence of a Pontarch would show that Pompeiopolis was in the province Pontus, but this reported inscription is a suspicious authority.

83. Part of the interior of Paphlagonia was given by Pompey to the descendants of Pylaimenes ; but we cannot be certain as to the situation or limits of their territory. Marquardt assigns to them the country round Olgassys, with the cities Pompeiopolis, Gangra, and Andrapa, about which I have already spoken. Pliny, VI., 2, speaks of gens Paphlagonia, quam Pylaemenia aliqui dixerunt, inclusam a tergo Galatia, without naming any town in it.

84. The preceding paragraphs show how difficult it is to determine the eleven politeiai of Pompey's province Pontus; the following are certain—Amisos, Sinope, Abonouteichos-Ionopolis, Amastris, Tion, and Herakleia, and perhaps we may add Dadybra,§ Sora, Krateia, Pompeiopolis, and the town which was afterwards called Hadrianopolis.

* A temple dedicated to Zeus Bonitenos, similar to the ἱερὰ τοῦ ὄρους τούτου (Olgassys) πανταχοῦ καθιδρυμένα, has recently been discovered by M. Doublet, ' Bull. Corr. Hell.,' 1889, p. 311.

† 'Sitzungsber. Berl. Akad.,' July, 1888, p. 863 ff.

‡ It is dated in the year 178, and mentions M. Aurelius without adding θεός, which proves that he was still living.

§ Either Dadybra or Sora may be Sebaste Paphlagoniae, which struck coins in the second and third centuries after Christ, and which Mr. Head, ' Hist. Num.,' p. 434, can hardly be right in identifying with Sivas, the ancient Sebasteia Armeniae. Ptolemy has both Sakora and Sakorsa, one of which should probably be corrected to Sora. Krateia and Tion were reckoned to be Paphlagonian, not Bithynian, Justin, Novel. xxix. Kuhn and Marquardt are wrong on this point. See Addenda about the coins of Sebaste.

Some coins of Hadrianopolis add the title ΣEB. This might suggest that it is to be identified with Sebaste Paphlagoniae, but coins of the latter city occur under Caracalla, while Hadrianopolis began to coin under Hadrian. If any of the above places be found hereafterwards to be unsuitable for the list of Pompey's politeiai, Timolaion might be suggested : it struck coins in the time of Mithradates, and may have been ranked as a city by Pompey, though it disappeared from history soon afterwards.* Mantineion has no claim to rank among the eleven politeiai : it is mentioned by Socrates, 'H. E.,' 2, 38 ; it was in Honorias (Act. Sanct., Aug. 24, Martyr. S. Tation), and is mentioned along with Claudiopolis.†

85. Amisos, which belonged to the province 63–56 B.C., was made a free city by Caesar, passed through various vicissitudes, and was liberated by Augustus from the tyrant Straton in 30. ‡ It was perhaps nominally free when Strabo wrote (19 A.D.), but was certainly attached to Bithynia-Pontus in 111–3, when Pliny governed the province (ad Traian., 92, 93, 110). It was still a free city then.

It is usual to give B.C. 33 as the era from which the Pontic city Amisos reckoned its chronology, and to say that the tyrant Straton was expelled in that year. But Strabo (p. 547) implies that Straton was put down by Augustus μετὰ τὰ 'Ακτιακά. Eckhel, II., 349, supposes that Straton must have been put down by Antony in 33, and that Augustus only confirmed their freedom. It is, however, not quite safe to set aside Strabo's authority in this style. When we investigate, we find that the authority is a coin of Diadumenianus with the date CMΘ. Now let us follow Strabo implicitly : we shall suppose that the people of Amisos, in gratitude for their deliverance by Augustus from the tyrant, adopted as their era the victory of their deliverer at Actium on Sept, 2, 31. The usual beginning of the Asian year was the autumn equinox. Then the year 1 of Amisos ended Sept. 21, 31 B.C., and the year 249 would end Sept. 218 A.D. Diadumenianus reigned nearly six months in 218, and we might therefore very naturally have his coins with date CMΘ.§ The result is the same if we suppose that Amisos followed the Roman fashion and began its year with January. The era 31 must therefore be substituted for 33 B.C. at Amisos.

84. From B.C. 7 onwards several Paphlagonian cities, possibly even Pompeiopolis, were included in Galatia. Hence the governors of Galatia are said in some inscriptions to be governors of Paphlagonia ; but it is

---

* Wrong ! Timolaion did not strike coins. See Addenda.

† Vit. S. Autonomi, in *Act. Sanct.*, Sept. 12, where the words ἐπ ἰτὸ Μαντίνειον καὶ τὴν Κλαυδιούπολιν οὗτος ἐπέπλει cannot be taken as a proof that either place was on the coast.

‡ Strabo, p. 547.

§ A coin of Aelius Caesar is dated PΞΘ : the year 169 ends 21st Sept., 138 A.D., and Aelius Caesar died on Jan. 1, 138. A coin of Galba is dated PA, but was apparently struck after his death as it reads ΘΕΟC CEBACTOC. Eckhel seems to err in thinking that the years were reckoned to start from the era : I think that the current year in which Actium was fought was reckoned. See Addenda.

not correct to infer, as is sometimes done, that the whole of Paphlagonia was attached to Galatia at the time in question.* Marquardt's words, p. 359, n. 10, must not be understood in the wider sense, when he quotes Ptolemy to illustrate this phrase in inscriptions. Ptolemy assigns to Galatia even the entire coast of Paphlagonia, including Abonouteichos and Sinope. Pliny certainly proves, ad Traian., 90–2, that Amisos and Sinope were attached to Bithynia-Pontus in A.D. 111–3. The question may be raised whether Ptolemy has been inaccurate, putting the whole of Paphlagonia into the province Galatia when he should only have put a part of it, or whether his authority may be accepted that the remainder of the country was attached to Galatia between 113 and 160. The fact that Ptolemy generally gives a very accurate account of the bounds of the Roman provinces† tells in favour of the latter view, which Marquardt adopts, p. 351. It is possible that the widening of Galatia to include the Paphlagonian coast took place in Trajan's reign, as a compensation for the separation from Galatia of Cappadocia, Pontus Galaticus and Cappadocicus, and other districts, which were made a distinct province.‡ But either this arrangement was again disused and the older system reintroduced about 160–200 A.D., or else we must admit that Ptolemy is entirely in error, for Abonouteichos used the Pompeian era in A.D. 210.§ Fresh evidence, which would almost certainly be discovered by a careful epigraphic exploration, is needed to clear up all these doubtful points.

85. It may be mentioned that Marquardt, p. 359, rightly observes that Gangra, &c., were added to Galatia in B.C. 7, but on p. 491 he retains by mistake the old view that they were added to Bithynia-Pontus in that year. Inscriptions give the proof that Amaseia was governed by the legate of Galatia, Pomponius Bassus, in A.D. 98, and by the legate of Cappadocia, Arrius Antoninus, in the middle of the second century. An inscription of Andrapa (Iskelib) also mentions Pomponius Bassus; and the description of the Galatian roads, which is given below, shows that these towns along with Gangra are critical points in the military system of roads.

86. The boundary between Bithynia - Pontus and the province Galatia can be more accurately fixed on the western side. The river Hierus or Siberis divided them, according to Pliny, v., 149. This would leave Juliopolis-Gordoukome and Dadastana to Bithynia, Laganeia to Galatia: but Ptolemy assigns even Laganeia, which is about a dozen

---

* For example they are also said to be governors of Phrygia, but only a very small part of Phrygia was actually attached to Galatia.

† Except where, as in Lykaonia and Cilicia Tracheia, he goes wrong through combining authorities of different dates.

‡ This probably took place finally under Trajan, see ' C. I. L.,' iii. Supplem. No. 6819.

§ Hirschfeld in ' Berl. Jahresb., 1888, p. 887.

miles east of the Hierus, to Bithynia.* In Bithynia there were xii. civitates, according to Pliny, v., 143. They may be enumerated as Nikomedeia, Nikaia, Chalcedon, Kios-Prusias (ad Mare), Apameia-Myrleia, Caesareia-Germanica-Helgas, Prusa (ad Olympum), Prusias (ad Hypium), Bithynion-Hadriana-Claudiopolis, and Juliopolis. There remain two: one of these is Daskylion, which is expressly included among the XII., though it did not strike coins; the other is probably Dia or Diospolis, on the coast between Daphnousia-Thynias and the mouth of the Sangarios.† Dia struck coins in the time of Augustus, and must therefore have been a civitas,‡ but it seems to have sunk into decay and to have struck no coins later than Augustus. Its territory must have been poor and confined, and its importance can never have been great. The bishopric Daphnousia, in later time included the territory of Dia. It became a bishopric earlier than 879,§ but probably later than 787. It probably was instituted at the same time with the group of bishoprics, Tataion, Noumerika, and Maximianai; and the elevation in dignity of Juliopolis, under the new name Basileion, probably took place at the same time. A bishop of Noumerika, named Constantine, is mentioned at the Council of 869; and Ignatius Juliopolis, or Ignatius Basilii, occurs at the same Council. This change in the whole district along the east side of the Halys was therefore probably due to Basil, and must in that case be dated 867 or 868.

87. The southern and western boundaries of Bithynia were modified in the end of the third or the fourth century. Laganeia and Juliopolis were transferred to Galatia, a change which is older than the death of Jovian, 364,‖ and is also implied in the Jerusalem and Antonine Itineraries, (A.D. 336 and 300–30). Apollonia and Hadriani were taken from Hellespontus and added to Bithynia, and a territory near Bolat on the south-west of Hadriani was erected into a bishopric of Bithynia under the name Neocaesareia or Eriste.

88. The history of Bithynia-Pontus in the fourth century presents some difficulties. Bithynia and Paphlagonia are given as separate

* Pliny similarly gives the Rhyndakos as the border between Asia and Bithynia, yet both Apollonia and Hadriani, which are east of the river, belonged to Asia (H. N. v., 142). We must therefore follow Ptolemy and include Laganeia in Roman Bithynia. On Juliopolis v. Plin. ad Tr., 77.

† Marquardt (following Kuhn, with some changes, but not improving on him) omits Prousa, Caesareia-Germanica, and Dia, giving in their stead Tion and Krateia. Now Herakleia ἐν Πόντῳ is included in Roman Pontus as is clear both from the name and from the express testimony of Strabo, p. 544; and Tion, which is east of Herakleia, must necessarily also be in Pontus, and is, moreover, assigned by Pliny to Pontus or Paphlagonia. Marquardt's statement that Prousa was a kome till Trajan's time is incorrect; Prousa coined money from Nero onwards. Justinian, 'Novel. XXIX.' assigns Krateia to Paphlagonia.

‡ This proves that Kuhn is wrong in inferring from Ptolemy that the territory of of Chalcedon extended to the river Hypios. But see Addenda.

§ Antonius Daphnousias and Damianus Daphnutii both occur at the Council of 879.

‖ Ammian. XXV., 10.

	Ptolemy.	Civil Arrangement, A.D. 100.	Civil Arrangement, 297–380.
...ΕΠΟΛΕΙΤΩΝ	Claudiopolis	Bithynia XI.	Bithynia
...ΠΥΠΙΩ	Prousa p. Hypio	Bithynia XII.	,,
...ΗΛΟΝΤΩ	Heracleia Ponti	Pontus I.	,,
...ΤΙΑ	Tion	Pontus II.	Paphlagonia
...ΚΡΙΟΠΟΛΙΤΩΝ	Krateia Flaviopolis	Pontus III.	,,
...ΑΔΡ · ΣΕΒ	..	Pontus IV.	,,
ΓΑΓΓΑΦ · / ΓΕΡΛΩΣ · ΑΡΧ · ΠΑΦ	Gangra	Galatia	,,
ΣΕΒΑ · ΠΑΦ · ?	Sakora? Sakorsa?	Pontus V.	,,
ΑΒΩΝΝ, ΙΩΝΟΠΟΛΕΙΤΩΝ	Abonou Teichos	Pontus VI.	,,
..	..	Pontus VII.	,,
ΑΜΑΣΤ(ΜΗΤΡΟΠΟΛΕΙΤΩΝ)	Amastris	Pontus VIII.	,,
ΠΟΜΠΕΙΤΩΝ · ΜΗΤ · ΠΑΦΛ ·	Pompeiopolis	Pontus IX. ?	,,

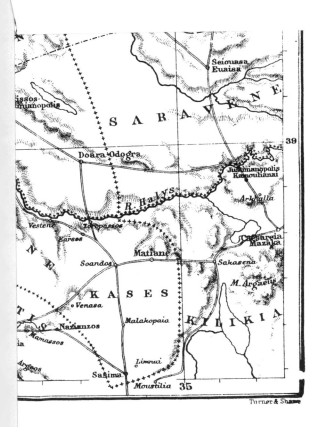

Seiouasa
Euaisa

SARAUENE

issos-
imanopolis

39

Doara Odogra

Justinianopolis
Kamoulianai

R. Halys

Arkelia

Vesten

Icorporiso

Caesareia
Mazaka

Harses

Matiane

Soandos

Sakasena

M. Argaeus

KASES

Venasa

NAZIANOS

Malakopaia

KILIKIA

Mamassos

in

Argeos

Limnui

Sasima

Moustilia

35

Turner & Shaw

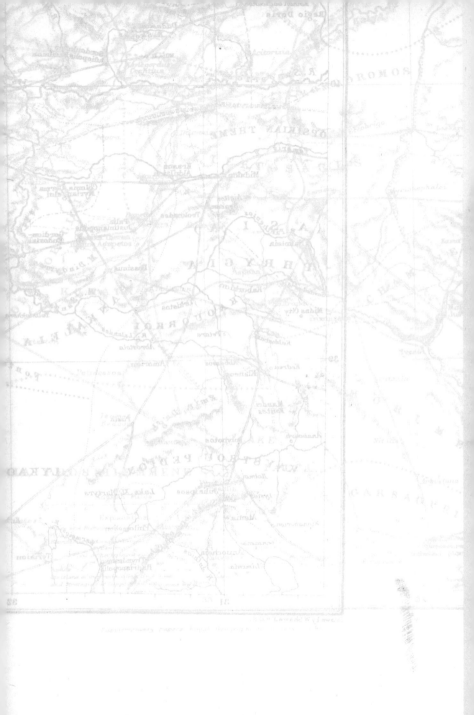

provinces in the lists not only of Polemius Silvius but also of the older Verona MS.; yet we have about A.D. 341 a consularis Ponti et Bithyniae, C. I. L. VIII., 5348.   But the probability is that the name Pontus here denotes only the city Heracleia in Ponto, which had formed part of the Roman Pontus, and does not include the entire province Pontus.*   It is quite consistent with the existence of two provinces, Bithynia including a small part of Roman Pontus, and Paphlagonia including Tion, Krateia, Hadrianopolis, and all the country up to the Halys (see Addenda).

89. Theodosius I., some time before Polemius Silvius's list (which dates about A.D. 386), made a new province Honorias, by taking out of Bithynia Prusias (ad Hypium), Herakleia, and Claudiopolis, and out of Paphlagonia Krateia, Hadrianopolis, and Tion.

90. About 536 A.D., Justinian united Honorias and Paphlagonia into one province, with twelve cities; but the metropoleis of the two separate provinces, Claudiopolis and Gangra-Germanicopolis, still continued both to be metropoleis, and the ecclesiastical constitution was unchanged (Novel. 29).   These changes in the arrangements of the provinces are illustrated by the accompanying Tables of Bithynia and Paphlagonia.

91. Two important roads, not counting the road to Ankyra and the path which skirts the sea, crossed Bithynia and Paphlagonia.   The first of these, which played a great part in the Mithradatic wars, passes through Pompeiopolis (Tash Keupreu); the other passes through Krateia and Gangra.

G.—The Byzantine Military Road.

The chief routes from Constantinople to the East are as follows† :—

1. The Pilgrims' Road.— This road is described more frequently than any other in Asia Minor.   It is given almost complete, and with very little interruption in the Peutinger Table.   It is described in full in the Antonine Itinerary, and with even greater detail in the Jerusalem Itinerary.   Many references occur to it in Byzantine writers, especially of later date; and in the section Constantinople—Ankyra it is still one of the most important trade-routes in the country.   It is described below.

2. Malagina, Dorylaion, Polybotos, Philomelion, Ikonion, and thence to Cilicia either by the Gates, or over one of the Tauros passes.— This is still much used as a post road, and in the Byzantine period was used especially in later time.   It is probably the one which Romanus in A.D. 1030 followed, when he marched from Constantinople to Syria by Philomelion (Cedren. II., 91).   The Crusaders under Conrad took this road (Cinnam. p. 81).   Alexius Comnenus went as far as Philo-

---

* These honorary inscriptions often seek to add dignity by giving the name of a country as governed by the official concerned, when in reality his province included only a small part of the country.   Heracleia was then in Bithynia.

† It is uncertain to which of the following routes we should assign Khelidon, a river or the road from Constantinople in partes Orientis, 'Act. Sanct.,' March 26, p. 677.

melion, and his march is described in some detail by Anna (Vol. II., p. 324). This route is not so good between Dorylaion and Ikonion as the following, and is rarely referred to until a late period. It is perhaps given in the Peutinger Table, but it only rose to importance after Ikonion became the Seljuk capital and a great road-centre.

(3.) Malagina, Dorylaion, Amorion, and the Cilician Gates.—This road is perhaps the easiest and most direct for single passengers or small parties, yet few examples of its use can be found; and it has hardly been recognised (so far as I have observed) by modern writers. Beyond Amorion there is a choice of routes, either by Laodicein Combusta and Ikonion,* or by Archelais, or direct across the plains west of Hassan Dagh towards Tyana. The latter route is the shortest, and the line of beacon fires which was maintained by the Iconoclast Emperors to give warning of Saracen invaders passing the Gates passed along it, but, owing to the want of water it is not practicable for armies but only for small parties. Moreover the country is so sparsely inhabited, and villages are so distant from each other that travellers without a guide may readily stray. Hence, though much the shortest way, it was not the ordinary " Pilgrims' Road." It was, however, sometimes used by pilgrims on foot, e.g. by S. Sabas, who died at Amorion while making the pilgrimage from Byzantion to Palestine.†

In the year 791 Constantine VI. advanced by this road as far as Anydroi Pyrgoi on an expedition against Tarsos. He turned back from Pyrgoi, and it is uncertain which of the possible routes he intended to take. This march has been referred to (see p. 346) as proving the position of Pyrgos or Pyrgoi ; ‡ possibly the difficulty of watering the army, if the season were dry, may have caused the premature and inglorious end of the expedition.

This route is given in great part in the Peutinger Table, and I believe that the original intention of that map was to give the road in full with the two branches to Ikonion and to Archelais. A slight dislocation has occurred in the southern part, and a rather more serious one in the north, where the intention was to represent the road from Dorylaion as going to Amorion and there forking to Dokimion and Synnada, to Laodiceia Katakekaumene, and perhaps § to Pyrgoi, but in place of this the road goes direct from Dorylaion to Dokimion, and a separate road goes from Dorylaion to Amorion.

---

* This is the araba route of the present day from Konia to Eski Sheher (Dorylaion) and Constantinople.

† ἐξέρχεται τοῦ Βυζαντίου ἐπὶ Παλαιστίνην, πεζῇ τὴν πορείαν ποιούμενος · καὶ δὴ φθάσας τὸ Ἀμόριον ἐτελεύτησε (Sabae Vita in Coteler. Eccles. Graec. Monum. III., p. 369).

‡ Theophan., p. 467, where Di Boor has πύργους in place of Πύργους, and in the index gives the name under Anydroi. The above description shows that he is mistaken in describing it as near Tarsos.

§ It is doubtful whether Pyrgos on the Table is a Latin accusative plural, or a nominative singular.

4. Nikaia, Linoe (Aine Göl), Kotiaion, Akroenos (Afiom Kara Hisar), and Ikonion.—This road is described by Cinnamus,[*] p. 4C, on the march of Manuel Comnenus; and Alexius Comnenus traversed it on his return march from Ikonion. It became important only at a very late period as an alternative route between Constantinople and Ikonion, when the latter was the Seljuk capital. It is not given in the Peutinger Table.

5. Dorylaion, Pessinus, along the west shore of lake Tatta to Archelais.—This route is given in the Peutinger Table, with no interruption, but with several interpolated names. It is not a useful route, and I know no historical example of its use.

6. The preceding are the great routes to Cilicia; but when the intention is to go to Ankyra, Tavium, Caesareia, Armenia, or Kommagene, the pilgrims' route is on the whole the best for light travellers, but it traverses a mountainous country, and although the natural interest that belongs to it has caused its importance to be much exaggerated, it was not one of the great through routes of the Byzantine Empire. The military history for many centuries depends on another road, longer but more useful and easy. This road went by Nikaia and Dorylaion, crossed the Sangarios by the bridge Zompos, and the Halys at the modern Tcheshnir Keupreu, and then forked to Sebasteia and Armenia, to Caesareia and Kommagene, and to the Cilician Gates.

This great military road of the Byzantine Empire was maintained with the utmost care for many centuries. It fell into disrepair under the weak sovereigns who succeeded Heraclius, and who brought the Empire to the verge of ruin. But under the vigorous rule of the Iconoclast Emperors the defences and communications of the Empire were again brought to the perfection in which they had been left by Justinian in the sixth century, and although we can trace the history of this road only in obscure passing references, there is no doubt that in general attention was paid to its maintenance ·until the eleventh century. Almost all the military expeditions of the vigorous emperors passed along this road. In the emperor's progress from Constantinople, he found the contingent of troops furnished by the different provinces awaiting him at stated points near the roads. These stated points were called ἄπληκτα: they were no doubt large standing camps, such as the old Romans called *Stativa*. They are enumerated by the Emperor Constantine Porphyrogenitus in the tenth century.

This main military road of the Empire was longer than the pilgrims' road. Its advantages lay in its greater ease and in its passing near the most convenient military stations for the defence of the provinces. But when these advantages disappear, when all roads fall alike into neglect, and when a foreign army which had no contingents to draw from the provinces invaded the empire, then the directness of the pilgrims' route

* The route is Pithekas, Akrounos, Philomelion, p. 38.

must again bring it into prominence.   Such has been the case since the eleventh century.

The course of the road was determined by considerations of easy concentration of the forces of the different provinces along the road, and it was defended at intervals by strong fortresses.   Those which I have seen are as a rule of the same general character.   They are perched on lofty precipitous rocks, which are of immense natural strength, but which could not be provisioned against a long siege, though they were practically impregnable against a short siege.   Such fortresses were well suited to the desultory character of the invasions to which Asia Minor was exposed from Sassanian or Saracen armies: these were, as a rule, mere predatory expeditions, which retired at the end of autumn.   A series of forts which could not be captured except by blockade and starvation formed an admirable system of defence against such enemies. Hence these forts became the nucleus of new cities, and their importance grew steadily during the Byzantine period, while cities in defenceless situations were deserted or reduced to mere villages.   Even cities whose strength depended on artificial fortifications and disciplined garrison troops and the observance of proper precautions, were not suited to protect a country, which was often ruled by careless and incompetent emperors, and whose defences were therefore often allowed to fall into disrepair.

Although the great stations on the road are expressly described by Constantine in a passage which I shall quote and emend below, I am not aware that any modern writer has connected this passage with the road, or has shown its extreme importance for the understanding of Byzantine military history.   It is therefore necessary to prove my theory, step by step, as regards both the route and the importance of the " Byzantine Military Road."

7. With regard to the time when this road was first organised, we observe that no less than four different cities, founded by Justinian and named Justinianopolis,* besides a paved causeway many miles in length, which was constructed by him, occur on this road.   Four separate points showing his work may be taken as sufficient proof that he organised the whole route, and its creation may be fairly adduced as one of the most striking proofs of the skill with which he planned and renovated the government of Asia Minor.†   I shall now proceed to discuss the road in detail, point by point, so far as the evidence I have been able to collect reaches.

Starting from Constantinople, an emperor using the road might either

---

* I have regarded it as certain that all these foundations date from Justinian I.; even where they are not attested by Procopius, most of them can be proved to have existed before Justinian II., A.D. 685.

† The road towards the east, on which he took care to maintain the postal service in high order, though he neglected it on other roads according to Procopius ('Hist. Arc.', 30), was certainly this road.

cross the Bosphorus and take the land route from Chalcedon to Aigialoi and cross the ferry to Kibotos, or he might take ship to some harbour such as Helenopolis, or Prainetos, or one of his private landing-places * on the south coast of the Gulf of Astakos. It has been already remarked that Helenopolis was the usual starting-point of the land road, and that the great series of buildings with which Justinian beautified it was part of his general scheme for this great road. Kibotos was close to Helenopolis. In later time at least the emperors themselves usually landed at Pylai, but this involved a détour, and was practised by the emperors alone. Romanus in 1076 is mentioned as an exception : perhaps being in a hurry he took the direct and usual course, and landed at Helenopolis. Hence the road went to Nikaia.

From Nikaia the road apparently went to Leukai on the Sangarios.† It passed first a village Gaita, which bears the same name as a Phrygian village on the horse road between Philomelion and Ikonion. We hear more than once about Christians from the neighbourhood of Philomelion being settled in Bithynia, and perhaps the name may have been carried in this way.‡

8. PITHEKAS is the next point mentioned on the road. There was a bridge beside it (τὴν κατὰ τὸν Πιθηκᾶν γεφύραν, Anna, l. c.). Strong fortifications at this place are mentioned by Nicetas Choniata.§ Haase, in the art. *Phrygia*, in Ersch and Gruber's 'Allgem. Encyclop.,' p. 274, inaccurately supposes that Pithekas was in the neighbourhood of Philadelpheia. Manuel Comnenus, marching from the lower Rhyndakos, crossed the Mysian Olympos (Keshish Dagh) before reaching Pithekas. He strengthened the fortifications in order to protect himself against the Turks of Konia. This shows how widely the Seljuk power was extended at the time. Only in the later years of his life did Manuel seize and fortify Dorylaion. In his earlier years Dorylaion was completely in Turkish power, and Manuel always in his earlier campaigns preferred the road by Kotiaion (which also passed through Pithekas). Kotiaion was further west and longer in the Christian possession than Dorylaion.‖

ARMENOKASTRON is perhaps one of the forts in the neighbourhood of Pithekas, which have just been mentioned (cp. F. 69). Anna Comnena mentions it on the march of Alexius between Pithekas and Leukai.

* These have been described above (F. 53) in discussing the road to Nikaia.

† Anna Commena, XV., vol. II., p. 322.

‡ The village south of Philomelion is still called Agaït; it is mentioned by Cinnamus, p. 42. Christians were brought in this way by Manuel Comnenus some years later, and settled at Pylai in Bithynia. Alexius also brought back Christians from Philomelion.

§ τὰ περὶ τὸν Πιθηκᾶν ἐρύματα (Nicet. Chon., p. 71; cp. Cinnam., p. 38).

‖ It is clear that in the disgraceful treaty of 1074 between Suleiman and the Emperor Michael, Dorylaion and Sugut, but not Kotiaion, were included in the country recognised as Seljuk. I have discussed the southern frontier in the American 'Journal of Archæology,' 1886, and have shown that Apameia-Celaenae, but not Soublaion, was included in the Seljuk country.

LEUKAI retains its name as Lefke. It is beside the junction of the river Gallos with the Sangarios. The suspicion suggests itself that the bridge of Pithekas, just mentioned, is the bridge over the Gallos, and that Pithekas, Leukai, &c., are all in the same neighbourhood. The fortifications by which Manuel strengthened the district of Melagena (Nicet. Chon., p. 71) would then be identical with τὰ περὶ τὸν Πιθηκᾶν ἐρύματα (ib.).

9. Malagina, Melagina, Melagena, Melangia, or Mela, are different names given to the first great station on the military road. It was an ἄπληκτον, where troops from the surrounding country concentrated to await the emperor's arrival, and to accompany his march to the east. Unfortunately the account of the ἄπληκτα given by Constantine, our sole authority, is so confused and inaccurate that its value is greatly impaired. He makes the troops of the Thrakesian and Anatolic Themes concentrate at Malagina; he omits to tell what troops concentrated at Dorylaion, the second ἄπληκτον, and he repeats the Anatolic Theme as concentrating at Kaborkion, the third ἄπληκτον. We are therefore obliged to trust to our own judgment in the matter. The Optimate troops would naturally concentrate at Malagina, the Opsikian and Thrakesian would concentrate at Dorylaion, the Domesticus Scholarum would come either to Dorylaion or to Kaborkion, the Anatolic troops would come to Kaborkion, so would the Seleukeian troops.

10. It will be convenient as a preliminary to our whole investigation to give here the text of this most important passage of Constantine, vol. I., p. 444 :—

Εἰσὶ τὰ ἄπληκτα· πρῶτον ἄπληκτον εἰς τὰ Μαλάγινα, δεύτερον τὸ Δορύλειον, τρίτον εἰς τὸ Καβόρκιν, τέταρτον εἰς Κολώνιαν, πέμπτον εἰς Καισάρειαν, ἕκτον εἰς Ἀρμενιακοὺς εἰς τὸν Δαζιμῶνα· ὅτε ὁ στρατηγὸς τῶν Θρακησίων καὶ ὁ στρατηγὸς τῶν Ἀνατολικῶν ὀφείλουσιν ὑπαντᾷν τῷ βασιλεῖ εἰς τὰ Μαλάγινα. ὁ δομέστικος τῶν σχολῶν καὶ ὁ στρατηγὸς τῶν Ἀνατολικῶν καὶ ὁ στρατηγὸς Σελευκίας ὀφείλουσιν ὑπαντᾷν τῷ βασιλεῖ εἰς τὸ Καβόρκιν· ὅτε εἰ μέν ἐστι τὸ ταξείδιον εἰς Ταρσὸν, τὰ λοιπὰ θέματα ὀφείλουσιν ἀποσωρεύεσθαι εἰς Κολώνιαν, εἰ δὲ πρὸς τὰ μέρη τῆς Ἀνατολῆς, ὀφείλουσιν ὑπαντᾷν τῷ βασιλεῖ ὁ μὲν Καππάδοξ καὶ ὁ Χαρσιανίτης καὶ ὁ Βουκελλάρις εἰς Κολώνιαν, ὁ δὲ Ἀρμενιακὸς καὶ ὁ Παφλαγὼν καὶ ὁ Σεβαστείας εἰς Καισάρειαν. ὅτε τὰ Ἀρμενιακὰ θέματα ὀφείλουσιν ἀποσωρεύεσθαι εἰς Τεφρικὴν εἰς τὸν βαθὺν Ῥύακα. The text is evidently in a very bad state, and I believe that the passage is to be restored as follows: my reasons will be given in detail below. The fourth ἄπληκτον is not εἰς Κολώνειαν, but εἰς Σανίαναν. Then the writer continues: (ἰστέον) ὅτι ὁ στρατηγὸς τῶν Ὀπτιμάτων ὀφείλει ὑπαντᾷν τῷ βασιλεῖ εἰς τὰ Μαλάγινα, ὁ στρατηγὸς τῶν Ὀψικίων καὶ ὁ στρατηγὸς τῶν Θρακησίων εἰς τὸ Δορύλαιον, ὁ δομεστικὸς τῶν σχολῶν καὶ ὁ στρατηγὸς τῶν Ἀνατολικῶν καὶ ὁ στρατηγὸς Σελευκείας εἰς τὸ Καβόρκιον· ὅτι, εἰ μέν ἐστι τὸ ταξείδιον εἰς Ταρσὸν, τὰ λοιπὰ θέματα ὀφείλουσιν ἀποσωρεύεσθαι εἰς Σανίαναν, εἰ δὲ πρὸς τὰ μέρη τῆς Ἀνατολῆς, ὀφείλουσιν ὑπαντᾷν τῷ βασιλεῖ ὁ μὲν

Καππάδοξ καὶ ὁ Χαρσιανίτης καὶ ὁ Βουκελλάρις καὶ ὁ Παφλαγὼν εἰς Σανίαναν, ὁ δὲ ᾿Αρμενιακὸς καὶ ὁ Σεβαστείας εἰς Καισάρειαν, εἰ δε εἰς Τεφρικὴν,* τὰ ᾿Αρμενιακὰ θέματα ὀφείλουσιν ἀποσωρεύεσθαι εἰς τὸν Βαθὺν ῾Ρύακα.

Reiske, in his commentary, suggests that this, with the rest of the first part of the Appendix to lib. I. de Cerimoniis Aul. Byz., was written during the fourth or fifth century, and is not the work of Constantine Porphyrogenitus; he argues that the term Καῖσαρ denoting the emperor had been disused in favour of Βασιλεύς before his time. This opinion cannot be correct, for the passage implies the division of the empire into Themata in place of provinces, and the language is of a much later type than the Greek of the fifth century. It is, however, highly probable that Constantine used such an older document, and that some of his errors are made in the attempt to accommodate this authority to the changed circumstances of his time. This document may have been early, for Constantine has probably adopted from it the term Καῖσαρ. If Koloneia is not a mere clerical error, it must come from the older document: the military importance of Koloneia Archelais must have disappeared when Mokissos was recognised as the great city of western Cappadocia by Justinian, but Constantine, finding the name in one of his authorities, retained it (see Addenda).

11. I shall now discuss the various forms of the name Melagena and the chief places in which they occur, and prove that they all denote one single place. Their identity has rarely or never been observed, and the situation of the place has not even been guessed at.

MALAGINA was a very important station on the road to Dorylaion.[†] It is very frequently mentioned in the Byzantine wars.

In the year 786 the Byzantine troops advanced against the Arabs as far as Malagina. In the year 798 the Arabs made a rapid incursion, penetrated as far as Malagina, and captured the horses of Stauracius, the court favourite, and the emperor's own saddle (προμοσέλλαν). The royal stables at Malagina (required for the imperial post service) are mentioned in the route described by Edrisi, from Amorion to El Khalidj (see under SANTABARIS), and on this occasion the Arabs evidently captured them with all the horses.[‡] In 858, also, the Arabs are said by some authorities to have again captured the imperial post-horses at Malagina (τὴν βασιλέως ἱππότιν συναγωγήν, Genes., p. 114).[§] These stables were the great horse-station of Asia Minor, and are frequently mentioned in the Appendix to Book I. of Constantine's ' Ceremonies of

---

* On the frequent expeditions against the Paulicians, referring especially to the campaigns of Basil, who broke their power.

† In the narrative of events preceding Concil. Nicaen. II., Mansi, XII., p. 992, cum fecissent isti viam usque ad Malagenam (ἕως τῶν Μαλαγίνων).

‡ Weil, ' Gesch. der Khalifen,' II., 157, note, and Muralt both speak of Mangana here; Mangana is a very different place, beside Constantinople.

§ Compare Theoph. Contin., p. 198. Symeon Mag. (p. 660) mentions that Malagina was in the Opsikian Theme.

the Byzantine Court,' where their whole organisation is described (pp. 459, 476, 486).

In 803 Bardanes, who had rebelled against Nicephorus, advanced to Chrysopolis on the Bosphorus, but retired immediately as far as Malagina : he was strategos of the Anatolic Theme, where he had rebelled, and towards which he naturally retired again. His march, therefore, must have been towards Dorylaion (Theophan., p. 479).

The Paulicians, under Chrysocheir, penetrated as far as Malagena in 872 (Genes., 114). All the recorded campaigns of the Paulicians pass along the military road.

12. The forms Melangia and Melagina or Melagena, as already recognised by Ducange, are clearly equivalent to Malagina ; but I add some proofs of the position of Melangeia on the same road. Constantine, bishop of Melangeia, is mentioned as late as 1269 by Pachymeres (vol. I., p. 102). Melagina is mentioned as an archbishopric in an unpublished Notitia Episcopatuum, in the Bibliothèque Nationale, Paris. It is given, last in order, as No. 39, among the ἀρχιεπισκοπαί. This Notitia belongs to the same class as Parthey's No. X. It is in a MS. marked No. 960, a *codex bombycinus* of the end of XIII or beginning of XIV century ; and it begins on fol. 89 rᵒ. The reference of Pachymeres seems to imply that the bishop of Melangeia was already raised to this dignity : he is mentioned along with the bishops of Ankyra, Ephesos, &c.

Melangeia is also mentioned as on the road from the Bosphorus to Dorylaion. Conrad crossed by the ferry Damalis, and advanced towards Philomelion by Melangeia and Dorylaion (Cinnam., p. 81). The emperor Manuel Comnenus, 1175 A.D., crossed at Damalis, advanced through Melangeia, where he collected the troops which concentrated there from Bithynia on the east, and from the districts along the Rhyndakos * on the west, *i.e.* the Optimate and Opsikian Themes, and then proceeded to Dorylaion. Melangeia here is shown to be on the same road as Malagina,† and like it to be an ἄπληκτον, where the troops of the Optimate Theme met the emperor on his march. There can, therefore, be no doubt of the identity of the two places.

After the preceding and following paragraphs were finished, I observed that Zonaras asserts the identity of Melangeia and Malagina, saying that the latter is the more rustic name.‡

13. The form Melagina seems to have led to another corruption Melaina. Melaina is mentioned by Ducas as a village on the road from Amasia towards Prousa (ἔγγυς που Προύσης, p. 129). I think there can be no doubt that Melaina = Melagina, § and we have thus a proof that

---

* Cinnam., p. 294 (cp. pp. 36, 127).

† The form Μαλάγγινα sometimes occurs for Μαλάγινα.

‡ Zonaras, III., p. 129 (Basel, 1557).

§ Melagina becomes Melaina, either through the operation of popular etymology, seeking a word with a meaning, or through the tendency of modern Greek pronunciation to weaken g before i into y.

the place was at the crossing of the roads from Prousa to the east and from Nikaia to the south, which exactly confirms the conclusion to be drawn from the fact that Malagina was an ἄπληκτον where the Optimate troops concentrated. After Dorylaion had passed into Turkish hands Melagena was the natural ἄπληκτον for the Opsikian troops also.

14. Mela, which does not occur in Hierocles, is mentioned as a bishopric in all the Notitiæ. It must, therefore, probably have risen to this rank after 530 A.D. In the Council held at Constantinople in A.D. 680, the bishop of Mela was present, and the names Mela and Justinianopolis Nova are used as equivalent. Mela therefore was refounded by Justinian and raised to the rank of a bishopric. Procopius, though he wrote his account of the buildings of Justinian not earlier than 560 A.D.,[*] does not refer to the building of Justinianopolis Mela, but the passage in which he describes the building and paving of the road from Bithynia into Phrygia may fairly be connected with the foundation of the city, and may serve as a proof that the city was situated on the road.[†] It may, of course, be confidently assumed that the road described by Procopius is the imperial post-road to Dorylaion, the great artery of communication with Phrygia. Procopius mentions his care of the road to the east (Hist. Arc., 30).

15. The situation of Mela is further determined by the usual entry in the Notitiæ, Μοδρηνῆς ἤτοι Μελῆς. Mela was sufficiently near Modra or Modrene, for the two to be included in one bishopric. Modra was situated on the upper waters of the Gallos. If the text of Strabo (p. 543) is to be trusted, the Gallos joined the Sangarios a little over 300 stadia, nearly 40 miles, from Nikomedeia, and this distance, as Leake mentions, proves that the Gallos is the river which flows past Leukai,[‡] rising in the little Lake Aine Göl ("Mirror Lake"). The probable inference then is that Modra was about the village Aine Göl, and Mela about the point where the imperial highway crossed the river Gallos. Strabo knew the distance from this point, the junction of the Sangarios and Gallos, to Nikomedeia, from an itinerary, and hence he

---

* He refers to the Sangarios bridge as in process of building. It was begun in 560.

† Ἔστι δέ τις ἐν Βιθυνοῖς ὁδὸς ἐς τὰ Φρυγῶν ἤθη ἐνθένδε ἰόντι, ἔνθα δὴ ἀνθρώποις τε ἀναρίθμοις καὶ ζῴοις ἑτέροις χειμῶνος ὥρᾳ διολωλέναι ξυνέβαινε · γεώδης γὰρ ὑπεράγαν ἡ χώρα οὖσα, μὴ ὅτι ὄμβρων ἐξαισίων καταρραγέντων ἢ χιόνων πολλῶν ἐπικεχυμένων τε καὶ διαλυθεισῶν ἐν ἐσχάτῳ, ἀλλὰ καὶ ψεκάδων ἐπιπεπτωκυιῶν, ἂν οὕτω τύχοι, ἐς τέλμα βαθὺ καὶ ἀπόρευτον ξυνισταμένη, τὰς τε ὁδοὺς τεναγώδεις ἐργαζομένη, τοὺς τῇδε ἰόντας ἐκ τοῦ ἐπὶ πλεῖστον ἀνέπνιγεν. ἀλλὰ καὶ τοῦτον αὐτός τε μεγαλοφροσύνῃ ψυχῆς καὶ ἡ βασιλὶς Θεοδώρα τὸν κίνδυνον τοῖς παριοῦσι διέλυσαν. ἐς ἡμέρας γὰρ ὁδοῦ ἥμισυ εὐζώνῳ ἀνδρὶ λίθοις παμμεγέθεσι σκέπας τῇ λεωφόρῳ ἀπεργασάμενοι ἐπὶ στερρᾶς τῆς ὁδοῦ παριέναι διεσκευάσαντο τοὺς τῇδε ἰόντας (Procop. Aedif. V. 3).

‡ Texier says that this river runs from Aine Göl, and Kiepert's later map agrees. His older map makes the river of Aine Göl run south of and parallel to the river of Leukai. Texier says that the river of Aine Göl is called Bedre Tchai: he would probably have observed that the name Bedre is the ancient Modra, but for his extraor dinary error about the site of Modra, which he places at Mudurlu. Kiepert follows him in this, and is obliged to put the Gallos east of the Sangarios.

gives it,. though there is really a much shorter interval between the Sangarios and Nikomedeia further north. But Strabo had no statistics of this shorter distance, for the route Ankyra-Nikomedeia, along which it might be measured, was of no importance in his time, whereas the route from Nikomedeia and Nikaia to Leukai, Dorylaion, Kotiaion, Smyrna, and Ephesos, must have been a most important road then (see E. 12).

The inference just drawn as to the situation of Mela cannot be considered quite certain; the conditions would be fairly well satisfied by a situation between Lefke and Vezir Khan, 10 or 12 miles further south. But the description which Leake gives of the situation and surroundings, combined with the importance of Lefke, show that Mela is to be sought not far from it, probably at some more defensible point.

16. The natural route from Prousa to Amasia would pass by Lophoi down the Gallos and across the Sangarios to join the other road from Nikomedeia to Amasia. A point in this neighbourhood would also be a good meeting-place for troops concentrating from the Optimate Theme. Malagina, Melagina, or Melaina, is therefore to be placed in the same place as Mela-Justinianopolis, and the importance of the city is to be connected with its situation at a meeting-place of roads. All Justinian's foundations owe their importance and lasting character to the skill with which they were placed. He simply recognised and gave precision and name to the places which by the force of natural circumstances were attaining importance amid the steady improvement and development of the northern parts of Asia Minor in the two centuries after the foundation of Constantinople.

In the name Malagina the termination -ινα should really be -ηνά ; it is adjectival and extraordinarily common in Anatolian names. Μελῆς, Μελινῆς, and Μελινῶν (all genitives), in the Notitiae, have lost the γ, like the form Melaina. Like Μελιτήνη in Cappadocia it is really an adjectival form, denoting the district, in which there was no true city. Μαλάγινα has altered its character and accent when it became a noun. The native name must have been Melag-a, and the adjectival character of the name Melagina or Melangia, as denoting a district and not a single town, is proved by a passage in Cinnamus (p. 127), where he speaks of Manuel as living at a place (χῶρος) named Metabole ἐν Μελαγγείοις.

Leuke or Leukai (the White Town) is to be considered as a village in the district Malagina, and perhaps popular wit or popular superstition sought a definite purpose in opposing the name to the ill-omened Melaina (Black Town).*

Modrene was the scene of a battle described by Nicephorus Patriarcha, p. 68.

17. Angelokome is by Texier (As. Min., p. 91) and Von Hammer identified, on account of the resemblance in name, with the modern Aine Göl.

---

* Compare Greek ΜαλοϜείς, ΜαλοϜέντα, Apple Town, in Latin Maleventum, changed to Beneventum.

This view is not consistent with a passage of Anna Comnena, according to which Angelokome would seem to have been situated on one of the rivers that flow out of Mount Ida. Anna (vol. II., p. 280) mentions that the Turks crossed a river Barenos between Kyzikos and Parion. This river, which must be either the Granikos or the Aisepos, flows out of Mount Ibis, where rise also the Skamandros, the Angelokomites, and the Empelos. The Angelokomites is obviously called after the town (often mentioned in late Byzantine time) past which it flows. Similarly the Barenos is obviously the river that flows by Baris, a town mentioned in all the Notitiae (sometimes as Sasabaris) and by Hierocles.* Other considerations incline us to place Angelokome as far east as possible, which would show that it was on the Aisepos, and Baris on the Granikos. It may, however, be doubted quite reasonably whether Anna's geography is trustworthy, when she makes the Angelokomites and Skamandros rise in the same mountain. Perhaps she has confused the two mountains, Ida and Olympos. † The enumeration of towns near Nikaia captured by the Turks, which is given by Pachymeres, ‡ seems conclusive. Belokome is Bilejik, Angelokome is Aine Göl, Anagourdes and Platanea are unknown villages in the direction of Melagena. It would not be correct to say that Aine Göl, which means "Mirror Lake," a natural and poetical name for a lake among the mountains, is got by popular etymology from the Byzantine name Angelokome. The fact seems to be that Belokome and Angelokome are Greek representatives of the Turkish names Bilojik and Aine Göl; and that these two places, having been for some time in the hands of the Turks, are designated by their Turkish names, while Melangeia, further north and close to Nikaia, has still its Greek name, which is retained even by Edrisi.§ Then the Angelokome that gave name to the river, would be a different place from this later Angelokome, a name coined out of the Turkish Aine Göl, and Anna's account of the four rivers flowing from Mount Ida (Ibis) may be accepted: her Empelos remains doubtful, perhaps the Satnioeis.

18. Modra or Modrene is by Texier placed at Mudurlu, far away on the other side of the Sangarios, though he agrees with Leake's identification of the Gallos. His sole ground is the modern name, which he considers to be a modification of the ancient name. But Mudurlu is a

* Hierocles has the form Βαρίσπη, a scribe's clerical error. Wesseling, however, wrongly suggests 'Αρίσβη as the proper reading. Βαρίσπη arises from a dittography, Βαρις παριον being written βαρις παπαριον, and the words being afterwards wrongly divided. Compare Βαρίς, ethnic Βαρηνός, in Pisidia. See D 3, 13, C 33, which shows that the Barenos was the Granikos.

† Other similar errors are given, under Mopsouestia Ciliciæ and just below in connection with Melagena.

‡ νῦν μὲν Βηλόκωμα, νῦν δ' 'Αγγελόκωμα, νῦν δ' 'Αναγουρδὴς καὶ Πλατανέα καὶ τὰ Μελάγγεια καὶ τὰ πέριξ πάντα (vol. II., p. 413).

§ See the route given under Galatia Salutaris, Santabaris: there Mulawwen perhaps corresponds to Bilejik-Belokome.

good Turkish name, and has no connection with Modra. Kiepert in his latest map follows Texier.

19. Gallos, which appears as a bishopric, united with the other places, Kadosia and Lophoi, must probably be placed on the Gallos, if there is an arm of that river which rises far away to the west. Gallos-Kadosia was in Bithynia Prima, subject to Nikomedeia, while Modra was in Bithynia Secunda, under Nikaia, which included the whole south-eastern part of the province from Aine Göl and the Nicene lake. Gallos-Kadosia is to be looked for north-west of Aine Göl, and the boundary of the ecclesiastical provinces passes between Kadosia and Aine Göl.

20. The operations of the year 1113 * are very hard to understand, but, after fixing the site of Malagina, it becomes possible to put them more precisely. The Turks who were ravaging Mysia divided at Kyzikos. One division under Mahumet retired through Lentiana and Poimanenon (Maniyas), and thence doubtless along the Rhyndakos towards Kotiaion and Dorylaion, the latter of which was entirely in the hands of nomadic Turkish tribes. † The emperor sent orders to Kamytzes to march against the Turks. He must have gone through Prousa and round the north side of Mount Olympos (Keshish Dagh) till he reached Aorata, obviously in the Rhyndakos valley at a point near Poimanenon. Here he attacked the Turks suddenly, dispersed them, and recaptured all their booty, but, instead of retiring on Poimanenon, he lingered at Aorata, and the Turks, rallying in a plain beneath Aorata, surprised him in turn, defeated his army, and captured himself with all the spoil. In the meantime the emperor had crossed the ferry from Constantinople to Damalis, and marched in three days to Aigialoi,‡ at the narrowest part of the entrance to the gulf of Astakos or Nikomedeia, whence he crossed the ferry to Kibotos on the south side of the gulf, and then again took the land-road to Nikaia. When he learned in Nikaia of the ill success of Kamytzes, he advanced by a different road to intercept the Turks. He went by way of Malagina and Basilika. Basilika is described as a narrow and difficult glen on the (south-eastern) skirts of Olympos : it is probably to be sought somewhere about Inn Ongu in crossing the watershed. § He then

---

* Anna Comnena, vol. II., p. 279 ff.

† This is mentioned in the survey of the history of Dorylaion, given by Nicetas and Cinnamus, when Manuel set about refounding the city.

‡ The hurry which Anna mentions does not correspond well with the three days between Damalis and Aigialoi (Alexius, however, was unwell), for Leake only gives 12 hours, 36 miles, from Scutari to Malsum, which must correspond to Aigialoi. One might feel tempted to identify Kibotos with the modern Ghevse, the ancient Kibyza or Δακίβυζα, but Dakibyza was on the north side, 9 miles west of the ferry, whereas several passages in Anna show clearly that Kibotos was on the south side (not far from Helenopolis-Drepanon).

§ See Addenda to p. 236.

descended to Alethina, which must be between Kotiaion and Dorylaion. Meantime Mahumet had already reached the neighbourhood of Dorylaion, but Alexius, ignorant of this, advanced on Akrokos, in the direction of Kotiaion. He came upon the other division of the Turkish army, which had advanced from Kyzikos over the river Barenos or Granikos, by Parion, Abydos, Adramyttion, and returned by the Kaikos valley through Khliara (which was east of Pergamos) and Germe (called by Anna, Karme). Its further march must have led by Synaos (now Simav), Aizanoi, and Kotiaion, until they were suddenly attacked by Alexius. During the battle the Byzantine rear-guard was suddenly attacked by Mahumet, who, learning of the emperor's arrival, had collected a force of the nomad Turkmens round Dorylaion, and followed in pursuit of the Byzantine army. Alexius was thus caught between two forces, but still he gained the victory after suffering considerable loss. He then retired to Constantinople.* The description of this route, when compared with Edrisi's account of the road Amorion-Kotiaion-Chalcedon (H 25), shows that Alexius followed the road by Bilejik (Mulawwen) to Kotiaion.

21. The route between Malagina and Dorylaion is nowhere described carefully, but I find a probable reference to it in a passage of Anna Comnena, pp. 312–315.

The Castle of Saint George was near the Ascanian lake, west or north-west of Nikaia. The Turks penetrated to it in the year 1116, while Alexius was at Aer (Eribolos, ten miles south of Nikomedeia). He at once advanced to Nikaia and the castle of Saint George, and even to Sugut,† which lies south of Malagina on the road to Dorylaion. The regular modern road to Dorylaion passes through Sugut, though there is another way through Bilejik, and this passage of Anna makes it probable that the ancient road took the same course.

The Castle of Saint George was on the lake of Nikaia, a little to the west or north-west of the city. It must be distinguished from the Castle of Saint Gregory on the south side of the gulf of Astakos or Nikomedeia (Pachym., II., 103), though the Bonn translation of Anna always renders Gregory instead of George.

22. Justinianopolis-Mela is several times at the Council of 680 A.D. called Nova Justinianopolis Gordi, which probably means of the country

* Anna's reference to Philadelpheia shows her vague idea of the situation.

† Κωμόπολίν τινα Σαγουδάους ἐγχωρίως καλουμένην. The fact that the Turkish name Sugut, "willow," was already so attached to this place that Anna uses it and calls it the native name, is a striking proof of the extent of the Seljuk power along the Dorylaion route. The Kotiaion route was not so completely in their hands during this or the following reign. Sugut soon after became famous as the original home of the Ottoman Turks in Asia Minor: Ἔστι Σογούτη παρὰ Μυσίαν κώμη οὕτω καλουμένη εὐδαίμων καὶ ποταμὸς παρ᾽ αὐτῇ οὕτω καλούμενος....καλοῖτο δ᾽ ἂν αὕτη Ἰτέας κώμη. It is about 250 stadia from the Euxine, according to Laon. Chalcoc., p. 13.

Gordos.   I have elsewhere * connected this with the names of the bishoprics Gordoserboi in Bithynia, subject to Nikaia, and Gordorounia, or Gordorinia, in Phrygia Salutaris, and with Gordou Kome, the old name of Juliopolis, in Galatia; and have drawn the conclusion that the country along the Sangarios (especially the left bank) from Leukai upwards for a great distance, was called Gordos.

23. The river Melas, which is mentioned by Pachymeres as a branch of the Sangarios near the bridge built by Justinian over the Sangarios, can hardly be connected with Mela-Malagina. No such river is indicated in the maps, though it is expressly mentioned by Pachymeres (II., p. 331).

24. Atzoula is an unknown place on the unexplored course of the Sangarios south of Nikaia.   Botoniates, in 1078, wished to go from Kotiaion to Constantinople, but knew that the Turks, having concluded an agreement with the Emperor Michael, were trying to intercept him. He had only a small company with him, and they avoided the direct roads and went by by-paths.   Thus they reached safely Atzoula on the Sangarios, which is said to have been 200 miles from Nikaia : the distance is such an absurd exaggeration as to suggest the correction εἴκοσι for διακόσια.† Atzoula is probably the same place that is called Azalas by Anna, II., 79, and Nic. Bryenn., 34; Azalas seems to be on the hills that lie between Nikaia and the Gallos. Anna gave the distances from Nikaia in stadia, but the number is lost.   There was a monastery Alypos on the south side of Azalas.

25. It may be laid down beforehand that all the ἄπληκτα must have afforded suitable camping-ground for great armies, where water and food for men and horses were easily procured, and that all must have been natural centres, easy of access from the districts whose troops concentrated there; in short, each ἄπληκτον is likely to have been a natural road centre. We cannot, however, be certain that each ἄπληκτον was actually on the road, for a place at some distance from the road might be a more suitable standing-camp for an army.

Melagena might fairly be supposed to be a gathering-place for part of the Opsikian Theme, as it certainly was later in the time of Manuel. But as Dorylaion was in the Opsikian Theme, I have made the troops concentrate there.   The division between the Themes is very confused and difficult in this part of Bithynia.   According to Constantine the line of division between the Optimate and Opsikian Themes began on the coast between Helenopolis and Pylai, and passed between Nikomedeia and Nikaia.   South of Nikaia the Opsikian touches the Buccellariote

---

* 'Cities and Bishoprics of Phrygia,' part II., § LXXXIII. The situations mentioned there must be slightly modified, since I have now been forced to place Justinianopolis-Mela further north than I did in that paper.

† Niceph. Bryenn., p. 119. Astytzion on the Scamander (*i.e.* "townlet"), where Theodore Lascaris kept his treasure, is to be distinguished from Atzoula (Pachymer., I., 68).

Theme, which extended as far west as Modrene. If Modrene was in the Buccellariote Theme, the line of division must have passed between Nikaia and Lefke, and Melagena would be in the Buccellariote Theme. It seems, however, to be an absurd division for military purposes, that the great military road should pass through first the Optimate Theme at Helenopolis, then the Opsikian Theme, then the Buccellariote Theme, and then again the Opsikian Theme at Dorylaion. We must, therefore, take the other sense of Constantine's words,* that Modrene was the frontier town of the Opsikian, and that the Buccellariote begins at the east side of Modrene, *i.e.* at the river Sangarios. The line dividing the Opsikian and Buccellariote Themes runs from the Sangarios about the junction of the Gallos to a point east of Midaion. The entire military road from Pylai to Dorylaion and Midaion then lay in the Opsikian Theme. Thereafter it touched the Buccellariote Theme almost at its southern frontier, where it bordered on the Anatolic Theme near Kaborkion.

26. The Opsikian Theme included probably the entire Troad, it touched the Thrakesian Theme on the north side of the Kaikos valley, and further east it extended southwards to include the castle of Koula, which is several times mentioned by the Byzantine writers. Koula was the Turkish name, and was adopted even by Byzantine writers after it had passed into Turkish hands. Pachymeres (II., 426, ff.) describes how, in 1306, Roger, with his Catalans, marched by Germe, Khliara, and Aulax, to Philadelpheia, whence he made an excursion to Koula, which he captured, and then returned to Philadelphia. The castle Phourni, which he captured on the same excursion, is probably Magidion, near Saittai. But the Byzantine name for Koula was Opsikion, as we may argue from the fact that it was included in one bishopric with Maionia, three hours to the west of Koula. Moreover, Magidion (beside Saittai) and Opsikion are mentioned as πλαγίως ἐγκείμενα from Khliara, Pergamos, and the country down to the Cayster valley (Georg. Acropol., p. 30).

The word Koula is explained by Ducange ('Notæ in Alexiad.,' p. 621) as a term applied by the Greeks to all acropoleis. But the fact that the acropolis of Antioch on the Orontes was called Koula by Anna (II., pp. 89, 90), and Kala by Scylitzes,† shows that it is simply the Arabic Kale or Kala, which has been adopted by the Turks as their commonest term for a strong place. I have explained the term fully, because Prof. H. Kiepert ‡ criticised my brief statement to the same effect ('Cit. and Bish. of Phryg.,' part II., § cvii.), and considers that Koula is an old Turkish word, meaning "city." I quite grant that this is so, but it

---

* Of the Buccellariote Theme, ἔστιν ἀρχὴ....ἀπὸ μὲν τῆς κωμοπόλεως Μοδρηνῆς ἀρχόμενον.

† ἐνὸς τῶν πρὸς δύσιν τῆς Ἀντιοχείας πύργων Καλὰ τοὔνομα (Scylitz. in Niceph. Phoc., quoted by Ducange (l. c.).

‡ In a letter which he kindly sent me on the subject.

means really " fortified city," and is taken from the Arabic. It is still used in Turkish in the sense of a single house standing apart among the fields away from a town, and therefore like a castle. The boundary of the Opsikian Theme, passing south of Koula, ran north-east to Meros (now called Kumbet), and a point east of Midaion on the Tembris.

27. The next important point which is mentioned on the road was the famous city of Dorylaion, an ἄπληκτον, where the troops of the Thrakesian and Opsikian Themes met the Emperor: it is still a Turkish military station.

It is mentioned that Scholarii, the guards commanded by the *Domesticus Scholarum*, were stationed in Nikomedeia, Kios, Prousa, Kyzikos, Kotiaion, Dorylaion, and one other place, until the time of Justinian, who removed them from the first six stations, and placed them in the cities of Thrace.* But though the Scholarii were removed, there can be no doubt that Dorylaion still continued to be a military station. In the time of Constantine Porphyrogenitus, however, the Domesticus Scholarum seems to have been stationed in Anatolic Phrygia, as he meets the Emperor at the third ἄπληκτον, Kaborkion; moreover, Joannes Kurkuas, the famous general who reconquered the country from the Halys to the Tigris, was Domesticus.

Dorylaion fell into the hands of the Seljuk Turks in the latter part of the eleventh century,† along with the line of the military road to a point further north than Sugut, but the line of road to Kotiaion by Malagena, Basilika, and Alethina, still remained in Byzantine possession, and attained great importance in the campaigns of Alexius (1115), John, and Manuel Comnenus. At last, in the year 1175, Manuel made a great effort to break the Turkish power, and reopened two of the old military roads, one by Soublaion in the south of Phrygia, the other by Dorylaion. He advanced to Dorylaion by the ferry Damalis, collecting his troops at Melangeia. Cinnamus gives an interesting account of the situation of Dorylaion, its former importance as one of the very greatest cities of Asia, the delightful climate (which is even yet praised in the country), the fertile soil, the river full of fish,‡ the numerous population, the baths, and of its utter destruction by the Turks. About 2000 nomads camped in the neighbourhood of the deserted city. Manuel did not rebuild the old city, but selected a new site at a little distance. The site which he chose was apparently that which is now called Karadja Sheher, a deserted fortress about six miles south-west of Eski Sheher (Dorylaion). It is a fortress of the later Byzantine style, built on an

---

* Theophanes, p. 236.
† Probably in the year 1074, as already stated.
‡ Fish swarm in the Tembris, but I was disappointed with those which I tried to eat: the flesh is soft, tastes like mud, and proved uneatable to a very hungry man. I found that the natives also considered the fish that were brought me hardly fit for food.

almost isolated spur of the plateau that borders the Tembris valley on the south, of great natural strength, but difficult to supply with water. After the defeat at Myriokephalon, in the following year, Manuel promised to destroy the new city, and, though he broke his word, he could not retain his hold on it, and it went to decay.

28. The imperial estate, called Tembrion in the Opsikian Theme, whence fishermen were taken to accompany the Emperor's expeditions, and catch fish for his table,* may have been beside Dorylaion or Midaion. The river Tembris flows past both cities. It is called Thybris by Cinnamus, who mentions also that the Bathys (which must be a tributary of the Tembris) flowed past Dorylaion.

The Byzantine writers give interesting accounts of the Turkish nomads who inhabited the plain of Dorylaion when Manuel reoccupied the city. Anna Comnena calls them Turkmens (τῶν κατὰ τὴν Ἀσίαν οἰκούντων Τουρκομάνων, vol. II., p. 284). I add other two passages : ὅσοι πολυθρέμμονες ὄντες ἀναδιφῶσι πόας τὰς λειμωνίτιδας† καὶ τούτων ἕνεκα τῶν οἰκείων ἠθῶν ἀπανιστάμενοι παγγενεὶ τὰ Ῥωμαίων ἐπεισίασιν ὅρια. (Nicet. Chon., p. 156). τότε δὲ Πέρσαι ἀμφὶ δισχιλίους περὶ ταύτην (the plain of Dorylaion) νομάδες ὡς ἔθος ἐσκήνουν (Cinnam. 295).

29. From Dorylaion the road perhaps followed the line of the old Roman road to Pessinus as far as Trikomia-Troknada. It is mentioned that the Emperor Basil II., in the year 880, when returning from an expedition into Kommagene, passed through Midaion. Presumably he travelled along the military road. Were it not for this passage, I should have supposed that the road went along the modern track direct to Troknada (Kaimaz) ; but the terms in which Midaion is mentioned do not permit the supposition that on this occasion Basil diverged a little from the direct road for some special reason in order to visit it. When he reached Midaion he halted, reviewed his troops, distributed rewards, and dismissed them to their winter quarters.‡

30. Troknada was the nearest point on the road to the third ἄπληκτον, Kaborkion, and probably the troops who had collected at Kaborkion joined the emperor when he reached Troknada. The distance is about twelve or fifteen miles. Kaborkion, a bishopric of Phrygia Salutaris in the latest class of Notitiæ, was probably in the Anatolic Theme. It was the place where the troops of the Anatolic and Seleukeian Themes collected, together with those commanded by the Domesticus Scholarum. Its situation at the great fountains of the

* See last note, p. 212. The estate is expressly mentioned as τοῦ χωρίου τοῦ Τέμβρη (Const. Porph., I., p. 488). But, since the above was in type, I have observed that this place (which is called Tembrion, Tymbrion, or Tembrieion by Stephanus) is the imperial estate called Eudokias by Hierocles, see E. § 27.

† This expression adds probability to the identification given below (see Galaiia, Santabaris) of Edrisi's Libadhia on a navigable stream with Dorylaion.

‡ Cedren., II., p. 216; Theophan. Contin., p. 283. Krasos was also on the Military Road (see p. 435), which probably then went to Justinianopolis.

Sangarios has been described, CB, § LXXIV.   The splendid water-supply in a thirsty land, and the fine fertile plain around made it an excellent camping-ground for an army.   It is still a good horse-breeding centre, an imperial estate, and a military station.

31. The road went on to a very strong and important fortress, Justinianopolis Palia, situated at Sivri Hisar, whose lofty twin peaks afford an impregnable citadel.   Dr. Mordtmann was first led by the name to suggest this situation: the course of the road proves his acute suggestion to be correct.   Its strength as a fortress, and its situation on the road soon made it the chief city of Galatia Salutaris.   It became first a bishopric, and afterwards the actual metropolis and the residence of the metropolitan bishop, though he still retained the title 'bishop of Pessinus.'   It still retains its rank as chief city of a Sanjak, and is an important centre of roads and commerce (see Galatia Salutaris).

32. The course of the road across Galatia is very uncertain.   The rarity of references to Ankyra in the military history of the Byzantine Empire, combined with the fact that it lies to the north of the direct route and that the road Sivri-Hisar-Ankyra is waterless except at the crossing of the Sangarios, suggests that the military road passed to the south of Ankyra.   In that case there can be no doubt that it went by Beinam (Gorbeous), where it joined the new road from Ankyra to Justinianopolis-Mokissos and Cæsareia, still one of the most important routes in Anatolia.   This road went nearly straight east to the Halys, which it crossed at the bridge now called Tcheshnir Keupreu, and besides which was probably situated the fortress Saniana, the military centre of the Turma Saniana.   The route from Sivri Hisar to Gorbeous (Beinam) is very difficult to trace.

33. The bridge Zompos or Zompi spanned the Sangarios at the point where the road crossed the river.   This point must have been south of the modern Kawunji Keupreu and near the mouth of the Ilidja Su, if the view which I take of the subsequent course of the road is correct.   Widely different views, varying from near the source of the Sangarios (Texier) to near its mouth (Ritter), have been expressed about the situation of this bridge, which is of great importance in Byzantine military history owing to its situation on the military road.   It will, therefore, be convenient at this point to examine the question of the Byzantine bridges over the Sangarios, Pontogephyra, Zompi, and perhaps Tantaendia.   The first of these was built by Justinian, A.D. 560, to replace a bridge of boats (which was frequently destroyed by floods) on the important roads from Nikomedeia to Ankyra and to the whole of the north provinces.   This bridge is described by Procopius (de Aedif., V., 2) as still building while he was writing his book.   Justinian diverted the course of the river to build it.   The fame of this bridge grew as time passed, and it still stands, a really great work, described by Texier as 429 metres long and composed of eight arches.   Pachymeres (II., 330)

mentions its true name Pontogephyra, and says that it no longer spanned the Sangarios but a smaller stream called Melas, as the Sangarios had changed its course. The Sakaria still flows some distance to the east of the bridge. The name Pontogephyra, apparently a hybrid, Greek and Latin combined, was corrupted to Pentegephyra, and explained as bridge of five arches, though according to Texier it is of eight arches.* This error occurs in Cedrenus (I., 678), and Theophanes (p. 234). Agathias composed an epigram on the bridge, which is quoted by Zonaras (III., p. 53) and Constantine Porphyrogenitus (de Them., p. 27). The latter, misunderstanding his authority, says the epigram was engraved on a stone in the bridge, and the misstatement has often been repeated.

34. Ritter, in his ' Erdkunde von Asien,' vol. XX., p. 558, identifies this bridge of Justinian with the bridge Zompi, but this is a quite mistaken view.† The situation of Zompi is defined with sufficient clearness by the many references that occur to it. At first sight something is to be said for Texier's view‡ that the bridge of Zompi is Tchandir Keupreu, a few hours below the great springs at Tchifteler in which the Sangarios rises. Anna Comnena refers to it as lying east of Santabaris (Bardakchi) and Amorion, and Nicephorus Bryennius speaks of it as near the sources of the Sangarios. Texier declares it to be a stone bridge of Byzantine work, and the case seems very complete in his favour. In 1883 I made a long détour in order to see the bridge; and in 1886 I again crossed it. It seems to me to be a Turkish bridge, built to carry the important route from Sivri Hisar to Azizie (the earlier Turkish Jirgin) and Afiom Kara Hisar. A road to the east from Dorylaion could not possibly go by Tchandir Keupreu, and, if it be Zompi, then the military road must have crossed the Sangarios by a different bridge. But a passage in Michael Attaliota (p. 184) forces us to look elsewhere for Zompi. In the year 1073 the Caesar John marched (evidently along the military road) from Dorylaion to the east, and crossed the bridge called Zompos, which spans the Sangarios, and connects the Anatolic and Cappadocic Themes. Now, I have stated above that the military road did not even touch Tchifteler (Kaborkion), where are the fountains of the Sangarios, but keeps away to the north of it without touching the Sangarios. But, even supposing that it did make the détour to Tchifteler, it would never make a further détour down the right bank in order to need a bridge to cross by some 12 miles down. It would go straight across from Tchifteler to Sivri Hisar (Justinianopolis). Moreover, it cannot be supposed that the Cappadocic Theme extended to the sources of the Sangarios at this time. It might, of course, be argued from Constantine's

* I am assuming Texier's account to be correct. But possibly he is wrong, and the bridge has five arches. In that case Pentegephyra would be correct, and Pontogephyra the corruption.

† There seems to be here some strange misconception of the great geographer, as in the same sentence he speaks of the plains of Dorylaion on the east of the Sangarios.

‡ Texier, ' Asie Mineure,' p. 391.

description of the Cappadocic Theme that it could not have reached to any part of the Sangarios, but was confined to the east side of the Halys; but his description applies to the older form of the Theme, and about 890 the Cappadocic Theme was actually extended as far west as the mountains east of Sivri Hisar (Gunusu Dagh, the ancient Dindymos ?).

35. It is necessary at this point to discuss the limits at different periods of the Cappadocic Theme. Constantine identifies the Cappadocic Theme, which was one of the three divisions of the great Armeniac Theme, with the old province Cappadocia Secunda; but this is a mere slip; for in the earlier part of his account he defines it clearly as adjoining Lykaonia on the one side and reaching to Caesareia on the other, and in another direction bordering on the Buccellariote Theme on one side and reaching to Loulon and even up to Podandos on the other side ('de Them.,' p. 19). But his description of the Buccellariote Theme shows that it extended to the Halys, and that it was divided from the Cappadocic Theme by the Halys. A passage, however, in his treatise 'de Administrando Imperio' (p. 225) shows clearly that, though originally the Buccellariote Theme did extend along the Halys as far south as the frontier of the old Cappadocian province near Parnassos, yet a modification took place subsequently. About the year 890 four military districts of the Buccellariote Theme, Bareta, Balbadon, Aspona, and Akarkous, together with three of the Anatolic Theme, Eudokias, Saint Agapetos, and Aphrazeia, were transferred to the Cappadocian Theme. These seven districts comprise all the southern part of Galatia, from Aspona, near the Halys, to the Sangarios and even to Eudokias, and are called the Turma Kommata.† The bridge Zompi crosses from Eudokias to Saint Agapetos or Myrika, and apparently either a third change must have occurred and Eudokias been again attached to the Anatolic Theme or else Michael refers to the fact that the Anatolic Theme included all the country south of the Sangarios, and must have come close up to Zompi.

36. Of these seven bandai or topoteresiai, Eudokias, Saint Agapetos, Aphrazeia, and Aspona, have (H, 5-12) been placed approximately or exactly. The precise sites of Bareta, Balbadon, and Akarkous, can hardly be fixed, but Akarkous is probably a false reading for Akarbous and is a variant of Gorbeous.‡ Bareta and Balbadon would then comprise the central parts of the Haimane (Bareta on the north

---

* τὴν τῶν 'Ανατολικῶν καὶ Καππαδοκῶν ἐπιζευγνύει ἐπαρχίαν (Mich. Attal., p. 184).

† Kommata is possibly the Latin *comata*.

‡ Gorbeous, Akarbous, compare Loulon, Halala, which have been identified in another part of this book. K for B is a common error; compare Ikria for Ibria in Not. I., VIII., IX. I misinterpreted Ikria in my 'Cities and Bishoprics of Phrygia,' part I., but put it correctly in the Table, part II. Since then, I find my correction confirmed by the Bodleian manuscript, Baroc. 185, fol. 16, which reads ἰυρίων, and which invariably writes υ for β.

Balbadon on the south), and Akarbous and Aspona similarly the eastern Haimane up to the Halys. Akarbous would be a fort commanding the military road, and similarly we may look for Bareta or Balbadon on or near the military road at a point south of Ankyra, and near the road from Ankyra to Perta and Archelais Colonia.

A comparison of the account given (K 15) of the Kharsian Theme shows that this later Cappadocic Theme must have been practically confined to these seven bandai. It was bounded on the north by the Buccellariote Theme, which is mentioned A.D. 1035 by Cedrenus, II., p. 514, and Glycas, p. 588, as still in existence, on the east by the Halys and the Kharsian Theme, on the south and west by the Anatolic Theme. Its importance, in spite of its small size, lay in its being on the line of the great road.

It is certainly true that the expression of Michael Attaliota about Zompi connecting the Anatolic and Cappadocic Themes suggests that the river separated the two Themes, and a great river is certainly the natural boundary between two military districts, just as the Halys was on the east. But on the other hand Eudokias seems necessarily placed at Yürme, and the baths of Saint Agapetos equally necessarily at the Hamam near Kadi Keui. Eudokias borders on Germa, and even if we could place Eudokias east of the Sangarios, separated by that river from Germa,* it would then be almost necessary to place Saint Agapetos at Yürme, and the difficulty would still remain.

In 1068 Romanus Diogenes, marching to the east by the usual road *via* Helenopolis, crossed the Sangarios by the bridge Zompos, and afterwards the Halys.† This passage also proves that Zompi was on the military road.

37. Another bridge called Tantaendia, evidently over the Sangarios, or perhaps one of its tributaries, the Tembris or the Siberis, is mentioned in the life of Theodorus Sykeota.‡ It lay between Colonia Germa and Sykea, and must be either over the middle course of the Sangarios, south of Sykea and Lagania, or over the Tembris near Germa. It is just possible that it is identical with the bridge over the Siberis built by Justinian (Procop., 'Ædif.,' V. 6).

38. To cross Galatia with a large army from east to west, there are only two roads which afford a water-supply. One of these would keep along the Tembris (Porsuk Su), cross the Sangarios, and ascend the Ankyra river. The military road appears not to have taken this course, and it must in all probability have taken the other. In that case, from Justinianopolis

---

* The position so far north is, however, impossible, for the seven bandai are clearly the southern part of Galatia. The Anatolic Theme, to judge from Constantine's description, could never have included Eudokias, unless it was pretty far south; and nothing is left for the Buccellariote, if the Anatolic extended to the river of Ankyra, which in that case would be the northern border of Eudokias.

† Scylitz., p. 639, and Attal., p. 139.

‡ Act. Sanct., April 22nd, p. 53.

it went to Eudokias, crossed the Sangarios south of the present Kawunji Keupreu, ascended the Ilija Su, which flows with a fine stream throughout the summer * from the central Haimane. The road would pass under the walls of Kizil Hissar Kale, which I suppose to be Aphrazeia, and which overhangs the river. It would then cross by Bareta or Balbadon to Gorbeous-Akarbous, and descend a stream which flows eastwards towards the Halys.

39. The Halys must have been crossed by a bridge, and Tcheshnir Keupreu is admirably situated, where the river is narrowed to enter a gorge in the mountains. A bridge over the Halys is indeed never mentioned by Byzantine writers; but it can hardly be the case that the Turks were the first to construct a bridge there.†

In A.D. 905, Samonas, the Saracen favourite of Leo VI., on pretence of going on a visit to his own monastery Speira, which was situated in Damatry beside Constantinople, fled to his native country, and, in order to avoid pursuit, hamstrung all the post-horses as he passed. He was, however, refused permission to cross the Halys, and was in consequence overtaken by his pursuers. A doubt might be raised whether this refers to the passage of the Halys at Tcheshnir Keupreu, or to the other crossing between Justinianopolis-Mokissos (Kir Sheher) and Caesareia. He had already long passed Speira, and was going onwards towards the east, when he was arrested, so that it was clear that he was fleeing. He then pretended that he was going to the Timios Stavros, the Holy Cross, at Sirichas or Sirachas.‡ When we remember that one of the fortresses in southern Galatia which we have (K 12–6) seen reason to place on the military road, was called Timios Stavros, there can be no doubt that Samonas was arrested at Tcheshnir Keupreu, and then pretended that he was going to the Holy Cross for religious purposes. The incident incidentally confirms in a general way the situation which has been assigned to Timios Stavros.

40. Another place on the road west of the Halys was Ara. In A.D. 906 Eustathius Argyrus was banished to his own house in the Kharsian Theme, but on his way died at Ara, and was buried at Spynin, a high point beside Ara.§ His sons, however, exhumed the body and carried it to the family monastery of S. Elizabeth in the Kharsian Theme. There is no clue to the exact position of Ara and Spynin.

41. There must certainly have been a fortress near the bridge to protect the crossing of the Halys. This fortress, as I shall try to prove, was Saniana.

In the first place, the defending fortress was on the east side of the

* I have gone along it in the middle of September.

† The present bridge may be only a repaired Byzantine bridge: it has a single pointed arch.

‡ Sirichas Leo Grammat., p. 278; Theophan. Contin., p. 369; Sirachas, Cedren., II., p. 264.

§ ἐς τὸ Σπυνὶν τοῦ Ἄρα τὴν κωνυφήν (Theophan. Contin., p. 374).

Halys, for Romanus Diogenes, in 1068, built for the first time a fort on the west bank at the crossing (Attal., p. 146).

In the second place, the three bandai in the south of Galatia beyond the Halys, which once belonged to the Buccellariote Theme, but in 890 were transferred to the Kharsian Theme, were united in the Turma Saniana. During the following century Constantine mentions that the Buccellariote Theme extended to the fortress Saniana The fortress Saniana is also mentioned in the year 824 as being surrendered by the insurgent chief who occupied it. Now it is clear that the Buccellariote Theme extended to the Halys, and it is therefore probable that the limiting town was on the Halys. Moreover, the principal fortress of a Turma may very suitably be placed at such an important point as the crossing of the Halys and a triple fork of the military road.

Another argument may be drawn from Strabo (p. 562), who mentions Sanisene apparently as a frontier district on the south of Paphlagonia.* Just as we find the two forms Pimolisa and Pimolia, or Kolose and Koloe, used to designate the same town, so Sanisene and Saniana are clearly the same name. Now it is certainly impossible to place Saniana as far north as Strabo implies Sanisene to have been; but remembering how vague were the limits of countries in Strabo's time,† we may, perhaps, consider that Sanisene was partly absorbed in Galatia, and partly left in Paphlagonia. In that case Sanisene would be originally a province or district along the Halys on both banks, south of Pimolisene, extending as far south as Tcheshnir Keupreu, near which stood the Byzantine fortress Saniana. Originally, of course, Saniana was an adjectival form, but it has, like Malagina, become a noun.

42. Now it is obvious that the bridge of the Halys would be a convenient ἄπληκτον for the Buccellariote troops. Constantine, however, says that the Buccellariote troops always met at Kolonia, i.e. Archelais. It is, however, a patent absurdity that when the emperor is marching to the east, the Buccellariote troops should concentrate 100 miles south of the road, and 60 miles south of their southern frontier, in order to join him conveniently. Substitute Saniana for Kolonia, and the description is clear and accurate. The order of enumerating the ἄπληκτα is then natural. Saniana is then the place where all the eastern themata meet the emperor if his march is towards Cilicia. But if he is going towards Kommagene the Buccellariote, the Paphlagonian, and the Kharsian troops meet at Saniana, while the Cappadocian, Armeniac, and Sebasteian ‡ meet at Caesareia.

---

* The text seems not satisfactory. The meaning probably is that southern Paphlagonia (ruled by several kings) was divided into Timonitis on the Bithynian frontier, and the kingdom of Gezatorix including Marmolitis and Sanisene and Potamia : omit one καί (see Addenda).

† He quotes the proverbial uncertainty, "the bounds of Phrygia and Mysia."

‡ One necessary transposition is here made between Paphlagonian and Cappadocian.

Yet another argument might be brought to show the utter absurdity of the reading Kolonia. A glance of the map will show that if Kolonia were an ἄπληκτον, it would in every case be by far the most convenient for the Seleukeian, and sometimes for the Anatolic troops, yet these troops go to Kaborkion : on the other hand, as the ἄπληκτα have been corrected, Kaborkion is the proper ἄπληκτον for them.

43. At Saniana the military road forked, and one branch went straight east, probably through Myriokephaloi, Timios Stavros,* Basilika Therma, Siboron, Hypsela, Agrane or Agriane, Sialos, Bathys Rhyax, and Sebasteia towards Armenia. This part of the road will be discussed below. It only remains to add that Justinian fortified several points on the road in Armenia, Satala, Koloneia, and Theodosiopolis, and built the walls of Sebasteia (Procop., Aedif., III.).

44. It is to be observed that the last ἄπληκτον is Dazimon, but that the troops who must have assembled there are said to meet the emperor, not at Dazimon, but at Bathys Rhyax. The situation of these two places, as fixed L 20, explains this peculiar language. Dazimon is the splendid plain called the Kaz Ova, west of Tokat. The Armeniac troops collected here, and when the emperor was approaching, they came to meet him at Bathys Rhyax, which is mentioned as a convenient place for going off the road into the Armeniac Theme.† Bathys Rhyax has been placed at Sialos or Siara, now Yeni Khan, where the roads from Tokat and from the west meet before they go on to Sebasteia. Thirty miles beyond Bathys Rhyax, and therefore near Sebasteia, was a hill by the road called Κωνσταντίνου Βουνός.‡ (See p. 267.)

45. The other branch of the road, going south-east from Saniana, passed through Justinianopolis-Mokissos, now Kir Sheher, which, from its refoundation by Justinian, has continued down to the present day to be one of the chief cities of eastern Anatolia. I have described, in discussing the roads east of Ankyra, the alteration that occurred in the roads across north-western Cappadocia in the fourth and fifth centuries, and the consequent rise of Justinianopolis to importance.

46. At Justinianopolis the road again forked, one branch went south by Zoropassos (Yarapson §), Soanda (near Nev Sheher), through the Turma Kases or Kasin in the plain of Venasa (about the modern Melegob and Hassa Keui), to Tyana and the Cilician Gates. During the centuries of Saracen warfare, the country between the Gates and the Halys was

---

* Such names as [Π]λώτινος for Troknades, S. Agapetos for Myrika, &c., show the influence of religion on nomenclature in Byzantine time. Another fort, called Myriokephalon, stood on the important Kleisoura, leading east from Soublaion.

† Compare Genesius, pp. 122-4, which is quoted in fixing the position of Agrane and Bathys Rhyax.

‡ Genes., p. 124.

§ The name is always given in the maps, Arebsun; but the spelling Yarapson corresponds far more closely to the local pronunciation. The initial y is always audible.

almost continually infested by Saracen bands. Hence on such an expedition the whole Byzantine army was collected by the time the emperor reached Saniana. It would have exposed the army to be cut off in detachments if it had concentrated further south.

It is possible that the old pilgrim's road along the left bank of the Halys may appear to some readers to be a preferable route. In that case the fork would occur at Akarbous, and an expedition against Cilicia would pass through the fortress Aspona (also a bishopric), would touch the Halys and pass through Parnassos and Nyssa, would then diverge from the Halys and join the other route at Soanda. But in addition to the arguments which have already led us to the view given above, I may add that the utter desolation of this route and the almost complete failure of Byzantine ruins on it, seem irreconcilable with the idea that it was one of the greatest imperial roads throughout the Byzantine period.

47. When the emperor was marching towards Kommagene or Melitene, it was most convenient that the Armeniac, Sebasteian, and Cappadocian troops should meet in Cæsareia. The march led from Justinianopolis-Mokissos south-east to the Halys, which it crossed by the bridge described below (L 2), and probably then passed through Justinianopolis-Kamoulianai to Cæsareia. The road from Cæsareia, across the rivers Karmalas or Onopnictes (Zamanti Su) and Saros to Arabissos (Yarpuz) and Germaniceia (Marash), has been described N 1; but it will be convenient to add here a note on the chief campaigns against the Arabs. In Section R. I have described the chief passes across Taurus, and corresponding to these Kleisourai there are in the Saracen Wars two chief lines of attack, used at different periods. The Arab armies at some periods cross by the Cilician Gates, at others they come from the Anti-taurus region. In the former case the operations take place chiefly on the road by Tyana, partly also on that which leads through Heraklea-Kybistra and Lykaonia. In the latter case, they take place on the roads that lead north and west from the river Saros. As a general rule, the operations of the period before 840 are on the Cilician route, and after 840, under Michael and Basil, they are almost always on the Kommagenian route.

H. Cities and Bishoprics of Galatia Salutaris.

This province was formed between 386 and 395 by the emperor Theodosius (Malalas, p. 348),* by taking the south-western part of Galatia, with the bishoprics Germa, Myrika, Eudokias, Pessinus and Petinessos or Pitnisos, and adding to them a part of Phrygia Salutaris, containing the bishoprics Amorion, Orkistos, Klaneos and Troknades.

* 386 is the approximate date given for Polemius Silvius, who mentions only one province, Galatia: 412-3 is the date given by Seeck to the 'Notitia Dignitatum,' which mentions two Galatias.

GALATIA SALUTARIS.

Roman Imperial Coins.	Hierocles, about A.D. 530.	Councils of 431, 451, 536, 553.	Councils of 680, 692.	Notitia VIII, IX.	Councils of 787, 879.	Notitia I.	Notitia III., X.
ΠΕΣΣΙΝΟΥΝΤΙΩΝ	1 Πισινοῦς	Pessinus	Pessinus	1 Πισινοῦντος	I. Pessinus	1 Πισινούντων ἤτοι Ἰουστινιανουπόλεως	1 Πισινοῦντος
..	..	..	..	8 Παλιας	..	8 Σπαλείας	8 Σπαλείας
..	..	Orkistos, 451	Ὀρκισοῦ	..	..	7 Ὀρκιστοῦ, Ὀρκισθοῦ	7 Ὀρκιστοῦ, Ὀρκισθοῦ
..	2 Ρεγεμαυρέκιον	Petinessos, 451	..	5 Πιτανισσοῦ	..	4 Πιτανισσοῦ	3 Πιτανισσοῦ
..	3 Πηγριμηγούς	..	..	..	..	..	..
ΑΜΟΡΙΑΝΩΝ	4 Ἀμόριον	Amorion, 451	Ἀμορίου	2 τοῦ Ἀμορίου	II. Amorion, 787, 879	II. 1 Ἀμορίου	II. 1 Ἀμορίου, Ἀμωρίου
..	5 Κλάνεος	..	Κελανίου	3 Κλανέου	Κλανέου, 787	II. 4 Κλανέου, Κλάθεος	II. 4 Κλανέου, Κλαθεοῦ
..	6 Ρεγετνακάδη	Troknades, 451	Τροχυάδων	6 Τροκνάδων	Τροκνάδων, 787	5 Τροκνάδων	5 Τροκνάδων
..	7 Εὐδοξιάς	Eudoxias, 451	Συρυάδων	4 Εὐδοξιάδος	..	3 Εὐδοξιάδος	4 Λωτίνου
..	8 Μυρικιόν	Μυρικηρών Θερμαί, 451	Θερμῶν τοῦ Ἀγ. Ἀγαπίου	..	..	6 Συροδέων, Συνοδίου	6 Συνοδέων, Συνοδίου
Colonia Germe	9 Γέρμια	Μυριάγγελοι, 553	..	7 Γερμοκολωνίας	..	6 Γερμοκολωνείας	2 Γερμοκολωνείας
ΦΙΛΟΜΗΛΕΩΝ	(Pisidia)	..	..	(Pisidia)	..	II. 2 Φιλομηλίου	II. 2 Φιλομηλίου
ΔΟΚΙΜΕΩΝ	(Phrygia S.)	..	..	(Phrygia S.)	..	II. 3 Δοκιμίου	II. 3 Δοκιμίου
..	(Phrygia S.)	..	..	(Phrygia S.)	..	II. 5 Πολυβότου	II. 5 Πολυβότου
..	(Phrygia S.)	..	..	..	II. Pissia, 879	II. 6 Πισσίας	II. 6 Πισσίας

Pessinus was made the metropolis of the new province. The name "Salutaris" was perhaps due to the hot springs, which abound in western Galatia and eastern Phrygia, and which have always been great medicinal resorts. See p. 437. A comparative list of the bishoprics is given in the accompanying Table.

1 and 2. PESSINUS and JUSTINIANOPOLIS.—This pair of cities is so closely connected that they must be treated together. Sivri Hissar, the modern capital, has succeeded to the honours of Pessinus, and is in great measure built out of the ruins of the Græco-Roman city. A church of S. Sophia at Pessinus, and a church of the Holy Angels outside the walls, to which the bishop George went forth, are mentioned in ' Acta S. Theodori,' April 22, p. 52. Two inscriptions of Pessinus, still unpublished, mention fine garments (two fibulatoria, two pairs of δίμιτα), sent as a present to the Emperor Trajan: it was doubtless this kind of cloth that is mentioned as being made in Galatia and as forming an important article of trade, in the Greek geographical tract published by Gothofredus (Geneva, 1628, p. 24), and dated by him A.D. 347–8. The pig was held to be an unclean animal at Pessinus, according to Pausanias, VII., 17, 10.

The situation of Pessinus has long been known at Bala Hissar, about 12 miles S.S.E. of Sivri Hissar. Texier publishes a beautiful plan of the ruins of Pessinus; but his plan is almost a pure invention, and has only the very faintest resemblance to the features of the place. The city sank into decay as Justinianopolis (Sivri Hissar) rose to importance; but it has always been inhabited, and the present inhabitants appear to me to be descended from the ancient population with not more than a very slight admixture of Turkish blood.

Justinianopolis was refounded by the emperor Justinian. Its older name seems to have been Palia or Spalia,* but the spelling varies so much that the correct form is quite uncertain. As Mordtmann† first divined, Justinianopolis is the impregnable fortress of Sivri Hissar. It was evidently built as one of the chain of strong places on the Byzantine military road,‡ and its military importance soon made it the real centre of the province. In Not. I., dated A.D. 883, we have the entry ὁ Πισινούντων ἤτοι 'Ιουστινανουπόλεως, which proves that it had definitely become the metropolis of the province, and the archbishop of Pessinus was now merged in the metropolitan of Justinianopolis. Yet, in all the Notitiæ, even in Not. I., which alone preserves in one of its entries the truth, Justinianopolis is mentioned as separate from Pessinus and ranking last among the bishoprics subject to that metropolis. When

* It is possible that Spania, which also occurs, is the best form. See p. 163.
† I am glad to have the opportunity of quoting Dr. Mordtmann, who did much good work, with few positive correct identifications. His papers are buried in old journals, especially ' Münchener Sitzungsber.' and ' Gel. Anzeiger.'
‡ See G 31.

founded by Justinian it was made a bishopric, and placed at the end of the existing list of bishoprics; but when it became (probably about 700 A.D.) the real centre of the province, the Archbishop of Pessinus transferred his residence to the fortress, and, while continuing to bear the title ὁ Πεσσινουντίων ἤτοι 'Ιουστινιανουπόλεως), became practically the archbishop of Justinianopolis.*

Justinianopolis is wholly ignored in the Councils, because it was not founded when the Councils before 553 were held; and when the later Councils were held the metropolitan of Pessinus is identical with the bishop (archbishop) of Justinianopolis. Only in the Council A.D. 553 he might have appeared, but of the whole province only Pessinus and Germa were represented in that Council.

3. GERMA, a colony of Augustus, Colonia Julia Augusta Fida Germa, is often called Germokoloneia in Byzantine documents. All writers have hitherto accepted Leake's view that it was situated at Yürme, and that "yürme" is the modern pronunciation of "germe." I have shown, J, § 1, that the view is mistaken, that conclusive epigraphic evidence places Germa near Masut Keui, on the lower course of the Tembris, and that the road-system of Galatia demands this situation. The derivation of Germe from the Phrygian correspondent to Greek θερμός, Sanskrit *gharmas*, Latin *formus*, is probable; but it is not known whether any hot springs existed nearer than Mousgon.

Hierocles has the name Γέρμια, which he gets according to a practice common with him from the ecclesiastical ὁ Γερμίων (ἐπίσκοπος). The same form occurs in the Latin translation of the 'Acta S. Theodori' and occasionally in the ecclesiastical lists.

4. MYRIANGELOI was a name given to Germa in Byzantine times: its origin is obviously from the chief church, which must have been dedicated to the "hosts of angels."

Germia of Galatia is regularly mentioned as an archbishopric in several of the Notitiæ of all classes.† Germokoloneia is regularly mentioned in the same Notitiæ as a bishopric subject to Pessinus. We might believe that the archbishopric is the same place as the bishopric, which had been left uncorrected in its old place, when it was elevated to be an archbishopric. Such examples of carelessness in keeping the registers are common, and in this case the double name facilitated the error. But the remarks, p. 322, show that Germia the archbishopric is perhaps in Bithynia.

Two monasteries at Germa are mentioned at the second Council of

---

* I have shown that the same occurred (1) at Perga and Attalia: see "Antiq. of S. Phrygia," in 'Amer. Journ. of Arch.' 1888, *s.v.* Perga; (2) at Prymnessos and Akroenos, "Cit. and Bish. of Phrygia," in 'Journ. of Hell. Stud' 1887, *s.v.* Akroenos; (3) at Kolossai and Chonai; and at numerous other places.

† Γέρμια Γαλατίας, Not. I., II., VI., X.; Γέρμια Γαλατίας πρώτης, Not. VIII.; Γέρμια Γαλατίας δευτέρας, Not. VII.

Nicæa, A.D. 787: Σέργιος ἡγούμενος τῶν Γερμίων and Ἰωάννης πρεσβύτερος τοῦ Ἁγίου Σεργίου τῶν Γερμίων.

5. EUDOXIAS is a name given to some town or village of Galatia in honour either of the mother or of the daughter of Theodosius II. It belongs to a large group of city names, which seem all to belong to the period of Valens, Theodosius I., and Pulcheria Augusta: in Phrygia Pacatiana, Valentia, Eudokias, Theodosia, and Pulcherianopolis; in Pisidia, Theudosiopolis (Eudoxiopolis in Hierocles); in Asia, several different places were named Theodosiopolis, and Arcadiopolis occurs; and many other examples might be collected.

Eudoxias and Germa were conterminous bishoprics, as is shown by a passage in the life of S. Theodorus Sykeota.[*] There was a feast of the Virgin *in Musgi oppido*, at which it was customary for the bishops of Germa and of Eudoxias to be present. Musgum was, therefore, probably a village on the frontier of Germa and Eudoxias, and the Christian custom perpetuated an old religious connection of both cities with some holy spot between them. Such a connection is not likely to have existed between cities on opposite sides of the Sangarios, and no other territory in Galatia Salutaris, conterminous with Germa, remains, except on the south of that city and on the east of Pessinus.

There is, therefore, every probability that Eudoxias was situated at Yürme, where there are considerable remains of a Byzantine bishopric, and in that case

6. MOUSGON was probably situated at the fine hot springs about six miles N.N.W. of Yürme.

7. SYNODION. It appears that the bishopric which is named (in genitive case) Συννάδων, Συνοδέων, Συνοδίου in the late Notitiæ III. and X., and in the Council of Constantinople, 692, must be identified with Eudoxias; but the reason of the name is quite unknown, unless it be derived from this great gathering at the hot springs ̣ad Musgi oppidum.

8. GORDION. The famous city Gordion is apparently to be identified with Eudoxias. Manlius, after crossing the Sangarios south of Pessinus, marched in one day to Gordion; and Alexander the Great, marching probably by the same road to Ankyra, passed through Gordion. It was an important commercial city of the early period, and the situation at Yürme explains this importance, because it is on the "Royal Road" from Pessinus to Ankyra. The identification seems fairly certain, for there is absolutely no other city within a day's march of the place where Manlius must have crossed the Sangarios.

9. AKKILAION is wrongly identified with Eudoxias, and the frontier of Asia consequently pushed too far east, in the map attached to my "Cities and Bishoprics of Phrygia," part II. The false situation assigned to Germa by all authorities and accepted by me, threw the whole

---

[*] 'Acta Sanctorum,' April 22nd, p. 47.

topography of the district into confusion. Akkilaion has now been properly placed on the Tembris, between Midaion and Germa. So long as Germa was placed at Yürme, since Eudoxias was certainly adjoining it, there was no alternative except to place Eudoxias on the lower Tembris. Then Akkilaion and Eudoxias were side by side, and, as Akkilaion never occurs as a bishopric, I supposed them to be actually included in one bishopric. The name Akkilaion, like Midaion from Midas, Dorylaion from Dorylas, Tataion or Tottaion from Tatas or Tottes, is obviously derived from a personal name Akkilas, and there can be little doubt that this is a variant of the very common Phrygian personal name Akylas.* Akkilaion is perhaps Gratianopolis, on which see C. B., LXXXIII., Act. Sanct., Apr. 22, p. 42, and Conc. Ephes., A.D. 431, where Philadelphus, bishop of Gratianopolis, was present. Akkilaion was in the province Asia, as is clear from its coins.

10. MYRIKA. The situation is proved with certainty by the hot springs, mentioned in a signature at the Council of Chalcedon. Besides the hot baths between Germa and Eudoxias, the only others known in Galatia Salutaris are at the Merkez of the Haimane, near Kadi Keui, at the head-waters of a stream which flows into the Istanoz Su not far above its junction with the Sangarios.† The exact form of the name is uncertain; the adjectives formed from it are Μυρίκιος and Μυρικηνός. Hierocles has Μυρικίων, which is apparently adapted from a list of bishoprics (ὁ Μυρικίων). In one entry at Council. Chalcedon ‡ we read " Elpidio (episcopo) Thermensis majoris," which implies a distinction from some other Thermæ of less importance.

11. SAINT AGAPETOS. In the later Notitiæ and in the Council. Quinis. A.D. 692, the bishopric changes its name, and is called after Saint Agapetos, to whom its church was doubtless dedicated. This seems to have been a real case of change of name, and not a change of situation. The common phrase with the double name (connected by ἤτοι) does not occur, but the new name is substituted for the old one and the entry is Θερμὰ τοῦ Ἁγίου Ἀγαπητοῦ.

An important passage of Constantine Porphyrogenitus (' de Admin. Imp.,' p. 225) is clear and readily intelligible, when Eudoxias has been placed in its proper position. About 890 the bandai or topoteresiai of Eudokias, Saint Agapetos, and Aphrazeia were transferred from the Anatolic to the Cappadocic Theme, and the latter (with four additional bandai) was made to include all the territory now called Haimane, bounded by the Halys on the east, lake Tatta on the south, and the

---

* For the variations between i and u in Phrygian cp. Siblia and Soublaion, kakin and kakoun, &c.; see my paper on the Phrygian inscriptions in ' Zeitschrift für vergleichende Sprachforschung,' 1887, and Fick, ' Ehemalige Spracheinheit,' connects Akrisias and akristis with the root krus.

† The flow of the water is wrongly indicated in some of Kiepert's maps of this country.

‡ Ed. Labbe, p. 87.

mountains between Sivri Hissar and Yürme (which are now called Gunusu Dagh, probably the ancient Dindymos *) on the west.

The seven bandai constituted the Turma Kommata.† The general situation of this Turma, as it has now been placed, is confirmed by a passage in Genesius, p. 122, who says that the Paulicians of Tephrike under Chrysocheir advanced as far as Ankyra and Kommata (μέχρι 'Αγκύρας τῆς πόλεως καὶ αὐτῶν τῶν Κομμάτων ‡). The Paulicians besieged or captured Ankyra, and even the military stronghold Kommata. It is doubtful whether this word is here to be understood as a definite fortress, the centre of the Theme, but more probably it denotes only the whole military district, with seven divisions and seven fortresses.

12. APHRAZEIA. Nothing is known about it, except that it must have been a fortress adjoining Saint Agapetos, and in the Anatolic Theme. Probably it was the fine fortress now called Kizil Hissar Kale, on a hill about three or four hours south-west of the hot springs of Myrika. On the termination -άζιος, -αζία, in Phrygian, Lycian, etc., see Kinch in Zft. f. Numism, 1889, p. 192.

13. PETINESSOS or PITNISOS. Its situation in the salt desert west of lake Tatta between Lykaonia and the Haimane is made clear by Strabo (pp. 567–8). The exact situation remains to be discovered by exploration of the southern frontier of Galatia. I have as yet made only one rapid journey across from Myrika to Philomelion. The site of Pissia (Piri Begli) would suit the indications of Petinessos fairly well, but a site further to the east would agree still better with Strabo. It seems difficult, in consistence with the order of Hierocles, to put any other bishopric on the Lykaonian frontier of Galatia Salutaris.

14. TROKNADES, a people with an apparently Gaulish name, inhabited the country on the northern or left bank of the Sangarios. Their chief town was apparently situated at Kaimaz (See C. I. L., III. Supplem., No. 6997). Hierocles has the name Regetnakade, i.e. Regio Troknades. In Not. III., X., we find instead of ὁ Τροκνάδων the strange name of ὁ Λωτίνου: this is probably derived from the name of a saint —perhaps Plotinus, like Saint Agapetus for Myrika.§

* Strabo, p. 567, gives the name. He also agrees (p. 626) with Herodotus in giving the name Dindymos to Murad Dagh, where the Hermos rises. A third Dindymos lay over Cyzicos. Kybele is often named Dindymene, for which the variant Zizimene is known (compare Nazianzos, Nadiandos), which suggests that Dindymos and Didyma are two forms of the same name (see Athen. Mittheil., 1888, p. 237). The reading Didymos in Ptolemy therefore need not be altered to Dindymos.

† Perhaps comata, as a title of some body of troops; the Latin word may have been misunderstood and turned into τά Κόμματα; cp. Perikommata Lydiae.

‡ The Bonn text prints κομμάτων without a capital.

§ Examples of this are numerous, and prove the power of the Church in the country; so we have Myriangeloi for Germa, and probably this cause has produced many modern names: Elias has given his name to Adada, Stephen to Maximianopolis (see my Antiquities of Southern Phrygia'); Aitamas (ἅγιος Θωμᾶς) is a Mohammedan village three hours east of Nigde; Yogounnes ('Ιωάννης) is the ancient Scioua;

On the whole, then, the probability is that Pitnisos was the bishopric of the district now called Djihan-beg-li, and that its territory was conterminous with that of Psebila-Verinopolis on the east and Amorion on the west, and that it reached to the regio Orkistena, the Sangarios and Aphrazeia on the north. This gives an enormous stretch of very sparsely inhabited country; but no doubt the territory of Amorion stretched far away to the south and east of the actual city. Considerable remains occur at Tcheltik, but I should prefer to connect Tcheltik with Amorion and to place Petinessos further east.

15. TRIKOMIA is mentioned by Ptolemy, and occurs in the Peutinger Table between Midaion and Pessinus. It is an old observation that the distances place it at Kaimaz.* It is not certain whether Trikomia is a Grecised form of Troknada, or whether three villages of the Troknades were actually united in one state (see my "Cities and Bishoprics of Phrygia," part ii., § xcv.). The Regio Trocnadensium was originally in Roman Asia and Byzantine Phrygia, and was, doubtless, transferred to Galatia, along with Orkistos, between 386 and 395.

16. ORKISTOS. The site, discovered by Pococke, is at Alikel Yaila. Alekian is the name given by Pococke and Mordtmann, and it is understood, though not commonly used, by the people of the district. It was part of the diocesis Asiana in A.D. 331,† and must, therefore, have belonged to Phrygia. In A.D. 451 it was in Galatia Salutaris. There can be little doubt that it was transferred from Phrygia to the new province of Galatia Salutaris at its formation, probably about 386–95 A.D. (See AMORION.)

The territory of Orkistos extended to the eastern skirts of the Phrygian mountains. An inscription found at Baghlije, the ancient Petara, shows that it was in the territory of Orkistos, unless the stone has been carried: Θεὸν Κόμμοδον 'Ορκιστηνῶν ὁ δῆμος καὶ ἡ γερουσία (Athen. Mittheil., 1889, p. 91).

The name "Orkistos" does not occur in Hierocles, though all the Notitiæ mention it as a bishopric, and it was elevated to the rank of a city in A.D. 331. The name in Hierocles which seems to correspond to it is Ῥεγεμαυρέκιον, i.e. Ῥεγεὼν Αὐρέκιον. In this name αυ is to be taken

---

Yonuslar ("Johns") is the ancient Vasada. Ayassaluk took the place of Ephesos, which was early deserted: Ayassaluk is ʽΑγίου Θεολόγου, from the great church of S. John, built by Justinian, and not ʽΑγιος Λούκας, as Mr. Wood, followed by Prof. G. Hirschfeld, thinks.

* Kaimaz cannot, as is usually said, be a survival of the old name Trikomia: because (1) Trikomia was not the popular name, but Troknades; (2) Kaimaz is a good Turkish name, occurring elsewhere: it means, "it does not slip." Names of this class are found occasionally: e.g., Et-yemez, "he does not eat flesh;" Bulduk, "we have found."

† Compare the great inscription, the Charter of Orkistos, which may now be read more correctly in Bruns, 'Fontes juris Romani,' or in a paper by Mommsen in 'Hermes,' 1887, p. 317, and which will soon appear as No. 6997 in the Supplement to C. I. L., iii.

as a rendering of ο; and ε is inserted between two consonants. The name is then equivalent to 'Ρεγεὼν "Ορκιον, *i.e.* " the region of the tribe Orkoi."

17. ORKOI. The Orkaorkoi are mentioned three times by Strabo (pp. 567, 568, 576) as inhabiting the vast treeless plains on the eastern frontier of Phrygia. The reference in p. 568 seems to place them north of Pitnisos, and that in p. 576 south of Pessinus, while that in p. 567 implies that they are between the Galatian Tektosages and Phrygia. The gieat plains extending along the right bank of the Sangarios from its source are the locality indicated by these references. Now, the name Orkaorkoi, if the form is correct, is a reduplication; and within the district where Strabo places them, is the city Ork-isto-s, which is obviously a sort of superlative of the tribal name. Instead of Orkistos Hierocles gives 'Ρεγεμαυρέκιον, *i.e.* 'Ρεγεὼν "Ορκιον. In the north of the country of the Orkoi or Orkaorkoi, at the source of the Sangarios, I have proved that there was situated a bishopric, Kaborkion, *i.e.* Καου-όρκ-ιο-ν, which probably contains the same tribal name with a prefixed word.* Thus our investigation brings together on the map these three words, occurring in such different periods of history and with such slight topographical indications, and when they are brought together they are found to contain the same tribal name.

The great inscription, the Charter of Orkistos, mentions that the town had once been a station (*mansio*) where four roads met, but that recently these roads had sunk into decay. At the time, A.D. 331, it is quite true that the old Roman road-system was in a state of transition. Roads leading to Constantinople were now taking the place of roads leading to Rome.

The coincidence between the words of the inscription and the known facts of history is so striking that we must accept the conclusion that the position of Orkistos was more important under the Roman system of roads than under the Byzantine system. But it seems difficult to accept the account which the Orkisteni give of the former importance of their town except after large allowance for exaggeration due to local patriotism; for most of the evidence accessible to us tends to show that no great roads of the Roman period could go by way of Orkistos. It is quite clear that no road mentioned in the Peutinger Table passed through Orkistos. The only routes which naturally pass through Orkistos are (1) a route from Pessinus straight to the west like the " Royal Road "; (2) a route from Amorion northwards through the Troknades (Kaimaz) to Midaion and Bithynia or Juliopolis and Paphlagonia. Neither of these is very important, but they seem to be meant in the petition of the Orkisteni, in which the four roads were enumerated, but which is now imperfect. Three are mentioned in the part that remains to us :—

---

* It has even occurred to me that OPKAOPKOI in Strabo is a corruption of KAOΥOPKOI. Compare also my "Cities and Bishoprics of Phrygia," ii. § lxxiv.

(*a*) The road to Pessinus, xxx. miles. This is an over-estimate, for the modern track can hardly be more than 25 miles. The only way in which the distance xxx. could be made up is that the road made a détour to a bridge over the river. This bridge must have certainly been on the direct road between Pessinus and Amorion, which is a far more important route.

(*b*) The road to "civitas . . . . . aitanorum xxx. miles:" the first letters of the name are lost, but Mommsen's restoration [Mid]aitanorum seems to be very probable, although (1) Midaion is very much more than 30 miles from Orkistos; (2) the order of enumeration seems to require here a road to the south-east, between the Pessinus road and the Amorion road.

(*c*) The road to Amorion.

There can be little doubt that the fourth road led to Nakoleia.

It is clear that the route Pessinus-Orkistos-Nakoleia corresponds on the whole to the "Royal Road," and that the route Amorion-Orkistos-[Trikomia-]-Midaion is the other of the only two routes, which, as I have said, can pass through Orkistos. It is, on the whole, true that these routes lead in a westerly and south-westerly direction, and therefore they are more encouraged by the set of trade to Ephesos and Rome than to Constantinople.

We must, then, accept the evidence of the inscription that these two roads were considerable trade-routes under the Roman empire, even although no other evidence confirms their existence. But I think that a milestone, which was long a puzzle to me, so long as I accepted the Peutinger Table as a fair picture of the Roman road-system, becomes intelligible as soon as we accept the road Pessinus-Orkistos-Nakoleia as a Roman road. In 'C. I. L.,' iii., Supplem. No. 7169, a milestone will shortly be published which I copied in 1884; it is in a cemetery 1½ miles S.W. of Altyntash. It gives the number Λ E, i.e. 35, and there seems no possibility of understanding this except as the distance from Akmonia. But a road from Akmonia to Altyntash cannot end there; it must go on over the Phrygian mountains towards the east, and would finally reach Orkistos and Pessinus.

18. AMORION: the site near the village Hamza Hadji was proved by Hamilton.* Amorion was in the Roman Province of Asia, and at one time took the name Vipsania. During the fourth century it must have been part of Phrygia, for it could not have been included in Galatia when Orkistos was in Phrygia. Between 386 and 395† therefore it must have been transferred along with Troknades, Klaneos and Orkistos to form the newly created province Galatia Salutaris.

---

* The plain stretching to the east is still called Hadji Omar Ova, which is perhaps a reminiscence of Amorion. Hamilton calls the now quite deserted site Hergan Kale; no name except Kale was known to any of the surrounding villagers to whom I talked.

† When Theodosius made the new province Galatia II., see p. 221.

In the feeble parody of the fine system of defence organised by the older Byzantine emperors, which was kept up in the eleventh century, the district between Amorion and the Sangarios was dignified with the name of the "Theme Cappadocia." This Theme and that of Khoma were, under Alexios Komnenos, entrusted to a toparches Bourtzes (Anna, I., 171) ; and the country towards the Sangarios was under his government (Anna, II., 325, 327).

Pankaleia appears to have been a name applied to the wide plain east of Amorion: the only reference to it is: κατὰ τὴν Παγκάλειαν.... ἱππήλατον τοῦτο πεδίον, τῷ 'Αμορίῳ προσέγγιον, Leo Diac., p. 170. But Cedrenus (II., p. 431), describing the same battle, says : ἡ Παγκάλεια πεδίον ἀναπεπταμένον τε καὶ ἱππήλατον, ἔγγιστά που τοῦ ποταμοῦ "Αλυος κείμενον. Byzantine writers often speak so loosely that it is difficult to decide in this case, but Leo Diaconus describes the events of this period with infinitely greater topographical accuracy than Cedrenus, and is to be preferred in this case. Moreover Zonaras also confirms Leo, saying that the battle took place near Amorion.

Amorion was fortified in the reign of Zeno (474–91; Cedren. I., 615). It had an eventful history during the Arab wars. It was captured A.D. 666 by the Saracens under Yezid, and recaptured by Andreas, general of the Emperor Constans in the same year (Cedren., I., 763, Theophan., 351). It was again besieged unsuccessfully by the Saracens in A.D. 716, 778, and 789.* In the first siege it was saved by the vigour of Leo the Isaurian, afterwards emperor, who fortified it so strongly that it was able to resist the Arabs for a long time. But it was captured by the Saracens, A.D. 838, through the treachery of a citizen, and the most splendid city of the East† was reduced to ashes.

Monasteries at Amorion are mentioned at the Second Nicene Council, 787 A.D.: Βασίλιος μοναχὸς τοῦ 'Αμορίου τῆς ἁγίας Θεοτόκου, and Θεόδωρος ἡγούμενος τοῦ 'Αμορίου.

Amorion became a very important city under the Iconoclast Emperors in the eighth century, and was infamous among the orthodox for its heresies.‡ It was three days' journey from Dorylaion (Cedren., II., 132).

19. LALANDOS was a district of Amorion, as is proved by the two inscriptions which I have published in the 'Revue des Études Grecques,' 1889, p. 21. I have there established the probability that Amorion was divided into a series of local tribes (φυλαί), and that the district Lalandos belonged to the tribe of Zeus (Φυλὴ Διός). The mystic

* Theophanes, 386, 452, 470.

† ἡ τῶν ἑῴων διαπρεπεστέρα (Cedren., II., p. 137).

‡ 'Ιουδαίων καὶ 'Αθιγγάνων καὶ ἑτέρων ἀσεβῶν πλῆθος ἐκπάλαι τῶν χρόνων ἐγκατοικίζεται· καί τις δὲ αἵρεσις ἐκ τῆς ἀλλήλων κοινωνίας καὶ διηνεκοῦς ὁμιλίας ἐπιφύεται (Cedren., II., p. 69). On Eudoxius, bishop of Amorion under Leo the Armenian (813–20 A.D.), see 'Act. Sanct.,' March 8, p. 788.

worship of Mithras flourished here, according to an inscription, as early as the first century after Christ.

20. ALANDRI FLUMEN, mentioned by Livy, XXXVIII. 17, is probably, as I have shown in the same place, to be corrected Lalandi Flumen. But the old correction "Alandri fontes" in Livy, XXXVIII. 15, is definitely to be rejected : the MSS. read " Mandri fontes," and a series of fountains, near a village still called Mandra, exist on the route of Manlius, which Livy is describing.

At some unknown time later than the Council of Constantinople (in Trullo) in 692 A.D., and earlier than the second Council of Nikaia in 787 A.D., Amorion was raised to the rank of an independent bishopric (αὐτοκέφαλος), and ceased to be subject to the metropolitan of Pessinus, or rather of Justinianopolis. In the later *Notitiæ* Amorion appears as metropolis of a district carved out of Phrygia Salutaris, Pisidia and Galatia, the bishoprics in which are given as

Notitia I., Γαλατίας δευτέρας.	Notitia III.	Notitia X.	Hierocles and Not. VII., VIII., IX.
ὁ τοῦ Ἀμορίου .	τῷ Ἀμορίου Φρυγίας	﹛τῷ Ἀμωρίῳ τῆς﹜ Φρυγίας . .﹜	Galatia Salutaris.
ὁ Φιλομηλίου .	α'. ὁ Φιλομηλίου . .	ὁ Φιλομηλίου .	Pisidia.
ὁ τοῦ Δοκιμίου .	β'. ὁ τοῦ Δοκιμίου .	ὁ Δοκιμίου . .	Phrygia Salutaris.
ὁ Κλάγξ . .	γ'. ὁ Κλανεοῦ . .	ὁ Κλαθεοῦ . .	Κλάνεος Galatia Salutaris
ὁ Πολυβώτου .	δ'. ὁ Πολυβότου . .	ὁ Πολυβότου .	Phrygia Salutaris.
ὁ Πισσίας . .	ε'. ὁ Πισσίας . . .	ὁ Πισσίας .	Not mentioned.

This new district was formed under Amorion as metropolis a considerable time after Amorion was made *autokephalos*, for the order of enumeration at Concil. Nicaen. II. (A.D. 787) shows clearly that Amorion was independent, but that the bishoprics afterwards subject to it were still in their original connection. The reference to the dignity of Amorion in 858 A.D. is indecisive as to its exact position whether as αὐτοκέφαλος or as metropolis with subject bishoprics. In that year the Patriarch Photius sent the archbishops of Amorion and Khonai as envoys to Rome, dignifying the latter for the first time with the title of archbishop* : this implies that Amorion was already an archbishopric. Khonai and Amorion are both metropoleis in the later *Notitiæ*, but not in the earlier, viz. VII., VIII., IX.

In the above list, Philomelion (Ak Sheher), Dokimion (Itchja Kara Hisar), and Polybotos (Bolowodun, as Leake detected) are well known and their situation makes it plain that, as in several other cases, the whole set of bishoprics formed a well-marked district along the roads leading from Amorion to the south and the west. This consideration is important in determining the situation of the two remaining bishoprics, Pissia and Klaneos.

* 'Vit. S. Ignatii,' in Mansi, 'Act. Concil.' XVI. p. 235.

21. PISSIA was probably situated at Piri-bey-li on the road from Amorion to Philomelion, about twelve hours from the latter and six from the former. The remains here are sufficient to mark it as a place sufficiently important to be the seat of a bishop, and its situation on the road between Philomelion and Amorion proves that it must belong to the same local group of bishoprics. This last consideration shows that my former view was wrong, and that Petinessos cannot be placed here. According to my former view Pissia was placed at Bayat between Dokimion and Amorion, but closer study shows that Klaneos was in all probability situated at Bayat.

22. KLANEOS (usually Κλάνεος *) is placed by Hierocles between Amorion and Troknades. This order points to a situation north, north-west, or north-east of Amorion, and agrees admirably with a situation on the road from Amorion to Dokimion. On this road there are two places where a bishopric might be placed—at Geume, and at Bayat. The latter place, at the crossing of this road with the important post-road Constantinople-Dorylaion-Ikonion, is in all probability the site of Klaneos. Geume is a place of much less consequence, and the inscriptions that are found there have probably been brought from Amorion, though, being on an important road, it was always a village of some consequence, and a coarsely-built mediæval ruin, perhaps of a church, stands half an hour west of it. The topography of the Bayat valley must detain us a little.

23. KEDREA is proved in a former paper to be the name of the fine old Turkish fortress about two miles west of Bayat.† It is mentioned by Anna Comnena (XV., vol. II., p. 324) on the march of Alexius by Dorylaion to Philomelion. He followed the regular and unmistakable post-road by Bardakchi, Khosrev Pasha Khan, and Bayat. After Dorylaion, Santabaris is the next place mentioned on his route. It must be either Khosrev Pasha Khan or Bardakchi: the only other place on the road is Seidi Ghazi, the ancient Nakoleia. There is no distinct proof which of these two places was Santabaris, but as that place was near Nakoleia, and as Kakkabokome was at Khosrev Pasha Khan, I have placed Santabaris at Bardakchi.

* It is sometimes accented Κλανεός, and many other varieties occur, the most remarkable of which is Κλάγξ, a form which proves that none of the Greek spellings represent the true character of the name.

† "Prymnessos and Metropolis" in the 'Mittheilungen Athen.,' 1882. I am glad to be able to point to the identifications of Kedrea, Akroenos, and Augustopolis, as conclusively proved, in this my first attempt to discuss the complicated problem of Phrygian topography, written when I had little knowledge of the country, and was impeded by a false idea of the line of the roads, by a false reading of the distance of Prymnessos on a milestone, and by the false situation proposed by previous scholars for Lysias. The account given in that paper of the march and return of Alexius seems to me still to be quite correct. The line of march is again referred to, and Ampous and other places fixed, in my ' Cit. and Bish. of Phrygia,' Part II., § 40.

From Santabaris Alexius sent one of his generals, Kamytzes, against Kedrea,* and another, Stypeiotes, against Amorion. Kedrea is described as a πολίχνιον ἐρυμνότατον, which suits admirably the fortress Assar Kumbet Kale. Kamytzes, finding Kedrea deserted by the Turks, forthwith marched against Polybotos. The emperor, learning of his success, proceeded to Kedrea and Polybotos. No doubt is left by this description as to the situation of Kedrea.

Kedrea is mentioned by Edrisi,† under the form Kidros, as a station one day's journey from Amorion on an alternative route to Nikaia. The route is thus given :—From Amouria

1 day to Kidros
1   „   river of Maderi
1   „   Castora
1   „   Massissa village
1   „   Libadhia, on a navigable river
1   „   Batransia, "bourg bien peuplé"
1   „   river of Mastara
1   „   Nikaia

The name Libadhia might make us inclined to place it at Sugut, but as the river of Mastara must be the Gallos, there seems no room for Batransia between. Moreover the navigable river can hardly be any other except the Tembris, so that Libadhia must rather be identified with Eski Sheher, while Batransia would correspond to Sugut. Between Kidros and Eski Sheher it is certainly difficult to place three stages, i.e. four days' journey. The distances are seven hours to Khosrev Pasha Khan, seven to Seidi Ghazi, and nine to Eski Sheher. Nikaia to Dorylaion, 28 hours, is a three days' journey, so that Dorylaion to Kidros, 23 hours, can hardly take four days. Probably the road is not a direct one. ‡

It is difficult to determine whether the valley of Bayat belonged to Byzantine Phrygia or Galatia. It could hardly, during the early Byzantine time, be included in any of the Phrygian bishoprics except perhaps Dokimion. After the group of bishoprics subject to Amorion was separated from Phrygia and Galatia Salutaris, the valley of Bayat must have been included in this group.§ Only two possibilities remain ; either it was now for the first time raised to the rank of a separate bishopric under the name Pissia, or it had all along been the bishopric

---

* Anna uses the name Kedrea twice, and Kedros once.

† Transl. Jaubert, II., p. 305.

‡ One of the difficulties in using the Arab geographers lies in the extraordinary zigzags which they give as routes. I have found them practically useless.

§ Its position marks it as a place of importance in Byzantine time, and its relative importance would certainly increase in the later Byzantine period.

Klaneos. Now Klaneos is put by the order of Hierocles in this part of Galatia, and there seems no room for a bishopric between Dokimion and Amorion unless it includes the valley of Bayat, while the name Pissia seems required for a bishopric south of Amorion, and it therefore seems necessary to place Klaneos at Bayat. Moreover, Bayat seems to be the only place in this country which could have been important enough to be a bishopric, and as situated at a crossing of two great roads it is likely to have been the seat of a bishop.

24. ETSYA was a village in the valley of Bayat, which is known only from the following inscription, copied by me in 1884, and verified in 1886. It is before a house in Bayat.

ΕΤΣΥΗΝΟΙΔΙ   'Ετσυηνοὶ Δι[ὶ
ΓΑΛΑΚΤΙΝΩΚ   Γαλακτίνῳ κ-
ΑΤΑΕΠΙΤΑΓΗΝ   ατὰ ἐπιταγὴν
ⅢΠΟΛΛΩΝΟΣΥΓ   'Α]πόλλωνος ὁ[π-
5 ⅢⅢΚΑΡΠΩΝΕΥΧΗΝ *   ἐρ] κάρπων εὐχήν·

The god to whom this dedication is made is the same who is mentioned in the following inscription, also of Bayat, which I copied in 1884: †—

Διὰ Μεγίστῳ Καρποδότῃ Σ[ω-
τῆρι 'Ολυνπίῳ Γάϊος Γεμίνι-
ος Οὐάλης εὐξάμενος καθ[ι-
ἑρωσεν.

This second inscription belongs to the fourth century, as the very rude lettering and the name of the dedicator shows. Zeus the Milk-god is novel; the adjective γαλάκτινος, milky, occurs elsewhere. The religion in the two inscriptions is that of a pastoral and agricultural community.

At one time I thought that a letter might have been lost at the beginning, giving the name [Π]ετσύα, which might be the Byzantine Pissia; but when I revisited Bayat in 1886 to verify this conjecture (which I printed in the 'Athenische Mittheilungen,' 1885, p. 348, as convincing), I found that it could not be sustained. No letter is lost, and the balance of argument is against Pissia having been situated here.

25. SANTABARIS (Bardakchi) is very rarely referred to. The accounts given of Theodorus Santabarenus in the life of Photius, and in the life of S. Nicolaos, show that it was near Nakoleia, and therefore within Byzantine Phrygia.‡

A route between Amorion and Malagina, given by Edrisi,§ furnishes a probable proof that Santabaris must be further north than Khosrev

---

* HN in lines 1, 3, and 5, and NE in 5, are *liée*.

† I published it in the 'Athenische Mittheilungen,' 1882, p. 134, from an incomplete copy by Sir Charles Wilson. I now give the complete and accurate text. In the other inscription of Bayat (Beyad), p. 126, for Χλ[ιά?]μου read Χάρμου.

‡ Zandapa of Mysia mentioned by Theophanes belongs to Moesia on the Danube.

§ Transl. Jaubert, II., p. 305.

Pasha Khan, and therefore must be at Bardakchi, where there are great remains. Edrisi gives the route from Amorion as—

15 miles to village of fish, and 2 to river	=	17
12 „ to Fandj	=	12
15 „ to Calahi-el-Ghabe (of the Forest) . . .	=	15
12 „ to Jew's Fort, and 18 to Sendaberi . . .	=	30
30 „ to Merdj djama el Melik Baderwana . . .	=	30
5 „ to Gharoboli, and 3 to Churches of the King	=	8
25 „ to Mulawwen (Bilejik)	=	25
15 „ to El-Agradh, and 15 to Meladjena . . .	=	30
5 „ to King's Stable	=	5
30 „ to El A'bra	=	30
24 „ to El Khalidj	=	24
	Total	226

Many of these names are uncertain, but the route appears to be one from the Canal (el Khalidj), i.e. the Bosphorus, to Amorion by a circuitous route through Melagena (Meladjena), Basilika, Dorylaion, and Santabaris. Thence it goes to Amorion by a zigzag route, perhaps through Sivri Hisar, and across the Sangarios (river of fish). Jew's Fort may be Tchifteler: Tchifut means a Jew, Tchifte, a pair.[*] Merdj djama would then be Dorylaion, Churches of the King would be Anna Comnena's Basilika. The passage in which Anna mentions Basilika and Alethina (vol. II., p. 281 ff.) has been discussed (G 20). The omission of Nikaia before El A'bra is remarkable: El A'bra must be at the ferry from Kibotos to Aigialos.

26. POIMANENON is mentioned as a place on the road from Santabaris to Amorion. Stypeiotes occupied it when detached towards Amorion, as was described above under Kedrea. No other reference occurs to the place, but the text is clear. It is doubtful whether it was in Byzantine Phrygia or in Galatia Salutaris. The name is interesting, as constituting another link between central Phrygia and Hellespontine Phrygia. The town of Poimanenon (now Maniyas) in Mysia is well known.

27. PETARA is proved to have been at Baghlije by an inscription, which I have published in my 'Cities and Bishoprics of Phrygia,' II., § LXX. It was probably actually a village in the territory of Orkistos, according to an inscription found in the village, a dedication to Commodus by the Orkistenoi (see No. 16).

28. ABROSTOLA is mentioned only in Ptolemy and in the Peutinger Table. The latter gives it twice, on the road between Amorion and

---

* Fandj then is Pessinus, and Calahi-el-Ghabe the strong castle (Kale) of Sivri Hisar. Jaubert must be wrong in taking Agradh as Aorata, which is in quite a different direction. See Addenda.

Pessinus, and on the road Amorion to Archelais. One, at least, of these positions must be wrong, for these two roads go from Amorion in quite different directions. The error must arise from bad drawing of the lines representing the roads, a frequent cause of error in the Table.* Ptolemy's authority is in this case valuable; for his lists, though in many respects bad, are generally so correct in assigning the cities to the Roman provinces, as to show that he used an excellent authority, perhaps an official list of the cities of each province. Abrostola is in the province of Asia, and it is not possible to bring it into the province of Asia except by placing it between Amorion and Pessinus on the right side of the Sangarios. The total distance from Amorion to Pessinus is about thirty Roman miles, and I should expect to find Abrostola either on the left bank of the fine stream that rises at Bunar Bashi, two or three miles east of Amorion (VI miles from Amorion, and XXIV from Pessinus, as in the Table), or on the right bank of the Sangarios (XX miles from Amorion, XI from Pessinus). I consider the former position more probable.

J. Roman Roads in Galatia and Northern Phrygia.

I. The Road from Dorylaion to Ankyra is given in the Antonine Itinerary as :—

> Dorylaion XXX Arcelaio XX Germa XXIV † Vinda XXXII Papira XXVII Ancyra.

Modern views as to the course of this road have always been distorted by a false idea, started by Leake, as to the site of Germa. It is supposed that Germa still retains its name as Yürme or Yüreme, and that the road makes a détour to the south in order to pass through it. But for this misapprehension, no doubt could exist in the mind of any person as to the natural course of this road : it must descend the Tembris (Porsuk Su) to the Sangarios, cross the Sangarios, and then go straight to Ankyra, passing a little to the north of Basri. This is both the easiest and the shortest route.

Now, there is no evidence to place Germa at Yürme, for the resemblance of the names is purely accidental. Yürme is a Turkish village name, which I have several times found elsewhere, and there

---

* To avoid an argument which is likely to be advanced against me, I may say that at first I tried to reconcile the two positions by supposing that a road went from Amorion to Archelais along the east coast of lake Tatta, and that at the point where this road passed nearest to Pessinus it was joined by a road from Pessinus, and that Abrostola was the point of junction. Were this road a real one, it would partly reconcile the positions given to Abrostola on the Table. But I had to give up this view when I visited the country east and south of Amorion. In the first place the road from Amorion to Archelais is an important route both now and in ancient time, it passes along the western skirts of the Salt Desert; and in the second place Ptolemy is decisive, for he places Abrostola in Phrygia and in the Roman Province Asia.

† The reading XXXII. also occurs for XXIV. in the Itinerary, pp. 201. 202.

is no reason to think that the modern word is a survival of the old name Germa.

The remains at Yürme are not those of a Roman Colonia, as Germa was, but of a Christian city of the early Byzantine type.* On the other hand, the Latin inscriptions found at Masut Keui on the lower Tembris leave no doubt that Germa was situated in that neighbourhood ('C. I. L.,' III., 284–6): they give the Latin name of Colonia Julia Augusta Felix, known also from coins. Moreover, other epigraphic evidence as to the course of the road has been discovered at various points, and probably only the fact that the modern roads follow different routes has prevented the discovery of much further evidence. We already have:—

(1) An inscription which I found at Basri, and which will be published 'C. I. L.,' III., Supplement, No. 6770. It is a dedication to Julius Maximus Cæsar, A.D. 235–8, by the soldiers of a Roman cohort, probably a detachment stationed at Basri. A military station must be on a Roman road: and several other inscriptions show that Basri is near an ancient site, which must clearly be Vinda.

(2) An inscription found on an ancient bridge, about three hours west of Balyk Koyunji, and published by me, " Inscr. de la Galatie," in 'Bull. de Corresp. Hellénique,' 1883, p. 22. It records the building of the bridge by a bishop Paul, probably him that was bishop of Ankyra in A.D. 579.

(3) A milestone of Aurelian, copied by Domaszewski five hours west of Angora on the road to Sivri Hissar ('C. I. L.,' III., Supplem., No. 6902).

(4) A milestone four hours west of Angora ('C. I. L.,' III., 317).

(5) A milestone one hour west of Angora ('C. I. L.,' III., 316).

The situation of Papira is still unknown: it is to be looked for in the country near Balyk Koyunji.

The distance from the point where I suppose Germa to be (near Masut Keui, but perhaps lower down the river) to Dorylaion is more than fifty miles. But the road must pass through Midaion (see below), and there can therefore be no doubt that one station is omitted, and that the road must be restored on the authority of the Peutinger Table as—

> Dorylaion xviii Midaion xxx Akkilaion xx Germa xxiv Vinda (Vindia) xxxii Papira xxvii Ankyra.

The distance from Germa to Ankyra is here too great. There must be some error in the numbers, but it is uncertain where the correction should be made. If one of the numbers be diminished by x. the result would be nearly correct, for the sum of distances station to

---

* Among the ruins is the best preserved façade of an early church that I have seen in Asia Minor. None of the inscriptions are Latin, and many are of the Byzantine period.

station is of course greater than the direct measurement given on the milestones from Germa to Ankyra, which was apparently about LXIII.

II. The road from Pessinus to Ankyra is given in the Antonine Itinerary as:—

Pessinus XVI Germa XXIIII Vinda, &c. as before.

The previous exposition shows what must have been the course of this road: it went north from Pessinus (Bala Hissar) to Germa on the lower course of the Tembris. A milestone has been preserved from the road Pessinus-Germa. It was copied at Mülk by Hamilton; and I have in vain, in 1883, searched through the village for it. As the road has now been determined, the position of this stone is quite natural, but according to the old view as to the site of Germa, its position is quite inexplicable. It is LXXI. miles from Ankyra, giving the distance Ankyra-Germa about LXI. to LXV., which is about the actual distance from a point near the mouth of the Tembris to Ankyra.

III. The road from Dorylaion to Pessinus is given in the Peutinger Table as—

Dorylaion XXVIII Midaion XXVIIII Tricomia XXI Pessinus.

Coins of Midaion show that it was situated on the river Tembris (Porsuk Su). The remains at Karadja Eyuk on the south bank of the river, about eighteen miles from Dorylaion, must be those of Midaion,* and the number in the Table must be diminished by x. Tricomia is apparently to be identified with Kaimaz, which was the chief centre of the tribe Troknades ('C. I. L.,' III. Supplem., No. 6997); and the Greek name Trikômia was probably applied to it as a union of three villages.† The distances from Kaimaz to Bala Hissar and to Karadja Eyuk are correctly given in the Table.

A mere cross-road from Midaion to Pessinus would be too unimportant to find a place in the Table. There can be no doubt that this is only a part of a great through route, which is rightly given in the Table as leading to Archelais Colonia. The rest of the stations have been discussed under Lykaonia. The roads in the Peutinger Table were originally drawn by one who thought of all roads as radiating from Constantinople, and in this case he had in his mind a road leading from Constantinople by Dorylaion, Pessinus and Archelais to the Cilician Gates. Similarly he had in his mind another road by Dorylaion, Amorion, Laodicea Combusta, to Ikonion and the south coast; but in both cases the line is broken in the copy that remains to us as the Peutinger Table.

---

* 'Cities and Bishoprics of Phrygia,' in 'Journal of Hellenic Studies,' 1887, § lxxx., where I have omitted to state that the distance XVIII. is a correction.

† 'Cit. and Bish.,' § xcv.

IV. The road from the Bosphorus to Ankyra is given in our authorities as follows :—

Peutinger Table.	Antonine Itinerary.	Jerusalem Itinerary.
Constantinopolis ..	Byzantio	Constantinopoli
Calcedonia	Calcedonia IIII	Calcedoniam
		mutatio Nassete VII.
	Panticio XV	mansio Pandicia VII.
		mutatio Pontamus XIII.
Livissa XXXVII ..	Libissa XXIIII	mansio Libissa VIIII.
		mutatio Brunca XII.
Nicomedia XXIII ..	Nicomedia XXII	civitas Nicomedia XIII.
		mutatio Hyribolum X.
Eribulo	Libo XXI	mansio Libum XI.
		mutatio Liada XII.
Nicea XXXIII	Nicia XXIII	civitas Nicia VIII.
		mutatio Schinæ VIII.
	Mœdo Orientis XVI	mansio Mido VII.
		mutatio Chogeæ VI.
		mutatio Thateso X.
Tateabio XL	Tottaio XXVIII	mutatio Tuta'o VIIII.
		mutatio Protunica XI.
		mutatio Artemis XII.
Dablis XXIII	Dablis XXVIII	mansio Dablæ VI. '
		mansio Ceratæ VI.
	Cenon Gallicanon XVIII	mutatio Finis X.
Dadastana XL ..	Dabastana XXI	mansio Dadastana VI.
		mutatio Trans monte VI.
		mutatio Milia XI.
Iuliopoli XXIX ..	Iuliopolim XXVI	civitas Iuliopolis VIII.
Valcaton XII		
Fines Cilicie X ..		mutatio Hyeronpotamum XIII.
Lagania XXVIII ..	Laganeos XXIV	mansio Agannia XI.
		mutatio Ipetobrogen VI.
Mizago XXXVIII ..	Minizo XXIII	mansio Mnizos X.
		mutatio Prasmon XII.
	Manegordo XXVIII	
		mutatio Cenaxem palidem XIII.
[Ancyra] XXVIII	Ancyra XXIIII	civitas Anchira Galatia . . . .

As I have never traversed any part of the road, I cannot speak about it in detail. As far as Nikomedeia it follows the direct road to the East through Pandik. From Nikomedeia, instead of going straight on along the lake Sabandja to Geive, the road makes a détour to Nicæa. The reason probably is that it was common to take ship to the coast opposite Nikaia, land at Prainetos, and take the land-route through Nikaia. Probably the two roads *viâ* Nikomedia and *viâ* Nikaia would meet at Geive, which may be supposed to be close to Tottaion.

TOTTAION is an important name. It appears in Ptolemy as Πα-ταούιον, obviously a fault for Ταταούιον. Hierocles has Ῥεγετάταιον, and Tottaion, Tataion, Tateabion occur indiscriminately in the ecclesiastical lists. The name therefore contains the sound of digamma, which is commonly omitted in Greek writing, but is sometimes given as ου or β.*   The name is formed from a common personal name Tatas or Tottes, like:—

Dorylaion	from	Dorylas.
Kotyaion	„	Kotys.
Kadoi (for Kadooi)	„	Kadys.
Otroia (Otrya)	„	Otreus.
Otroos	„	Otreus.
Anaia	„	Anes.
Attaia	„	Attes.
Akkilaion	„	Akylas.

DABLIS is probably to be sought near Terekli as indicated in Kiepert's old map.

DADASTANA was the border town of Bithynia and Galatia, in the latter province. The emperor Jovian died there in 364 A.D., when marching towards Constantinople along this road.† The Itineraries agree about the boundaries between the provinces, but Ptolemy places Juliopolis, Laganeia, and Dadastana, as well as Dableis and Tatavion, in Bithynia. Apparently, therefore, the boundary of Galatia was altered when the new arrangement of the provinces, attributed to Diocletian, came into existence. Ptolemy's apportionment of the cities among the Roman provinces is in general far more correct ‡ than the positions which he assigns to the cities.

The discrepancy between the authorities in regard to the section Dableis-Dadastana is probably to be explained by the omission of a station in the Jerusalem Itinerary between Fines and Dadastana.

JULIOPOLIS was certainly situated by the river § a little west of Nalli Khan: it is described at greater length below. Twelve miles east of Juliopolis the road crossed the river Siberis (Hierus in Pliny,|| Hycronpotamum in the Jerusalem Itinerary). The village of Sykea or Sykeon was situated at the crossing of the river, and Justinian built a bridge over the stream (Procop. 'Aedif.,' V., 4). Theodorus Sykeota was born there in the sixth century, son of a woman of loose character, who made a profit from the travellers along the road (Act. Sanct., April 22, p. 32). Anastasiopolis was situated twelve miles east of Sykea, and must therefore be a Byzantine name of Lagania, which

---

* So Sanaos or Anava has the ethnic Sanabensis in some ecclesiastical lists.

† Ammian., XXV., 10, 12; XXVI., 8, 4. Zosimus, III., 34, p. 173, says τῆς Βιθυνίας ἐν Δαδαστάνοις, retaining the old Roman division of Bithynia and Galatia.

‡ Isolated exceptions occur: Sagalassos he puts in Lycia, but Lycia and Pamphylia were one province. Strategia Antiochiane he gives in Cappadocia, misled by an authority of older date.

§ Its ancient name is Scopas or Scopius.

|| Ἱερός is a Greek form, adapted from the native name to give a word with a meaning. The omission of an initial σ and of a digamma are natural in Greek.

occupies the same position in the Itineraries.* The Peutinger Table falsely inserts two stations between Juliopolis and Lagania.

Half-way between the river Siberis and Bei Bazar the site of Lagania Anastasiopolis must be looked for. The little *mutatio* called Petobroge, which bears a Gallic name like Eccobriga, Allobroges or Allobriges, &c., has now become the chief town of the district, Bey Bazar, unless better maps prove Lagania to be there.

Mnizos was apparently situated near where the road crosses the Emir Tchai. Manegordos, which is a more probable form than Malogardis, was in all probability situated near Girindos about midway between Mnizos and Ankyra: inscriptions have been found there. It is omitted in the Jerusalem Itinerary, where it should probably be inserted after Prasmon. Lake Cenaxis should be easily found (see K 1). The distances in this part of the road seem too great. Girindos is at most 20 miles from Ankyra. Mizago in the Peutinger Table is the result of mixing up Mnizo and Manego[rdo]; compare Comitanasso mixed of Coropasso and Parnasso.

This road of course became far more important after Constantinople became the capital of the eastern empire, and it is still a great trade-route. But even before 330 its existence can be traced. As soon as Nicomedia was made by Diocletian into one of the four capitals of the Roman world and the seat of one of the four rulers, the road must immediately rise into great importance. It is described in the Antonine Itinerary, which belongs to the period 300–330 A.D.† But its chief interest lies in its being the natural land-route for pilgrims from Europe to the Holy Land. The cheapest way for western pilgrims to reach Jerusalem on foot was by way of Constantinople, then along a road of the Roman system to Nicomedia (or occasionally by ship to Nicæa), and thence through Ankyra (Angora) and Tarsos. This road is in some respects the most interesting of all the later roads of Asia Minor: it was carefully kept up, and the stations and halting-places continued to be the same as they were in the time of Constantine. In the sixth century after Christ the publica regii cursus via is referred to (Act. S. Theodori Sykeotae).

K. CITIES AND BISHOPRICS OF GALATIA PRIMA.

It would perhaps have been a better arrangement to discuss these cities along with those of Pontus, but there is also a certain convenience in keeping the two Galatian provinces together. The basis of a topographical discussion must as usual be sought in the Byzantine lists.

* Wesseling has observed this correctly.

† Compare *præfatio* to Parthey and Pinder's edition. It is written from the point of view of a person who thinks Nicomedia the capital. Dr. C. Miller ('Die Weltkarte von Castorius,' p. 119) gives the date as 300, which seems to me too early.

GALATIA PRIMA.

Hierocles c. 531 and Conc. Chalced. 451.	Notitiæ i., VII., VIII., IX.	Notitiæ III., X., XIII.
1. Ἄγγυρα * μετρόπολις.	1. Ἀγκύρας.	1. Ἀγκύρας.
2. Ταβία.	2. Ἀτταβίας, Ταμίας.	2. Ταβείας.
3. Ἀσπόνα.	4. Ἀσπόνης.	4. Ἀσπώνης.
4. Κίννα.	7. Κήνης. Κίνης.	7. Κίννης.
5. Ρεγεναγαλία.	8. Ἀναστασιουπόλεως.	8. Ἀναστασιουπόλεως.
6. Ρεγέμνηζος.	6. Μίζζου. Μνίζου.	6. Μείζου.
7. Ἡλιούπολις.	3. Ἡλιουπόλεως.	3. Ἰλιουπόλεως ἤτοι Βασιλαίου.
————	5. Βηρινουπόλεως.	5. Μηρινοχιπόλεως ἤτοι Σταυροῦ.
————	————	9. Καλουμένης. Καλούμνης.

1. ANKYRA. The situation of Ankyra has never been a matter of doubt: it is still called Enguri. A nunnery named Petris at Ankyra is mentioned in Acta S. Theodori, April 22, p. 38. Saint Plato was executed *in Campo Amoeno* outside the walls of Ankyra, under Maximian, praeside Agrippino (Act. Sanct., July 22, p. 234). The lake mentioned in the passio S. Theodoti, cap. 2, near the city, may be the Cenaxis palus of the Jerusalem Itinerary (Act. Sanct., May 18).

2. TAOUION, TAVIUM. The vexed question as to the site of Tavium has been set at rest by the discoveries of Prof. J. R. S. Sterrett. The situation at Nefez Keui, proposed by Texier, was long accepted: but Prof. G. Hirschfeld in 1883 published an elaborate memoir in the 'Sitzungsberichte' of the Berlin Academy, in which he attempted to prove that Tavium was situated at Iskelib on the west side of the Halys. Prof. Kiepert replied † to this memoir, but tried to place Tavium in the valley of Alaja, about 20 miles north-east of Nefez Keui. Their reasoning did not alter my opinion, and I asked Prof. Sterrett to hunt very carefully through the country about Nefez Keui for evidence. His search produced the evidence of a milestone that Nefez Keui was the site of a *caput viæ*, and no other city in this part of the country but Tavium could have been a *caput viæ*.

3. ASPONA was situated on the road from Ankyra to Parnassos. Its precise situation cannot be determined without more careful examination of the country. The description of this road which has been given (p. 255) shows where it must be looked for. Its territory must have included all the southern part of Galatia *cis Halym*, touching the territory of Ankyra on the north, Cappadocia, lake Tatta, and Lykaonia on the south, and perhaps Myrika on the west.

* The spelling and accentuation are clearly true to the local pronunciation, as is shown by the modern form Enguri.

† 'Gegenbemerkungen zu Prof. Hirschfeld' in the 'Sitzungsberichte' for Jan. 1884.

4. MNIZOS was about 50 miles from Ankyra, and is to be looked for about 25 miles west of Girindos (Manegordos).

5. LAGANIA (Regenagalia, *i.e.* regio Lagania, in Hierocles) was re-named Anastasiopolis, evidently under the Emperor Anastasius (A.D. 491–518). Churches of Saint George and of the Archangel are mentioned in it (Acta S. Theodori, April 22, p. 46).

6. SYKEON was a village on the Siberis, 12 miles west from Lagania, and the imperial highway (publica regii cursus via) passed through it. There was in it a church of Saint Gemellus.

7. JULIOPOLIS was the name given to the older Γόρδου Κώμη. It again changed its name in the later Byzantine period to Basilaion or Basileon. In Not. X., XIII. it occurs as Ἰουλιόπολις ἤτοι Βασίλειον, as a bishopric subject to Ankyra. In Not. II., X., XI., XII. (which belong to the late Byzantine period), Βασίλαιον or Βασίλεον appears, not as subject to the metropolis Ankyra, but as an independent (αὐτοκέφαλος) bishopric. Not. X. therefore contains two separate bishoprics named Basileon, and Parthey on this ground distinguishes them (see his index, *s. v.*). But a passage from a Novella of the Emperor Alexius Comnenus (A.M. 6595, A.D. 1086) * shows that this is incorrect. The bishops of Heracleia and Ankyra appealed to the XII. Canon of Chalcedon, which provided that the metropolitan bishop of a province should retain his rights over any bishopric in his diocese which might be raised in dignity (τιμηθείσῃ ἐκκλησίᾳ), in order to prevent the province from being dismembered (τὸ μὴ κατατέμνεσθαι τὴν μίαν ἐπαρχίαν εἰς δύο). Alexius decided that the emperor might do as he chose in the way of raising bishops to a higher rank, and that when he did so they ceased to be in any way subject to their former metropolitan, and were referred straight to the patriarchal church at Constantinople. It appears therefore that there is only one church Basileion, and that even after it became autokephalos and independent, the Notitiæ remained uncorrected and enumerated it among the bishoprics subject to Ankyra, as well as in its proper place of dignity.

Basileion is evidently named in honour of one of the emperors Basil. Now Notitia II. appears to contain the list of metropolitans and *autokephaloi* in the order of precedence fixed by Leo the Wise (886–912); it follows that Juliopolis had changed its name not later than his reign, and therefore that it was called after Basil I. (867–86). But as Notitia I., which is dated in 883, does not contain Basileion, that name might appear to have been introduced either in the last year of Basil I.,

---

* Lib. II. Nov. iv. in Leunclav., ' Jus Græco-Romanum,' p. 130 : διαλαμβάνον ὡς τῆς μητροπόλεως τοῦ Βασιλαίου καὶ τῆς μητροπόλεως Μαδύτων χηρευουσῶν .... διανέστησαν οἱ μητροπολῖται, ὁ Ἡρακλείας καὶ ὁ Ἀγκύρας, καὶ εἰπεῖν · μὴ ὀφείλειν τὰς τοιαύτας ἐκκλησίας, κἂν ἐτιμήθησαν τῷ τῆς μητροπόλεως ἀξιώματι, παρὰ τοῦ μέρους τῆς μεγάλης ἐκκλησίας ψηφισθῆναι ἀλλὰ παρ' αὐτῶν · διὰ τὸ τὴν .... ἐκκλησίαν τοῦ Βασιλαίου ἐπισκοπὴν εἶναι τοῦ Ἀγκύρας.

or more probably under Leo (886–912), being given in memory of his father. But the name Basileion occurs at Conc. 869, and this is an example of the frequent omission to correct Notitiæ up to date. It is evident that some changes were introduced in the city simultaneously with the change of name, and that its importance was raised. In the later historians Basileion is not unfrequently mentioned. The reason why Juliopolis became so much more important in this later time is probably to be found in the fact that the great military road, which will be described below, was not maintained so carefully, and the direct road from Constantinople to Ankyra would in that case become more important, and with it Juliopolis, as a half-way station, must rise in consequence.

The original name of Juliopolis recurs in a late document of the Eastern Church, where a monastery ἐν τῷ χωρίῳ τῆς Γορδίου Κώμης is said to be under the control of τοῦ Μητροπολίτου τοῦ Φαγίτζη.

8. Petobriga was a village on the road 12 miles east from Lagania. It is mentioned as Petos or Peton in the Acta S. Theodori, April 22, p. 55.

9. Kinna. After all the other bishoprics of Galatia are placed there remains a great district west of Ankyra, in the north-western part of the rich corn-growing district now called Haimane. The order of Hierocles seems to show that Kinna is to be placed there, but the exact situation can be determined only by further exploration.

Kinna is to be sought in the country between Mnizos, Myrika, Ankyra, and Gorbeous (Beinam). A passage in the 'Acta S. Theodori,' April 22, pp. 45–6, agrees with such a situation, but is too vague to afford any accurate evidence. Theodore, returning from a pilgrimage to Jerusalem, after entering the borders of Galatia, stopped at a monastery called Druina (apud Druinorum monasterium). Here it was soon found out who the visitor was, and he healed various sick people. He then went to bless a neighbouring monastery of S. Stephen. Then Amiantus, bishop of Kinna, heard of his presence, and induced him to visit Kinna. He returned from Kinna to Druina, and thence proceeded on his road to Anastasiopolis. The question is by what road Theodore would travel. None of the names mentioned make this certain. In the fourth or fifth century the probability would have been all in favour of the usual pilgrims' route by Ankyra and Parnassos. But this road had in his time (600 A.D.) ceased to be an important one, and the road by Ankyra and Mokissos (Kir Sheher) had supplanted it. But the difference is not important in this case. The roads coincide between Sykea and Gorbeous (Beinam), and the probability is that Druina lies north of Gorbeous, between it and Anastasiopolis.

10. A great number of places, generally near Sykeon and Anastasiopolis, are mentioned in the Acta S. Theodori. Such are Dugaria (p. 45), Euchraes (p. 46) or Eucraa (p. 55), Reace (p. 44), Tzidrama (p. 35); Euarzia, 8 miles from Sykeon, is perhaps the same as Euchraes (p. 44),

Buna or Bunas and Hynia (p. 55). Pidrum was a town in the territory
of Juliopolis (called by a common Byzantine error Heliopolis), near
which was a place Ambrena with an *oratorium Archangeli* (p. 49).*
Buzæa was in the territory of Gratianopolis in the regio Gordiana,
outside the bounds of Galatia (p. 42).† Trapezus was 10 miles from
Sykeon (p. 36). Area, 8 miles from Sykeon, was a pagan holy place,
protected by Diana. Alectoria (pp. 52 and 57) was clearly near Sykeon.
Araunia was a town five miles distant from Sykeon on the road to
civitas Sebasta, which is a translation of πόλις Σεβαστή, and may mean
either Ankyra or Constantinople. An archipresbyteros Andreas lived
at Araunia. Scudra was beside the Sangarios not far from Sykeon
(p. 60). Xeroniaca was a valley near Sykeon (p. 43). Oppidum Sandi
is within a day's journey of Sykeon (p. 54), and oppidum Permetaniæ
is a little further away but in Galatia (p. 55). Permetania seems to be
the same as Permetaia (p. 43). Æantium seems to be near Permetania
(p. 57). The hill Brianea (p. 43) with a monastery of S. Theodorus
(p. 54) was eight miles from Sykeon. Konchas, a small town, and
Enistratus, a village, were also near Sykeon (p. 38). Mazamea or
Mazania, on the upper Siberis *sub climate Mnozeniæ*, possessing a church
of S. Euenicus (p. 40), was evidently in the territory of Mnizos. The
Siberis must drain a large area, since one of its branches rises in the
territory of Mnizos. Places to whose situation no clue is given are Potamia
Galenirum (p. 43), Apocomensis vicus (p. 43), Mons Draconis (p. 43).
The Psilis is a river of Bithynia, west of the Artanes. Oppidum
Æantium and oppidum Silindiconense‡ (p. 57) are perhaps in Galatia :
Colonossus regione Lycaoniæ (p. 43). *In Caria fluvius Copas* is probably
a false reading (p. 44) : the river Scopas or Scopius flowed past
Juliopolis into the Sangarios. Iopolis (p. 35), 15 miles from Sykeon, is
clearly a mistake for Juliopolis.

The 'Acta' of Theodore Sykeota are very important, as giving a picture
of the state of north-western Galatia in the end of the sixth century.§
Unfortunately only a Latin translation is published in ' Acta Sanctorum,'
and the names and perhaps also the sense have been sometimes very
badly represented ; but we may believe safely that all topographical
details are faithful. All the places which we know from other sources
are mentioned with correct descriptions, though sometimes under
distorted names—Mnizos, Petobriga (called Peton), Anastasiopolis,
Juliopolis, and the rivers Siberis and Scopas. The numerous topo-

---

* Pidrum must be in the Buccellariote Theme, and is to be distinguished from
Pidra, an unknown place in the Anatolic Theme, τοῦ ['Ανατολικοῦ] θέματος ἐπί τινι τόπῳ
Πίδρᾳ προσονομαζομένῳ, Genes., p. 8; κώμην Πίδραν κατονομαζομένην ὑπὸ τὸ θέμα τελοῦσαν
τῶν 'Ανατολικῶν (Theophan. Contin., p. 6).

† Gratianopolis is a temporary name of some town, perhaps Akkilaion : see H 9.

‡ Silindiconense must surely be a mis-translation of Σιλινδοκώμη ; compare Κακκαβο-
κώμη, &c. It is unfortunate that the Greek original is not accessible. With Silindos
compare Lydian Silandos. Apocomensis vicus must also contain the element -κώμη.

§ Theodore died A.D. 613. See Addenda.

graphical details which we cannot control by independent testimony may be accepted with confidence for the country within a moderate distance; but, in regard to remoter cities, the author's geographical knowledge is defective. For example, he has no idea of the distance from Amorion to Sozopolis (p. 53), but he knows that the road from Sozopolis to Sykeon passes through Amorion, Germa, and over the bridge Tantaendia.

One other probable reference to Kinna is to be found in the 'Acta S. Theodori' (p. 44). Theodore was made bishop of Anastasiopolis in succession to Timotheos, and by order of the bishop of Ankyra he was consecrated by the bishop of Kinara. The word Cinara in the Latin version is certainly incorrect, and, as the bishop in question was under the jurisdiction of Ankyra, he must be of Kinna.* This certainly suggests that Kinna was not distant from Anastasiopolis, or was even an adjoining bishopric. The previous indications, combined with this, place Kinna about Balyk Koyunji, or even nearer the Sangarios, and assign to it the territory which is bounded by Myrika, Germa, Anastasiopolis, Mnizos, Ankyra, Aspona.

KADOSIA, the bishop of which was brought to Theodore (p. 53) on a litter to be cured of his sickness, belongs not to Galatia, but to Bithynia. We find the entry Γάλλου ἤτοι Καδοσίας, or Δοσίας in the earliest Notitiæ, and at the Council held 680 A.D., George bishop of Galos or of Kadosia was present. In the later Notitiæ, I., III., X., XlII., the entry is always Γάλλου ἤτοι Λόφων (see p. 182).

11. VERINOPOLIS rose to importance in the Byzantine period. It is not mentioned by Hierocles, and yet it was evidently refounded and renamed before his time during the lifetime of the empress Verina. The late Notitiæ mention it along with Stavros, showing that these were two neighbouring towns included in one bishopric. These were two fortresses, which became important stations in the Byzantine military system, but had apparently not been raised to the rank of a bishopric when Hierocles made his list, about 530 A.D. In all probability they became a bishopric in the re-organisation of the Byzantine empire by Justinian within a few years after Hierocles wrote. The history of the Byzantine changes in the comparative importance of Anatolian towns from the time of Justinian onwards turns on military considerations. The forts (τοποτηρησίαι), situated on military roads, often in different situations from the Roman cities, grew into bishoprics and finally often into the capitals of provinces. Any place which became a

---

* Compare Hierocles's Lysinara in Pamphylia. Both names have been formed in the same way. The expression ὁ Κινέων, or Λυσινέων, ἐπίσκοπος, written with the common mis-spelling Κιναίων, Λυσιναίων, has been misread Κινάρων, Λυσινάρων and interpreted "Bishop of Cinara, Lysinara." The expression really means, in accordance with the almost universal formula, "Bishop of the people of Cina, Lysinia."

bishopric after Hierocles is presumably a fortress of the Byzantine type, situated on a high, precipitous hill.

The great importance of Euagina as a meeting-place of roads becomes apparent in our examination of the Roman roads leading east from Ankyra. Though I have not visited its site at Göne, I have heard in the country great reports of ruins near it. How, then, shall we account for its apparent omission in the Byzantine lists? We must believe that, if any town in Eastern Galatia grew into a bishopric in Byzantine time, that town was probably situated at Göne. In short, everything points to the conclusion that Verinopolis was the name given to Euagina when it began to rise, in the growing development of this district, to be a place of importance (see p. 261).

12. STAVROS is apparently of equally late development. Notitiæ III., X., XIII., which alone mention it, are the latest class of lists, and the only other reference which I have found to the place dates about A.D. 890. I therefore understand that Stavros was on the military road of Justinian (whose course is discussed in sect. G), and that it became important only after the formation of that road. Being united with Verinopolis in a single bishopric, Stavros must have been not far distant from it, and is to be looked for a few hours to the south.*

13. MYRIOKEPHALOI is apparently another of the fortresses of Justinian on the great military road. The name occurs also in Phrygia, denoting a fortress east of Soublaion on a military road, which also was organised by Justinian.† Myriokephaloi was west of Stavros. Verinopolis, Stavros, and Myriokephaloi were three fortresses, which together formed the Tourma Saniana. They belonged to the Buccellariote Theme, but were, about 890, transferred to the Kharsian Theme. They may be safely taken to include the whole southern part of the province Galatia on the east side of the Halys. The important passage of Constantine Porphyrogenitus ('de Admin. Imp.,' 225), which mentions the modifications of 890, will be more fully considered below.

14. KALOUMNE is named as a bishopric in the latest class of Notitiæ. It is perhaps the same place that is mentioned under the name Kadêmna as a bishopric of Phrygia Salutaris in Not. I: Kademna and Alopex are certainly quite erroneously appended at the end of the list. Nothing is known about it. Was it Kotch Hissar? (see Addenda).

15. Before concluding the discussion of Galatia Prima it is necessary to attempt to define the limits at different times of the Kharsian Theme. Constantine Porphyrogenitus says the name was derived from some general named Kharsios, who flourished when the Theme was formed in the time of Justinian or some other emperor: this derivation is

---

* We find "Pessinus or Justinianopolis" as a single bishopric: the distance between Bala Hisar and Sivri Hisar is four hours (about 12 miles). Stavros is also called Timios Stavros, and was a name of the place called also Sirichas or Sirachas, G 39, 43.

† See 'American Journal of Archæology,' 1888, p. 282.

obviously a mere guess of Constantine's. It has been stated above that the name is probably derived from the town of Garsi or Karissa, at the important road centre of Alaja.* Originally this place, called τὸ Χαρσιανὸν κάστρον, was one of the bandai or topoteresiai of the vast Armeniac Theme. Then the Theme was divided into three parts, and the name Kharsian was given to the central one. The boundaries of this Theme vary considerably. In the time of Michael (843–867 A.D.), there was only a Kleisourarch of Kharsiana, so that as yet it hardly ranked as co-ordinate with the great Themes.†

In A.D. 730 Moslemah invaded Cappadocia and captured the Kharsian fortress. ‡ The passage shows that the fort was in Cappadocia rather than in Pontus.

In 832 Theophilus defeated the Saracens at Kharsianon. §

In A.D. 860 a battle took place at Porson in the district Abysianum on the borders of the Armeniac and Paphlagonian Themes, about 500 miles from Amisus, and some of the defeated Arabs escaped across the Halys, but were soon afterwards captured in the Kharsian Theme (Genes., p. 99).

The Strategoi of the Kharsian Theme and of the Armeniac troops are mentioned under Basil I., and Agrane and Siboron are said to be in the Kharsian Theme, while it is implied that at Siboron there was ready access to the Armeniac Theme. ‖

When Joannes Kurkuas began his career (under Leo VI.) the bounds of the empire on the east were the Kharsian Castle, the town of Hypsela, and the Halys: he carried its bounds to the Euphrates and the Tigris (Theophan. Contin., p. 427). Here the distinction is made between the fortress Hypsela and the central Kharsian fortress, and the line indicated agrees admirably with the lower Halys, Alaja, and the lofty rock Mushalem Kale.

In A.D. 887 the town Hypsela in the Kharsian Theme was captured by the Saracens.¶

In the year 906 Leo VI. exiled Eustathius Argyros to his house in Kharsiana. On his way thither he was poisoned at Ara, and buried at Spynin (εἰς τὸ Σπυνὶν τοῦ Ἄρα τὴν κορυφήν). His sons exhumed his body and carried it to the family monastery of S. Elizabeth in the Kharsian Theme.**

* ἡ πόρτα τοῦ Χαρσίου at Constantinople (v. Theophanes passim) was opposite Blacherna, and perhaps hence gets its name (as if Καρσίου).

† I find mentioned in Michael's reign the Armeniac, Buccellariote, Koloneian Paphlagonian, Thrakesian, Anatolic, Opsikian, and Cappadocic Themes, and the Kleisourarchai of Seleukeia and Kharsiana.

‡ τὸ Χαρσιανὸν κάστρον (Theoph., p. 409; Cedren., i. p. 800).

§ κατὰ τὸ Χαρσιανόν (Cedren., ii. 123; Contin., p. 114).

‖ τόν τε τοῦ Χαρσιανοῦ καὶ τὸν τῶν Ἀρμενιακῶν [στρατηγόν] (Cedren., ii. 210 Genes., 122).

¶ ἡ κατὰ τὸ Χαρσιανὸν διακειμένη πόλις ἡ Ὑψηλή (Cedren., ii. 250, cp. Theophan Contin., 354). The Bonn text of Cedrenus prints ὑψηλή as an epithet. (Finlay, by a misprint, has Hysela for Hypsela.)

** Theophan. Contin., 374 Cedren., ii. 269.

Another reference may be quoted to this older form of the Kharsian Theme. " S. Eudokimos—genus quidem duxit e Cappadocibus—electus ut præesset parti exercitus Cappadocum et moraretur circa id quod vocatur Charsianum." *

16. About 890 occurred a reorganisation of the eastern Themes, and five topoteresiai which constituted *Galatia trans Halym* were transferred from the Buccellariote and Armeniac Themes to the Kharsian Theme. At the same time the southern parts of the Cappadocic Theme, viz., the Tourma Kases (which probably includes Tyana and the plain of Venasa) and the topoteresia of Cæsareia and Nyssa, were also transferred to the Kharsian Theme. The Cappadocic Theme now included the country from the mountains near Sivri Hissar (Dindymos) to the Halys, and the Kharsian Theme all the country from the Halys to Cæsareia on the east and Loulon on the south.†

For topographical purposes it is important to observe that the topoteresiai of Tavium and Komodromos, which had belonged to the Armeniac Theme, and which included the northern parts of *Galatia trans Halym*, were added to the Tourma Kharsiana, while the three topoteresiai which had belonged to the Buccellariote Theme, and which included the southern parts of *Galatia trans Halym*, constituted the Tourma Saniana. The Tourma Kharsiana, therefore, was the north-western part of the Kharsian Theme, and this confirms the view already stated that Garsi or Karissa, situated at Alaja, was the original centre from which the name Kharsia spread over the entire Theme. Originally it was only a part of the Armeniac Theme; then this great Theme was divided iuto three, Cappadocic, Kharsian, and Armeniac, and finally the reorganisation which I have just described was made.

An objection may be urged that Alaja, where I have placed Kharsia, falls more naturally into the Buccellariote than the Kharsian Theme. But originally the line of division was made between the Armeniac and the Buccellariote, and in that case the line of separation between Göne and Alaja is not so surprising. Moreover, the arrangement of 890, which united Kharsia with Tavium and Komodromos, clearly requires a close geographical connection between them.

Another Tourma of the Kharsian Theme was named Kymbalaios. It was perhaps the country about Kir Sheher, to the east and north.

The powerful castle on the lofty isolated rock of Mushalem Kale must have been a very important point in the Saracen wars, and was perhaps centre of another Tourma or at least a Topoteresia. It is

---

* Act. Sanct., July 30, p. 312.

† It is after this enlargement of the Kharsian Theme, in A.D. 978, that Basilika Therma is mentioned (Cedren., ii. 431) as in the Kharsian Theme. See Constant. Porph., 'de Admin. Imp.,' p. 225.

referred to only in A.D. 887 * as Hypsela. This Hypsela must be distinguished from the town of the same name, which appears as a bishopric of Pontus Polemoniacus in the latest Notitiæ, unless (as is probable) geographical connection is violated.

17. DILIMNIA, which occurs in the Jerusalem Itinerary, x miles from Ankyra on the road to Parnassos, under the form Delemnia, and which is perhaps corrupted to Olenos in Ptolemy, is also mentioned in an inscription, published by Domaszewski, in the Archaeolog. Epig. Mittheil. aus Oest., IX., 1885, p. 115. It was a village situated perhaps at the northern end of the Lake Mohan Göl, or on the hill between it and Ankyra.

18. MALOS (Μαλός) was a place a little over 40 miles from Ankyra,† on the western bank of the Halys. Theodotus came to the place at the time when the remains of Valens (τοῦ ἐν Μηδικῶσιν διὰ πολλῶν ἐλθόντος μαστίγων) were thrown into the Halys. Theodotus saved them, and carried them to a rock on the bank, about two stadia ‡ from the village. There were there grass and trees (δένδρα ἀρκεύθινα καὶ βοράτινα), and at morn the sound of grasshoppers and the song of nightingales. Several of the brethren by chance found him here, and were sent to bring the presbyter from the village. The presbyter, coming out of church at the sixth hour, saw them coming, and the village dogs barking and troubling them; he went with them, and was told by Theodotus to prepare on the spot a receptacle for the relics (Act. Sanct., May 18, IV., p. 165).

Of the three roads that lead from Ankyra to the Halys, the one that is probably meant here is that which goes to Kalejik (Eccobriga). The distance from Angora is at present given as 13 hours, and may be fairly reckoned as 40 Roman miles. The distance by the straightest road due east, to the Halys and Tavium, is decidedly less than 40 miles.

19. PROSEILEMMENE was a term applied to a district of Galatia, south of the three Gaulish tribes (ὑπὸ τὰ εἰρημένα ἔθνη), and north of the Bizenoi and the part of Lykaonia containing Petinessos, Egdaumana, Kinna, &c. The name is probably to be explained on the analogy of Epiktetos Phrygia, § as indicating the entire district of Lykaonia which was added by Pius (p. 377) to Galatia. Ptolemy ‖ is the only author that mentions this name. The Bizenoi inhabited what Pliny calls Lycaoniae partem Obizenen (V., 32, 147). Probably the Greek form

* See also Theoph. Contin., p. 427.

† ἀπῳκισμένον σημείων μικροῦ πρὸς τεσσαράκοντα.

‡ The term stadia probably means miles; compare Anna's statement as to the distance of Basileia from Nikaia, and see also L, 5.

§ Compare Strabo, p. 563, who says that the name Epiktetos given to Hellespontine or Little Phrygia dates from the Attalids.

‖ Wilberg in his note gives the strange derivation of προσειλημμένη from προσειλεῖν instead of προσλαμβάνω.

of this name should be Οὐιζηνοι, and the name of the town Οὐύνζελα given by Ptolemy twice, in Galatia among the Tektosages and in Pisidia, is connected with it. The contradiction, which on this theory is involved in placing Οὐύνζελα among the Tektosages, is due to the fact that Ptolemy uses a different authority for his paragraphs about the tribes in the different provinces from the one which he uses to make his lists of cities. It is, however, possible that Οὐύνζελα among the Tektosages is a fault for Οὐύνδια.

20. The boundaries of the Roman Province Galatia varied greatly at different times. The province was formed on the death of Amyntas in B.C. 25. The bounds towards the north and west have already been discussed. On the south it included the whole of Pisidia, with Milyas and Kabalis, and must have reached down almost to the southern limits of Taurus, where it rises from the coast lands of Pamphylia. Komama and Kolbasa, colonies of Augustus, must have belonged to it, and prove how far it extended. When Vespasian instituted the province Lycia-Pamphylia, he must have detached a great part of Pisidia from Galatia to make the new province; and the southern frontier of Galatia then took the line indicated by Ptolemy, including the valley of Apollonia, but not that of Konane, Seleuceia, and Baris. Further east Neapolis, Amblada, and the Orondeis, with Misthia and Pappa, were left to Galatia, but the south-eastern end of Bey Sheher Lake, with Karallia, Kolybrassos, Lyrbe, &c., along with all the parts south of this line, were assigned to Pamphylia. That this enlargement of Pamphylia belongs to the re-organisation by Vespasian is shown first by the fact that no other occasion seems reasonable for the change from the older arrangement, which prevailed as late as Nero ('C. I. L.,' III., Supplem., No. 6872), to the later arrangement, which at Komama had come into force as early as 141 A.D., when Voconius Saxa became governor of Lycia-Pamphylia;* and secondly by the date in an inscription of Palaiapolis Pisidiae, which appears to be reckoned from 74 A.D. as era.†

The boundary on the south-east will be treated under T, 47.

21. The boundary between Galatia and Cappadocia is indicated by the list of bishoprics and by the discussion of the strategiai of Cappadocia. The limits of the Roman province on this side varied greatly. In 70 A.D. Cappadocia was placed under a consular legatus Augusti, and at some time not later than 78 it was united with the province Galatia. This arrangement lasted until the time of Trajan, but in the later

---

* See Benndorf, &c., 'Reisen in Lykien,' ii., p. 132, 'C. I. L.,' III., Supplem., 6885.

† Marquardt assigns the year 74 as a probable date for Vespasian's reorganisation of Lycia-Pamphylia, on the authority of Suetonius and Eusebius; see 'Staatsverw.' i., p. 376. This date is now confirmed by the above-mentioned inscription, which is commented on A. S. P., D. 16, and in Addenda to p. 194, and which proves that the new system began with the governor who was sent in the summer of the year 74.

years of that emperor * the vast province had been divided, and Galatia was entrusted to a praetorian legatus (as it had been before 78), while Cappadocia was governed by a consular legatus (as the united provinces had been since 78). Previous to 78 B.C. Pontus Polemoniacus, Pontus Galaticus, and part of Paphlagonia, were connected with Galatia. This had been arranged apparently in the years 7 B.C. and 63 A.D. Hence the inscription of Sospes, ' C. I. L.,' III., Supplem., 6818, gives an enumeration of the country governed by a legatus of Galatia, which was true between A.D. 63 and A.D. 78, and probably was never before or afterwards true : the enumeration is Galatia, Pisidia, Phrygia, Lycaonia, Isauria, Paphlagonia, Pontus Galaticus, Pontus Polemoniacus. Of these eight countries, the first five were the original province of B.C. 25, Amyntas's kingdom : Paphlagonia and part of Pontus Galaticus † were added in B.C. 7, and Pontus Polemoniacus was added in A.D. 63.

In the period 78–100 ‡ the combined province is Galatia, Cappadocia, Pontus, Pisidia, Paphlagonia, Lycaonia, Armenia Minor (' C. I. L.,' III., 312, 318). The omission of Isauria and Phrygia here is due to their being only small districts, included under the terms Galatia and Pisidia.

When under Trajan at some uncertain date the province was again divided : Pontus Galaticus and Polemoniacus went with Cappadocia, as is proved by inscriptions of Arrius Antoninus at Amaseia and of Arrian at Sebastopolis, as well as by the inscription of an unknown governor of Galatia, 'C. I. L.,' III., Supplem., 6819, which enumerates the countries governed by him as Galatia, Phrygia, Pisidia, Lycaonia, Paphlagonia ; the contents of this inscription date it under Trajan, and probably in the second half of his reign.

A further change in the list of countries ruled by the governor of Galatia is indicated by ' C. I. L.,' III., Supplem., 6813, where the enumeration is only Galatia, Pisidia, Paphlagonia. The omission of Phrygia is doubtless due only to the fact that so little of Phrygia was included in the province ; it is here summed up under Pisidia. But the omission of Lycaonia is clearly to be connected with the enlargement of the province Cilicia so as to include the three eparchiae Cilicia, Lycaonia, Isauria, which took place under Antoninus Pius (see p. 378).

22. The following Table gives the changes in the dimensions of the Roman province Galatia :—

* ' C. I. L.,' III., Supplem., 6819. The refinements of change described by Marquardt, p. 362, must probably be discarded, for Sospes has to be substituted for Sollers, and the date for the government is uncertain: ib. 6818. Still it is not definitely proved that the provinces were united between 88 and 96. On the date of 6818, see the following remarks.

† See Addenda.

‡ The period may be proved to be longer by further discoveries. It may be noted that ' C. I. L,' III., Supplem., 6818, must probably date between 70 and 78, if the Sarmatian expedition referred to is that of 70 A.D. The date 90 or 92 for the expedition, approved by Mommsen, ' Hermes,' III., 115, and Marquardt, p. 362, cannot, in view of the preceding exposition, be accepted.

25 B.C.—7 B.C.   Gal. Pisid. [Phryg.] Lycaon. [Isaur.].*

7 B.C.—63 A.D.   Gal. Pisid. [Phryg.] Lycaon. [Isaur.] Paphlag. Pont. Gal.

63 A.D.—78 A.D.   Gal. Pisid. [Phryg.] Lycaon. [Isaur.] Paphlag. Pont. Gal Pont. Polem.

78 A.D.—100 A.D.   Gal. Pisid. Lycaon. Paphlag. Pont. [Gal. et Polem.] Capp. Arm. Min.

100 A.D.—140 or 150 A.D.   Gal. Pisid. [Phryg.] Lycaon. Paphlag.

140 or 150 A.D.—297 A.D.   Gal. Pisid. [Phryg.] Paphlag.

23. The exact boundary-line on the eastern side cannot be fixed, but the description of the cities and bishoprics shows approximately the line that separates Galatia from Pontus Galaticus and Cappadocia.

24. About the end of the third century the province was divided among three new provinces, Paphlagonia, Galatia, and Pisidia, and, about 386–95, Theodosius subdivided Galatia into two, taking part of Phrygia to form the western province, with the metropolis Pessinus. The two Galatias were distinguished sometimes as Prima and Secunda, sometimes as Great and Little,† Galatia.   The name Salutaris was often applied to Pessinuntine Galatia, as to eastern Phrygia.   An ecclesiastical division, which was probably made in the ninth century, but which was never a civil division, may also be noticed.   The cities south and west of Amorion were placed under it as metropolis ; as the old civil division into provinces had long since been disused and Themes been substituted, no regard was paid in this new arrangement to the boundary between Phrygia and Galatia.

L. ROMAN ROADS FROM ANKYRA TO THE EAST.

1. First, I take the roads Ankyra-Archelais and Ankyra-Cæsareia : the former appears in four forms in our authorities as follows:—

Antonine Itinerary, p. 205.	Jerusalem Itinerary.	Antonine Itinerary, p. 143.	Peutinger Table.‡
Ancyra	Ancyra	Ancyra	[Ancyra.]
	Dilimnia X. ..		
G·rbeous XXIV. ..	Gorbeous XI. ..	Corbeunca XX. ..	Corveunte X.
Oι ·ologiaco XVIII.	Rosolodiaco XII.	Rosolaciaco XII. ..	
	Aliassus XIII...		Garmias XIII.
§Aspona XX.	Aspona XVIII...	Aspona XXXIII. ..	Aspona X.
	Galea XIII. ..		
	Andrapa IX. ..		
Parnasso XXII. ..	Parnassos XIII.	Parnasso XXIV. ..	Aspasi XII.
Nysa XXIV... ..	Iogola XVI. ..	Ozzala XVII.	
Osiana XXXII. ..	Nitalis (?) XVIII.	Nitazi (?) XVIII. ..	Nita...zo XXXI.
Saccasena XXVIII.	Argustana XIII.		
Cæsareia XXX. ..	Colonia Archelais XVI.	Coloniam Arcilaida XXVII.	[Archelais] XXX

* Names in brackets are small districts which might be omitted in an inscription without causing any doubt as to bounds.

† Theophan., p. 71.   The sense of τῶν κάτω Γαλατῶν, *Act. Sanct.*, May, vol. i., p. 730A, is doubtful.

‡ In the Peutinger Table the stations are put in the reverse order, so that Corveunte is next to Archelais.

§ The Antonine Itinerary in both cases perhaps omits a station between Aspona and Parnassos.

Few roads have been so much discussed as this, which forms a part of the pilgrim route from Europe to the Holy Land. The central critical point is the determination of the site of Parnassos, which has been variously placed, by Hamilton (whom Kiepert follows), at Kotch Hisar on the salt lake Tatta, and by Mordtmann at Kir Sheher on the opposite side of the Halys. I believe that the argument given below (p. 298) is sufficient to determine within narrow limits the situation of Parnassos, so that I need not spend time in examining and stating the arguments which might be brought forward against older views. Parnassos was on the right bank of the Halys, between Tchikin Aghyl (pronounced Tchikinal) and Kessik Keupreu.

Tho first part of the course of this road is not doubtful. It went along the east side of Mohan Göl to Gorbeous, near Beinam.* The exact situation of Gorbeous is unknown, but the route is clearly marked, and, moreover, I saw in 1886 a part of the old pavement, Roman or Byzantine, beside Aghaboz. The road went on in a fairly straight line to the Halys at Tchikin Aghyl, which is situated at the point where the river makes a bend to the north from its previous course, W.N.W. A little above Tchikin Aghyl there are fords, and I doubt whether any other ford exists on the Halys till we reach the upper part of its course. The situation of Parnassos on the Halys is certain, but the arguments given below do not suffice to place it accurately without much closer examination of the country than has yet been made. But as we know from Polybius that Parnassos was at a crossing of the river, and as it is in the last degree improbable that a bridge existed there in the time of Polybius, it seems probable that Parnassos was situated at the fords. Moreover, according to my route in 1886, the distance from Aghaboz to Tchikinal † is, in an air-line, 60 statute miles; and, according to my estimate, the distance by road is 69 statute miles. Now, the distance from Gorbeous to Parnassos is 78 Roman miles according to the Jerusalem, and 68 according to the Antonine, Itinerary. There is therefore quite satisfactory agreement in regard to distance if Parnassos is placed a few miles higher up the river than Tchikin Aghyl. The intermediate stations must be placed according to the distances given in the authorities. The discrepancies between the four different accounts afford a convincing proof how little we can trust to any one. The Jerusalem Itinerary is probably the best authority in this case.

According to this view the boundary between Cappadocia and Galatia was near the place where the Kara Señir Dagh approaches close to the Halys about six miles north of Tchikin Aghyl.

2. At Parnassos the road forked. One branch went by Ozizala, Nitalis, and Argustana to Archelais Colonia. The other went by

* I should look for Gorbeous somewhere between Beinam and Aghaboz.

† Tchikin Aghyl is commonly pronounced in this way, as the guttural usually disappears between vowels in Turkish.

Nyssa to Cæsareia. There is a natural probability that it would in the latter part of the way coincide with the road Archelais-Soandos-Sadakora-Cæsareia, and I shall examine the latter stages below. Nyssa was on the river Halys, as I will show in detail below.

We see, then, that under the Roman Empire the road from Ankyra to Cæsareia never crossed the Halys, but skirted it for a long way through Parnassos and Nyssa. This is not the shortest road, but it avoids a double crossing of the Halys, a river which is liable to great winter floods. As long as Rome was the capital, and all imperial business camé from and went to Rome, intercourse between Ankyra and Cæsareia was confined to provincial intercourse, and the inhabitants probably used the short road when it was open and the Roman road in winter. But when Constantinople became the capital, the road between Cæsareia and the capital passed through Ankyra: intercourse along the road must have grown enormously, and the shorter path must have become much more important. Moreover, civilisation was spreading and intercourse increasing rapidly at this time in these parts of Asia Minor. The inconvenience of having the direct path blocked in time of flood must have been felt with growing impatience, and at last caused formal ǀrepresentation to the Emperor. A lucky accident has ˙ preserved to us the contemporary record. A letter or petition addressed to the Emperor Theodosius has been attributed to Basil of Cæsareia, and been transmitted to us probably through this mistake.* The writer describes the great floods in the Halys and its tributary the Kara Su, which had rendered the Halys impassable and so cut off communication between Cæsareia and the three provinces, Galatia, Paphlagonia, and Helenopontos. Tillemont,† the only writer, so far as I know, who has commented on this document, has strangely misunderstood it. He says that the intention of the letter is to beseech the Emperor to restore a bridge across the Halys, which had been carried away by the recent inundation. But the writer only says that the swollen waters rendered the Halys impassable and cut off all communication across it. He entreats the Emperor to build a bridge and set free the traffic from dependence on the uncertain crossing of the river.‡

3. It is n⟨ ⟩ known whether Theodosius complied with this request and built a bridge; but later history implies the existence of an easy communication across the Halys, and it is highly probable that the bridge was built soon after this letter was written, the first since the old bridge on the "Royal Road."

* It is published in Cotelier, ' Eccles. Græc. Monum.,' II., p. 97.

† Tillemont, ' Mémoires pour servir à l'histoire de l'Eglise,' IX.

‡ Incidentally he mentions that there was no ford over the Halys. Traffic was dependent on a ferry. There is a ford over the Halys during the late summer near Tchikin Aghyl, in Galatia, which I have crossed, but I know of no other on the central part of the river's course. There are bridges near Cæsareia and a ferry at Yarapson.

A new era in the history of Cappadocia began when the bridge over the Halys was built. Before that time the road from Ankyra to Cæsareia avoided the uncertain crossing and followed the course of the Halys. Parnassos, situated on the Halys at the point where this road intersected the road leading from Colonia Archelais and the south-west countries to Tavium and the countries of Pontus and Armenia, had hitherto been an important town, frequently alluded to as a crossing-place of the Halys, but it henceforth lost its importance, and at last disappeared from existence. The road from Ankyra to Cæsareia sought a new route, taking the short road, which involves two crossings of the Halys. This new road opened up the country north of the Halys. The modern Kir Sheher is situated at a point on the road, where paths from the north, from Colonia Archelais, and from Tyana and Cilicia converge. This point became a very important one as soon as the direct road from Ankyra to Cæsareia was formed, and Kir Sheher is still, and must have been for many centuries, one of the greatest commercial centres of Cappadocia. Accordingly, about a century and a half after Theodosius, the emperor Justinian recognised the change that had been wrought in the country, formed the whole north-western half of Cappadocia, which had hitherto been subject to Tyana, into a new province, and made Mokissos its metropolis under the name Justinianopolis. From what has just been said, it follows that Mokissos must have been situated at Kir Sheher.

4. Ankyra to Tavium and Amasia, and Ankyra to Gangra and Amasia Authorities (a) Peutinger Table.

[Ancyra] xxxvi Acitoriziaco xxxiii Eccobriga xxv Lassora xvii Stabiu. Tavio xiii Tonea xxx Garsi xxx Amasia.

Gangaris occurs on a road Nicomedia-Gangaris-Amasia, but this Amasia is separate from the Amasia of the other road, and Leake has already observed that a confusion seems to have occurred between Amasia and Amastris; the stations Otresa and Virasia, given on this road, do not aid us here.

(b) Antonine Itinerary (p. 203).

Ancyra xxiiii Bolegasgus xxiiii Sarmalius xx Ecobrogis xxiiii Adapera xxiiii Tavia.

These roads are so confused and corrupted that a certain restoration is at present impossible. The following may be given as the most probable, though the stations are in several cases uncertain. I give some weight to the evidence of Ptolemy, as far as (1) his division into provinces, (2) his quotation of names; but the situation in which he places the names on his map cannot, in the beginning of our investigation, have any weight whatsoever.

Prof. G. Hirschfield, in his paper on Tavium, differs in regard to this last point, and contends that Ptolemy's map may be used as an important and even decisive criterion in cases where our other authorities differ; but his contention is disproved both by Prof. Kiepert's 'Gegenbemerkungen,' and by the ascertained inaccuracy of the positions which he maintained and supported by the authority of Ptolemy.*

I do not, of course, contend that Ptolemy's positions have absolutely no value, but for our purpose, in an unknown country, they would be more injurious than helpful. After the investigation has established a number of results, Ptolemy may be used more freely; but at present the extent to which I value his authority must be restricted within the limits stated above.

The most valuable evidence about these roads is a set of Trajan's milestones, which reveal a system of roads planned about the end of the first century.

5. It is not certain from the evidence that there was a direct road along the shortest line from Ankyra to Tavium; other routes, which are still often used, go by Kalejik and by Gorbeous (Beinam). But there is a natural probability that there was a direct road between two such important cities. A milestone at Orta Keui ('C. I. L.,' III. Supplem. 6901) is now situated on a road which went due east up the river from Ankyra, and its position can hardly be explained unless there was such a direct road.†

Now a road from Gangra-Germanicopolis to Ankyra, though it is omitted in the Peutinger Table, is necessary, and is mentioned in the tale of Saint Callinicus, who walked from Gangra to Ankyra, a distance of 70 stadia, shod with iron spikes: when he had gone 60 stadia he reached Matrica, where he called forth a fountain which still flows.‡ If we read miles for stadia, we get a fair approximation to the distance viâ Kalejik, where two milestones are known, and through which the modern road—and, doubtless, also the ancient road—to Gangra passes. Kalejik is about xxxvi miles from Gangra. By a direct road it is indeed not so much as xxxvi miles from Ankyra, but two milestones of Trajan and of Hadrian found at Kalejik read xxxv and xxxviii, and it does not admit of doubt that these distances are measured from Ankyra. § They can be accounted for only by a détour: the road joined the road Tavium-Ankyra some distance out of the latter city. The distances xxxvi and xxxiii on the Table close to

* Professor Hirschfeld still adheres to his opinion, 'Berliner Wochenschrift,' 19 Mai, 1888, p. 629:—" In Ptolemaios glaube ich eine Kontrolle für die Richtigkeit der Tafel gefunden zu haben ('Monatsber. Berl. Akad.,' 1883, 1260 f.)."

† Inscriptions are, of course, often carried. Milestones, from their shape and cumbrous size, are less often carried, and, as a rule, only to be used as gravestones in the cemetery of a town.

‡ Act. Sanct., July 29, p. 41. On stadia in the sense of miles, compare F 73.

§ 'C. I. L.,' III., 309, asserts that Ancyra cannot be the *caput viæ*, as the real distance is not so great as the numbers; but the supplementary part of III., 6898, gives up the objection.

Ankyra seem so appropriate to this road, that I accept them and restore

Ankyra xxxiiii Acitoriziaco xxxvi Gangra.

Acitoriziacum,* then, was a station near Kalejik, perhaps a little to the north or north-east.

6. The road Ankyra-Tavium is given both in the Itinerary and in the Table: they agree in a station Eccobriga, and Lassora may be identical with Adapera (Δ and Λ being interchanged in a Greek original). If we follow the Table and read xviii between Lassora and Tavium, Lassora would be at Ishakli, and Eccobriga a little east of Yakshi Khan, xxvi miles from Lassora. There remains only about 43 miles to Ankyra, in which distance there cannot be room for more than one station.

We must follow the Itinerary, and restore

Ankyra xxiiii Sarmalius xx Eccobriga xxiiii Lassora xviii Tavium.

One station too many, Bolegasgus, with the same distance xxiiii, is given in the Itinerary: it indicates either a transference or a corruption. Lassora is probably Ptolemy's Laskoria, and must be corrected accordingly. Matrica, with its fountain, should be looked for about ten miles from Ankyra towards Gangra.

7. The milestones of the road constructed by Trajan are found at Amaseia, Iskelib, and Kalejik, and the distance at Iskelib is, as Professor G. Hirschfeld rightly saw, reckoned from Amaseia. It is therefore not open to doubt that the road Ankyra to Gangra went on to Iskelib, Tchorum, and Amaseia. It may be thus completed :—

Gangra xlv Iskelib xxvii Tchorum † xx Etonia xxx Amaseia.

8. There is a milestone of Trajan at Tavium, which was therefore included in the same construction as Amaseia, Iskelib, and Kalejik. The road Ankyra-Tavium went on to Sebasteia and to Amaseia, forking at Tavium, as is clearly given on the Table. The latter road must pass by Alaja, an obvious Roman site; geographical considerations leave no doubt that this is the route. Thence it goes by Hadji Keui, or else falls into the Iskelib-Amaseia road at Tchorum. The former course is more natural, and suits the distances given in the Table :—

Tavia xiii Tonea xxx Garsi xxx Amasia.

It would at first appear that Tonea is at Alaja, and Garsi at Hadji Keui. But Ptolemy puts Etonia in Pontus Galaticus and Karissa, which is obviously equivalent to Garsi, in Galatia: and though his authority is not high, still it has some weight. Moreover, it is perhaps confirmed by the Byzantine records. This country north of the Ak Dagh and east of the Halys was the Turma Kharsiana. The name Kharsiana is an

---

* Probably a corrupt name.

† Eukhaita was situated at Tchorum (p 319); Andrapa at Iskelib.

adjective, derived from a town Kharsia, which we can hardly refuse to identify with Garsi of the Table. Ptolemy's form Karissa looks like a Grecised form of the name. Now, the Theme seems more likely to be named after an important point like Alaja than such a place as Hadji Keui. The important and central situation of Alaja so impressed Professor Kiepert, that he wished to place Tavium there ('Gegenbemerkungen zu Prof. G. Hirschfeld' in 'Berlin Sitzungsber.,' 1884.) Moreover, Hadji Keui was certainly not in Kharsiana, but in the Armeniac Theme (using Armeniac in the narrower sense). I therefore place Karsia near Alaja, * Etonia at Hadji Keui, and restore

Tavium VII Tomba XXIII Karsia XXX Etonia XXX Amaseia.†

In regard to Ptolemy's placing Etonia in Pontus Galaticus, I quite admit that decisive authority cannot be attached to his geographical separation between Galatia, Pontus Galaticus and Pontus Polemoniacus. He places Amaseia, Sebastopolis (Sulu Serai), Choloe and Pida (which are between Amaseia and Neocæsareia), and Komana Pontica in Galaticus, and yet Zela, equally with Neocæsareia and Sebasteia, is in Polemoniacus.‡ But on the whole, the towns which he places in Polemoniacus are further east, those in Galatia further west, than those of Pontus Galaticus. Hence, though there are one or two exceptions, and though his authority is not conclusive, yet his assignment of the cities to the several provinces must be accepted, unless distinct reasons can in any case be brought against it; and all other considerations tend to confirm him in this case.

9. Tavium to Zela, Sebastopolis, Komana, Sebasteia, Neocæsareia.
Authorities (a) Peutinger Table.

Tavium XXXVI Rogmor § XXXVI Aegonne XXVIII Ptemari XXVI Zela XXXII Stabulum XXII Seramisa XV Neocæsareia.

Tavium XVI Tomba XXII Eugoni Ad Stabulum XXII Mesyla XV Comana Pontica continued to Nikopolis.

Tavium XVI Euagina XXIIII Saralio XXII Zama XXXV Aquas Arauenas continued to Cæsareia Mazaca.

No connection with Sebasteia is shown in the Table.
(b) Antonine Itinerary
given in detail below.

---

* I place the town two or three miles N.W. of the village Alaja.

† Another example of the stations on a road in the Peutinger Table being given in the wrong order may be found in Ankyra-Archelais. It was facilitated by the assonance Tomba Tonea, see § 10.

‡ After the above remarks have been long in print, further study makes me add that I now see no ground to doubt Ptolemy's accuracy here: the frontier line is confirmed by Strabo, p. 559, and may be safely accepted. His lists of Pontus Galaticus, Cappadocicus, and Polemoniacus, are perhaps taken from a high authority.

§ The fault is a characteristic one: Tavium [T]rocmor[um] is divided into two stations and the number xxx. is given twice.

In regard to these roads, which are obviously very corrupt, it is essential to observe the importance of the point now called Göne, where there are said to be nι nerous remains (I have not visited it, but speak from report heard in the neighbourhood at Alaja and Terzili Hamam). Göne is on the ordinary road Yuzgat-Sivas, which must coincide with one of the two ancient routes Tavium-Sebasteia.

10. In regard to the road which goes due east from Tavium, the Peutinger Table in the triple

> Tavium xxxvi [T]rogmor[um] xxxvi Ægonne to Zela.
> Tavium xvi Tomba xxii Eugonia to Komana.
> Tavium xvi . . . . Euagina

repeats and confirms itself. I have mentioned that the sum of distances station by station is always greater than the total distance measured straight along the road. Ægonne, Eugonia, Euagina, 36 miles from Tavium, may be unhesitatingly identified with the modern Göne. The roads to Zela and to Komana Pontica must naturally agree for part of the distance, and fork at Göne. From Ægonne to Zela the distances seem accurate in the Table, and Ptemari is confirmed by Ptolemy's Pleumaris.

> Ægonne xxviii Pleumaris xxvi Zela.

The name of the intermediate station Tomba, though suspiciously like another station Tonea on another road, and not confirmed by Ptolemy, is certainly to be accepted on account of the modern Tamba Hassan. The modern village is on a different road, between Tavium and Alaja (Karissa), but the name may have shifted on the Peutinger Table. On account of this probable confirmation, I would gladly assume a transposition in the Table, putting Saralos (Saralio on the Table next to Tavium on the eastern road, and Tomba between Tavium and Karissa. The name of the station at Göne is variously given Ægonne, Eugonia, Euagina, Fuagina, Eudagina.*

The form Eugonia seems to be a mere attempt to give a Greek form with a meaning to a native name; the hot springs suggest such a form. The resemblance to the modern name Göne is apparently accidental; Göne is elsewhere known as a Turkish name. The true native name is probably more correctly reproduced in Euagina.

11. The road Tavium-Sebastopolis (Sulu Serai) -Sebasteia is a road of the first importance. It is given in the Itinerary up to Sebastopolis as:—

> Tavium xxx Magoro xxiiii Daorano xl Sebastopolis.

This is obviously utterly corrupt: the road must pass through Euagina, which is omitted; and Magoro or Mogaro, and Dorano, are clearly corrupt names, beyond the reach of emendation. It is just possible that Rogmor, as a separate station on the Table, i. e. [Tavium T]rogmor[um],

---

* The last has been transferred to the Sebasteia-Cæsareia road. Euagina, falsely written Fuagina, has produced Ptolemy's Φουιβάγινα, which affords an interesting proof that Ptolemy used some Latin authority.

has arisen from the same error that produced Magoro. The station Seramisa or Sermusa occurs twice on the Table: if its real situation was between Euagina and Sebastopolis, it might readily be transferred on the one side towards Komana, on the other side towards Cæsareia. Ptolemy's Sermouga, which bears obviously the same name, is so placed by him as to agree admirably with this position. I restore the road:

Tavium xxxvi Euagina xxiiii Sermousa * xxvi Sebastopolis.

12. Beyond Sebastopolis the road is given in the Antonine Itinerary:

Sebastopolis xxiiii Verisa xii Siara xxxvi Sebasteia.

The distances on this road are far too great for the direct distance from Sebastopolis to Sebasteia. We must therefore either correct them, or assume that the road is circuitous. The latter alternative is correct. Verisa is a station on the important trade-route Sebasteia-Komana-Amaseia-Amisus. The road Tavium-Sebastopolis-Verisa is intended to form a junction with this great trade-route. The road Sebastopolis to Sebasteia probably went direct through Siara (Yeni Khan), but the Itinerary, depending on a map not perfectly accurate in proportion, gives what is really a circuit as the direct road.

13. The inter-relation of these roads, and the origin of the errors in our authorities cannot be understood without the restoration of one of the great trade-routes. The existence of this trade-route as a Roman road, though not attested by a single trace in the Itinerary or the Table, is vouched for (1) by a milestone, which I copied in 1881, at Ahmed Serai, between Amaseia and Amisos.† It is marked KΓ, 23, but the *caput viae* is uncertain, and it has perhaps been carried.‡

(2) Komana was on an important trade-route from the interior of Asia, (ἐμπόριον τοῖς ἀπὸ τῆς Ἀρμενίας ἀξιόλογον Strab. 559), which has been briefly referred to above.

(3) The road from Amaseia to Komana is described in the Acta of Saint Basiliscus, who was led on foot along it by the soldiers. He passed through a village, Cumialis, reached a village, Dacozae or Daknai or Dakai, where he stayed a night. He crossed the Iris by a bridge *ad locum Varismorum*,§ and reached a village Saos or Saon. At this point it is mentioned that it was the third day since he had eaten. He spent a night at a village, and on the next day at the fourth hour reached Komana. The bridge was evidently near Turkhal; and the road was much the same as the modern road Tokat to Amaseia.

---

* Sermusa xvi. and Seramisa xvi. on the Table.

† I published it in Journal of Philology, 1883, p. 156. It is No. 6894 in 'C. I. L.,' III., Supplement.

‡ It is one of the smaller kind of milestones, and is now built into the wall of a house. The older milestones are larger than the later.

§ Can this be a corruption or mistranslation for "the bridge on the road to Verisa"—Varismorum for Verissorum? The present text would then be due to the misunderstanding of the story by the writer.

The course of this road cannot be doubtful. It is clearly marked by nature, and is still one of the important trade-routes of Asia Minor, passing by Sivas, Yeni Khan, Bolus, Tokat, Turkhal, Amaseia, Ladik, Ahmed Serai, Amisus. A milestone at Ahmed Serai, marked KΓ, proves the line of the Roman road is closely followed by the modern road. The ancient names have already been given for the most part, Sebastein Siara (corrupt), Verisa, Dazimon (in the territory of Komana Pontica, which lies on the river a little off the direct road), Ibora, Amaseia. Laodiceia lies slightly off the modern route, but the détour is very slight, and the ancient road must have passed close to it.

14. The road Zela-Neocæsareia in the Table is obviously false, for it must pass through Komana Pontica. One of the stations, Seramisa, has already been referred to another road. The probable and natural route is by Turkhal (Ibora), after which it coincides with the road mentioned above to Komana. Komana is given in another line on the Table without any connection to Neocæsareia. But a road from the west to Neocæsareia must pass through Komana, and the arrangement in the Table, which makes Komana a terminus, is obviously absurd. As Ibora, an important point on the road, is never mentioned in the Table, full as it is in this part, the suggestion is natural that it is the station, Stabulum, which is given twice—Zela-Stabulum-Neocæsareia, and Tavium-Stabulum-Komana.

The roads from Zela and from Sebastopolis to Neocæsareia may be thus restored :—

Sebastopolis xxiv Verissa xx Komana xxi Neocæsareia.

and

Zela 15 Ibora 24 Komana 21 Neocæsareia

15. The road given in the Table as

Amaseia xv Palalce xii Coloe x Pidis xvi Mirones x Neocesaria

seems to be nearly correct. Ptolemy has Coloe as Χολόη ἢ Χολόγι, and Pidis as Πίδα ; and he puts them between Amaseia and Neocæsareia on his map. Colonel Stewart (of Khartum memory) gave me the following route from Amaseia :—

5 miles, Zane (Sene K., Kiep.), cross Yeshil Irmak by bridge.

13½, Gusgus Kilisse.

26, Kalagalla (1090 feet above sea-level) in Tash Ova.

32½, Kizilduan, Greek village.*

37, Kushuff.

43, Fidi.

49½, Heunk (Herek, Kiepert).

73, Niksar.

Gusgus Kilisse corresponds to Palalce, Kalagalla to Koloe, and Pida to Fidi ; but the distance of Pida is wrong, and it is necessary to read xx

---

* Kizil Doghan, Red Falcon, must be the real form of the name.

instead of x. The x before Neocæsareia also seems a very small stage. If we read xv we should have the whole distance, stage to stage, 78, which corresponds very well to Colonel Stewart's estimate, 73 English miles. The measurement direct from Amaseia to Neocæsareia would, of course, be less than the total, reckoned stage by stage.

Mirones seems corrupt. It is perhaps Ptolemy's Mesorome of Pontus Polemoniacus, which the Table also gives as Mesorome, on the road Sebasteia-Nikopolis.

16. A road in the Antonine Itinerary which, at the first glance, is most suspicious is

Tavium xxi Corniaspa xxv Parbosena xxv Sibora xx Agriane
xxx Simos xl Sebasteia.

Kiepert has suggested that Sibora is identical with the bishopric Ibora, and at first sight the identification appears so natural that it must be accepted (*Gegenbemerkungen zu Hirschfeld über Tavium : Berl. Sitzungsber.*, 1884, p. 57). Now, Ibora is fixed at Turkhal on the Iris by unexceptionable evidence, so that this identification of Sibora and Ibora would prove the road to be quite erroneous. But the road is corroborated as regards Corniaspa, Sibora, and Agriane by passages hitherto unnoticed by geographers, and it must be accepted as a correct description of the real path.

Korniaspa was a district within the borders of Cappadocia, but so close to the Galatian frontier, that Eunomius, who was born at Oltiseris, a village of Korniaspa, was scornfully called by Basil a Galatian (Greg. Nyss. *c. Eunom.*, pp. 259, 281). As Korniaspa is, according to the Itinerary, just xxi miles from Tavium, the two passages confirm each other completely. Now Euagina and Karsia are, according to Ptolemy, in Galatia, therefore it is not possible to reach Cappadocian territory in xxi miles from Tavium, except by going south. The road on which Korniaspa is situated must, then, be probably the direct road Tavium-Cæsareia. Now a point on that road which is xxi miles from Tavium would be about xxv from Aquæ Saravenæ (Terzili Hamam). The second station on the road is Parbosena (vv. ll. Barboscena, Pardosena), which seems to be a form of Tarbasthena,* mentioned by Gregory Nyssenus (*c. Eunom.*, p. 263). Now Korniaspa is the name of a district, and we may conclude that Tarbasthena is also the name of a district. Aquæ Sarvenæ is obviously the name of a single place, and the possibility is suggested that Aquæ Sarvenæ was a bath in the district of Tarbasthena, which became the chief town of the district, and, as will be shown below, seat of the bishopric.

17. In the year 873 the Paulician leader Chrysocheir invaded the Byzantine dominions and penetrated as far as Ankyra (μέχρις Ἀγκύρας τῆς πόλεως καὶ αὐτῶν τῶν Κομμάτων, Genes., p. 122). As he returned he

---

* Compare Perbena-Trebenna, Tarbassos-Corbasa-Colbassos.

was cautiously followed by Joannes Domesticus, who carefully concealed his movements and kept a day's journey in the rear.* At length Chrysocheir encamped at Agrane in the Kharsian Theme, and John remained at Siboron. These places must, therefore, be on some road leading from Ankyra to the Paulician capital Tephrike, and Siboron must be a good day's journey west of Agrane. This precisely agrees with the Antonine Itinerary, in which Sibora is xxv miles west of Agriane on a road leading from Tavium to Sebasteia.

18. This Sibora, or Siboron, on a road from Tavium to Sebasteia, must be different from Ibora, a bishopric of Helenopontus. The road on which it was situated was apparently the direct route from western Galatia to Tephrike (passing of course by Sebasteia). Basilika Therma was on the road, as may be gathered from a passage in Cedrenus, which shows that Basilika Therma was in the Theme of Kharsiana, and on a road leading to the east. In the year 978 Phokas was defeated by Skleros at Amorion. He retired in good order into the district of Kharsiana (τὸν λεγόμενον Χαρσιανὸν κατειληφώς). Skleros followed him, encamped at Basilika Therma, and challenged him to a second battle. Phokas was again defeated and fled into Iberia (Cedren. II., 430-2). This account leaves only two possible positions for Basilika Therma, at Göne and at Terzili. Now Basilika Therma was a bishopric of Cappadocia Prima, and we can hardly suppose that Cappadocia extended so far north as Göne, and moreover, it has been shown that Ptolemy's authority places Göne in Galatia. Basilika Therma must, therefore have been situated at Terzili Hamam, as I conjectured years ago,† judging from the importance of the remains there and from the popularity of the baths with the Christians of Cæsareia.

19. This road became a most important one in the Byzantine Empire. It was part of the military road from Constantinople to Sebasteia and Armenia, and was in constant use throughout the Byzantine campaigns. It crossed the Halys at Tcheshnir Keupreu, and was of course the great road of the Thema Kharsianon. The Kleisourophylax of that Theme was probably stationed on the military road, and in that case there can be little doubt that the lofty castle now called Mushalem Kale, which must have been a central point in the defence of Kharsiana, was his head-quarters, and on the military road. It is probable that it is the " Lofty Castle " (Ὑψηλή) mentioned in the Saracen wars.

It is probable that Sibora was the city beside Mushalem Kale. It became a bishopric in later Byzantine time, not apparently before the ninth century. This is precisely the period when we hear most about

---

* This is probably the true explanation:—Genesius says, διαστηματίζων μίλιον ἕν. Theoph. Cont., p. 272, and Cedrenus, ii. 209, have ἀπό τινος διαστήματος. John's movements were unknown to Chrysocheir, and there must therefore have been some considerable distance between them.

† 'Bulletin de Correspondance Hellénique,' 1883, p. 304.

the military importance of this road. There can be little doubt that during the troubled Byzantine time the city at Mushalem Kale was the chief town of the district. Moreover, it is near the mines now called Ak Dagh Maden, and derived additional importance therefrom. In that case, for xxv of the Itinerary between Parboscena and Sibora we must read xxx or even xxxv.

/ 20. In the above quoted passages of Genesius, &c., the further course of the road is thus described. John sent part of his army to follow Chrysocheir μέχρι τοῦ Βαθυρύακος, and to observe whether he detached any troops to operate in the Kharsian or the Armeniac Theme. Chrysocheir [starting from Agrane?] in the evening encamped on the slopes of the hills* (ἐσκήνωσε κάτω, Genes.; κατὰ τὴν τοῦ ὄρους ὑπώρειαν, Cedren.), while the Byzantine troops encamped on a ridge overlooking his camp, at a wooded difficult spot called Zôgoloênos. At dawn the imperial troops suddenly attacked the Paulicians, some of whom were attending to the baggage animals (τὰ φόρτια τοῖς ὑποζυγίοις ἐκούφιζον), entirely defeated them, and pursued them 30 miles (ἀπὸ τοῦ Βαθυρύακος ἕως τοῦ κατωνομασμένου Κωνσταντίνου βουνοῦ).

Bathys Rhyax, or Bathyrrhyax, is also mentioned by Constantine Porphyrogenitus as one of the ἄπληκτα on the great military road which we have described (see G.). It should therefore be looked for at a junction of roads where troops from different quarters could conveniently concentrate on the military road, to be in readiness to swell the army as it marched eastwards. This consideration places it in the valley about Yeni Khan, a very important point.

21. Now, all roads from Sivas towards the west or north must pass through Yeni Khan, as Sir C. Wilson asserts positively after long familiarity with the country. It follows, therefore, that the roads from Sebasteia to Verisa and to Agriane must have coincided as far as Yeni Khan. In that case, considering the frequent corruptions in the itineraries, it would seem probable that Simos is a false reading, and is in some way to be identified with Fiarasi and Siara of the other road.†
The distances, xxxvi in two cases, xl in the third, are rather too great; xxx is the utmost distance of Yeni Khan from Sivas.

22. The road from Mushalem Kale to Yeni Khan is 16 hours (by Kara Kaya 10 hours). This confirms the Itinerary, and Agriane must be looked for about Ekkayi. The road is to be restored

> Tavium xxi Korniaspa xxv Tarbasthena [x]xxv Sibora xx
> Agriane xxx Siala xxvii Sebasteia.

* Accoi .ng to another account, the Paulicians reached the place called Bathyrrhyax in the evening, and the Byzantine troops encamped on a hill above them.—Theophan. Contin., p. 272. [No statement here shows how long the detached troops followed the Paulicians.]

† Perhaps ΣΙΑΛΟΣ has become ΣΙΜΟΣ. Sialos and Siara are practically identical. Fiarasi is probably caused by a correction si being added to a false form Fiara.

From the preceding exposition it may be inferred that an important road, already shown in part, has to be completed as follows :—

Amasia xxxii Zela 20 Sebastopolis 24 Siala or Siara 27 to 30 Sebasteia.

23. The road Sebasteia–Nikopolis–Satala, &c., is quite unknown to me by actual inspection, and, as it is unusually well described in our authorities, I need not go through the task of applying the ancient statements to the modern maps. I have no new material to contribute, and I content myself with quoting the description of one march along the military road from Constantinople to Armenia. In the year 1069 the Emperor Romanus marched from Helenopolis on the Bosphorus, crossed the Sangarios by the Bridge Zompos, crossed the Halys, and avoiding Cæsareia, came to an excellent camping-place named Cool Fountain (Κρύαν Πηγήν) and thence to Sebasteia.* After crossing the Halys on this march he traversed·the province of Kharsiana (τῇ τοῦ Χαρσιανοῦ ἐπαρχίᾳ) (Mich. Attal., pp. 145–6; Scylitz., p. 690). At Sebasteia two roads parted, and again converged in the theme of Coloneia : Romanus took the left road. At last he reached Theodosiopolis, and finally Manzikert. On his return he passed through Theodosiopolis, then through Coloneia, then through Melissopetrion (κάστρον δὲ τοῦτο ἐπί τινος λόφου κείμενον), then advancing into the Armeniac Theme, he encamped at Dokeia (Mich. Attal., p. 168).

The castle of Kara Hissar, near the line of this road, is a Byzantine not a Roman stronghold. It is once called Μαυρόκαστρον (i.e. Kara Hissar): τοῦ Μαυροκάστρου φρούριον, εἰς ἕνα τῶν Ἀρμενιακῶν τόπων ἐπὶ λόφου κείμενον ὑψηλοῦ καὶ δυσκατεργάστου (Mich. Attal., p. 125; cp. Scylitz., p. 679). It is perhaps Koloneia.

M. ROMAN ROADS IN CENTRAL CAPPADOCIA.

1. The Peutinger Table gives a road :—

Tavium xvi Euagina xxiiii Saralio xxii Zama xxxv Aquæ Aravenæ xx Dona xx Sermusa xvi Siva xxii Cambe xvi Mazaca Cæsareia.

The distance from Tavium viâ Aquæ Sarvenæ (Terzili Hamam) to Cæsareia is not more than 120 miles: the distance on this road is 191 miles. The road is therefore much too long.

Prof. E. Hirschfeld has discussed this road at length in his paper on TAVIUM in ʿBerlin. Sitzungsberichte,ʾ 1883, p. 1260, and has come to the conclusion that it is the surest guide amid the tangled and

---

* This description becomes much clearer from the discussion of the Byzantine military road ; after crossing the Halys he avoided Caesareia, i.e. he took the left fork of the road, not the right : before Sebasteia he came to a fine camp at Cool Fountain, i.e. the camp at Bathyrrhyax. At Sebasteia he took the left road to Zara, not the right hand road to Tephrike.

contradictory accounts of the roads and stations in the border-lands of Pontus, Galatia, and Cappadocia, inasmuch as it is guaranteed by two independent authorities, Ptolemy and the Peutinger Table. But Prof. Kiepert in his 'Gegenbemerkungen' has proved that Hirschfeld's view of this road is mistaken, and as it depends on a theory of the site of Tavium which is definitely disproved, I need not discuss it.

I have (see L 18) shown that the Aquæ Saravenæ were the hot springs now called Terzili Hamam. The road of the Table, then, is not a direct road, but a détour. Euagina is at Göne, and we have therefore a part of a great north route from Cæsareia viâ Aquæ Saravenæ, Euagina, and Karsia (Alaja), to Amaseia and Amisos. Sir C. Wilson informs me that this is at present the great road from Caesareia to Amisos : it is the only road that is practicable for arabas, and must always have been a great trade-route. It passes through Tchorum (Eukhaita). It is possible that from Alaja there was a connection viâ Iskelib and Boiabad to Sinope, which is a junction of four roads on the Table; but this difficult mountain path cannot have been important.

The road on the Table needs further correction. Between Euagina and Tavium a station is omitted; and between Euagina and Cæsareia the numbers are far too great. Zama is a town of Khamanene, and cannot possibly be on this road. It has been transferred from the road Tavium–Mokissos, which is defective in the Itinerary and omitted in the Table. Saralos (Saralio) is, I believe, transposed (see L 10), and we have

Tavium XVI Saralos XXII Euagina XVIII Aquæ Saravenæ.

Between Aquæ and Cæsareia the distance is given as 94 miles, which is too much. The stations, however, cannot be correct, for Dona (Dora) can hardly be separated from Ptolemy's Odoga or Dogra, which is evidently the Doara of the Byzantine lists. This was one of the bishoprics in Cappadocia Secunda under Tyana, and afterwards in Tertia under Mokissos, and cannot therefore possibly be placed on the road between Cæsareia and its subordinate bishopric Aquæ (i.e. Basilika Therma), for that road must have been wholly in Cappadocia Prima. Moreover, such a number of short distances as are given on this road is unusual in the Table, and most improbable in a country like Cappadocia, thinly peopled, with few cities, and only slightly civilised. Dona has therefore been transferred from another road, probably Cæsareia–Mokissos.

Sermusa is given a second time in the Table as Seramisa, between Zela and Neocæsareia, and it is clearly identical with Ptolemy's Sermouga in Pontus Galaticus. The other position in the Table must therefore be preferred, and there remains

Aquæ XX Siva XXII Cambe XVI Cæsareia.

Siva is the modern Yoannes (Kiepert), or Yogounes, where the name of the saint to whom the church was dedicated seems to remain. Kambe is

Kemer. The only correction needed is xxxii for xxii between Siva and Cambe.

2. The Antonine Itinerary gives a road from Tavium by Therma, Soanda, &c., to Cæsareia. The mention of Soanda proves that this is not a direct road (per compendium), but a circuitous road by Soanda. Soanda is known as a station between Archelais and Cæsareia. The mention of Therma gives a further clue. Therma denotes the hot springs of Kir Sheher (Mokissos), and the Itinerary is really giving the route Tavium to Mokissos, and thence by Soanda to Cæsareia; but the loss of several names at the beginning has obscured the account.* The two roads cannot meet except at some point near Nev Sheher, where therefore Soanda must be placed. The route Mokissos to Soanda must certainly go by Hadji Bektash (Dogra) and Zoropassos. An intermediate station is omitted. A comparison of this road with that from Nyssa to Cæsareia shows a remarkable similarity. They are thus represented :—

Nyssa.	Therma.
Osiana, 32.	Soanda, 18.
Sakasena, 28.	Sakoena, 32.
	Ochras (Acras v.l.), 16.
Cæsareia, 30.	Cæsareia, 24.

There can be little doubt that the road from Nyssa to Cæsareia passed by way of Nev Sheher, and about that point it would join the road Archelais to Cæsareia. Thirty-two miles is about the distance from the position we have given Nyssa to Nev Sheher.† Osiana then must be about Nev Sheher, where we have placed Soanda, and it seems necessary to consider Osiana as a corruption of Soanda.

The next station on each road appears in a great variety of forms in the MSS.—Siccasena, Saccasena, Accasena, Sacasena, Seccasena, and Sacena, Sacona, Saconna. There is great probability that all are corruptions of one name, and the distance 28 or 32 suggests that the station was near Inje Su, which is an important junction of roads. But a few miles north-east of Inje Su are the ruins called Viran Sheher, and near them Major Bennet tells me there is a village Suksun, which has preserved the actual name Siccasena. Hence we may confidently identify the site of this station as Viran Sheher, and prefer the distance 32 between Soandos and Siccasena. ‡

From Viran Sheher to Cæsareia is too short a distance for the numbers on the Itinerary. Even if we correct xxx to xx, the estimate

---

* Another example of names omitted in this Itinerary is in the road Ankyra to Dorylaion. Prof. Kiepert has rightly seen that this route is likely to have been given in some of the Itineraries, but makes the error of identifying Aquae Sarvenae as Kir Sheher, and thus applies the wrong names to the road, see his ' Gegenbemerkungen zu Prof. G. Hirschfeld.'

† The total from Parnassos to Soandos (56 Roman miles) agrees well with the actual distance from the situation a few miles above Tchikin Aghyl to Nev Sheher.

‡ Strabo's route by Sadakora takes a more southern path, see p. 306.

seems great enough, as the distance can hardly be more than sixteen English miles : but the numbers in the Itineraries can never be pressed. It is clear that Ochras or Acras is inserted here wrongly; and it also is evidently a corruption. Perhaps it is [Od]ogra misplaced, and then the road is to be restored

> Tavium—Zama xviii Therma xviii Odogra xvi Soanda xxxii Sakkasena xv Cæsareia.

It has been suggested above that Zama belongs to this road.

3. The direct road Tavium to Cæsareia is apparently omitted in the ancient documents, but in reality every station on it is given :—

> Tavium xxi Korniaspa xxvi Siva [x]xxii Kamoure xvi Cæsareia.

4. The road Sebasteia-Cæsareia is given in the Antonine Itinerary as :—

> Cæsareia xxvi Eulepa xxiiii Armaxa xxviii Marandara xxx * Scanatus xxviii Sebasteia: total cxxxvi,

and in the Peutinger Table as :—

> Cæsareia xiii Sorpara xiiii Foroba xiiii Armaza xvi Eudagina xxxii Magalasso xxxii Comaralis xxii Sivastia.

The total distance is about cxxv miles,† which agrees fairly well with the Antonine Itinerary. The road passes through Palas, obviously an ancient name: we shall see that it is probably the bishopric Aipolioi. Eulepa seems to be another form of the same name : ‡ the consonants being transposed as in Capatiana for Pacatiana, Morea for Romea (i. e. 'Ρωμαία), &c. The distance is fairly correct: Palas is about xxx miles from Cæsareia, but the ancient site may have been different from that of the modern village, a common phenomenon.

Armaxa is guaranteed also by the Table; and is probably a correct name. Marandara is also given as Malandara and Marandana. It is perhaps Ptolemy's Mardara. Eudagina is Euagina transferred to a wrong road. Comaralis is Carmalis, and belongs to a different road (O II). On Scanatus see O II. Magalassos is perhaps a form of Dagalassos, Ptolemy's Megalossos, between Sebasteia and Nikopolis.

N. ROMAN ROADS OVER ANTI-TAUROS.

1. In the roads between Cæsareia and Melitene, the Antonine Itinerary is extraordinarily full, but so full of contradictions and errors that it was quite unintelligible till a series of milestones threw light upon them. §

---

* V.l. xxxviii., which is more likely to be corrupt. Cæsareia xvi. Eulepa also occurs

† According to Major Bennet: Sivas 13 Yildiz Su 7 Sarai 23 Karadj Euren 25 Tchepne 11 Stone bridge over Halys 12 Palas 30 Kaisari.

‡ Palas, of course, is an accusative form. Aipolioi is grecised to get a form with a meaning.

§ The first was discovered by Mr. Clayton in 1881; I added several in 1882; and Mr. Sterrett has copied and published a fine series.

Strangely enough, the continuation of the great Roman highway, Ephesus and Cæsareia to the Euphrates, is quite obscured and only part of it is given in the course of a different road.   There are two possible routes for this road.   (1) The first is

Cæsareia 24 Zerezek 10 Zamanti Su 30 Kara Kilisa.

This is the most important of the modern roads which cross Anti-Tauros from Caesareia.   It is practicable for wheeled traffic throughout, and in all probability it is the route which was taken by the Roman road from Kokussos or Komana to Caesareia.   The only other route which can be thought of goes by Mardin and Tomarza.   There it forks, having a choice of routes over Anti-Tauros; the southern route goes by Keuseli (where it is joined by a road from Ferak Din, Argya Sheher, &c.) over the Gez Bel, past Rumlu, to join the Komana-Kokussos road south of Keklik Oglu, while another route goes by Suwagen (Σεβάγηνα) on the Zamanti Su, crosses Anti-Tauros by either the Dede Bel, or the Geuk Bel, or the Kuru Bel, to Elimenli and Komana (Shahr-Dere-si).

I can trace no probable reference to the Tomarza route in ancient writers, and the identification of Arasaxa as Zerezek (mentioned first, I think, by Major Bennet, many years ago) seems to prove that the Roman road followed a more northern route.

The precise route east of Zerezek is by Kulete, over Zamanti Su, near a recently built Mohajir (i.e. Refugee) village, past Tass, over Anti-Tauros by the Kuru Tchai pass to Kara Kilisa on the Saros. Thenceforward the road coincides with the road from Sebasteia and Ariarathia to Kokussos or to Komana.   There is indeed a path leading more directly to Arabissos, Melitene, and the Euphrates, by Tovla, Tcharshak, and Dali Kavak, to Maragos and Tanir (Tanadaris).   It is about 24 miles from Kara Kilisa to Maragos: but the path is quite impracticable for wheels, and cannot have been used as the Roman road.

(2) The other road is

Caesareia 26 Karadai* 6 Ekrek 8 Yere Getchen 4 Zamanti Su 24
Keui Yere 15 Maragos 4 Khurman Kalesi 7 Tanir 12 Arabissos.

This is also still a road of some importance, and wheeled traffic can traverse it.   It crosses Anti-Tauros, between Zamanti Su and Keui Yere, by the pass called Yedi Oluk,† which is also the pass leading from Azizie (Ariaratheia) to the Saros valley.   This road has also a continuation direct towards Tanir and Arabissos, which is just barely practicable for wheels.   It is probably the trade-route which Strabo describes as leading by Erpa, on the Karmalas, to the Euphrates at Tomisa, which is doubtless, as Kiepert puts it, due east of Melitene.   It is more difficult to decide whether the Roman military road followed

---

* Karadai is about a mile north of Zerezek
† There is an alternative pass more to the west by Kavak Tepe, not ¦practicable for wheels.

this route or took the pass by Kuru Tchai. The numbers that are given certainly suggest that Codusabala was at Keui Yere, and that the road Kokussos-Caesareia coincided with the road Kokussos-Ariaratheia for a greater distance than is possible by the Kuru Tchai road. Moreover, the frequent appearance of Ptanadaris (Tanir) in the Antonine Itinerary proves that it must have been a station of some consequence; it is always put by the Itinerary on the wrong road, but the explanation of the mistake would be easy if there were two roads, Codusabala-Kokussos-Arabissos and Codusabala-Ptanadaris-Arabissos. We may then probably say that a Roman road went along the Yedi Oluk route that has just been described. The road is described in the Antonine Itinerary as :—

Caesareia xxiiii Arasaxa xxiiii Codusabala.

The mention of Arasaxa is not conclusive, for, although I have not given Zerezek on the Yedi Oluk road, yet that place lies hardly a mile south of the shortest path, and may quite well be taken on the road. It is clear that either the second xxiiii must be corrected to xliiii, or that a station has been omitted. Strabo gives the station Erpa on the Zamanti Su, and we may conjecturally insert it. The whole road might then be restored as follows :

Cæsareia xxiiii Arasaxa xix Erpa xxiiii Codusabala xxviiii Ptanadaris (Tanir) xxii Arabissos.
The Peutinger Table gives
Cæsareia xxiiii Sinispora xiiii Arasaxa x Larissa xxiii in Cilissi xx Comana.

I give this as a typical example of corruption.

Sinispora xiiii must be eliminated : Sinis is perhaps Sinis near Melitene and *pora* is perhaps Erpa. In Cilissi should be in Cilicia, and belongs to the road through the Cilician Gates to Tarsos.* But, in regard to Larissa, the Peutinger Table is confirmed by Michael Attaliota in describing the march of the Emperor Romanus, who, in the year 1067 starting from Constantinople, marched by Cæsareia and came to Larissa (ἦγεν εἰς τὴν Καισάρειαν, εἶτα καὶ τῇ Λαρίσσῃ προσέμιξε) : then, advancing further, he encamped at some distance from Melitene (Mich. Attal., p.123). Larissa is also often mentioned as a Turma, originally belonging to the Cappadocian Theme, but transferred by Leo VI. in 890 to the Theme of Sebasteia.

This weighty coincidence must be accepted, but the distance x. from Arasaxa is probably too small, and in the present state of the Table it is impossible to say anything more definite about the position of Larissa,

---

* The roads on the Peutinger Table from Komana to Melitene and to Samosata, though very long, do not contain one correct station : e. g. Catabola is Kastabala, brought from the road Iconium-Pylae Ciliciae-Tarsos; Arcilapopoli is Archelais Colonia, transferred here from the road Laodicea-Cæsareia ; Sagalasso and Sama are Dagalassos and Zara, brought from the road Sebasteia-Nicopolis.

than that it was on the direct road to Melitene, not very far east of Arasaxa and probably near Erpa on the river Karmalas.

Maroga, now Maragos, was also on this road XII miles from Tanadaris, but I omitted it in the list given above in order to retain one more number from the Itinerary.

The possibility must of course be left open that both the Kuru Tchai route and the Yedi Oluk route were used by the Romans, and Larissa may have been on the former, Erpa on the latter.

2. The rest of the Anti-Tauros roads would be quite unintelligible without the recently discovered series of milestones. In studying the milestones the first principle to observe is that stones in the cemetery of a town are carried from all quarters : hence the milestones of Kokusos vary from PΛ to PMΔ. But five miles east of Göksun the number PKB occurs, and 12 miles north the number PΛH occurs, and 17 miles north the number PMΔ. The distance Kokusos to Melitene along the Roman road then must have been in all probability 127 Roman miles. The distance of Arabissos cannot be determined so certainly, but is near 100.

In the roads which are given in the Itinerary, the most striking feature is the constant introduction of Ptanadaris. There can be little doubt that Ptanadaris is Tanir, and in that case it is introduced in the most absurd and impossible way. It belongs to the road Arabissos-Cæsareia, and should be eliminated from all other roads. If we cut it out we have the road in the Itinerary Melitene to Arabissos 104 M. P., Arabissos to Kokusos 28 M. P. Now, the sum of separate distances, station to station, is always greater than the direct distance from end to end. We may therefore conclude that the following stations are accurately given in the Itinerary :—

Melitene XXVIII Arca XXI Dandaxina XXIIII Osdara XXVIII Arabissos. Osdara must be looked for between Demirji and Alhazli.

What route did the Roman road follow between Melitene and Arabissos? Mr. Sterrett says that between Albistan (12 miles east of Arabissos) and Malatia " no milliaria were found. I am wholly unable, to account for this fact, as there are only two possible roads from Albistan to Melitene, one of which we traversed on the way out, and the other on our return. It may be safely affirmed, however, that the Roman road did not go by way of Köz Agha and Pulat, since this whole road is much too difficult. Had the Roman road gone this way it could not have avoided the abrupt pass of Ola Kaya, and it is exactly this pass that makes it necessary to look for it elsewhere. The only other route is that by way of Derinde, and thence down the Tokhma Su to Malatia."

There is, however, another road, apparently unknown to Mr. Sterrett, of which I have been told by Major Bennet, who has traversed it. It passes through Arga, crosses the mountains in a nearly direct line, and reaches the valley of the Sogutlu Irmak near Alhazli. The road may be thus described:—Arga, 3600 feet above sea-level, at 8 miles crosses summit 4680 feet, at 14 miles crosses summit 6270 feet, and soon after another summit 6250 feet, at 30 miles reaches Sogutlu Irmak, at 66 miles reaches Arabissos. By this road the distance, Arca to Arabissos, would be about 70 Roman miles: let us say 71 miles. We have the distance Melitene to Arca 28 M.P., and from Arabissos to Kokusos 28 M.P., giving a total Melitene-Kokusos of 127 miles. The Roman road then must have followed this route. The road was formerly an excellent one, practicable for wheeled carriages; but it has in recent years fallen into disuse and disrepair.

3. To understand the rest of the Itinerary it is necesary to observe the exact position of Komana, which lies in a glen right off the main road, and can be reached only by a détour from the direct road. The direct road Kokusos-Sebasteia passes by Kemer 24 miles, Keui Yere 35, to Azizie about 55, and thence to Tonosa and Sebasteia. The distances Azizie-Tonosa and Tonosa-Sebasteia seem about 42 Roman miles. Kemer is certainly a Roman site, and if so it must be Sirica : placing Coduzabala, by conjecture, near Keui Yere. The road, then, may be

Kokusos XXIIII Sirica XII Coduzabala XX Ariarathia XLII Tonosa XLII Sebasteia.

The direct road Kokusos-Komana diverges at Yalak from the road Kokusos-Sirika : measuring along this road, the distances are about

Kokusos XXVI Komana VI Sirica XII Coduzabala.

But it is more probable that there was only one Roman road to Komana diverging at Sirica : the distances then would be

Kokusos XXIV Sirica VI Komana VI Sirica XII Coduzabala, &c.

Between Sirica and Komana the milestones P N B and P N Γ (152 and 153 are found) about two or three miles from Sirica. These agree so well with the latter system of measurement, that it may be provisionally adopted. If hereafter milestones be found between Sirica and Ariarathia, reckoning without the détour to Komana, so as to give about 162 miles Melitene to Coduzabala, the proof will be complete.

4. A Roman road of great importance led direct from Arabissos to Sebasteia. There can be no doubt about the course of this road. It passed Aristil 5, Khurman 7, Kashanli 14½, Almali 18, Görun 39.* The rest of the distance can be calculated only roughly, but if, as is probable, it passed by Kangal, it would be about 80 Roman miles. Between Kangal and Arabissos it must coincide with the road Nicopolis-Arabissos, given in the Itinerary (181–3) :—

Arabissos XXVII Tonosa XXV Zoana XXIII Gundusa XXX Eumeis XVIII Zara XX Dagalasso XXIV Nicopolis.

* Görun retains the name of the ancient Gauraina.

Between Sebasteia and Kangal it is perhaps given in the Itinerary (177) :—

Sebasteia xxiiii Blandos xxviii Euspœna xxiiii Aranis xxviiii Ad Prætorium xxxii Pisonos xxii Melitena.

The direct road Sebasteia-Melitene passes through Kangal, but the distances in the above route are so much too great as to show there is some error. If, however, we suppose that Euspœna is Kangal, and that x has been added between Euspœna and Sebasteia, we have a fair approximation to the proper distance, which is about 40 from Sebasteia to Kangal, 100 from Kangal to Melitene.

5. The roads are too corrupt, and the localisation of every point too uncertain, to justify any scheme of reconstruction. It is sufficient to show here what the routes must have been. But a few words must be devoted to the extraordinary corruption of the road Arabissos-Nicopolis-Satala. It is represented as a direct road, and yet it passes through Tonosa; but the name Tonosa* is certainly false. If we suppose an intermediate station on the way to Görun, we should have the following road :—

Arabissos xviii near Almali xxiii Gauraina xxxviii Euspœna.

Gundusa is perhaps Ptolemy's Godasa, and Doana Ptolemy's Dagona, and Eumeis is surely a corruption of Camisa. It may, however, be doubted whether there was any direct road Euspœna-Camisa. The system of defence was probably content with the road Euspœna-Sebasteia-Camisa-Nicopolis.

6. As to the road Satala-Melitene, which completed the circle of military roads within the province Cappadocia, I cannot speak, but I may add the following note about one station, given as Arauracos, 45 miles south of Satala.

Arauraka is mentioned also: (1) in a gloss on Theophanes (p. 7, l. 19, Di Boor), ὁ ἅγιος Εὐστράτιος ὁ ἀπὸ τῆς Ἀραυρακινῶν ὁρμώμενος πόλεως ; (2) Ptolemy has the name in the form Σαράβρακα ἤτοι Σαλαμβρία ; and (3) Constantine Porphyrogenitus de Thematibus, p. 31, calls it Arabraka.

Arauraca seems too close to the name of the Gallic tribe Rauraci to be unconnected with it, yet no ala or cohors Rauracorum is known which might have been stationed there as ala Auriana was at Daskousa, legio xii at Melitene, legio vii at Samosata.

This road is given in the Itinerary as

Satala xvii Suissa xxviii Arauracos xxiv Carsagis xxviii Sineruas xxviii Analiba xvi Zimara xvi Teucila xxviii Sabus xvi Dascusa xxxii Ciaca xviii Melitena.

Kiepert places Satala at Sadagh, seven geographical miles north-east of Melik Sherif, and 15 east of Sehabhan Kara Hisar. Legio XV

* It has been corrupted through recollection of Tonosa between Sebasteia and Ariarathia.

Apollinaris was stationed here ('C. I. L.,' III. Supplem., 6744). Daskousa was on the banks of the Euphrates opposite Penga. Ala II. Ulpia Auriana was stationed here ('C. I. L.,' III., Supplem., 6743).

Ptolemy assigns Daskousa, Zimara, Sinibra to Armenia Minor on the banks of the Euphrates, and mentions Analibla west of the Euphrates in Armenia Minor. He puts Ciacis (which he seems to have derived from an itinerary where it was given as an ablative), and Dagousa (which is probably a dittography of Daskousa), in Melitene.

7. Three passes, leading across the eastern part of Tauros into Kommagene, can be traced in the ancient records, one from Kokussos to Germanicia, a second from Arabissos to Germanicia, which is far more frequently mentioned and evidently much more important, and a third leading direct south from Melitene to Samosata. These three passes correspond with the three chief modern routes, Guksun to Marash, Albostan* to Marash, which is by far the most important, and Malatia by Pulat to Adiaman and Samsat. The statement of these facts leaves little doubt that Marash is near the ancient Germanicia. But, as this situation has been disputed by Ritter and Kiepert, I must examine it more closely. Kiepert, having sacrificed all the north-western part of Kommagene to the two Strategiai Saravene and Laviansene, which he follows Ptolemy in misplacing, is obliged to set Germanicia and other Kommagenian towns much further south and east than their true position. First, however, I may describe some of the marches of Byzantine emperors across Tauros.

8. The march of Basil from Caesareia into Kommagene, in 877, is described in great detail by Cedrenus II., p. 213, and Theoph. Contin., p. 278. It is the same route which Romanus Diogenes afterwards took in A.D. 1068 (Scylitz., p. 671). After leaving Caesareia, the advanced guard captured Xylokastron (Psilokastron, Cont.), and Phyrokastron (Paramokastellon, Cont.). Then the castle of Phalakron surrendered.† The Saracen army fled before the emperor, who captured Kasama (Kaisos‡ or Katasamas, Cont.), Karba (Robam or Endelekhone, Cont.), Ardala (Andala, Cont.), and Erymosykea (Erymosykaia, Cont.). Then Basil crossed the rivers Onopniktes and Sardos (Saros, Cont.), and arrived at Kokussos or Koukousos, whence he penetrated through the defiles of Tauros, cutting his way through the forests, by Kallipolis and Padasia to Germanicia. He chose this uncommon route evidently because the regular route by Arabissos was in the hands of the Saracens.

---

* This pass has been described to me, and its importance most strongly emphasized, by Sir Charles Wilson, Colonel Chermside, and Major Bennet. Albostan, "the Garden," has taken the place of the ancient Arabissos, as the northern key to the pass : the site of Arabissos is the modern village Yarpuz, which retains the ancient name.

† This place, whose name is given in the same form by Cedrenus and Contin., must be distinguished from the mountain Phalakron, mentioned by Constantine Porph., de Them., p. 31, as on the northern or north-western frontier of the Theme Koloneia.

‡ On Kaisos as an Arab personal name, see Muralt, p. 151, 307. See p. 280.

All the forts which are mentioned on this passage must be strong-holds commanding the roads between Caesareia and Erpa, for they are all mentioned before the Onopniktes (Karmalas). Melitene and even Arabissos appear to be at this time in the hands of the Saracens.

After devastating the outskirts of Germanicia, but not venturing to attack the walls, within which the Arabs remained, Basil besieged Adata in vain, and finally returned to Caesareia.

9. To appreciate fully the evidence of this campaign, it is necessary to examine the frontier between the Arab and the Byzantine power at this time. It is hardly possible to fix the exact date when Germanicia passed into the Saracen power.* The Byzantine records are silent, till in 745 Theophanes mentions that it was recaptured by the Christians. On this subject we may collect the following facts. In 668 Arabissos and Melitene were both still in Byzantine hands : Arabissos was a military station and residence of the Kleisourarch who guarded the eastern passes of Tauros (Theophan., p. 350). The Arab historians declare (see Weil, 'Khalifen,' I. 471) that Marash was evacuated by the Greeks in 695; but this was perhaps only a temporary withdrawal, as in 700 the Greeks defeated the Arabs near Samosata. But most probably the campaign of 700 was a single great effort, and Kommagene now passed into Saracen hands. In 712 Theophanes, p. 382, apparently implies that Melitene was outside of the dominions of Philippicus. Amaseia was conquered in the same 'year, and in 726 Caesareia of Cappadocia was taken. In 716 the theatre of war was about Amorion, Akroenos, and even Pergamos. In 717 the Arabs crossed by Abydos into Europe, and even besieged Constantinople. But this rashness cost them a severe defeat. It is practically certain that at this time the passes of Tauros were entirely in Arab power. The Kharsian fortress was captured in 730 by the Arabs. But from this time their power diminished. In 740 they were defeated at Akroenos, and were trying to capture Tyana, which they had taken in 708, but which must again have passed under Christian power. In 746, according to Cedrenus, II., 7, and Theophanes, p. 422, Constantine Copronymos, taking advantage of the dissensions among the Arabs, captured Germanicia and laid waste Doulichia (i.e. the country near Doliche). In 752 he captured Melitene and Theodo-siopolis, in Armenia. The great pass was thus in Christian hands for some years, till in 770 Germanicia was recaptured by Al Mansur, and incorporated in Palestine, i.e. Syria.† In 778 a great Byzantine army

* The dates given by different authorities vary considerably. I follow Muralt for convenience in every case where he mentions the events.

† Finlay wrongly understands that the inhabitants were transported to Palestine : μετεποιήθη εἰς Παλαιστίνην is Theophanes's way of saying that it was separated from the Byzantine sway, and made part of the Arab dominions. Palestine ought to be translated Syria here.

besieged it in vain. The Arab historians say that at this time they captured Adata (Hadath, Weil, II., p. 98), but Theophanes does not mention this fact. We may, however, safely assume that the northern entrance to the pass had been held by the Christians since 746 at latest. In the next year the Saracens restored the fort Hadath, and made an unsuccessful attack on Dorylaion and on Amorion. In 780 they captured Semalouos in the Armeniac Theme. The tide of conquest now turned once more, and the Greek arms were probably never seen again in eastern Cappadocia till Basil's expedition in 880. Basil did not venture to advance by the usual route, which was doubtless strongly defended. He advanced by Kokussos, and opened up an unused and undefended route. He ravaged the country up to the walls of Germanicia, and closely besieged Adata.

10. These references show that Adata was nearer the Byzantine frontier, and more accessible to them than Germanicia; in other words, Adata was a fortress a little north of Germanicia defending the pass to Arabissos. Basil's plan was a bold stroke to capture the Syrian end of the pass, even though the northern end was not yet in his power; but he was not successful. A foolish prophecy and legend is related in connection with the siege (Contin., p. 280). Adata, the famous city (περιβόητος), remained in Saracen hands till 946, when Bardas, the general of Constantine, captured it. Melitene, called a city of Syria, i.e. of Saracen land, had previously been taken by John Kourkouas, in ᴜ34 (Theoph., 416).

11. Adata and Germanicia are, therefore, two distinct places, but not far from each other on the same great eastern road. They were no doubt, under the same bishop, who may have been styled ὁ Γερμανικείας ἤτοι ᾿Αδάτων. Hence Glykas, p. 549, makes the mistake of actually identifying them.*

Weil, II., p. 98, is probably wrong in inferring from the Arab geographers that Hadath was south of Marash.† The preceding reasoning is confirmed by the enumeration of Mohammedan border-fortresses, Malatia, Hadith, Marash, Harunie, Kenisa, Ainzarba, Massissa, Adana, and Tarsos.‡ Heraclius in 640, evidently marching by the pass that leads to Arabissos, passed Adata after Germanicia.§

12. Almost all the military expeditions which we can trace as crossing eastern Tauros, most probably followed the route Arabissos-Germanicia. So in 668 Andreas, the envoy of Constans, returned from Damascus by Arabissos and Amnesia.‖ Unfortunately no account gives a list of names

---

* Γερμανικόπολίν τινα λεγομένην ᾿Αδατα, p. 549.

† They give Hadith between Marash and Membitch.

‡ Istakhri, liber climatum, translated by Mordtmann, Hamburg, 1845, pp. 33, 38, 42, 44, quoted by Ritter, Kleinasien, ii. 57.

§ Theophanes, p. 313, where the reading ᾿Αδανα must be corrected.

‖ If Amnesia is connected with the river Amnias, we may say, with confidence, that he returned by Sebasteia, Eukhaita, Pompeiopolis, Kastamon, &c.

along the road ; either the northern or the southern end of the pass being always omitted. But the military importance of Arabissos (see p. 311) and the frequent military references to Germanicia, show that they were the two critical points on the great Tauros pass. The Antonine Itinerary does not give any road across Tauros, except that which cro-ses the eastern pass from Melitene to Samosata : but it is evident, from its Syrian routes, that Germanicia was a critical point on the great road to the east.

13. From Marash two important roads lead to the Euphrates and Edessa, one by Samosata, the other by Doliche and Zeugma. These two roads are given in the Antonine Itinerary as—

(1) Germanicia xv Catabana xvi Nisus xiiii Tharse xiii Samosata leg. vii. xii Edessa.

(2) Germanicia xx Sicos Basilisses x Dolicha xii. Zeugma xx Bemmaris xxv Edessa.

These routes are most probably correct, but the numbers are wrong : such small numbers are improbable in Syrian roads, and the Antonine contradicts itself, giving on the next page—

Germanicia xv Sicos Basilisses xv Dolicha xiiii Zeugma.

14. The evidence of Ptolemy is certainly in favour of placing Germanicia at Marash. He places it further west than any other city of Kommagene. Though Ptolemy's authority is not high, it counts for something when it agrees with all other indications from ancient authors. The order of Hierocles and of the Notitiæ, practically the same, gives no clear evidence, but puts Germanicia among the five northern cities of Kommagene.

15. Germanicia was formerly placed at Marash. Ritter * mentions that several writers of the Middle Ages held this opinion, and that the Armenians call Marash Germaniki. But he and Prof. Kiepert identify Marash with Antiocheia ad Taurum, while they consider that Germanicia must have lain further south or east.

In the first place, Ritter and Kiepert have to answer the question, what was Marash called in the early Byzantine period. They trace its history down to Ptolemy under the name Antiocheia, and then resume it towards the beginning of the ninth century under the name of Marash : had it no importance and no Byzantine name in the intermediate period ? It certainly existed, and must always have been an important place, as it commands the southern entrance to the most important pass across the eastern part of Taurus. It is known † to the later Byzantine writers by its native name Maras : this probably proves that the native name had been preserved in local usage, while officially the city bore a name of the Græco-Roman type, and that the

* 'Kleinasien,' ii. p. 47.

† Marash is mentioned as Μαράσιον by Cinnamus, 216 ; and as Μαράσιν, Anna, ii. 115 (see Ducange's note, p. 633). Similar examples are Χάρποτε ἐν Μεσοποταμίᾳ κείμενον, Cedren., ii. 419 ; Sis, v. FLAVIAS Ciliciæ.

native name at last expelled the official title.* I believe that this official name was Germanikeia. Ritter, who maintains that it was Antiocheia, is bound to show what Byzantine bishopric included within its bounds this city of Antiocheia.

In the second place, Ritter gives as one of the reasons for placing Germanicia further south than Marash, that Stephanus says it was in Euphratesia, "also im Süden von Kommagene dem Euphrates näher gerückt." But according to the provincial division of Diocletian Euphratesia bordered on Melitene, and even Perre is included in it, and is named by Hierocles next to Germanicia : Euphratesia included the whole of Kommagene, and Kommagene extended to the borders of Melitene and Kataonia. Perre is well known to have been beside the modern Adiaman, north of Samosata.

Again, Altyntash Kale, where Kiepert would place Germanicia, is pronounced by Puchstein to be a purely mediæval ruin, without any trace of ancient importance. Its situation and its remains are both alike inadequate to explain the importance of Germanicia, and the route Germanicia-Zeugma-Edessa in the Itinerary is ridiculous if Germanicia is at Altyntash Kale.

16. Almost the only reference to a third route crossing Taurus from Melitene to Samosata is the account of the military road in the Antonine Itinerary.

Melitena xii Maisena xxviii Lakotena xxvi Perre xxiii Samosata.

This route is fairly certain. It goes by Elemenjik, Khan Bunar, Viran Sheher or Surghy (near which Lakotena must be placed), and Adiaman (Perre). We should gladly place some of Ptolemy's names on this road. Maisena or Maiasena does not seem a correct name, and Lacotena should perhaps be altered with some MSS. to a Cotena. But some new evidence is needed before any conjectures are justifiable.

In Theophanes, p. 350, it is shown that the ordinary route from Damascus to Melitene was not by this pass, but by that of Arabissos. This pass is mentioned along with that of Germanicia and Adata in the treatise de Velit. Bell. Niceph., p. 250, where the names Melitene, Kaloudia, Kaësoun, and Daoutha, are connected with it. Kaësoun must be distinguished from Kaisos (see § 8).

17. The road from Kokussos to Eastern Cilicia is given in the Peutinger Table as follows :—

Cocuso xviii Laranda xviii Badimo xxii Praetorio xxii Flaviada xviii Anazarbo.   Total 98 miles.

This is a route of considerable importance : it has been described to me by Colonel Stewart and Major Bennet.

* Prakana replaced the official Diocæsareia in Isauria about 787, and so Kardabounda and Sibilia replaced those of other Isaurian cities.

Miles.

Guksun, 4500 feet above sea-level.

6. Adji Alma plateau, 5690 feet.

13. Kara Kilisa ruin, 5400 ; then cross cañon of river Saros, exactly 1000 feet deep.

21. Hancha Dere, 3900 feet.

31. Hadjin, 3200 feet, near Badimon.

40. Geuk Su (Saros), 2300 feet.

47. Kiraz Bel, 5130 feet.

54. Tapandere, 3000 feet, near Praetorium.

68. Girgen Su, 940 feet.

76. Sis,* 500 feet, Flavias.

90. Anazarba.

113. Osmanie.

124. Geuz Khane (Epiphaneia, Bennet).

130. Reach sea.

O. CITIES AND BISHOPRICS OF CAPPADOCIA.

Generally, the lists of Hierocles and of the *Notitiæ Episcopatuum* form the best starting-point for the discussion of the topography of a province. I annex a comparative table of these lists, but it is of little use in this case, because the organisation of Cappadocia was apparently very peculiar. The other provinces were for the most part divided into cities, each possessing a certain territory ; a few districts or demoi mentioned in each province form exceptions. But Cappadocia was divided into large districts, in each of which there were many villages, or even towns. The district under the Bishop of Cæsareia was so large in the fourth century, that he had fifty *chorepiscopi* to help him. The name of the district often differs from that of the most important town known in it, and sometimes the bishop gets his title from the town (Sasima, Basilika Therma, Doara), while the district in which that town is situated is mentioned by other writers under its own name. Hence many of the names in Cappadocia have an adjectival form (Melitene, Sakasena, Sobagena, Sebagena, &c.). Kuhn, Verfassung des römischen Reiches, ii. p. 231 ff., gives an excellent account of the Cappadocian political system. Strabo says there were only two cities—Greek cities in a Cappadocian country, according to Philostr., Vit. Apoll., i. 4— Eusebeia (Cæsareia) and Eusebeia Tyana, but it would appear that at least Archelais and Ariarathia should be added as centres of Hellenistic organisation. Elsewhere there were no citizens, no assemblies, no city magistrates.†

* Other distances are Sis to Adana 44, Adana to Missis (Mopsouestia) 15, Adana to Ayas 34, Missis to Osmanie, 35.

† Παχείᾳ τῇ γλώττῃ καὶ ὡς Καππαδόκαις ξύνηθες, ξυγκρούων μὲν τὰ σύμφωνα τῶν στοιχείων, συστέλλων δὲ τὰ μηκυνόμενα καὶ μηκύνων τὰ βραχέα.—Philostr.,Vit. Soph., ii. 13

CAPPADOCIA PRIMA ET SECUNDA ET TERTIA.

Coins, or Early Authorities.	Concilia 325-381-451 451, 458 Ep. ad Leonem 458.	Hierocles.	Concilia, 692, 787, 879.	Notitiæ, I. VII. VIII.	Notitiæ, III. X. XIII.
ΚΑΙΣΑΡΕΙΑΣ, or ΕΥΣΕΒΕΙΑΣ	I. Cæs., 325, 381, 431, 451, 458	I. 1 Καισάρεια	I. Καισαρείας, 787, 879	I. 1 Καισαρείας	I. 1 Καισαρειάς
Aquae Saravenae (Peut., Ptol.)	Therma, 451, 458	I. 3 Θερμά	I. Βασιλικῶν Θερμῶν, 692, 787	I. 2 Βασιλικῶν Θερμῶν	I. 4 Βασιλικῶν Θερμῶν
Nyssa (Anton., Ptol.)	I. Nyssa, 381, 451	I. 2 Νύσσα	I. Νύσσης, 692, 787 / I. Καμάχης, 692	I. 3 Νύσσης / I. 4 Μεθοδιουπόλεως (Θεοδοσιουπ.) Ἀρμενίας	I. 2 Νύσσης
Cambe (Peut., Ptol.)	..	..	Ἰουστινιανουπ. Καμουλ. (bis), 553. / I. Καμουλιανῶν, 692, 787, 879	I. 5 Καμουλιανῶν	I. 3 Καμουλιανῶν
Seioua (Peut., Ptol.)		..	I. Κισκισσῶν, 692, 787	I. 6 Κισκισοῦ	I. 5 Κισκισοῦ
Sibora (Anton.), Soroba (Ptol.)		..	I. Τιβεριάδος, 692	..	I. 6 Εὐαισσῶν, Ἀοισῶν
Arasaxa (Anton., Peut., Ptol.)		..	..	..	I. 7 Σεβεριάδος
Eulepa (Anton.)		..	..	..	I. 8 Ἀραθίας
Podandos (Anton., Ptol.)		I. 4 Ῥεγετσοδανδός	..	..	I. 9 Αἰπολίων
ΤΥΑΝΩΝ, ΕΥΣΕΒΕΙΑΣ	I. Tyana, 325, 381, II. 451, 458	II. 1 Τύανα	II. Τυάνων, 692, 787, 879	II. 1 Τυάνων, Χριστουπόλεως	II. 1 Τυάνων, Χριστουπόλεως
ΚΥΒΙΣΤΡΕΩΝ	I. Cyzistra, 325, II. Cybistra, 451	II. 3 Κύβιστρα	II. Σασίμων, 692	II. 2 Κυβίστρων	II. 2 Κυβίστρων
Faustinopolis (under Pius)	II. Justinopolis, 458	II. 2 Φαυστινούπολις	II. Φαυστινουπόλεως, 692	II. 3 Φαυστινουπόλεως	II. 3 Φαυστινουπόλεως
Siala (Ptol.)	II. Asumae, 458	II. 5 Σάδισμα / II. 8 Ῥεγεκουκουσός	II. Σασίμων, 787	II. 4 Σασίμων	II. 4 Σασίμων
Therma (Anton.), Mokissos (Polyb.)	..		III. Μοκησσοῦ, 536, 553, 692, 787, 879	III. 1 Μοκησσοῦ, Ἰουστινιανουπόλεως	III. 1 Μοκησσοῦ, Ἰουστινιανουπόλεως
Nazianzos (Anton., Ptol.)	I. Nazianzos, 381, II. 451, 458	II. 4 Ναξιανξός	III. Ναξιανζοῦ, 536, 692, 879	III. 2 Ναξιανζοῦ	III. 2 Ναξιανζοῦ
Garsauira (Strab.)	I. Colonia, 325, 381, II. 451, 458	..	III. Κολωνείας, 692	III. 3 Κολωνείας	III. 3 Κολωνείας
Parnassos (Polyb., Anton.)	I. Pharnaci, 381, II. Paterni, 451, 458	II. 6 Παρνασός	III. Παρνασσοῦ, 536, 692, 787	III. 4 Παρνασσοῦ	III. 4 Παρνασσοῦ
Odogra (Ptol.), Dona (Peut.), Ochra (Ant.) Snarios (Strab., Anton.)	II. Doala, 458	II. 7 Ῥεγεδάρα	III. Δοάρων, 692, 787	III. 5 Δοάρων, Δαώρων	III. 5 Δοάρων, Δαώρων
			..		III. 6 Ματιανῆς

It is impossible to group the different towns and villages under the bishoprics to which they were subject, as evidence is altogether wanting. I therefore prefer to discuss Cappadocia under the *Strategiai*. The classification into bishoprics, however, often gives important evidence in particular cases, and I shall often have to appeal to the Byzantine divisions, an account of which is necessary as a preliminary.

In the winter of 371-2 the Emperor Valens divided Cappadocia into two provinces, with the intention of injuring Basil, Bishop of Cæsareia, by reducing the size of the province subject to him ecclesiastically. Podandos, a mere hamlet, was first made metropolis of the new province, Cappadocia Secunda, but afterwards Tyana was made the metropolis. Then arose a struggle between Anthimos, Bishop of Tyana, and Basil, the latter trying to retain his authority over Anthimos and the other bishops of Secunda, the former claiming to be independent and Metropolitan in his province.

Cappadocia Secunda was again divided into two by Justinian about A.D. 536. He made Mokissos the capital of Cappadocia Tertia,* giving it the name Justinianopolis.

The account which Strabo gives of the ten *Strategiai* differs very much from the position assigned to them by Ptolemy. Kiepert follows Ptolemy, and places Laviansene and Saravene south of Melitene on the frontier of Kommagene, along the Euphrates. I shall follow the authority of Strabo, and in tracing out the map after him I hope to show so many incidental confirmations as to prove that he is more to be trusted than Ptolemy. Strabo divides the *Strategiai* into two groups of five each. The first lie in a series extending along the southern side of Cappadocia (i.e. towards Taurus), from the Euphrates on the east to Lykaonia on the west; they are Melitene, Kataonia, Kilikia,† Tyanitis, and Garsauritis. The other five extend along the northern side, from the eastern limits of Cappadocia to the Galatian frontier; they are Laviansene, Sargarausene, Saravene, Chamanene, Morimene.

Pliny (vi. 3) agrees partly with Strabo, partly with Ptolemy: Cappadociæ pars prætenta Armeniæ majori, Melitene vocatur; Commagenæ, Cataonia; Phrygiæ, Garsauritis, Sargarausene, Cammanene; Galatiæ, Morimene.

Ptolemy agrees fairly well with Strabo as regards the general position of Tyanitis, Garsauritis, Kilikia, Chamanene, Kataonia, and Melitene, though even in their case he has frequently made serious errors; but he has placed Sargarausene where Saravene should be (Pliny makes the same error ‡), and Mouriane (i.e. Morimene) where

* I find no instance of this title in ancient documents; both Mokissos and Tyana being called metropoleis of Secunda Cappadocia.

† I distinguish Kilikia as the *Strategia* of Cappadocia, Cilicia as the country south of Taurus.

‡ The error is probably due to the likeness of the two names: Σαραυηνή a΄ Σαρ[αργ]αυ[σ]ηνή.

Sargarausene should be, and has put Saravene and Laviansene in Kommagene, either omitting most of their territory, or putting it in Armenia Minor. His map of Cappadocia and Armenia Minor is therefore inexact to a degree entirely beyond his representation of the other provinces of Asia Minor. The reason appears to be that the *Strategiai* were an antiquated institution, belonging to history, not to political reality. He could therefore not have access to Roman official lists, but was obliged to trust to the maps. The authority which he followed appears to have given him in most of the *Strategiai* the names of several of the chief towns.* These he places together, sometimes first, in his list of the cities of the *Strategia*, and their known position disagrees in many cases with the situation which he assigns to it, while it agrees perfectly with the situation which Strabo assigns to it. He then added a few other towns in each *Strategia*, which he derived from the authority of existing maps or itineraries of the district where he placed the *Strategia*, and which therefore seemed to him to agree with his position for it.

I. GARSAOURIA is fixed by Garsaoura, which has been recognised by Leake as the old name of Colonia Archelais, now Ak Serai. It therefore bordered on Lykaonia. Ptolemy, Strabo, and Pliny are agreed in this position.

The cities of Garsaouria are given by Ptolemy as

Φρέατα	Διοκαισάρεια
Ἀρχελαΐς	Σαλαμβρία ἡ καὶ Σαράβρακα
Νανεσσός	Τετραπυργία.

PHREATA is never mentioned elsewhere. The immense depth of the wells in the plain of Hassa Keui and Malakopaia may have caused the name. But this plain seems to belong to Morimene, and wells are characteristic of many villages† in the plains of Cappadocia and Lycaonia. Very deep wells existed also at Savatra (Strab., p. 568.)

ARCHELAIS was founded, as its name denotes, by Archelaos, king of Cappadocia. Leake has shown that it is the same as Strabo's *komopolis* Garsauira (p. 537, 539) on the great eastern highway, and we might infer that the foundation of Archelais is later than Strabo's time, were it not that his information can be traced down to 19 A.D., whereas Archelaos died and Cappadocia was made a Roman province in A.D. 17. Probably therefore Strabo's information about Garsauira was not up to date. Strabo mentions that, though a mere komopolis in his time, it had been formerly a metropolis. It was made a Roman colony by Claudius.‡ It struck no coins under the empire, a remarkable character

---

* I shall show under ISAURIA that Ptolemy gives a name to the eleventh Strategia which could be used only during the reign of Antiochus IV., A.D. 37; his authority on the *Strategiai* must therefore have been living at that time.

† Most of the places mentioned by Ptolemy are mere villages. Strabo mentions that there were only two cities in Cappadocia, Mazaka, Tyana (p. 537 : see p. 281).

‡ Pliny, 'Nat. Hist..' vi. 3, who makes the mistake of placing it on the Halys.

which it shares with Claudius's other colony Claudiopolis in Cilicia Tracheia (Byzantine Isauria). It was an important city throughout Byzantine history, and even more important under the Seljuks of Konia. Nicetas Choniata mentions that it was called Τάξαρα by the Turks in the twelfth century. Τάξαρα is apparently a Greek writing of the Turkish Ak Serai.* It is very often mentioned in Byzantine authorities as Κολώνεια.

NANESSOS must be the same place which is called Momoasson in the Jerusalem Itinerary, 12 miles east of Archelais on the road to Tyana. It still retains its name in the form Mammasun, about three hours east of Ak Serai, and this form shows that the Itinerary is more accurate in the name than Ptolemy.

DIOCÆSAREIA was the name given under the Roman Empire to the small town of NAZIANZOS, the birth-place of Saint Gregory Theologos Nazianzenos. Many passages prove the identity: e.g.

Γρηγορίου μνήσαιτο τὸν ἔτρεφε Καππαδόκεσσιν
'Η Διοκαισαρέων ὀλίγη πόλις.—Greg. Naz. Poem., p. 1121 Migne.

About 376–80 A.D., Diocæsareia, for some act of insubordination, was threatened with degradation from the rank of a city. Gregory interceded successfully on its behalf with Olympios, the governor of Cappadocia Secunda (Greg. Naz., Ep. 141.)

By the Emperor Romanus Diogenes (1067–71) Nazianzos was raised to the rank of a metropolis (Scylitz., p. 705 [845]).

Nazianzos was on the road to Tyana, 24 miles † from Archelais. It still retains its name as Nenizi, six hours east of Ak Serai. In the Jerusalem Itinerary it is corrupted to Anathiango, and in the Antonine it is written Nantianulus. Philostorgius (ap. Suidam, s. v. Γρηγόριος) mentions that it was a station on a Roman road (σταθμός).

The forms Ναδιανδός and Ναζιανζός are given as equivalent by Philostorgius (Hist. Eccles., viii. 11).

KARBALA was the name of a village in the territory of Nazianzos, beside which was an estate ARIANZOS, the hereditary property of Gregory Nazianzen. It still retains its name in the form Καλβαρή in Greek, and Gelvere in Turkish. Gelvere is a Christian village, 2½ hours south of Nenizi, containing numerous rock cuttings (churches, houses, &c.), and a church full of relics of S. Gregory Nazianzen. The inhabitants are all aware that Nazianzos, the city of their saint, was at the Turkish Nenizi.

In some references a doubt is left whether Karbala was the village, and Arianzos the estate, or vice versâ; but it is distinctly mentioned in one passage (see Mansi, Act. Concil. ix., pp. 256, 258), that Arianzos was

---

* Compare Cinnamus, who has 'Ακσιαρη aud Πέγσιαρη; Turkish, Ak Sheher and Beg Sheher. Taxara is for τὸ 'Ακ Σαρά : compare Chalcocond., p. 243, who speaks of Konia as Τοκόνειον. See also p. 279, 290, and Addenda.

† XII. + XII. M.P. The distances are seemingly rather too great.

a farm (*prædium*) in the district of Nazianzos, belonging to Gregory Naz.,* whére he was born. The expression κτῆμα ἐν 'Αριανζοῖς occurs. At Arianzos a festival of the holy martyrs on the twenty-second of the month Dathousa is mentioned by Gregory Nazianzen (Ep. 125). This village Karbala is called τοῦ χωρίου Καπραλέως (Greg. Naz. Ep., 308), where the spelling either varies or the reading is corrupt; Gregory writing to the governor [of Cappadocia Secunda], says that when the latter happened to be present [at Nazianzos], Gregory had the opportunity of talking with him (παρούσης τῆς τιμιότητός σου, διελέχθην): he was at the time living on the family property at the village Karbala.

SALAMBRIA, or SARABRAKA, is a very doubtful place. Sarabraka cannot be separated from Arauraka (i. e. Arabraka †) of Armenia Minor, whose position is assured by the Antonine Itinerary (208 and 216) as 50 miles (or 47 miles) west of Satala on the road to Nikopolis. Two alternatives are open: either that Ptolemy has misplaced Sarabraka, or that the identification of Salambria and Sarabraka is incorrect. Salambria seems to be the same as Salaberina, which is placed on the Peutinger Table between Archelais and Tyana, but which cannot belong to that road, all whose stations are well known.

TETRAPYRGIA seems to occur twice on the Peutinger Table, once as Tetra, between Kybistra and Cæsareia, and again as Tetrapyrgia, between Ikonion and Pompeiopolis. Either situation is irreconcilable with Ptolemy, but neither has the slightest real weight, and the last place in one of Ptolemy's lists has equally little weight: hence we may say that nothing is known of Tetrapyrgia except the name. The Acta Sanctorum ‡ aids us by preserving the record of a station Tetrapyrgia in northern Syria. Probably this station has been falsely transferred to Cappodocia; though it is possible that two places of the name may have existed. There was also a Tetrapyrgia in the Cyrenaica.

To these we may add

ARGUSTANA, XVI. miles north of Archelais on the road to Parnassos. Argustama is a more probable form.

CHUSA, XII. miles west of Nazianzos, on the road to Tyana: the name is suspicious.

The towns or villages of Garsaouria are

Colonia Archelais (Garsauira)	Nazianzos Diocæsareia
Mammassos	Karbala
Arianzos	Chusa
Argustana (Argustama)	Mataza ? (see (KILIKIA).
Nora or Neroassos (see KILIKIA).	Argos or Argaios (see LYKAONIA).

---

* Cf. Greg. Naz., Ep., 203, 125.

† The form Arabraka is used by Constant. Porph. *de Them.*, p. 31.

‡ I cannot give the exact reference, which I have lost for the time. The name of a Syrian Tetrapyrgia occurs also Act. Sanct., Jan. 26, p. 341, but another more specific reference occurs. See below, p. 357.

II. Morimene is described by Strabo (p. 537), as the part of Cappadocia which adjoined Lake Tatta: and (p. 534) as the western *strategia* on the northern side of Cappadocia. He also says that Venasa is a district of Morimene (p. 537), and I shall prove below that Venasa was the plain of Melegob. Hence we see that Strabo makes Morimene the district along the southern bank of the Halys, from the frontier of Galatia to Melegob. It is bounded by Galatia, the Halys, Kilikia, Tyanitis, Garsaouritis.

Pliny agrees, saying that Morimene is on the Phrygian border (*prætenta Phrygiæ*, VI. 3).

Morimene is called by Ptolemy Mouriane, and placed between Kataonia and Armenia Minor. Some of the towns which he places in it, however, demand a very different situation, exactly in the position Strabo places Morimene. This proves that Ptolemy had access to an authority which gave a more accurate account of the *Strategiai* than he himself has produced. His list is

Σίνδιτα	'Αράσαξα
Κόταινα	Γαρνάκη
Ζοροπασσός	Καρναλίς
Νύσσα	

Sindita and Kotaina are, according to the principle laid down above, perhaps derived from Ptolemy's authority on the *Strategiai**, and are, therefore, towns of the real Morimene. If so, they are either absolutely unknown otherwise, or else the names are corrupted. It is useless to advance conjectures such as that Sindita may be Soanda, and Kotaina may be [Mala]kopaia, as they cannot be proved. (See also Lacotena or a Cotena, N, § 16.)

Zoropassos has retained its name as Yarapson (Arebsun on Kiepert's map), on the southern bank of the Halys: the ferry over the Halys on the direct road from Nev Sheher (Soandos) to Hadji Bektash (Doara) and Kir Sheher (Mokissos) is at this point, which is, therefore, of some consequence.

Nyssa is fixed on the bank of the Halys by the description of Gregory, bishop of Nyssa. In Epistle VI. he describes his return to Nyssa about A.D. 378. He passed through Earsos and Vestene and down the course of the river (which can be no other than the Halys), through a number of villages, which lay close to each other along the stream, to Nyssa: Nyssa was on the road from Cæsareia to Parnassos. If, as is probable, Gregory was coming from Cæsareia, his road led through Soanda (Nev Sheher), and thence through Earsos and Vestene: from this point he mentions that his road led down to the riverside. Vestene, then, must be near Tuz Keui. Nyssa is to be looked for 24 miles from Parnassos, on the south bank of the Halys, about 10 miles above Kessik Keupreu. I

* They come at the beginning of his list, but see Sargarausene, Saravene, and Laviansene.

have observed in this neighbourhood a great many curious cuttings in the rocks at the river's brink.

Nyssa was not far from the Galatian frontier : hence Gregory says (Epist. p. 1075 Migne), οἱ πρόσχωροι τῆς ἐμῆς Ἐκκλησίας Γαλάται. The garden on the banks of the Halys, from which Gregory wrote his twentieth epistle, was doubtless beside Nyssa; and he mentions that the name VANOTA was Galatian, and that it deserved a name more in accordance with its beauty than a mere Galatian word.*

Nyssa, though away from the proper territory of Cæsareia, and in Cappadocia Secunda, was retained by Gregory for the diocese of his brother, Basil of Cæsareia, at the time of the dispute between Basil and Anthemius (see p. 100). It was also included in the same Turma with Caesareia, obviously for defence of the south bank of the Halys. This Turma was transferred to the Kharsian Theme about 890 by Leo VI.

ARASAXA has retained its name as Seresek or Zerezek,† six hours east of Cæsareia. Its situation cannot be reconciled with the real Morimene of Strabo and Pliny, but it suits exactly the Mouriane of Ptolemy on the east of Kilikia. This, therefore, is a clear example of a name inserted by Ptolemy from a map or itinerary to suit his position of Mouriane. It belongs really to Kilikia.

KARNALIS and GARNAKE are otherwise unknown. Their position after Arasaxa makes it probable that they have been taken by Ptolemy from an itinerary as lying in the district which he considered to be Mouriane.

Karnalis may be a mistake for KARMALIS, and be connected with the river Karmalas, now Zamanti Su. It must then be derived from an Itinerary, and must have been a station beyond Arasaxa, at a crossing of the Karmalas, either on the road Cæsareia to Komana and Melitene, or on the road Komana to Sivas. Now the Peutinger Table has Comaralis on the road Sivas to Cæsareia. Comaralis may safely be corrected Carmalis. The stations on this road in the Table are all false, with the exception of Armaxa (see p. 270); and Carmalis has been transferred from some other road.

In order to place Karmalis, it is necessary first to examine the evidence about the river Karmalas. The Karmalas is supposed by Kiepert to be the Tokhma Su, a tributary of the Euphrates, flowing through the *Strategia* Melitene. This opinion is contrary to two passages of Strabo. In p. 539 Strabo mentions that a temporary obstruction of the upper Karmalas produced floods in Cilicia, in the districts near Mallos; and in p. 537 he says that the Karmalas traverses Cilicia as

---

* Therefore the Cappadocians scorned the Galatians. So the heretic Eunomius complained, as of an injury, that Basil had called him a Galatian, whereas he was a Cappadocian of Oltiseris, a village in the district of Korniaspa, near the Galatian frontier of Cappadocia.—' Greg. Nyss. c. Eunom.,' pp. 259, 281

† So far as I know, Major Bennet was the first to notice this survival of the ancient name.

well as Cappadocia. These passages point unmistakably to the great river, now called Zamanti Su, which rises far in the north of Cappadocia, and, uniting with the Saros, flows into the sea near Mallos. It is true that the river Pyramos passed close to Mallos, whereas the Zamanti and Saros are a little further off. But the lands on the latter river may very well be described by Strabo's words, τῶν Κιλίκων τινὰ χωρία τὰ περὶ Μαλλόν, and there is no other river except the Zamanti Su which can by any possibility correspond with Strabo's description (p. 537, 539, 663): " The Karmalas was a river of Sargarausene, which flowed into Cilicia, and it was crossed at the small town, Erpa or Erpha, by the road from Cæsareia to Melitene."

In the ninth century the Karmalas bore the strange name, Onopniktes. In Cedrenus (II. 213-4) and Theophan. Contin. (p. 278-80), a march of Basil from Cæsareia to Kokussos is described. He crossed the rivers Onopniktes and Saros. There are only two rivers on this march, the Zamanti Su, or Karmalas; and the Saruz Su, or Saros.

The modern name Zamanti Su is perhaps derived from the fortress, Tsamandos, which is sometimes mentioned by Byzantine historians (e.g. Cedrenus II. 423). Its situation is uncertain, but references suggest that it was in the region of Cappadocia through which the Zamanti Su flows; and we may now say with confidence that it was situated on the river. The name Zamanti Su, when compared with Gediz Tchai, Gebren Su, Porsuk Su, clearly means " the river that comes from the town Zamanti;" and the name Tsamandos or Zamanti, as applied to a fort or town, must have survived into the Turkish period. There are two places which might very naturally give name to the river; one now bears the name Azizie, having been recently made the seat of a *kaimakam* for the Circassian country, and re-named after the Sultan Abdul Aziz.[*] It is situated in a very remarkable, impressive, and important situation, where a magnificent series of fountains rise from the hills that fringe the Zamanti Su, and form a stream which much more than doubles the water of the river. It might well be that the river derived its name from this fountain. Similarly the Sakaria is considered to rise in a vast series of fountains near Tchifteler, and not in any of the long streams which join these fountains within a few miles of their source. Another place that might give its name to the river is Viran Sheher, through which the Zamanti Su flows a little distance from its source.[†] One or other of these must be the site of Karmalis. Now Tsamandos was on a lofty hill, which is quite inconsistent with Viran Sheher, but may suit Azizie: therefore Karmalis was probably Viran Sheher.

---

[*] Its older name appears to have been Bunar Bashi (Ritter, ' Kleinasien,' ii. 139).

[†] Kiepert and Ritter make the Zamanti Su rise at Bunar Bashi, and place Viran Sheher on the Saruz Su. This is an error, and is corrected in Kiepert's latest map. The water that flows through the centre of Viran Sheher flows to Azizie. Ainsworth makes Viran Sheher a Turkish fortress, but on this opinion see pp. 290, 1.

There is, indeed, another possibility, that Karmalis may have been the older name of a place, which, in Byzantine times was called Tsamandos. Perhaps even Zamanti may be a foreign name, probably adapted from the Turks by the Byzantine writers: though the other examples known to me of Turkish names employed by the Greek historians are all later.* In that case both Tsamandos and Karmalis might be the names for the modern Azizie. But this view seems to me very improbable. Tsamandos has something of a native Anatolian sound about it. There is indeed an identification, which, if it were possible, would decide against the latter alternative. Strabo (540) mentions a fort Dasmenda. Dasmenda is exactly the sort of form that might be modied by later pronunciation into Tsamand-os. But Strabo places Dasmenda much further west, in Chamanene, at the western extremity of the ridge which bounds Cappadocia on the north, and it is therefore quite impossible that Dasmenda could be on the Zamanti Su. It is, however, quite possible that there might be two places Dasmenda, just as we have two places Komana, two places Metropolis in Phrygia, two places Ankyra &c., and this is the view to which I incline.†

The probability is, then, that Karmalis was at Viran Sheher: if so, it would be beside the station *ad medium* of the Antonine Itinerary, half-way between Tunusa and Ariarathia, and it would be either in Laviansene or in Sargarausene. A fortress called Dasmenda or Tsamandos was at Azizie, and the magnificent fountains there led to the river being called Zamanti Su.

The list of places said, by Chamich, II., 53, to have been given to Gaghik, about 1064, in return for the district of Vanand (with its capital Kars), comprises Amaseia, Komana, Larissa, and Tsamandos, as Finlay mentions. Finlay himself says that it was only the district round Tsamandos that was given, and he apparently includes Sebasteia ‡ and Larissa in that district. I have not access to the authorities necessary to follow out this line of reasoning. On Larissa, see p. 272.

It ought to be added that Viran Sheher is said by Ainsworth § to be a Mohammedan fortress, of later construction even than Byzantine. He identifies it with Edrisi's Shohaïr, placed by Rennell 18 geographical miles from Tonosa, and 57 from Kaisari. The opinion at which Sir Charles Wilson and I arrived in 1882 was very different. We observed a cross in relief on one of the gateways, certainly coëval with the

---

* Τάξαρα for Ak Serai, Τζυβριτζὴ κλεισούρα, Τζυβρηλιτζημανί in the twelfth century, Ἀκσιαρη and Πέγσιαρη, Μαράσιν, Σίς, Τοκόνειον, Χάρποτε, Μέμπετζε (Leo Diac., 71).

† The variety in termination is, of course, quite common. The prefix Das appears in Dasmenda, Dastarkon, Dasteira. Cf. Mous in Mousbanda, Moustilia; Las in Laskoria.

‡ He wrongly calls it Sebaste. Tsamandos is also mentioned in Attal., pp. 121–22 (Tsamantos), and Const. Porph., de Them. Lycand.

§ Joun. of R. Geograph. Soc., 1840, x. p. 314.

building. The place must be Byzantine, but its open situation on comparatively level ground, marks it as rather a rendezvous (ἄπληκτον) for troops than a kastron for frontier defence. According to the Byzantine style, kastra were built on lofty and hardly accessible rocks.

Rennel, 'Western Asia,' II., p. 169, mentions that the Arab geographers say that Zapetra bore also the name Zamaneni. He therefore identifies it with Tzamandos, and places it between Marash and Samosata; * and he considers that the description of Tzamandos as being on a high steep hill, which would be quite inconsistent with the situation he assigns, is "heightened."

Constantine Porphyrogenitus describes Tzamandos as being on the frontier of the Theme Lykandos. The question, then, is to determine the situation of this Theme. Lykandos was a country previously desert, and uninhabited (in other words, made unsafe by Saracen depredations, but not completely and peacefully under Saracen rule), which was made a Theme by Leo VI., about 890 A.D. † This suggests the Anti-Tauros region, rather than Kommagene, which was never trod by a Byzantine army from 745 till 877, and then only for a single raid. The pass into Kommagene was not definitely gained for the Christians till 946 (see N. 10). In the 'Treatise de Velitat. Bell. Niceph.,' p. 250, Lykandos and Cappadocia are said to be divided by Tauros from Cilicia: it is there implied that certain passes cross Tauros from Cilicia to Lykandos and Cappadocia. Now, as the pass to Germanicia and Adata is mentioned as different, the passes which are meant must be the important one from Anazarbos and Sis (Flavias) to Hadjin (Badimon) and Kokussos, and possibly also the difficult passes from Cilicia to the country immediately south of M. Argaios. Lykandos then probably included whatever the Byantine troops held east of the Zamanti Su, and perhaps also the country immediately west of the Zamanti Su and south of M. Argaios.

Lykandos was the name also of a city in the Theme. It is mentioned as being three days' journey from Cæsareia, and in Cappadocia.‡ A town like Komana is three good days' journey from Cæsareia, and we can hardly reckon Lapara-Lykandos as further distant. Moreover, it is implied that this place was in A.D. 976 in Byzantine possession, and it is highly improbable that any part of Kommagene was at this time in Byzantine hands. Leo Diaconus also says Lapara was on the Armenian frontier.§ Bardas, after his victory at Lapara, A.D. 976, immediately proceeded to Tzamandos. The description suits a site near Komana as Lapara, and Azizie as Tzamandos admirably; and Lapara is described

---

* He seems to mean the ruins called Altyntash Kale.

† Compare Const. Porph., de Them. Lycando, with de Admin. Imper., § 51.

‡ διὰ τριῶν ἡμερῶν καταλαμβάνει τὴν Λαπάραν· τόπος δὲ οὗτος μέρος τῆς Καππαδοκίας, τὸ νῦν λεγόμενον Λυκανδόν, Cedren. II., 422; compare Const. Porph., ll. cc.

§ μεθόριον τῆς χώρας τῶν Ἀρμενίων, p. 169.

as being a rich country, which suits the upper Saros valley. Constantine, 'de Admin. Imper.,' p. 228, also speaks of the kleisoura that
lies between the city Lykandos and Tzamandos. This is the well-
known and important pass by which the Roman road crossed from
Ariarathia to Koduzabala, and we may therefore confidently place
Lapara-Lykandos in the valley near Keui Yere and Koduzabala.

It would be long to discuss the other references to Tzamandos,
such as Scylitzes, p. 677 (cp. Attal., p. 121). But the description of the
campaign of Romanus Diogenes, in 1068, shows clearly the situation of
the Theme Lykandos. His design was, after spending the summer in
Lykandos, to cross into Syria in the autumn. In pursuance of this plan
he entered Syria by the pass from Kokussos to Germanicia, which therefore leads from Lykandos into Syria (see Attal., 104 ff. ; Scylitz., 669 ff.).

VENASA is a district mentioned by Strabo in Morimene (p. 537).
There was at Venasa a sanctuary of Zeus (ἱερὸν τοῦ ἐν Οὐηνάσοις Διός),
which possessed 3000 hierodouloi and a large and fertile country,
producing 15,000 talents annual revenue to the priest. The priest held
office for life, and ranked next to the priest of Komana. In a former
paper ('Bulletin de Corresp. Hellén.,' 1883, p. 322) I published an
inscription relating to the worship of this deity: Μέγας Ζεὺς ἐν
οὐραν[ῷ ἔστω?] εἰλεώς μοι Δημητρίῳ. It was engraved on a flat stone
lying on the top of a hill near a village called in Turkish Suvermez
and in Greek Φλοητᾶ. A well and a hole with traces of building around
exist on the hill-top, which commands a splendid view of the plain.
Being embarrassed by the erroneous position for Morimene, accepted by
Kiepert on the authority of Ptolemy, I there stated that this inscription
could not refer to the Zeus of Venasa. But when Morimene is rightly
placed, the greater part of this plain is in it, and then the inscription
may be taken as evidence that Venasa was the ancient name of the
plain. This position is confirmed by a quaint and interesting episode
in the history of the Christian Church in Cappadocia.

A certain Glycerius was ordained by Basil as deacon of the church
of Venasa (Οὐήνεσαν, Σύννασαν, Οὐήνατα). He misbehaved in this capa-
city, and despised the authority of his presbyter, of the chorepiscopus,
and of Basil himself. At last he took the opportunity of a great
gathering at Venasa (σύνοδος, obviously the Christian substitute for the
old festival τοῦ Διὸς τοῦ ἐν Οὐηνάσοις), when a great multitude was collected from all quarters, and before the whole assembly he brought
forward a band of virgins, who followed his ministrations, and danced
in public. Finally he fled from Venasa, accompanied by his devotees,
and sought refuge in the diocese of Gregory. Basil, finding that
Glycerius had thus gone beyond the sphere of his own authority, wrote
to Gregory and begged him to send back the women to their parents,
and if possible also to force Glycerius to return. But Gregory rather
took the part of Glycerius, and evidently considered that he was truly

religious; and finally Basil agreed to overlook the past entirely if they would all return.

The episode is quaint and interesting. It is clear that Glycerius introduced something of the wild enthusiasm of the old Cappadocian religion, analogous to Montanism in Phrygia, and there is much probability that if the mildness of Gregory had not prevailed over the persecuting energy of Basil, the movement might have grown stronger. Apparently a little judicious leniency quieted the disturbance.

For topographical purposes it is necessary to discover who was the Gregory into whose diocese Glycerius fled. Tillemont considers that either Gregory of Nyssa or Gregory of Nazianzos is meant. But the tone of the letter is not what we might expect if Basil were writing to either of them. It is not conceived in the spirit of authority in which Basil wrote to his brother or to his friend. It appears to me to show a certain deference, which, considering the resolute, imperious, and uncompromising character of Basil,* I can explain only on the supposition that he is writing to the aged and venerable Gregory, Bishop of Nazianzos. Then the whole situation is clear. Venasa was in the district of Malakopaia, or Suvermez, towards the limits of the diocese of Cæsareia. The adjoining bishopric was that of Nazianzos. Venasa being so far from Cæsareia, was administered by one of the fifty *chorepiscopi* whom Basil had under him,† and the authority of Basil was appealed to only in the final resort. Glycerius, when Basil decided against him, naturally fled over the border into the diocese of Nazianzos.

The great plain which extends from Sasima nearly to Soandos is full of underground houses and churches, which are said to be of immense extent. The inhabitants are described by Leo Diaconus as having been originally named Troglodytes.‡ Nicephorus traversed their country A.D. 963, during his march along the Byzantine military road viâ Tyana to the Cilician Gates. Kasin (see p. 250 and p. 356) may therefore be probably placed in this valley. For example, every house in Hassa Keui has an underground story cut out of the rock; long narrow passages connect the underground rooms belonging to each house, and also run from house to house. A big solid disc of stone stands in a niche outside each underground house door, ready to be pulled in front of the door at any alarm.

SASIMA (the length of i is proved by the line quoted below) was on the road between Nazianzos and Tyana. The distances point certainly to Hassa Keui. At this the road to Soandos diverged

---

* Seen especially in his behaviour to Gregory Nazianzen in the matter of the bishopric of Sasima. I find it necessary to explain for the benefit of classical scholars that Gregory Naz. was son of Gregory, Bishop of Nazianzos.

† Tillemont, ' Mém. p. servir, &c.,' ix., p. 120.

‡ Τρωγλοδῦται τὸ ἔθνος τὸ πρόσθεν κατωνομάζετο τῷ ἐν τρώγλαις καὶ χηραμοῖς καὶ λαβυρίνθοις, ὡσανεὶ φωλεοῖς καὶ ὑπιωγαῖς, ὑποδύεσθια.—Leo Diac., p. 35.

from the road to Archelais.   The situation is well described by Gregory
Nazianzen ('Poem.,' p. 1059, Migne):

> Σταθμός τίς ἐστιν ἐν μέσῃ λεωφόρῳ
> Τῆς Καππαδοκῶν, ὃς σχίζετ' εἰς τρισσὴν ὁδόν,
> Ἄνυδρος, ἄχλους, οὐδ' ὅλως ἐλεύθερος,
> Δεινῶς ἀπευκτὸν καὶ στενὸν κωμύδριον,
> Κόνις τὰ πάντα, καὶ ψόφοι, καὶ ἅρματα, κ.τ.λ.
> Αὕτη Σασίμων τῶν ἐμῶν ἐκκλησία.

An absolutely unhistorical modern legend about St. Makrina is
related at Hassa Keui.   Recently a good-sized church has been built in
the village, evidently on the site of an ancient church; it is dedicated
to St. Makrina, who, as the village priest relates, fled hither from
Kaisari to escape marriage, and to dedicate herself to a saintly life.
The underground cell in which she lived is below the church.

Basil, during his conflict with Anthimus of Tyana, made an attempt
to retain the district within his diocese by raising Sasima to be a
bishopric, and consecrating his friend Gregory Nazianzen as bishop.
The attempt was frustrated, partly by the reluctance of Gregory to live
in such an unpleasant place, and partly by the determined opposition of
Anthimus, supported by the civil authority.   Sasima was always
attached in subsequent time to Tyana.

Near Sasima there was a place called LIMNAI, which Anthimus
occupied, in spite of the opposition of Gregory Nazianzen, during the
quarrel with Basil.   The incident is described by Gregory Nazianzen,
Ep. 50, where Λίμναι is usually regarded as a common noun; but there
was - no reason why Anthimus should occupy the marshes, and great
reason why he should seize a village Λίμναι in the district of Sasima
(κατέσχε Λίμνας).   This is the village, one hour east of Hassa Keui, now
called Göljik in Turkish and Λίμνα by the Greeks of the district.*

This obscure village Limnai is once referred to in the contradictory
accounts given of the exile of the usurper Basiliscus and his wife
Zenonis.   As several of the original authorities are not accessible to me,
I quote Valesius (ad Theodor., Lect. I. 36): "De loco in quo Basiliscus
tyrannus interiit, dissentiunt antiqui scriptores.   Marcellinus quidem
in Chronico, et ex illo Jordanes in libro de Successione Regnorum,
Basiliscum in oppido Cappadociæ Limnis periisse tradunt, quibus con-
sentit Auctor Chronici Alexandrini; sed Victor Thunonensis in Chronico
Basiliscum Sasimis Cappadociæ mortuum esse scribit cum uxore ac
liberis.   Quod quidem propius accedit ad scripturam Theodori nostri
(Βουσάμοις).   Theophanes vero in Chronico pag. 107 Basiliscum una
cum uxore et liberis Cucusum Cappadociæ deportatum fuisse scribit."

The seeming contradiction now disappears almost entirely with the
above exposition of the situation of Limnai.   All the authorities are

---

* See my paper in 'Bull. de Correspond. Hellén.,' 1883, p. 324.

agreed except Theophanes, who must be in error. In Theodorus Lector the name is corrupted from Σασίμοις to Βουσάμοις.[*]

The greater part, probably the whole, of this plain belonged to Morimene, except perhaps Sasima and Moustilia. Sasima was apparently included in Strategia Tyanitis by Ptolemy, in whose list it has been corrupted; the first syllable has dropped, and ΣΙΜΑ has become ΣΙΑΛΑ.

MOUSTILIA of Ptolemy's Kilikia is the modern Misti, of the same valley, part of the bishopric of Sasima.

Since the position of Morimene has been recognised, we may place in it the following.

SOANDA or SOANDOS (corrupted Osiana in the Antonine Itin., p. 206) was the point where the roads from Parnassos and from Archelais to Cæsareia met;[†] it must therefore have been situated not far from Nev Sheher, a situation which must in all periods have had some local importance. We might have expected a bishopric in such a fine and central position; and in the latest Notitiæ, III., X., XIII., a bishopric, MATIANE, occurs under the metropolis Mokissos. Matiane has still retained its name as Matchan, a small village a few miles east of Nev Sheher, beside one of the most striking groups of rock-cut houses, churches, and tombs that exist in Asia Minor. Matiane and Soandos are practically one bishopric.

Soandos must be read in place of Scandos, which is mentioned as a village of Cappadocia subject to Cæsareia, three miles from Moutalaska. (Σάβας πατρίδος μὲν ὑπῆρχεν Καππαδοκίας χώρας Μουταλάσκης τε κώμης ὑπὸ μητρόπολιν τελούσης τὴν Καισαρέων). A monastery called Flavianæ was 20 stadia from Moutalasca. (Compare Vita Sabæ in Cotelier, Eccles. Gr. Monum., iii., p. 222-3). The monastery was perhaps among the wonderful rock remains of Matchan, which is called Martchan in some maps.

The fact that it was subject to Cæsareia proves that this Scandos of Cappadocia should not be identified with the Scandis mentioned by Justinian, Novel., XXVIII., as a town among the Lazi, in the most eastern parts of Pontos, beyond Trapezous.[‡] The place Scanatus, mentioned in the Peutinger Table, near Sebasteia, on the road to Cæsareia, is probably a misplacement and misspelling of Justinian's Scandis.

MALAKOPAIA is mentioned in the Saracen wars at the end of the eighth century. It retains its name as Melegob. The late Dr. Mordtmann observed this in an interesting paper.

OZIZALA is given in the Antonine Itinerary as Ozzala, in the Jerusalem Itinerary as Iogola, and in the Peutinger Table Nitalis Ozizala have perhaps been run together into Nitazo. The correct form is given in some letters of Gregory Nazianzen to his friend Amphilochius

---

[*] Σάσουμα was, δου -ss, a real variety of Σάσιμα (in which iota is long): compare Siblia and Soublaion. Sousama and Bousama may be corruptions: the latter is a mere clerical error. Asuma for Sasuma, see p. 282.

[†] See p. 269.

[‡] See also Procopius, B. Pers. II., 289; B. Goth. IV., 526.

(Ep. 25 to 27).   There is some friendly joking in the letters, turning on the fact that Ozizala abounded in vegetables, while Nazianzos was a corn-growing district.   It was 16 or 17 miles south of Parnassos.   While it must be left in doubt whether Parnassos, was in Chamanene or in Morimene, there can be little doubt that Ozizala was in Morimene.

An estate, which belonged to the family of Amphilochius, in the territory of Ozizala, is frequently referred to.   Its original native name is unknown : it was renamed EUPHEMIAS after a brother of Amphilochius who died there.   The father of Amphilochius, however, was born at Nazianzos (Greg. Naz., *Poem.*, p. 1121, 1151).   Gregory Nazianzen went (from Nazianzos) to pay a visit to Gregory Nyssenus, and stopped by the way at Euphemias (Ep. 197).   Basil (Ep. 217) writes to Amphilochius of Iconium, delighted at the prospect of seeing him again.   If Amphilochius comes to the house at Euphemias (εἰ καταλάβοις τὸν οἶκον τὸν ἐπ τῆς Εὐφημιάδος), it will not be difficult for Basil to go there, and moreover, he may at any rate be obliged to go to Nazianzos.

NITALIS is given in the Jerusalem Itinerary, 34 miles south of Parnassos.   The Antonine has Nitazi, and the Peutinger Table has Nitazo, which seem to be corruptions arising from the next name Ozizala. The towns or villages of Morimene are :

Nyssa.	Vestene.
Zoropassos.	Earsos.
Soanda.	Malakopaia.
Ozizala.	Venasa.
Euphemias.	Sasima.
Matiane.	Limnai.
Nitalis.	

Parnassos is doubtful : it may be either in Morimene or in Chamanene, probably in the former.

III.   CHAMANENE is placed in much the same position by Strabo and by Ptolemy, adjoining Galatia on the west and the north.   Pliny's expression *Phrygiæ prætenta* may be interpreted in the same sense.   It is uncertain whether Strabo considered that Chamanene was confined to the right bank of the Halys, or whether he considered that it embraced some territory on the left bank north of Morimene.   But as Ptolemy begins with Zama and Andraka, he has probably got them from his authority on the Strategiai, and in that case Chamanene lay on both sides of the Halys.*
Ptolemy's list of towns in Chamanene is

Ζάμα.	Οὐάδατα.
Ἄνδρακα.	Σαρούηνα.
Γαδίανα (v. l. Γαδάσηνα).	Ὄδωγρα.

---

* The position of Chamanene on the Galatian frontier explains the words of Basil, κἀμοί τίς ἐστι κτῆσις περὶ Χαμανηνήν, in a letter addressed to *Censitori*, apparently *Censitori Galatiæ*.   In Ep. 313, also addressed to a Galatian official, he says, ἔστι γὰρ κἀμοὶ οἶκος ἐν Γαλατίᾳ.

ZAMA is placed by the Peutinger Table on the road between Tavium and Cæsareia, but more probably it was a station close to the Galatian frontier, between Tavium and Therma-Mokissos. No other reference to it is known to me.

ANDRAKA is called ANDRAPA in the Jerusalem Itinerary. It was 12 miles north of Parnassos, on the frontier of Galatia and Cappadocia. A city of Paphlagonia is also known of the name Andrapa; Ptolemy has it ῎Ανδραπα ἡ καὶ Νεοκλανδιόπολις, and it was the birthplace of a saint named Hesychios (Act. Sanct., March 6th, p. 456). The correct form of the Cappadocian name is uncertain.

GADIANA is an adjectival form, and Gadia may be the Galea of the Jerusalem Itinerary; Galea was 9 miles north of Andraka or Andrapa, on the Galatian side of the frontier. Perhaps Ptolemy is wrong in assigning it to Cappadocia, or else the frontier may have varied at different times. It is probably to be identified with Strabo's Kadena, the capital of the usurper Sisines, as Nora-Neroassos was his treasure-fortress (Strab., p. 537). The two places are therefore probably not far distant from each other : see KILIKIA.

OUADATA is mentioned only by Ptolemy. The name seems corrupt. Ouadata appears to have been taken by him from an itinerary which placed it on a road south of Andraka. In that situation Ozizala lay, and delta for zeta is allowed by the form Nadiandos (see NAZIANZOS). It is possible that ΟΔΙΔΑΛΑ has been corrupted into ΟΥΑΔΑΛΑ and ΟΥΑΔΑΤΑ.

SARVENA is by its name identified with Aquæ Sarvenæ* of the Peutinger Table, and marked as a part of the neighbouring *Strategia* of Saravene. I have elsewhere (*Bulletin de Correspondance Hellénique*, 1883, p. 320) identified it with the Byzantine bishopric Βασιλικὰ Θερμά, and placed it at the hot springs now called Terzili Hamam.

ODOGRA is probably the same as Doara which became a bishopric in the fourth century. It is also probably the same as Dona (to be corrected Dora) in the Peutinger Table on the road between Cæsareia and Tavium. The following considerations enable us to localise it near Hadji Bektash :—

(1) When Cappadocia was divided by Valens in A.D. 371-2 into two provinces, Prima and Secunda, Doara was in the latter under the metropolis Tyana.† It could not, therefore, be situated on the most direct road from Cæsareia to Tavium, for that road seems to have been entirely in the *diœcesis* of Cæsareia, but must have lain on a road that goes further to the west, i.e., on the road that goes by Kir Sheher (Mokissos). Previous to this it had been subject to Cæsareia, and Basil, Bishop of Cæsareia, did not give it up without a struggle. He made it a bishopric, and consecrated, by the hands of Gregory Nazianzen, the first

---

* Aquas Aravenas in the Table: see above, pp. 265, 268.
† See Mansi, 'Acta Concil.,' ix., p. 258.

Bishop, in 373 A.D., in the hope that he would attach the see to his side in his controversy with Anthimus, Bishop of Tyana.* The passage just quoted from the *Acta Conciliorum* shows that he did not succeed, and that Doara continued to be under Tyana, and that its Bishops were consecrated by the Metropolitan of Tyana.†

When about 436 A.D. Justinian raised Mokissos to the rank of a metropolis (*metropolitana jura dedisset*), he named it Justinianopolis and placed Doara, Nazianzos, Parnassos, and Colonia Archelais under it (Mansi, l.c.).

(2) An incident in the church history of the fourth century confirms the situation assigned to Doara.‡ In A.D. 383 a certain Bishop Bosporius was accused of heresy. It is mentioned § in the business of Council v. (Constantinop., A.D. 553) that this Bosporius was Bishop of Doara. Tillemont, however (Mém., &c., IX., p. 533 and 727), rejects this testimony on the ground that no other reference to a Bosporius of Doara occurs, and considers that the person meant is the well-known Bosporius, Bishop of Colonia. But the fact that an obscure Bishop of Doara should rarely be mentioned has nothing surprising in it, and a consideration of the circumstances shows that Tillemont is wrong. At the request of Gregory Nazianzen Amphilochius, Bishop of Iconium, came as far as Parnassos in order to befriend Bosporius. In coming to Parnassos Amphilochius necessarily passed through Colonia; and if Bosporius had been Bishop of Colonia, he would have stopped there. He went on, however, towards Doara, until he came to Parnassos, on the road from Iconium and Colonia to Doara. Here he was close to the diocese of Bosporius, at a central and important city by the crossing of the Halys. The only other road to Doara would have gone round to Zoropassos.

The exact site of Doara can hardly be determined. It was probably either Mudjur or Hadji Bektash. The latter is the central establishment of the Bektash Dervishes, once such a powerful body; and the continuity of religious history suggests that it is the modern representative of the old bishopric of Doara.

PARNASSOS, a town of great importance, has been very variously placed by geographers. Mordtmann, in a paper that contains much interesting matter, has put it at Kir Sheher (Mokissos-Justinianopolis). Hamilton, followed by Kiepert, has placed it at Kotch Hisar, a village near the Salt Lake, Tatta. According to this view, the road follows the shortest line across country from Ankyra to Archelais, but makes a long détour so far as concerns the way from Ankyra to Cæsareia. I shall prove that the road between Cæsareia and Tyana ran along the southern bank of the Halys for a long distance, and that Parnassos was situated

---

* See Greg. Naz., or. 13, or 'Vita Basilii' in the Migne edition, I., p. 95, where Tillemont's errors ('Mémoires, &c.,' ix., p. 394) are made clear.
† Ordinationem Episcoporum Tyanensis episcopus faciebat.—Mansi, ix., 258.
‡ Greg. Naz. Ep. 184.
§ Acta Concil., v., p. 477.

on the river, at a point where the road from Colonia Archelais, Iconium and the south-west in general to Pontus, Eastern Galatia and the northeast in general crossed the river. In the thirsty country of Cappadocia it was convenient to keep close to the only river which flowed perennially.

I know no authority which expressly places Parnassos on the river, but it can be proved that the road to Galatia touched the Halys about 12 to 20 miles north of Parnassos, and that Nyssa, which was 24 miles from Parnassos on the way to Cæsareia, was also on the river.

The first point is proved by a passage of Polybius (xxv. 4, 8, 9). When Pharnakes invaded Cappadocia, Eumenes and Attalos advanced into Galatia against him. From Galatia they reached on the fifth day the Halys, and on the sixth day Parnassos. Ariarathes, king of Cappadocia, presumably marching from Cæsareia, joined them at Parnassos, and the combined armies entered the territory of Mokissos.* Parnassos was the natural *rendezvous* for the armies coming from Galatia and from Cæsareia, for it is given as a station nearly half-way on the road from Cæsareia to Ankyra. The only fords of the Halys known to me are a little above Tchikin Aghyl, and Parnassos was probably beside them.

The second point is proved in the discussion of Nyssa (see NYSSA). Parnassos then being situated on the direct road between two points on the Halys, must also have been on the Halys. At Parnassos the roads from Cæsareia and from Archelais met. There can be no doubt, as a glance at the map shows, that a road here crossed the river, and went to Tavium and to Pontus in general, by Therma or Mokissos. The situation is further determined by Polybius's statement just quoted, which shows that Parnassos adjoined Mokissos, now Kir Sheher (see JUSTINIANOPOLIS MOKISSOS).

The exact point where Parnassos stood can only be determined by an actual inspection of the localities,† but we may approximately fix it. The army of Eumenes and Attalos must have reached the Halys somewhere near Tchikin Aghyl, and next day they marched to Parnassos, which was therefore about 10 to 20 miles further on. This would bring us to a point on the river opposite Mokissos. Again, the distances given are, Parnassos to Ankyra, 84 M.P. or 99 M.P.‡; Parnassos to Cæsareia, 114 M.P. A point on the Halys beside Tchikin Aghyl would be about half-way from Ankyra to Cæsareia. The uncertainty of the numbers in the Itineraries must, however, prevent this argument from having any great value.

* Παραγενόμενοι δὲ ἐκ Καλπίτου πεμπταῖοι πρὸς τὸν Ἅλυν ποταμόν, ἑκταῖοι πάλιν ἀνέζευξαν εἰς Παρνασσόν. Thence ἦλθον εἰς τὴν Μωκισσέων χώραν (the reading Μωκισσέων is an old correction of the text).

† In a very hurried journey I crossed the ford and went on by Tchikin Aghyl to Ankyra.

‡ The Jerusalem Itinerary makes it 99 M.P., and is probably more correct. The Antonine has 84. I have shown that the distance Parnassos to Cæsareia is probably to be reckoned 10 miles shorter.

In the discussion of the roads it has been shown that the changes of the fourth century tended to reduce the importance of Parnassos. It ceased to be a road-centre, and became a mere station on the road from Archelais Colonia to Justinianopolis Mokissos; and it was so near the latter that it gradually sank into decay, and has now ceased to exist.

JUSTINIANOPOLIS, refounded by Justinian, and made metropolis of a large division of Cappadocia, was one of the chief cities of Cappadocia in the Byzantine period. Kir Sheher, a city in a fine situation, is the modern metropolis of the same division of Cappadocia. The description given by Proçopius of Justinianopolis so accurately represents Kir Sheher, that when I read it I recognised the situation immediately: ἦν δέ τι φρούριον ἐν Καππαδόκαις Μωκησσὸς ὄνομα ἐν μὲν τῷ ὁμαλεῖ κείμενον, σαθρὸν δέ, ... ὅπερ Ἰουστινιανὸς βασιλεὺς καθελὼν, τεῖχος ᾠκοδομήσατο κομιδῇ μέγα ἐς τὰ πρὸς ἑσπέραν τοῦ πάλαι φρουρίου, ἐν χωρίῳ ἀνάντει τε καὶ λίαν ὀρθίῳ καὶ ἀμηχάνῳ προσελθεῖν (de Ædif. V. 4). There is in the outskirts of Kir Sheher, a very large mound, apparently artificial, with high steep sides, and a large extent of level surface on the top,—a Mound of Semiramis, similar to that of Tyana.

Independently of this description, which is too vague to be absolutely convincing, our consideration of the road-system has shown that Mokissos-Justinianopolis was situated at Kir Sheher, and that its central importance was due to the revolution of the road-system, caused by the transference of the governing centre of the Empire from Rome to Constantinople.

The insignificance of Mokissos as a city, previous to the re-foundation by Justinian, is proved by its title in Hierocles, Ρεγεκουκουσός: it was a mere *regio* without any central town. The same is the case with the neighbouring Doara, called Rege-Doara in Hierocles.

Under the emperor Michael Palæologus, when Mokissos had long been *in partibus infidelium*, the Bishop of Mokissos acted also as Bishop of Prokonnesos.*

The towns of Chamanene are:—

Parnassos?   Therma or Mokissos Justinianopolis
Andrapa or Andraka   Zama
Galea or Gadia   Doara, Dogara, or Odogra.

IV. SARAVENE has had all its towns taken away by Ptolemy, who has placed it away down on the Euphrates with the cities—

Juliopolis, on the Euphrates.
Barzalô, on the Euphrates.
Serastere
Lakriassos
Enteleia
Adattha.

* ὁ Μωκησσοῦ προεδρεύων τότε τῆς ἐκκλησίας Προικοννήσου κατὰ λόγον ἐπιδόσεως.— Georg. Pachym., i., p. 286.

These are, so far as known, towns either of Melitene or of Kommagene. Ptolemy apparently felt that the towns mentioned in his authority on the *Strategiai* as belonging to Saravene were inconsistent with the position on the Euphrates which he assigns to Saravene, and therefore omits them entirely, or transfers them to Chamanene.

Adattha or Adata is frequently mentioned as near Germaniceia by the Byzantine writers.

In the year 880 the emperor Basil advanced from Kokusos, clearing the road as he went. Having reached Callipolis and Padasia, he himself cheered his men by marching on foot through the difficult defiles beyond. Thus he reached Germaniceia, ravaged the country round, but not venturing to besiege the city, he proceeded to Adata and laid siege to it. He could not capture Adata, but having destroyed a little town named Geron (Geronta) in the neighbourhood, returned again over Mount Argæus to Cæsareia, and thence by Midaion to Byzantium.* The pass through which Basil marched seems to have been that which leads from Guksun direct to Marash (Germaniceia): the usual road across Taurus into Kommagene was from Arabissos by Albostan to Marash: it was probably in the hands of the Saracens, and Basil took another route. Cedrenus (p. 214) and Theophan. Contin. (p. 278-80) agree in all respects in the description of Basil's campaign in Euphratesia or Kommagene. He vainly besieged Adata (Adapa in the Bonn text of Cedrenus †), which was long afterwards captured by his son Constantine, took a little fort named Geron or Geronta, and returned over Mount Argæus to Cæsareia.

Hadath, a fort between Marash and Membitch is frequently mentioned by the Arab writers. It must be the Ἄδατα of the Byzantine historians (v. Weil, Khalifen, ii. 98, and Edrisi, Jaubert, ii. 139.)

The position of Saravene is determined by Strabo, who puts it on the north side of Cappadocia between Khamanene and Laviansene. The position of Basilika Therma has been fixed in the examination of the roads at Terzili Hamam. These baths therefore were in Saravene, and must therefore be the Aquae Saravenae. We may then safely assign to Saravene the towns on the road Tavium to Cæsareia viâ Aquae Saravenae, in so far as they do not belong to Galatia in the north, and to Kilikia in the south. Saravene was in great part in Cappadocia Prima under the Byzantine Empire. It was then bounded by Galatia on the north, Laviansene on the east, Kilikia on the south (the Halys probably being the boundary), and Khamanene on the west. The boundary with Khamanene apparently lay east of Zama and Doara. The whole country of Ak Dagh was in Saravene.

* The conclusion of this march shows that the direct road from Cæsareia to Dorylaion, Nikomedeia, and Constantinople passed near Midaion.—Theophan. Contin., p. 280-2.

† Finlay, in his 'History,' ii., p. 246, makes the mistake of fancying that Adana of Cilicia is the place in question. Glycas (p. 549) actually identifies Adata and Germanicopolis, but this is erroneous.

SIBORA is obviously identical with the bishopric Seberias, or Seuarias, of the later *Notitiæ*, called Tiberias at the Council of A.D. 692. Sobara, placed by Ptolemy in *Strategia Kilikia*, is probably the same place ; it occurs last in his list, and is therefore not got from his authority on the *Strategiai*. Probably it is really in Saravene. Seuarias looks like a form adapted so as to suggest a meaning in Greek, a common reason for the modification of Anatolian names ; it was construed as the " town of Severus."

It would appear that this district must have been subject to Cæsareia, and when seven new bishoprics were added to the four original bishoprics under Cæsareia, one of them must have been up in this remote district. Sibora, being the town near the mines, would be the most important in the district, and therefore the seat of the bishopric.

BASILIKA THERMA, KORNIASPA, OLTISERIS, PARBOSENA or TARBASTHENA, SIBORON or Sibora, AGRANE or AGRIANE, have all been fixed in the examination of the road-system.

SIOUA or SEIOUA has in the same place been fixed at Yogounnese or Yoannes. Ptolemy places it in *Strategia Kilikia*, but it is more probable that Kilikia did not extend across the river Halys. The Halys forms the natural boundary both of Morimene and of Kilikia.

The regiones or villages of Saravene are

> Basilika Therma or Aquæ Sarvenæ.
>
> Korniaspa.
>
> Oltiseris.
>
> Tarbasthena, or Parbosena.
>
> Sibora, or Siboron.
>
> Agrane, or Agriane, and Siara (see p. 308).
>
> Sioua, or Seioua ; or Euaisai, or Euasai (see KILIKIA).

V. LAOUINIANE is placed by Ptolemy on the Euphrates between Melitene and Saravene. He places Korne, Meteita and Claudias on the Euphrates, and then adds in the country west of the Euphrates :

Καπαρκελίς.	Σαβάγηνα (see VII Σοβάγηνα).
Ζιζόατρα.	Νοσαλήνη.
Πασάρνη.	Λαύστασα.
Κίζαρα.	

There is a certain probability that one or two of these, probably those at the beginning, are derived from his authority on the *Strategiai*, and the rest are inferred from his view of the situation of Laviniane. The three on the Euphrates are of course inferred in the latter way. It may be suspected that Caparcelis (Caparceis?) is an ablative (compare Ciacis, N 6). The place is, like Tetrapyrgia, transferred erroneously from Syria. The Itinerary gives Capareis 16 miles from Epiphania on the road to Beroea, but ' C. I. L.,' III., Supplem., 6814, shows probably that the name begins Caparc.

Strabo gives the name as Laviansene (Λαουιανσηνή), and places it at the north-eastern extremity of Cappadocia (p. 540), bordering on Kolopene and Kamisene (p. 560), and containing the head waters of the Halys, inasmuch as that river rises in Cappadocia (p. 546). It therefore included the country south and south-east of Sebasteia, and was bounded on the west by Saravene, on the south and sóuth-west by Sargarausene and Melitene, on the east by Lesser Armenia. In Ptolemy this whole district is included in Lesser Armenia.

The roads from Sebasteia to Cæsareia, and to Ariarathia, were probably for the most part in Laviansene. On the foimer were the bishopric Aipolioi (the latter probably within the bounds of Kilikia), and the stations mentioned in the Antonine Itinerary, Armaxa and Malandara or Marandana. On the latter were Tonosa and Karmalis (the latter probably within the bounds of Sargarausene).

VI. KILIKIA was fixed by the situation of the capital Cæsareia-Mazaka, and Ptolemy agrees with Strabo about it. It was probably bounded on the north by the Halys, and on the west by the Karmalas (Zamanti Su, see KARNALIS).

Ptolemy gives the following list of towns in Kilikia.

Μουστιλία.	Κύζιστρα.
Σίουα (ἢ Σείουα).	Ἐβάγηνα (ἢ Σεβάγηνα).
Κάμπαι.	Ἄρχαλλα.
Μάζὰ ἢ Μάζακα ἢ καὶ Καισάρεια.	Σόβαρα.

MOUSTILIA has retained its name in the form Misti. It must have been the next station to Andabalis on the road from Tyana to Cæsareia. It lies on the borders of Morimene at the edge of the district Venasa.

CÆSAREIA-MAZAKA. The old name Μάζακα is said to be derived from Mosoch the ancestor of the Cappadocians (Philost., 'Hist. Eccles.,' IX. 12'; Joseph, 'Antiq.,' I., c. 7, p. 136). The city was refounded by Claudius, who gave it the name of Cæsareia: the refoundation is no doubt coincident with the same Emperor's foundation of Colonia Archelais, and marks a general reorganisation of Cappadocia and Lykaonia.* Other writers say that Tiberius gave the name Cæsareia: that is, perhaps, a less trustworthy account, founded on the fact that Tiberius made Cappadocia a Roman province, and, aided by the prænomen Tiberius, which is common to both Emperors (Euseb., Chron., in A.D. 21, and Hieron., Chron., p. 184; Eutrop., Vit. Tib., p. 77). Socrates ('Hist. Eccles.,' V. 4) is the only authority who vouches that Claudius gave the name Cæsareia, and modern writers have always accepted the authorities in

* Compare Claudiopolis Colonia in Cilicia Tracheia, Archelais Colonia in Cappadocia, Claudio-derbe, Claud-iconium, Claudio-laodicea in Lykaonia, which attest a wide reorganisation of this part of the empire by Claudius. The date was probably 41.

favour of Tiberius. But Socrates is confirmed, not only by the proofs of a general reorganisation by Claudius in 41, but also by the evidence of coins. The name Cæsareia never occurs on coins of the city earlier than his time : those which read ΕΥΣΕΒΕΙΑΣ ΚΑΙΣΑΡΕΙΑΣ belong probably to his reign,* before the new title had ousted the old.

The name of Cæsareia was taken from the city, and it was expunged from the list of cities (ἐκ τοῦ καταλόγου τῶν πόλεων) by the Emperor Julian, who hated it on account of the strength of the new religion in it. The whole city was Christian (πανδημεὶ Χριστιανίζοντας) ; and the great temples of Zeus Poliouchos and Apollon Patroos had long ago been destroyed (Sozom., ' Hist. Eccles.,' v. 4).

When Basil was engaged in the struggle with Anthimus of Tyana he raised a number of places to the rank of bishoprics. These were, however, for the most part not recognised as having the rank of πόλεις. They are omitted by Hierocles, except Sasima, Doara, and Podandos. But in the sixth and later centuries the number of bishoprics increased. The earlier Notitiæ give more than Hierocles, and the later Notitiæ add still more. The steadily growing importance of Cappadocia under Byzantine rule accounts for the steady growth in the number of bishoprics. It will facilitate the subject to examine the whole list here at once. The bishoprics subject to Cæsareia are given in the accompanying Table (p. 282).

These bishoprics would naturally be situated on the great lines of road which connected Cæsareia with other important centres. So, for example, we have found that Matiane on the road to Archelais Colonia, and Sibora, an important fortress on the military road from Constantinople to Sebasteia, appear as bishoprics in these later Notitiæ.

KAMOULIA can hardly be distinct from Kemer, for Kamoulia and Kamouria are equivalent forms. Now Kemer has been shown in the discussion of the roads to be the site of Kambe : β in the Byzantine lists and in Greek later than the second century commonly takes the place of ου, and Καμούη (or possibly Καμούρη) may be corrupted to Cambe in the Peutinger Table and Κάμπαι in Ptolemy. Ptolemy has Kamouresarbon (cp. Gordo-serba) in Pontus Cappadocicus.

In the lists of Concil. Constant., 553 A.D., Kamoulianai is called Justinianopolis.

KISKISOS still retains its name as Kisken, a government centre, seat of a Mudir, south-east from Mt. Argæus.

EUAISSAI, EUASAI, EUOISAI, may, perhaps, be Ptolemy's Σείουα, Siva in the Table, which has been placed on the road Cæsareia-Basilika Therma at Yogounes. A bishopric seems very suitably placed on this road : the church must have been sacred to St. John, probably the Evange-

---

* I am indebted for this statement to Mr. Head, who has kindly given me his opinion on the point.

list, many relics of whom are still shown in an Armenian monastery east of Cæsareia. The place retains the name of the saint.*

Seioua or Siva may probably have lost a final -sa, and Seiouasa approximates closely to such a form as Euasai or Eubisa.† The initial S is dropped also in the following name, and the equivalence of υ and ου appears also in Σαύατρα, Σαούατρα, Σόατρα. Basil of Cæsareia, Ep. 251, writes to the inhabitants of this town as Εὐαισηνοί, Εὐασινοί, Εὐβισηνοί, in Latin Evaseni or Evaiseni. The contents of this letter, e.g. the influence which Eustathius of Sebasteia has tried to exercise on the Evaiseni, the allusions to Galatia, Amaseia, Zela, suggest a situation in the northern part of Cappadocia : and the later Notitiæ show that it was subject to Cæsareia. Basil's letter also shows that it must have been a place of some consequence in the fourth century, which establishes the probability that it was situated on an important trade-route, such as that which leads from Cæsareia to Euagina, Eukhaita, and the coast.

Yogounnes, where we place Euasai, must be in all probability in Saravene, not in Kilikia, unless the latter extended north of the Halys.

SEBAGENA or EBAGENA is probably the modern Suwagen near the crossing of the Zamanti Su, east of Tomarza, on the road from Cæsareia by Tomarza and the Kuru Bel to Komana. We may confidently assume besides Σεβάγηνα the forms Σενάγηνα and Σεουάγηνα, in which the resemblance to Suwagen or Seuagen is unmistakable.

THEODOSIOPOLIS ARMENIAE is a clear example of a city attached ecclesiastically to the metropolis of a distant province. Justinian made it the capital of his Armenia Prima, but his redistribution of the provinces was long disregarded by the ecclesiastical lists.‡ Notitiæ VII., VIII., IX., and I., continue to attach Theodosiopolis to Cæsareia, and only in the late Notitiæ III., X., XIII. is his arrangement followed, and Theodosiopolis ceases to be under Cæsareia, though, owing to the incompleteness of these lists in the eastern districts, it is not given as an Armenian metropolis.

The bishopric of Nyssa, as compared with Sasima and Doara, exemplifies the way in which an ecclesiastical connection might arise between a bishopric and a distant metropolitan. Nyssa was more clearly than either Sasima or Doara a part of Cappadocia Secunda ; it always retained its ecclesiastical dependence on Cæsareia, but politically it must have been subject to Tyana from 372 to 536 and afterwards to Mokissos. All three were apparently places to which Basil consecrated bishops during his contest with Anthimus and the civil power. His bishop

---

* So we find a village Aitamas, now purely Turkish, some distance east of Nigde : Aitamas = Ἅγιος Θωμᾶς. See pp. 220, 227.

† B shows the consonantal value of u.

‡ Some instances of confusion between Justinian's arrangement and the usual ecclesiastical order are quoted, p. 326 Theodosiopolis is Kamacha-Ani.

of Nyssa, his own brother Gregory, was ejected by the dominant Arians, but the eminence and vigour of Gregory secured his reinstatement and triumphant return. Basil's appointment was thus successful, and the connection always continued. His appointment at Sasima was unsuccessful: Gregory Nazianzen would not maintain the contest, and Sasima passed under the metropolitan of Tyana. At Doara, in like fashion, Basil's nominee was expelled, and apparently never reinstated (Ep. 239; Gregory Naz., Or. 13, consecrated Basil's bishop).

The other connections of this kind which can be traced with more or less probability are:—

> Podandos of Cappadocia Secunda with Cæsareia.
> Argiza of Hellespontus with Ephesos.
> Amblada of Pisidia with Iconium.
> Lamos of Cilicia with Seleuceia.

AIPOLIOI seems to have retained its name as Pallas on the road Cæsareia-Sebasteia. Eulepa in the Antonine Itinerary seems to be situated at Pallas, and to be a transposed form of the same native name, which is hellenised Aipolioi to give a word with a meaning in Greek.

ARATHIA is perhaps ARASAXA, mis-written on the analogy of Ariarathia.

ARMAXA, MALANDARA or MARANDANA, were stations on the road between Sebasteia and Aipolioi.

KYZISTRA. As to the other names in Ptolemy's list, Leake has suggested that the road of the Table, Tyana xxxvii Andabalis xv Scolla xxii Cibistra ix Tetra—Cæsareia, is a real road, and that Cibistra must be corrected to Cizistra on the authority of Ptolemy. This is paying too great deference to the authority of the Table. I regard Cibistra as simply transposed from another road, and feel great doubt whether any road Tyana-Cæsareia was given by the ultimate authority from which the Table was derived. Such cross-roads existed, but are out of keeping with the scheme of the Table, which gives only great through-routes. Kyzistra, mentioned as a bishopric at the first Council of Nikaia, is merely an error for Kybistra, and a similar error may be suspected in Ptolemy.

SEBAGENA, or, as it might have been written, Σεουάγηνα or Σευάγηνα, still retains its name as Seuagen; see p. 305.

ARKHALLA is still called Erkelet.

SOBARA is unknown, unless it be Sibora in Saravene. The Peutinger Table has Foroba on the road Cæsareia-Sebasteia: it is out of place, and is perhaps also a corruption of Sibora.

SAKASENA has retained its name as Suksun, beside the ruins named Viran Sheher. It is corrupted to Sacœna in one place in the Antonine Itinerary, and given more correctly in another. It was the first station on the road to Soandos.

SADAKORA is mentioned by Strabo as on the road between Soanda (about Nev Sheher) and Cæsareia. It is probably the same place that is mentioned by Philostorgius as DAKORA or DAKOROA. Eunomius, the heretic, had an estate there. He was sent by Eutropius to reside in retirement at Cæsareia, but being unpopular there on account of his enmity to Basil, the late Bishop of Cæsareia, he was allowed to go to his property at Dakora. There he died, and his body was removed to Tyana.* Philostorgius gives no clue to the exact situation of Dakoroa, but Sozomen, who calls it Dakora, says it was a village of the territory of Cæsareia πρὸς 'Αργαίω.† Sozomen, but not Philostorgius, says that Eunomius was born at Dakora (πατρίς· κώμη δ' αὔτη Καππαδοκίας Δάκορα). This is probably merely a false inference of Sozomen from such words as occur in Philostorgius, τοὺς ἑαυτοῦ ἀγρούς. Eunomius, as Gregory Nyssenus mentions, was born at Oltiseris, a village of Korniaspa on the borders of Cappadocia towards Galatia.

DEMAKELLA (or Makellon), a place near Cæsareia Capp., where Gallus and Julian were sent to be educated, Theophan., p. 35. Sozomen more correctly calls it Makellon, and says it was an imperial estate with baths and splendid fountains.

According to Vitruvius, VIII., 3, "est in Cappadocia, in itinere quod est inter Mazacam et Tuanam, lacus amplus," in which reeds or wood are petrified in a day. It is not known what Vitruvius is here alluding to.

I add here a list of places, of which we know only that they were in Cappadocia.

MOGARISSOS is mentioned only in the biography of Saint Theodosios: κώμη τις ἤνεγκε τὸν μακάριον, ὄνομα Μογαρισσὸς κατὰ τὴν τῶν Καππαδοκῶν χώραν κειμένη [vv. ll. Magariassos, Mogariassos, Môgarisos, Marissos], ἣ τότε μὲν τοῖς πολλοῖς ἄγνωστός τε καὶ ἄσημος ἦν, νυνί δὲ καὶ πᾶσι σχεδὸν δι' αὐτὸν γνώριμος. (Metaphrastes, I., p. 469, ed. Migne.)

APENZINSOS is mentioned only in the will of Gregory Nazianzen: τὸ κτῆμα τὸ ἐν 'Απηνζινσῷ, property of Euphemius, wrongly occupied by Meletius.

KANOTALA is mentioned only in the will of Gregory Nazianzen: ὠνὴν τοῦ χωρίου Κανοτάλων.

MATAZA, an estate belonging to Philagrius, a friend of Gregory Nazianzen and of his brother Cæsarius. There is no clue to its position, except that it was far enough from Nazianzos to require a journey for the one to visit the other, but near enough to require an apology when Gregory came to Nazianzos but did not visit Philagrius. (Greg. Naz., Ep. 30–6, 92.)

NAVILA (μέχρι Ναΰλων), a place near enough to Nazianzos for Gregory to go there on a visit, but far enough for the visit to be a matter of some difficulty. (Ep., 204–6.)

---

* Philostorg., x. 6.—Δακοροηνοὶ δὲ τοῖς ἀγροῖς τὸ ὄνομα. Cf. xi. 5.

† This expression is misunderstood by the writer in Smith's 'Dictionary of Christian Biography' (s.v. Eunomius), who says that Dakora was under the shadow of Argæus. Cæsareia ad Argæum is the distinguishing title of Cæsareia-Mazaka.

Borissos, a village (κώμη) of Cappadocia, where Karterios and Eulampion, the parents of Philostorgios the historian, lived. (Philost. H. E., ix. 9.

Getasa: τὰ Γήτασα τὸν ἀγρὸν τοῦ θεοφιλεστάτου ἐπισκόπου Μελετίου. (Greg. Naz. Ep., 99.)

Nora or Neroassos has been placed by Hamilton at Zengibar Kalesi. Sterrett also says, " There can scarcely be a doubt but that the higher peak of Zengibar Kalesi is Nora." But the only distinct topographical statement about Nora is that it was on the borders of Lycaonia and Cappadocia, which requires a situation very much further west. Moreover, Strabo mentions that Sisinas kept his treasure in it, and that Kadena was his capital. Now Kadena is probably on the western frontier (see Chamanene). Moreover, the context in Strabo shows that Argos and Nora were a pair of forts on the western frontier, and he goes on, " Garsauira also is on the Lycaonian frontier." Nora was probably further north than Argos, perhaps on the skirts of Ikejik Dagh, or at Halva Dere on the northern spurs of Hassan Dagh.

The following names occur only in the Peutinger Table, and are untrustworthy:—Scolla, Asarinum, Pagrum.

The towns and villages of Kilikia then are

Cæsareia Mazaka.	Arasaxa.
Saccasena.	Sebagena.
Sadakora, Dakora.	Kiskisos.
Arkhalla.	Aipolioi.
Kamoure, Kamoulia.	Demakella, Makellon.

VII. Sargarausene (or Sargabrasene) is placed by Ptolemy on the Galatian frontier, and by Pliny on the Phrygian frontier, which may be treated as almost an equivalent definition. Ptolemy's error may have been produced by the similarity of the names Σαρανηνή and Σαργαυρασηνή, for he has placed the latter exactly where he should have placed the former.

Strabo places Sargarausene on the side of Cappadocia towards Taurus, between Kataonia and Kilikia. Its exact relation is fixed by the course of the Karmalas, which flows through it, and by the town Erpa or Erpha on the road from Cæsareia to Melitene at the crossing of the Karmalas. The towns named by Ptolemy agree with the situation as defined by Strabo. The boundaries, then, are: on the north Laviansene, on the east and south Melitene and Kataonia, on the west Kilikia.

Ptolemy gives the following towns in Saragausene:—

Φίαρα.	Σαβαλασσός.
Σαδάγηνα.	Ἀριαράθιρα.
Γαύραινα.	Μάρωγα.

Phiara may perhaps be the Siara or Fiarasi of the Itinerary, at Yeni

Khan, north-west of Sivas.* In Ptolemy's map Phiara appears in this position, north-west of Sebasteia. If the identification is true, Phiara must have been placed here by Ptolemy, not from his authority about the *Strategiai*, but by inference from his conception of the position of Sargarausene.

SADAGENA seems to be a false reading for Sobagena, which, as Professor Sterrett has discovered, is the fortress now named Khurman Kalesi. Here, again, Sobagena is doubtless the name of the district, and Khurman is probably the ancient name of the fortress still preserved. The inscriptions which enabled Professor Sterrett to fix the site of Sobagena and Sarromaëna are so important for topography that I quote them here: I received, two years before Professor Sterrett travelled, a copy of these inscriptions from Major Bennet, and reached the conclusions stated here before Professor Sterrett's copy was known to me. They are engraved on a rock near Khurman Kalesi to the north-west.

(1) Διχθαδίης κώμῃσι Φιλιππίου 'Αρσινόου τε
οὗτος ἀρίγνωτος Πρείων ὄρος ἀστυφέλικτος.
ἔπλετο δ' 'Αρσινόῳ μὲν ἐδέθλια Σαρρομάηνα,
τῷ δ' ἄρ' ἐπὶ προχοῇσι δύω ποταμῶν Σοβάγηνα.

(2) 'Εννέα τοι πέτρηθεν ἐπὶ κρήνην Σοβαγήνων
καλλίροον στάδιοι Κόρακος ποταμοῖο παρ' ὄχθας.

The inference drawn by Professor Sterrett is clearly correct, that Korax was the old name of Khurman Su.

MAROGA retains its name as Maragos or Malagos. In regard to this I have to differ from Professor Sterrett,† who infers from the above inscription that "it is clear that Sarromaëna must have occupied the site of Maragos, which name may even be a corruption of Sarromaëna." As to the name, it seems to me obvious that Maragos is the ancient Maroga, and that it cannot possibly be a corruption of Sarromaëna. But it is not impossible that the position of Sarromaëna may be reconciled with this identification, if it be the name of a district and not of a town. The termination marks it as an adjectival form. Sarromaëna, then, was the district on the Maragos Tchai, containing the small town or village Maroga.

GAURAINA has retained its name as Görun or Gurun. It is situated on the Tokhma Su, near the borders of Melitene, and on the important road direct from Sebasteia to Arabissos. Not far east of Gauraina is the modern Derende, which Kiepert ingeniously conjectures to be a form of the ancient Dalanda.‡ But there are two objections, neither of them conclusive, but having some slight weight. (1) Ptolemy places Dalanda

* Like φουβάγηνα (p. 261) it seems to be derived from a map with Latin names. It probably was in Saravene, which Ptolemy confuses with Sargarausene. See p. 266.

† 'Epigraphical Journey in Asia Minor,' p. 232, a work full of material gathered with much labour and skill, in the ' Papers of the American School at Athens,' iii.

‡ Ibid., p. 305, where Delendis is given. The form given by Ptolemy is Dalanda.

on the Euphrates, but he may err in position. (2) It is doubtful whether the reading Dalanda occurs in any MS.

SABALASSOS may be the same town, which is named Codu-sabala* in the Antonine Itinerary. Codusabala was situated between Komana and Ariarathia on the upper waters of the Saros about Kizil Bunar or Keui Yere.

ARIARATHIA is fixed by a consideration of the Roman roads of eastern Cappadocia. It was situated at Azizie. It derives its name from one of the Kings Ariarathes (333 to 97 B.C.), and probably dates from the second or third century B.C. It owed its importance to its situation on the high road from Komana to Sebasteia, Komana Pontica, and Amisus. In the eighth or ninth century after Christ the name Tsamandos, perhaps, came into use, having been popularly preserved from ancient time† ; just as Prakana, obviously the old Isaurian name, supplanted Diocæsareia in the eighth century.

Ariarathia is mentioned by Gregory Nazianzen in a letter (Ep. 310) written to the governor [of Armenia Secunda].

The towns which we can assign to Sargarausene are— .

Ἥρπα or Ἥρφα.	Σοβάγηνα.
Ἀριαραθία, Τζαμανδός (= Δάσμενδα ?)	Μάρωγα and Σαρρομάηνα.
Καρμαλίς (perhaps in Laviansene).	Koduzabala or Σαβαλασσός.
Ἀράσαξα (more probably in Kilikia).	

VIII. KATAONIA is extended by Ptolemy in the most absurd fashion to include Mopsoukrene in Cilicia, between Tarsos and the Pylæ Ciliciæ,‡ Dalisandos in Lycaonia, and Claudiopolis in Isauria. It is traversed by the Saros, and extends south to the mountainous region of Tauros and Amanos (Strab. 521, 527), in which lies the border between it and Cilicia and Kommagene. The Karmalas probably bounded it on the west, dividing it from *Strategia* Kilikia. In a larger sense Kataonia included Melitene, as Strabo mentions (p. 533), and he uses the term in this wide sense (528) when he says that once Akilisene of Armenia was reckoned as part of Kataonia. It included the Anti-tauros with Komana.

Ptolemy enumerates in Kataonia the following cities (I omit Κύβιστρα, Κλαυδιόπολις, Δαλισανδός, Παδνανδός, Μόψου Κρήνη) :—

Καβασσός.	Κόμανα.
Τύννα.	Ταναδαρίς.
Τιραλλίς.	Λεανδίς.

---

* The varieties of reading are great : doduzabala, coduzabala, doducabala, guduzabala, doduzalaba, coduzalaba, codozalaba, codozabala, codolaba.

† See above, KARNALIS or KARMALIS, O, II.

‡ The reason lies in the great extension given to Cappadocia for a time after 17 B.C., when the Eleventh Strategia, extending from the Isaurian coast to Kybistra, was added to it.

KABASSOS. There is some temptation to alter this name into Ko-kussos. The confusion of K and B is frequent, and Kokussos (now Guksun) was a very important station on the Roman road in Kataonia. But Kabassos is mentioned by Stephanus Byzantius as a village of Cappadocia [on the road] between Tarsos and Cæsareia. He probably refers to a road by Sis, and not to the direct road through the Cilician Gates, to Cæsareia, for Kabassos is also mentioned as a bishopric of Cilicia Secunda (see p. 386).

TYNNA and TIRALLIS are entirely unknown.

LEANDIS is no doubt identical with Laranda of the Antonine Itinerary, 18 miles from Kokussos on the road to Anazarbos. Mr. Sterrett, in his ' Preliminary Report of a Journey in Asia Minor,' p. 19, places it at Kilissejik, five hours west* of Kokussos, but in his complete account of the journey† seems to have given up the identification. I think, however, that it is quite right. Kilissejik is on the road Kokussos to Anazarbos, about 13 miles from Kokussos. Major Bennet tells me that the name is Kara Kilisa.

TANADARIS, the Ptandari of the Antonine Itinerary, has retained its name in the form Tanir.

ARABISSOS is not mentioned by Ptolemy, though it was a very important place. It was the military centre of Kataonia, and a station for troops, and has retained its name as Yarpuz. In modern time, the central point of the district has changed from Yarpuz to Albostan,‡ a few miles south east; but the importance which now attaches to Albostan, as guarding the entrance to the most important pass by far across Tauros into Kommagene, formerly belonged to Arabissos. The pass. which is most frequently mentioned in the Byzantine frontier wars, is that from Arabissos to Germanicia or Adata (see N. 12, O. 4), and one or other of these towns must correspond to the modern Marash. The latter name occurs in Byzantine history in the form Μαράσιν, Μαράσιον.

In the year 640 A.D., Heraclius, starting from the country about Amida and Martyropolis (about the sources of the Tigris), crossed the river Nymphios, and reached the Euphrates at a point where there was a bridge of boats. The enemy had destroyed the bridge, but he succeeded in crossing by a ford in the month of March. He passed through Samosata, and crossed Tauros by Germanicia and Adana (error for Adata).§ Afterwards he crossed the Saros by a bridge; he must therefore have taken the regular road Arabissos to Cæsareia, on which alone there is likely to have been a bridge. He then turned north to Sebasteia (Sivas).

* By a slip Mr. Sterrett says " south-east."
† ' Papers of the American School at Athens,' vol. ii., p. 239.
‡ Al Bostan, the Garden.
§ Πάλιν τὸν Ταῦρον ὑπερβὰς εἰς Γερμανίκειαν ἀφίκετο, καὶ περάσας τὴν Ἄδανα ἦλθε πρὸς. τὸν Σάρον.—Theophanes, 313. Read Ἄδατα (see SARAVENE).

Andreas, the envoy of the emperor Constans, went from Damascus to Melitene. When he reached Arabissos, he met the Kleisourophylax and instructed him to keep watch for Sergius, the envoy of the rebel Sapor, on his road back from Damascus; Sergius, while returning through the Kleisourai, was found and taken prisoner, and carried to Andreas, who had gone to Amnesia. The pass here alluded to must certainly be the pass from Marash to Albostan, and it is plain that the officer charged with its defence resided at Arabissos (Theophan., p. 350). Amnesia is otherwise unknown, unless it be connected with the river Amnias beside Pompeiopolis in Paphlagonia.

The military importance of Arabissos is also attested by a passage in the life of Saint Eutychius ('Act. Sanct.,' April 6th, p. 564); accidit ut ii quibus Moderatianæ legionis commissa erat cura venirent ex Arabisso (to visit Eutychius at Amaseia).*

It was placed in Armenia Secunda at the reorganisation of the provinces by Diocletian,† and Justinian (A.D. 536) changed the name of the province to Armenia Tertia, without altering its limits.

BADIMON and PRÆTORIUM on the road from Kokussos .to Anazarbos, which went by Kiraz Bel, Tapan Dere and Flavias (now Sis). See N. 17.

DASTARKON is mentioned by Strabo as (p. 537) washed by the river Karmalas, and in the Strategia Kataonia. It must be sought on the Zamanti Su below Ekrek. Dastarkon was the seat of the Kataonian Apollo, who was reverenced over all Cappadocia. It was on a lofty rock surrounded by the river. Das-tarkon (cp. Dasteira Dasmenda) contains an interesting name, seen also in Tarkondimotos, Tarquinius.‡

AZAMORA is mentioned along with Dastarkon in such a way as to leave its position doubtful between Melitene and Kataonia.

Osdara, 24 miles east of Arabissos, near Alhazli.

SIRICA, on the Saros, six miles east of Komana. This Sirica can hardly be identical with Siricha, which seems to be situated nearer the Halys. Samonas, on pretence of going to his monastery Speira, which was in Damatry, fled from Constantinople to Melitene. Just before crossing the Halys, he was seized by Nicephorus Kallonas; he pretended that he had come on a pilgrimage to the cross in Siricha (ἐι τῷ Σιριχᾷ, Theophan. Contin., 369. See G. 39). It may, however, be identical with Stephanus's Σάριχα, πόλις Καππαδοκίας.

* Arabessoi, mentioned by Menander, p. 395, cannot be the people of Arabissos they belong to Armenia, further east.

† Cf. Philostorg. ap. Suidam, s.v. Εὐδόξιος: ἐξ Ἀραβισσοῦ τῆς Μικρᾶς Ἀρμενίας.

‡ An example of this name has been misunderstood, both by Professor Sterrett, who publishes it ('Wolfe Exped.,' No. 181), and by W. Gurlitt, in 'Berl. Phil. Wochenschr.,' 1889, p. 730. Sterrett corrects his copy to Τάρκυν[α] Βέρραν: Gurlitt corrects to Ταρκυνδέρραν. The copy is correct, Ταρκυνδβέρραν, where β is to be understood (as often) as equal to digamma. Compare ἘστϜεδιυνς for Ἀσπένδιος.

The towns of Kataonia are :—

Komana.	Leandis, Laranda.
Sirica.	Kokussos.
Tanadaris.	Badimon.
Arabissos.	Prætorium.
Osdara	

IX. Melitene is placed similarly by Strabo and by Ptolemy. It is bounded on the east by the Euphrates, on the north by Lesser Armenia, on the west by Sargarausene and Kataonia, and on the south by Kommagene.

Perhaps some of the towns assigned by Ptolemy to Laviansene and even Saravene should be included in Melitene ; the remainder belong either to Kommagene or to Kataonia, but they are for the most part so little known, that it is impossible to place them.

According to the reorganisation of Diocletian, Melitene became the metropolis of Armenia Secunda, a province which is góverned by a præses in Notit. Dignit. (ab. 413 A.D.) and in Hierocles. Justinian, Novella xxxi., named the province Armenia Tertia, made its governor a *Comes Justinianeus*, and remodelled the organisation in various ways ; the passage gives an interesting account of the province :—Ad hæc tertiam Armeniam instituimus, eam quæ prius secunda dicebatur, in qua principatum tenet Melitena urbs insignis in pulchro solo clementique cælo posita, neque multum distans a fluentis Euphratis fluvii. Hanc nos in præsentia et augendam et ad formam spectabilium traducendam putavimus : præsidem quoque hujus comitem Justinianeum nominandum, dandosque ipsi pro annonis solidos 700, eius assessori solidos 72, et cohorti eius solidos 360, et ut omnia habeant quæ eiusmodi thronorum propria sunt. Et qui prius Cohortales nominabantur, tum omnia faciant quæ etiam prius, et maxime circa publicam exactionem occupentur ; tum ad Comitianorum appellationen transeant, perinde omnibus eis conservatis ac si Cohortales existerent. Urbes vero ei partim Arcam et Arabissum, partim Ariarsatheam, et alteram Comanam (quam etiam Chrusam appellant), et Cucusum subdidimus, quas et prius habebat e sex omnimodo consistens urbibus.

An excellent species of wine, οἶνος Μοναρίτης, is said by Strabo to grow in Melitene (p. 535). He also says that Melitene was the only part of Cappadocia that abounded in fruit-trees, and modern travellers also speak of the orchards.

Melitene should perhaps strictly be called Melita, it was the central city of a district Melitene ; but the form Melita never occurs. The city was not in existence in the time of Strabo : it gradually grew up as the centre of the people Melitenoi and the country Melitene. Hence the name is strictly an adjective, ἡ Μελιτηνὴ πόλις. It still retains its name under the form Malatia.

The strength of the fortress is often praised by Byzantine historians :—
τὸ ἐπίσημον καὶ ἐξάκουστον καὶ πάνυ ὀχυρὸν καὶ δυνατὸν κάστρον, Μελιτινὴν
ὀνομαζόμενον, or again τὸ ἀήττητον καὶ ἀμάχητον κάστρον, Theophan. Contin.,
p. 415; Cedren. ii., p. 263. According to Mr. Sterrett* there are now
two towns, Old Malatia, which was abandoned during the Turco-
Egyptian war, which occupied the site of the ancient city, and New
Malatia, seven or eight miles to the south-west.

Ptolemy assigns to this Strategia the following towns: on the
Euphrates Δάγουσα (read perhaps Δάσκουσα), Σίνις κολωνία, Μελιτηνή;
and further west, Ζωπάριστος, Τιταρισσός, Κιάνικα, Φουσιπάρα, Εὐσιμάρα,
Ἰασσός, Κιακίς, Λεύγαισα, Κάρμαλα, Σημισός, Λαδοινερίς.

Dascusa at Penga ('C. I. L.,' iii. Suppl. No. 6743). Sinis Colonia,
probably Pisonos of the Itinerary, xxii miles from Melitene, on the
road to Sebasteia. Kiakis is Ciaca of the Itinerary, xviii miles north
of Melitene on the Euphrates (Craca of the Table). Semisos seems,
perhaps, to correspond with Maisena (i.e. Mesena) of the Itinerary.
Probably Ptolemy gets such names as Leandis, Ciacis, Caparcelis†, from
an itinerary in which ablative cases were used, as sometimes in the
Peutinger Table. The following names also occur in Basil, and may be
referred to Armenia Minor: a district Orpanene or Orphanene, with two
villages, Korsagaina and Attagaina (Ep. 278): Phargamous, where a
great meeting in honour of certain martyrs was held every year (Ep. 95).
Ptolemy does not mention Arca, now called Arga, a Roman station and
a bishopric, which must have belonged to Melitene.

X. TYANITIS will be most conveniently discussed along with Lycaonia
and the Kleisourai or passes over Taurus.

XI. The precise boundaries of the Roman province Cappadocia can
hardly be fixed more accurately than results from the description of the
Strategiai. One of the boundaries towards Galatia, near Parnassos, is
given exactly. Again, Pliny says that the river Kappadox divided the
provinces. This river is probably one of the tributaries on the right,
i.e. east, bank of the Halys, for no tributary on the west bank seems to
suit the description. Pliny's words must not be pressed, for he gives
the Rhyndakos as the boundary of Asia, and the Siberis or Hieros of
Galatia, but the frontier only approximates to these rivers. Hence
Kiepert is probably right in giving the name Kappadox to the Delije
Irmak. Lake Tatta was apparently part of the western frontier.

Hassan Dagh was for the most part in Cappadocia, but it is doubtful
whether the western end did not extend into Lykaonia. Kybistra
certainly, and Kastabala probably, were included in Cappadocia. The
Pylæ Ciliciæ were the southern limit, and probably a line along the
great ridge of Tauros marks the frontier. The eastern Strategiai

---

* Epigraph. Journ. in Asia Minor, in 'Papers of the American School of Athens,
ii. 330.

† On Caparcelis, probably a Syrian town, see p. 302.

are assigned by Ptolemy to Armenia Minor, but Armenia Minor and Cappadocia were one Roman Province. The bounds of Cappadocia on the east and north cannot be indicated more precisely than is done in the discussion of the Strategiai. Several of the cities which Ptolemy assigns to Armenia Minor, in the narrow sense, certainly belong to the Strategiai.

The bounds of Cappadocia on the north must have varied at different times. The district of Sibora, Korniaspa, and Basilika Therma, can hardly have been reckoned in Cappadocia by Strabo, who mentions (p. 540) that the boundary between Cappadocia and Pontos was a mountain chain, which extended parallel to Mount Tauros (i.e. east and west) from the western extremity of the Strategia Khamanene to the eastern parts of the Strategia Laviansene. This chain is certainly the ridge which in its central portion is called Ak Dagh, and which towards the west forms a watershed between the Halys and the Delije Irmak, while towards the east, under the name Tchamli Bel, it closes in the northern side of the upper Halys valley. The southern provinces of Pontos, which border on Cappadocia, are Zelitis, Kolopene, and Kamisene. The situation of these provinces is accurately indicated on Kiepert's map: Zelitis is fixed by the capital Zela, now Zille; Kamisene by the fortress Kamisa, a little way east of Sebasteia (Sivas) on the road to Satala and Nicopolis; and Kolopene by Sebastopolis (Sulu Serai) and Sebasteia (Sivas) which Pliny places in it, vi. 3.* The mountain ridge is therefore a boundary between Pontos and Cappadocia only in a loose and general way; as in truth it is not a single well-defined ridge, but a broad irregular elevation. The Halys, which flows along the southern side of the mountain ridge, is understood by Strabo to flow from east to west: it rises in Cappadocia close to the frontier of Kamisene in Pontos, flows through Kamisene, and then for a long distance traverses Cappadocia (Strabo, 546).

Roman Cappadocia probably extended much farther north than the bounds assigned by Strabo. Probably the Byzantine bounds, which are indicated by the situation of Korniaspa, Basilika Therma, and Sibora, are much the same as the Roman bounds. Ptolemy even includes Phiara in Cappadocia; but this is perhaps not true, if his Phiara is identical with Siara-Fiarasi of the Antonine Itinerary.

It is necessary to describe briefly the themes into which the eastern parts of Asia Minor were divided in later Byzantine times, beginning probably from the reign of Heraclius, 610–41. By far the most important of these themes, during the eighth and following centuries, was the Armeniac, while those names which indicate a situation still further east, Khaldia and Mesopotamia, were of small size and little importance. But this cannot always have been the case. Apparently the design

---

* Strabo says Megalopolitis, the district round Megalopolis-Sebasteia was conterminous with Kolopene.

of Heraclius was similar to the scheme of defence of the early Roman empire. The large provinces of the earlier empire had been controlled by generals who commanded armies, exercised great power, and had the defence of the eastern frontier in their trust. The emperors, from the end of the third century onwards, carried out a different policy. They made the provinces small and multiplied their number. They greatly increased the number of provincial governors and diminished correspondingly their individual power. The government was more centralised and less was trusted to the commanders of the provinces. With a series of weak emperors this policy reduced the empire to the verge of ruin. The vigour of Heraclius restored it; and his policy inaugurated a new system of military governors, ruling over vast districts and commanding large bodies of troops.

The names Khaldia and Mesopotamia were used in the tenth century, but Khaldia denoted the country near Trapezous. In the ninth century Khaldia included Keltzene, but Leo VI. transferred Keltzene to the theme Mesopotamia.* Comparing the known history of the theme Cappadocia, which was originally the country of that name, afterwards the country between the Sangarios and the Halys, and at last, in the time of Alexius Comnenus, only the plains round Amorion, we may believe it probable that the name Khaldia had changed in a similar way its denotation as the boundaries of the empire shrank. Under Heraclius the name Khaldia may have denoted the south-eastern frontier theme, and may have had some pretension to be geographically true. It is not impossible that Khaldia and Armeniaca were the two frontier themes of Heraclius, but evidence is too scanty to give confidence to any opinion.

Mesopotamia, on the other hand, is said to have been instituted for the first time by Leo VI.,† who took Kamakha from Koloneia, and Keltzene from Khaldia, to form it.

It is probable that the Armeniac theme, in the same way, got its name from the fact that it included Armenia and the northern part of the eastern frontier. But in the tenth century it had ceased to include any of Armenia, and denoted the countries of Cappadocia and Pontus, and extended even west of the Halys, to include Dokeia and Andrapa. The themes were purely military divisions, and their names denoted sections of the army. These sections retained their old name as they were driven back from their old stations, and soon their names were applied to the districts in which they were stationed within the narrowed limits of the empire.

The shrinking of the Byzantine bounds ceased. The Iconoclast emperors stemmed the tide of Mohammedan invasion : the Macedonian

---

* The chief authority on the themes is Constantine Porphyrogenitus, both in his treatise de Thematibus, and in the fiftieth chapter of his ' de Admin. Imper.'

† Const. 'de Adm. Imp.,' p. 226 ; τῷ τότε καιρῷ Θέμα οὐκ ἦν.

dynasty rolled it back. The great general, John Kourkonas, advanced the frontier of the empire from the Halys to the Tigris.* New themes were created out of the newly conquered districts; and their gradual creation marks the gradual advance of the Byzantine arms. The remarkable account of the transference of the name Cappadocia, which is given, p. 216, 250, on the authority of Constantine, is not the consequence of an arbitrary defiance of geography by the Emperor Leo VI. It marks one of the first stages in the reorganisation of the reconquered country. The centre and south of Cappadocia had been either in Saracen hands or exposed to continual inroads, and the name of the country had been carried west of the Halys by the soldiers who had been stationed in it. Leo VI. did not carry back the name to its old country. He arranged that the name should continue to denote the country and the soldiers between the Halys and the Sangarios. The Kharsian Tourma in the north of Cappadocia and the south of Pontos, on the other hand, had not so utterly ceased to exist, and the name had been extended to include the country as it was conquered; and Leo arranged that it should denote all the country up to Cæsareia on the east, and to Tyana on the south.

The theme of Koloneia must have been originally a part of the Armeniac theme, if we can trust the statement of Constantine, p. 21, that Neocæsareia was in the Armeniac theme, for that city certainly was afterwards in the Theme Koloneia (id., p. 31). This theme is older than 860 (Theoph. Contin., p. 181).

Sebasteia was similarly formed into a new theme out of part of the old Armeniac theme, at some time later than 860. Originally it was only a turma of the Armeniac theme, and it became a theme under Leo VI., when the turma of Larissa was placed under it.

The theme of Lykandos was also originally a part of the Armeniac theme, before it passed into the hands of the Saracens. This is implied by Theophanes, who mentions no other theme to which it could belong, and speaks of Sapor, general of the Armeniac theme, as residing at one time in the parts round Melitene (p. 350). He also speaks of Kokussos as a city of Cappadocia (p. 124), and Cappadocia was in the Armeniac theme. Lykandos was formed into a theme under Constantine later than A.D. 913.†

P. THE PONTO-CAPPADOCIAN FRONTIER.

1. With regard to the topography of the provinces along the Black Sea, Honorias, Paphlagonia, and Pontus, I am glad to be able to resign

* The expression, which is slightly exaggerated, is taken from Theophan. Contin., p. 427.

† Finlay wrongly says it became a theme under Leo VI.; see Const. ' de Adm., p. 228.

the difficult task to Prof. G. Hirschfeld, who made a long journey through them in 1883. Hierocles' list in Honorias agrees exactly, even to the order of enumeration, with the Notitiæ. In Paphlagonia he gives six cities, whereas the Notitiæ give only Gangra, Ionopolis, Dadybra and Sora; but of the two which Hierocles adds, Amastris was made an autokephalous archbishopric about A.D. 800 between the date of Hierocles and of the oldest Notitiæ,* and the same was the case between 536 and 553 with Pompeiopolis. Justinian (Novel., xxix.) restored the original unity of Paphlagonia, out of which a part had been taken to form Honorias; but adds that it would be pedantic to give back to Bithynia the cities Prousias, Herakleia, and Claudiopolis, which had been taken from it to complete Honorias: these cities, therefore, continued attached to Paphlagonia. The ecclesiastical division into two provinces continued as before, for the principle was now established that the Church should not follow the political changes of organisation. We may infer that Hadrianopolis, Tios and Krateia were in the eastern part of Honorias. The Parthenios was probably the boundary between Honorias and Paphlagonia in the narrow sense, and possibly Hadrianopolis was at Safaramboli, unless that be the site of Germia-Theodorias.

2. The accompanying table includes the provinces that bound Cappadocia on the north. It is unnecessary for my present purpose to examine them completely, and I have travelled so little in them that I could not venture to do so. But with regard to a few towns which lie near the Cappadocian frontier and have been used in discussing the roads, it is necessary to prove their position.

3. EUKHAITA was a bishopric of Helenopontos. It was always considered a city of that province (Justinian, Novell., xxviii.), and its bishop was originally subject to the metropolis of Amaseia ('Act. Sanct.' Feb. 7th, p. 24). It was made *autokephalos* apparently at an early time: hence Hierocles, who simply took the lists of bishops in Helenopontus under Amaseia, omits it. This honour was probably accorded to it, at least partly, on account of the great sanctity of its patron saint Theodore, who killed a dragon in the district of Eukhaita.† It was a station on some road; hence, when Eutychius was recalled from Amaseia to Contantinople, his journey lay through Eukhaita and Nicomedia ('Act. Sanct.,' April 6th, p. 565). He travelled probably viâ Tchorum and Gangra. This route is the most direct, and its use is proved by the following incident.

During an invasion of the Huns into Pontus and Cappadocia,

---

* Notitia VII. is incomplete, but it does not mention Amastris in the archbishoprics, and doubtless agreed with Hierocles.

† The Acta Theodori (Feb. 7th) contain little or no local colouring. His history is divided between Eukhaita, Nikomedeia, and Heracleia [Pontica], which is said to be a city near both the others!

Eukhaita was on the point of being captured, and Macedonius fled from Eukhaita to Gangra (Theophan., p. 161);* this points very probably to Tchorum as the site of Eukhaita.

HELENOPONTUS, PONTUS POLEMONIACUS, ARMENIA PRIMA.

Hierocles.	Notitiæ I. VIII. IX.	Notitiæ III. X. XIII.
Ἀμασία	I. 1 Ἀμασείας	1 Ἀμασείας
Ἴβωρα	4 Ἰβύρνων	4 Ἰβόρων ἤτοι Πιμολίας
Ζῆλα	7 Ζηλῶν (om. viii. ix.)	7 Ζηλῶν
Σάλτον Ζαλίχην	6 Ζαλίχου ἤτοι Λεοντουπόλεως	6 Ζαλίχου ἤτοι Λεοντοπόλεως
Ἄνδραπα	5 Ἀνδραπόδων	5 Ἀνδράπων
Ἄμισος	2 Ἀμισσοῦ	2 Ἀμινσοῦ
Σινώπη	3 Σινώπης	3 Σινώπης
—	II. Εὐχαίτων	II. Εὐχαίτων
Νεοκαισάρεια	1 Νεοκαισαρείας	I. 1 Νεοκαισαρείας
Κόμανα	5 Κομάνων	4 Κομάνων
Πολεμώνιοι	4 Πολεμωνείου	3 Πολεμωνίου
Κερασοῦς	3 Κερασοῦντος	2 Κερασοῦντος
Τραπεζοῦς	2 Τραπεζοῦντος	II. Τραπεζοῦς.
—	—	5 Ἀλύας
—	—	6 Ῥιζαίου
—	—	7 Κόκκου
—	—	8 Εὐνίκου
—	—	9 Ἀραδάση
—	—	10 Μαρτυροπόλεως
—	—	11 ὁ Ὑψηλός
Σεβάστεια	1 Σεβαστείας	1 Σεβαστείας
Νικόπολις	3 Νικοπόλεως	3 Νικοπόλεως
Κολονία	5 Κολωνίας	5 Κολωνείας
Σάταλα	4 Σατάλων	4 Σατάλων
Σεβαστούπολις	2 Σεβαστουπόλεως	2 Σεβαστουπόλεως
—	6 Βηρίσσης	6 Κηρίσσης

4. Since the preceding paragraphs were in type an article has appeared in the 'Bulletin de Correspondance Hellénique,' 1889, p. 297, on Eukhaita. It is written by M. Doublet, who, however, merely expresses the opinions communicated to him by M. l'Abbé Duchesne. He argues from an inscription of Safaramboli that Eukhaita was situated there. But the inscription on which he founds this opinion merely shows that the church at Safaramboli was dedicated to Saint Theodorus

* Compare Cedren., i., p. 633 : τὴν Ἀρμενίαν ἐξέδραμον, Καππαδοκίαν τε καὶ Γαλατίαν καὶ Πόντον ληϊζόμενοι, ὡς καὶ τὰ Εὐχάϊτα μικροῦ παραστήσασθαι· ὅθεν καὶ φυγὼν ὁ ἱερὸς Μακεδόνιος σχεδὸν κινδυνεύων εἰς Γάγγραν διεσώθη.

and that the city was, according to the commonest of Byzantine customs, spoken of sometimes as the "city of Theodorus." It does not prove that the city was officially designated Theodoropolis, but merely that in a religious dedication the city was called after its patron saint. It is not improbable that Theodorus was worshipped as patron saint of more than one city in the north : the legend connected with him does not confine his influence to a single city.* The further proof is still wanting that Safaramboli was within the bounds of Helenopontos, in which province Eukhaita was included. A glance only at the map is needed to show that Safaramboli was far west of Helenopontus, and near the boundary of Honorias and Paphlagonia ; surely M. Doublet had never consulted the map when he proposed the identification.

5. In the first place, Eukhaita was a city of Helenopontos. Notitia I. gives under the αὐτοκέφαλοι, as No. ξβ', Ἐπαρχίας Ἑλενοπόντου ὁ Εὐχαΐτων. Now there are perhaps, I admit, some rare cases where, through some unknown ecclesiastical bond, a bishopric is attached to some province in defiance of geographical situation ; but this is not a case in point, for Eukhaita, though not subject to the Metropolitan of Helenopontos, is said to be a city of the province. Moreover, it happens that the government list of the cities of Helenopontos under Justinian is known,† and Eukhaita is among them.

Secondly, the bounds of Helenopontos are settled by those of Paphlagonia, which included Gangra, Pompeiopolis, and Ionopolis. The western boundary of Helenopontos was, therefore, east of these cities. It may be defined still more exactly. Helenopontos included three cities on the west side of the Halys, viz., Sinope, Leontopolis, commonly called Zalikhos or Saltus Zalichenus, and Andrapa, which is by Ptolemy said to bear also the name Neoclaudiopolis. The last of these is identified by Kiepert with great probability ‡ as the modern Iskelib. The second

---

* Compare, *e.g.*, the invocation to the Archangel Michael at Akroenos, ῥῦσον τὴν πόλι(ν) σου; see Prymnessos and Metropolis in 'Mittheil. Athen.,' 1882. It happens that from single passages we know that both Germia and Koloneia were known occasionally by the name of their patron Theodorus: at Conc. Const., 553 A.D., Joannes episcopus Colonensium sive Theodoriadis civitatis: on Germia, see § 6. Similarly the fact that Safaramboli (Hadrianopolis, or perhaps Germia) was protected by the patron saint Theodorus is known from this inscription only.

† "Helenopontum quidem octo urbes implent, hoc est Amasia, Ibora, Euchaita, insuper et Zela et Andrapa et Aegeum ad climacas, hoc est gradus, situm, Sinopa et Amisus, antiquæ urbes, sed et Leontopolis, quæ et ipsa jam inter urbes numeratur : aliæ vero quinque Polemoniacum Pontum continent : Neocæsarea, et Comana, Trapezus et Cerasus et Polemonium : Pityus enim et Sebastopolis inter castra potius quam urbes numerandæ sunt" ('Novella' xxviii.) The Latin text has a curious mistranslation, αἵ γε πρὸς τοῖς κλίμασι κείμεναι Σινώπη τε καὶ Ἀμισός being rendered "Aegeum ad climacas ": on κλίμα see Isauria.

‡ Kiepert in 'Sitzungsber. Berl. Akad.,' 1884, in his 'Gegenbemerkungen zu Professor G. Hirschfeld.' The latter identified Tavium with Iskelib. I find no definite passage to localise Andrapa, but general considerations make me accept Kiepert's assignation with confidence. A city is wanted at Iskelib and there seems no other to

is obviously the glen of the little river Zalekos, 210 stadia west of the Halys. * Sinope is well known. A line between these three and the three eastern cities of Paphlagonia marks the bounds of Helenopontos on the east. The assignation of Dokeia to it in the following paragraph, if correct, marks it still more narrowly.

Thirdly, Eukhaita was in the Armeniac Theme.† It is absolutely impossible to think that the Armeniac Theme, which included the whole of Cappadocia from the Cilician Gates to the Black Sea at Amisos should extend so far west as Safaramboli, leaving to the Paphlagonian Theme the little corner between that and the borders of the Buccellariote Theme, which extended to the sea at Herakleia. I need not linger to enforce this point. It is, however, obvious that, if Dokeia was in the Armeniac Theme, it must have been in Helenopontos, and in that case we may say that it must have been very close to the frontier. Dokeia, now called Tossia, is recorded to have been in the Armeniac Theme: ‡ it was occupied by Romanus Diogenes on his return from captivity in 1072. Alexius Comnenus returned from Amaseia by Dokeia (said to be in Paphlagonia), Kastamon, and Herakleia (Niceph. Bryen., p. 92).

Fourthly, Eukhaita was probably east of the Halys. The passage quoted above from Theophanes shows that in A.D. 508, when the Huns were ravaging Pontos and Cappadocia and Galatia, Macedonius fled from Eukhaita to Gangra. If Eukhaita were at Safaramboli, he would be going right into the hands of the foe in fleeing to Gangra. He was at some place such as Tchorum, and then naturally escaped westward to Gangra. Moreover, the words of Theophanes suggest that the Huns did not cross the Halys, and therefore that Eukhaita, which they besieged, was on the east side of the river.

These passages show that Eukhaita was on a road from Amaseia to Nikomedeia, in easy communication with Gangra, and east of the Halys. Tchorum is the site that suggests itself from a study of the map, without actual knowledge of the country.

6. The only passages known to me that tell in favour of MM. Duchesne and Doublet are (1) that quoted in § 3, footnote, from 'Acta S. Theodori;' but the biography appears to me, as I have there

place there except Sora and Andrapa. Sora was probably further west, and M. Doublet is probably right in identifying it as the modern Zora, half a day south-east of Sapharamboli (a very loose and inaccurate way of describing the situation), Bull. Corr. Hell., 1889, p. 311 : we must therefore abandon Mannert's proposed identification of Sora with Kastamon, the modern Kastamuni (Nicet. Chon., 28 ; Cinn., 13–15). Andrapa was clearly in this neighbourhood. ἐξ αὐτῆς τῶν Ἀνδραπηνῶν γῆς ὁ μακάριος (Ἡσύχιος) ἐκφύς (Act. Sanct., Mar. 6, p. 456).

* M. Doublet says (l. c., p. 297), " Je n'ai malheureusement pu identifier ni Ibora ni Zaliche."

† Theophanes, p. 489, mentions that Leon, governor of the Armeniac Theme, was at Eukhaita with the military chest: De Boor rightly infers that Eukhaita was in the Theme.

‡ Οὗτος ἐκ γένους τῶν Ἀρμενιακῶν ἦν ἀπὸ Δόκιαν χωρίου Δαρβιδοῦν (Theophan. Contin., p. 426). For Δόκιαν perhaps read Δοκιανο..

stated, to want local colouring, and therefore not to be written by a person who knew the district. It is really one of the most contemptible documents in the entire 'Acta Sanctorum.' * It is quite clear that nothing whatsoever was known about Theodore except his name and a tale that he had slain a dragon. He was worshipped in several places in Paphlagonia and Pontos, and the legend brings them together: he killed a dragon at Eukhaita and he lived at Herakleia. The example of Makrina at Sasima, and of the coffin of Seidi Ghazi at Nakoleia, show how readily stories about saints, Christian or Mohammedan, grow up at places where they are worshipped. †   (2) A quotation given in § II. of the Bollandist preface to 'Acta S. Theodori' may also be held to favour MM. Duchesne and Doublet: the bishop of Hadrianopolis, seeking for Alypios, καταλαμβάνει τοῦτον ἐν Εὐχαίτοις ἤδη τῆς πανηγύρεως τελουμένης Θεοδώρου τοῦ Μάρτυρος. These two references do not seem to me worth weighing against the arguments which have just been stated.

Again, even if it be admitted that Safaramboli bore the official name Theodoropolis, this does not agree with Eukhaita, for M. Duchesne himself states that the name Theodoropolis was given to Eukhaita 969–73 on the occasion of a victory over the Russians, but this inscription belongs to the fifth century. We must look for some place which was called by religious people by the name of S. Theodorus in the fifth century. Germia perhaps fulfils this condition, and may possibly have been situated at Safaramboli.

Germia is mentioned as a metropolis in Notitiæ I., II., VI. VII., VIII., X., generally as belonging to Galatia, in VII. as belonging to Galatia Prima, and in VIII. to Galatia Secunda. This might appear conclusive as to its situation. But in the Quinisexta Synod, A.D. 692, there occurs among the archbishops at the beginning of the list Μωϋσῆς ἀνάξιος ἐπίσκοπος τῆς Θεοδωριατῶν ἤτοι Γερμιατῶν [πόλεως] τῆς Βιθυνῶν ἐπαρχίας. Besides him we find, among the bishops of Hellespontus, Παῦλος τῆς Γερμηνῶν πόλεως τῆς Ἑλλησποντίων ἐπαρχίας. Now Germocolonia, a well-known city of Galatia Secunda, mentioned in all the Notitiæ as a bishopric subject to Pessinus, cannot be the same as this Germia, for the former bears the religious name Myriangeloi, the latter of Theodorias. Except the name Garmias in the Peutinger Table between Ankyra and Parnassos (which is certainly an error, as this road is very well attested by other authorities), I see no other reference to this Germia. If we can trust the lists of the Council in preference to the Notitiæ, Germia might be situated at Safaramboli. It is true that Safaramboli is rather to be assigned to Paphlagonia than to Bithynia; but Justinian expressly says (Novel. XXIX.) that Claudiopolis

---

* Three versions, all equally poor, are published under Feb. 7.

† "Portaverunt eum ab Heraclia in Euchaita" (Add. p. 894 D.). On Makrina, see SASIMA. It is, of course, an insult to Mohammedanism to speak of the worship of Seidi Ghazi: the dervishes, indeed, who kept up the memory of Seidi Ghazi, are below the standard of Mohammedanism, but even they cannot be said to worship Seidi Ghazi

and Herakleia were, strictly speaking, Bithynian cities, and Safaramboli, therefore, is not far east of the boundary between Bithynia and Paphlagonia. A certain vagueness always existed, as is well known, in regard to the boundaries of provinces other than the Roman official divisions. Still, I lay no stress on the identification, except that it is not impossible. I on the whole prefer the conjecture that Hadrianopolis was at Safaramboli.* But Germia, certainly in the seventh century, and probably in the fifth century,† bore, religiously, the name of S. Theodorus, and the evidence is not conclusive against Germia being at Safaramboli. Eukhaita is recorded to have received the name Theodoropolis in the tenth century, and the evidence appears to be conclusive that it was east of Gangra, and probably east of the Halys.

The frequent references to Eukhaita show its importance. Why, then, is it omitted by Hierocles and all older writers, as well as by the modern geographers? ‡ Under the Roman empire the district in which Eukhaita was situated was not penetrated by the Græco-Roman civilisation: hence the silence of writers older than Hierocles is only natural. But the growth in importance of the cities along the north of the Anatolian plateau is one of the most marked features during the two centuries 350–550, and during this time Eukhaita became one of the πόλεις of Helenopontos. If Hierocles had used a government list of cities, he could not have omitted it: the reason why he has omitted it must be that he followed the ecclesiastical lists, in which this city, being αὐτοκέφαλος, was not given among the bishoprics under Amaseia. The earliest proof that Eukhaita was αὐτοκέφαλος is at the Council of A.D. 680, where the order clearly implies that Leontopolis and Kotrada in Isauria, as well as Eukhaita, are metropolitan bishoprics.

There is one other possible situation for Eukhaita. It may have been, not on the road Amaseia-Gangra, but on the more northern route, Amaseia-Vezir Keupreu-Tash Keupreu (Pompeiopolis), &c. But the flight of Macedonius to Gangra certainly suggests the southern route.

Some MSS. of the later Notitiæ § give four bishoprics as subject to Eukhaita, viz. Gazala, Koutziagros, Sibiktos and Bariane. Of these Gazala might perhaps be identified with Gazelon (chief town of the district Gazelonitis), which is conjecturally placed by Kiepert at Vezir Keupreu. But the majority of MSS. assign these bishoprics to the metropolis Neai Patrai in the Peloponnesus, and add τῷ Εὐχαίτων θρόνος

* If the situation for Sora assigned by M. Doublet is correct, Hadrianopolis must be further west, for it was in Honorias; and Safaramboli seems a peculiarly suitable site. Kastamuni was in Paphlagonia, as it was separated from Honorias: it may be that Dadybra and the later Kastamon were a single bishopric.

† The incidental allusion proves that the name was current among the people, and, therefore, of some antiquity.

‡ M. Duchesne is, I think, almost the first writer since Le Quien who has mentioned it.

§ Not. X., and a Paris MS.

ὑποκείμενος οὐκ ἔστι, and Nilus Doxapatrius agrees with them. It is, therefore, more probable, so far as the evidence of the Notitiæ goes, that these four bishoprics belong to the Peloponnesus : perhaps some authority on the topography of Greece will decide the question.

After the preceding paragraphs are in print I find further confirmation in Act. Sanct., June 5, p. 586, where a quotation is given from Acta Theodori Tironis of Amaseia, to the effect that a noble matron Eusebeia transported the body of the martyr "in possessionem suam, quae distat a civitate Amasia via unius diei, in locum qui vocatur Euchaita." Tchorum strictly is two days' journey from Amaseia, but an estate within the territory of Tchorum might quite well have been a day's journey distant. On the same page another quotation is given from a MS. Vita S. Barbarae, ἦν δὲ ἐν τῇ χώρᾳ τῇ ᾿Ανατολικῇ, τῇ καλουμένῃ ῾Ηλιουπόλει, ἀνὴρ κατοικῶν ἐν χωρίῳ ἐπιλεγομένῳ Γελασέοις ὡς ἀπὸ μιλίων δεκαδύω Εὐχαίτων. There is no city named Heliopolis, which is evidently an error. If we correct to [Οὐ]ηρι[ν]ουπόλει, we have placed Verinopolis at Geune, and a farm in the northern part of the territory of Verinopolis might very well be twelve miles from Tchorum. The two passages prove that Tchorum was Eukhaita.

With regard to the four bishoprics, Mr. Tozer informs me that he can trace none of the names in Greece. The probability therefore is, either that they must be assigned to some third metropolis, or that they belong to Eukhaita. The district which would naturally be subject to Eukhaita is the country along the Halys on the east. The northern part of this country bears the name Gazelonitis, and its chief town may perhaps occur as one of the four bishoprics.

7. The ancient city at Safaramboli, then, was not Eukhaita : I leave it to Prof. G. Hirschfeld to specify its name with certainty.[†] The modern name, is perhaps, derived from Θεοδωρίαν πόλιν. It is a very common occurrence that the modern name of a city should follow that of the patron saint. Θ becomes S, as in Ayasaluk from ῞Αγιο Θεολόγο : the dissyllables Θεο and ίαν are regularly run together into one syllable in the common pronunciation of Greek : the only difficulty is the change of δ to f, but the modern pronunciation of δ[‡] solves much of the difficulty. The accusative form is the common one, e.g. in Baliamboli, Παλαιὰν πόλι(ν).

8. It will be useful to give at this point a comparative table of the changes introduced into the provinces of this district by Justinian (Novel., xxviii., xxxi.). From it we see that Zela was on the

---

* I have no opportunity of consulting the original. Theodorus Tiro is postponed from Feb. 17 to November in ' Act. Sanct.' M. Duchesne, who quotes from ' Acta Theod. Tir.,' does not appear to have noticed this important passage, which demolishes his topographical theory.

† Before I noticed the reference to Germia Theodorias, I had thought of Hadrianopolis.

‡ English th in that.

frontier of the older Helenopontos adjacent to Armenia Prima (Sebastiana); Komana on the frontier of Polemoniakos adjacent to Armenia Prima Sebastiana; Satala, Nikopolis, and Colonia on the eastern frontier of Armenia Sebastiana, forming a convenient new province with Trapezous and Kerasous of Polemoniakos.[*]

PONTOS AND ARMENIA.

Justinian's Re-organisation.		Older Byzantine Arrangement.
Armenia Prima	Bazanis or Leontopolis	Unknown
,,	Theodosiopolis	Cappadocia Prima
,,	Trapezous	Pontos Polemoniakos
,,	Kerasous	,,
,,	Satala	Armenia Prima
,,	Nikopolis	,,
,,	Colonia	,,
Armenia Secunda	Sebasteia	,,
,,	Sebastopolis	,,
,,	Komana	Pontos Polemoniakos
,,	Verisa	Armenia Prima
,,	Zela	Helenopontos
Helenopontos	Amaseia urbs	,,
,,	Amisus urbs	,,
,,	Ibora urbs	,,
,,	Eukhaita urbs	,,
,,	Andrapa urbs	,,
,,	Sinope urbs	,,
,,	Leontopolis urbs	,,
,,	Neocæsareia urbs	Pontos Polemoniakos
,,	Polemonion urbs	,,
,,	Pityous phrourion	,,
,,	Sebastopolis phrourion	,,

The confusion caused by the fact that Armenia Sebastiana was Prima before Justinian and in the Notitiæ. Secunda in the civil

* Justinian, Novel., xxxi., formed a new province of Armenia Prima with the metropolis Leontopolis. He adds: Urbes illi adsignavimus, Theodosiopolim, quam etiä prius habuit: Satalam, et Nicopolim, Colonea quoque ex prima (ut ante vocabatur) Armenia assumpta: item Trapezunte, et Cerasunte ex Polemoniaco prius dicto Ponto. He made Armenia Secunda out of parts of the old Prima and of Pontos: Secundum vero ordinem tenere iussimus eam Armeniam quae ante prima dicebatur, in qua caeteras praecedit Sebastea urbs, attributa illi, et Sebastopoli, quam prius quoque habuit, et insuper Commana ex Polemoniaco prius Ponto dicto; et Zela ex Helenoponto: neque non Berisa. Armenia Tertia was the old Secunda unchanged; see O. 2. Armenia Quarta was formed out of various tribes, including the districts Tzophanene, Anzethene, Balabitene, etc. It contained the city Martyropolis and the castle Kitharizon.

division after Justinian, is often apparent in the ecclesiastical lists :
e.g. at Synod of 680, Verissa Secundæ Armeniæ; and Notitia I. speaks of
Armenia Quarta (evidently that of Justinian, for it mentions Kitharizon,
though it places Martyropolis, part of his province, in Mesopotamia),
and yet it has no Armenia Tertia.

9. SEBASTOPOLIS, also called Heracleopolis, was situated at Sulu Serai.
This is proved by an inscription on the Roman bridge beside the town,
which has been published by Renier (' Rév. Archæolog.,' 1877, p. 200)
and by Roehl (' Beiträge zur griech. Epigraphik ') from a copy so bad
that their transcripts differ widely. It was afterwards published by me
from the accurate copy of Sir Charles Wilson (' Journal of Philology,'
1883, p. 154). It is erected by the archons, senate, and people of
Sebastopolis Heracleopolis, under the governor of Cappadocia, Arrian
(the historian), A.D. 137.

10. AMASIA, AMISOS, SINOPE, NEOCÆSAREIA, KOMANA, SEBASTEIA, have all
retained their ancient names with more or less modification to the present
day. Komana is now a small village on the Iris, above Tokat, which is
said to be called Gömenek : I have not seen it. Strabo (p..557) mentions
that the Iris flowed through the city of Komana. Sebasteia was called
Megalopolis after Pompey, and under the early empire took the name
Sebasteia. Its walls were rebuilt by Justinian.

11. IBORA. The position of Ibora can be determined with approximate
accuracy by the letters of Basil and Gregory Nyssenus. The family
estate where they were born, where they often went to live, and where
their sister Macrina died, was on the banks of the Iris, at a village
Annesoi. The road by which Gregory returned from Annesoi to Nyssa
after the death of Macrina passed through Sebastopolis, which was
apparently not far distant. In his youth Basil retired from the world
to live as a hermit close to Annesoi, but on the opposite side of the Iris.*
It is frequently mentioned that Annesoi was in the diocese of Ibora.
Emmeleia, the mother of Basil, Macrina, and Gregory, had brought the
remains of the Forty Martyrs to Annesoi and built a church there to
receive them.† Hence, when the Bishop of Ibora died, Gregory took
temporary charge of the church, as he felt to be his duty.‡ Here
delegates from Sebasteia, the metropolis of Armenia Secunda, came to
visit him. Now Ibora was a bishopric on the frontiers of Pontus, and
not far from Dazimon (Tokat); therefore it was probably that bishopric
of Pontus which adjoined Sebasteia.

Gregory Nazianzen (Epist. iv.) describes the hermitage to which

---

* Basil Epist., 3 and 223.—ἐπὶ τῆς μονῆς τῆς ἐπὶ τῷ Ἴριδι ποταμῷ.

† Κώμης τῆς ἐμοὶ προσηκούσης, ἐν ᾗ τὰ τῶν τρισμακαρίων τούτων ἀναπέπαυται λείψανα,
ἔστι τις πολίχνη ἡ γείτων, Ἴβωρα καλοῦσιν αὐτήν.—(Greg. Nyss., in 'Quadr. Mart.,'
p. 783.)

‡ Ἴβωρα πόλις ἐστὶ τοῖς ὁρίοις τοῦ Πόντου κατῳκισμένη, ἔχουσα πρὸς ἡμᾶς ἐξ ἀρχαίου
.... ἐπιῤῥήτως.—Greg. Nyss., ' Epist.,' p. 1075. κατὰ τὸν προσήκοντα τῆς παρ' αὐτοῖς
ἐκκλησίας ἐπεμελήθημεν.

Basil retreated as situated in a narrow glen among lofty mountains, which keep it always in shadow and darkness, while far below the river foams and roars in its rocky, narrow, precipitous bed. (Ep. iv.) This description can hardly refer to any other part of the river than the rocky glen below Turkhal. Ibora cannot be placed further down, because it is the frontier bishopric of Pontus towards Sebasteia; and further up there is no rocky glen until the territory of Komana is reached.

Gregory Nyssenus, in his treatise on Baptism (πρὸς τοὺς βραδύνοντας εἰς τὸ βάπτισμα, iii. p. 415, Ed. Migne), speaks of Komana as a neighbouring city.* Tillemont, thinking that the treatise was written at Nyssa, infers that Nyssa and Komana were near each other. The truth is, that Gregory must have written his treatise at Annesoi. We may therefore infer that the territory of Ibora adjoined that of Komana on the east and that of Sebasteia on the south, and touched the Iris from the boundary of Komana down to a point below Turkhal. The boundary was probably near Tokat, and Ibora itself may have been actually situated at Turkhal.

If this reasoning be correct, how are we to explain Basil's letters 86 and 87. A certain presbyter's corn had been seized by the public officers (τῶν τὰ δημόσια διοικεῖν πεπιστευμένων) at Verisa (ἐν Βηρίσσοις, ἐν Κηρίσσοις). Letter 86 is written to the governor of the province in which Basil had been born and brought up (τῷ ἄρχοντι τῆς πατρίδος and τῷ ἡγεμόνι), i. e. the governor of Pontus, and complains of the conduct of the officials at Verisa. The second is addressed to the officer under whose instructions the officials of Verisa claim to have acted: this officer is informed that Basil has already written to the governor of the province, and is exhorted to compel restitution of his own accord, as Basil will otherwise take the matter into the court of justice. From the expressions used in the second letter, it is certain that this officer was stationed at no great distance from Basil's residence, Annesoi. The writer of the note in Migne concludes that therefore Annesoi was in the district of Verisa. This is incorrect. Verisa was one of the towns in the district administered from Ibora, where the chief civil and ecclesiastical officers of a "city and bishopric" resided. The farm from which the corn of Dorotheos, brother of Basil,† co-presbyter with the officer of the Ibora district, had been seized, was in Verisa, in the district of Ibora.

In the task of explaining the false inferences hitherto drawn from these two letters, we have at the same time gained a valuable indication of the site of Verisa.‡

---

* ἐπὶ τῆς Κομαναίων [i. e. Κομανέων] πόλεως ταύτης ἀστυγείτονος (p. 423).

† ὁ ποθεινότατος ἀδελφὸς Δωρόθεος: not an actual brother of Basil, but rather a friend, called emphatically "my very dear brother."

‡ The notes in Migne explain the first letter as written to the officer in Verisa, the second as to the *praeses* of Cappadocia !

It might seem inconsistent with the situation assigned to Ibora that Basil sometimes speaks of it as near Neocæsareia (Niksar). In Epistle 210, Basil writing from Cæsareia in Cappadocia to the people of Neocæsareia, may very well say that he will be near them when he goes to Annesoi, even though Annesoi is beside Turkhal. Epistle 216 is to be interpreted in the same way. On a circular journey for church purposes, Basil came from the south-west to Dazimon (the Kaz Ova between Tokat and Turkhal), and then visited his brother Peter, whom we may assume to have been living on the family property at Annesoi. The first and more natural interpretation is that Peter, the brother of Basil, lived at a place further up the Iris than Dazimon, in the direction of Neocæsareia (Bas. Ep. 216 διὰ τὸ προσεγγίζειν τοῖς κατὰ Νεοκαισάρειαν τόποις). But on more careful consideration it is obvious that after the troubles in Dazimon, Basil went to take a holiday with his brother Peter, and therefore he did not necessarily continue his journey onward from Dazimon. The expression of neighbourhood to the district of Neocæsareia is doubtless only comparative: Basil's usual residence was Cæsareia. Moreover, as Ibora has now been placed, its territory probably touched that of Neocæsareia.

As Ibora is now placed, its situation also suits the statement of Procopius, Hist. Arc., p. 111, that Amaseia and Ibora were both destroyed by an earthquake under Justinian. The most correct form of the name is Ἴβωρα.

The place to which Naucratius, brother of Basil and Macrina, retired, and where he died, was three days' journey from Annesoi, in a wooded hilly district on the Iris. It must have been three days' journey down the river towards Amasia, as this distance measured up the river would take us beyond Komana far into the province of Polemoniacus (Greg. Nyss., vit. Macrin., p. 967).

Araxius was bishop of Ibora at the time when Macrina died; the date of her death is by some authorities given as July 19th A.D. 380, by others November—December 379. Another bishop, Uranius, probably earlier, is mentioned in 'Act. Sanct.,' April 6th, p. 553 (qui Ibororum cathedram exornavit ibique conditus est).*

The territory of Ibora extended perhaps as far as the Halys. In Not. III. occurs ὁ Ἰβόρων ἤτοι Πιμολίας (with the variant Πιμολίσσης) Pimolissa and Ibora were therefore two towns under the same bishop According to Cedrenus, ii., 626 and 642, Pimolissa was a fortress on the Halys (τὸ φρούριον τὴν Πημόλισσαν. πέτρα δὲ ἡ Πημόλισσα παρὰ τὸ χεῖλος κειμένη τοῦ Ἅλυος ποταμοῦ), and Strabo refers to the district of Pimolisa as situated next to Chiliokomon, in the northern part of the

---

* Uranius, along with Meletius and Seleucus, bishops of Amaseia, built a monastery at Amaseia. Meletius and Seleucus were buried there (ib.). The monastery is mentioned by Theophanes, p. 228. It was named Flavia ('Act. Sanct.,' ib p. 561).

territory of Amaseia, but extending to the river Halys.* Kiepert's position for Pimolisa at Osmanjik seems highly probable.

12. VERISA or VERISSA was originally in the diocese of Ibora. It was afterwards dignified as an independent bishopric under the Metropolis of Sebasteia in Armenia Prima.† This makes it probable that the territory of Ibora was inconveniently large, and the southern part, with the town of Verissa, was constituted an independent city and bishopric. This took place after the time of Basil and before 458 A.D. Verissa was assigned to Armenia Prima both in the Notitiæ and in the Epistola Prov. Armen. I. ad Leonem.

These considerations unite in pointing us to the site of Bolus, which fulfils all the conditions; and we see that Bolus actually is the modern form of Verisa. Two passages quoted in L. 13 and P. 12 perhaps mention the direct road from the sea-coast as passing through Verisa.

12. DAZIMONIS was the name of the rich plain now called Kaz Ova, through which the Iris flows after passing through the middle of Komana (Strab., p. 547). Dazimon, which seems to have been a fortress, must have been the modern Tokat, with its strong castle. In the year 860 the Emperor Michael led an army against the Saracens, encamped in an open grassy plain Cellarion ($\chi o \rho \tau o \phi \acute{o} \rho o \nu \ \pi \epsilon \delta \acute{\iota} o \nu$) in the district called Daximon.‡ To understand the events that follow, it is necessary to know what had been the previous movements of the Saracens. The Byzantine writers give no information on this point, but Finlay infers from the Arab historians that they were returning from Sinope. Instead of marching by the regular road ($\tau \hat{\eta} s \ \tau \epsilon \tau \rho \iota \mu \mu \acute{\epsilon} \nu \eta s \ \acute{o} \delta o \hat{\upsilon}$) which led to Zelisa (perhaps a mistake for Belisa, a form intermediate between the older Berisa and the modern Bolus §), they turned aside and marched to Chonarion. Chonarion was near the Byzantine camp, and in the battle which followed Michael was defeated, and fled six miles to a rugged hill called Anzês. The Saracens after vainly attacking Anzês, retired to a grassy plain named Dora ($\check{\epsilon} \gamma \nu \omega \ \pi o \rho \rho \omega \tau \acute{\epsilon} \rho \omega \ \chi \omega \rho \acute{\eta} \sigma \epsilon \iota \nu$ Theoph. Contin., p. 179; cf. Genes., p. 93).

In the year the Saracen army was encamped at Daximon ($\kappa a \tau \grave{a} \ \tau \grave{o} \nu \ \Delta a \xi \iota \mu \hat{\omega} \nu a$), Theophilus collected an army from all quarters and encamped

---

* Compare also Niceph., p. 143, Teubner edition.

† Hierocles, if his list is quite complete, considers Verissa as a part of Ibora; but Justinian (Novella, A.D. 536) mentions it as an independent city of Armenia under Sebasteia, and it is given under Sebasteia in Epist. ad Leonem in 458. Justinian placed Zela and Komana in the new province of Armenia Secunda along with Sebasteia, Sebastopolis, and Verisa, but the ecclesiastical division remained as before. Probably Hierocles is defective, and ought to contain Verisa.

‡ Καὶ καταλαβών τινα χῶρον ᾧ ἐπώνυμον Δαξιμών, ἐκεῖσε σκηνοῦνται εἴς τι λιβάδιον κατωνομασμένον Κελλάριον.—Genes., p. 92. Perhaps ξ should in this word always be corrected to ζ, but the same variation occurs in the name Moxeanoi of Phrygia (Ptolemy and an inscription), who are MOZEANOI on coins.

§ Perhaps it may be preferred to consider Zelisa as an error for Zela, but the story will be equally intelligible.

at Anzes (κατὰ τὸν Ἀνζήν). A battle took place immediately : Theophilus was defeated and fled to Chiliokomon, near Amasia (Genesius, p. 67–8; Theophan. Contin., p. 127–8; cp. Strab., p. 561).

It is clear from the Arab accounts (Weil, Chalifen ii., p. 312) that the Saracens had invaded Anatolia by way of Melitene.* At Anzes Theophilus could ascend a hill and survey the Saracen army in its position.

Dazimon (τῷ Δαζιμῶνι) is mentioned as a town or a district of Pontus, visited by Basil (Ep. 212, 216) on a circular tour, in order to counteract the Arian influence of Eustathius, Bishop of Sebasteia. It was therefore near enough to be under the influence of Sebasteia, and the context shows that it was quite close to Ibora (see IBORA). The situation at Tokat illustrates admirably the circumstances related in the letters. Dazimon was not a bishopric; it must have been subject to the Bishop of Komana. In the Byzantine wars it must have become far more important than Komana, and the title ὁ Κομάνων ἤτοι Δαζιμῶνος might be expected, if the lists were completely true to historical fact.

13. Eudoxiana is placed by Kiepert at Tokat.† The only reference to Eudoxiana that I have observed is in the Latin version of Ptolemy, where it is inserted between Sermuga and Comana in Pontus Galaticus. This could be accepted only as a Byzantine interpolation in the text: some city must be meant which temporarily took the name. But Wilberg's supposition that Eudoixata or Eudoxata of Armenia Minor is meant is very probable. The latitude and longitude of Eudoxiana are hardly consistent with Pontus Galaticus, and agree almost exactly with those assigned to Eudoxata.

Q.—LYKAONIA AND TYANITIS.

1. The roads of Lykaonia and of southern Cappadocia will be most conveniently treated together, and I have therefore separated the discussion of the southern part of Cappadocia from the rest of that country. In the vast level plains of Lykaonia and southern Cappadocia, roads may run in any direction. We therefore get no help from the natural road-lines in determining the sites of cities, but on the contrary we must first fix the cities and then lay down the roads that connect them.

Lykaonia was first formed into a separate province about 371–2 A.D. For some time previously it seems to have been divided between Pisidia and Isauria.

In later Byzantine times Lykaonia was entirely included in the Anatolic Theme. This is mentioned by Constantine (de Them.), and his

---

* The fortress Loulon, which commanded the road through the Cilician Gates, was at this time in Byzantine hands. From Melitene the Arabs would probably advance through Sebasteia.

† In C. I. G., 4184, the statement also appears.

LYKAONIA.

Roman Coins. (Coins of the Κοινὸν Λυκαόνων are asterised.)	Ptolemy.	Councils of 325 and 381.	Council of Chalcedon, 451.	Hierocles, ab. 530.	Councils of 680, 692, 787, and 879.	Notitia VII., VIII., IX.	Notitia I.	Notitiæ III., X., XIII.
COL · AEL · HAD · ICONIENSI ·	Ikonion	Ikonion, 325, 381	Ikonion	Ἰκόνιον	Ikonion, 680, 692	I. 1 Εἰκωνίου	1 Ἰκωνίου	I. 1 Ἰκονίου
COL · IVL · FEL · GEM · LVSTRA	Lystra	Lystra, 325, 381	Lystra	Λύστρα	600–700 (Le Quien), 879	2 Λύστρων	2 Λύστρων	2 Λύστρων
...	Misthion (Orondeon)	Misthia, 381	Mistheia	Μίσθεια	Mistia, 692	6 Μισθίων	II. Μηνθείας	II. Μ[ί]σθεια καὶ Κολώνεια
Amblada Galatiae	Amblada (Pisidiae)	Amblada, 325, 381	Amblada	Ἄμβλαδα	Amilanda, 692, 787	4 Ἀμβάδων	4 Ἀμβάδων	4 Ἀμβλάδων
..	Ouasada	Passalonensis, 381	Ousada	Οὐάσαδα	Aasada, 692, 879	3 Οὐασάδων	3 Οὐασάδων	3 Βασάδων
*ΔΑΛΙCΑΝΔΕΩΝ	[Homonades, Str.]	Comanadensis, 325, 381	Homonada	Οὑμάναδα	Soumanada, 692	5 Νουμανάδων	5 Ὀνομανάδων	5 Μαναδων
*ΙΛΙCΤΡΕΩΝ	..	(Ylistra, 431)	Ilistra	Ἴλιστρα		15 Ὑλλίστρων	14 Ἡλίστρων	12 Ὑλίστρων
⁓CΕΒ·ΛΑΡΑΝΔΕΩΝ· ΜΗΤΡΟΠΟ·	Laranda ..	Laranda, 325 (Isaur.)	Laranda	Λάρανδα	Larandos, 879	7 Λαράνδων	6 Λαράνδων	11 Λαράνδων
*ΚΛΑΥ·ΔΕΡΒ·	Derbe	Barathra, 325 (Isaur.)	Derbe	Δέρβαι	Derbe, 692	9 Δέρβης	8 Δέρβης	
*ΒΑΡΑΤΕΩΝ	Barattha	(Isaur.)	Βαράγγων	Βαρατή	Barata, 680, 692	8 Βαρέτων	7 Βερέτης	15 Βαράτων
*ΥΔΗC·ΙΕΡΑC	[Hyde, Pliny]	Udisenus, 381	Side	Ὕδη		10 Ὕδης (om. VII.)	9 Ὕδης	{ 13 Πασσάλων / 14 Τιβασσάδων }
ΜΗΤΡΟΠΟΛΕΩC· ΙCΑΥΡΩΝ	Isaura	Isaura, 381	Isauropolis	Ἰσαυρόπολις				
*CΑΟΥΑΤΡΕΩΝ	Korna	Kotna, 381	Korna	Κόρνα		11 Σαυάτρων	10 Σαβάτρων	7 Σαβάτρων
..	Savatra	Sobara, 381	Savatra	Σάβατρα	Perta, 787	16 Πέρτων	15 Πέρτων	16 Πέρτων
..	Perta	Perta, 381	Persa	Πέργτα		12 Πέρτου	11 Κάνου	8 Κάνης
..	Kanna	Kanna, 381	Kanna	Κάρνα				9 Εὐδοκιάδος
..	Egdaumana	..	Ὑδμαυτοῦ	Γλαύαμα		14 Γαλβάνων, Γαλμάνων	13 Γαλβάνων ἤτοι Εὐδοκιάδος	10 Πύργου
..	..	..	..	Ῥίργνον	Psibela, 680; Berenoi, 692	13 Βηρινουπολιο-ψιανῶν	12 Βηρινουπόλεως	6 Ψιβήλων

Ptolemy adds Ἀδοπισσός, Χασβία, Παραλαΐς, Ξεωνάτα, Ἀρβίσταμα, Κόγγουστος. Notitia VIII. gives Μίσθεια twice, as an archbishopric and as a simple bishopric. Concil. Nicaen. gives Ikonion, Ambluda, Homonada to Pisidia, Lystra, Barata, Laranda to Isauria.

statement is confirmed by another authority, who mentions that the Anatolic Theme bordered on Cilicia.*

I now discuss the cities in detail, taking first Lykaonia and then the southern part of Cappadocia, and finally the passes across Taurus. The foundation of such a discussion must as usual be a comparative table of the ancient lists; see p. 331.

2. ICONIUM. The site of Iconium has never been uncertain; it has preserved an unbroken history and a single name down to the present day.

According to tradition Sosipatros, one of the Seventy Disciples, was bishop of Iconium, and was succeeded by Terentius, also one of the Seventy ('Act. Sanct.,' June 20th, p. 67). Cornutus, bishop and martyr, in Act. Sanct., Sept. 12.

Iconium was selected by the Seljuk sultans as their capital, moved partly by its central situation, and partly perhaps by the amenity of its surroundings, unusual in Lycaonia. The gardens and orchards on the west and south-west of Konia are still a pleasant feature; they depend on irrigation, of course. The irrigating channels are mentioned in Nicetas Choniata, p. 542 (τὰ τῶν κήπων ταφρεύματά τε καὶ τοὺς διώρυχας, οἳ συνεχεῖς εἰσι περὶ τὸ Ἰκόνιον).

3. LYSTRA is proved to have been at Khatyn Serai by the following inscription, found on the site now called Zoldera, a mile north of the village, by Prof. Sterrett ('Wolfe Expedition,' p. 142): Divum Aug(ustum) Col(onia) Iul(ia) Felix Gemina Lustra consecravit d(ecreto) d(ecurionum). This situation for Lystra was conjectured by Leake in 1820, but subsequent writers had inclined to other views, till Prof. Sterrett's discovery confirmed Leake's guess.†

Artemas or Artemius, one of the Seventy Disciples, is said to have become bishop of Lystra in the first century (Act. Sanct. June 20th, p. 67).

4. MISTHIA or MISTHEIA. The evidence with regard to this city is scanty. It was on a Roman road, for it is mentioned by Anon. Ravenn. It was in the territory of the Orondeis, who had another city named Pappa. Misthia was in Lykaonia, and Pappa was in Pisidia; therefore, the territory of the Orondeis was divided by the boundary between Byzantine Pisidia and Lykaonia, and the two cities must have lain near each other on the frontier. These conditions point unmistakably to the north-eastern extremity of the Bey Sheher Lake. For Misthia there is practically no choice; it must have been situated at the site called

---

* De Velit. Bell. Niceph. Phok. præf. (p. 185 Bonn).—ἐν τοῖς γειτονοῦσι τῇ Ταρσῷ θέμασι, τῇ τε Καππαδοκία καὶ τῷ Ἀνατολικῷ. Still later Seleukeia became a separate Theme, between Cilicia and the Anatolic Theme.

† My own error as to Khatyn Serai ('Bulletin de Corresp. Hellén.,' 1883, p. 318) was due to my observing that the ruins were evidently those of a Roman colony; and as it was not known in 1883 that Lystra was a colony, the proof seemed complete that Lystra could not have been situated there. A year later the first evidence was published that Lystra was a colony, viz. a coin belonging to M. Waddington. MM. Radet and Paris identify Zosta with Lystra (Bull. Corr. Hell., 1886, p. 511).

Monastir between Khiak Dede and Kirili Kassaba, on the Roman road Antiocheia-Neapolis(Kara Agatch)-Misthia-Karallia(Bey Sheher). The mile-stones at Khiak Dede, Kirili Kassaba, and near Bey Sheher, also the inscription of a στατιωνάριος * at Kirili Kassaba, prove the course of the Roman road.

Misthia is very rarely mentioned. It was captured by the Arabs in 712, but probably not long retained by them (Theoph., p. 382). In the reign of Leo (about 900 A.D.) a Saracen army invaded the Anatolic Theme, and laid siege to the castle of Misthia (τὸ κάστρον Μισθείας), but were obliged to retire when they heard of an inroad made by the Byzantine general Nicephorus Phokas into Cilicia. The castle of Misthia may be situated on one of the hills beside Monastir, or may even be the actual city Misthia.†

Misthia is given in the earlier Notitiæ VII., VIII., IX., as a bishopric under Iconium. But in all the rest it is an archbishopric.‡ It was apparently raised in dignity at the same time as the neighbouring Neapolis of Pisidia, and this must have taken place not later than the middle of the eighth century.

5. VASADA and Misthia were adjoining bishoprics, so that it could be a question to which of them certain ground belonged.§ The northern territory between Misthia and Iconium still remains without a bishopric, and at Yonuslar there are the remains of a large and fine church. Yonuslar was therefore the centre of the bishopric which extended over this hilly but well-watered and, in many parts, very fertile region, and its ancient name must be Vasada. Yonuslar means Jonases or Johns. This suggests that the church was dedicated to St. John, and that, as is very often the case in Anatolia, the religious name has supplanted the civil name in popular use, and has thus passed into the modern language. See also pp. 220, 227, 305.

Saint Eustochios belonged to Ousada [read Ouasada]. He was baptized by Eudoxios, bishop of Antiocheia. He then removed to Lystra, where he converted Gainos, his cousin, with his entire household. He was arrested in the time of Maximian, carried before the

* Published by me in 'Bulletin de Corr. Hellén.,' 1883, p. 316.

† The Byzantine habit of making castles on precipitous rocks suggests that this *kastron* was not on the actual site of Misthia, but on some lofty site. It is even possible that the *kale* about a mile west of Selki Serai is meant: it stands on a lofty hill, and is of great natural strength. I did not ascend it, and saw no traces of walls through a glass, but the natives of Selki asserted that it was an ancient fortress. Theodore of Misthia, Cedren., II., 398. I do not know why Misthia and Koloneia are united in Notitia X, unless it be that Koloneia was *in partibus infidelium* and the title was conjoined with Misthia.

‡ In Not. VIII. it occurs twice, first as an archbishopric, and then as a bishopric under Iconium. This is an example of a common kind of error in these registers, arising from carelessness in correcting them.

§ τὸν ἀγρὸν ἐκεῖνον, τὸν ὑποκείμενον τῇ Μηστείᾳ, ᾧ ἐπεκηρύχθη ὁ ἄνθρωπος, κέλευσεν Οὐασόδοις ὑποτελεῖν.—Basil. Ep., 118 ; quoted by Wesseling *ad loc.* Read Οὐασάδοις.

præses Agrippinus, and finally sent to Ankyra, where he was executed (Act. Sanct., June 23. p. 472).

6. AMBLADA, according to the order of Hierocles, is beside Misthia and Ouasada; according to the Notitiæ, it is beside Homonada and Ouasada. These indications would be excellently satisfied by a situation at or a little to the north of Selki Serai, if there were any indication of ancient life there. None, however, is known to exist, and this district belongs to Misthia, while other reasons point to a situation for Amblada, further west, beyond Misthia. Amblada is placed both by Ptolemy and by Strabo (p. 570) in Pisidia; the latter mentions it as on the frontier of Phrygia and Pisidia, and the former as being (with Apollonia, Antiocheia, and Neapolis) in that part of Pisidia which still remained in his time attached to the province Galatia. These particulars are sufficiently explicit to warrant us in placing Amblada on the eastern side of the Limnai (Egerdir Göl) near Galandos.* This situation is confirmed by the statement of Strabo that Amblada was renowned for its wine; now the shores of the Egerdir Lake have always been renowned for their grapes, and, in reply to my questions, the inhabitants of Antiocheia (Yalowaj) and the neighbourhood unanimously declared that the country about Galandos was covered with vineyards, and supplied grapes to their markets. In the middle ages it was said that thirty-six different species of grapes were produced on the southern shores of Egerdir Lake.† On the other hand, grapes, though not altogether wanting, are very little grown on the east side of Bey Sheher Lake, about Misthia and Selki Serai, which furnishes a new reason against the attempt to place Amblada there. I have, therefore, no hesitation in placing Amblada at some place not far from Galandos on the eastern side of Egerdir Lake. Philostorgius, Hist. Eccles., V. 2, mentions that Amblada was in an unpleasant and unhealthy situation, that the soil was barren, and that the inhabitants were rude and uncultivated. The name occurs in a great variety of forms, Amlada, Amblada, Ampelada, Anpelada, Amilanda, &c.; the native form was probably Mlad-a, or Mlad-os, which is hellenised in various ways. The name occurs also as Blaundos, or Mlaundos, or Blados, or Phlaudos in Lydia. Many members of the Society called Xenoi Tekmoreioi ‡ belonged to Amblada, and this fact suggests that it was not far from the north-east end of the *Limnai* (Hoiran Göl). This situation makes it difficult to explain why the

---

* I placed Amblada here in a paper published in 1883 (' Journ. Hell. Stud.,' vol. iv., p. 37). Professor Sterrett, who explored the district, mentioned (on my request that he should examine for the purpose) that there were no traces of ancient life there, in his Preliminary Report. This forced me to retract my opinion (' Mittheilungen des Instituts zu Athen,' 1885, p. 349), but since then he has published both Greek and Latin inscriptions found by himself in the district (' Wolfe Expedition,' pp. 277–8).

† Ritter, ' Kleinasien,' ii., p. 484, after Hadji Khalfa.

‡ See Sterrett, ' Wolfe Expedition,' p. 240, and my paper in ' Journ. Hell. Stud.,' 1883, p. 23 ff.

bishop of Amblada was under the metropolitan of Ikonion; but the examples of Argiza and Theodosiopolis (E. 2 and p. 305) show that bishops sometimes were connected with a distant metropolitan, for some unknown reason. The situation of Pappa and Misthia, in Ptolemy, seems to be south and east of the district which contains Amblada, Neapolis, and Antiocheia; and, when Ptolemy confirms other evidence, he may be accepted as valuable.

7. HOMONADES were a tribe occupying the mountainous region east and north of Trogitis (Seidi Sheher Lake). This situation is clearly demanded by the description of Strabo, as on the Pisidian border, on the north-eastern side of Cilicia Tracheia, and near Isaura (pp. 668, 679), and as adjoining the territories of Selge and Katenna * (pp. 569, 570) among the mountains of Taurus.

There can hardly be any doubt that the inscription (Sterrett, 'Wolfe Expedition,' No. 240), in which the Demos of the Sedaseis speak of ἡμᾶς καὶ τοὺς ὁμοεθνεῖς ἡμῶν, proves that the Sedaseis were one of the demoi into which the ethnos of the Homonades was divided. This inscription was found at Namusa, in the district which has just been assigned to the Homonades.

No coins of the Homonades are known, and this failure can hardly be an accidental one, due merely to the deficiency of our collections. The reason, I think, lies in the subdivision of the ethnos into smaller parts. Hence in later time the Homonades are enumerated in the lists both of Pamphylia and of Lykaonia; some of their villages or towns were in one province, some in the other. One of these towns was, as I believe, Dalisandos, which was a member of the Koinon Lykaonon, and which must therefore be distinguished from the other Dalisandos, a member of the Dekapolis of Isauria in the valley of the Ermenek Su. In a paper recently published in the 'Athenische Mittheilungen des Instituts,' I have argued that Dalisandos was situated at Fasiller, and this localisation seems to me to be correct; but I had not then learned that a second Dalisandos must be assumed in Isauria. I then thought that a border city might have been mentioned in both provinces, but I now find that the authorities for placing Dalisandos or Lalisandos in the Dekapolis are conclusive.

The Homonades, being thus broken into small demoi or towns, formed no political unity and did not strike coins. Dalisandos did, and perhaps such places as Kolybrassos have also developed out of mere villages or demoi of the Homonades. Strabo's account makes them extend from Katenna and Selge on the west to Cilicia Tracheia on the south-east and Lykaonia on the east; and strictly taken this would imply that Lyrbe and Karallia also were towns of the Homonades, not to mention Gorgorome. Possibly even Parlais, if I have correctly

---

* Selge at Sürk has long been an accepted position, and Professor G. Hirschfeld detected Katenna in the modern name Godena.

assigned it, was a colony founded on the edge of their territory by Augustus in order to keep down this people who were in his time a real danger to the pacified provinces. Similarly Lystra on their eastern frontier served the double purpose of a fortress against the Isaurians and the Homonades.

8. ILISTRA retains the ancient name in the form Ilisera.

9. LARANDA is still called Laranda by the Christian population, as well as Karaman, which is the official and usual name.

10. DERBE. In fixing the site of Derbe, the first preliminary is to understand what is meant by Ptolemy's 'Strategia Antiochiane,' which he places in Cappadocia, and which contains the four towns Derbe, Laranda, Olbasa, and Mousbanda. In studying any statement of Ptolemy, the first essential is to determine his authority. In this case there can be no doubt that he refers to the same historical fact as Strabo does (p. 535), when, after describing the ten *Strategiai* of Cappadocia, he adds that in the first century before Christ there was an eleventh strategia consisting of part of Lykaonia, Cilicia, and Cappadocia (προσεγένετο δ᾽ ὕστερον παρὰ Ῥωμαίων ἐκ τῆς Κιλικίας τοῖς πρὸ Ἀρχελάου καὶ ἑνδεκάτη στρατηγία, ἡ περὶ Καστάβαλα καὶ Κύβιστρα μέχρι τῆς Ἀντιπάτρου τοῦ λῃστοῦ Δέρβης)*. This, like the other *Strategiai*, had ceased to exist long before the time of Ptolemy; but we may accept his list as a valuable testimony as to its limits. His list contains only four names, Derbe, Laranda, Olbasa, and Mousbanda; but Appian and Strabo both add Kastabala, and Strabo also adds Kybistra. Of these, Olbasa, or rather Olba, according to the necessary correction of M. Waddington ('Voyage Numismat.,' s.v.) and Mousbanda, are cities of Byzantine Isauria, which was in earlier time called Cilicia Tracheia. Laranda has been already mentioned, and the situation of Kybistra at Eregli is certain. Accordingly, the general position of this eleventh Strategia is certain. It extends from the original frontier of Cappodocia at Kybistra westward and southward as far as Derbe (μέχρι Δέρβης, Strabo), which must therefore be west of Laranda. Considering the frontier line and the position of Ilistra and Laranda, there is hardly any choice left. Derbe must be placed about Zosta.† The situation agrees admirably with the order of Hierocles and Not. I., VII., VIII., IX. It is demanded also by another passage in Strabo (p. 569), who defines Isaurica as containing the two Isauras and many other villages, and proceeds: τῆς δ᾽ Ἰσαυρικῆς ἔστιν ἐν πλευραῖς ἡ Δέρβη. His next words, μάλιστα τῇ Καππαδοκίᾳ ἐπιπεφυκός, refer to the fact that it was on the frontier of the eleventh strategia, an external addition which had been attached to Cappadocia.

* He refers to the same district (p. 537) as τὴν ἐπίκτητον (i. e. στρατηγίαν): τὰς δ᾽ ἐπικτήτους οὐ συναριθμῶ ταύταις, (1) τὰ Καστάβαλα καὶ τὰ Κύβιστρα, (2) καὶ τά, &c. Appian (Bell. Mithr., 105) merely says, "several cities of Cilicia Tracheia, among which was Kastabala."

† This situation was first suggested by Professor J. R. S. Sterrett.

Strabo (p. 535) is clear that this district of Kybistra, Kastabala, Derbe, &c., was in the province Cappadocia, constituted by Tiberius A.D. 17, when the last king Archelaus died, but in later time Derbe and Laranda appear as part of Lykaonia, cities of the Κοινὸν Λυκαόνων. It is not recorded when they were transferred from Cappadocia to Lykaonia, but it is highly probable the title Claudio-Derbe was instituted by Claudius, when he arranged the transference, A.D. 41. Afterwards, when Cappadocia and Galatia were united by Vespasian, the whole of Lykaonia was included in this vast province. Hence Ptolemy is confused in his division of Galatia and Cappadocia, putting part of Lykaonia in the one province and part in the other. The *Strategia Antiochiane* he derived from an old source; for there is no probability that the Roman province was administered according to the *Strategiai*.* If the Romans had kept up this division, Ptolemy's list of the cities in the *Strategiai* would probably not have been so bad as it is.

11. BARATA is very rarely alluded to. The following is the only reference known to me in literature. A saint, named 'Joannes in the Well,' lived in Kybistra with his mother Julia and his sister Themistia. He chose the life of a hermit, and with his mother's consent went out at the age of thirteen to live in the wilderness (τὴν ἔρημον οἰκῆσαι γῆν). An angel met him and guided him, and he went a journey of one day till he found a well, in which he lived ten years. Then a certain Chrysias, ὧν ἐν τῇ ὕλῃ τῶν Βαρατέων,† was brought by an angel forth into the wilderness and buried Joannes (Act. Sanct., March 30th, p. 830 and *add.* 43).

The locality is clear. Joannes went forth from Kybistra (now Eregli) into the plains north-west, which lie between Eregli, Kara Bunar, and Kara Dagh. Barata must be one of the towns on the edge of this desert, and the order of the Byzantine lists, which place it along with Laranda, Derbe, and Hyde, is more in favour of a site in the Kara Dagh, while Hyde was at Kara Bunar, and S. Joannes lived in the treeless level plains between them.

The Peutinger Table confirms this situation. It mentions Barata fifty miles from Iconium on a road leading to the east. This coincidence of authorities places Barata at Bin Bir Kilisse or Maden Sheher ‡ in Kara Dagh.

If I am correct in placing Hyde at Kara Bunar, the order of the Byzantine lists points conclusively and inexorably to this site for Barata; but the conjectural position of Hyde is too much in need of external confirmation to be able to afford any support to other identifications.

---

* Kuhn, 'Stadtsverfassung des röm. Reiches,' considers, on the contrary, that the Roman administration was conducted according to the strategiai.

† One might suspect "Υδη for ὕλη, for there are no trees in Lycaonia, and Hyde was in this country. Perhaps the original text was "Υδη [πλησίον] τῶν Βαρατέων.

‡ Maden Sheher means "City of Mines." No mines are now known.

Still it is important that these positions should in their entirety confirm the order of Hierocles.

As this site, though rather famous, has been very little explored, I may briefly mention the remarkable series of churches, which are well worth a careful examination by students of ecclesiastical antiquities. Sir C. Wilson and I copied the following inscription, which ran along the side walls of the nave of one of these churches: a syllable or two were engraved over the keystone of each of the arches. The remaining part of the inscription began from the east end.

+ΤΟΚΟΛΛΗΠΙΝ	τὸ κολλῆ[γ]ιν
ΕΝΚΟΙΝѠ	ἐν κοινῷ
ΕΥℨΑ	εὐξά-
ΜΕΝΟΙ	μενοι
ΕΤΕ///////	ἔτε[ι ..

The inscription must have begun at the west end, on the left hand as one entered the church, and, after running the whole length of the church, continued on the right side, back to the entrance.*

On the walls of a church, outside the ancient city, there are a number of pilgrims' marks, all of the same type.

ΕΥΧΗΝΗϹΙ	εὐχὴ Νησί-
ΟΥΤΙΒΕΡΙΟΥ	ου Τιβερίου.
ΕΥΧΗΤΕΥΚΡΟΥ	εὐχὴ Τεύκρου
ΠΑΠΙΟΥ	Παπίου.
ΕΥΧΗΝΕΥ	εὐχὴν Εὐ[γενίου?].

Similar inscriptions from Bin Bir Kilise are given by Davis, p. 310,

ΕΥΧΗΙΝ · · · ·	εὐχὴ ᾽Ιν[γενούας?]
ΕΥΧΗΔΟΜΕΤΙΟΥ	εὐχὴ Δομετίου.

and by MM. Radet and Paris, 'Bull. Corr. Hell.,' 1886, p. 512, which may perhaps be restored [εὐχ]ὴ Γεορ[γίου κὲ Ζώ]ης [κὲ] παντὸς [οἴκου αὐτῶν].†

I should be glad if some attention could be given to these ruins, which are perhaps the most interesting in Asia Minor for church antiquities.

12. UBINNACA, in the Peutinger Table, near Archelais, is certainly a corrupt form. Hyde suggests itself as perhaps the original name. According to the following restoration of the Roman road, Hude and Canna were adjoining stations, and their names may have been corrupted into the single Ubinnaca.

* The correction κολλῆ[γ]ιν seems necessary, but the reading seemed clear on the wall. I do not understand in what sense κολλῆγιν, a well-known form = collegium, is to be taken, unless it be "the church of a collegium."

† The three other inscriptions from Bin Bir Kilise, published on the same page, are badly explained, and perhaps not well copied. One seems to begin αὕτη ἡ κατ(οί)κ(η)σ(ι)s Μ(ω)υ[σ]ῆs τοῦ ᾽Ιάσσονος. Another ends μην(ὶ) Νοέβρου ι'. The third begins [ὁ δεῖνα....]ου ἰδίο[ι]s ἀναλώμασι, &c.

13. HYDE. Of this city nothing is known. Pliny says it was a city of Lykaonia, situated on the borders of Galatia* and Cappadocia, and it struck coins as a member of the Koinon Lycaonon. Hierocles mentions it after Derbe and Barata, and Notitiæ I., VIII., IX. have it also after Barata and Derbe, and before Savatra and Kanna. These considerations agree well with the neighbourhood of Kara Bunar. Now Notitiæ III., X., XIII. omit Hyde and mention Thebasa. It is a natural supposition that the omission of Hyde was not accidental, but that Hyde was merged in Thebasa.

14. Alterations were frequently made in the situation of cities during the Byzantine period † : in such cases the lists sometimes, but not always, give the names of the old and the new site side by side. I shall now proceed to show that everything recorded about Thebasa points to a situation in the country about Kara Bunar.

In Not. III., X., XIII., Passala and Tibassada ‡ occur as 13 and 14. There can be little doubt that these two names are a dittography, and that they denote the strong fortress Thebasa in Lycaonia. Thebasa is said by Pliny, v., 27, to have been a Lykaonian city, situated in Tauros. It is also mentioned in the account of the Saracen inroads during the eighth and ninth centuries, when it was a critical point. It was, therefore, situated on one of the roads by which the Saracens were in the habit of invading the Byzantine territory, i.e. it was one of the two roads which met at Podandos (one by way of Tyana, the other by Herakleia-Kybistra), and went south to Tarsos through the Cilician Gates. § Herakleia-Kybistra was another of these critical points at the time ; Malakopaia (north of Tyana) another.

Thebasa belonged to Lycaonia, whereas Herakleia-Kybistra was part of Cappadocia at all times; therefore Thebasa must have been further west, and perhaps on the direct road thence to Iconium. We should then look for it in the neighbourhood of Kara Bunar ; there are there both water and suitable points for fortification. A convenient water supply in this dry plain was of course an object of the first importance for the Saracen invaders.

It was a pleasant confirmation of my work that, when independent reasoning had led me at different times to place Thebasa and Hyde as I have done, I then observed that the result explained the omission of Hyde in Not. III., X., XIII. We have one of the numerous cases of

---

* He uses the name in the sense of the province Galatia, in which Lykaonia was included.

† I.e. a new centre grew up, and the mass of population collected there.

‡ Tibassada; with the termination compare Tymbriada, a form of Tymbrias. ΠΑΣΣΑΛΑ = ΤΙ[Β]ΑΣΣΑΔΑ.

§ Loulon was in Saracen hands at the time when Thebasa is mentioned, and consequently invasions were as a rule made through the Cilician Gates (see below).

correspondence between a city in the low ground, Hyde, and a strong fortress on a rock, Thebasa. Corresponding examples are—

> Prymnessos and Akroenos
> Kolossai and Chonai
> Pessinus and Justinianopolis-Palias

It is possible that some MS. Notitia may yet be found with the entry Ὕδη ἤτοι Θήβασα.

15. It must be acknowledged that the above conditions are not very definite, and that they would be fairly well fulfilled if Hyde and Thebasa were situated further north-west at Kara-ang-Kapu, where there is a very strong castle on a lofty hill, rising on three sides right out of the Lycaonian plain, and close to the Cappadocian frontier. This might seem to suit the position of Ubinnaca on the Peutinger Table much better; for Ubinnaca there seems to be placed on a road from Archelais to Tyana, passing west of Hassan Dagh, and therefore through Kara-ang-Kapu. The only difficulty in the way of this is that Argos or Argeos seems to be the name of the castle above Kara-ang-Kapu, and that I feel very doubtful whether a road west of the Hassan Dagh can ever have been in use. My opinion, after traversing the road, was that it can at no time have been the route from Archelais to Tyana, and that no Roman road passed through this rocky, dry, and barren country on the western skirts of the Hassan Dagh. Moreover, it is hardly an admissible supposition that a city striking coins could have existed in such a miserable situation as Kara-ang-Kapu.

The conditions would not be well fulfilled if Hyde and Thebasa are supposed to have been situated at Ambararassi: (1) I think there is no hill there which could become a Byzantine fortress: (2) Kastabala was more probably situated there; (3) the corruption Ubinnaca in the Peutinger Table then remains unexplained.

Thebasa was fortified by Nicephorus A.D. 805, along with Ankyra and Andrasos. In 806 Harun-al-Rashid occupied Tyana, and built a mosque there; he then captured Herakleia, Thebasa, Malakopaia, Sideropalos, and Andrasos, which in the Arab account are given as Herakleia, Sakaliba (Byzantine Λοῦλον, called by Joan. Chald. Hisn Assakaliba, the bulwark of Tarsos), Dabesa (apparently Thebasa), Safssaf, Kunia or Malkunia (apparently Malakopaia), and Dsu-l-kala.* As soon as Harun

---

* As I quote this list, I may here give a discussion of the names, which might more suitably be given below in R. In this list Safssaf and Dsu-l-kala seem to correspond to Andrasos and Sideropalos. Safssaf means " willow," and in Turkish Sogud (Suyut), which has the same meaning, is a common village name.

Safssaf was taken by the Saracens in a raid, A.D. 797, when Harun penetrated as far as Ankyra (Weil, ' Gesch. d. Khalif.,' ii. 470). Theophanes mentions a raid of the Saracens in 796, which reached Amorion (p. 470). The two are possibly the same,

retired, Nicephorus refortified the same places, and even ravaged Cilicia about Mopsouestia and Anazarbos; but Harun again sent an army, and once more captured Thebasa.

Theodosius, bishop of the Catholic Church in Ide, signed the will of Gregory of Nazianzos. He is, doubtless, Bishop of Hyde.

Pliny mentions the Thebaseni in Galatia, i.e. the Roman Province, which included Lykaonia. Mordtmann, not observing this, distinguishes the Galatian from the Lykaonian Thebasa, and identifies the former with Pteria ('Münch. Sitzungsber.,' 1860, p. 178, ff.).

Here is the most convenient place to discuss the south-western corner of Cappadocia, which is properly a part of Strategia Tyanitis, but is by Ptolemy separated from it. It contains two cities, Kybistra and Kastabala.

16. KYBISTRA was situated where the modern Eregli stands, in an open well-watered situation, a very city of orchards. Such a situation was not suited for the troubled times of Byzantine warfare, and during the eighth and ninth centuries we often hear of a fortress Herakleia, which is proved to have been close to Kybistra, and united with it in one bishopric by an entry in Notitia X., 96: τὰ Κύβιστα ἤτοι τὰ Ἡρακλέους. The name of the fortress has been preserved in the modern form Eregli; its precise site is to be looked for on some hill in the neighbourhood.

Kybistra is mentioned by Cicero (ad Fam., xv. 4) as in Cappadocia, near the boundary of Cilicia, and not far from Taurus.

Herakleia-Kybistra was captured by Harun in 805, and by Almamun in 832 A.D.

Kybistra-Herakleia was originally a bishopric under the metropolis Tyana, but it was formed into an archbishopric under the Patriarch Constantine (1059-64, Not. X. 96). It is mentioned in the list of arch-bishoprics in Not. X.* and XI. This event probably marks the recognition by the Church of the fact that great part of Cappadocia now passed into Mohammedan hands, but Kybistra still remained in Byzantine possession, and it therefore became an archbishopric; though the names

but I prefer to distinguish them, for my principle is (p. 345) to follow our authorities as far as possible, and not try forcibly to identify every raid mentioned by Arab historians in the unceasing frontier wars with some event described by Byzantine writers. We shall therefore regard the obvious resemblance of the names Sideropalos and Dsu-l-kala as accidental; we shall distinguish the raid on Safssaff and Ankyra from that against Amorion, and take the former as a probable proof that Safssaff was on the road from the Cilician Gates to Ankyra. Andrasos (p. 368) then was not Safssaff, and must therefore be Dsu-l-kala. Cf. Theophan., p. 482; Weil, 'Gesch. d. Khalifen,' ii. 160; Edrisi Jaubert, ii. 301. But see Addenda.

* It therefore occurs twice in Not. X., as an archbishopric, 96, and as a bishopric, 129, a typical instance of the carelessness with which these registers were kept. The actual words of Not. X., 96, might apply to another Constantine, 1153-5, but the explanation given in the text shows that this date is unsuitable, as Cappadocia was entirely in Turkish hands at that time. Nazianzos was made an archbishopric by Romanus Diogenes 1067-71.

of Tyana, &c., were retained as bishoprics, yet they were really *in partibus infidelium*.

In the year 1069 Romanus IV. advanced from Sebasteia (Sivas) against the Turks who were ravaging Lykaonia. He came as far as Kybistra-Herakleia (τῆς λεγομένης Ἡρακλέους κωμοπόλεως). The road which he took must have been by Cæsareia and Tyana. Here he heard that the Turks, after capturing Ikonion, had gone away; and he altered his plans, and sent part of his forces into Cilicia.

17. KASTABALA. Ptolemy mentions KHASBIA in Lykaonia: this is an obvious corruption; and Kastabala is the probable correction. Strictly, Kastabala ought to be in his *Strategia Antiochiane*, but different authorities are followed by him in the lists of Antiochiane and of Lykaonia.

Kastabala is mentioned by Pliny, VI. 3, without any precise indication of locality, as a city of Cappadocia. It is mentioned by Ptolemy in the corruption Khasbia as of Lykaonia. It must therefore have been on the frontier west of Kybistra, which was always reckoned in Cappadocia, and east of Laranda. This agrees with Strabo, who twice mentions Kastabala (p. 535 and 537) along with Kybistra, as a pair of towns, not far from Tyana, but nearer Mount Tauros. When Kybistra is fixed at Eregli, it is a natural and probable conclusion that Kastabala is at Ambararassi.

Another Kastabala was situated on the Pyramos, and bore also the name Hieropolis. The lucid statement of M. Imhoof-Blumer (*Monnaies Grecques*, p. 353) points to a different conclusion from that which he draws. The coins which he there describes were probably all struck by a city of Cilicia proper, situated near the river Pyramos: the exact site of the city still remains to be discovered, and the Antonine and Jerusalem Itineraries are unfortunately confused and inaccurate in this part. I should look for it on the Pyramos near Osmanie.

A cutting conducts the road across the rocks immediately beyond Kastabala, two miles before reaching the end of the lake, and about 19 miles from Kybistra.

Katabatala (τὴν τῶν Μανιχαίων πόλιν), which was captured by Basil's generals (A.D. 876) at the time when he himself was taking Loulon and Melouos, can hardly be Kastabala (Theophan. Contin., 278), but is more probably in Armenia, near Tephrike, Argaous, and the other Paulician cities (Lokana, Tauras or Taras, Amara: Theoph. Cont., 267, 278, Cedren, ii. 154, 207).

If Kastabala was a fortress in this situation, why is it never mentioned as an important point in the Saracen wars? The reason is, I think, as follows:—Kastabala was a fortress of the kind which was usual in the time of the Greek kings and of the Roman empire, conveniently situated near a great road, and depending for its strength mainly on artificial fortification. But almost all the fortresses which were important in the

Saracen wars were perched on lofty and hardly accessible rocks; such were Loulon, Khonai, Akroenos, Sozopolis, Justinianopolis - Palias, Kharsianon Kastron, and many others. Kastabala was not sufficiently defensible, and fell into decay early in the Byzantine period.

18. ISAUROPOLIS is mentioned by Hierocles and at the Council of Chalcedon (A.D. 530 and 451). It is never mentioned in any of the Notitiæ. But Zeno, providing in one of his laws that every city should have the right to be seat of a bishop made a special exception of Isauropolis, which went along with Leontopolis.* Leontopolis is mentioned as an autokephalous diocese in the Notitiæ.

Isaura was situated on the high and strong hill now called Zengibar Kale; it was discovered by Hamilton. MM. Radet and Paris wrongly infer, from an inscription which they have published in ' Bull. Corr. Hell.,' 1887, p. 67, that Isaura was a Roman colony. The words on which they rely, Ἰσαυρέων ἡ βουλὴ καὶ ὁ δῆμος οἵ τε συμπολιτευόμενοι Ῥωμαῖοι, do not, as Professor Mommsen informs me, justify such an inference.

Hilarius, bishop of the Catholic Church τῆς κατὰ Ἰσαυρίαν (not ἐν, which is used in the same passage with regard to the town of Hyde [Ἴδη]), signed the will of Gregory of Nazianzos.

19. KORNA is mentioned by Ptolemy and by Hierocles, and a bishop of Korna (Cotnensis) was present at Concil. Constantinop. 381, and another at Concil. Chalced. 451. It never occurs in the Notitiæ. The order of Hierocles suggests a position either between Derbe, Isauropolis, and Lystra, or a little to the west of Iconium; the authority of Ptolemy leans in the same direction. No other evidence is known to me. No reason for its disappearance after Justinian's time is known: it may have been merged in another bishopric. Similarly, Isauropolis disappears from all lists later than Hierocles. It is possible that the two phenomena are connected, which would lend additional probability to the situation of Korna near Isauropolis.

20. SAVATRA, or SOATRA, is fixed with a degree of certainty unusual in Lycaonia: it was on the direct road from Laodicea Katakekaumene to Archelais, as has been shown above; it was not far from Archelais-Garsaoura (Strab., p. 568); it was in the waterless Lycaonian plains, supplied by deep wells with water which was sold. These indications point clearly to the ruins, four hours south-west from Eskil,† which are extensive. It cannot be so far east as Sultan Khan or Eshaya, where there are abundant springs of water: and it can hardly be further west than the site above-mentioned, since it was not far from Archelais.

Professor Sterrett has placed Savatra at Obruklu; but that situation contravenes the conditions, for it is not on the road Laodicea to Archelais,

---

* The law is quoted above, in the introduction.

† I examined these ruins in 1886, when travelling with Mr. H. A. Brown. We took the straightest possible road from Tyriaion and Laodiceia Katakekaumene to Archelais.

and it derives its water, not from wells, but from a lake; moreover, Obruklu would rather be called near Iconium than near Archelais.

21. KOROPASSOS, a Lycaonian village, 120 stadia from Archelais on the road to Savatra, Laodicea, and Ephesos (Strab., p. 568, 663). It is also mentioned in the Peutinger Table in the corrupt form Comitanassos, which perhaps results from a confusion with Parnassos on a neighbouring road. It should easily be found between Sultan Khan and Ak Serai. Koropassos is probably to be read in place of the corrupt name Adopissos, which Ptolemy places precisely in this north-eastern corner of Lycaonia.

Koropassos is to be distinguished from the city Koropissos of Ketis in Isauria (Cilicia Tracheia), whose situation is discussed below.

22. KANNA is placed by the order of the Byzantine lists in north-eastern Lycaonia, in the neighbourhood of Savatra and Perta. Ptolemy agrees, placing it near Adopissos to the south. These considerations point to the south-western skirts of Hassan Dagh, south of Kara-ang-kapu, on the hill over which is the great fortress Argos. A bishopric is required for this district, and all the conditions agree with the view that Kanna was that bishopric.

23. ARDISTAMA is placed by Ptolemy in the north-western part of Lycaonia. It still retains its ancient name in the form Arissama (which should probably be spelt Arrissama), north-west of Kara Bunar, and not very far from Kara-ang-kapu. It was not a bishopric, being probably merged in Kanna (or possibly in Hyde).

24. PERTA is by an examination of the very uncertain road Archelais-Pessinus placed at Eskil, but, in the uncertainty as to the number and order of the stations on this road, the possibility must be left open that it was situated at some other site in the north part of Lycaonia. It is apparently intended in the Table to be 32 miles from Archelais. A situation near Eskil would agree admirably with the order of Hierocles. The Notitiæ always place Perta last, which prevents any inference from their order.

25. GLAUAMA appears to be the correct form of a name which appears as Egdana, Γλαύαμα, Γάλβανα, Γάλμανα, Γάλβανος, Ἐκδαύμανα. In the Notitiæ it appears always with the addition EUDOKIAS (ἤτοι Εὐδοκιάς). An examination of the road Archelais-Pessinus on the Peut. Table leads us to place it at Inevi, and the order of Hierocles and of the Notitiæ favours a situation on the northern frontier of Lycaonia; but, considering how very uncertain are stations on this road, it must be left quite open to place Glauama at some other site on the west side of Lake Tatta.

The double name makes it probable that there were two sites included in one bishopric, and that Eudokias was a foundation of the fifth century, in a situation of the later type,* while Glauama was at a site of the Roman type.

26. VERINOPOLIS or PSEBILA is mentioned in the 'Notitiæ,' but not in

* The favourite Byzantine situation was on a lofty or a precipitous hill.

Hierocles.   Theodosius, bishop τῆς Βηρηνῶν πόλεως, τῆς Ψιβήλων πόλεως, was present at Concil. Constantinop. iii., A.D. 680, and at Concil. Quinisext. A.D. 692.   The city must be distinguished from Verinopolis or Stauros in Galatia Prima, of which the bishop Stephanus was present at the same Council, 692.

Verina was wife of the emperor Leo (457 to 474), and we should expect that Verinopolis was raised to the rank of a city and bishopric during that period, or else during the reign of Zeno, husband of her daughter Adriane, when she retained some influence (474 to 491 A.D.). It ought in that case to be mentioned by Hierocles; its failure may be due to the loose way in which the ecclesiastical registers were kept.

Leontius of Sibila, Sibilla, or Sibêla signs among the Isaurian bishops at Concil. Nicæn. ii., A.D. 787. This place seems to be the same as Sybala or Syballa, mentioned in Isauria by Notitiæ III., X.   The question arises whether this Isaurian bishopric can be identified with the Lycaonian Psebila or Psibela ; and, considering how loosely the lists were kept, the mere fact that Notitiæ III. and X. mention both, does not absolutely disprove their identity. If they are identical, the city must be placed on the frontier of the two provinces. Le Quien takes this view. It is indeed clear that Sibila was in the northern part of Isauria (see T, 24), and therefore near the Lykaonian frontier ; but my rule is to accept the authority of the Notitiæ where no clear reason is seen to discredit them. It is therefore more probable that Notitiæ III. and X. are to be followed, and in that case the order of all Notitiæ suggests a situation for Psebila in the northern part of Lykaonia. No other evidence is available, but it is worth while to allude to the possibility that the otherwise unknown Pegella, mentioned in the Peutinger Table north of Perta, may be a corruption of Psibella.

The frontier between Byzantine Galatia and Lykaonia lies between Glauama and Petinessos.   Now, the furthest north point to which Lykaonia can ever have extended on the west is between Atlan and Piri-Bey-li (the latter in Galatia Amoriana), therefore it is very unlikely to have extended further north on the east side than Inevi. The country and the roads near Lake Tatta are almost unknown, only a part of it having been seen by Ainsworth.

27. SEIOUATA, placed by Ptolemy in the north-west of Lykaonia, is otherwise unknown. Possibly it is a corruption of Saouatra, which is wrongly given by Ptolemy in Isauria : he also gives Olba and Antiocheia twice.

28. PYRGOS occurs on the Peutinger Table between Savatra and Iconium, or perhaps between Savatra and Laodiceia. A bishopric of Pyrgoi is mentioned, Not. III., X., XIII. Hierocles has Πίργον. which is probably a corruption of the same name, and his order would suit admirably a situation in the north-western part of Lykaonia. Now the great extent of territory north and north-west of Laodicea seems to require a bishopric,

and in this quarter, a little off the road Sauatra-Laodicea, is a place Orbugh,* which seems to preserve the ancient name. The town Anydroi Pyrgoi, disguised in Theophanes, p. 467, according to the text and index of De Boor, as Anydroi, on a road leading from Amorion to Cilicia, is evidently the bishopric in question: it was clearly situated in this district.

Another place named Pyrgos is mentioned by Tagenon on the march of Frederick Barbarossa from Iconium to Laranda. The details of the march are as follows :—

May 23. Went out of Iconium to a hortus regius, and stayed there in plenty. This hortus is one of the gardens described above.

,, 26. Started thence and came to XL Fontes.

,, 27. Reached large stream of potable water; the stream is now called Tcharshembe Su.

,, 28. A large village, with vineyards.

,, 29. Pyrgos.

,, 30. Laranda, quae dividit Ciliciam, id est, Armeniam, a Lycaonia. Thence they crossed the mountains after reaching some Christian villages, and on the mountains the Prince of Sibilia came to meet them : est autem Sibilia castrum munitissimum, et Marchia Christianorum . . . defensatur.

June 6. Bridge over Selephica stream; they cross, and thence difficult road lies before them: the bridge must be over the river south of Mut.

,, 10. Selefke. The Emperor is drowned.

This route seems to follow the modern track from Konia by Cassaba, near Ilisra, to Laranda, and Pyrgos must be Cassaba, the walls of which are still a remarkable monument. We cannot identify this Pyrgos with the Byzantine town (see Addenda).

It is most convenient to allude at this point to the Strategia Tyanitis, and the cities which it contains.

29. TYANA has long been known at Kiz Hissar, called by some writers Kilisa Hissar. It is certainly a various form of Xenophon's Dana ; the two varieties being attempts to represent in Greek an Anatolian name.†

30. CÆNA and HALALA-FAUSTINOPOLIS, are to be looked for at due distances on the road from Tyana to the Cilician Gates. Faustinoplis must be near Pashmakji ; it derived its name from the elder Faustina, who died there.

31. ANDABALIS is still called Andaval, 16 miles north of Tyana on the road to Sasima, Cæsareia-Mazaka, Colonia Archelais, and Mokissos.

---

* It is called Obruklu in maps, but Orbugh approximates nearer to the local pronunciation, and the Salname has Obruk. Obruk is a Turkish word meaning water-jar, and perhaps the true old form Orbugh (Πύργος) has been modified by popular etymology so as to give a name with a meaning.

† Called also Eusebeia, and Colonia Antonina.

32. PASA or PASPASA was near Tyana. Gregory Nazianzen (Ep. 163), mentions a certain George, with the epithet Πασπασηνός,* and Euphrantes, bishop of Tyana, stated at Concil. v., that this George was head of the monastery of Pasa, 12 miles from Tyana (Acta Conc. v., pp. 447–8, Mansi, ix. 258).

33. XANXARIS. The hot baths of Xanxaris† are mentioned only by Gregory Nazianzen, who visited them in A.D. 381. He was residing at Arianzos, his farm near Nazianzos; and he speaks of his visit to the baths as having led him rather far from home (περαιτέρω προήγαγεν). His visit to the baths gave him the hope, almost the certainty, of meeting Olympius, the governor—this, of course, means governor of Cappadocia Secunda.

This proves that the baths of Xanxaris were a usual resort of the people of Tyana, and were not very far from that city. They are still a favourite resort of the inhabitants of this district; they are situated between Bor and Nigde, a little off the direct road (on the north side, I think), and are called simply "the Hamam."

At the baths there was a monastery, and Gregory mentions that the head was much troubled τῇ τοῦ δρόμου φροντίδι, which seems to imply that he had to look after the service of post-horses on the public road. The Hamam lies beside the road from Tyana to Andabalis, and must be about 10 or 12 miles from Tyana; the monastery, therefore, is evidently that of Pasa. Beside Andabalis was an imperial estate, where the fine Cappadocian horses were bred, called "equi Palmatiani" in the fourth century after Palmatius, who apparently was the lessee or superintendent of the estate. Pasa or Xanxaris was apparently on this estate.

34. BAZIS, given by Ptolemy in Tyanitis, is an interesting word. The feminine personal Cappadocian name Bazeis is certainly connected with it. It is derived from Old Persian baga, "god," Phrygian Bagaios, "Zeus," and is the seat of Zeus Asmabaios, near Tyana, described by Strabo, p. 537; Philostratus, Vit. Apoll., i. 4; and Ammianus, xxiii. 6.

35. DRAGAI: Δράται and Δάγραι are the readings of Ptolemy. Comparing Tracias of the Peutinger Table, we see that Δράγαι is probably the correct reading. It was situated near Tyana, on a Roman road; but the Table is here so confined, that we may hesitate to accept its authority that the road in question led from Tyana to Archelais. This seems to be false, for we know all the stations on this road very well, it being described, stage by stage, in the Pilgrims' route.‡ But I shall proceed to show that Dragai is probably the name of the imperial estate near Andabalis, and therefore lay on the road from Tyana to Archelais.

---

* Var. lect. Πασπασινός, Παπηνός, Παστηνός, Πασσηνός. See Addenda.

† Some edd. read Ζανζαρίδος, Greg. Naz., Ep. 125, 126.

‡ The view I formerly took, that the Table shows a road going from Tyana to Archelais by Canna and Dragai on the west side of the Hassan Dagh, seemed to me to be untenable when I traversed that road (see HYDE).

Drizes or Drizion is several times mentioned by the Byzantine writers, and, if it can be proved to be in this neighbourhood, the various forms of the name may be identified as renderings of a single native name.*

The first reference to Drizion or Drizes might perhaps seem on a cursory glance to demand a situation further south. In the year 975 John Tzimiskes returned from Syria to Constantinople : on the march he was extremely annoyed to see that the rich estates, Longias and Drizes, which had been recovered from the Saracens by long and bloody wars, had been seized by the chamberlain Basil.† But most authorities speak of Anazarbos and Podandos instead of Longias and Drizes, and it would therefore appear that Longias was an estate near Anazarbos, and Drizes near Podandos. Longinias is elsewhere recorded ‡ to have been a Cilician estate, and probably Longinias should be read for Longias in Leo Diaconus. As to Drizes there is no possibility that a rich and fertile estate existed in the pass of Podandos, and we must look for it at the north end in the plain of Tyana. The details show that these two estates had formerly been imperial property, illegally seized by Basil, and hence arose the anger and bitter reproaches of the emperor against him. The imperial estate of Drizes may probably be identified with the Villa Palmati, which was near Andabalis, probably lying between it and Tyana (see Addenda).

The position which I have assigned to Drizes is confirmed by the only other reference which I have been able to find to that unimportant place. In 964 Nicephorus marched against Cilicia, taking with him the Empress Theophano and her children. He left Theophano outside of Cilicia ἔν τινι φρουρίῳ Δριζίῳ καλουμένῳ. This shows that Drizion was not far from the Cilician frontier, and near or on the road to the Pylæ, through which he entered. The Byzantine military road, by which he must of course have marched, passed by Tyana ; and at Dragai, or Drizion, a few miles from Tyana, perhaps as being a more pleasant country retreat than the large city Tyana, he left his wife to wait his return (Theophan. Contin., 361). Another account says that he encamped some time in Cappadocia before entering Cilicia (τῇ Καππαδόκων ἐναυλιζόμενος χώρᾳ), and returning after his expedition, spent the winter in Cappadocia, preparing for the next campaign (Leo Diac., 51 ; cp. Zonaras, ii. 201).

36. PODANDOS is well known, and frequently referred to by the Byzantine writers. It occupied a very important position in a deep valley in front of the Cilician Gates (τῆς οἰκουμένης τὸ βάραθρον, Basil., Ep. 14).

Podandos has retained its name as Bozanti. Comparing the equivalent forms Nadiandos and Nazianzos (Philostorg., Hist. Eccles., xii. 7),

* Compare Baga and Bazis, Dragai and Drizes.

† Leo Diac., p. 177.

‡ I have read about Longinias in Act. Sanct., but have unfortunately destroyed the reference which I made at the time, but which afterwards seemed too trivial for preservation. Cinnamus, p. 180, mentions it as a place near Anazarbos. See also Anna, ii., p. 126, and Ducange's note, p. 636.

we see that the " z " in Bozanti indicates an ancient variety in the name. The *regio Podandus* is mentioned by Hierocles, but never occurs as a bishopric, and it is indeed difficult to see where amid the mountains of Tauros could be the population that would require a bishop. Moreover after Cappadocia was divided by Valens into two provinces, Prima and Secunda, Podandos must have been politically in Secunda; but during the struggles that followed, the bishops of Cæsareia retained, for at least a short time, ecclesiastical jurisdiction over the district of Mount Tauros, and Anthimus saw the revenues of the monastery of Saint Orestes in Tauros carried past Tyana to Cæsareia. It is quite probable that they marked this jurisdiction by consecrating a bishop of Podandos, the central point of the Tauros region, but before the earliest "Notitia," this bishopric had disappeared. Podandos had been taken by the Arabs as early as the seventh century. In 530, Hierocles, being under the influence of the ecclesiastical lists of his time, placed Podandos in Cappadocia Prima: had he followed the civil lists, he would certainly have put it in Secunda, for, when Cappadocia was divided in 371–72, Valens made Podandos the capital of Secunda, but soon changed the capital to Tyana.

37. SIALA is mentioned in Tyanitis by Ptolemy. It has been already discussed in Cappadocia, where I have mentioned that ΣΙΑΛΑ is probably a corruption of [ΣΑ]ΣΙΜΑ, a city and bishopric some miles north of Andabilis.*

38. BAGADAONIA is described by Strabo (p. 539) as a plain in the very south of Cappadocia, underneath the very shadow of Tauros, barren, the haunt of wild asses, hardly producing a single fruit-tree. The description applies, not to the plain of Tyana, as has usually been understood, but to the plains north and north-west of Kybistra. Stephanus mentions Bagadaonia as the southernmost part of Cappadocia.

The only other reference to this district is in Nicephorus Bryennius, p. 63, where the name is Gabadonia. In 1073 Isaac and Alexius Comnenus advanced from Iconium to Cæsareia, and they were defeated by the Turks not far from Cæsareia. Alexius escaped with difficulty, and reached after some wandering τὸ ἐν Γαβαδονίᾳ πολίχνιον. This town, mentioned apparently as a familiar place, is in all probability the well-known fortress of Herakleia-Kybistra. Alexius must have tried to escape in the direction of Iconium.

R. THE PASSES OVER TAURUS.

1. At this point it will be most convenient to describe the passes of Mount Taurus, which were under the general charge of the Kleisour-arch, or Guardian of the Passes, in the Byzantine system of frontier defence. The chief passes over Taurus are the Pylæ Ciliciæ, through which led the main road from all parts of the plateau of Asia Minor to

---

* Compare Siara or Simos of the Itineraries, near Sebasteia.

Cilicia in all periods of history. The regular approach was by way of Tyana, as we know from Xenophon and from all later authorities; but there are other two approaches, from Kybistra and from Cæsareia. Other passes, all more or less difficult, lead direct from Lycaonia, to the coast at Anemourion, at Kelenderis, and below Seleuceia. The most important of these is the one which is frequently mentioned as the pass of Andrasos or Kylindros, i. e. the pass leading viâ Andrasos, or Adrasos, to Kelenderis.

The treatise on the tactics of Nicephorus Phokas, the results of his experience in a long course of successful war against the Saracens, enumerates in chap. 23 the chief passes by which the Saracen armies could retire from a foray in Byzantine territory into their own country, i. e. Cilicia or Commagene. They are (1) the passes which lead into the Anatolic Theme out of the Theme of Seleuceia, crossing from Cilicia into Cappadocia or Lykandos, (2) the passes crossing from Kommagene to Melitene and Arabissos, (3) the Armenian passes beyond the Euphrates.* The first head includes the pass of Adrasos, the Cilician Gates, and the pass from Anazarbos and Sis by Hadjin to Komana and to Kokussos.

2. In the expedition made by Nicephorus (before 960 A.D., see under MISTHIA *Lycaoniæ*) into Cilicia, he advanced by the pass of MAURIANON, ravaged the country towards Adana, marched down as far as the sea, and encamped on the banks of the Kydnos, beyond the bridge on the road to Adana. The Saracens who were besieging Misthia, hearing of the raid, raised the siege, and marched in all haste to intercept the Byzantine army on its return. But Nicephorus having stayed only a day or two in Cilicia, retired in safety by the pass of KARYDION. There cannot be the slightest doubt, from the places in Cilicia mentioned, that Nicephorus advanced through the Cilician Gates. The Saracens returned from Misthia, by way of Vasada, Konia, Eregli, towards the Gates to intercept him. Nicephorus, however, had already retired in safety. What, now, was the pass by which he returned? I have no doubt he retired through the Cilician Gates. A few miles north of the Gates, the road divides into three; the left leads to Kybistra, the central to Tyana, the right direct to Cæsareia-Mazaka.† Now Nicephorus cannot have advanced by Kybistra, for, as he must have traversed Lykaonia to reach that pass, there was every chance that the Saracens would hear of his raid too soon, and be able to intercept him. Moreover, it is expressly mentioned that the Anatolic and Opsikian troops were left to

---

* P. 250.—δι' οἵας γὰρ ὁδοῦ διελθεῖν βουληθῶσιν, ἀπό τε τῶν ἐν Σελευκείᾳ κλεισούρων καὶ τοῦ τῶν Ἀνατολικῶν θέματος, καθὰ τὰ Ταυρικὰ ὄρη τήν τε Κιλικίαν διορίζουσι Καππαδοκίαν τε καὶ Λυκανδόν· πρὸς τούτοις δὲ καὶ τὰ παρακείμενα Γερμανίκειάν τε καὶ Ἀδατὰν, καὶ τὸ Καησοῦν καὶ τοῦ Δαουθᾶ, Μελιτήνην τε, καὶ τὰ Καλούδια· καὶ τὰ πέραθεν τοῦ Εὐφράτου ποταμοῦ κ.τ.λ.

† The Cæsareia road separates from the other beside Podandos (Bozanti Khan); the other two fork at Takhta Keupreu, six miles further north.

oppose the Saracen invasion, so that the troops with Nicephorus must have been mainly those of the eastern Themes, Kharsiana, Armeniaca, &c. Hence Nicephorus must have advanced by one of the other passes, and certainly by the regular military route by Tyana, which, therefore, is the pass Maurianon. On his return the pass of Kybistra is obviously even more out of the question than on the advance; hence the name Karydion remains for the pass leading to Kaisari by Bereketli Maden.

After writing out this argument, I turn to my map, and find that the road from the Pylæ Ciliciæ to Cæsareia passes by Bozanti Khan (Podandos) and Funduklu; Funduklu is the Turkish translation of Καρύδιον.*

The point where the passes Maurianon and Karydion forked was perhaps called Gytarion or Typsarion. In 1068 the Byzantine army crossed the passes of Mount Tauros from Cilicia, ἐξιοῦσι δ' ἡμῖν εἴς τι χωρίον τῆς τοῦ Ποδαντοῦ κλεισούρας ἐκτός, Τυψάριον καλούμενον. The emperor went thence direct to Constantinople; hence there is every probability that Typsarion is not on the Eregli pass, but on the direct road from Podandos to Tyana. Mich. Attal., p. 121.

Scylitzes, p. 677, differs from Michael as to the name and the position,—εἴς τι χωρίον τῆς Ποδανδοῦ κλεισούρας, Γυτάριον κατονομαζόμενον.

At this point the army heard reports from Melitene: there is therefore only one point which suits all the conditions,—that point is where the direct road from eastern Cappadocia joins the Tyana-Tarsos road. Here news would naturally reach the army; and it is a point out of the pass in one sense, yet it would be equally correct to say that it is in the pass.

The pass Maurianon was guarded by the strong fortress Loulon, which had been captured by Basil in 878, and the route was therefore open to Nicephorus.

3. LOULON, called SAKALIBA or Hisn Assakaliba by the Arabs, was a frontier fortress of primary importance in the Saracen wars. It commanded the main pass leading north from Tarsos, and its possession was a critical point. Its critical importance is often mentioned,† and the references, if taken strictly, would show that Loulon was close to Tarsos; but a study of its history shows clearly that this is quite impossible, and

---

* The three roads may be thus given, with approximate distances:—(1) Pylæ 12½ Podandos 4½ Yosunlu 2 Funduklu 5½ Kamushli Khan 3¼ Soldakli 12¾ Kaya Alti 8½ Kavlak 5¼ Frenk 2½ Enehil 3¼ Ashlama 5 Gerdeliz 3 Arapli 8 Develi Kara Hissar 19½ Indje Su 19 Kaisari. (2) Podandos 3 Ak Keupreu 3 Takhta Keupreu 19 Pashmakji (near Faustinopolis) 13 Tyana. (3) Takhta Keupreu 13 Tchifte Khan 11 Ulu Kishla 12 Tchapan 15 Eregli (Kybistra) 20 Kastabala. Most of these estimates I owe to Major Bennet.

† τὸ πλεῖστα τὴν Ῥωμαικὴν ἐπικράτειαν ὠφελοῦν ὀχυρώτατον κάστρον (Theophan. Contin., 277), the bulwark of Tarsus (Jo. Chald.), φρούριόν τι τῇ Τάρσῳ ἀγχίθυρον ἐπί τινος ὑψηλοτάτου λόφου καὶ ἐρυμνοῦ (Cedren., ii. 174); ἔρυμά τι καὶ φρούριον τῇ κατὰ Κιλικίαν Τάρσῳ πλησιάζον καὶ γειτονοῦν (Theophan. Contin., 197).

that Loulon was much further north.   It commanded the most important route to Tarsos, and was thus the key which opened and closed the road to Tarsos.   This great road must of course be the road from Tyana through the Cilician Gates.   Over the actual Gates themselves there are the remains of a fortress, and it is possible that is Loulon; but even this position, 40 or 50 miles from Tarsos, seems too far south to suit history, and I should look for a site nearer Tyana.

4. The Thema of Lesser Cappadocia, which lay south of Kharsiana, bordering on Lykaonia and Buccellarii and including Cæsareia-Mazaka, extended on the south as far as the fortress of Loulon, and even to Podandos.*   The terms imply that Loulon was north of Podandos.

5. Loulon is mentioned as the first point in the line of beacon fires, by which news of a Saracen invasion was telegraphed to Constantinople ; this line of communication was discontinued by the Emperor Michael (842–57) in one of his foolish freaks (Theophan. Contin., 197).   It is impossible that a point on the southern slope of Taurus towards Tarsos should be the beginning of this line.   This shows that it must have been situated on the northern skirts of Taurus, and its commander was charged with the watch of the passes.   The beacon fire must have been lighted on some peak south of Faustinopolis, and we might look for Loulon in this neighbourhood.†

The description of the line of beacons is the critical passage to fix the site of Loulon.   The second beacon, on the hill of Argaios or Argea (i.e. Argaia), might at first sight appear to be Argaeus beside Cæsareia-Mazaka, the loftiest mountain in Asia Minor.   But it is obvious that such a line for the beacons is quite impossible, not to mention that a fire, even as far north as Tyana, could not be visible on Argaeus. General considerations made me quite certain that one of the beacons must be on a peak of Hassan Dagh, and in 1886 I went round the western side of the mountain.   At the extreme western or south-western end, an almost isolated peak rises direct from the plain of Lykaonia about 1000 feet.   The summit commands a wonderful view : to

* Constant. Porph. de Them., p. 19.—μικρὰ δὲ Καππαδοκία ἡ νῦν χρηματίζουσα εἰς θέμα, ἥτις ὅμορός ἐστι Λυκαονίας καὶ διαβαίνει μέχρις αὐτῆς Καισαρείας, πλατύνεται δὲ ἕως ἀρχῆς τῶν Βουκελλαρίων, καταλήγει δε πρὸς ἀνατολὰς μέχρις αὐτῆς Ῥοδεντοῦ καὶ τοῦ φρουρίου τοῦ καλουμένου Λούλου καὶ αὐτῆς Ποδενδοῦ.   If, as I think probable, Ῥοδεντοῦ is a mistaken form for Ποδενδοῦ, perhaps suggested by a Latin form Podentos, the inference in the text that Loulon was north of Podandos cannot be pressed.

† The line of beacons is given as follows (Theophan. Contin., 197):—διὰ φανοῦ δηλοῦσιν τοῖς κατὰ τὸν Ἀργαῖον βουνόν, καὶ οἱ αὖθις τοῖς κατὰ τὴν Ἰσάμον, καὶ οἱ τοῖς κατὰ τὸ Αἴγιλον, καὶ τοῦτο τοῖς κατὰ τὸν Μάμαντα πάλιν βουνόν· εἶτα τοῦτον ὁ Κύριζος διαδεχόμενος, καὶ αὖθις τοῦτον ὁ Μώκιλος , ἐκ τούτου δὲ ὁ τοῦ ἁγίου Αὐξεντίου Βουνὸς τοῖς ἐν τῷ μεγάλῳ παλατίῳ κατὰ τὸ ἡλιακὸν τοῦ Φάρου ἐπὶ τούτου διαιταρίοις ἀφωρισμένοις ἐν βραχεῖ ἐποίει δὴ φανερά.   The same stations are given by Cedrenus, ii., 174, Loulon, Argaios hill, Isamos hill, Aigialos (sic), Mamas, Kirkos, Môkillos, hill of St. Auxentios, and the palace.   Constantine Porphyr. (de Cerim., i. app., p. 491) gives them as Loulon, Αἰγέας βουνός, Samos, Aigilon, Olympos, Kyrizos, Μούκιλος ἐπάνω τῶν Πυλῶν, hill of Saint Auxentios, and the palace.

the north lies the great salt lake Tatta, backed by the hills of Galatia ; south extends the huge wall of Taurus, and between lies the hollow Lykaono-Cappadocian plain. A fire at the northern end of the pass would be clearly visible on this peak of Hassan Dagh, and the view extends thence far away north-west in the direction of Constantinople over a perfectly flat plain, on the horizon of which one or two peaks are visible. As the third peak from Argaios is Olympos, obviously the Mysian mount, it is impossible to place Argaios too far to the south, while the evidence about Loulon being the bulwark of Tarsos restricts us to a point not too far removed from Taurus. Not a shadow of a doubt can remain in the mind of any one who ascends the peak which I have described and surveys the country round, that it is the only point which makes the short line of beacons a possibility. On this peak are the ruins of a strong fort, whose masonry seems to be in part Hellenic and in part Byzantine restoration. Standing here, and thinking of Strabo's expression, " Argos, a lofty fortress towards Taurus," * I recognised that the Byzantine name Argaios is the same as Strabo's Argos, the latter form being only a little more græcised.

When Argaios is thus fixed, it would be an easy matter for an explorer to discover the next points, Isamos and Aigilos. The name Argaios, which is given to two of the most striking mountains in Cappadocia, is probably a Cappadocian word meaning mountain. From Argaios the view extends to the mountains north of the salt lake Tatta. If we put Isamos at some peak in the desert west of the north end of the lake, Aigilos must be looked for somewhere near Troknades, perhaps between Kaimaz and Dorylaion, in a point of the hills south of the Tembris. It is more difficult to flash the news across the broken country between Dorylaion and Constantinople, and hence more beacons are needed in the latter half of the way. See F. 56.

6. It has now become clear that Loulon is a fortress commanding the pass between the Cilician Gates and Tyana. Now precisely in this pass lies the bishopric Faustinopolis ; the city of Faustinopolis was built by Marcus Aurelius and named after the Empress Faustina, who died there. Its original name was Halala. It appears probable that the second syllable of Halala is long, and that it is the same word as the Byzantine Loulon.

7. Loulon is called by the Arab historians Sakāliba, or Assakaliba. Prof. Robertson Smith informs me that the word means " Sclavonians," and that, " according to Belādhorī, p. 150, many Sclavonians were placed by the Caliph Merwan II. along the frontiers." Hisn Sakaliba, therefore, is the Castle of the Sclavonian guards." Theophanes, p. 348, mentions, that in 664 5000 Sclavinoi joined the Saracens, and were settled in Seleukobolos near Apameia. In 691, 20,000 Sklaboi, who had been

* P. 537, in describing the Cappadocian fortresses, ὅ τε Ἄργος ἔρυμα ὑψηλὸν πρὸς τῷ Ταύρῳ.

enrolled in the Byzantine army, deserted and joined the Arabs (Theoph., p. 366).

8. Loulon was captured by Harun-al-Rashid, when the Saracen power, reviving under the Abbasside Khalifate, was a second time beginning to press hard on Asia Minor. According to Weil (' Gesch. der Khalifen,' ii., p. 160) the Arab historians place the capture in 805,* but the Byzantine historians do not mention it at all; and the history of the wars from 782 onwards makes it probable that Loulon was in Saracen hands during them. The Saracens could not invade by the Cilician Gates unless this fortress were in their hands. It was probably taken in 782, or soon after.

Loulon remained in Saracen hands at least as late as 811. We do not hear when it was recovered by the Byzantines; but Weil mentions that, after capturing Herakleia-Kybistra in 831, the Khalif Al Mamun in 832 besieged Loulon unsuccessfully for a hundred days. In 833 Le began to rebuild and fortify Tyana, perhaps to aid his designs against Loulon; but he died in this year, and his successor gave up the intention of refounding Tyana. It is apparent that if Al Mamun was not master of Loulon in 831, he cannot have invaded by the pass which it commands, but must have crossed Taurus by another way to attack Herakleia-Kybistra and Tyana.

The great invasion by Motassem in 838, when Amorion was captured, must have passed through the Cilician Gates, and Loulon was probably captured as a preliminary. But still, in the campaigns of 856–63, the Saracens seem always to invade by the passes leading from Kommageno to Kataonia, which makes it probable that Loulon was then a Byzantine possession. It is recorded that Michael (843–67) discontinued the line of beacons from Loulon to Constantinople,† and apparently Loulon passed into the power of the Saracens between 863 and 867 (Cedren., ii. 174).

9. In A.D. 878 Basil captured Loulon, " which had been, by the neglect of preceding emperors, allowed to pass into the hands of the Saracens, and was held by them as a fortress, strong both by natural situation and by its garrison." Thereupon the fortress Melouos voluntarily surrendered (τὸ Μελοῦος κάστρον, Theophan. Contin., 277–8). It is highly improbable that Basil penetrated into Cilicia at this time, for the Saracens were still too strong; and this fact confirms our previous conclusion, and shows that both Melouos and Loulon must be placed on the north side of Taurus. About the year 900 it can be proved that Loulon was still in Byzantine hands,‡ and it probably remained in their power till the Turkish conquest.

* The other fortresses captured at the same time were Thebasa (Dabesa, Arabic), Andrasos (Dsu-l-kala), Malakopaia (Kunia or Malkunia), Sideropalos (Safssaf). Loulon is not mentioned by Theophanes, but is mentioned by the Arab historians.

† Muralt, ' Essai de Chronogr. Byzant.,' i., dates this event in 866.

‡ See the description of the inroad made by Nicephorus Phokas into Cilicia about 896, quoted above in describing the pass.

10. MELOUOS, or MELOE. It is clear from the passage just quoted that Melouos was a frontier fortress on a pass of Taurus. There can be no doubt that it is identical with the Meloe mentioned in Isauria by Hierocles and the Notitiæ. The references to it may be taken to imply that it was on an important pass; and it was probably on the pass from Laranda by Adrasos and Germanicopolis to Kelenderis. Adrasos was further south than Meloe, to judge from the general probabilities of the Byzantine allusions. Hierocles mentions them together, and apparently Melouos has still retained its name as Meliss Tepe, while Adrasos was probably on the Kalykadnos, a few miles further south. The evidence is more fully discussed below.

Melouos cannot be the same place that is called Semalouos by Theophanes (p. 453), which was besieged for a whole summer by Harun-al-Rashid, and captured in September 780, for Semalouos was in the Armeniac Theme. But perhaps Melouos is to be identified with Milos or Milios (see § 11).

I add here a few fortresses which are mentioned during the Saracen wars, apparently in these parts, but which cannot be placed exactly with our scanty information.

11. Milos. In 781 Irene sent all the Asiatic troops to guard the *kleisourai*, and prevent an invasion of the Saracens. A battle took place at Mêlos or Milos * in which the Byzantine troops gained a complete victory, according to Theophan. (p. 455); while the Arab historians say merely the Saracens did not venture to face the great Byzantine force. Milos is, therefore, in or near one of the *kleisourai* leading from Cilicia across Tauros.

12. Koron is mentioned in Theophan. Contin. (p. 360, etc.), as having been captured by the Saracens in the year 892. No clue to its situation is given, except that it was a fortress of Cappadocia. It was in Cappadocia Secunda under Tyana (Constant. Porph. de Them., p. 21). This suggests that it was either in the plain of Venasa, or more probably at the ruined fortifications now called Viran Sheher, some hours south-east of Ak Serai (Colonia Archelais), on the outskirts of Hassan Dagh.

13. Tyropoion is occasionally mentioned as a strong fortress; but in the few casual references to it hardly any clue is given to its situation. When Phokas, who had rebelled against the emperor John Tzimiskes, A.D. 971, and had occupied Cæsareia, found that Sklêros was advancing from Dorylaion against him, and that his own followers were deserting him, he fled to Tyropoion (Cedren., ii. 390, cp. 443). Romanus Diogenes, being dethroned in 1072, and being defeated at

---

* Muralt, 'Essai de Chronogr. Byzant,' vol. i., quotes also the form Milios from another authority, to which I have not access. Milios has a singular resemblance to Melouos or Meloe, the Isaurian fortress and bishopric; for great varieties exist in the forms of proper names in these late times. It is, therefore, not improbable that Milos is to be identified with Melouos.

Dokeia (now Tossia) in the Armeniac Theme, retired into Cappadocia, occupied a fort Tyropoion, ἐπὶ λόφου κείμενον ὀχυροῦ, and finally retreated into Cilicia, [of course by the Cilician Gates]. The enemy, advancing against him, avoided the pass of Podandos (i.e. the Cilician Gates), and crossed Mount Tauros by one of the Isaurian passes.* These passages show that Tyropoion lay in the country south-west of Cæsareia, and between Dokeia and mount Tauros.

After this was in type, the identification of Dipotamon has shown me that Tyropoion is Tyriaion (see PHRYGIA).

14. Μασαλαιός or Μασαλαιών is mentioned by Theophanes (389–90) as in the Anatolic Theme. The only other reference to it known to me is 'Act. Sanct.,' April 3, App. p. xxx, where it is mentioned as a fort in the μέρη τῆς Ἀνατολῆς, to which Saint Nicetas was exiled. Being in the Anatolic Theme it cannot have been in Cappadocia. It may have been either in Lykaonia or Phrygia, but the events narrated by Theophanes agree better with a position in Lykaonia on the road from Cilicia to Akroenos. A town Theodosiana, otherwise unknown, is to be sought on the same road nearer Akroenos.

15. Kopidnados, where the Saracens were victorious in 788 (Theoph., 463), in the Anatolic Theme, is possibly the same as Apadna in Isauria, where Justinian built a monastery (Procop., Aedif., V., p. 328).

16. Kasin, a great cave or underground stronghold, called Matmurah by the Arab historians, which was captured by the Saracens in 776, by smoking out the inhabitants. There can be little doubt that Kasin was in the plain of Venasa, about Sasima and Malakopaia; great underground residences are a special and peculiar feature of this plain, which lies on the direct road north from the Gates.† In 776 the Saracen invasions were beginning anew, and as yet they did not penetrate very far into Byzantine territory. The Arab accounts, indeed, say that they captured Ankyra in this year; but the Byzantine authorities do not confirm this; and it appears incredible, unless there be some place near the frontier whose name is confused by the Arabs with Ankyra of Galatia. Some other references at this time certainly are more naturally interpreted of an Ankyra in the south of Cappadocia, but perhaps they are only mistaken references to the Galatian Ankyra.

Kasin is clearly the same as the military district Kases, transferred from the Cappadocian Theme to Kharsiana about 890. This fact implies a situation south of the Halys, as I have shown in speaking of the Theme Kharsiana.

---

* Διὰ τῆς τῶν Ἰσαύρων εἰς ταύτην ἐνέβαλεν, δυσεξόδευτοι δ' ὄντες καὶ τραχεῖς καὶ ἀνάντεις καὶ λίαν στενόποροι οἱ διατειχίζοντες τῶν ὁρῶν αὐχένα ἐς τὴν Κιλικίαν οὐ μετρίαν ἐποίουν οὐδ' εὔοδον τῷ στρατῷ τὴν εἰσέλευσιν (Mich. Attal., p. 174).

† Theophan., 449; Weil, 'Khalifen,' ii., 97. It is possible that Kasin is a corruption of Sasima, midway between the old form and the modern Hassa Keui.

S. ROMAN ROADS IN LYKAONIA AND TYANITIS.

After thus fixing the cities of these districts, it becomes possible to attempt to trace the roads.

1. The road from Iconium to the Cilician Gates is not given in a direct and complete way in the Table, but it cannot have been omitted, and most of the stations on it are given in a scattered way. It may be restored from the fragments, taken in conjunction with the following road, as

> Iconium 50 Barata 21 Kastabala 20 Kybistra 54 Podandos (*Paduando* in the Table) 13 Pylæ Ciliciæ (*fines Ciliciæ* in the Table)—[Mopsoukrene (omitted on the Table)] —Tarsos.

It is probable that the Tetrapyrgia, which is mentioned twice in the Table, as Tetra between Cibistra and Mazaca, and in full as Tetrapyrgia on the road Iconium-Claudiopolis, has been transferred here from Syria. Tetrapyrgium is mentioned in the tale of Saint Sergius,* who was carried from castrum Barbalissos (on the Euphrates) to castrum Soura, and then made to run, shod with iron nails, to castrum Tetrapyrgium, a distance of nine miles, and thence nine miles more to castrum Ruzaphata. The latter place is obviously Resapha, afterwards called Sergiopolis. Procopius (Bell. Pers., ii., p. 99) says that Sergiopolis was 126 stadia from Soura, and was situated in the southern part of the *campus Barbaricus*, which must obviously be the territory of Barbalissos.

2. A road is given in the Peutinger Table:—

> Iconium L Barata XXXIX Tyana.

The course of this road is determined by the probable situation of Barata at Bin Bir Kilisse. It is therefore really the road to the Cilician Gates, from which the road to Tyana forks at Kybistra. There seem to be some stations omitted: Kastabala and Kybistra, which lie immediately east of Barata, are mentioned in the Table, but on wrong roads.† The road then is to be restored.

> Iconium L Barata XXI Kastabala XX Kybistra XXXIX Tyana.

---

* This reference should be added to O. 1, where I was unable to insert it.

† It puts Kybistra between Tyana and Cæsareia-Mazaka, Kastabala between Komana-Capadociæ and Melitene. Another view is taken by the older geographers. Leake, followed by Kiepert, &c., corrects the Cibistra of the Table to Kyzistra, which is mentioned by Ptolemy in the *Strategia Kilikia*, and accepts the road Andabalis-Kyzistra-Tetra-Cæsareia as a real one. I believe that Cibistra must be understood to be the important station Kybistra in a false position. I am very doubtful also whether Ptolemy's Kyzistra is to be accepted as a real city, for in the Nicene Council, A.D. 325, Kyzistra is given as a bishopric, which proves that it is merely an error or a various form, due to local pronunciation, of Kybistra. Ptolemy, misled by the variation in the name, puts one in *Strategia Kataonia*, and one in *Strategia Kilikia*: in a similar way he doubles Olba as Olbasa, and puts one in *Ketis*, the other in *Strategia Antiochiane*, being ignorant that the latter includes *Ketis*.

3. The road from Iconium to Seleukeia of Isauria coincides with the last to Barata. Then it passes by Laranda (omitted on the Table), ad fines, Koropissos in Ketis (Coriopio on the Table), Claudiopolis (omitted on the Table), where it forks, one branch (probably not mentioned on the Table) going to Kelenderis, the other to Seleukeia. The Table makes this road go to Pompeiopolis instead of Seleukeia. This is probably a mere fault of drawing complicated by the triple occurrence of this city in the Table, twice Pompeiopolis, and once Soloi. This road then may be restored:

> Iconium ʟ Barata—[Laranda]—Koropissos—[Claudiopolis]— Seleukeia.

At Seleukeia it joined the coast road, given on the Table (after some corrections are made) as

> Selinus — Anemourion — Arsinoe — Kelenderis — Seleuceia — Korykos—Pompeiopolis-Soloi—Zephyrion—Mallos—Aigai— Issos—Alexandreia κατ' Ἰσσον—Rossos.

The Katabola on this road, beside Issos, seems to be transferred from the road Issos by Kastabala to Kommagene.*

4. The next road went:

> Iconium xx Lystra (Taspa on the Table) xxiiii Isaura (Isaria)

This road may have gone on by Germanicopolis and Anemourion to join the coast road, but, considering the difficulty of the country south of Isaura and the late date at which it was civilised, the probability is that it went no further than Isaura.

5. The next road has almost wholly disappeared from the Table. There remains only the coast end. It must have passed by Dalisandos (? Fassiller), Karallia (Bey Sheher), Parlais, and Katenna (Godena). It will be again referred to below.

6. There remain four roads whose existence is probable or certain (1) Iconium to Vasada (Yonuslar) and Misthia (Kirili Kassaba), where it joined the road Antiocheia-Neapolis-Misthia-Karallia: this is a probable route, but is omitted in the Table. (2) Iconium to Laodicea Combusta: this road is certain, but is confused on the Table with a route of very doubtful character from Iconium to Archelais, which seems to be described as

> Iconium xx Pyrgos xxiii Savatra,

the continuation to Archelais being missed. Such a road, however, is impossible, for it would not go by Savatra, but would join the road Laodicea-Archelais either at Sultan Khan or at Koropassos. Moreover, it is in the last degree improbable that a direct route Iconium-Archelais could have been of such importance at this period as to find a place in the Table. Such a route rose to importance only when Konia became

* See above, Kastabala.

the Seljuk capital, and Ak-Serai-Archelais, one of their chief cities, was connected by a direct road with the capital.

(3) The Table gives a road Laodiceia-Caballucome-Savatra. This road also is quite falsely given, for we are fortunately able to place Caballucome with definite certainty on a different road. Joannes Cinnamus comes to our aid, and mentions Κάβαλλα (which is evidently the same as Καβαλλουκώμη *) on the direct road from Iconium to Philomelion.

6. The passage of Cinnamus (p. 42) is as follows :—Manuel advanced against the Turks of Iconium by way of Akroenos (Afiom Kara Hissar), where he defeated part of their army, the rest being with the Sultan Masut at Philomelion. The Sultan retreated to a place Andrachman (ἐπί τινα χῶρον Ἀνδραχμᾶν Περσικῶς [i.e. in Turkish] ὠνομασμένον). Manuel now advanced to Hadrianopolis, and encamped at Gaita (still called Aghait), where he again defeated the Turks, and the Sultan fled to Iconium. Manuel advanced again to Kaballa, while the Sultan relied on the defence of the mountains which separate Kaballa from Iconium. Kaballa, therefore, could not be on the road Iconium-Laodicea-Tyriaion-Philomelion, as that road goes through the plain the whole way; and there is no alternative except to place it on the Tchigil road; and the coincidence of name and the existence of remains point to the situation of Kaballa at Tchigil. The difficult pass Τζιβρηλιτζημανί by which Manuel continued his march is either the crossing of the mountains a few miles west of Iconium, or the pass beside Devrent Keui. The road from Tchigil to Konia traverses both. Manuel did not advance beyond Tchivrelitzemani,† but retired by the road that leads to Lake Pasgusa, formerly called Skleros. This lake is the ancient Karalis, Bey Sheher Göl, and Skleros is evidently a Byzantine variant of Karalis.

Kabala is also mentioned by Cedrenus ‡ as a fortress above Iconium (φρούριον ἄνωθεν τοῦ Ἰκονίου διακείμενον).

The only other reference to Kabala which I have observed is in A.D. 824, when Choireas, governor of Kabala, was implicated in the insurrection of Thomas against Michael II. Kabala is an important point in the Byzantine military system, for the governors of Kabala and Saniana are both in situations of great power § (see SANIANA in Galatia).

7. Colonel Stewart describes this route, Ak Sheher to Eleveras 5, to

* Compare Kakkabas or Kakkabokome, see my 'Cities and Bishoprics,' pt. ii. sec. lxviii.

† Nicetas Choniata (p. 72) says he laid siege to Iconium, but this is a pure exaggeration. But even Cinnamus's account suggests that he came very close to Iconium, and his line of retreat suggests that he advanced beyond the junction of the road Misthia-Vasada-Iconium with the road Philomelion-Kaballa-Iconium; the junction is between the two passes described in the text.

‡ Cedren., ii., p. 266. Georg. Mon., Sym. Mag., and Theoph. Contin., all mention the name Kabala, in telling this incident, the flight of Andronicus from Leo IV., in 908, but do not specify its situation. Cp. Zonaras, II., p. 180, ed. Par.

§ Cedren., ii., p. 90; Theophan. Contin., p. 71.

Aghayit 7, to Freis * 9, to Doghan Hissar 17, to Rus 21, Tchir (correct form Tchigil) 29, Derwent 37, Kavaklu 48, Konia 64½. Hence we may restore the road on the Table as

> Philomelion xxx Kaballa xxxvi Iconium.

8. After putting this road on the restored Table, we have also to form the connections Iconium-Laodiceia and (4) Laodicea-Savatra-[Koropassos]-Archelais, both of which may be taken as quite certain. One other Lycaonian or Cappadocian road is represented in the Table—

> [Archelais] xx Salaberina xvi Cæna xvi Tracias xvi Tyana.

Salaberina is unknown. Cæna is given by the Jerusalem Itinerary on the road from Tyana to the Cilician Gates, and has therefore been falsely transferred to its place in the Table. Traciae was an imperial estate near Andabalis, 16 miles from Tyana on this road.

The road Iconium by Kara Bunar to Tyana is described by the late Colonel J. D. H. Stewart as:—

> Iconium 12 Dedem 7½ Karkhu (stone bridge over a stream) 7 Ismii 11 Yerekli Devrent 15 Kara Bunar 21 Bektek 7½ stone bridge over a stream 11 Tchayan (15 Tyana).

This road falls at Bektek into the road from Kybistra to Tyana, and there is no reason to think that it ever was a Roman road.

9. A fragment of the Table still remains unaccounted for—

> Iconium xx Pyrgos xxiii.

and probably some of the far too numerous names between Pessinus and Archelais belong to roads in the west of Lycaonia. It is quite possible that there was a station Pyrgos between Laodiceia and Savatra, and it may be assumed as certain that one or more stations were mentioned on the road which is given as

> Amorium xx Laodicea.

The existence of this last road is certain.

10. The road Archelais-Pessinus appears on the Table thus:—

> (Archelais) xii Comitanasso (i.e. Coropassos, mixed with Parnassos on another road) xx Perta xx Conguso xx Pegella xx Egdava xv Vetisso xx Bagrum vii Tolosocorio xxiiii Abrostola.

Of these, Abrostola may be at once dismissed as being Phrygian in the province Asia,† and Vetisso seems to be the same as Ptolemy's Οὐέτεσσον in Galatia. The distances on this road may be estimated as follows:—

> Archelais xii Coropassos 20 Eskil 35 Inevi 70 Sangarius bridge 25 Pessinus.

---

* Sterrett gives this name Reghiz; the correct form is Egri Göz, "Squint Eye," but the pronunciation approximates to Ereghoz.

† Abrostola is given by Ptolemy as in Phrygia, and there seems no reason to doubt his statement, which gives a valuable clue to its situation.

On the road as it appears in the Table a station Congoustos is given, but Ptolemy places it far west, and it probably belongs to one of the western roads. There remain, then—

Archelais XII Coropassos XX Perta (Eskil) XX Pegella XX ΓΛΑΥΑΜΑ (Inevi).

Here the road forks, one branch goes to Ankyra: the other, which is shown on the Table, goes to Pessinus and Dorylaion. We may restore its course as—

ΓΛΑΥΑΜΑ XV Pitnisos XX Bagrum — Tolistochora XXIIII Pessinus.

T. CILICIA TRACHEIA OR ISAURIA.

1. The map of Isauria, though much improved by Professor Sterrett's journey in 1885, is still too uncertain to permit anything like a proper study of the ancient topography. As I have never travelled in any part of the country, I cannot do more than put down a few notes about scattered points. The beginning of a study of the country should be made from the great roads which lead across Taurus from Laranda to Kelenderis, to Anemourion, and to Seleuceia. The first of these was a Roman road, and it must in all ages have been an important route between Iconium and the sea. But the other roads are also of import-ance. In ancient time the road Laranda-Seleuceia apparently passed by Claudiopolis, but another road has recently been made practicable for wheeled vehicles in furtherance of Said Pasha's scheme to connect Konia with a harbour on the coast. It goes direct from Laranda through Maghra, and traverses a desert country. A study of the list of Hierocles has led me to the belief that he arranges his cities with an eye to these roads. This view can be proved only by a careful exploration of the country, which still remains to be made. Professor Sterrett's exploration in 1885 was very far from exhaustive : he traversed none of these roads, and, though he acutely detected several ancient names in the modern village names, yet no epigraphic evidence to fix any city * was added by him. In brief terms my view is that the three chief roads are—

(1) Laranda Koropissos Claudiopolis Kelenderis.
(2) Claudiopolis Diocæsareia Seleuceia.
(3) Laranda Melouos Adrasos Germanicopolis, where it forked, one path leading to Kelenderis, and one near Eirenopolis to Anemourion.

The grounds on which this view is based are rather difficult to put clearly.

2. The following statistics as to these roads were given me by the late Colonel J. D. H. Stewart.

* Astra and Artanada were not cities.

(1) Akliman (harbour of Seleuceia) to Mut (Claudiopolis), 54½ miles.*

Akliman, sea level.

10½ alt.   2100 feet.
22½ Geuk Belen.
31¼ Noghreen, 1700 feet.

38 Zehne.
45¼ Tareveliler.
54½ Mut, 1000 feet.

(2) Mut (Claudiopolis) to Karaman (Laranda), 51 miles.

Mut, 1000 feet.

9½ alt. 4650 feet.
14 Summit, alt. 5250 feet.
20 Restel Yaila.

31 Watershed, 1500 feet.
44½ Fusandeen.
51 Karaman.

(3) Kilindria (Kelenderis) to Ermenek (Germanicopolis), 59 miles.

Kilindria or Gulnar, over
    Selli Pass.
17 Eleribas, 3300 feet.

26 Tash Oglu, 4500 feet.
46 Zeve, 2896 feet.†
59 Ermenek, 4442 feet.†

(4) Ermenek (Germanicopolis) to Karaman (Laranda), 59 miles.‡

Ermenek, 4442 feet.

16 Kanish Boghaz.
19 Boundary of Vilayet Konia.
30 Bostan Su Keui in Kaza
    Khadim.

31½ Bostakchi Su.
36½ Meliss Tepè.
47 Boyalar.
59 Karaman (Laranda).

Another estimate by Colonel Stewart, taken from another journey, is—
Kilindria to Ermenek, 63¼ miles, time, 25 hours, 10 minutes.
Ermenek to Meliss Tepe, 48¾ miles, time 16 hours 3 minutes.
Meliss Tepe to Karaman, 5 hours.

(5) Laranda to Selefke viâ Maghra.*

Laranda.

21 alt.   5500 feet.
29 alt.   6100 feet.

50½ Maghra, 4590 feet.
(?) Akliman.

Colonel Stewart could not give me any estimate of the roads Akliman
to Maghra, and Kilindria to Mut. The latter is stated by Leake as
18 hours, and the former by my friend Mr. Hogarth as 11 hours §,—
about 40 to 45 miles. The road Ermenek-Anamur (Anemourion) seems
to be very little used now, and can never have been a route of any real
consequence.

3. The most direct road from Laranda to Kelenderis passes through
Mut, and it is generally agreed that Leake is right in identifying Mut
as the ancient Claudiopolis, which is described by Theophanes as lying
in a plain between the two ridges of Taurus (μεταξὺ τῶν δύο Ταύρων ἐν

---

* I think that Colonel Stewart's estimates of distance are too small, owing to his
reckoning that a horse's pace is slower than I believe is the case. His time of march is
Akliman-Geuk Belen 9 hrs. 20 mins., Geuk Belen-Mut 6 hrs. 30 mins.

† Heights of Zeve and Ermenek taken according to boiling-point.

‡ Time, Ermenek to Karaman 22 hrs. 55 mins.

§ Eleven hours in an araba going down hill.

πεδίῳ κειμένης p. 138). The description is understood by Leake to denote the Kalykadnos valley, which is obviously correct. The identification, though universally accepted, is a mere guess, founded neither on actual knowledge of the country nor on positive evidence. The story of Papas (§ 7) might suggest that Diocæsareia was at Mut, but at present I refrain from making a change.

4. Claudiopolis was a colony of Claudius.[*] No coins of this city are known. Perhaps, like Archelais in Cappadocia, also a colony of Claudius, and Colonia in Lesser Armenia, it had not the right of coinage; for the entire failure of its coins, colonial or otherwise, can hardly be due merely to our imperfect knowledge. The situation of the colony was chosen where the great route from the north enters the valley of the Kalykadnos.

5. Ruins are mentioned by Leake at a khan on the road from Mut to Laranda; but at the present day there is not even a village on the road. I shall proceed to show that Koropissos was situated on this road, perhaps at the ruins observed by Leake.[†] The Peutinger Table places Koropissos (under the form Coriopio) on this road, and the situation is probable, for both the importance of this city with its coinage, which is rich in comparison with other cities of this mountainous district, suggests a situation near a great road, and its title, Metropolis of Ketis, agrees. The precise limits of the district Ketis cannot be determined, but the following considerations enable us to place it approximately.

6. Ketis, according to Ptolemy, contains the city of Olba in the interior, and extends along the coast from Anemourion to beyond the mouth of the Kalykadnos. Basil of Seleuceia, according to the interpretation of M. Waddington, seems not to agree with this, for he says that the river Kalykadnos rises in the recesses of Ketis (ἀπὸ τῆς Κητίδος μυχαιτάτων χωρίων); unluckily it is quite uncertain whether the name Kalykadnos was given to the northern or the southern branch of the river. M. Waddington assumes that the Kalykadnos was the southern branch, and this is also the opinion of Ritter and of Kiepert [‡]; if so, Basil is in flat contradiction with Ptolemy, who clearly makes Selentis the country where that branch rises. But I believe that Basil's words [§] must be understood to refer to the northern and much longer

---

[*] Deduxit coloniam Claudius Cæsar, Amm. Marc., xiv., 25.

[†] I find a note that Mr. Davis mentions the ruins of an ancient city at Kestel. between Laranda and Mut: this may be the site of Koropissos, and the remains mentioned by Leake may come from it.

[‡] Kiepert in his latest map has changed his opinion, and agrees with the view here stated.

[§] Καλύ(κα)δνος ὄνομα τῷ ποταμῷ, ἐρχομένῳ μὲν ἄνωθεν πόθεν ἀπὸ τῶν τῆς Κητίδος μυχαιτάτων χωρίων, παραμείβοντι δὲ χώρας καὶ πόλεις συχνὰς, κἂν τῇ πρὸς ἡμᾶς πορείᾳ παραλαμβάνοντι καὶ ἑτέρους ποταμοὺς ἐκ τῶν ἐφ' ἑκάτερα χώρων καὶ τόπων ἐπεισιόντας (I. p. 275 P.) It receives Ermenek Su on right and Maghra Su on left. M. Waddington, making Ermenek Su Kalykadnos, has to face the difficulty that it receives no affluent of any consequence from the right.

branch of the river, and that the name Ketis is applied to the eastern parts of Isauria or Tracheia Cilicia, on both sides of the river Kalykadnos from its source to its mouth. According to this interpretation, Basil and Ptolemy are in perfect agreement. Three cities of Isauria, Koropissos, Olba, and Philadelphia, are proved by the legends on their coins to have been situated in Ketis, and Ptolemy agrees about Olba, but omits Koropissos, and puts Philadelpheia in Lalassis.

7. Olba was situated (1) in Ketis, (2) not very far from Seleuceia, to which it is said to be ἀστυγείτων πόλις, (3) in the mountainous tract above Soli (Strab., p. 672). These references demand a situation east of Claudiopolis, and north or north-west of Seleuceia. Another argument, of a somewhat complicated character, may be drawn from the legend on a coin of Diocæsareia, ΔΙΟΚΑΙϹΑΡΕΩΝ ΟΛΒΟϹ. The native name of Olba was apparently Ourba, or Orba.* The form Olba was grecised to suggest the sense given by the analogy of ὀλβία, ὄλβιος, ὄλβος. Vying with the name Ὄλβα, Diocæsareia invented the above legend. Such competition in legends is very common in the coinage of Anatolian cities. This explanation has any probability only if Diocæsareia and Olba are neighbouring towns : Hierocles mentions them side by side. Where, then, was Diocæsareia ? Diocæsareia is known to have been another name for the Isaurian Prakana from the lists of bishops present at the Second Nicene Council in 787 A.D., when Manzon is mentioned as bishop, sometimes of Diocæsareia, sometimes of Prakana. Now Prakana was captured by the Turks of Iconium, A.D. 1144, and restored to the Byzantines by terms of the treaty of 1147 (Cinnam., 39 and 66; Nicet. Chon., 68). Seleukeia was in Byzantine hands throughout this reign, and Prakana must therefore be further up the country on the boundary between Byzantine and Seljuk territory, which, however, at this period, is quite uncertain, but the circumstances suggest that Prakana was between Seleukeia and Lykaonia, and a frontier town, and it is expressly said by Nicetas to be not far from Seleukeia (τῆς Σελευκείας ἐχόμενα ἵδρυται, p. 68). His authority is confirmed in this case by the order of the Byzantine lists, which always connect Diocæsareia with Olba, Claudiopolis, and Hierapolis. I should look for Prakana on the lower Kalykadnos between Claudiopolis and Seleukeia, and near it, but east of the river, also Olba, which would thus be in the mountainous district above Soli.

Diocæsareia is also proved to have been on the Kalykadnos by the fact that it was one of the cities of the Decapolis, whose limits and cities will be treated below. Saint Papas was forced to run from Laranda to Diocæsareia and Seleukeia before the horses, ' Act. Sanct.,' Mar. 16, p. 420. The road was probably viâ Claudiopolis.

8. Another proof of the situation of Ketis is derived from the legend on coins, ΠΟΛΕΜΩΝΟΣ ΒΑΣΙΛΕΩΣ [ΟΛΒΕ]ΩΝ ΛΑΛΑΣΣΕΩΝ ΚΑΙ

---

* Ourbanopolis in Acta S. Bartholomæi, Aug. 25th; Ourba, with v. l. Orba, in Theophanes. Olba ἀστυγείτων πόλις, Basil of Seleuceia in Vit. S. Theclae.

KENNATΩN. These three countries must have adjoined each other. Now the district Lalassis seems to be fixed with certainty on the upper waters of the Ermenek Su by Prof. Sterrett's acute observation that Lakhlas has preserved the old name Lalassis.

9. Kennatis is known only from coins, as bordering on Ketis and Lalassis. We may perhaps infer that some of the Byzantine bishoprics, which are unknown to the numismatic lists, were cities which grew up in Kennatis during the gradual progress of civilisation in Cilicia Tracheia in the third to the fifth centuries. It probably included the region between Ketis and Lalassis, and may have formed part of the Decapolis. Kennatis and Lalassis were made independent for a time, as is proved by a coin struck under Domitian with the legend KOINON ΛΑΛΑΣΕΩΝ ΚΑΙ Κ[ΕΝ]ΝΑΤΩΝ. These indications, vague in themselves, leave little or no doubt as to the general situation of Ketis, east of Lalassis and Kennatis, and along the course of the Kalykadnos.

10. The third city of Ketis is Philadelpheia. No evidence remains of situation except (1) what can be derived from the order of the Byzantine lists, and (2) the fact that it is not one of the cities of the *Decapolis Isauriæ*, i.e., it is not on the Ermenek Su.* Hierocles places it next to Eirenopolis.

11. EIRENOPOLIS has retained its name as Irnebol to the present day, opposite to Germanicopolis (Ermenek) on the south side of the Ermenek Su valley. It is called Isnebol on Kiepert's map, but Prof. Sterrett† has observed the proper form, Irnebol, though his identification of Irnebol as Neronopolis is impossible, because there is no such city recorded in Isauria or Cilicia Tracheia. Neronias, which occurs as a name of Eirenopolis, is referred by all lists which mention it to the other Eirenopolis of Cilicia Campestris nearAnazarbos and the Pyramos; and I think that all coins ΕΙΡΗΝΟΠΟΛΕΙΤΩΝ belong to the latter and not to the Isaurian Eirenopolis. Leake's attribution of Eirenopolis to the coast of Cilicia Tracheia was founded on a coin reading ΙΡΗΝΟΠΟΛΕΙΤΩΝ ΖΕΦΥΡΙΩΤΩΝ; but this coin cannot be accepted as genuine, depending only on the testimony of Vaillant; and moreover Leake's situation is disproved by the evidence given above that Irenopolis was on the Ermenek Su.‡

Philadelphia then is to be placed probably north of the Ermenek Su, on the road from Germanicopolis to Laranda, and in the country of Ketis.

13. This city Eirenopolis must be carefully distinguished from the Cilician city, Eirenopolis, a bishopric of Cilicia Secunda, an inland city, to be looked for not very far from Anazarbos. In all probability the

---

* I shall prove in a following paragraph that the name Decapolis was given to the district along the Ermenek Su and the Kalykadnos below the confluence.

† 'Wolfe Expedition' in Papers of Amer. School of Athens, iii. p. 84.

‡ It is one of the cities of the Decapolis, or valley of the Ermenek Su. Isnebol, about which Prof. Sterrett (l.c., p. 81) makes no suggestion, is probably Zenonopolis Isauriæ.

coins which read ΕΙΡΗΝΟΠΟΛΕΙΤΩΝ simply, belong to the Cilician city. Its era on coins is A.D. 52. It was on a river, probably the Pyramos, as a coin shows the Good Fortune of the City with a river-god at her feet.

14. All evidence as to the situation of Ketis therefore agrees with the Peutinger Table in regard to Koropissos, and it may be considered very probable that Koropissos was on the road between Claudiopolis and Laranda, probably near Kestel.

15. Koropissos, metropolis of Ketis, must have been an important town. It appears as a bishopric at the Nicene Council, A.D. 325 ; but it is not mentioned either by Hierocles or in the Notitiæ. The only explanation can be that it is concealed under another name. It is not improbable that Hieropolis is the name that replaces Koropissos : that the metropolis should also be the holy city of Ketis is quite in accordance with the analogy of the cities in this district, where the dynasts were priests.

16. The Decapolis of Isauria is mentioned, and the ten cities Germanicopolis, [Dio]Cæsareia, Eirenopolis, Neapolis, Lauzados, Zenopolis, Dometiopolis, Titiopolis, Claudiopolis, Dalisandos, are enumerated by Constantine Porph., Them., p. 36. In the life of Gregory Decapolita Isauricus the expression occurs μία τῶν τῆς Δεκαπόλεως, τῶν πρὸ τῆς Ἰσαυρίας, πόλις ᾗ ὄνομα Εἰρηνόπολις (quoted in ʻ Act. Sanct.,ʼ April 18th, p. 583 : but the day of this Gregory is Nov. 20th). The expression πρὸ τῆς Ἰσαυρίας suggests that they were all in the same district, and this is corroborated by Constantine's remark that they were " over Seleukeia," i.e. higher up the river in the inner country. The title Decapolis is obviously applied to a well-marked district in which there were ten cities. This district must have been along the Ermenek Su. Many of the ten cities are placed there by other evidence, and for the rest the same locality is fixed by this title.*

Of the ten cities, Claudiopolis and Germanicopolis have been fixed at Mut and Ermenek by Leake, and in the preceding paragraphs it has been shown that Diocæsareia, Eirenopolis, Zenopolis,† and Domitiopolis were on the Ermenek Su.

17. Dalisandos is mentioned by Stephanus Byzantius as an altered form of the older Λαλισανδός. The connection of Λαλισανδός with the name of the people Λαλασσεῖς is too obvious to be passed by. But another Δαλισανδός which is mentioned among the bishoprics of Pamphylia, must be distinguished : it cannot possibly be situated among the Lalasseis, for it was a member of the Koinon Lykaonon, and must therefore have been situated near the plain of Lycaonia and on the frontier of Pamphylia. It seems impossible to avoid the conclusion that there were two cities Dalis-

* Another Decapolis is found in Palestine, a third in the Katakekaumene of Lydia. To the Isaurian Decapolis belong Gregorius Isaur. Decapolita and Theodorus Decapolita (Smith's Dict., 34).

† The proper form Zenonopolis is commonly abbreviated Zenopolis.

andos. One belonged to the Koinon Lykaonon, and was afterwards attached as a bishopric to Pamphylia Prima. It was perhaps situated at Fassiller on the Roman road from Iconium to Karallia and Side. The other was properly Λαλισανδός, and was a town of the Lalasseis on the southern arm of the Kalykadnos : the order of the Byzantine lists and the fact that it was included in the Decapolis alike demand this position.*,

18. Three cities, Titiopolis (with coins), Neapolis, and Lauzados, remain, and may confidently be assigned to the Ermenek Su valley, and Prof. Sterrett has once more well observed that Lauzados has retained its name to the present day as Lavdha. As to Titiopolis, the order of Hierocles causes some difficulty (see § 31).

19. The Decapolis gives important negative evidence. All cities not included in it are not on the Ermenek Su from its source down to Claudiopolis: and none of the three cities of Ketis are included, therefore Ketis was not the district on the Ermenek Su, which consequently cannot be the Kalykadnos. Again the evidence is conclusive that Lalassis was the district along the upper Ermenek Su. Finally, all cities omitted from the Decapolis are to be sought in other parts of Isauria.

20. Comparing the order of Hierocles with the list of the Decapolis we find confirmation of our previous results, and a suggestion of more. Diocæsareia is on the lower Kalykadnos above Seleuceia, and Olba is next to it but away from the river, perhaps on a branch road Koropissos-Olba-Seleuceia. Next comes Claudiopolis on the middle Kalykadnos, and then Hieropolis, which we have identified with Koropissos and placed north of Claudiopolis on the road to Laranda. Then Hierocles gives three cities of the Ermenek Su, and thereafter three cities of the north, Philadelphia, Meloe, and Adrasos.

21. It has been shown above that Melouos or Meloe (Môlôê in Hierocles) was situated on one of the passes leading from Lycaonia into Cilicia, and that the ancient name Melouos remains under the modern form Meliss Tepe nearly twenty miles south-west of Laranda.

22. Hierocles mentions Adrasos and Meloe side by side. This order suggests that Adrasos is to be looked for on the same road, and the inference is confirmed by the accounts given of the great Byzantine victory of 960 A.D., over the Saracens, which was fought in the kleisoura leading to Kelenderis or Kylindros. This battle is twice referred to, though the name is not mentioned, in 'Niceph. Phok. de Velitat. Bell.,' præf. and c. 3, p. 191. The latter passage tells that the Saracens were defeated when, on finding one pass blocked (perhaps the pass leading direct to Claudiopolis) they made a détour to take another. Some of

---

* This Dalisandos was πόλεως εἴδωλον ἔτι καὶ ὄνομα ἐν τοῖς ἀφανέσι μὲν καὶ ἀνωνύμοις ἀπερῥιμμένη in time of Basil, bishop of Seleuceia 448–458, ed. Migne, p. 580.

the authors who mention this victory give the name as Andrassos or Adarassos.;* but one account describes it more accurately, and says that the Byzantine army occupied τὴν κλεισούραν τὴν οὕτω καλουμένην, and attacked the Saracens as they were returning through the Kleisoura from a plundering expedition.† The Kleisoura Kylindros is the great pass that led to the coast at Kelenderis (a name subjected to great variations by Byzantine writers). The name, therefore, may be given to one or other of the two routes from Laranda to Kelenderis, the one passing by Claudiopolis, the other by Meloe (Meliss Tepe) and Germani-copolis. The order in Hierocles leaves no doubt that Adrasos is on the latter road, and it is confirmed entirely by Notitiæ III., X., and less thoroughly by Notitia I.

23. Next in Hierocles comes Sbide (misspelt Zeede). We should therefore look for it in the north, and perhaps on the same road, or at least in the same district as Meloe and Adrasos. This presumption is confirmed both by the order of the ecclesiastical lists, and by a passage of Theophanes. In A.D. 475 the Emperor Zeno, with his wife Ariadne, were expelled from Constantinople by his mother-in-law Verina, and her brother Basiliscus. They took refuge in Ourba (v. l. Ὄρβα) of Isauria, the native country of Zeno Trascalisseus. Orba is described as φρούριόν τι ἰσχυρόν. Here Illos and Trokoundos laid siege to them, whereupon they changed their quarters to Sbida or Sbide, where they were pressed by the enemy till 477. This suggests a situation for Sbida more inaccessible than Olba or Orba, and therefore suits a position among the mountains west of the Kalykadnos, and north of the Ermenek Su.

The name Sbida suffers many transformations in the ecclesiastical documents, but the best form seems to be Sbîda. The variants Zeede, Sbide, Sbeda, occur; it frequently is spelt as a trisyllable,‡ Syneda [for Sybeda], &c.

Ibidinge, mentioned at Synod. Quinisexta, seems to be for Sibidinge, and to be the name Sibide with a suffix, which occurs in the Isaurian name Ninilingis (Theophan., p. 138). This Isaurian suffix perhaps corresponds to -nda or -dda in other parts of Asia Minor.

Sibidoṇda (Phrygia)	Sbida (Isauria)
Attoudda (Phrygia)	Attaia (Lydia), Atys
Aloudda (Phrygia)	Alia (Phrygia), Ala, " horse "
Klannoudda (Lydia)	Kelenai (Phrygia).§

* These variations of the name Adrasos occur in the ecclesiastical lists also.. On the Arab name Dsu-1-kala, applied to Adrasos, see p. 341 and Addenda.

† Anon. Vat. 60 b. quoted in notes to ' Velitat. Bell. Niceph.'

‡ Compare the Phrygian Sibidounda, which obviously contains the same word with the common Anatolian suffix, "onda."

§ Kelenai is usually called Kelainai, to suggest a meaning in Greek: but the coins and inscriptions always give Zeus Keleneus.

24. The principality of Sibilia on the borders of the Mohammedan and Christian territory, which is mentioned on the route of Barbarossa in 1190, is clearly to be identified with Sibela (which is not in Hierocles). Immediately after leaving Laranda the Crusaders entered the territory of the Christian Armenians, and the prince of Sibelia, who had the control of their road, came to meet them. Unfortunately the details given of the march between Laranda and Seleukeia are insufficient to show what route Frederick followed; but it is at least clear that Sibelia was in the northern part of the mountain country.* Sibyla, which was captured by Kilij Arslan in 1156 along with an unknown town Punura,† is evidently the same place : Manuel in reprisal made an expedition into Cilicia; the Armenians of Cilicia evidently took Sibyla between 1156 and 1190. The probable limits of Seljuk power at this time agree with the conclusion that Sibyla or Sibilia was between Laranda and Mut. It was either near Koropissos or possibly a late name given to that city.

The possibility, already referred to under Psebila of Lykaonia, that a city on the borders of Isauria and Lykaonia was assigned to both provinces, as Sibila in Isauria, and as Verinopolis-Psebila in Lykaonia, must for the present be left open. But this seems to me not to be probable.

25. Mousbanda is mentioned by Ptolemy as a town of Strategia Antiochiane. There can be little doubt that it is an equivalent form to the Bousmadis (Βούσμαδις, ᾿Ισαυρικὴ πόλις) of Stephanus Byzantius. The bishops of Mousbada (sic) and Sibilia or Sibela were both present at the Second Council of Nicæa A.D. 787. Musbanda must be identified with Musanda, mentioned along with Anemourion and Korakesion by Pliny, V. 93 (Myanda is the common reading there, but Musanda has manuscript authority). Forbiger is perhaps right in identifying Myanda with Mandane, given in the Stadiasmus (see Leake, p. 203) between Anemourion and Kelenderis near Sykai. It is remarkable that Sykai and Mousbada are both bishoprics in 787, and have each a bishop named Sisinnius. Some of the lists of 787 omit Sykai, but so many lists mention both bishoprics that the occasional omission of one of them is probably accidental. One of the two is probably equivalent to the bishopric Anemourion, which is not mentioned in any of the lists.

26. Leontopolis was very near Isauropolis, for Zeno ordered, in exception to the usual rule, "one city, one bishopric," that Leontopolis

---

* I use, not the original authority about Sibelia, viz. Tagenon, but the account given by Ritter, 'Kleinasien,' ii. 317, and the brief reference of Von Muralt. [But, since the preceding was printed, I have had the opportunity of reading Tagenon. I give the itinerary on p. 346, and have no doubt that Frederic marched by way of Claudiopolis.]

† Cinnam., p. 176. The index gives the name as Punsura.

and Isauropolis should have the same bishop. It was doubtless the modern Siristat, and may be the town mentioned as the birthplace of Conon ('Act. Sanct.,' March 5th, p. 360); *ex villa Bidana* [κώμη Βιδανή] *oriundus*, and one MS. adds xviii. stadia ab urbe Isauria.

27. KARDABOUNDA, a bishopric in the Second Council of Nicæa (787 A.D.) is the native name of some bishopric, which commonly bears a Græco-Roman name. The cities which have retained their Græco-Roman name till the present day, Zenopolis, Domitiopolis, Eirenopolis, are of course excluded by this fact.

28. LAUZADOS. Continuing the list of Hierocles we find, after Sbida, that he mentions two cities of the Decapolis, Neapolis and Lauzados. He has in his list traversed the Ermenek Su valley from east to west; the presumption then is that the two cities are on the head-waters of the Ermenek Su, and in this neighbourhood Prof. Sterrett has acutely detected Lauzados in the modern Lavdha.

29. NEAPOLIS may probably be the Ninika, which Ptolemy places in Lalassis, and may be localised at Lakhlas (Lalassis) in the same neighbourhood.

30. The principle of Hierocles's enumeration has now·become clear. He first enumerates the coast cities, then he traverses the valley of the Kalykadnos to the junction, and thereafter continues along the Ermenek Su. After each group of cities along the river he mentions the cities on the road which traverses the country from north to south, and reaches the river in their neighbourhood. One difficulty occurs in this list.

31. TITIOPOLIS is a city of the Decapolis, and must therefore be on the Ermenek Su, or else on the lower Kalykadnos. Either in this single case there is a dislocation in Hierocles, and Titiopolis is misplaced, or else Titiopolis was situated on the mountains between the Ermenek Su and the coast.

32. A comparison of Hierocles with the Notitiæ reveals some remarkable omissions in his list. The most striking of these is the failure of Domitiopolis and Zenopolis, two cities at the upper end of the Ermenek Su valley, which have both retained their name to the present day. Domitiopolis is mentioned by Ptolemy, Zenopolis certainly is named after Zeno the Isaurian (474–91),* and was therefore in existance when Hierocles wrote. These cities are probably omitted only because, in the earlier Byzantine period, more than one city in the narrow upper valley were united under one bishop, and Hierocles is greatly under the influence of the ecclesiastical lists of his time. The other omissions are clearly due to the fact that the towns lay in mountain tracts west and

---

* His Isaurian name was Traskalisseus or Tarasikodisa Rousoumbladeotes : the second word is perhaps an ethnic from a local name Rousoumblada, which is compounded with a name like Amblada.

north-west of the Kalykadnos, and were of slight consequence, except Leontopolis-Isauropolis, which Hierocles assigns to Lykaonia.* The Klimata of Kasai, Bolbosos, Kostras, and Banaba, are only districts and not cities.† Kodaka of Notitiæ III., X., is probably a corrupt name.

33. KOTRADA is not mentioned by Hierocles. The Notitiæ give it as an independent archbishopric, and this arrangement has probably misled Hierocles, and made him omit the city; similarly he omits entirely the important cities Eukhaita of Helenopontus and Kotiaion of Phrygia Salutaris for the same reason.

34. It is unfortunately impossible to attach much weight to Ptolemy's description of these districts. He seems to confuse Lalassis with Selentis ‡ Tracheia, which, as he says, contains five cities, Seleuceia, Diocæsareia, Philadelpheia, Domitiopolis, and Kaystros. Of these, Domitiopolis is on the upper Ermenek Su, Philadelpheia to the north in Ketis, Seleuceia and Diocæsareia on the lower Kalykadnos, and Kaystros on the coast. Kaystros is given in the ecclesiastical lists as Kestros.

35. Ptolemy mentions Eirenopolis in Lakanis, which should be perhaps Λακανατίς. Coins were struck between 40–70 A.D., with the legend ΛΑΚΑΝΑΤΩΝ, and, as the name is not found in later time, it is clear that one or more cities were founded, whose names are substituted for that of the people. It will be shown below that Lakanatis lies south of the Ermenek Su. Ptolemy places Lalasis east of Ketis instead of south-west, and mentions in Lalasis a city Ninika, but the name is not found elsewhere.

36. Some additional light is thrown on the topography of Isauria (or Cilicia Tracheia) by a study of its history. M. Waddington has made it highly probable ('Mel. Numism.', ii., p. 121) that from 43 till at least 29 B.C., a principality extending from Iconium to Olba was held, first by Queen Aba 43–39, then by M. Antonius Polemon. Now we know that a part of Cilicia Tracheia was given by Augustus to Archelaos in 20 B.C., and Strabo defines this part as embracing ἡ Τραχεῖα περὶ Ἐλαιοῦσσαν Κιλικία καὶ πᾶσα ἡ τὰ πειρατήρια συστησαμένη, p. 535; τὰ ἐν τῇ Τραχείᾳ Κιλικίᾳ ἐν ᾗ τὴν Ἐλαιοῦσσαν νησίον εὔκαρπον συνέκτισεν Ἀρχέλαος ἀξιολόγως, p. 537. For some years previously we know that Amyntas possessed the whole of Lykaonia, including Derbe, and parts of Isauria. He must have taken Iconium from Polemon of Olba, and Derbe he seized from Antipater. When he died, in 25 A.D., most part of his kingdom was made

* A law of Zeno mentions that they were under one bishop.

† The term Klima perhaps denotes a slope towards the sea (compare Justinian, Novel. xxvIII., αἵ γε πρὸς τοῖς κλίμασι κείμεναι Σινώπη τε καὶ Ἀμισός), but the ordinary sense 'regiones' is quite probable.

‡ Selinuntis would be a more correctly formed name.

by the Romans into the province of Galatia, but apparently Derbe, Laranda, and Cilicia Tracheia were given to Archelaos, as has been shown above (see DERBE.)

37. The Cappadocian part of Archelaos's vast kingdom was taken by the Romans at his death in A.D. 17; but part of Cilicia was left to his son, Archelaos, comprising the otherwise unknown people named Klitai.* Archelaos II. was still reigning A.D. 36 (Tac., Ann. vi. 41.). There is no record as to what was done by the Romans with the rest of Cilicia Tracheia in A.D. 17, and even the full extent of the first Archelaos's kingdom is unknown. Now, fortunately, Strabo, in calling this extra-Cappadocian territory of Archelaos ἐνδεκάτη στρατηγία and ἐπίκτητος, has given us the means of identifying it with Ptolemy's Στρατηγία ᾿Αντιοχιανή ; and we thus learn that it embraced also Olba and Mousbanda ; in short, we may safely infer from a comparison of Strabo and Ptolemy that it included Ketis, and all the coast and the eastern interior parts of Cilicia Tracheia. The western part of the interior of Tracheia was not included in this *Strategia*, for about 11–15 A.D. this western region (not, however, including Olba†) was governed by a dynast Ajax. His realm included the districts Lalasis and Kennatis, which were, as we have seen, along the Ermenek Su. We have no more information about Kennatis and Lalassis till A.D. 41.

38. How much of Cilicia Archelaos II. retained is unknown, but it is not impossible that he was allowed to retain great part of the Cilician territory that his father had held. Seleukeia, however, strikes Imperial coins under Tiberius, and must, therefore, have been temporarily or permanently attached to the province. But the Romans appear to have taken little or no interest in the country. In A.D. 38 we again get a glimpse into the condition of the country. In that year a district, including Cilicia Tracheia and part of Lykaonia, was given by Caligula to Antiochus IV. and Iotape. Coins prove that his dominion extended from Elaioussa-Sebaste westwards to Anemourion, and northwards to Lykaonia.‡ There is, therefore, every probability that this was practically the same province of Cilicia Tracheia which had belonged to Archelaos, and this conclusion is made quite certain by the fact that Ptolemy calls the Eleventh *Strategia* of Cappadocia, which consisted of part of Lycaonia and Cilicia Tracheia, and which had belonged to Archelaos, by the name Antiochiane. This name evidently dates from the year 38, when it was governed for the first and last time by a king Antiochus. In this

---

* Can Klitai be an error for [La]kanatai or Kennatai?

† M. Waddington maintains that it did include Olba, but the coins omit Olba. Strabo's account does not expressly include it, and Ptolemy asserts the contrary.

‡ He struck coins at Anemourion, Lakanatis, and Sebaste, and also with the legend ΛΥΚΑΟΝΩΝ, according to a coin recently acquired by the British Museum, as Mr. Head informs me.

year Antiochus probably founded the two cities, Germanicopolis and Philadelpheia, naming them after his imperial benefactor, Caligula Germanicus,' and his own wife, Iotape Philadelphos. This adds a slight additional probability that Philadelpheia was situated on or near the road leading from Germanicopolis to Laranda. Soon afterwards Antiochus lost favour, and was deprived of his kingdom.

39. In 41, Claudius again restored the kingdom to Antiochus and Iotape, who ruled until 72 A.D. It would appear that any part of Lykaonia which had previously been included in the realm of Antiochus was henceforth attached to Galatia; Ikonion henceforth strikes coins with the name Claudeikonion. At the same time Derbe and Laodiceia receive the title Claudioderbe and Claudiolaodiceia, though no coins are known till a later date. The central part of Cilicia Tracheia also was not restored to Antiochus, but was given* to Polemon of Pontus in exchange for the Bosporian part of his own kingdom. His new kingdom included Ketis, Kennatis, and Lalassis. The foundation of the colony Claudiopolis belongs to the same reign, and perhaps even to the same year (Claudiopolis quam deduxit coloniam Claudius Cæsar, Ammian. xiv., 25). The foundation of a colony shows that the Romans were now taking more interest in this remote mountain district.

40. Claudiopolis is situated at the lower end of the central Kalykadnos valley, before the river enters the narrow mountain gorge which conducts it to the coast-lands, and this situation suggests that it was on the frontier between Ketis which was given to Polemon, and the coast-lands which were given to Antiochus. Kennatis and Lalassis on the Ermenek Su, part of Ketis in the north, all belonged to Polemon; the coast-lands belonged to Antiochus and Iotape; the middle and lower Kalykadnos valley from Claudiopolis to the sea, attached to the Roman province Cilicia, extended like a wedge between the two kingdoms. It is remarkable that Claudiopolis, like Claudius's other colony, Archelais of Cappadocia, struck no coins.

41. In 74 Vespasian united part of Cilicia Tracheia to the province of eastern Cilicia. He still left to the daughter of Antiochus, named Iotape, and to her husband Alexander a small kingdom, consisting of an island (Josephus, Ant. 18, 5, 4, says merely νησιάδος τῆς ἐν Κιλικίᾳ).

It has been generally agreed that this means Elaioussa, but the possibility that it was Iotapa may be considered. Iotapa began to strike coins under Hadrian. It was on the coast west of Selinus, and may possibly have once been an island, as Elaioussa also is now

* Our authority (Dio Cass., 59, 12; 60, 8) says only "part of Cilicia"; it is a very probable conjecture of M. Waddington that a coin ΠΟΛΕΜΩΝΟΣ ΒΑΣΙΛΕΩΣ which reads [ΟΛΒΕ]ΩΝ ΛΑΛΑΣΕΩΝ ΚΑΙ ΚΕΝΝΑΤΩΝ, specifies the district of Cilicia assigned to him. It is probable that [ΚΗΤ]ΩΝ rather than [ΟΛΒΕ]ΩΝ should be restored in this case.

joined to the coast.* This part of the country was apparently left out of the empire as a frontier district till the time of Trajan or Hadrian.

42. It is uncertain what was the fate of Ketis at this time. Perhaps certain autonomous coins of Olba belong to this period. Under Antoninus Pius Olba struck imperial coins, and was therefore included at that time in the empire, as part of some province. That this province was Cilicia appears clear from Ptolemy, who assigns Ketis with Olba to Cilicia.† But as Philadelpheia of Ketis strikes imperial coins under Trajan and Koropissos under Hadrian, Ketis must have been united to Cilicia not later than the very beginning of the second century.

43. The upper part of the Ermenek Su valley was left autonomous for some time longer, as a sort of frontier district. Under Domitian a coin of the KOINON ΛΑΛΑϹΕΩΝ ΚΑΙ Κ[ΕΝ]ΝΑΤΩΝ occurs (Head, ' Hist. Num.').

44. Imperial coins are not known of any of the cities included in the district, which we have been examining, earlier than Trajan. Those of Syedra indeed begin under Nero, but Syedra was in Pamphylia Provincia, which was organised much earlier. Seleuceia coined imperial money under Tiberius, and therefore must have been in a Roman province for some time during his reign; and with Claudiopolis Colonia it was in a Roman district from A.D. 41 onwards. The Irenopolis which struck numerous coins, was probably a city of Cilicia Campestris, not far from Anazarbos, and near the Pyramos. Sebaste-Elaioussa strikes imperial coins under Augustus.

45. It may be convenient to bring together, in brief terms, the most probable facts with regard to the government and bounds of Cilicia Tracheia and Lykaonia in the Roman period.

B.C. 67. The Teucrid dynasty of priest-kings of Olba rule a considerable principality after the destruction of the Isaurian or Cilician pirates. Aba, daughter of Zenophanes, married into the family, and finally succeeded in seizing the power.

B.C. 43. Aba is confirmed queen of Olba by Antony and Cleopatra.

B.C. 39. Aba is deposed. M. Antonius Polemon, probably a member of the Teucrid family, becomes king: his power extends even over Iconium, besides Olba, Lalassis, and Kennatis.

B.C. 29. Polemon still reigning.

B.C. 29–27. Amyntas seizes Iconium and part of Isauria, and also takes Derbe from Antipater Derbetes.

B.C. 25. Amyntas' kingdom left to the Romans Augustus soon after gives to Archelaos, king of Cappadocia, the eleventh strategia,

---

* The island Iotapa, νῆσου Ἰωτάβης, Conc. A.D. 556, seems to be in the Erythræan Sea.

† His second mention of Olba as part of the eleventh *Strategia* Antiochiane is due to his use of an old authority for the *Strategiai*.

including Kybistra, Derbe, Ketis, and great part of the coast of Tracheia. The rest of Lykaonia and the country Isauria in the narrow sense are attached to the province Galatia.

The western parts of the interior of Tracheia, including Kennatis and Lalassis, seem to continue to be an independent kingdom under members of the Teucrid dynasty; probably a king named Teucer reigns about this time.

A.D. 11–13. Ajax, son of Teucer, begins to reign over Kennatis and Lalassis.

A.D. 15–17. Fifth year of Ajax.

A.D. 17. Archelaos dies, and the Romans take possession of Cappadocia, but leave to his son, Archelaos II. [part at least, or, more probably, the whole of] his kingdom in Lykaonia and Cilicia Tracheia. Kybistra, however, probably is taken as part of Cappadocia.

A.D. 15–37. Seleuceia strikes imperial coins, and must therefore be in Roman possession, as part of the province Cilicia during some part at least of the reign of Tiberius.

A.D. 36. Archelaos II. still reigning.

A.D. 38. Part of Cilicia Tracheia and Lykaonia (obviously the same territory that was called the eleventh strategia) is given to Antiochus IV. and Iotape Philadelphos by Caligula Germanicus. Antiochus founds the two cities Germanicopolis and Philadelpheia, and strikes coins— ΛΥΚΑΟΝΩΝ, ΛΑΚΑΝΑΤΩΝ, ΑΝΕΜΟΥΡΙΕΩΝ, ΣΕΒΑΣΤΗΝΩΝ. The strategia acquires the name Antiochiane.

A.D. 38–40. Antiochus loses favour, and is deprived of his kingdom, the disposal of which is uncertain.

A.D. 41. Antiochus is again made king of part of Tracheia, including only the coast-lands. Derbe is attached to Lykaonia. Iconium, Derbe, and Laodiceia receive the title Claudian. Claudiconium begins to strike coins. Kennatis and Lalassis, whose fate since 17 A.D. is uncertain, are now formed, along with the interior of Ketis, into a kingdom which is given to Polemon, king of Pontus. The colony Claudiopolis is founded, and probably the eastern part of the Kalykadnos valley, from Seleuceia to Claudiopolis, is attached to the Roman province Cilicia.

A.D. 63. End of the kingdom of Pontus. The Pontic part of Polemon's kingdom is attached to Galatia: the fate of the Cilician part is unknown. Olba seems to have become independent, as autonomous coins exist of style later than Ajax, 11–15 A.D. Kennatis and Lalassis also independent.

A.D. 74. Vespasian adds part of Cilicia Tracheia to the province Cilicia, including probably Ketis and Lakanatis. Philadelpheia strikes imperial coins under Trajan, Coropissos under Hadrian. Olba bears the titles Hadriana Antoniniana, but no coins earlier than Antoninus are known.

A.D. 82–96. Coins of the Koinon of Lalasis and Kennatis.

A.D. 117–138. About this time the province Cilicia, including Tracheia, is an imperial province, under a prætorian legatus Augusti; its previous government is not certain, as it was perhaps under the governor of Syria.

A.D. 138–161. Lykaonia and Isauria are separated from Galatia and attached to Cilicia; the governor of " the three eparchiai " is a consular legatus.* Tarsos assumes the title, " metropolis of the three eparchiai." This arrangement perhaps lasts till Isauria and Cilicia are divided into separate provinces in the latter part of the third century. Still later, Cilicia was divided into Prima and Secunda by Honorius.

46. The remarks of M. Clerc, 'Bull. Corr. Hell.,' 1887, p. 351, give a different account of the division of the provinces. On account of an inscription reading — Καρμινίου ᾿Αθηναγόρου ἀνθυπάτου Λυκίας καὶ Παμφυλίας καὶ ᾿Ισαυρίας, he maintains that, after the time of Pius, Isauria was separated from Cilicia-Lykaonia, and attached to Lycia-Pamphylia; and that it was again separated from the latter and attached to the former by Severus. This view seems wrong, because Cilicia and Lykaonia are not continuous with each other, but are separated by Isauria (which must from this time onwards be understood in the larger sense of Cilicia Tracheia). It also seems unnecessary, for a part of Isauria always belonged to Pamphylia Provincia; and it was characteristic of such honorary inscriptions to give additional honour by a long enumeration of names of countries governed by the official in question, even though he governed only a small part of some of the countries. (See Addenda.)

47. With regard to the boundary between the new province Cilicia-Isauria-Lykaonia and the province Galatia, it seems probable that the entire Koinon of Lykaonia was included in the former province, while the other cities which did not belong to the Koinon were attached to Pisidia, except Lystra, Parlais, Iconium, which were in Lykaonia, but, being Roman colonies, could not stoop to enter a union of native cities. This may be inferred from the list of Ptolemy, who is later than the new arrangement. He still includes, in the

* M. Clerc, in 'Bull. Corr. Hell.,' 1887, p. 351, says a "legat praetorien," but the inscription of Etrilius Regillus Laberius Priscus, 'Bull. Corr. Hell.,' 1885, p. 435, shows that he was a consular legatus. M. Clerc's remarks contain an inaccurate account of the facts described in the text following. It appears possible that the change was coincident with the accession of Pius. Pactumeius Clemens was praetorian legatus in the last year of Hadrian, 138. He was made consul in his absence in the week that Hadrian died, and was continued as legatus of the new emperor. Possibly his unusual consulship in absence was owing to the new system of consular legati being now inaugurated. M. Waddington first fully explained the "three eparchiai," but dated the arrangement from the reign of Severus, 'Bull. Corr. Hell.,' 1883, p. 290. Mr. Sterrett's copy of the Etrilius inscription ('Wolfe Expedition,' No. 189, and Appendix), which seems to be more complete than that of MM. Radet and Paris, shows that Etrilius was legate for the second time, which implies that he had previously been legatus and had come back to the province a second time.

province Galatia, Tyriaion, Laodiceia, Vasada, and the cities on the west of Tatta, from Savatra northwards. But his account is certainly partly wrong. He is right in saying that a μέρος τῆς Λυκαονίας belonged to Galatia,* and in separating from it another part, which, on the whole, is the south-eastern district of Lykaonia. But he is clearly wrong, at least as regards Lystra, Savatra and Isaura, in the line of demarcation between these two parts; and he is also wrong in assigning the south-eastern half to Cappadocia. The origin of the latter error lies in his use of an old authority on the Cappadocian strategiai: this authority, writing after the eleventh strategia had been formed about 25 B.C., † described the whole of them as constituting the eleven divisions of Cappadocia. Ptolemy, finding in one authority that the eleventh division of Cappadocia included part of Lykaonia, and in another authority that Galatia included another part of Lykaonia, was betrayed into his absurd division, which was never true at any period of the history of the provinces.

48. It may be added that this same view explains how Ptolemy assigns so many Cilician cities to Strategia Kataonia. He had the view that Cappadocia included a considerable part of Cilicia Tracheia and Isauria. He used an authority who gave no complete lists of cities in the several strategiai, as has already been shown; and he did his best to apportion the cities according to the map which he had constructed.

49. The coins, then, are probably our best authority. I should conjecture that Pius organised a Koinon of the part of Lykaonia, which he assigned to the province Cilicia-Isauria-Lykaonia, similar to the Koinon of Cilicia, which had existed since the reign of Augustus. No coins of the Koinon are known earlier than the time of Pius; and though this does not constitute any real argument in cases like Derbe, which struck no coins until that time, it does in the case of Savatra, which struck coins from Trajan onwards, but only began to add ΚΟΙ. ΛΥΚΑΟΝΙΑC in the time of Pius. Moreover, there was evidently a general impulse to coinage of the Koinon under Pius and Marcus, when the coins of all the cities begin.‡

50. The following Lykaonian cities strike coins, but not of the Koinon, Iconium, Laodiceia, Lystra, and Parlais. Lystra, Parlais, and Iconium were Coloniae Romanae before the time of Pius, and thus were of a more honourable rank: Laodiceia almost certainly continued to be in the province Galatia, as Ptolemy declares. It became probably a Colonia Romana under Maximin.

* It may have been at this time that the title προσειλημμένη, which has not been rightly understood by any geographer, was given to the Galatian part of Lykaonia.

† Either this authority wrote after the eleventh strategia received the name Antiochiane, or perhaps a marginal note added the title Antiochiane to a writer who described the eleven strategiai of the kingdom of Archelaus.

‡ The emperor on the coin of Hyde is not mentioned by Mr. Head, 'Hist. Num.,' p. 595; Barata, Dalisandos, Derbe, Ilistra, and Savatra begin under Pius or Marcus.

51. Towards the end of the third century the province Galatia was broken up into Paphlagonia, Galatia, and Pisidia, and the province Cilicia-Lykaonia-Isauria was broken up into Cilicia and Isauria. The new province Isauria included also the southern part of Lykaonia : the new province Pisidia included the north-western part of Lykaonia. The line of division between Isauria and Pisidia in the first half of the fourth century must probably have been much the same as the dividing line which Pius drew. But any hope of aid from a comparison of the later line with the older is frustrated by the fact that (1) the authorities for the later division are both scanty and unsatisfactory; the chief authority, viz. the list of Bishops present at the First Nicene Council, though a useful document, is not to be implicitly depended on in details; (2) slight modifications of the boundary-line may have taken place.

52. Ptolemy assigns Savatra to Galatia: this is certainly wrong, because it struck coins of the Koinon Lykaonon. He also places Savatra* in Isauria, which is absurd. He assigns to Galatia the three cities of Isauria, Lystra, Isaura, and Savatra, yet gives Parlais and Iconium to Cappadocia (for which name we must of course substitute Provincia Cilicia-Isauria-Lykaonia). One or other of these assignments must be wrong, and possibly all are wrong, for Iconium is put in Pisidia by the Nicene lists. Isaura is proved to have been in the province Cilicia-Lykaonia-Isauria by the inscription dedicated to Etrilius, 'Bull. Corr. Hell.,' 1885, p. 435, and Parlais can hardly have been in any province except either Pisidia or Pamphylia. It is, however, remarkable that, in the case of Parlais, Ptolemy is confirmed by the Nicene lists. These lists are given below V. 7 : a comparison with Ptolemy shows that the points of uncertainty are only (1) Iconium, (2) Pyrgos, (3) Parlais, and (4) Vasada.

53. It is not improbable that both Ptolemy and the Nicene lists are right about Iconium. It may probably have been metropolis of Lykaonia among the three eparchiai, and afterwards have been made metropolis of the new province Pisidia-Lykaonia.† Pyrgos was perhaps not a bishopric at this early time; nothing is known about it. Parlais is treated at length under Pisidia. Ptolemy puts Vasada in Galatia, which naturally implies that it was afterwards in Pisidia, but which

---

* Mr. Sterrett's correction of Σαύατρα to Ἄστρα in Isauria can hardly be accepted. I ought perhaps to say that I originally suggested it to him, and it was ascribed to me in his proofs; but I afterwards came to recognise that it is not justifiable to correct all Ptolemy's errors, and I requested Mr. Sterrett either to cut out the correction or else not to ascribe it to me, as I could no longer believe in it.

† I am not aware that there is any distinct proof of what was the metropolis of Pisidia in the first half of the fourth century, whether Antiocheia or Iconium. The order of the Nicene list suggests that Iconium was metropolis; perhaps there may have been two metropoleis in the province, as there were from an early period in the case of Bithynia and of Pamphylia.

throws all the more difficulty in the way of assigning Parlais to Lykaonia-Isauria-Cilicia. It is doubtful whether Vasada is mentioned in the Nicene lists. Theodorus Vasagadensis or Vialbitanus is given in Isauria, but it may be preferable to understand [Vi]albitanus as indicating Olbianus, and Vasagadensis as a corruption arising by assimilation to the preceding Cumanadensis. But in Conc. Antioch., A.D. 341, Theodorus Vasadensis is a bishop of Isauria. We have therefore a clear contradiction between Ptolemy and the fourth century lists.* If we follow the latter, we may suppose that Vasada was a little further south than Yonuslar, between that and Karallia, and was actually included in Isauria up to 361–2. Probably Vasada originally included the country between Karallia, Dalisandos, and Misthia, while Misthia extended across to embrace even Yonuslar, and the 118th letter of Basil quoted above orders the presbyter of Yonuslar to be in future placed under the bishopric of Vasada. This ecclesiastical change would be one of the consequences of the formation of the new province Lykaonia. Yonuslar was more conveniently attached to Vasada; but, being on the road from Misthia to Ikonion, it had hitherto been in the same province with them, but henceforth it could be attached to Vasada, which was now in Lykaonia also.

54. M. Camille Jullian† conjectures that Isauria was separated from Cicilia as early as the time of Probus, 276–82 A.D. He rightly remarks that it included part of the upper plateau with the cities Lystra and Laranda, and that the name Isauria, which originally was applied only to a small district between Cilicia Tracheia and Lykaonia proper, was subsequently extended over the whole of Cilicia Tracheia. The limits of Isauria-Lykaonia in 138–61 were as follows, if we follow Ptolemy in all cases where he cannot be proved to be wrong, i.e. in all cases except Savatra, Lystra, Parlais, and Isaura.‡ The frontier did not touch Bey Sheher Lake at all. It included Dalisandos (Fassiller), and may possibly have touched Trogitis (Seidi Sheher Lake). It left Vasada to Galatia, but included Iconium, and ran obliquely north to include Savatra and probably to touch Tatta. This province gradually came, as M. Jullian remarks, to bear the single name Isauria, and, perhaps as early as 276–82, Isauria was separated from Pisidia. The bounds were modified at this time, but the exact details are reserved to V. 7.

55. SELEUCEIA. The site is well known. A temple of Apollo Sarpedonios, who sends birds to destroy locusts, is mentioned there by Zosimus, p. 50. According to Basil of Seleuceia, there was a temple

* It is possible that in the rectification of the frontier, when Iconium, according to our hypothesis, was made metropolis of Pisidia, Vasada was transferred to Isauria; then Ptolemy also might be correct.

† 'Revue Historique,' 1882, May–August, p. 331.

‡ Ptolemy must have used an authority for Roman Galatia of older date than 138, and trying to accommodate it to the new state he made various errors, keeping Parlais, Isaura, and Lystra.

and oracle of Sarpedon on the side towards the sea, and a temple of Athena on the Acropolis.* Saint Thekla settled on a hill opposite both temples, on the south of the city, and no doubt her church afterwards stood there.

56. Lamos must have been situated on the river Lamos, still called Lamas Su. Its coins bear the legend ΛΑΜΟΥ ΜΗΤΡΟΠ ΛΑΜΩΤΙΔΟC. This situation causes a geographical difficulty, for two Cilician cities, Elaioussa and Korykos, are further west than Lamos, which is always assigned to Byzantine Isauria. The ancient city was situated not on the coast, but some distance up the river; it is placed by Ptolemy in the interior, and never mentioned in the Peripli. Perhaps the situation up the country may explain the geographical inconsistency. There are, however, other difficulties in this position of Lamos, which I cannot resolve, but must leave to the consideration of explorers. This position is quite inconsistent with the order of Hierocles, who places Lamos between Anemourion and Antiocheia. His order is confirmed (1) by the lists of Chalcedon and of Epistola ad Leonem: the latter places Lamos and Kharadra † in one bishopric, and the former mentions only Kharadra, omitting the name Lamos entirely: (2) by the epithet in the lists at Chalcedon Ἀκάκιος ἐπίσκοπος Ἀντιοχείας τῆς Λαμωτίδος. The situation of Antiocheia is known, and, if it was in Lamotis, then Lamotis must have lain between Ketis and Selentis: (3) by the omission in all the Peripli of any city Lamos on the coast where the Lamos river was situated, though Strabo does mention the river and city between Elaioussa and Soloi.

These facts point to the view that Lamotis was a district on the coast, next to Selentis or Kennatis, containing three cities, Antiocheia, Kharadra, and up the country Lamos. In that case there ceases to be any geographical inconsistency in assigning Lamos to Isauria, Elaioussa and Korykos to Cilicia.‡

57. Kharadra or Kharadros is placed with certainty by Strabo and the Peripli between Anemourion and Antiocheia.

The exchange of prisoners, which Basil arranged with the Saracens of Tarsos, (A.D. 945), took place on the river Lamos, probably the Isaurian river (Theoph. Contin., 443). Muralt mentions another in 845. Strabo makes this river the boundary of Cilicia Tracheia and Campestris.

58. Antiocheia. There were two cities of this name in Isauria. The

---

* These temples may be fairly inferred from his words τῷ δαίμονι τῷ Σαρπηδόνι, τῷ καταλαβόντι μὲν τὴν ἐπὶ τῆς θαλάττης χήλην, and δαίμονι Ἀθηνᾷ, ἥ . . . . κατειληφυῖα τὸν ἐπώνυμον αὐτῆς πύργον. The oracle of Sarpedon is implied in the words διὰ χρησμολογίας. See Nic. Chon., 29 ; Cinnam., 16, 179 ; Anna., II., 121.

† Latmi et Calendri.

‡ Ptolemy's map also becomes more accurate on this view of the situation of Lamos. There is great need for exploration of this country. If no rivers flow into the Ermenek Su from the south, there must be rivers flowing into the sea in this district, and where there are rivers there are probably cities.

most important is a city on the coast between Selinus and Anemourion, on the hill Kragos. It is described by Theophanes (p. 139) as ἐπί τινος ὄρους κειμένην ὑψηλοῦ κατὰ τὴν μεσημβρινὴν τῆς χώρας θάλασσαν.

59. The other Antiocheia is known only from an inscription, discovered by Mr. Davis; it was situated high up on the Budjakche Tchai.

60. SEBASTE is given in Byzantine lists as a bishopric of Cilicia Prima between Soloi-Pompeiopolis and Korykos. But we find also that

61. JULIO-SEBASTE is given in Byzantine lists as a bishopric of Isauria between Antiocheia and Kestroi. It seems necessary to distinguish these two as separate cities. Sebaste includes the small island Elaioussa, which is close to it. It was founded by Archelais (20 B.C. to 17 A.D.), and struck autonomous coins under Antiochus and Iotape (38 to 72 A.D.), as well as imperial coins from Augustus to Volusian. Julio-Sebaste is not mentioned except in the ecclesiastical lists. It is probably to be identified with the Isaurian Nephelis.

62. SYKE, which occurs as a bishopric at the Council of 787, must also be the native name of one of the cities, which in the official lists bear official names of the Græco-Roman type. Theophanes (p. 445) mentions that it was a castle of Isauria with a harbour, with a difficult kleisoura leading towards Tarsos. Leake quotes references to it from Athenæus (iii., 14),* Geographus Ravenn., Stephanus, and Scylax as amended by Gronovius, and places it between Anemourion and Kelenderis.

63. In 1119 A.D. John Comnenus captured Philadelphia, and in 1120 Sozopolis, and then advanced to Attaleia, taking Hierakoryphites and other fortresses near Attaleia. He thus opened up a road lying through Byzantine territory to Isauria and Cilicia which was used in several expeditions by himself and his son Manuel. In 1180, on the death of Manuel, it was once more blocked by the Turks, who captured Sozopolis and other smaller places, and held Attaleia under a long blockade (Nicet. Chon., 340).

In 1141 John Comnenos marched by this circuitous route, Sozopolis, Lake Pasgousa, and Attaleia, into Cilicia, where he died, and his son Manuel returned to Constantinople by a direct march across Lykaonia, sustaining no loss from the Seljuks of Konia.

In 1137 John Comnenus invaded Cilicia, where the Armenian prince Lebounes or Leon had allied himself with the Latin princes of Antioch. The emperor must have advanced through Pamphylia by the road just described. Lebounes had even attacked Seleuceia, which was still part of the Byzantine empire. The emperor captured Mopsouestia, Tarsos, Adana, Anazarbos, and marched on Baka; the garrison retired to Antioch, and the Byzantine army also followed them thither, postponing Baka. From Antioch the emperor marched into "upper Syria," captured

* Leake gives 111, 5, and the error is copied in Smith's 'Dictionary of Geography.'

Piza, passed by Berrhœa, took Hama and Khabarda and Seser. He then returned to Cilicia, and captured Baka and Kapniskerti.

In A.D. 1155 Manuel Comnenus made a great expedition to Isauria and Cilicia. On the way, ἐπειδὴ πρὸς τῇ Μικρᾷ Φρυγίᾳ ἐγένετο,* he defeated the Turks of Iconium. He then marched through Pamphylia, and left the heavier troops at Attaleia, while he himself with the light troops marched by the coast road to Seleuceia, ordering the governor of the province Isauria, Alexius Casianos (ὃς τὴν Σελευκέων τότε διεῖπεν ἀρχήν Cinnam., 179) to hold the troops of the province in readiness. He marched to Seleuceia and thence into Cilicia, and captured the strong fortress of Lamos (ἐρυμνὸν μάλιστα ὄν). Thereafter he took Kistramos and Anazarbos, Longinias, and finally Tarsos. Returning, Manuel took the shorter road to Constantinople through Lykaonia in place of the longer road by Pamphylia (Cinnam., 190). He evidently took the road Seleuceia-Diocæsareia, and passed by Laranda,† and caused much alarm to the Turks; but he acted peaceably, and did his best to restore confidence to the Mohammedan population. At Kotiaion he was attacked by the Turks and suffered some loss. Nicetas (p. 134) describes this expedition "into Armenia" briefly,‡ and mentions the heavy losses incurred on the homeward march.

This gives some conception of the extent of the Seljuk empire at this period, from south of Laranda to about Kotiaion.

64. PAPYRION is a fortress frequently mentioned by Theophanes and other authorities during the troubled reign of Zeno, who kept a treasure in it. Theophanes says it was in Cappadocia; but his own account, and that of others, leaves little or no doubt that this is a mistake, and that it was in Isauria, and probably in the north-western part. It seems to be mentioned in an inscription published by Sterrett, where we have with a slight correction of the impossible published text, Ταράσιν Μανέου καὶ Ζῆζιν Παπο[ρι]νδεῖς, i.e. natives of Paporion.§ The inscription, then, proves, when correctly interpreted, that Astra and Paporion were neighbouring towns, in the very part of Isauria where Papyrion is placed by the historians.

65. ASTRA and ARTANADA, whose names were previously unknown, were discovered by Sterrett at Tamashalik and Dulgerler.

* Probably about Laodiceia ad Lycum.
† Called Ἄρανδα in the published text of Cinnamus.
‡ Adana and Tarsos are described as πρόσχωρα τῇ κάτω Ἀρμενίᾳ.
§ 'Wolfe Expedition,' p. 49. Prof. Sterrett's punctuation and interpretation are in several respects wrong: the sense is "Mathoun built at his own expense and brought workmen: Tarasin and Zezin, of Paporion, and Loukios of Astra fitted up." Sterrett's text is ΠΑΠΟΠΝΔΕΙϹ. He proposes the correction ΠΑΠΠΟΡΟΝΔΕΙϹ, which gives an interpretation geographically improbable, and which seems unfair to his own accuracy as a copyist. ΠΝ is a very natural error for ΡΙΝ, if part of the curve of Ρ were obliterated, so that, by the very slightest alteration of his copy, we have an excellent and probable reading. I suggested this to him, but he preferred the published text.

66. KOTRADA is an almost unknown town of Isauria, and yet so important as to be a metropolis or archbishopric. The order proves clearly that it had attained this rank before the Council of A.D. 680.* It was either in the north-west part of Isauria, or more probably near the western coast. It seems to be mentioned twice in Not. I., first as a metropolis (Κοτιάδων for Κοτράδων), and next as a bishopric of Isauria as τὸ κλίμα Κοστράδος: such double mention is a common phenomenon in the Notitiæ.

67. The four Klimata, Kassa, Banaba, Bolbosos, and Kostras,† are probably four districts on the Pamphylian frontier, see p. 417.

68. NAGIDOS is known as an important city striking numerous coins of the fifth and fourth centuries B.C. It then disappears from numismatic lists. The reason must be either that it changed its name, or that its inhabitants were taken to swell the population of some new city founded by the Diadochi.

69. ANEMOURION near Nagidos struck coins under Antiochus IV. It retains its name as Anamur.

U. CILICIA.

For the sake of completeness, I add here a few notes on Cilician cities. In general the topography of Cilicia is in a much more advanced state than that of any other province of Asia Minor. Tarsos, Pompeiopolis-Soloi, Korykos, Adana, Mallos, Zephyrion, Anazarbos, Mopsouestia, Aigai, Alexandreia, Rossos, are all satisfactorily discussed and placed by Leake.‡

BISHOPRICS OF CILICIA PRIMA AND SECUNDA.

A.D. 451.	Hierocles A.D. 530.	Notitia I.
I. 1. Tarsos.	1. Tarsos.	1. Tarsos.
2. Pompeiopolis.	2. Pompeiopolis.	2. Pompeiopolis.
3. Sebaste.	3. Sebaste.	3. Sebaste.
8. Korykos.	4. Korykos.	4. Korykos.
4. Adana.	5. Adana.	5. Adana.
6. Augusta.	6. Agousia.	6. Augustopolis.
7. Mallos.	7. Μάλχος.	7. Mallos.
5. Zephyrion.	8. Zephyrion.	8. Zephyrion.
II. 1. Anazarbos.	1. Anazarbos.	1. Anazarbos.
6. Mopsouestia.	2. Mopsouestia.	2. Mopsouestia.
9. Aigai.	3. Aigeai.	3. Aigeai.
2. Epiphaneia.	4. Epiphaneia.	4. Epiphaneia.
8. Alexandreia.	5. Alexandreia.	7. Alexandreia.
5. Rosos.	6. Rosos.	10. Rosos.
4. Eirenopolis.	7. Eirenopolis.	5. Eirenopolis.
3. Flavias.	8. Flavias.	6. Flavias.
7. Kastabala.	9. Kastabala.	9. Kastabala.
		8. Kabissos.

* At this Council it is also clear that Leontopolis of Isauria and Eukhaita are metropoleis.

† The text is wrongly given by Parthey and Pinder, p. 85. The manuscript, Biblioth. Nat. Paris, No. 1310, has the correct form, τὰ δὲ κλίματα· Κασσῶν· Βανάβων· Βολβοσοῦ· Κοστράδος.

‡ Rhosos or Rossos is omitted in Leake's index, but given on p. 218.

SEBASTE of Cilicia has been distinguished above from Julio-Sebaste of Isauria. It was founded by Archelaus, and afterwards struck coins with the portraits of Antiochus IV. and Iotape.

AUGUSTA is placed by Ptolemy in the district Bryklike of Cilicia west of Charakene (which contains the city Flaviopolis) and north of Lamotis. The Byzantine lists mention it in Cilicia Prima, between Adana and Mallos. These references agree with the customary view that Augusta lay between the Saros and the Pyramos; but no evidence known to me proves its exact position. Coins of Augusta with the legend AVΓΟVCΤΑΝΩΝ are dated by an era, 19–20 A.D., showing that it was refounded and renamed Augusta in that year.

KORYKOS is placed by Leake, and after him by Kiepert, on the coast west of Lamos and Elaioussa. Lamos is regularly assigned to Byzantine Isauria, while Korykos and Elaioussa are given in Cilicia. Leake's situation is certainly at least approximately correct, and this must be accepted as a case of violation of geographical arrangement in the Byzantine ecclesiastical division. A few isolated cases of a similar character are known, e.g. Amblada Pisidiæ, Argiza Hellesponti, Theodosiopolis Armeniae. But see p. 380.

Korykos was founded by Attalus, according to Eustathius (ad Dionys. Perieg. 855, p. 161 a, Steph.) It was a Byzantine military station in the Cibyrrhaiote Theme (στρατοῦ ἄρχοντα τῶν Κουρικιωτῶν τῆς ὑπὸ Κιβυρραιωτῶν χώρας, Niceph. Patr., p. 45).

Korykos (called Κούρικον) was a dismantled place in the time of Alexius Comnenus, though formerly very strong (ἐρυμνοτάτη). He reoccupied and fortified both it and Seleuceia, which was six stadia* distant. This estimate of distance is decidedly too small (Anna, II. p. 120).

ZEPHYRION, the bishopric of Cilicia Prima, has been properly distinguished by Leake from the Isaurian promontory of the same name. Its coinage is considerable, but (as was stated above) the coin of Irenopolis-Zephyrion is either forged or misread.

MOPSOUKRENE is fixed on the road from Tarsos to the Cilician Gates by many authorities. The Itineraries place it XII. miles from Tarsos. Theophanes says it was the first stage out of Tarsos (ἐν Μαμψουκρήναις πρώτῃ μονῇ ἀπὸ Τάρσου, p. 46). The name is often written Mampsoukrene, compare Mampsista for Mopsouestia and Thampsioupolis for Themissonioupolis.

CHRYSOBOULLOS, a place near Tarsos, in the direction of the pass of Podandos (Pylæ Ciliciæ), is mentioned by Cedrenus (II., 217).

Baltolibas, the fountain of Balton, is mentioned only by Scylitzes (p. 684). The Turkish troops, who had been pillaging Iconium (having crossed the Euphrates near Melitene, and advanced through Cappadocia) in A.D. 1069, crossed into Cilicia διὰ τῶν τῆς Σελευκείας ὀρέων, where they were harassed by the Armenian inhabitants. In Cilicia they heard that

---

* Stadia is, no doubt, used here in the sense of miles, see F, 73.

a Greek army was waiting for them at Mopsouestia, and, after a short rest at Baltolibas, they crossed Amanus (τὸ Σαρβαδικὸν ὄρος) into the country of Aleppo.*

FLAVIOPOLIS, placed by Ptolemy in the district of Cilicia called Charakene, continues to be mentioned in all Byzantine lists as a bishop-ric Flavias.† It is given in the Antonine Itinerary as the first station (xx. m. p. distant) from Anazarbos on the road to Kokussos. This leaves no doubt that it is to be identified with the modern Sis. The name Sis or Siskia is the old native name, which was for a time replaced by the title Flavias, but which returned into use in the later Byzantine period. In A.D. 704 the Arabs besieged Sis (τὸ Σίσιον Κάστρον) in Cilicia, but were defeated by a sudden advance of Heraclius.‡

MOPSOUESTIA is called Mampsista or Mansista in Byzantine times, Mansis in older Turkish, and Missis at the present time. The name is given as Mamista by Anna Comnena (II. 126, cp. Ducange's note, II., p. 637) and Glycas, and even Malmistra, &c., by Latin writers. It is said by the Byzantine writers to have been situated on the Saros: τέμνεται γὰρ ἡ πόλις αὕτη μέσον τῷ Σάρῳ ποταμῷ ὡς δοκεῖν δύο πόλεις εἶναι (Cedren. II., 362). This fact leads Anna Comnena (II., p. 138) to speak of the two cities of Mopsos, one destroyed and one standing, divided by the river Saron (ποταμῷ Σάρωνι): Ducange has given the correct inter-pretation of this passage.§ In the face of these clear statements we are rather surprised to remember that in reality it was situated on the river Pyramos, not on the Saros.

MALLOS was situated on the height at the mouth of the river Pyramos at the modern Kara Tash. The river has altered its course since ancient times. A low range of hills stretches along the coast north-east from Kara Tash. The Pyramos, which formerly passed on the west side of this range, now joins the sea at the opposite end several miles east of its old course; but its former channel with the bridge that crossed it can still be traced. Inland from Mallos is the famous Aleian plain. The coast-land south of the range of hills is all a recent formation from the river, which is rapidly filling up the bay of Ayash. As at Tarsos and Anazarbos, the chief magistrate of Mallos bore the name, common among Dorian states, δημιουργός.‖

AIGAI, has retained its name as Ayash, i.e. Αἰγάς. The temple of Asclepios there was destroyed by Constantine at the same time as the

* Cp. Attal., 135–8; Zonar. xviii., 12.
† Forbiger ('Alte Geogr.,' p. 290) distinguishes Flaviopolis from Flavias because Ptolemy's position disagrees with the other authorities. But if every city which Ptolemy puts differently from other authorities were made a separate city, the result would be a serious increase in the number of places in Asia Minor.
‡ Muralt incorrectly says the Arabs took Sis, cp. Theoph., p. 372, and 'Act. S. Tarachi,' Oct. 11.
§ A good deal about Mopsouestia is found in Mansi, 'Act. Concil.,' ix., p. 276. ff.
‖ See my paper in 'Journal of Philology,' 1882, p. 143.

temple of Aphrodite at Aphaka (Theophan., p. 24). The god is called on its coins ΘΕΟΣ ΣΩΤΗΡ. Its coins have the legends ΑΙΓΕΑΙΩΝ, ΑΙΓΕΩΝ, ΑΙΓΑΙΩΝ. It was an important naval station under the Romans, as is proved by coins with the legend ΝΑΥΑΡΧΙC and as is natural from its situation. A bridge over the Pyramos between Mopsouestia and Ægæ is mentioned on the coins of both cities.

EPIPHANEIA is mentioned by Cicero (ad Fam. xv. 4) as in Cilicia one day's journey from Amanus. Pliny mentions that its original name was Oiniandos (cp. Oinoandos of the Kibyratis). It has not been satisfactorily placed, but certainly could be placed readily by a careful examination of the country; but I cannot add anything to Leake's remarks. Kiepert places it in the same general situation as Leake. Major Bennet puts it at Geuz Khane eleven miles on the road from Osmanie to Piyas.

EIRENOPOLIS has already been placed approximately in discussing the Isaurian city which bears the same name.

KABISSOS, which does not occur in Hierocles, is given in Not. I. as a bishopric of Cilicia Secunda, and is mentioned by Ptolemy as Kabassos in Kataonia. Stephanus quotes the statement of Apion that Kabassos was a village of Cappadocia between Tarsos and Cæsareia-Mazaka. The city Kabessos, mentioned in Iliad xiii., 363, is sometimes (but of course wrongly) identified with the town. The authorities are not explicit enough to fix the position of the place, but it must have been on the frontier of Cilicia Secunda and Cappadocia (see p. 311).

RHOSSOS or ROSOS. The situation is clearly indicated by Strabo and by a passage in ' Acta Sanctorum,' Jan. 11, p. 678 : " Rosus est oppidum Ciliciæ, dextra ei qui navigat in Pontum Cilicium. Hujus ad orientem et meridiem est mons altus, spatiosus et umbrosus." On this mountain stood the monastery called " in Scopulo," between Rosos and Seleuceia.

PINDENISSOS, a city of the Eleutherocilices, captured after a regular siege by Cicero (ad Fam. xv. 4, ad Att. v. 20). The name seems to be a mere local variety of the Pisidian or Pamphylian Pednelissos, which occurs in many different forms, approximating to Pentenissos.

BAKA, a fortress of Cilicia, is mentioned by Nicetas Chon., pp. 29, 33, Cinnamus, pp. 18, 20.

Anna Comnena gives much information about Cilicia, and mentions the rivers Sarôn and Hermôn (II. 138, 241), meaning probably Saros and Pyramos.

I add a few references to the ' Acta Sanctorum ' :—

1. DEMETRIAS was the name of an estate (κτῆμα) in the district of Tarsos, on the southern slope of a mountain (' Acta S. Zenaidis,' Oct. 11).

2. Many particulars about Anazarbos, Mansista (i.e. Mopsouestia), and Siskia occur in the ' Acta S. Tarachi ' (Oct. 11).*

3. SS. Claudius, Asterius, and Neon, Isaurians, connected also

---

* " Numerianus Maximus præses provinciæ, coss. iterum Diocletiano et Maximiano ! "

with Laranda, were executed at Ægæ, under Lysias the Præses, on August 23, " coss. Augusto et Aristobulo." It is true that in the third century Laranda and Isauria were subject to the governor of Cilicia.

4. Maximus præfectus at Pompeiopolis Ciliciæ, v. ' Acta S. Calliopii,' April 7, p. 660 (date under Maximian).

5. S. Julianus, son of a senator of Anazarbos, suffered at Ægæ Ciliciæ, when Marcianus was præses provinciæ; the time is variously reported as under Decius, Gallienus, or Diocletian, and the narrative is utterly without local colour. March 16, p. 421.

6. An estate-named Lara or Laras in the Latin text, but Ῥάδαμνος in the Greek, about six miles from Anazarbos, is mentioned, ' Acta S. Marini,' Aug. 8.

7. At Anazarbos, under Diocletian, Pelagius praeses, Febr. 5, p. 663.

8. S. Pelagia of Tarsos, without local colour or verisimilitude, May 4, p. 459.

9. S. Zenobius, under a dux Lysias, with some information about Cilicia, Oct. 30.

V. CITIES AND BISHOPRICS OF PISIDIA.

1. No province of Asia Minor is so difficult in respect of topography as Pisidia. The first difficulty, which as yet is insuperable, is to attain any certainty as to the correspondence between Hierocles and the Notitiæ. Hierocles uses the temporary names Eudoxioupolis and Justinianopolis, which do not occur in the Notitiæ and cannot be appropriated with certainty; and his corrupt name Themisonios is also quite uncertain. The lists of Chalcedon, which often clear up the obscurities of Hierocles, give five bishops of Pisidia simply by name, without their dioceses, so that they are practically useless, and the signatures of the ' Epistola ad Leonem' are so few, and the names of the bishops are so changed in the seven years since the Council of Chalcedon, that this aid also fails. Further exploration is needed, and without the discovery of new documents no progress seems possible. The accompanying Table of the bishoprics is therefore uncertain in several correspondences, and the discussion that follows is in several places little more than a statement of difficulties.

2. I have divided the Notitiæ into two classes for Pisidia, but strictly speaking there are three. The oldest class consists of VII. and VIII., which have Neapolis as a bishopric, omit Mallos, Tityassos, Parlais, Siniandos, and Bindeos, and give Atenia.* Of these, VII. is clearly the older, as it mentions Konana under the temporary title Justinianopolis, which Hierocles also uses. The second class consists only of IX.: it agrees with the older class in respect of Neapolis, Mallos, Tityassos,

* Bindeos I identify conjecturally with Theudosioupolis, a bishopric in 458. It did not strike coins because it was an imperial estate.

Siniandos, and Atenia, but adds Bindeos and Parlais. The latest class consists of I., III., X., XIII., which are identical in spite of slight differences due to mere clerical blunders. These omit Atenia, give Neapolis as an archbishopric, and add not merely, like IX., Bindeos and Parlais, but also Mallos and Tityassos.

At first sight we might conclude that Hierocles here gives a list of the governmental districts of Pisidia, and that gradually some of these were raised to the rank of bishoprics, Bindeos and Parlais between the time of Notitiæ VIII. and I., Mallos and Tityassos still later. But the Councils prove that this opinion is erroneous. Sinethandos is a bishopric in 451 and 458; Parlais in 325, 381, 451, and 458; Mallos in 458; even Tityassos and Bindeos* are found in 692, before the date of the oldest Notitia, and it seems, therefore, almost certain that every place mentioned by Hierocles was a bishopric in his time. The only places which are not proved to have been bishoprics before 530 are:—Dabinai or Sabinai, known only from the Tekmoreian lists in the third century and Hierocles in the sixth; Atenia, known only from the Tekmoreian lists, Hierocles, and the early class of Notitiæ; Baris, which was an important city, striking coins, and mentioned in all Notitiæ; Timbrias, which is not proved to be a bishopric till 680, but which struck coins and is in all Notitiæ; Tityassos, which struck coins; and perhaps Bindeos, on which see p. 387. All cities which struck coins may be assumed to have been bishoprics before 530; hence only Atenia and Dabinai remain in doubt. Atenia is known only from older authorities and has no place in later authorities. The inference, therefore, is that it was a decaying place, which was a bishopric in earlier time, and afterwards disappeared. Dabinai is the only remaining difficulty, and certainly the probability is against its having ever been a bishopric. It was probably united with another town in one bishopric, and Hierocles gives them as two separate towns; several of the Notitiæ do the same with Mesotimolos and Blaundos in Lydia. Hierocles' list in Pisidia is, therefore, identical with the list of bishops of his time, after uniting Dabinai with Limnai or with Atenia; and one of his names, ὁ Τιμβριάδων (ἐπίσκοπος), is obviously transcribed from a list of bishops, while another is probably to be understood as an adjectival from [ὁ] Θεμισόνιος [ἐπίσκοπος].

3. One of the first problems that confront us is to fix the bounds between Pisidia, Lykaonia, and Pamphylia, in the Byzantine time. In the early part of the fourth century, Pisidia extended much further to the east, and included the north-western part of Lykaonia. In 371-2 the new province of Lykaonia was formed by taking parts from Isauria and Pisidia and probably also from Pamphylia. The only way to fix the frontier where the three provinces meet is to discuss the situation of the cities that must have adjoined the frontier. All three provinces probably

* See footnote on previous page.

touched the lake of Bey Sheher, which was in ancient times called Karalis. The Byzantine name was, perhaps, Pasgousa or Poungousa; but the application of this name is not quite certain. The only doubt which can arise is whether this name should not be applied to the more westerly double lake, Hoiran Göl and Egerdir Göl, the ancient Limnai.*

Lake Pasgousa or Poungousa has always been considered to be Bey Sheher Lake; and the evidence seems conclusive, yet not quite satisfactory. John Comnenus, in 1142, marched by this lake, and captured the islands in it, which were inhabited by Christians who from long intercourse with the Turks had adopted many of their customs. The point which decides most authorities to identify Pasgousa with Bey Sheher Lake is that the islanders could go to Ikonion and return the same day. But this is unsatisfactory, for the eastern coast of Bey Sheher Lake is over sixty miles from Iconium by road, and the statement as it is given is therefore impossible, and cannot fairly be used as an argument in favour of the identification, though, of course, it is not such a great exaggeration about Bey Sheher Lake as about Egerdir Lake. A stronger reason is that Skleros is said to have been the older name of this lake: it can hardly be doubted that Skleros is the old name Karalis altered by the etymological tendency in order to get a name with a meaning in Greek. This reason seems conclusive, and yet the circumstances recorded suggest the Limnai rather than Bey Sheher Lake. The emperor was opening up a road to Attaleia, which had for some time been entirely cut off from land-communication with Constantinople. He advanced by Laodicea and Sozopolis, both of which he had to recapture from the Turks. Bey Sheher Lake lies quite away from any probable road from Sozopolis to Attaleia, whereas it would be a very natural road to go by Egerdir, and, in passing, to capture the two islands near it. This consideration, however, cannot weigh against the preceding reasons, and therefore Pasgousa, or Poungousa, must be accepted as the Byzantine name of Lake Karalis. But the geographical accuracy of the later historians is not always perfect.

Incidentally the first campaign of John gives a striking example of the manner in which Byzantine Christians were treated by the Seljuk Sultans and by their own emperors. The inhabitants of the islands hated Byzantine rule, and preferred the Turks; and John was obliged to reduce them by force of arms (Nicet. Chon., 50; Cinnam., 22)

Manuel returned from Ikonion by way of Lake Poungousa (formerly called Sklêros). When he reached the head-waters of the Mæander, he considered he was beyond the enemy's country, and went out to enjoy the pleasure of hunting. He found, however, an encampment of Turks while he was away from camp. This shows the bounds of Seljuk and Byzantine dominion in the year 1146 (Cinnam., 59).

* On the name, see below, LIMNAI.

4. The situation of Misthia, Vasada, and Amblada shows that the north eastern and eastern shore of the lake Karalis belonged to Lykaonia.

5. KARALLIA must be placed on lake Karalis. It is in Pamphylia, and, as the northern and eastern shores of the lake belonged to Lykaonia, and the western shore must apparently have belonged to Pisidia, it must have been situated on the southern shore. There were probably two cities, one at the south-eastern end of the lake, where the river runs out of it to lake Trogitis, and the other near the south-western end.* As the latter is more likely to be Parlais, the former must be taken as the site of Karallia. Its modern name is Bey Sheher. Bey Sheher has been an important city throughout the Turkish period, being named as one of the six † chief cities of Hamid in the fourteenth century.

Bey Sheher and Ak Sheher are named by Ducas (p. 204) as captured from Karaman by Murad : their names are given, κατὰ τὴν τῶν Τούρκων γλῶτταν, as Ἀκσιαρη and Πέγσιαρη.‡

Karallia was by older authorities placed at Kirili Kassaba, the name being supposed to have remained. The name Kirili may perhaps be connected with the ancient Karalis,§ but it is primarily the name of the whole territory along the east side of the lake, and the market-town of this territory is Kirili Market. The name of the lake may have been given to the territory, and the name of the territory, according to the Turkish division, was given to its market-town.

6. PARLAIS or PARALAIS. The references to this city are very con- tradictory. Ptolemy places it in Lykaonia, the Notitiæ place it in Pisidia, Hierocles does not mention the name, and in the Councils the phrase " Paralais Lykaoniæ " occurs several times. It was one of Augustus's Pisidian colonies, and must, therefore, have been an important town on a Roman road.

Formerly, when I discovered that Khatyn Serai was the site of a Roman colony, and it was not known that Lystra was a colony, the conclusion seemed inevitable that Parlais was at Khatyn Serai: I was forced to this opinion against various considerations, the order of Hierocles and the authority of Leake, which pointed out Khatyn Serai as the site of Lystra. Afterwards M. Waddington, and later M. Imhoof- Blumer, published coins which showed that Lystra was a Roman colony ;

---

* This site has been seen by no traveller, but has been reported to Sterrett and to myself.

† The six are Ak Sheher (Philomelion), Bey Sheher, Kara Aghatch (Neapolis), Yalowatch (Antiocheia), Seidi Sheher (Lyrbe (?) Kolybrassos (?)), and Sparta (Baris): see Ritter, 'Kleinasien,' II., 461.

‡ Implying the common dialectic variety Shahr for Sheher. The final η represents the Turkish ending in -i. For other examples of Turkish names in Greek compare p. 209, p. 290.

§ I do not, however, think so ; first, because it is uncertain whether the name Karalis was used in later Byzantine time (see § 3); and secondly, because Kirli is a common Turkish name.

and then Mr. Sterrett discovered an inscription which proved Colonia Lystra to have been situated at Khatyn Serai. Parlais remains to be placed on another site.

Kiepert has recently conjectured that Parlais has retained its name as Barla, on the west coast of Egerdir Göl. This I think impossible because—(1) it does not account for Ptolemy's attribution to Lykaonia : though Ptolemy's authority is, of course, slight in such a matter, owing to his frequent errors, yet he is confirmed by the phrase " Parlais Lykaoniæ " at some of the councils; (2) it does not account for the attribution of Parlais to Isauria in the Nicene Council; (3) Barla lies in a nook between the mountains and the lake, a place which could never have been of the slightest military importance. The Roman colonies founded by Augustus were planted for military reasons and connected by military roads. The idea that a military road could ever have wound along the crooked and narrow west bank of the Limnai can only appear ridiculous to any one who has seen the country. These colonies were certainly founded on one scheme and all connected with the military centre, Colonia Antiocheia Pisidiæ. The only way of reaching Barla from Antiocheia is by a very circuitous road round the lake, a road which has in many places only just room to pass between the mountains and the water. The aim of the colonies was to control the mountaineers of Pisidia and Isauria; but colonists at Barla would be cut off from the world and utterly useless. Kiepert's conjecture must, therefore, be rejected.

The problem is to find a site adjoining at once Pisidia, Isauria, and Lykaonia. Such a site can be found only at the south end of lake Karalis, or between Karalis and Trogitis. The series of Roman mile-stones, of large size, but none with any visible traces remaining of inscription, leading down the east side of Karalis and as far as Trogitis, also point to the existence of an important military road here, and a colony is to be looked for on an important military road. Moreover, an Augustan colony is wanted on the Pisidian frontier, between Lystra on the east and Kremna on the west, to complete the scheme of Augustus. Finally, the Latin inscriptions of this neighbourhood are more numerous than usual, and Latin inscriptions always indicate the presence of Romans. These considerations seem conclusive. There remains only the difficulty of selecting the exact site. Paralais was in Byzantine Pisidia, and that province can have included only the western and south-western shore of Karalis. Ruins named Uzumla Monastir are reported near the south-western extremity. These ruins are close to the important route from Antiocheia and Ikonion to the coast at Side, and the situation appears to be admirably adapted for striking in several directions. At the same time the form " Paralais " has, as others have suggested, perhaps arisen from the situation on the lake. Coins have the form "Parlais;" but popular derivation, aided by the natural tendency to develope a vowel sound between the two consonants, sought a form that gave some possible meaning in Greek.*

The principle enunciated in the preceding paragraph that, in the central and eastern parts of Asia Minor, "Latin inscriptions always indicate the presence of Romans,"† appears to be an important one. Latin was very little known in the country, and Latin inscriptions are rare : the educated classes wrote in Greek, and the uneducated spoke only the native language, with perhaps a smattering of Greek. But it is quite unjustifiable to argue, as MM. Radet and Paris do in 'Bull. Corr. Hell.,' 1886, p. 511, that "la présence d'une inscription Latine à Zosta" (in the midst of several Greek inscriptions) "semble indiquer l'existence d'une colonie romaine." If this argument were allowed, we should have far more than a hundred Roman colonies in the country. The proper argument to prove the existence of a Roman colony has been stated by me in 'Bull. Corr. Hell.,' 1883, p. 318, where it is inferred, from the fact of four inscriptions out of seven at Khatyn Serai being Latin, that a colony must have existed there. My inference has since been justified by Professor Sterrett's discovery; and, in general, it may be maintained that, if the majority of the inscriptions found on a particular site are Latin, and if more than four or five in all are found, the site is that of a Roman colony. The converse, however, cannot be maintained, that in all colonies the majority of the inscriptions are Latin.

7. An indication of the position of Parlais may be derived from a less certain source, viz., the Acta Concil. Nicæn., A.D. 325. The lists of this council are older than the formation of a separate province of Lykaonia. The boundaries of Pisidia, and Isauria, and Pamphylia were then very different from the later bounds, and Parlais belonged to Isauria. It is, however, true that there are several cases in which the bishoprics at the Council of Nicæa are apparently assigned to the wrong province; but, in almost all cases, those which are wrongly assigned are near the frontier. It may reasonably be maintained that the lists of this council are much more correct, and that they give us a better picture of the provincial organisation than such writers as Czwalina allow. For example: it is possible that before the province of Lykaonia was formed in 361–2 there was a single large province of Isauria, including the southern part of Lykaonia and the eastern part of Pamphylia, with such cities as Syedra, Homonada, Paralais, and with the metropolis Isaura. When, in 361–2, it was found advisable to divide further the large province of Isauria, all the Lykaonian cities were taken from it and from Pisidia. It was perhaps at the same time,‡

* I believe indeed that it was late before Greek became the language of the Pisidian people in general; but it was known to all educated people, and as a rule it is only the testimony of the educated that has come down to us.

† I.e., cives Romani, who are not necessarily Italians.

‡ The character of the changes, as they are described in the sequel, makes it probable that the redivision of Isauria took place all at once.

certainly it was later than A.D. 325, that Lycia-Pamphylia was divided into two provinces, Lycia and Pamphylia. In our oldest authority, the Verona MS., Lycia is omitted, which merely means that it was included, along with Pamphylia, in a single province. In 313 the same governor is given to both Lycia and Pamphylia.* It has been maintained that in the Verona MS. Lycia must be restored; but before correcting our authorities, it is better to try whether they cannot be justified. The lists of 325 divide the eastern towns of Pamphylia between Isauria and Pisidia, assigning Selge to the latter. When Pamphylia was separated from Lycia, parts were taken both from Isauria and from Pisidia to form the new province Pamphylia.

As Side had equal claim with Perga to be a metropolis, the ecclesiastical lists always separate Pamphylia Prima under Side and Pamphylia Secunda under Perga, though the civil organisation admitted only a single province.† Similarly Bithynia was divided for ecclesiastical, but not for civil, purposes between Nikomedeia and Nikaia. To compensate Pisidia for the loss of Ikonion, Amblada, Selge, &c., Paralais was added to it, and also Mallos, if I rightly place it in Mallos Ova. It was probably the unruly state of Isauria, and the difficulties it caused to the imperial Government, which led to its being reduced to a more manageable size. I add the lists of the three provinces as they existed in 325 : the bishoprics of Pamphylia and of Lycia are separated at the Council, but the part of Pamphylia that remains is too small to have been really a distinct province.

PISIDIA.

1. Eulalius Iconiensis (aft. Lykaonia).	Ikonion.
2. Telemachus Hadrianopolitanus.	Hadrianopolis.
3. Theodorus Uzelenis.	Zorzila.
4. Eutychius Seleuciensis.	Seleuceia.
5. Hesychius Neapolitanus.	Neapolis.
6. Uranion Selgensis, Sutenonensis.	Selge.
7. Apagamus, or Aramius, Lisiniensis, Limenensis.	Limnai.
8. Tarsicius Apamenus.	Apameia Cibotos.
9. Patricius Ambladensis (aft. Lykaonia).	Amblada.
10. Polycarpus Metropolitanus.‡	Metropolis.

* Cod. Theodos. 13, 10, 2.

† This division is implied by the order of Hierocles, in the Epistola ad Leonem, A D. 458, and in the lists of Conc. Chalced., A.D. 451. It is not recognised in the lists of Conc. Constantinop., A.D. 381.

‡ It may be doubted whether Polycarpus is not the metropolitan of the whole province and bishop of Antiocheia, for the metropolitan is not always put first (see the Isaurian list). But, on the whole, this view seems less probable, and perhaps Iconium may at this time have been either sole metropolis or one of two metropoleis, in the province Pisidia. Silvanus of Isauropolis is not called simply Metropolitanus, but in Isauro

PISIDIA—*continued.*

11. Acumedius, Academius Pariensis,*
    a Paro.   Pappa.
12. Heraclius Barensis.   Baris.
    Theodorus Usensis: dittography of 3.
13. Adon Byciæ Lycius.   Laodiceia.

PAMPHYLIA (united with Lycia).

Callinicus Pergensis.   Perga.
Euresius Termessenus.   Termessos.
Teuxius Cyrbenis, Siarbitanus.   Berbe.
Domnus Aspendius.   Aspendos.
Quintianus Seleuciensis.†   Sillyon.
Patricius Maximianopolitanus.   Maximianopolis.
Aphrodisius Magidorum.   Magydos.

ISAURIA.

Stephanus Baratthensis.   Barata.
Athenæus Zoropassenus, Corpissitanus. Coropissos.
Ethesius Claudiopolitanus.   Claudiopolis.
Agapetus Seleuciæ.   Seleuceia.
Silvanus Metropolitanus in Isauro.   Isauropolis.
Faustus Phuphenatensis, Phanemu-
    thiensis.   Panemouteichos? ‡
Antonius Antiochenus.   Antiocheia.
Nestor Syedrensis.   Syedra.
Hesychius Chorepiscopus.
Cyrillus Sidensis, Cumanadensis.   Side? Homonada?
Theodorus Vasagadensis,§ Vialbitanus. Vasada? Olba?
Theodorus Chorepiscopus, Anatolius
    Chorepiscopus.
Paulus Larandensis.   Laranda.
Quintus Chorepiscopus.
Tyberius Lystrensis.   Lystra.
Aquila Chorepiscopus.
Eusebius Paralais Lycaoniæ.   Paralais.

is added: compare the phrase of Hilarius, who signed the will of Gregory Nazianzen in the end of this century, τῆς κατὰ 'Ισαυρίαν καθολικῆς ἐκκλησίας. The Latin in Isauro is a bad translation of κατὰ 'Ισαυρίαν.

* The corruption is facilitated by the following Barensis.

† There is no Seleuceia of Pamphylia: Seleuceia of Pisidia and of Isauria both occur in their respective provinces.

‡ The name is a difficulty, as it would be expected to be in Lycia-Pamphylia with Sillyon, Aspendos, and Perga.

§ Vasagadensis has been corrupted by assimilation to the preceding name; but see App. M. 10. Probably Vasada is meant here, as it is supported by Conc. Antioch. A.D. 340.

If we accept, as far as possible, the evidence of the Nicene lists, we must say that when, about 276–82, Isauria was made a separate province, the frontier was modified from the line which it had followed since 138–161. Isauropolis seems to have been made the metropolis. Iconium was transferred to Pisidia, and in its stead Vasada was attached to Isauria. To give the new province sufficient extent, the eastern part of Lycia-Pamphylia was added to it, including Karallia, Parlais, Mallos, Lyrbe, Kolobrassos, Homonades, Syedra, probably Etenna and Katenna, and possibly even Side. But, in the tendency of the fourth century to diminish the size of the provinces, Lykaonia was created in 371–72 out of parts of Pisidia, Isauria, and Galatia, and Pamphylia was made a new province, distinct from Lycia. The frontier was again rearranged; Pamphylia was now made to extend even further than it had ever extended before,—even Dalisandos, which belonged to Lykaonia-Isauria from 138 to 276, being now attached to Pamphylia. The discussion of the bishoprics has shown the exact bounds of the provinces from this time onwards: but Amblada, which must have belonged to the civil province of Pisidia, had formed an ecclesiastical connection with Iconium between 276 and 361, and its bishop continued obedient to the metropolitan of Iconium.*

The first certain reference I have found to a separate province Pamphylia is in the epistle of the synod of Alexandreia, A.D. 363, where we find the enumeration, Pamphylia, Lycia, Isauria, Pontus, Cappadocia. But M. l'Abbé Duchesne infers, from the mention by Hilarius 'de Synod.' 63 (ii. 498) of ten provinces in the Dioecesis Asiana, that Lycia and Pamphylia were separated already in A.D. 358. If this be so, it becomes more difficult to follow the Nicene lists.

8. The list of the bishops of Paralais, as given in the Councils, proves its situation conclusively to have been close to Lykaonia, yet subject to Pisidia. They are—

325 Eusebius Paralais Lykaoniæ, in Isauria.
381 Patricius Paraliensis, in Pisidia.
431 Libanius Pari Lykaoniæ.
451 Libanius Parlai or Paralai in Pisidia.
458 Libanius Paralenus signs 'Epistola Synodi Pisidiæ.'
503 Libanius Parlai Lykaoniæ.
877 Anthimus Parlai.†

Why, then, is Parlais omitted by Hierocles? The omission is to be compared with those of Kotiaion and Eukhaita. Perhaps Parlais (which was evidently an important place, as its bishops were present so regularly at councils) was the head of a small district, transferred from Isauria to Pisidia in 371–2, but retaining an ecclesiastical isolation for

---

* This division may seem rather artificial, but I prefer to follow the Nicene list as far as possible; new evidence may be found to prove or disprove it.

† Georgius Galai in 692 is altered by Le Quien to Parlai; but [Sa]gala[s]i is more probably correct.

some time. Mallos and Tityassos may have been included along with it,
and the whole may gradually have been transferred to the metropolitan
of Antiocheia.*   Or possibly it was simply the title Parlais Lykaoniæ
which prevented Hierocles from giving it in Pisidia, and its omission in
the Lykaonian lists that prevented him from giving it in Lykaonia.

9. Hierocles begins with a group of six cities, which occupy the
country between the Limnai on the west, Karalis and the Lykaonian
frontier on the south, Sultan Dagh on the east, and the Phrygian frontier
on the north.   Of these—

ANTIOCHEIA is well known, and its remains are still very imposing.
Its walls, which gain additional elevation from taking advantage of a
rising ground, make it a very strong fortress of the Hellenistic and
Roman type.   A very remarkable rock cutting, nearly semicircular
in outline and of great size, perhaps marks the hieron of Men
Askaenos.   The river Anthios flows through the territory of
Antiocheia to the Limnai.† Ptolemy mentions Antiocheia twice : once
in Pisidia of Galatia Provincia, along with Apollonia, Amblada, and
Neapolis; and once in Phrygia Pisidia of Pamphylia Provincia. The
former list is apparently founded on a Roman official authority, while
the latter does not appear to be so, and can, therefore, not be relied on as
a perfect authority for the boundaries of the province.

10. NEAPOLIS is first mentioned by Pliny.   It occurs in Geogr.
Ravenn., which may be taken as a proof that it was on a Roman road.
Moreover, Hierocles is particularly fond of beginning his enumeration
of the cities of a province by giving those which lie on some important
road ; e.g. in Lydia : Sardis, Philadelphia, Tripolis ; in Lykaonia : Ikonion,
Lystra.   Ptolemy places Neapolis south of Antiocheia, and we may,
therefore, assume that it was on the Roman road, many of whose milestones are preserved from Antiocheia to Mistheia, Karallia, Parlais, and
the south coast at Side.   On this road is the important town of Kara
Aghatch, which is known to have been one of the six great towns of
this part of the plateau in the fourteenth century.‡

The earliest Notitiæ, VII., VIII., IX., mention Neapolis as a
bishopric under Antiocheia, but the later Notitiæ give it as an archbishopric.§   This dignity was probably given to it at the same time as
to Mistheia : the exact date is uncertain, but was before 838 A.D.   Its

* The discussion of the Akmonia district and the Khonai district in Phrygia, and
the Kormasa-Komama-Panemouteichos group in Pamphylia, give parallel instances.
Compare also Selge.

† ANTHIOS on coins : Kiepert gives Anteus.

‡ They are Ak Sheher (Philomelion), Bey Sheher (Karallia), Seidi Sheher (Lyrbe
or Kolybrassos), Isbarta, commonly pronounced by all natives Sparta (Baris), Yalowatch (Antiocheia), Kara Aghatch ; v. Ritter, ' Kleinasien,' II., 460.

§ Only Notitia I. mentions it as an archbishopric of Pisidia ; the others, II., X., XI.,
give it, like other archbishoprics, without indicating the province, and hence Parthey's
index divides the references to this city under two separate heads.

importance in later Byzantine time corresponds to that of Kara Aghatch in early Turkish time.

No coins of Neapolis are known.

11. ANABOURA. A people named Anaboureis are known from inscriptions and from Strabo. The first of these inscriptions was published by me in the 'Athenische Mittheilungen,' 1883, p. 71, and the number has since been increased by Professor Sterrett. The disappearance of the name Anaboura from all writers later than Strabo is due to its being replaced by Neapolis. I stated (*l.c.*, p. 76) that "some time between 19 A.D., the latest date mentioned in Strabo, and 75 A.D., about which time Pliny wrote the 'Historia Naturalis,' the name Neapolis displaced the name Anaboura. Either a new name was given to the old town, or a new town was built near the old one in a more suitable situation." Professor Sterrett has detected in the modern form Enevre * the old name Anaboura, and has thus proved that the second alternative is correct. The "New City" was built on the Roman road, but the old Anaboura continued to exist, and we might expect to find, if the Notitiæ were complete records of the actual state of the country, the entry ὁ Ἀναβουρέων ἤτοι Νεαπόλεως.

The name Anaboura also occurs in Phrygia. The northern part of Pisidia was certainly inhabited by a Phrygian people, speaking a Phrygian language, and Strabo undoubtedly considered that Antiocheia belonged to Phrygia,† and that the frontier between Phrygia and Pisidia was between Antiocheia and Anaboura.

Manes Ourammoes, who is mentioned in the inscription of Anaboura, quoted above, was probably a chief or king of the people before its final conquest by the Romans.‡

The territory of the Anaboureis probably lay north and west of that of the Orondeis. One of their inscriptions was found at Felle by Professor Sterrett. I copied it again in 1886. It is built into a Turkish aqueduct, the stones for which may have probably been brought from a distance. It is, however, not necessary to believe with Professor Sterrett that this stone has been brought from Enevre across the hills, a distance of nine or ten miles. It is equally probable that the territory of the Anaboureis was wide, and included several small towns or villages.

12. LIMNAI, SABINAI, and ATMENIA belong to the region of the double lakes called Limnai, and of their north-east and east side. The order of Hierocles is here confirmed by the evidence of the inscriptions of the ξένοι Τεκμόρειοι.§ Sabinai and Atmenia are good examples of the difficulty of determining from Byzantine lists alone the

* It is not a village, but a deserted ruin (Euren), 7 or 8 miles west of Karagatch.

† He speaks of it as Antiocheia πρὸς τῇ Πισιδίᾳ, p. 569.

‡ With the phrase of the Anabouran inscription, ὄντες ἀπόγονοι Μάνου Οὐραμμόου. compare the frequent βασιλέων καὶ τετραρχῶν ἀπόγονοι in inscriptions of Ankyra Galatiæ. I have discussed the probable sense fully in "A Study of Phrygian Art, II." in 'Journ. Hell. Stud.,' 1889.

§ See below, § 35.

proper form of a name. The forms Atmenia, Atenia, Atenoa, all occur; the natural conclusion from these would be that Atmenia is correct, and that a letter has been lost in the shorter forms. But the inscriptions show that Tenia was the form in the Roman period. So Sabinai is in all probability to be identified with the ethnic Dabeneus of the inscriptions.* Until some inscription reveals it, the true form of the name Sinethandos, Siniandos, Siniandros, Sitriandos will always be uncertain. Such examples render the identification of Alieros and Alastos less improbable.

13. PAPPA is mentioned by Ptolemy as one of the two cities of the Orondeis. The emperor Tiberius seems to have given it the rank of a city, and allowed it to take the name Tiberiopolis. A coin published by M. Waddington has the legend ΤΙΒΕΡΙΕΩΝ ΠΑΠΠΗΝΩΝ, and an inscription found at Antiocheia by Professor Sterrett reads: Τύχην εὐμενῆ τῇ Κολωνείᾳ, Τιβεριοπολειτῶν Παππηνῶν 'Ορονδέων βουλὴ δῆμος.† This inscription was obviously engraved on the pedestal of a statue of " the Good Fortune of Antiocheia," presented to the colony by the Pappenoi; and this presentation, combined with that of Lystra ‡ (τὴν λαμπροτάτην 'Αντιοχέων κολωνίαν ἡ λαμπροτάτη Λυστρέων κολωνία τὴν ἀδελφὴν . . . ἐτείμησεν) probably points to some special connection of Antiocheia as a metropolis with the whole set of Roman foundations of Augustus and Tiberius in the southern part of the province Galatia. These foundations had all certainly the object of holding the newly-conquered country, and of guarding it against the mountaineers of Isauria and the Homonades. They were connected by a system of roads, which radiated from Antiocheia as the military centre of the whole of southern Galatia.

The military colonies of Augustus, which were probably founded in B.C. 6 (C. I. L., iii., Supplem., No. 6974) were—

Colonia Julia Augusta Olbasa.
Colonia Julia Augusta Pia Fida Comama.§
Colonia Julia Augusta Felix Cremna.
Colonia Julia Augusta Parlais.
Colonia Julia Felix Gemina Lystra.
Colonia Cæsareia Antiocheia.

* On these two names see § 35, and my paper on " The Græco-Roman Civilisation in Pisidia," in ' Journ. Hell. Stud.,' 1883.

† This inscription gives the correct form of the name, and at the same time finally disposes of the idea that there was a city Oroanda. The following texts mention the tribe :—Polyb., xxii., 25 : ἐξαπέστειλε πρὸς τοὺς 'Οροανδεῖς; iv. 26 : χρήματα παρὰ τῶν Οροανδέων; Livy, xxxviii., 18 : " legati Oroandensium ;" ib. 37, " L. Manlio Oroanda misso," which implies the existence of a city, is probably a mistranslation from Polybius; ib. 39 : " ab Oroandis rediit ;" Plin., v., 24 : " oppida Oroanda, Sagalessos ;" but Sillig quotes one MS. Oronda and another Aronda; this is a false inference from the tribal Orondeis; Ptolemy has 'Ορονδικοί.

‡ Found at Antiocheia by Sterrett. I have since copied it again in 1886.

§ So Head, 'Hist. Num. ;' but a coin is quoted with legend : COL. IVL. AVG. G. I. F. COMAMENORVM, and another with G. F., which imply Gemina not Pia.

The preceding inscription, showing such a close relation between Pappa and Antiocheia, may be taken as a proof that Tiberius connected Tiberiopolis Pappa with Augustus's series of colonies, and, as Pappa occurs in Anon. Ravenn., we may conclude that it was on a Roman road from Antiocheia to the south or east. One important line seems required to maintain the connection of Antiocheia with Lystra Colonia and with Lykaonia and the east in general. This route leads straight east from Kara Aghatch (Neapolis) round the southern end of the Sultan Dagh to Doghan Hissar (near Hadrianopolis-Thymbrion), and thence south to Ikonion and Lystra, and east to Tyriaion (Ilghin). We may probably connect the foundation of Neapolis * with the formation of this road, and attribute a general revision and improvement of the organisation of Pisidia † to Tiberius. Similarly another wide-reaching reorganisation took place under Claudius, probably in his first year, 41 A.D., when Lykaonia was remodelled, and the foundations, Claudeikonion, Claudio-Derbe, Colonia Claudiopolis, Claudioseleuceia, Colonia Archelais, and Cæsareia were probably all made.

We thus have a clue to the situation of Pappa, on the road east of Neapolis and south-east of Antiocheia. Another clue is furnished by the situation of the tribe Orondeis with their two cities Misthia and Pappa. Ptolemy places Pappa to the east and south of Misthia : considering his vague ideas as to the comparative situation of the roads and cities, we may accept the statement as to the district, without that as to direction. The fact that Pappa is in Pisidia, while Misthia is in Byzantine Lykaonia, shows that Pappa was probably further north than Misthia. Pappa, then, is to be looked for between Neapolis and Doghan Hissar. Professor Sterrett's suggestion that Tcharyk Serai, one hour east of Kara Aghatch, was the site of Pappa, has, therefore, everything in its favour.

The preceding argument has shown why the inscription found by Professor Sterrett at Beldjez or Beldjighas cannot be taken as proof that Pappa was situated there, though it is the epitaph of a tomb constructed by Τειμόθεος Μεννέου Παππηνὸς χαλκεύς. Such inscriptions are sometimes erected by metoikoi, and Timotheos must have gone from Pappa to practise his trade in another city. Professor Sterrett also rightly rejects this inference.‡

14. Hierocles next passes to Paroreios Phrygia, part of which belonged to Byzantine Pisidia. The name of the first city in this district is of

* Above we dated it 19 to 76; we may now date it 19–37.

† A city Tiberiopolis also in northern Phrygia (Egri Göz or Amed). The institution of Cappadocia as a procuratorial province in 17 also belongs to Tiberius, but not the renaming of Mazaka (see p. 303).

‡ He, however, goes much too far when he takes this inscription as a proof that Pappa was not at Beldjez, and gives his III. 420 as a proof that Adada was not at Kara Bavlo (' Wolfe Expedition,' p. 283). This is exactly the contrary of what he should have inferred. Such occurrence of an ethnic in an inscription is always an indication,

quite uncertain form, Sinethandos, Siniandros, or Sitriandos.   It was, to judge from the order of Hierocles, probably situated at Khadyn Khan, where there are numerous remains.   I have published these in the 'Athenische Mittheilungen,' 1888, where I have stated the opinion that Sinethandos was in the Roman time only a *pagus* of the territory of Laodiceia.*   The other cities of this district, Tyriaion, Hadrianopolis or Thymbrion, and Philomelion, have already been discussed under sect. C., Nos. 58–62.   Hierocles then passes to the western part of Pisidia, beginning his list with Sozopolis.

15. APOLLONIA is proved by its rich coinage and by its numerous inscriptions to have been a very important city.   It was a foreign settlement of Lycian and Thracian colonists, and in all probability Professor Hirschfeld is right in regarding it as a foundation of the Pergamenian kings.†   The Thracian colonists may, perhaps, have been mercenary soldiers, who, under the name Traleis, formed a distinct part of the Pergamenian forces.   Some Lycians were, for some reason unknown to us, settled along with them   Apollonia then was a Pergamenian counterpoise to the Seleucid foundations Dokimion and Synnada.

16. SOZOPOLIS takes the place of Apollonia in the Byzantine lists. Professor G. Hirschfeld was the first to observe the correspondence as being probable, but had no proof to give.   For years I felt sure that he was right, but sought in vain to find any direct proof, though an indirect proof may be gathered from the campaigns of John and Manuel Comnenus.   At last I found the following passage in the 'Acta Sanctorum,' June 19, p. 813, in estimating the value of which we must remember that a pass leads across the mountains from Apollonia to Konana. S. Zosimus lived at Apollonia in the territory Sosopolis ('Απολλωνιάδος τῆς ἐν Σωσοπόλει) in the reign of Trajan.   He was seized by Domitian the præses,‡ who resided at Antiocheia, shod with iron shoes, yoked with the horses, and driven to Konana (εἰς τὴν Κανεωτῶν πόλιν, where read Κονανέων).   Another manuscript life of Zosimus says he was killed ἐν τῇ Κονανέων πόλει, whither the præses had gone after passing through Apollonia.   In this document the phrase occurs, ἦλθεν δὲ ἐν τῇ 'Απολλωνίᾳ

though not a conclusive proof, of the ancient name. The presumption from the inscription of Beldjez is that Pappa was situated there ; but general considerations lead us to reject this presumption.

* Siniandos is omitted in the earliest Notitiæ VII., VIII., IX. The others give it, so that the omission in these three is probably accidental.

† He, however, as I think, wrongly, understands Λύκιοι Θρᾷκες as meaning Thracians of Lycia ; it should be understood as equivalent to Λύκιοι καὶ Θρᾷκες, and as proving two classes of colonists in the city. The inscription quoted in E. 15 seems to prove this. The Θρᾷκες were probably Thracian mercenaries who had served in the Pergamenian army, where they were called Τράλεις (see Tralleis Asiae).

‡ The tale, therefore, first took literary form after the reorganisation of the provinces attributed to Diocletian ; but the local knowledge is a clear mark of a genuine popular tradition living in the country. The first account given in the text is quoted from the Menologion Basilii.

διὰ τῆς Σωζουπολιτῶν πόλει. These phrases show that the tale took literary form when the name Sozopolis had become common, and that of Apollonia was little known. It is not known at what period this took place, but the name Sozopolis occurs in all documents from the Council of Constantinople, A.D. 381, onwards. Probably Sozopolis is not merely another name for Apollonia, but a different city, so that the document just quoted is quite accurate in speaking of Apollonia as being in the territory of Sozopolis. Apollonia was a city of the plain having the peaceful character of the Pergamenian foundations.* Perhaps during the fourth century it was deserted, and Sozopolis was built on a lofty almost isolated hill projecting from the mountains on the south, the modern Olu Burlu. We can now have little hesitation in correcting Sterrett's Σοροπόλεως in No. 545 to Σο[ζ]οπόλεως.†

Sozopolis was an important place for pilgrimage in Byzantine times. There was a statue there of the Virgin from which oil exuded.‡ Theodorus of Sykea went on a pilgrimage to the church of the Virgin at Sozopolis, and his route by Germe and Amorion is described. He stayed forty days at Sozopolis, where Zoilus was the bishop. The church dated, according to tradition, from Mark, the cousin of Barnabas, who became bishop of Apollonias ('Acta Sanct.,' June 20, p. 67). The sacredness of Sozopolis as a place of pilgrimage is probably due in part to the fountain called Ayasman (i.e. ἁγίασμα) at Tymandos, a city in the neighbourhood.

Sozopolis passed into Turkish hands in accordance with the agreement made by Michael VII. with the Seljuks in A.D. 1074.§ It was recaptured by John Comnenus in 1120, and seems to have remained under the Byzantine power for some time. Sozopolis was besieged unsuccessfully by the Turks in 1142, but it remained probably in Byzantine hands throughout the reigns of John and Manuel Comnenus; but at last, in 1180, Sozopolis, Attaleia and Kotiaion were finally captured by the Turks on the death of Manuel. A Christian congregation, however, has preserved an unbroken continuance in it throughout the Turkish rule.

17. TYMANDOS was discovered by Professor J. R. S. Sterrett at Yassi Euren, four hours east of Olu Borlu (Sozopolis). It was raised to tho rank of a *polis* by some pagan emperor or emperors, most probably

---

* The precise site of Apollonia is probably at Olukman, which Sterrett describes, 'Wolfe Expedition,' p. 352, though he seems, like previous writers, to consider Olu Borlu the actual site of Apollonia.

† o for 'ω in an inscription dated A.D. 1069 need surprise nobody.

‡ "Oleo quod ex sanctæ puræque Dei Genetricis semperque virginis Mariæ Dominæ nostræ imagine solet scaturire Sozopoli" ('Act. Sanct.,' April 6, p. 560). It might be doubted in this example which Sozopolis is meant; but the route of Theodorus Sykeota, as given in the following sentence of the text, leaves no doubt that he went to Sozopolis of Pisidia ('Act. Sanct.,' April 22, p. 53).

§ According to the certainly correct inference of Finlay, there was such a treaty or at least agreement.

Diocletian and Maximian, to whose age the inscription seems to belong. Tymandos is mentioned by Hierocles and all the Notitiæ. It is not mentioned by any older writers, except Ptolemy, who gives it under the form Talbonda. This identification seemed always very probable to me, but it might probably seem to many critics to strain too far the possibilities of language. I regard the variation as merely one of the most extreme examples of the changes through which native names were liable to be forced when they assumed a Greek form. Other examples are Sagalassos and Selgessos, recorded by Strabo as equivalent, Selge and ΕΣΤΛΕΛΙΙΥΣ on coins, ΕΣΤΓΕΔΙΙΥΣ and Aspendos.* But fortunately I found a decisive proof, which sets this identification beyond controversy and makes analogies unnecessary.

18. TALBONDA is mentioned only by Ptolemy and at Concil. Constantinop. 448 A.D., where, in the Latin Version, occurs " Longinus reverendissimus episcopus Talbondanæ civitatis provinciæ Pisidiæ," while the Greek version has ὁ εὐλαβέστατος ἐπίσκοπος τῆς Τυμανδηνῶν πόλεως ἐπαρχίας Πισιδίας. The names Talbonda and Tymandos are here used as equivalent to each other.

There is a saint named Conon connected with Mandi or Manda in Pamphylia who may belong to Tymandos: the ecclesiastical lists often omit the first syllable of the name. But Mandi may be for Magydi. Another Conon of Bidane, 18 stadia from Isaura, is difficult to distinguish from this Conon ('Act. Sanct.,' March 6).

The beautiful spring in the hill south-east of Yassi Euren,† called Ayasman (ἁγίασμα) by the Turks, is still a place of annual pilgrimage for the Greeks of Olu Borlu (Apollonia). In the pagan time it seems to have been dedicated to Hercules Restitutor, as is shown by a Latin inscription (C. I. L., iii., Supplem., No. 6867): "Herculi Restitutori C. Iulius Hilario."‡

The permanence of the religious awe attaching to this and other such striking manifestations of the divine power is one of the most interesting features in the religion of Asia Minor.

19. METROPOLIS was placed in the Tchul Ovassi by G. Hirschfeld, the first traveller who explored the valley; but he afterwards deserted this view, and argued confidently that it was in the valley of Apollonia. The fact that it was on the great highway from Ephesos to Cæsareia would alone be sufficient evidence that the latter view is incorrect.

---

* Kormasa, Korbasa, Kolbassos and Tarbassos seem to me a certain case of equivalence; but others may doubt it.

† Sterrett discusses the proper form of this name at some length, and finally concludes that the first word is Yaztü, meaning "level." He has misunderstood the sharp dental sibilant. Redhouse's Turkish handbook gives *Yassi*, level. It is a common element in Turkish village names—Yassi Eyuk, Yassi Euren, Yassi Gümü.

‡ Ephem. Epigraph. V., 13054 from Sir C. Wilson's copy. Less correctly by Sterrett, ' Wolfe Exped.,' No. 559. On account of his difference in text I went back in 1888 and re-examined the inscription.

Kiepert's old map placed Metropolis with approximate accuracy. It is difficult to see why Metropolis was given to Pisidia under the Byzantine system. It naturally goes with Phrygia. It is closely connected by road with Synnada, while the mountain chain which in general bounds Byzantine Pisidia on the north divides it from the rest of that province. In spite of these considerations it was divorced from Synnada, and subjected to Antiocheia. In the 'Conc. Chalced.,' Heorticius, bishop of Metropolis, is so often called bishop of Nikopolis Pisidiæ, and even of Metropolis Nikopolis Pisidiæ, as to make it probable that the name Nikopolis was actually borne by Metropolis during the fifth century.*

20. APAMEIA was long one of the greatest cities of Asia Minor. Its decay dates from the foundation of Constantinople. Under the new system it was no longer on a great road, whereas so long as commerce tends to the west it is situated at a knot in the road-system. Professor G. Hirschfeld's discussion of the topography is generally satisfactory, but he is certainly wrong about the rivers. Mr. Hogarth has corrected him. Hirschfeld identified the Lidja as the Marsyas. Hogarth, with correct instinct, rejected the idea that "this melancholy stream, bubbling tamely out of a flat tract at the foot of a naked slope, and slinking away more like a drain than a river, could be the storied Marsyas." † This little stream is formed by tepid springs, called, therefore, by the generic name Lidja, and a coin of Apameia, which shows the four streams Mai(andros), Mar(syas), Or(gas), and Ther(ma), grouped around the patron goddess of Apameia (a deity of the Ephesian Artemis type), is a conclusive proof that the people of Apameia distinguished the hot springs from the Marsyas.

Professor Hirschfeld quotes in support of his identification of the Marsyas " ein paar Quellen, welche ganz nah seinem Austritte jetzt aus zwei Bogennischen aufsprudelnd alsbald in ihn fallen : " these springs he identifies as Κλαίων and Γελῶν. He has not observed that the two "Bogennischen" are simply two low arches to carry the Roman road over the hollow where the various hot springs rise. His supposition of a grotto having formerly existed at this place seems to me ‡ absolutely inconsistent with the surroundings. Hirschfeld also errs in giving the name Huda-verdi, "God hath given," to the principal stream. The name

---

* I devoted a paper to the "Metropolitanus Campus" in 'Journ. Hell. Stud.,' April, 1883. I have to add the following fragment of an inscription, which I copied on the actual site of Metropolis, half-way between Tatarli and Haidarli in October, 1883 : [ἡ βουλὴ καὶ ὁ δῆμος ἐτείμησεν Ἀ]ρ[τεμ]ίδωρον Σοσθένους τοῦ Ἀρ[τ]εμιδ[ώρ]ου σχ[ο]λ[α]στι[κ]οῦ, ἄνδρα ἐπίσημον καὶ ἐν πολλοῖς χρήσιμον γεγονό[τ]α τῇ πατρίδι, δόντα καὶ ἀργύριον εἰς ἀγῶνος δια . . . . . .

† Hirschfeld "Über Celainai-Apameia Kibotos," in 'Berl. Akad. Abhandl.,' 1876; Hogarth in 'Journ. Hell. Stud.,' 1888.

‡ I visited Apameia in 1881, 1882 (very hurriedly), and 1888, when I examined this point carefully, knowing Hogarth's unpublished opinion. In 1881 I had not read Hirschfeld's paper; but as I knew he had done the site very carefully, I paid no special attention to the topography.

Huda-verdi is restricted to a single fountain, which burst forth about 50 years ago (as I was told) at a point about 100 yards or more below the chief fountains of this stream, and a little above the highest mill. This new fountain gives fine drinking-water, which, if I remember rightly, *none* of the other fountains do, and hence is called Huda-verdi. Much of its water is kept separate, and carried off by a wooden pipe for the use of the town.

The supposed fountain Kallirhhoe at Apameia depends on Sestini's false reading of a coin; see Imhoof-Blumer, Num. Zft., 1884, p. 289.

Professor Hirschfeld's large scale map of Apameia is very good. It is to be regretted that we have no other map like it for any site in the interior of Asia Minor.* His small map of the Dineir and Dombai valleys, given on the same sheet, is not so good as it should be. His study of the history of Apameia-Celainai is very important.

Hierocles now passes to the southern parts of Pisidia, and goes along them from west to east. His first name is one of the great difficulties of the province.

21. EUDOXIOUPOLIS is never mentioned, except by Hierocles; but probably it is to be identified with Theodosioupolis,† mentioned among the signatures to the 'Epistola ad Leonem.' The order, Apameia, Eudoxioupolis, Sagalassos, Baris, suggests that Eudoxioupolis is to be placed at Kilij, near the north-eastern end of lake Askania, and near the modern town Ketchi Borlu. There can be no doubt that there was an ancient city and bishopric here, and equally little doubt that it was in Byzantine Pisidia.‡ The district seems to have been an imperial estate on the borders of Phrygia, and a boundary-stone of this estate has been described in E., 16. We cannot, therefore, place at Kilij any city that coined money, and if this is correct the only names of the Roman period that can be applied to it are Zorzila and Bindeos. Now Zorzila seems to be more probably situated elsewhere. Moreover, we have just seen that Theudosioupolis was the name given to this place in the fourth or fifth century, and Theudosioupolis may be identified with Bindeos, but cannot possibly be identified with Zorzila, for the two occur in the same lists, 458 and 530. Bindeos, therefore, may be placed at Kilij; its want of coinage is due to its being on an imperial estate. It received from one of the two emperors Theodosius the rank of a city and bishopric, but the old name Bindeos returns from 692 onwards. The modern name Fandas, 2 hours south of Kilij, at the other end of the valley, may contain the ancient name, but is certainly not the ancient site. The form of the name, which is always ὁ τοῦ Βινδαίου

* Even on the coast hardly any sites are decently mapped. M. Weber's map of Ephesos is one of the few exceptions.

† The form [Θ]ευδοσιούπολις might readily be corrupted Εὐδοξιούπολις.

‡ Sterrett, 'Wolfe Expedition,' gives several inscriptions, and I have copied additional ones.

(Βινδέου) ἐπίσκοπος, may be due to its being an imperial estate, and κτήματος may be understood. In that case Βινδαίου would be the genitive of an adjective, and Βίνδα, or some similar form, would be the name; but from want of any distinct authority I retain the name as Bindeos. Ptolemy gives in Pisidia both Beudos Vetus and Ouinzela. The former is transferred by error from Phrygia; the latter occurs also in Galatia.* I think that Beudos has been placed here by Ptolemy through confusion with Bindeos, and the mention of it along with Baris, Konane, and Seleuceia, suits admirably the situation just assigned.

22. SAGALASSOS it called Sagalessos by Pliny, and Selgessos is given as an alternative form by Strabo. Probably, therefore, the second *a* is a weak vowel that has developed between the two consonants, and Saglassos or Selgessos is closer to the native form of the name. The modern form is Aghlasun, which is the old accusative Σαγλασόν with the loss of initial s. Saglasos differs from Selge § only by the addition of the suffix -sa or -ssos, which is so common in Asia Minor. Similar examples are—

Prokonessos (Hellespontus).	Prakana (Isauria).
Thyessos (Lydia).	Thya-teira (Lydia).
Kidyessos (Phrygia),	Kadoi (Phrygia).
Halikarnassos (Caria).	Halikyrna (Bœotia).

Professor G. Hirschfeld, followed by Professor Kiepert in his latest map, makes Manlius march by Sagalassos. Livy says only that he laid waste "agros Sagalassensium," and I have shown in my " A. S. P." that the agri are the lands along the south side of lake Askania, which belonged to Sagalassos even down to the time of Diocletian. Professor Hirschfeld's error was entirely excusable until the inscriptions which show the wide extent of the Sagalassian territory were discovered; and if he had known this fact he would doubtless have recognised that Leake was correct in his idea of the march of Manlius. The route that Kiepert, in modification of Hirschfield, gives in his last map shows magnificent disregard of impassable mountains. Kiepert apparently saw that Hirschfeld's view that Manlius advanced into Pamphylia is irreconcilable with Polybius, who is clear that Manlius did not advance further than "near Termessos." But he clings to Hirschfeld's theory of the subsequent route, and makes Manlius cut along the ridges of Tauros north-east from Termessos. This via media is impossible physically: either Hirschfeld's theory or mine must be accepted.

* Ouinzela, given twice, is an error such as Ptolemy repeats in the case of Olba and Kormasa. It is, perhaps, to be identified with Vinda or Vindia of the Antonine Itinerary on the road between Dorylaion, Germa and Ankyra. This suits Ptolemy very well.

† The difficulty of rendering this name in Greek is shown by the older coins with legend ΣΤΛΕΓΙΟΣ, ΕΣΤΛΕLΙΙΥΣ; v. Imhoof-Blumer, ' Monn. Gr.,' p. 340.

23. BARIS retains its name as Sparta or Isbarta: Isbarta is the official spelling, Sparta is the invariable pronunciation.*

24. MINASSOS has retained its name to the present day as Minasun. It was discovered by Professor Sterrett, a little to the south-east of Sparta, and it is known also from coins reading

ΜΙΝΑΣΣΕΩΝ ΚΑΙ ΚΟΝΑΝΕΩΝ ΟΜΟΝΟΙΑ.

Its situation might be taken to prove that it was united in one bishopric with Baris, but the above coin indicates some old-standing connection between Minassos and Konane, and rather points to its being united with Konane. The point is difficult to decide.

At Conc. VI. Constant., A.D. 680, we find Κοσμᾶς Κονανῶν ἤτοι Μανούων, which we might correct to Μινασσέων, but in other entries we find Κοσμᾶς Καντάνων τῆς Παμφυλίων ἐπαρχείας and " Cosmas episcopus Conanensis Pamphyliæ." Κοσμᾶς Μανούων alone frequently occurs, and once " Cosmas Homonadorum." It is named regularly between Karallia and Korakesion. The probability, therefore, is that the bishopric in question is that which, under the name Μαναίων, Μανάνων, Μαναύων, Μαναύσων is mentioned in many Notitiæ, last in Pamphylia Prima. Konana or Kantana is obviously a mistake for Kotana (i.e. Katenna).

Ptolemy seems to mention Minassa under the form of Orbanassa, where the first syllable has probably come from an assimilation to Olbasa above.

25. SELEUKEIA SIDERA, at the ruins named Selef, near Baiyat, was discovered by Professor G. Hirschfeld. Claudioseleukeia is its name on coins.

26. AGRAI was united in one bishopric with Seleukeia. It was identified by Hirschfeld in the modern Aghras, three miles north of Seleukeia.

The first bishop of Seleukeia was Artemon, who, according to the tradition, was converted by Saint Paul on his visit to this city (' Act. Sanct.,' March 24, p. 474).

27. TIMBRIAS was situated on the river Eurymedon, whose name is mentioned on its coins. I suggested to Mr. Sterrett to look for it on the upper Eurymedon (the lower course of the river being excluded, as belonging to Byzantine Pamphylia), and he discovered no other possible situation except the valley of Yilan Ova, and rightly infers that Timbrias was situated there.

28. The next name is one of the puzzles in Hierocles; [ὁ] Θεμισόνιος

---

* Compare Burdur, the official form, Buldur the popular one. I am unable to understand why Prof. G. Hirschfeld says in a note in his paper on the route of Manlius in the Gratulationsschrift of Königsberg University to the Roman Institute that the modern form Isbarta proves that the ancient accent was Βαρίς, not Βάρις: εἰς Βάρίδα naturally becomes Isbarta; εἰς Βαρίδα could only become something like Isvrid, compare εἰς Νικομήδειαν, Isnimid, Ismid. The accented syllable remains, the unaccented syllables grow weak and often disappear.

(ἐπίσκοπος) is a form clearly derived, and certainly corrupted, from a list of bishops. The only name which could readily be corrupted in this way is Prostama. Attalus Prostamensis was present at Concil. Constant., A.D. 381. Prostama is obviously to be identified with Prostanna of coins. The most remarkable and frequent type on coins of Prostanna is the mountain ΟΥΙΑΡΟΣ. When in 1886 I traversed this district I came first in sight of the lofty peak of Egerdir rising above the intermediate hills, as we crossed from lake Askania to the valley of Baris, and when for days afterwards I saw what a remarkable feature it was in the view from many points of our route, I recognised it as Mount Viaros., Then I observed that Hierocles mentions the city between Timbrias and Konane, which exactly suits Egerdir. Finally the position and importance of Egerdir requires an ancient city to have been situated somewhere in the district naturally connected with it. On these grounds I propose the identification Prostanna—Egerdir with some confidence. I do not mean to assert that the two are on exactly the same site, for it is rarely the case that a modern city in Asia Minor occupies precisely the ancient site; but I consider that Prostanna was situated at the southern 'end of the Limnai.

If Prostanna was so important, why is it omitted from all the lists of bishoprics? Two possible reasons suggest themselves. It might have been constituted an archbishopric in the sixth or seventh century, and though it is never mentioned among the archbishoprics, the objection is not fatal, for these lists omit also Akmonia and other places. But in this case I think another explanation is more probable. The bishoprics of Limnai and of Prostanna were probably united in one at some time later than 381. The two naturally go together; Limnai includes especially the two islands close to Egerdir, and its religious importance would lead to the conjoint bishopric being named after Limnai. A thoroughly complete list would probably give both names, ὁ Λιμνῶν ἤτοι Προστανέων.

29. JUSTINIANOPOLIS is, as Wesseling saw, a temporary name of Konana. The evidence may be put more strongly than he gives it, since we have distinguished the classes of Notitiæ. VII. and VIII. give the same list of bishoprics: and they give the following:—

VII. 17 Tymandos, 18 Justinianopolis, 19 Metropolis.

VIII. 17 Tymandos, 18 Konana, 19 Metropolis.

30. KONANA was detected by Professor G. Hirschfeld in the modern Gönen. The name is frequently confused with Komama and Komana in the ecclesiastical lists, so that the task of separating the bishops of the various cities is by no means easy, and has not been satisfactorily done by Le Quien.

31. In the last two names Hierocles turned back westwards to complete the western district of Pisidia. He now goes on to complete the southern frontier by giving the cities in the south-eastern district of

Pisidia.   Mallos is probably to be looked for in the Mallos Ova, on the road from Parlais to Side.

32. ADADA is fixed at Kara Bavlo by the inscription found there by Mr. Sterrett ('Wolfe Expedition,' No. 420), though he himself draws, on p. 283, exactly the opposite inference.   Professor G. Hirschfeld and myself independently drew the same conclusion from the inscription when it was published.   In the games held at Kara Bavlo a competitor who was a citizen of Timbrias and of Adada gained the prize.   Timbrias and Adada then were probably neighbouring cities, and, as Timbrias has been fixed elsewhere, it remains to put Adada at Kara Bavlo.   The inference is, of course, not binding, but in the dearth of information it gives a clue to the situation which quite agrees with the order of Hierocles.

33. ZORZILA and Tityassos are quite uncertain.   In the last two numbers it is impossible to lay any stress on the order in Hierocles, as it is commonly his custom to insert at the end names omitted in the body of the list (e.g. Lydia, Phrygia Salutaris).   No other evidence is as yet available about either city.   The modern name Burdur or Buldur has suggested itself to me as a modification of Durzela, Zarzela, or Zorzila, and the march of Manlius which passed along the coast of lake Askania mentions a city Darsa in a position which suits Buldur very well.   I propose to correct Livy's text from Darsam to Darsilam, and see another form of the native name which is hellenised in so many ways.

Zorzila or Zarzela struck no coins.   It might certainly be expected that a city with the splendid situation and surroundings of Buldur would be rich enough to coin money.   But inscriptions come to our aid here, and show us that the territory along the southern shore of lake Askania belonged to Sagalassos.   Buldur, then, was only part of the "ager Sagalassensium," and could not strike coins as an independent city.   The identification, however, is quite uncertain; and further evidence is required.

34. Tityassos struck coins.   No evidence is known as to its situation, except the following inscription, in very rude letters, which I copied at Ilghin (Tyriaion) in 1883 : —

+ΑΥΡΗΛΙΟCΘΙ	+Αὐρήλιος Θί-
HoCTATIACCH	ηος Τατιασση-
NOCKEAΠTONIC	νὸς κὲ 'Απτόνις (i.e. 'Αφθόνιος)
ANECTHCAM	ἀνεστήσαμ-
ΕΝΤΗΓΛΥΚΥΤΑ	εν τῇ γλυκυτά-
ΓHHMωNMH	τῃ ἡμῶν μη-
TPIdOMNHC	τρὶ Δόμνης
EKTωNY AP	ἐκ τῶν ὑ[π]αρ-
	⌜χόντων αὐτῆς⌝.*

---

* In l. 1 Θ is very uncertain, and in l. 2 the second A is also doubtful.   Pisidian names have often many vowels together, as 'Ηουήιος, and here Θίηος.   Δόμνης shows the

It is possible that Τατιασσηνὸς is a badly spelt ethnic from Tityassos. If that be so, it would be an argument that Tityassos was in the east rather than the west of Pisidia, as inhabitants of a neighbouring city are more likely to have settled at Tyriaion than those of a city at the other side of the province.

Tituensis, assigned to Pamphylia at Conc. Constant., 381 A.D., is not a bishop of Tityassos. The two consecutive names Mydus Pentenessensis, Paneminensis, Midos Panemou, Heraclides Tituensis, Ptynsensis, Tychensis have been confused, and are to be restored—Midos Petnelissensis, Heraclides Panemoutichensis.

35. One of the most curious and important series of inscriptions that have been found in Asia Minor, are those of the Xenoi Tekmoreioi, which belong to the country on the north-west and west of Antiocheia. The first of these was found by Sir C. W. Wilson and myself in 1882, and was published by me in ' Journ. Hell. Stud.,' 1883. Prof. J. R. S. Sterrett in 1885 found a number of others, and in 1886 I revised the text of the whole series and added one or two more. Sterrett has published the entire series in his 'Wolfe Expedition,' incorporating or mentioning in his Addenda most of my corrections and additions. By some accident, however, I did not see the proofs of his text of the first inscription, which I had published in 1883, till too late; * and this inscription, which is by far the most important of the series, as being the only complete and the longest one, appears in his work in a very different form from what it has in my publication. Prof. G. Hirschfeld has very properly, in his review † of Sterrett's work, called attention to the variation, which throws some doubt on my restoration and interpretation of the opening lines: no interpretation of the opening lines is attempted by Sterrett, and I may say that none is possible with his text. The most serious divergence is as to the arrangement of the lines, and as to my distinction of two separate inscriptions. For example, Sterrett gives as lines 9 and 11 of his copy, what I make two halves of one line, and he prints the whole as one inscription, while I have interpreted it as two. The reason of the difference is that the first two or three lines and parts of others are on a fragment that has been broken off the column. Sterrett evidently did not, after putting the one fragment on the other, make a copy to show where the lines fitted on to each other. I did so in 1882, and in 1886 I again verified the arrangement, having the two parts of the column held firmly in their place, while I made a new copy; and I now state, as I

confusion of dative and genitive which begins in the third century and is quite common in the fourth century in the inscriptions of this district.

* I had with me in 1886 his manuscript copies of all except this one, compared them all in a most careful way with the originals, and sent to him my whole notes and remarks.

† Göttinger Gelehrte Anzeiger, 1888.

have already done in the ' Chronique d'Orient,' that my arrangement of
the lines and my distinction of two separate inscriptions is correct in
every point. It is now possible also, owing to the new inscriptions
which Prof. Sterrett has discovered, to restore the whole more completely
than I did in 1883.

36. The first inscription began as follows :—

$$'A\pi\acute{\eta}\gamma\gamma\epsilon\iota\lambda\alpha\nu \; \acute{\epsilon}\nu?] \; \tau\hat{\omega} \; \Delta\iota\pi\acute{\nu}\text{-}$$
$$\lambda\omega?, \; \acute{\epsilon}\pi\grave{\iota} \; \mathring{a}\nu\alpha\gamma\rho\alpha\phi]\acute{\epsilon}\omega\varsigma \; A\mathring{v}\rho.$$
$$\ldots\ldots\ldots 'O\nu\eta]\sigma\acute{\iota}\mu\sigma\upsilon$$
$$K\tau\iota\mu]\epsilon\nu[\eta\nu]\sigma\hat{\upsilon} \; \acute{\epsilon}\pi\acute{\iota}[\delta\sigma\sigma\iota\nu \; (\delta\eta\nu\acute{a}\rho\iota\alpha) \; \varsigma?]\tau\alpha',$$
5    $\cdot\acute{\epsilon}\pi\grave{\iota} \; \pi\rho\alpha\gamma\mu\alpha\tau\epsilon\upsilon?]\tau\sigma\hat{\upsilon} \; A\mathring{v}\rho. \; \Pi\acute{a}\pi\alpha\varsigma \; M\epsilon\nu\nu\acute{\epsilon}\sigma\upsilon \; T\upsilon[\ldots.$
$$\Phi\rho\sigma\nu\acute{\iota}\mu\sigma\upsilon \; K\alpha\rho\mu\eta\nu\sigma\hat{\upsilon} \; \delta\acute{\sigma}\nu\tau. \; (\delta\eta\nu\acute{a}\rho\iota\alpha) \; [\ldots$$
$$\kappa(\grave{\epsilon}) \; \acute{\epsilon}\pi\grave{\iota} \; \beta\rho\alpha\beta\epsilon\upsilon\tau\hat{\omega}\nu \; A\mathring{v}\rho. \; 'A\lambda\epsilon\xi\acute{a}\nu\delta\rho\sigma\upsilon \; \beta'. \; \Theta[\ldots\ldots$$
$$\kappa\alpha\grave{\iota} \; A\mathring{v}\rho. \; Z\omega\tau\acute{\iota}\kappa\sigma\upsilon \; M\epsilon\nu\epsilon\lambda\acute{a}\sigma\upsilon \; M\alpha\rho\sigma\iota\alpha\nu\sigma\hat{\upsilon} \; \delta\acute{\sigma}\nu\tau \; [\ldots.$$

In the patois which passed as Greek in this district about 200–50 A.D.
the above may be interpreted : "[There promised money ? in] the
Temple, when Aurelius ...., son of Onesimus, a Ktimenian (who
gave in addition * 6301 denarii), was clerk, and when Aurelius Papas†
Menneas Ty....,‡ son of Phronimus, a Karmenian (who gave ....
denarii), was (magistrate?), and when Aurelius Alexander, son of
Alexander, a Th......., and Aurelius Zoticus, son of Menelaos, a
Marsian (who gave ......), were Auditors;" then follow the names
of the persons who promised subscriptions.

After this inscription was engraved, a further explanation was added,
and had to be squeezed in at the top and at the right side after the ends
of the lines of the first inscription. The second inscription can be
distinguished easily, because it is engraved in smaller but more regular
and better formed letters.

$$\ldots\ldots\mathring{\epsilon}\tau]\sigma\upsilon\varsigma \; \epsilon[\rho' \; or \; \sigma']. \quad T\acute{\upsilon}\chi\eta\varsigma. \quad M\epsilon\gamma\acute{a}\lambda\eta \; "A\rho\tau\epsilon\mu\iota\varsigma.$$
$$\Xi\acute{\epsilon}\nu\sigma\iota \; T\epsilon\kappa\mu\acute{\sigma}]\rho\epsilon\iota\sigma\iota \; \acute{\epsilon}\pi\sigma\acute{\iota}\eta\sigma\alpha\nu \; \phi\iota\acute{a}\lambda\eta\nu$$
$$\kappa\alpha\grave{\iota} \; \mathring{a}\nu\delta]\rho\epsilon\iota\acute{a}\nu\tau\alpha \; \kappa\alpha\grave{\iota} \; \chi\acute{a}\lambda\kappa\omega\mu\alpha \; \kappa\alpha\grave{\iota} \; \pi\alpha\tau\acute{\epsilon}\lambda\lambda\alpha\varsigma$$
$$\kappa\alpha\grave{\iota} \; \lambda\iota\beta\alpha\nu\omega\tau\rho\acute{\iota}\delta\alpha$$
$$\acute{\epsilon}\kappa \; \tau\hat{\omega}\nu \; \mathring{\iota}\delta\acute{\iota}\omega\nu$$
$$\mathring{a}\nu\alpha\lambda\omega\mu\acute{a}\tau\omega\nu$$

The first line is very faint: I came to the conclusion that neither $\epsilon\mathring{\upsilon}\tau\upsilon\chi\acute{\eta}\varsigma$
nor $\mathring{\upsilon}\pi\grave{\epsilon}\rho \; \tau\acute{\upsilon}\chi\eta\varsigma$ had been engraved on the stone. The bare genitive
$T\acute{\upsilon}\chi\eta\varsigma$ is unexampled in my experience; but $\mu\epsilon\gamma\acute{a}\lambda\eta \; "A\rho\tau\epsilon\mu\iota\varsigma$ has since
then been detected as a formula of this religion.§

* $\delta\acute{\sigma}\nu\tau\sigma\varsigma$ is accidentally omitted.

† Papas is put in the nominative instead of the genitive; on the other $\delta\acute{\sigma}\nu\tau\sigma\varsigma$ is put
in the genitive, while in almost every case it ought to be in the nominative.

‡ If it were possible to understand that, by some fault of grammar, two persons
were meant, the restoration $M\epsilon\nu\nu\acute{\epsilon}\sigma\upsilon \; T\upsilon]\iota\tau\eta\nu\sigma\hat{\upsilon}, \; A\mathring{v}\rho.K\alpha\rho\iota\kappa\sigma\hat{\upsilon}?] \; \Phi\rho\sigma\nu\acute{\iota}\mu\sigma\upsilon \; K\alpha\rho\mu\eta\nu\sigma\hat{\upsilon}$ suggests
itself.

§ See my " Artemis-Leto and Apollo-Lairbenos," ' Journ. Hell. Stud.,' 1889.

37. Prof. Sterrett, in the map attached to his book, makes Tekmorion a town. It seems to me impossible to understand Xenoi Tekmoreioi in this way. I interpret this remarkable title as " the Guest-friends who use the sign (τέκμωρ)." The rather poetical term τέκμωρ is not unnatural in the artificial Greek of Pisidia. This association was united (according to the exposition given in my former paper, which need not be repeated here) in the worship of Artemis of the Limnai.

38. The point in this set of inscriptions which chiefly interests us at present is the geographical names, showing the homes of the members of the association.

Prof. G. Hirschfeld, in his review of Sterrett, and myself, have both written on the local names ; and in general we agree in recognising the Xenoi as being a purely native institution. The members have little or nothing of the Græco-Roman tone, and they belong as a rule to districts which are inhabited on the old Anatolian system (κωμηδόν), and not on the Græco-Roman system (κατὰ πόλεις). Where natives of cities which were centres of Græco-Roman civilisation are mentioned, such as Antiocheia, Julia, and Synnada, a village name is almost always added, showing that the person in question is ranked by his κώμη as well as by his πόλις : in this respect I am indebted to Hirschfeld's paper for full comprehension of the facts, for I had previously understood the expression Συνναδεὺς ὀικῶν ἐν Κανδρουκώμῃ as " a native of Synnada, who has settled in the village Kandroukome beside the Limnai."

39. The list of ethnics which Sterrett gives needs to be corrected in various points, and I shall therefore go over it in detail, trying to determine in each case the probable form of the village name.

Prof. Sterrett has corrected several faults of my first publication ; e.g. in l. 11 he has rightly substituted Καρμηνοῦ for my Καρ. Μ[ε]ν[έ]ου, and Κρανοσαγηνός for my Κράνος Ἀγηνός (compare Λύκου Κράνος of Phrygia). But he has followed my error in understanding Ἰμάηνος or Μάηνος as a personal name instead of an ethnic Ἰμαηνός.

Adada : a city coining money, and a bishopric.

Azara or Ezara : a village six hours east of Philomelion, still called Azari Keni.

Aiza , unknown village, compare Aizanoi and ἀζένα (accus.), " beard."

Akroenos : a local adjective, which came to be used as a place name, the modern Afiom Kara Hisar ; cp. Ganzaenos, Poimanenon.

Algiza : a village of the territory of Synnada, which bears the same name as Algiza or Argiza of Hellespontus. No Xenos comes from the Hellenised regions of the west coast except possibly Attaleia.

Algonia or Algounia : a village of the territory of Synnada.

Amblada or Anpelada : a city coining money, and a bishopric.

Anagos : village of territory of Synnada : omitted by Sterrett (373, 1).

Apollonia: Hirschfeld in his review of Sterrett misunderstands a correction of mine. The reading Ap[oll]onia is probable in 374, 8, Apollonia is pretty certain in 376, 1. Apollonia is a city coining money, and a bishopric.

Arasiza, Arkasta, Askara: unknown villages.

Archelais: a stranger from Archelais on the borders of Cappadocia and Lykaonia is probably to be understood in 366, 54.

Attaleia: must apparently be understood from 'Ατταλ[ην]ός which occurs twice, but it is not certain which Attaleia is meant.

Baro[ukl]ia: * Battea : Boalia: unknown villages.

Boitiniathes: was corrected by Sterrett to β'. Οἰτινιάθης, and by me in my second copy to β'. Οἰ[ε]ινιάθης for Οἰεινιάτης: see Oinia.

Daokome : Diatora : Doudada: unknown villages, the third is in a fragment which I could not find: Daokome is wrongly restored by Sterrett in 378, but occurs in 382.

Dabenai: in 366, 38 Sterrett reads ΔΑΡΗΝΟC, but both in 1882 and again in 1886, when I verified this point with special care, I read ΔΑΡΗΝΟΥC, with the notes that ΗΝ is in ligature, Ρ may be Β, for a fracture of the stone prevents certainty, and Ω. must be error for Є: I identify Dabenai with Hierocles' Sabinai in the same district, altering the text of Hierocles to Dabinai.

Eireumenia : Hermokome: unknown villages.

Ekk[ea]: uncertain reading.†

Esouakome: Soa, a village of the Prepenisseis, in northern Phrygia, is probably meant here. Compare Carian Soua-gela, " Tomb-King."

Ganzaenos: the ethnic has come to be used as a proper name in the modern Gondane, a village eleven miles west of Antiocheia.

Gardibia or Gardybia : Giza or Gisza (Carian gissa, " stone "): and Grekea or Trekea: † unknown villages.

Imaion or Maion: 'Ιμαηνός, hitherto misinterpreted by myself and Sterrett as genitive of a personal name, is an ethnic, formed from Ma, as Tataion is from Tatas, &c.: unknown village.

Julia : a city coining money, and a bishopric: a village " Aud . . ai " is mentioned (374, 33) in the territory of Julia.

[Kab]orkoi: this restoration I propose with confidence in 383, 6: this people inhabited the left bank of the Sangarios in the upper part of its course.

Kakoza : Kamarga : Karbokome : Karma or Kharma (378, 1) : Karsenda or Karseirda : Kelosnia : Kerasia : Klantea : Klela : Kleustia : Knouteina : Koundoza : Kousea : Kradra : Kranosaga : Ktimena or Khthimena : unknown villages.

---

* ΥΚΛ are all marked as uncertain in my revision of Sterrett's copy.

† Γ or Τ first letter. The suspicion suggests itself that 'Εκκ(εα)νός (where εα are marked very uncertain in my copy) is a fault of the engraver for Γρεκκεανός.

Kandroukome : Koumalettos or Koumalittos : villages of the territory of Synnada.

Kasonia : Katiena : villages of the territory of Antiocheia.

Kinnaborion : a village of the Karamyk Ova, afterwards a bishopric of Phrygia.

Lanka or Lankea : Lapeistra, Lapistra, or Laphystra : Laptokome : Lykiokome : Latmos : * unknown villages : the last cannot be identified with the Carian mountain.

Limenia : a village, probably connected with the Limnai, perhaps on the island at the north-western end.

Lykaones πρὸς ἔνδον, a tribe of Cutchuk Sitchanli Ova, south-west from Afiom Kara Hisar.

Mamouta † : Marallis or Marallita : Marsia : Mergnia : Mikkonia : Mono-kleros : Mordion : Mouza : unknown villages.

Malos πρὸς χῶμα Σακηνόν : Mallos, a village, afterwards a bishopric in the south-east of Pisidia.

Mandra : a village of the territory of Synnada : it is probably the village north-east from Surmene which is still called Mandra, near which are Mandri Fontes of Livy. This implies that the territory of Synnada extended far to the north.

Metropolis : a city striking coins, afterwards a bishopric.

M[i]sylos : identified by Hirschfeld with great probability in the neighbourhood of Tymbriada.

Nazoula : Neidos : Neophytos : unknown villages.

Oikea : Olympokome : unknown villages.

Oborai : a village of the territory of Synnada.

Oinia : a village of the Oinan Ova.

Pagada : Padia : Papaion : Patea : Peidra or Pidra : Peisda or Peisdia ‡ : Perokia : Peskenia, Peskeinia or Pesenia (obviously a fault of the engraver) : Polymarga : Plouristra (381, 7) or Proureistra : Ptagia : unknown villages : Pidra is mentioned as a village of the Anatolic Theme : Peskenia seems to be named after Pescennius Niger.

Peliganon or Piliganon : a village of the territory of Synnada.

Raita : Rekokome : Renbea : unknown villages.

Sagoue : unknown village. § The form resembles Lagoe or Lagbe in western Pisidia.

Simikka or Simmikka : Sourbia : unknown villages.

---

* Correcting Μειλάτμειος to Μείλα [Λά]τμειος : the engraver probably omitted one of the two consecutive syllables ΛΛ.

† Sterrett wrongly reads ΟΥΤΤ for ΟΥΤ (or possibly ΟΤΤ) in 366, 74.

‡ Padia also occurs 366, 58, where Παδιανός should be read, not Π[εισ]διανός.

§ Sterrett's Σαγουτηνός seemed to me certainly wrong y read. His Σαγουντηνός as a variant in his index is not justified by his text.

Synnada: a city with the villages Algiza or Algizoa; Kandroukome;
    Koumalittos; Mandra : Oborai; Peliganon; Anagos; Algounia.
Strouma (in 366 I read $\Sigma\tau\rho ov\mu[\eta]v\acute{o}s$) : i.e. "Stream-town," compare
    strom, Roma, and streit, stlis.
Tataion : Talimeta * : Tettha : Tenita, Tyita, Tyta, or Tita.
Tloua † : Tyrsa : Triglettia or Trouglettia : Totonia ‡ : unknown villages.
Chailiara (? I could not find this on the stone) : Pserkiokome : unknown
    villages.

40. LIMNAI.—I have assumed the truth of Prof. G. Hirschfeld's
excellent conjecture that the double lakes now called Egerdir Göl and
Hawiran (or Hoiran) Göl were in ancient time called Limnai. The
bishopric of Limnai, with which I have conjectured that the bishopric
of Prostanna (Egerdir) was united, seems, if my conjecture is right, to
prove this view completely. I find also in Conc. Nicaen. II., A.D. 787,
Ἐπιφάνιος ἡγούμενος τῆς Ἁγίας Θεοτόκου Λίμνας. § I cannot doubt that
the Virgin Mother of the Lake is the Christian representative of the
(Parthenos) Artemis, whose worship on the north-east coast of the lake
and all around we find to have been such an important cultus in ancient
time. At the present day, beside a Turkish village on the north-east
shore of the Hawiran Göl, named Kaziri or Ghaziri, in a country which
for centuries has been inhabited only by Turks, ‖ there is a shrine of the
Virgin, which is an object of pilgrimage for all the Christians of Pisidia
and Lykaonia. The Virgin of the Lakes was as important in ancient
time as her Christian successor is to-day. Hence, we can understand
the wide extent of country from which the Xenoi Tekmoreioi are
drawn.

In my former article I vainly spent much labour and conjecture in
the attempt to find a reference to the Limnai in the Tekmoreian
inscriptions, but Sterrett has supplied the desired name, Limenia, of the
settlement beside the lake or on the small island beside Kaziri. In
1886 I was very anxious to go out to this island, but the single boat
which had once belonged to the village had perished of neglect some

---

* In my former paper I altered this name by a bad conjecture to Talimeneus. It
occurs 366, 91, as Ταλιμετηνός (Sterrett Λ . . λιετμηνός); 366, 69, as Ταλιμεττηνός (Sterrett Ταλωεττηνός); and 366, 85 and 86 as Ταλιμετεύς. I succeeded in 1886 in reading
all these places correctly and with certainty.

† In 374, 49, I read ΤΛΟΥΗΝΟС ; Sterrett has ··ΟΥΗΝΟС, but transcribes incorrectly [Τυι]τηνός. Compare the Lycian Tlos.

‡ In 366, 48, probably read [Τωτ]ωνιά(νε)της : in 366, 74.

§ The nearest Christian settlement is in Apollonia (Olu Borlu), about 24 miles
distant : the next are at Konia and Sparta.

‖ A monastery exists to the present day on one of the islands in the Egerdir Lake,
where Hirschfeld found the fragments of the biography of Euthymius, recently published by De Boor.

years before, and had never been replaced: the villagers formerly cultivated the island, but now could not go out to it. This is a typical example of Turkish village life and manners.

W. Pamphylia, Caria, and Lycia.

1. In all lists of bishoprics Pamphylia is divided into two provinces, which I distinguish as Prima and Secunda.* Hierocles does not formally make any division, and none of the lists of the civil provinces, which are all earlier than Hierocles, distinguish two provinces Pamphylia. Hence, it has been concluded that the division of Pamphylia into two provinces took place later than Hierocles.† I have, in 'Athen. Mittheilungen,' 1885, p. 345, shown that this is incorrect, and that the division already existed in A.D. 458, and that it is implied in the order of Hierocles; but I did not then observe the true explanation of the facts. This division was a purely ecclesiastical division, and was not recognised in the civil administration. The same was the case in Bithynia, where ecclesiastical jealousy and dignity divided the province between the metropoleis of Nikomedeia and Nikaia. Similarly the later divisions of Phrygia Pakatiana, Pamphylia Secunda, &c., had certainly only an ecclesiastical, never a civil, existence, as is proved by the fact that in many cases, they were made after the introduction of the division into Themes, when the civil government was no longer arranged according to the old provinces.

In Pamphylia there were two metropoleis, Perga and Side, both of which claim that title on their coins under the empire, and which seem to have kept a certain rivalry with each other, like Smyrna and Ephesos, Tarsos and Anazarbos, Nikaia and Nikomedeia. Both Perga and Side are recognised as metropoleis in Concil. Ephes., A.D. 431. When the division of the bishoprics between the two metropolitans was made we have no means of judging. It is recognised in the list of bishops present at Chalcedon, which is arranged according to provinces, but this list is not so early as the Council, A.D. 451: the order of signatures ‡ at the Council is not decisive, but on the whole tends to show that the division was already recognised. The division certainly existed when the Epistle to the Emperor Leo was written in 458.

2. Hierocles knew that there was only one province of Pamphylia.

---

* I use these terms for convenience, on the analogy of Cappadocia Prima and Secunda, but like Bithynia Prima and Secunda, and other examples given in the text, they had never any real existence.

† E.g., by M. Waddington, in 'Rev. Numism.', 1883, p. 29.

‡ M l'Abbé Duchesne was the first, I think, to distinguish between the signatures, which are contemporary with the Councils, and the arranged lists, which are later; see Mél. Graux.

He made his list of the cities by transcribing first the ecclesiastical list of Secunda, then the ecclesiastical list of Prima. In doing so he made some faults, owing to misunderstanding of the forms : e.g. from the form ὁ δήμου Σαβαίων * (ἐπίσκοπος) he makes simply a name δήμοι Σαβαίων, and a marginal note δήμοι Ἴσβα added by a later scribe has crept into the text as a second place Δεμουσία.

3. He gives ASPENDOS under the name Primopolis. Primopolis or Priamopolis is the name under which Aspendos appears at Conc. Ephes., 431. The origin of the name, which is elsewhere unknown, is not certain. Possibly, as I have suggested about Hadriane Pamphyliae Secundae and Neronias Ciliciae, it was derived from a local saint (A S P, p 15). Philostratus (Vit. Apoll. I., p. 9[15]) calls Aspendos the third city of Pamphylia: he of course understands Side and Perga as the first two.

4. SIDE.—Notitiae VIII., IX. mention Zela before Side. This is obviously a dittography, arising probably from a form ΣΗΔΗ, corrupted to ΣΗΛΗ.

5. SELGE became an archbishopric in later times.

6. ISBA.—Le Quien takes the δήμου Σαβαίων of Hierocles as a corruption of Σεμνέων, but Hierocles has Σέρνα for Σέμνα or ˙Σέννα (see § 2). From his order he seems to have considered Isba in Pamphylia Secunda, whose cities he enumerates first of all :† hence I have conjecturally placed it on the frontier of the two livisions of the province, but evidence is absolutely wanting (A S P, p. 27). We are reduced to the argument that the ruins at Kiesme on the Eurymedon between Timbriada and Selge must belong to some ancient city, that it is difficult to see what city could be placed here except Isba,‡ and that the situation explains very well why Isba is assigned sometimes to Prima, sometimes to Secunda. The epigraphic evidence does not corroborate this view, but is not inconsistent with it.

MM. Radet and Paris have published an inscription § found at Kiesme, a decree by the people of Sillyon in honour of Kleon, son of Kleon. They therefore identify Sillyon as "le nom de la ville antique située sur l'emplacement des ruines de Kiesme." They are apparently ignorant, both that Sillyon is already identified in a very different part of the country, and that the custom is common for cities to pass a decree in honour of a citizen of a different city, and to have that decree erected in his city: compare C. I. G., 3818, a Prymnessian decree found at

---

* I.e. Σαβέων: the native name was probably Sba, which in Greek becomes sometimes Ἴσβα, sometimes Σάβα (compare Ispa of Laviansene or Armenia Minor).

† Either he follows an ecclesiastical list, which put Isba in Secunda, or there is some dislocation in the text.

‡ The arguments of Hirschfeld in his ' Reisebericht' prove that Pednelissos cannot be placed at Kiesme.

§ 'Bull. Corr. Hell.,' 1886, p. 500.

Nakoleia, which long led to an error similar to that which MM. Radet and Paris make about Sillyon. The other inscription which they publish from the same neighbourhood seems to give the old name of Kiesme, Μουλασσέων ὁ δῆμος. Moulassa may be compared with Mylasa or Mylassa of Caria. Now there is no bishopric Moulassa, and the people must have been included under some bishopric. I conjecture that Moulassa was part of the district Isba.

7. SENNA.—The bishopric Σεμνέων seems to imply a town Semna (or Semnos). There is here apparently an attempt to make the form give a meaning in Greek. The form Sesenniorum in 431 suggests that the true form is Senna, corrupted Serna in Hierocles. There is no clue to the situation of Senna, except in its relations with Kasai.

Le Quien mentions Nectarius Senneae twice, both as bishop of Sanaos in Phrygia, and correctly as bishop of Semneai (which is the form he wrongly infers from ὁ Σεμνέων), without noticing the inconsistency.

8. KASSAI or KASAI was apparently a bishopric adjoining Sennea, and sometimes united with it under one bishop. In 431 Nectarius Casorum, with the marginal note Sesenniorum, was present at the Council of Ephesos ; and the Greek lists generally use the form Νεκτάριος ἐπίσκοπος τῆς ἐν Σεννέα καθολικῆς ἐκκλησίας. Ignatius was bishop of Semnea in 869 and of Kassai in 879.* Against these facts must be set the evidence of Conc. Const. 553, when we have Conon Semneatanorum or Semneon and Cyriacus Casatanorum (Casatorum, Curatorum). Either at this time the two towns were temporarily under separate bishops, in accordance with the law of Zeno (474-91 A.D.) quoted in the introduction, or Semneon is an error for 'Ετεννῶν: the latter supposition is very improbable.

At Conc. Const., A.D. 536, we have Θεόδωρος Κασσατῶν (in Latin Carissorum.)† Kasai is mentioned also at the end of some of the Isaurian lists, where we have τὰ δὲ κλίματα· Κασσῶν· Βανάβων· Βολβόσου. The word κλίματα probably means ground sloping towards the sea, in which sense it seems to be used in Justinian.‡ From the character of the country it is probable that Kasai was on the slopes a little back from the sea on the frontier of Pamphylia and Isauria. This exactly agrees with Ptolemy, who mentions Laerte, Kassai, Lyrbe, Kolobrassos and Kibyra as Κιλικίας Τραχείας μεσόγειοι in the province Pamphylia. Laerte and Kibyra are known to have been close to the sea.

---

* Athanasius of Semnea and Ignatius of Kassai, in 879, are rival bishops, Ignatian and Photian.

† At Conc. Chalcea Marcellinus or Marcianus Coralliae or Carissorum occurs. In both cases Carissa is probably a pure error.

‡ αἴ γε πρὸς τοῖς κλίμασι κείμεναι Σινώπη τε καὶ Ἄμισος., Justin., Novel. xxviii., where the word seems to be used in the same sense; but in Act. Theodori Syceotae, p. 40 (in loco Mazaniae, qui est ad Siberim superiorem sub climate Muozeniae), it is used in the ordinary sense of "a region."

9. ETENNA and KOTENNA are very hard to separate. The following list gives most of the facts known about them.

{Troilus	Geonensis (Τενῶν corrupted to Γενῶν)	381
{Hesychius	Cantinensis (Kotenensis)	381
{'Ἀκάκιος	Κοτεννῶν	431
{Εὐτρόπιος	'Ἐτεννῶν	431
{Εὐγένιος*	Κοτεννῶν	451
{Εὐδόξιος	'Ἐτεννῶν	451
Φλαβιανὸς	Κοτενῶν (Cotenorum)	536
Κοσμᾶς	Καντανῶν ἤτοι Μανούων	680
Joannes	'Ἐτεννῶν	787
{Μακάριος	Κοτέννης	879
{Πέτρος	'Ἐταίνου	879
{Θεόδωρος	'Ἰτέας or 'Ἰτενίας†	879

Notitiæ VIII., IX., I., give only one of the two: Notitiæ III., X., XIII., give both, and so do four Councils. Polybius V., 73, mentions Etenna in Pisidia above Side. Strabo mentions the Katenneis in Pisidia adjoining Selge and the Homonades. M. Waddington, who does not notice that the ecclesiastical lists distinguish the two and mention them side by side, considers that Polybius and Strabo must refer to the same place, and that the true native form is Hetenna, in which the strong Pisidian H at the beginning was sometimes represented in Greek by K and sometimes dropped entirely. His arguments are (1) that Strabo places Katenna in a similar situation to that assigned by Polybius to Etenna; (2) "une preuve decisive" the Notitiæ give Kasa, Etenna, Orymna, and Hierocles gives Kasa, Kotana, Orymna.‡ These reasons have convinced Prof. G. Hirschfeld, who unhesitatingly assumes the identity of the two places in the second part of his 'Reisebericht' without even mentioning that some authorities have distinguished them.

The table given above shows that the signatures of the Councils of 381, 431, 451, and 879 prove the presence of two bishops, of Etenna and of Kotenna, at each of them; and Notitiæ III., X., XIII., mention the pair side by side. It is therefore not possible to accept the opinion of M. Waddington absolutely. At the same time I think that it is not entirely wrong. I am strongly disposed to accept the original identity of Etenna and Kotenna, but a distinction throughout the Byzantine period is clearly made out. Another example (below, § 12) will be given of the development of several cities out of a single tribe;

* Sometimes v. l. Εὐσέβιος.
† Peter and Theodore are probably rival bishops, Ignatian and Photian. See. p. 430.
‡ 'Voyage Numism.', p. 86.

and I think that the tribe Hetenneis was divided into at least two districts. The northern took the name Etenna, while the southern preferred the name Kotenna. The latter contained also a town Manaua or Banaba which grew to importance in Byzantine time, and was the seat of the Bishopric. Hence in 680 we have the signature Κοσμᾶς Καντανῶν ἤτοι Μανούων, and most of the Notitiæ omit Kotenna and give only Manaua or Manoua. But most of the Councils show the name Kotenna, Kantana or Kantina, and Notitiæ III., X., XIII., give three bishoprics, Tena or Kotenna, Etenna, and Manaua.

Hirschfeld has detected the site of Katenna or Kotenna in the modern Godena, and an inscription which he publishes shows that the people called themselves Κοτεννεῖς.

Le Quien confuses Konane of Pisidia with Kantana or Katenna Pamphyliae, and omits the former entirely from his lists. Komama Colonia is also a difficulty to him, and appears in his lists (as in Ptolemy) as Κόμμακον.

10. ERYMNA appears in almost all the lists as Orymna, and Hirschfeld has detected it in the modern Ormana. But the hellenised inhabitants called themselves 'Ερυμνεῖς, as appears from two inscriptions, one published by Hirschfeld, the other by MM. Radet and Paris:* in the second the word Erymneus has become a personal name, like 'Ιταλικός, Μακεδών, &c., but the form may be taken as a proof of the customary spelling, which, as usual, is adapted to give a meaning in Greek by the resemblance to ἐρυμνός.

11. MANAUA, to take the most probable form of many variants, is probably identical with the κλίματα Βανάβων in Isauria, and the same remarks apply to it as to Kasai. I have also spoken about it under Konane of Pisidia. The passages there quoted show that in A.D. 680 Manaua was united in one bishopric with Katenna. This shows that it adjoined Katenna, and we may therefore place it between Katenna and the sea on the sloping southern skirts of Taurus,†

12. DALISANDOS. The Notitiae give Homonades and Dalisandos as two consecutive bishops. I have little doubt that this is a mere error of division. Dalisandos, situated at Fassiller, was a village of the Homonades, which gradually acquired the rights of a city, and was admitted as one of the cities of the Koinon Lykaonon, but was also felt to be one of the cities of the Homonades. Similarly I think it not improbable that the whole territory between Lakes Karalis and Trogitis belonged, in the time of Strabo, to the Homonades, and that gradually Lyrbe Kolobrassos and Karallia, if I am right in the position which I

---

* Τιβ. Κλ(αύδιον), Κυρείνᾳ, 'Ερυμνέα, &c., υἱόν, Τιβ. Κλ(αυδίου) 'Ιταλικοῦ in an inscription of Aspendos, ' Bull. Corr. Hell.,' 1886, p. 161, where the authors misunderstand Κυρείνα, taking it in the accusative as the cognomen of Tiberius Claudius. The order is a bad imitation of the Latin Ti. Claudius, Ti. F., Quir., Erymneus.

† Le Quien omits Manaua entirely under Pamphylia Prima.

have assigned to them, acquired independent existence as cities, and Parlais was a colony founded to keep down that tribe, whose conquest proved too hard for King Amyntas and was only achieved by Quirinius.

13. MYLOME, MYRABE, or MYLA, is a striking example how difficult it is to discover the true name of a city mentioned only in Byzantine lists, (compare Siniandos-Sinethandos of Pisidia). Some MSS. read Μύλων, which suggests the Mylai of the Peripli; but this Mylai is far away towards the east part of the Isaurian coast and cannot be in Pamphylia. I believe that Kibyra is the place meant. This place gave its name to the Kibyrrhaiote Theme; and must therefore have been a great seaport. Now according to Ptolemy, Kibyra itself stood a little back from the sea, therefore Justinianopolis was probably a fortified harbour on the coast, founded by Justinian as more convenient than the tiny harbour of Attaleia. Hence it bears also the name Justinianopolis.

14. In regard to Pamphylia Secunda, I need say little, as I have recently discussed it in my 'Antiquities of Southern Phrygia and the Border Lands.'* As I have there shown, several corrections must be made in the list of Hierocles before it can be compared with other lists. He turns the single title Termessos Jovia et Eudocias into three towns : Μυωδία and Χωρία Μιλυαδικά are two versions of the same : so also are Μαξιμιανούπολις and Κτῆμα Μαξιμιανουπόλεως, Δεμουσία and Δήμου Σαβαιῶν. Perga, the metropolis, seems to have lost its importance during the Byzantine period, and Attaleia took its place as chief city of the province and residence of the metropolitan. The Notitiæ, however, continue to give Perga as the metropolis, but a note in Notitiæ IV., gives the truth (see ASP., D 4). The tiny harbour of Attaleia was used as late as the twelfth century (Anna, II. 113). The fortress Hierakoryphites is mentioned by Cinnamus, p. 7, as near Attaleia.

Between 787 and 869† Perga and Sillyon were united as one metropolitan bishopric. Sillyon had been made an autokephalos bishopric before 787, but in VII., VIII., IX., it is a simple bishopric subject to Perga, while in I., it is united with Perga.

After Pamphylia was in partibus infidelium, and Attaleia had become the chief (finally the sole) seat of Christianity in the district, the metropolitan of Perga was apparently identified with the bishop of Pyrgion or Dios Hieron. This seems the sole possible explanation of the entry, Parthey, p. 314, 60, Πέργη τὸ νῦν Πυργίν (i.e. Πυργίον). See Addenda, p. 430. Prokonessos in later time stood in the same relation to Mokissos, Monembasia to Side (Notitia XII., 14), &c.

---

* In ASP, D 16 (4), read κλυ[τόβουλο]ν for κλυ[τόπωλο]ν, as Dr. O. Crusius writes to me : ib., D. 19, (7), read ὤφιλεν, εἰ δὲ χερ[σ]ὶ, &c., as M. Waddington warns me in a letter, and Dr. Wolters in a later number of ' Amer. Journ. Arch.'

† Gelzer fixes the date more narrowly between 787 and 812.

‡ Gelzer only says earlier than 968. Cp. Act. Sisinnii, Sept. 8, p. 41.

15. In discussing the proper form of the name of the town which belonged to the δῆμος Λαγβέων or Λαγηνοί (ASP. D 14, and E), I did not properly explain the facts, but advanced alternative views. The Pisidian name had a form approximating to Lagwa ; compare Σαγουηνός in the Tekmoreian inscriptions. This form was Grecised sometimes as Λαγόη (probably also Λαγούη), which appears in Polybius and probably has been corrupted in Livy from Lagoen to Lagon, sometimes as Λάγβη (where β, as frequently, is substituted for an earlier ov) in Λαγβέων of an inscription, and in Λαγβηνός of an inscription and a coin, sometimes with the complete loss of the spirant as Λάγη, implied in the Byzantine Λαγηνοί.

16. In regard to Olbasa-Hadriane ASP., D 15, I may add another probable reference which I get from Le Quien. A certain Olympius, Ἀδριανουπόλεως ἐπίσκοπος τῆς Λυκίας, is mentioned as having confuted the error of Origen about the resurrection, in the scholia to cap. 7 of the work 'de Ecclesiastica Hierachia,' which is attributed to Dionysius the Areopagite. Le Quien understands that Hadrianopolis of Pisidia is meant ; but the error is perhaps of a different kind. Zosimus I., 69, speaks of Kremna as in Lycia, and Ptolemy assigns Sagalassos to Lycia : in both cases the Roman province Lycia-Pamphylia is the cause of the error, a city which strictly belongs to Pamphylia being spoken about as belonging to Lycia. So I understand that Olympius was bishop of Hadrianopolis of Lycia-Pamphylia. This explanation supposes that the original authority for the statement wrote before the middle of the fourth century, when Lycia and Pamphylia were separated.

17. The route of the consul Gneius Manlius Vulso in B.C. 189, has been discussed in stages in former papers, and alluded to in this work, pp. 135, 142, 143. It is therefore unnecessary to spend any time in repeating what I have said previously. The route from Ephesos by Magnesia, Hiera Kome, Antiocheia, Gordiou Teichos, Tabae, the river Kazanes, Eriza, Thabusion, Sinda, the river Kaulares, lake Karalitis, Mandropolis, Lagoe, Fountains of the Lysis, Kolobatos, Isinda, a point a little north of Termessos where he turned and marched north again, the river Tauros, Xyline Kome, Kormasa, Darsa, Agri Sagalassensium, and Aporidos Kome to Rhocrini Fontes, has been described in ASP. E. The readings are there proposed in the text of Livy Gordiu Teichos (doubted by Waddington), Kazanes (proved by Waddington), Lagoen, Rhocrinos Fontes.

The march from Aporidos Kome by Rhocrini Fontes, Metropolitanus Campus, Dinia-Khelidonia, to Synnada and Beudos Vetus, has been discussed in my paper 'Metropolitanus Campus' and in CB. LVII. Aporidos Kome is still called Baradis, and lies a few miles east of Bindaios-Eudoxiopolis.

The continuation of the march by Anaboura, Mandri Fontes, Abbassos, Lalandum Flumen, has been described in my paper ' Inscriptions Inédites d'Asie Mineure,' where the proposed readings **Mandri Fontes** and **Lalandum Flumen** are justified.

The march next led through the village Tyscon, where ambassadors from the Pisidian tribe Orondeis came to the Roman general, a fact which suits a situation a little east of Amorion, for the ambassadors would naturally come by Hadrianopolis, Pissia (Piri-Bei-li), and Amorion. The army then advanced to Plitendum and Alyattos apparently in two days, and after some delay to Cuballum : whence several days' march brought him to the Sangarios. The short distance from the sources of the Lalandos to the Sangarios shows that Manlius was advancing by very short marches, while he was trying the effect of negotiation on the Gauls. The river was crossed by a bridge, constructed by the army at a point south-east of Pessinus, south or southwest of Gordion. After this he must have again crossed the Sangarios, but as there was certainly a bridge already in existence on the road from Pessinus and Gordion to Ankyra, the passage of the river is not mentioned.

18. The frontier of Caria and Phrygia has been discussed in ASP, c. I give here a table of the bishoprics, but several of the correspondences are very doubtful, e.g. that of Eriza with Siza. There can be little doubt that in the Notitiæ the Roman name Sebastopolis is replaced by the original native name, but which of the names at the bottom of the Table corresponds to Sebastopolis is uncertain. Probably the decisive passage lurks in some ecclesiastical document. The same is the case with Χωρία Πατριμόνια (i.e. patrimonialia) with the dittography Κτῆμα φυλικαῖον, which from being a marginal note has crept into the text as Κο-κτημα-λικαί.

19. Besides the Carian cities mentioned in the table, coins were also struck during the Roman period by Kyon, Euippe, Euralion, Euromos, Hydrela,* Plarasa, and Bargasa. Of these, probably,

Euromos was under the bishopric of Mylasa,

Hydrela	„	„	„	Brioula in Asia,
Plarasa	„	„	„	Aphrodisias,

Except Kyon, the others are unknown, but it is certain that the importance and civilisation of the Carian coast was greatest in early times, and steadily decreased in the Roman and Byzantine period. Mr. W. R. Paton tells me that Roman imperial coins are very rare in his experience on the Carian coast.

20. KYON.—The situation of Kyon was discovered by MM. Cousin and Deschamps. It would be difficult to find a more carelessly written article on ancient antiquities than that in which they have described

---

* Hydrela, being on the north side of the Maeander, ought to be reckoned in Lydia, not in Caria. The same remark applies to Nysa, which must go with Magnesia, Tralleis, Mastaura and Brioula : all belong to Lydia, but some are wrongly assigned to Caria in numismatic works.

the city (' Bull. Corr. Hell.', 1887, p. 308). They give the name as Kûs, and, forgetful of Stephanus Byzantius,* they state more than once that the ancients never refer to the city, and they give absolutely no clue to the situation where they place the city, except that it is in the hills that separate the valley of the Marsyas from that of the Harpasos. They do not know whether or not Rhodes possessed the city in the time of Claudius, as if there could be any doubt on the point. They are even ignorant that coins of the city are well known. In a Journal which has done so much for the study of Antiquity as the Bulletin, such an article is not worthy of its position and surroundings, nor worthy of its subject.

Kyon must have lost importance, and been subordinated to some city of the plain: hence, it is not a bishopric.

21. Titakaza is known to me from two autonomous coins, one which passed through Mr. Lawson's hands, the other reported to me by the kindness of Prof. Th. Mommsen as having been recently acquired by the Berlin Museum. Mr. Lawson's coin came to him from the direction of the Caro-Pisidian frontier, and it has struck me that Tapasa in the Notitiæ may be a Byzantine modification of (Ti)takasa.

22. It is as yet impossible to draw the boundary between the Thrakesian, Kibyrrhaiote, and Anatolic Themes. The Kibyrrhaiote Theme included Miletos, and therefore began at the Maeander, which had always been the boundary between Caria and Lydia. All the coast lands from this point eastward belonged to the Kibyrrhaiote Theme; but there is no possibility of determining how much of the inner country was included in that Theme. The boundary must have run along some mountain ridges that lie east and west; but several lines are equally possible. Originally the coast, even up to and including Cilicia, belonged to the Kibyrrhaiote Theme. At a later time the Kleisourai of Seleuceia were formed into a Theme which appears to have included also all the coast-lands between Pamphylia and the Mohammedan frontier.

In a rough way we may say that Asia and Lydia belonged to the Thrakesian, Phrygia to the Anatolic, Theme: but the Lykos valley, with Hierapolis, Khonai and Laodiceia, must perhaps be united with the military administration of the coast-lands in the Thrakesian Theme, and separated from the Anatolic Theme. There can be no doubt that from some time between 692 and 787 Khonai was the chief military centre of that valley.

23. The order of Hierocles' enumeration of the Carian cities is clearly geographical; but two are out of place, Iassos and Bargylia. Their position is so peculiar, that it is almost necessary to suppose that a dislocation of the text has occurred. Orthosia, Harpasa, Neapolis, Hyllarima, and Antiocheia, must therefore be understood to form a geographical group; and probably Kyon falls under one of them,

* As Mr. W. R. Paton mentioned to me.

though until MM. Cousin and Deschamps give some better clue to the situation of the ruins they discovered, no certainty is attainable.

Of the numerous bishoprics added in the Notitiæ, some were doubtless originally included under better known bishoprics, e.g. Loryma under Knidos. Stadia or Stadeia, which is frequently mentioned in the Carian list at Concil. Nicaen. II, 787 A.D.,* may possibly correspond to Δετάβων or Μετάβων of the Notitiæ. Θεόπεμπτος Τροτολυκείας ἐπαρχείας Καρίας, A.D. 692, is a puzzle : perhaps the name of the bishopric consists of two names run together and corrupted.

24. I add a few notes on the authority of Paton. He has traced† the island Pserimos in Pliny, v. 36, in an inscription, and in the modern name Pserymo, an island between Kos and Kalymna. Pisye still retains its name as Pisi, called in some maps Kigi, a village near Mughla. Mughla is the ancient Mobolla. Bargasa perhaps lay east from Idyma. Termera was at Assarlik, where Sir C. Newton placed Souagela or Theangela. Theangela was at Kenier, where Kiepert's map puts Pedasa. Pedasa probably lay inland a little to the east-north-east. The Tripolis of the Chersonasioi Paton would identify as Akanthos, Bibassos, and Syrna, the last being expressly named by Stephanus. ‡

25. The principle of arrangement of the Lycian cities in the list of Hierocles is very similar to that which has been proved in Isauria. Hierocles begins on the east coast with Phaselis and comes westward. Where a road leads up from a coast-town to cities of the interior, he mentions the cities on this road before going further along the coast. Similarly in Isauria, after mentioning the cities on the coast, Hierocles makes the line of the Ermenek Su (Decapolis) the basis of his enumeration, and gives the cities from the mouth to the source ; but when any of these cities lies on a cross-road over Taurus he mentions the cities on that road before going further up the river.

26. In Lycia the relation between Hierocles and the ecclesiastical lists is very difficult. Hierocles omits several places, such as Rhodiapolis, which were important at all periods, coining money and appearing as

---

* Tabai also occurs in this list.

† 'Bull. Corr. Hell.,' 1888, p. 282. The usual texts of Pliny give the name Psyra; but Pserima and Pserema have MS. authority.

‡ Ponticoussa, "island of mice," near Pserymo, must be Pliny's Pinnecusa, the name being modified to give a meaning to the popular mind. Orak, where there are ruins, is probably Lepsimandros. Pliny omits Kedreai, the largest island in the Keramic Gulf. Mobolla, mentioned 'Bull. Corr. Hell.,' X., 488, is called Mogola by Constantine Porph., de Them., p. 38, who names it along with Pisye. On Theangela and Pedasa see Paton in 'Class. Rev.,' 1889, p. 139. The Tripolis of the Chersonasioi is a very doubtful term, founded solely on the words of Stephanus: χερρόνησος, πόλις ἐν τῇ κατὰ Κνίδον χερρονήσῳ. καὶ Τρίπολις. Paton adds from 'Arch. Delt.,' 1888, p. 112, the names Amos, Lei . . . . . . ; the sums given there prove that there were more than three cities in the Synteleia which, as Boeckh first saw, included all the peninsula except Cnidos. The Koinon Chersonasion long continued to exist: see Paton in 'Class. Rev.,' 1889, p. 423, and 'Bull. Corr. Hell.,' 1886, p. 423.

bishoprics during the fifth century and in the Notitiæ. Is the list of Hierocles defective? A civil list would not omit such a city as Rhodiapolis, so that the difficulty is not solved by supposing that Hierocles used such a list. I believe that the explanation in such cases is that Hierocles used as his authority an ecclesiastical list, in which, owing to the fact that Rhodiapolis and Korydallos were united under one bishop, the former was apparently not named, but there had arisen a corruption which had caused in Hierocles the extraordinary form Renkylias. A critic will desiderate some proof that these two cities were ever united in one bishopric. I can give no proof, but I can point to their situation, and I can appeal to another fact, which throws light on this case and strengthens my theory by analogy, while at the same time it shows what errors are caused to modern writers on topography by the neglect of this habit of uniting two cities under one bishop.

Petersen in the second volume of the Austrian Exploration in Lycia, p. 162, identifies Zenonopolis with Pinara. His sole reason is that, in Notitiæ I., VII., VIII., IX., the latter is omitted and the former occurs, while Hierocles and Notitiæ X., XIII., give Pinara, and omit Zenonopolis. But he has not observed that Theodorus, bishop of Pinara and Stauracius, bishop of Zenonopolis, were both present at the second Nicene Council, A.D. 787. Zenonopolis and Pinara are entirely distinct bishoprics and cities. Why then do so many Notitiæ omit Pinara? The reason is that Pinara and Sidyma were in the earlier organisation united under one bishop, as is proved by the entry at Concil. Seleuc., A.D. 359, Πινάρων καὶ Διδύμων.* This union existed in 451 and 458, but had been dissolved before 787, as appears from the signatures of the second Nicene Council. But it leads to the omission of Pinara in the four earliest Notitiæ. Three of these are indeed later than 787, but this merely proves what I have already so often urged, viz., that the lists of suffragan bishops often retain facts of a much earlier date than the lists of metropolitans and autokephaloi. This example may be used to support my theory both about Rhodiapolis and also about Mesotimolos-Blaundos in Lydia, and other places.

27. Besides the cities mentioned as coining money in the annexed Table, coins of Apollonia, Kalynda, and Masikytos, are also known. Apollonia was included in a Tetrapolis with Aperlai, Simena, and Isinda, and probably all were included in the bishopric of Aperlai. Apollonia was on an island, as Stephanus mentions, probably the island of Dolichiste, as M. Waddington says (Le Bas, 1290).

The coins with the legend ΛΥΚΙΩΝ-ΤΡ are commonly assigned to Trebenna. This is a mistake, for, as I have proved in 'Athen. Mittheilungen,' 1885, p. 343, Trebenna was a city of Pamphylia, not of Lycia. The coins in question therefore must be assigned to Trabala, not to Trebenna.

* Didyma for Sidyma; so often at Concil. Nicaen. II.

28. Tergasos, which occurs in Notitiæ X., XIII., also is mentioned at the Council of 879. There are several other remarkable resemblances between the latest class of Notitiæ and the late Councils, whereas Notitia VII. has several reminiscences of Hierocles.

29. Komistaraos in Hierocles obviously corresponds to Mastaura in the Notitiæ. I suppose that Κώμη Μάσταυρα has lost one of the syllables beginning with M, and that a form Μαστάουρα has been corrupted to [Μα]στάραος.

30. In Pamphylia I ought to add that Alastos, which is mentioned in three inscriptions, was situated somewhere not very far from Palaiàpolis; and when we find in the later Notitiæ the entry Παλαια-πόλεως ἤτοι Ἀλιεροῦ or Ἀλευροῦ or Ἀλεεροῦ, the suspicion arises that Alastos is meant. The variation in form is not greater than in some other cases (see pp. 398, 402); and such variations are so great that it is impossible to determine the exact form of any name which occurs solely in ecclesiastical documents.

ADDENDA.

P. 89 ff. The article by Gelzer in 'Jahrbuch für protestantische Theólogie,' XII., on "Zeitbestimmung d. griech. Notitiæ Episc.", did not come to my knowledge until January 1890, when I saw Hirschfeld's reference to it in his review of Sterrett's 'Wolfe Expedition' (which I unfortunately failed to observe before). This Journal is not in the Aberdeen University Library; and I owe to the Free Church College and to Principal Brown's kindness the opportunity of reading it. The following points are agreed on independently by Gelzer and myself :—

1. Notitia VII. is the oldest. Gelzer dates it at latest in the beginning of the eighth century.
2. Notitiæ VIII. and IX. are the next in age. Gelzer dates IX. A.D. 806–815, and VIII. a little later.
3. Notitia I. is next : it is, according to Gelzer, not later than 850.
4. III. and X. are much later : Gelzer dates the former about 1100, under Alexius Comnenus, and the latter towards 1200.
5. Any arrangement in 680 or 692 is to be ascribed to the system of Justinian.

It is impossible for me to find during the University Session the opportunity to study the subject with sufficient concentration to express an opinion about various points in Gelzer's article. During an occasional half-hour stolen from other work, I cannot bring together the facts in my mind, and the article is far too important to be lightly criticised. In a hasty perusal I have not been struck by anything which makes me wish to alter any statement in this book, though I learn from Gelzer how much still remains undone, yet capable of being done. If I had had the luck to know Gelzer's article a year ago, I should certainly have been able to do the work which is attempted in this book much more thoroughly. The method which he indicates of distinguishing different recensions of the same Notitia, is likely to give some interesting results. I add a few notes on points that have struck me in reading his article.

I am glad to be able to give one or two striking confirmations of his dates in the later periods of church organisation, but I have to express dissent on several points. (1) I do not think that he has proved sufficiently his scheme previous to Justinian; and I shall point out, in the following paragraph, a discrepancy between his scheme and the facts about Kios of Bithynia. I still retain my previously formed opinion that church organisation was in a very fluctuating condition before the time of Justinian, and that the order of dignity was not fixed decisively, except for a few of the higher metropoleis, until his reign. Some of the Chalcedonian lists which he quotes as authoritative, appear to me to be made up later than the time of the Council. (2) I do not think that he sufficiently appreciates the difference between the first and the second parts in each Notitia, or the fact that the first part may be proved to belong to a particular period, while the second part may retain unaltered statements that belong to an earlier date, though he admits at least one case of this kind. (3) He takes no account of the facts that have led me to the view that Notitiæ III., X., XIII., are founded on a different list (viz., a church list) from I., VII., VIII., IX., which are taken from a government list of bishops, varying in some respects from the church list. My view perhaps may be wrong, but the facts which lead me to it seem not capable of being explained by the mere fact that III., X., XIII., are later.

Gelzer argues that the first 14 autokephaloi bishoprics mentioned in Notitia VII. had that rank as early as 459, that the next 11 were raised to that rank between 459 and 536, while the following 7 were elevated by Justinian between 536 and 553; Bizya, Tomi, and Leontopolis are traced as early as 451. In most cases it is certain that Gelzer is right; but my view is that such distinctions were rather fluctuating and uncertain, and that order of dignity was unsettled, till Justinian. Kios according to Gelzer falls among the 11 that became autokephalos between 459 and 536. He has not observed that Julianus a Co, who is mentioned as a bishop of superior rank at Chalcedon, and who afterwards wrote in 458 to the Emperor Leo as an independent bishop, must be bishop of Kios. It is hardly possible that a bishop of the island Kos is meant; and, moreover, in the classified list of bishops appended to Act XV., he is assigned to Bithynia along with the bishops of Nikomedeia, Nikaia, Chalcedon, and Apameia. We have therefore a clear case of a bishop of Kios claiming in 458 the right to address a letter, as an independent autokephalos bishop, to the emperor. I consider this to be a proof of the fluctuating state of dignity and organisation at the time. Other proofs to the same effect I find in the position of Dorylaion and Kotiaion. Dorylaion appears to be autokephalos in 451; and I have argued in my papers in 'Expositor,' 1889, that Kotiaion claimed the same position. The Notitiæ nowhere, so far as I know, directly notice the fact that metropoleis must have been at some period formed in Phrygia (probably Akmonia) and in Pamphylia Secunda, as local groups of bishoprics are omitted in these provinces.

The views advanced by Gelzer about the later ecclesiastical organisation, seem to me, so far as I can at present judge, to be correct; and they make a great step in our knowledge of the subject.

He considers that important changes occurred shortly before 869, which are shown in Notitia I.; and that a still more sweeping series of changes was made by Leo VI., who completed a list of 50 metropoleis and 50 autokephaloi. Soon afterwards his list was altered by the elevation of Eukhaita to be a metropolis. Amastris and Khonai also were soon after made metropoleis; * and Gelzer quotes a Paris MS. (Coislinianus CCIX.) which gives only these 53 metropoleis. These facts throw light on the arguments I have brought forward to show that in later times certain bishoprics were subject to Eukhaita and Khonai. The same MS. gives also Asmosata as a metropolis: this was the case for a short time under Constantine, when Samosata was captured from the Arabs and incorporated with the empire for a few years. Gelzer attributes the elevation of Khonai to the importance of the Church of S. Michael, which he considers to belong only to the tenth and eleventh centuries: but Khonai was one of the chief military centres at this late period, and I attribute the Church of Michael already to the old Kolossai. It becomes known to us first in the tenth century, because we know practically nothing about Kolossai and Khonai till that period, when the military importance of the rock of Khonai makes it a centre for the wars of the period. It was doubtless a Tourma or a Topoteresia from the seventh century onwards, but we begin to hear of it only when the theatre of war lies in the district.

Gelzer's proof that Leontopolis was an autokephalos bishopric as early as 451, throws some light on the method of Hierocles. He learned from his authorities that Isauropolis-Leontopolis was a single bishopric, but by an error he put it in the wrong province. In the case of some archbishoprics, such as Eukhaita, he did not know in what province to place them, and therefore omitted them entirely.

Nakoleia was an autokephalos archbishopric in 862. Gelzer has no earlier date than 869. He also shows that a number of new metropoleis were created between 1035 and 1082: he has missed a fact that confirms his view in one case. Nazianzos was made a metropolis (p. 285) between 1067 and 1071. He states, p. 542, that the existence of Nazianzos as a metropolis cannot be proved earlier than 1166.

On p. 362 Gelzer errs in saying that the bishopric of Kotiaion occurs in no Notitia. It occurs in VIII. and IX., as subject to Synnada, but is disguised in the corruption Κυτίμιον (i.e. Κυτι[ά]ιον) or Κομίτιον. Had he known the date of the elevation of Amastris, which is proved in my text,

---

* Gelzer only says earlier than 968. Cp. Act. Sisinnii, Sept. 8, p. 41, and my p. 91.

p. 91, he would have a strong additional argument and an earlier fixed point as the latest possible date for Notitiæ VII., IX.

P. 94. At the Council of 879 we find that in a great number of cities there are two separate bishops. I assume throughout this book that these are bishops of rival parties, Ignatian and Photian. The fact and the hypothetical explanation which I advance have not, so far as I am aware, been mentioned (except in C. B., LIV.), and ought therefore to be scrutinised by critics. The following examples may be given of double bishops. Μιχαήλ Αγκυροσυνσῶν, Σισίννιος Συναοῦ, Εὐσέβιος Συναοῦ, Βασίλειος Συναοῦ, have to be distributed to two cities, Synaos and Sanaos. 'Αντώνιος Δαφνουσίας and Δαμιανὸς Δαφνουτίου,* perhaps belong to one place. So certainly 'Αναστάσιος Τυράου and Κωνσταντῖνος Τυραίου, 'Αντίοχος Μάκρης and Νικόλαος Μάκρης, Στέφανος Βινδαίου and Παῦλος Βινδαίων, Κύριλλος Λινόης and Βασίλιος Λινόης, perhaps also Μεθόδιος Δαδαλείας and Εὐστόλιος 'Αλδίλου. Κωνσταντῖνος Λαοδικείας probably belongs to Lykaonia, leaving Παῦλος and Συμεών to be bishops of the Phrygian metropolis. Other cases, such as Leo, Kerykos and Constantine of Neapolis, Theodorus and Theognostus of Apameia, may belong to different cities of the same name. Σάβας Κινηπόλεως and 'Αντώνιος Κίννης seem to me to be bishops of Kinna; but some may hold that Sabas was bishop of Konni or Kone.

P. 101. A warning to the same effect against identifying ancient sites by modern names that happen to resemble them, is given by Dr. Conrad Miller, 'Die Weltkarte des Castorius,' p. 121. But he carries his scepticism in this respect, and his belief in the Peutinger Table, to an extreme. The example which he quotes of a bad identification, which had caused unfair discredit to be thrown on the Table, viz., that of Scopi with the modern Uskub, is unfortunate. Mr. A. J. Evans has proved most conclusively (' Archæologia,' vol. xlviii., " Researches in Illyricum ") that Scopi was beside Uskub: the Peutinger Table needs much correction here, as it does in very many other cases. An identification founded on such close resemblance as Scopi and Uskub, and especially where the modern name is not a significant and usual Turkish word, may almost always be safely accepted.

P. 104 (A, 3). The mediæval name of Dios Hieron is said to be Pyrgi. See Miklosich and Müller, 'Acta et Diplomata,' II, cccxcvii., p. 104,†
τὸ Πυργίον ὅπερ ἐν τcῖς τακτικοῖς (i.e. in Notitiis Episcopatuum) Διὸς Ἱερὸν ὀνομάζεται. If the name Pyrgi still remains in use, this may give a clue to the situation. Πυργίον was apparently made the seat of the metropolitan of Perga, p. 420, after Pamphylia was almost entirely in partibus infidelium, and Attaleia had become the archbishopric and the chief (finally the sole) seat of Christianity in the province. The elevation of Pyrgion to be a metropolis took place between 1193 and 1199 (Gelzer, p. 547).

---

* Daphnoudion of Phrygia in the late Notitiæ is probably an error.

† I take the quotation from Gelzer: the book is not accessible to me in Aberdeen.

M. Fontrier, of Smyrna, in answer to my question, writes that Pyrgi is a village in the Kaystros valley, two hours south-east of Odemish, inhabited by Christians and Turks, now a poor place, but formerly important for silk produce. This site, so close to that of Hypaipa, can hardly be the exact position of Dios Hieron, but, although Pyrgion was put in the rank of Dios Hieron, it was probably a separate place. Still the story in Ducas, p. 83, that when Tchineit died suddenly at Ephesos he was at once carried to Pyrgion on the skirts of Mount Tmolos and buried, hardly suggests a situation so distant as Hypaipa. Perhaps the old Pyrgion and the modern Pyrgi are different places.

P. 105 (A, 4). There is every probability that the article of Schuch-hardt on the site of Kolophon ('Athen. Mittheil.', 1886, p. 398), which embodies also the opinion of Prof. Kiepert, has solved the long-standing problem of the site of that city. Kolophon was an inland city, 10 or 12 miles north of the coast. Notion was on the coast. In Roman time the site of Kolophon lost its importance, while the name was transferred to the site of Notion, and the latter name disappeared. Hence Pliny speaks of Notion as of a place that no longer existed. The disappearance of the old Kolophon and the change of name, is later than the Peloponnesian war, but earlier than the time of Cicero.

P. 113 (A, 27). Τὰ δ' ἐν 'Ασίᾳ περὶ Τράλλεις καὶ τὸν Χαρακωμήτην ποταμόν. For 'Ασίᾳ Schweighœuser prefers Λυδίᾳ, Kaibel Καρίᾳ. No change is needed, for the Province Asia is meant; but Λυδίᾳ is at least true, Καρίᾳ false. The name of the river (nomen suspectum, Kaibel) is clearly 'Αχαρακακωμήτης.

P. 118 (A, 42). It is remarkable that Marquardt should so entirely disregard the authority of Pliny, and make Tralleis, Philadelpheia, Eumeneia, and Cyzicos into separate conventus; and that he should be followed, and even the doubts that he himself expresses in some cases should be disregarded, by Monceaux ('De Communi Asiae') and others. The result is that entirely false tables have been constructed by the writers whom I have named to show that the same cities struck cisto-phori, were the seats of conventus, and enjoyed other honours. I have pointed out the true character of these honours in the 'Classical Review,' 1889. It is possible that such cities as Philadelpheia and Cyzicos may afterwards have been erected into conventus by a subdivision of the larger divisions mentioned by Pliny (C B, xxviii.).

I have given a tentative list of the peoples and cities in the conventus of Laodiceia, Apameia, Synnada, and Philomelion, C B, xxviii. The doubts there expressed as to the xxv peoples in the Laodicean conventus are partly resolved by the rectification of the frontier of the province (see above, E, 21) and the inclusion of Lagbe, Ormeleis, &c., in the province, and, therefore, in the Laodicean conventus. But the v. l. xxii. is more likely to be correct than the vulgate xxv.

P. 117 (A, 37). The proof about Aigai has recently been made quite complete by Dr. Schuchhardt in Bohn's work on the 'Antiquities of Aigai.' My reference to his opinion in my footnote is to his paper on the Macedonian Colonies, 'Athen. Mittheil.' 1888, p. 1.   He has now published an inscription, which proves that one of the twelve cities destroyed by the earthquake under Tiberius was situated at Nemrud Kalesi, and Aigai is the only one of the twelve that can possibly be placed there.

P. 117 (A, 39).   Khliara ought, on account of its position, to belong to the ecclesiastical province of Lydia, and its bishop to be subject to the metropolitan of Sardis.   But by the time that Khliara began to exist as a bishopric, the old provincial system had decayed, and the lists of the Notitiæ had no reality, and were worth only the paper on which they were written.   Sardis itself had lost all consequence, and so also had Ephesos, the metropolis of Asia.   At the present day the metropolitan of Ephesos resides at Magnesia (now called Manisa); but Ephesos, or rather Ayasaluk, was still an important place in the fifteenth century.   The fact that Khliara was made subordinate to Ephesos is only one of many facts that prove the utter disorganisation of the old ecclesiastical system towards the close of the Byzantine period.

P. 123 (B, 13).   At the criticism of Mr. Hogarth I add a note to explain more clearly the facts about Koula.   Koula was not an ancient site: the ancient city in whose territory it lay was situated at Sandal about three miles distant.   The inscription of the Katoikia Koloe was attributed by M. Tsakyroglos to Sandal, and he supposed that Sandal was Koloe, and that the name had (as in other cases) been transferred to the modern city at a little distance.   He disregarded the unvarying statement of the owners that the stone in question came from Kara Tash, on the grounds (1) that most inscriptions of Koula come from Sandal, which is itself also full of inscriptions, (2) that there is little intercourse between Kara Tash and Koula.   I have investigated the point carefully, and have no hesitation in saying, (1) that the Koloe inscription is of a different character from the Sandal inscriptions, (2) that there was formerly a brisk trade in madder root between Koula, which is a great seat of the carpet trade, and Kara Tash district, where the root grows, (3) that the statement of the owners of the stone is trustworthy, (4) that Koula is not the modern form of the name Koloe, (5) that Satala is Sandal, and the site of Koula was part of its territory. I should add that the inscription in question has been at Koula, in the possession of the same family, for more than thirty years.

P. 126 (B, 22).   The Masdyenoi seem to be Paphlagonian mercenaries from the town of Mastya, mentioned by Pliny, VI. 2, west of Kromna.   The Traleis or Thracians, and the Masdyenoi, were different classes of mercenaries employed by the Pergamenian kings.   The Macedonians, who got the citizenship of Pergamos at the same time with the Masdyenoi, were, according to Schuchhardt, the descendants of mercenaries settled by the Seleucid kings in different cities of Asia.

P. 127 (B, 26). Hamilton found at Göbek, a few miles from Suleimanli, an inscription Βλαυνδέων Μακεδόνων. Compare coins.

P. 135 (C, 2). Gelzer confirms my view that Hierapolis was made a metropolis by Justinian. He is disposed to consider that before its elevation it was already an autokephalos archbishopric. There is no evidence for this, but it is not improbable in itself. It may now, I think. be considered as an established fact that Justinian made Hierapolis metropolis over a group of bishoprics, and hence in 692 we find a distinction indicated between the Laodicean bishoprics, Ankyra, Tiberiopolis, Kadoi, Aizanoi, &c., and the Hierapolitan group, Mossyna and Attoudda (the others were not represented at the Council).

P. 135 (C, 3). The inscriptions of the Demos Thiounteon, in the territory of Mossyna, which I published in the 'American Journal of Archaeology' (ASP, Α. xii.) make it possible to fix the district where a species of variegated marble, used in ancient commerce for many centuries, yet practically unnoticed by modern writers, was quarried. It also gives the means of correcting the text of Strabo, p. 374. In an inscription of Hierapolis, C. I. G., 3915, the expression σορὸν Θιουντηνήν occurs, which Franz in his transcription alters to Δοκιμηνήν. M. Waddington, on Lebas, 1683, defends Θιουντηνήν. We now see that M. Waddington was right, and that the stone was found at Thiounta, 8 or 10 miles north of Hierapolis.

The colour of the marble sarcophagus, on which the inscription is engraved, is not described by M. Waddington, but the following passages show that the Thiountene stone was a variegated marble (ποικίλη λίθος). Constantine Porphyrogenitus ('de Cerim. Aul. Byz.,' p. 644, Bonn ed.) mentions that Eudokia, wife of Justinian II., and another empress, wife of Anastasius, were buried in sarcophagi of Hierapolitan stone. The sarcophagi of the splendid mausoleum which he is describing may be assumed to have been of beautiful and valuable stone. The material is here called Hierapolitan, not Thiountene; but it is natural that it should be called by the name of the great city which is not far distant, and to which doubtless orders from the outer world were sent, instead of the name of the obscure village where it was found. Similarly the marble found at Dokimion was always called Synnadic marble from the time of Strabo onwards, yet Dokimion was a city striking coins of its own, 32 miles from Synnada. Again, Strabo, p. 374, speaks of μέταλλα τῆς ποικίλης λίθου τῆς Σκυρίας, καθάπερ τῆς Καρυστίας καὶ τῆς Δευκαλλίας καὶ τῆς Συνναδικῆς Ἱεραπολιτικῆς. In the 'Journal of Hellenic Studies,' 1887 (CB., xxxi), I pointed out part of the cure for this passage, but in weighing the question as to which Hierapolis was meant, I came to the wrong conclusion. The original text was—

ΤΗϹ ΔΟΚΙΜΑΙΟΥΚΑΙΤΗϹΙΕΡΑΠΟΛΙΤΙΚΗϹ

A marginal explanation, Συνναδικῆς, was added, as the name Δοκιμαίου was strange, being confined to the immediate neighbourhood of the quarries, as Strabo mentions on p. 574.* The marginal note crept into the text in the wrong place. The name that precedes, being strange, was corrupted ΔΕΥΚΑΛΛΙΟΥ, and its gender corrected to ΔΕΥΚΑΛΛΙΑϹ.

The references to this marble belong to all periods, from the time of Christ till the tenth century. On every occasion that its use is mentioned, it is employed to make sarcophagi. Strabo mentions it as variegated, like Dokimian and Carystian marble. It was quarried at Thiounta, about 12 miles north-west of Hierapolis. In the neighbourhood it was called Thiountene, but in the world generally it was called Hierapolitan.

P. 136 (C, 25). On the name Τζυβριτζή, my friend, Mr. A. J. Evans, writes to me : " the Clisura is surely connected with the Turkish word for ' bridge,' as it appears in its Slavonic guise ' tchuprija.' " The proper Turkish word is Keupreu.

P. 136 (C, 27). I may add that the line of the road from Khonai to Homa is wrongly represented on my map in ASP. It must 'probably have gone past Tchardak, along the lake of Anava, and then by Bolatli across a low rising-ground in a direct line to Homa. I infer this from the description of the march of Frederick Barbarossa, an outline of which is given B 33. He marched along the lake of Anava and by the same Kleisoura, though there is a little confusion in the accounts. The place ubi fluvius Mandra oritur can hardly be Apameia-Celaenae, but must be some of the immense springs that rise between Homa and Dineir.

P. 138 (C, 33). I have never thought it necessary to give any proof that Ahat Keui is the site of Akmonia. The reasons advanced by Franz in his dissertation, " Fünf Inschriften und fünf Städte Kleinasiens," in support of the identification might be greatly strengthened by the evidence of other inscriptions and by general considerations.

P. 144 (C, 78). Nakoleia, as I have shown in C B, LXVII., was made an autokephalos archbishopric between 787 and 862 : Gelzer has no earlier date for its elevation than 869. Gelzer, p. 542, points out that Nakoleia was elevated to the rank of a metropolis between 1035 and 1066 : it appears as a metropolis at the Synod of 1066. No clue is known to the bishoprics that were subject to Nakoleia ; but it is not improbable that Santabaris was one of them. But the order of enumeration in 879 would almost suggest that Nakoleia was then a metropolis.

P. 140 (C, 53). Julia, the peaceful city of Roman time, is to be looked for in the lower ground, on the actual line of the road. Ipsos is to be looked on some higher and more defensible situation on the skirts of Sultan Dagh. Neither Tchai nor Sakli (Isakli, " the Isaacs ") seems to be an ancient site, but at Tchai ruins were reported to me as existing

---

* Even the inscriptions of Hierapolis, where Dokimian marble was used, employ the form Δοκιμηνή, which, according to Strabo, is incorrect.

in the Sultan Dagh. Careful examination of the district will doubtless reveal the exact site of both places. The battle of Ipsos must have taken place in the open plain, where Seleucus and Lysimachus met, but no conclusion can be drawn from this as to the site of Ipsos ; for the battle got its name from the city in whose territory it was fought, but did not necessarily or even probably take place within or beneath the walls. Mr. Hogarth has traversed the district more recently, but only in the same hurried way as myself, and will have something to say about it in ' Journ. Hell. Stud.,' 1890. Kaystrou Pedion must be the plain between Tchai, Sakli, and Bolowodun : the army of Cyrus halted in the plain without going up to the high-lying city of Ipsos, just as they traversed Keramon Agora without going to the hill-city of Akmonia.

P. 144 (C, 77). I have accidentally omitted to mention a village named Pontana or Pontanos, situated a few miles north-north-west from Meros (Kumbet), whose existence is proved by the following inscriptions which I copied in November, 1881 :—

    (1) At Gemütch—

MHIıι	$M\eta[\tau\rho\grave{\iota}$
ΠΟΝΤΑΝ	$\Pi o\nu\tau a\nu$-
HNH	$\eta\nu\hat{\eta}$
ΕΥΧΗΝ	$\epsilon\grave{\upsilon}\chi\acute{\eta}\nu.$

    (2) At Aginn (Ak Inn ?) : under a relief representing a bull's head—

ΠΟΝΤΑΝΙ-	$\Pi o\nu\tau a\nu[\eta$-
ΙΟΙΟϹΙΩ	$\nu o\grave{\iota}$ 'Οσίῳ
ΔΙΚ- ΩΕΥ	$\kappa\grave{\epsilon}]$ $\Delta\iota\kappa\acute{\epsilon}\omega$ $\epsilon\grave{\upsilon}$-
ΧΗΝ	$\chi\acute{\eta}\nu.$

P. 144 (C, 82). Krasos or Krassos was in the Opsikian Theme (Theophan. 414), and in the province Phrygia (Theophan. 481). On the other hand, Galen seems to place it in Bithynia, when he gives the list Νίκαια καὶ Προῦσα καὶ Κράσσου [πεδίον or πόλις]* καὶ Κλαυδιούπολις καὶ 'Ιουλιούπολις, ἀλλὰ καὶ Δορύλαιον ἤ ἐστι μὲν ἐσχάτη τῆς 'Ασιανῆς Φρυγίας. But it is perhaps more probable that Galen is wrong about the situation of Krasos. It was certainly on the Tembris east of Dorylaion, and perhaps Galen, like so many modern geographers, confused between the Tembris valley, which belonged to Phrygia, and the northern Sangarios valley parallel to it, which belonged to Bithynia. The two references in Theophanes show that Krasos was on the Byzantine military road, probably immediately east of Midaion ; and it is very probable that the inference given in my text is wrong, and that Akkilaion and Krasos are one place, or rather that Akkilaion strictly is the town (now Alpi), Krasos strictly the district, but the town is sometimes called by the district name.

          * Wesseling corrects to Κράτεια.

P. 144 (C, 83).   Any one who wishes to appreciate the importance
of Kotiaion in history must, in addition to what is said in this book and
in my " Cities and Bishoprics of Phrygia," consult the papers on " Early
Christian Monuments in Phrygia," which I published in the " Expositor,"
1888 and 1889.   These papers, begun with the intention of giving a
popular account of the subject, led me to views about the state of the
church in Phrygia under the Roman Empire, which, whether they
ultimately prove true or not, are at least so far as I know entirely new.
All that I have said about the unique position of Kotiaion seems to me
to be justified by my subsequent studies.   Kotiaion and Amorion must
have been the chief centres of heresy in Phrygia : hence arises the
peculiar position of both, first as autokephaloi, afterwards as metropoleis.   The question how far the bishoprics subject to each of them
shared in their views requires a wider investigation before an answer
can be given ; but in both cases I should attribute their elevation to the
rank of metropolis to the period of the Iconoclast emperors.   The earlier
orthodox emperors did not recognise their claim to be independent
(autokephaloi) church centres, a claim which was chiefly founded on
their importance as centres of the proscribed native forms of Christianity ; but the same qualification recommended them to the Iconoclast
emperors.   Kotiaion never appears as autokephalos in the Notitiæ, but
as metropolis in the latest Notitiæ.   Amorion appears as autokephalos
in Notitiæ VIII., IX., and at Concil. Nicaen. II., 787 ; but according to
my view they both maintained their position, unrecognised by the
government,* from the beginning, as Dorylaion did in 451.   Probably
some unknown episode of church history is the reason why Akmonia
and its group of bishoprics are separate from Phrygia Pacatiana in the
older Notitiæ (which I understand to be founded on a list of bishoprics,
kept for civil purposes in the palace), and united with it in the later
Notitiæ (which I understand to be founded on a church list).

P. 150 (C, 97).   But a passage of Procopius (' Bell. Goth.' III., p. 394)
states that Λύκου Κράνος was a mountain in Pisidia, and Λυκοκρανῖται
were the inhabitants of the district.   If this statement is not a mere
guess of Procopius to explain the curious name, we must reject the
view taken in the text that Λυκοκρανῖται was the name of a regiment.
Justinian transferred the soldiers called Lykokranitai (militum cohors,
De Boor's index) from Phrygia to Syria.   The name may be compared
with Ὄφεως Κεφαλή, whose existence on the northern frontier of Pisidia
has been made very probable by Prof. G. Hirschfeld (' Gött. Gel. Anz.',
1888, pp. 591-2).

P. 151 (C, 99).   I prefer to follow Malalas until some distinct proof

* The disagreement between the people of Kotiaion and the government is shown
by their murder of four successive bishops sent from Constantinople.   I feel no doubt
that Malalas rightly attributes the story to Kotiaion, and that the Paschal Chronicle
is wrong.   The people probably claimed the right to appoint a bishop for themselves.

is given that Phrygia was divided before the time of Constantine. It is sometimes said that Malalas places the formation of the new province in 333 A.D.; but he gives no date.

The latest derivation of the name Salutaris is that suggested by Ohnesorge, 'Die röm. Provinz-Liste von 297,' that parts of Galatia, Phrygia, and Palestine, were so called because they had been especially connected with the saving truths of Christianity : the parts of Galatia and Phrygia that had been visited by Paul were styled Salutaris.

P. 154 (D, 3). Subsequent consideration shows me that ἡ ἐξορία is only an adjective attached to Prokonnesos, which was on an island, and therefore, strictly speaking, outside of the frontier. There was a distinct province of the "Islands" in the Aegean; and the epithet Προικόνησος ἡ ἐξορία means that Prokonnesos, though beyond the strict frontier of Hellespontos, is included in it. The proper form of the name certainly is Προκονησσός, which is related to the Isaurian Prakana, as Σελγησσός (for Σαγαλασσός) to Σέλγη, and other cases : the variation of vowel in Prakana and Prokonessos may be compared with Attalos and Ottalos, Atreus and Otreus, Tatas and Tottes, Tataion and Tottaion. Προικό-νησος is a form due to popular etymology, seeking a name with a meaning in Greek.

P. 155 (D, 4). Prof. Kiepert, if I rightly understand him, considers the true form to be, not Kirmasli, but Kirmasti, i.e. Κρεμαστή.

P. 155 (D, 5). M. S. Reinach suggests, as I think rightly, that the second part of the name Hadrianoutherai is really the native word teira = " town " (as in Teira, Thyateira, Temenothyrai), and that the customary form and legend are due to the etymologising tendency. I should compare the Gallic Augustodunum for a similar hybrid compound of a Roman name and a native word, dunum, "hill."

P. 157 (D, 8). Two alternatives are open with regard to the birthplace of Aristides. (1) He was born at the estate in the territory of Hadrianoutherai among the people Milatai; and Philostratus and Suidas have wrongly given the name Hadrianoi in place of Hadrianoutherai : (2) he was born at Hadrianoi, but his regular home in life was on an estate at Hadrianoutherai. The former alternative seems to me to be correct ; for the priesthood of Zeus was held by his father, and he constantly refers to the altar of Zeus at his home. The reference to Hadrianoi in ἱερ. λογ., III., pp. 546–7, implies apparently a mere chance visit to a strange city, and is in a different tone from his references to the estate.

P. 159 (D, 13). Parthey, p. 318, 124, has a remarkable statement, Μονόλυκος ποταμὸς ὁ νῦν Βαρηνός. If the Barenos is not the Granikos, it must be a river not far distant (see D, 24).

P. 161 (D, 16). The transference of Hadrianoi from Mysia or rather from the Roman Province Asia to Bithynia is distinctly mentioned by Suidas, s. v. Aristides, Ἀδριανοὶ δὲ πόλις Μυσίας τῆς νῦν Βιθυνίας.

P. 162 (D, 19). Mannert (III., 605), on authority of the peripli places the river Artanas 300 stadia east of the river Rhebas, 150 stadia east of the promontory Melaina, 150 stadia west of the river Psilis, and 360 west of Kalpe. The emperor Constantine Copronymus settled a large body of refugee Sclavi on the banks of the Artanas (Theophan., p. 432).

P. 164 (D, 29). I have made three alterations of the text of Athenaeus as published by Kaibel, inserting syllables that have dropped out of the MSS.

P. 164 (E, 1). Since the frontier of Asia Provincia Romana has been rectified (see E § 21), the probability has occurred to me that the road Apameia-Kibyra lay entirely in the province, and therefore that there is no necessity to suppose (as I was obliged to do in ASP.) that a road ran from Apameia to Takina and Themissonion. Takina lies only three miles off the direct line of road from Apameia to Kibyra. We thus also escape a difficulty which was confessed in ASP., viz. that the road Apameia-Kibyra, whose existence is proved by a number of mile-stones, began and ended in Asia, yet traversed mainly a different province. The road lay entirely in Asia, when the frontier is rectified.

P. 166 (E, 4), compare p. 155 (D, 4). The inscription discovered by Dr. E. Fabricius, from which the site of Argiza is inferred, will be accessible in the supplement to C. I. L., III., before the present work is published. It was found at Balia (i.e. παλαία) Bazar Keul. The published maps are not sufficiently trustworthy to show whether this village, or the site whence the inscription was brought to the village, can be on the road from Pergamos to Cyzicos. I therefore retain the conjectural position given to Argesis on the road, and on the map, though I believe that Argesis is merely the ablative of Argiza. I have the firm conviction that everything which I have said about Poimanenon, Argiza, Ergasterion, &c., will have to be modified when the modern geography is pictured in a trustworthy map, but I also hope that the modifications required to adapt my words to the truth will be obvious to every reader. The view which I think most probable is that the Table has mixed up two roads :

(1) Pergamos [55 Ergasteria] Argiza-Poimanenon 35 Cyzicos.

(2) Pergamos-Adramyttion-Argiza-Poimanenon-Cyzicos.

P. 173 (E, 21). I cannot venture to be more precise as to the boundary between Karalitis and the sea. The river Indos of Pliny and Livy is rightly distinguished by Kiepert in his recent map from the Kalbis of Strabo and Ptolemy. The Kalbis lies within the Roman province Asia, and the Indos is probably the boundary between Asia and Lycia.

P. 173 (E, 22). With regard to the πραγματευταί, Mr. Pelham sends me a note, which shows that this Greek term is a rendering of actores (and not, as I have assumed in the text, of negotiatores). He compares Dig. 40, 5, 41. Στίχον καὶ Δάμαν τοὺς πραγματευτάς μου, οὓς οὐκ ἐλευθέρωσα . . . . quaero si paratis actoribus &c.: Plin., Epist. III., 19, eodem procuratore iisdem actoribus: Plin.. Paneg. 36, actori et etiam procuratori tuo: Cod. XI., 72, de conductoribus et procuratoribus sive actoribus praediorum fiscalium: ih., 73, actores sive conductores dominicos: Cod. Theodos., II., 31, servo, colono, conductori, procuratori, actorive. The *actor* was a slave charged with the *rationes*.

Mr. Pelham also writes to me: "*praepositi pagorum* are mentioned Cod. Theod. VII., 4, XII., 6, &c. They seemed to have replaced the old popularly elected *magistri*, had evidently some duties connected with the *annona*, and are coupled with *praepositi horreorum*. The office and its duties are discussed by M. Voigt, 'Drei Epigraphische Constitutionen Constantins' (Leipzig, 1860, p. 169): see also for the office as a *munus* to which *curiales* were liable, Kuhn, I., pp. 243, 244. There is no trace of it before the fourth century. The change from the elective *magister* to the *praepositus*, or praefectus (Orelli, 4025), has always seemed to me characteristic of the centralising tendencies of the empire."

P. 176 (E, 22). But the inference that Tymbrianasa was included in Galatia at the time when this boundary-stone was set up, is not certain. The 'governor and procurator of Galatia might be acting in the matter because Sagalassos was at that time in Galatia, and the boundary-stone was a limit between the provinces Galatia and Phrygia. I prefer, on the whole, for the reasons given in Addenda to E, 1, to suppose that these estates were in Asia from the first, and that Manius Aquilius constructed a road from Apameia to Cibyra, which ran along the southern frontier of the new province, keeping within it the whole way.

P. 181 (F, 15, 16). Ptolemy mentions Παταούιον as a city of Bithynia, and Mannert, Forbiger, &c., on his authority, speak of Patavium. The name must be corrected to Ταταούιον. It is often referred to, generally as Tataion or Tottaion, in the Itineraries, the Peutinger Table, and numerous Byzantine documents. The form Tateabio, which is found in the Peutinger Table, is an error for Tatabio (the ablative being used as in many other instances). The Phrygian personal names Tatas and Tottes are connected with Tataion and Tottaion, as Dorylas is with Dorylaion; compare Kotyaion and Kotys, Akkilaion and Akeles or Akylas, Attaia and Attes or Atys, Anaia and Anes. Tottes and Tatas are therefore only varieties of one name. The identity of Tataion and Tottaion is paralleled by Attalos and Ottalos, Atreus and Otreus (see p. 189), and is placed beyond doubt by the references quoted in the annexed table of the bishoprics of Bithynia. Ταταεύς or Ταταηνός occurs among the Xenoi Tekmoreioi, proving that a village Tataion existed also on the Phrygo-Pisidian frontier; and Παπαηνός proves there a village Papaion, connected with the divine and the personal name Papas.

P. 191 (F, 81, note). M. Theod. Reinach's note on the Roman
Bithynian era seems to me to be a retrogressive step. He places the
government of Bithynia by Pansa in B.C. 48–7, supposing that Pansa
was sent to govern Bithynia immediately after the battle of Pharsalia,
Aug. 9, 48 B.C. But (1) Cn. Domitius Calvinus was probably the official
who directed Caesar's interests in Asia and Bithynia in 48–7 ; (2) both
Pansa and Hirtius were able to report to Cicero about April 47 (Ep. ad
Att., XI., 14, 3) the language used by Quintus, which is a conclusive
proof that Pansa was not in Bithynia at that time. Probably Pansa
was left in Bithynia by Caesar during the summer of 47, or even after
the victory of Zela on Aug. 2, 47. Probably the coins were not struck
before the autumn equinox, when a new Bithynian year began. This
year was 236 according to the coins of Nikaia and Apameia. In the
year 46, Pansa returned to Rome (Cic. ad Fam., VI., 12, 2). We have
therefore the fixed point that the Bithynian year 236 corresponds to
47–6 B.C., and therefore the year 1 corresponds to 282–1 B.C. Some
event in the course of the last three months of 282 or in the first nine
months of 281, gave a reason for reckoning this the Bithynian year 1 ;
and Mommsen may well be correct in assigning as the reason the death
of Lysimachos and consequent triumph of the Bithynian dynasty. Still
the supposition is not absolutely excluded that the coins may have been
struck immediately before the equinox of 47, and that the year 236
began at the equinox of 48, which would make 283–2 the Bithynian
year 1.

P. 193 (F, 84). Probably one of the eleven civitates instituted by
Pompey in Pontus was Neapolis, which did not long survive him.
Strabo (p. 560) mentions that Pompey constituted Phazemon (about the
hot springs of Marsovan or Merzifon) a πόλις, and apparently made it
part of the province, but some time afterwards it was put under the
rule of kings.

P. 193 (F, 84). The authority on which Mr. Head, Hist. Num.,
p. 434, relies, when he mentions Sebaste Paphlagoniae as a city coining
money, is Mionnet (Suppl., IV., p. 570), who quotes five coins described
by Sestini. Of these, three read CEBACTH : the others read respectively
ΣΕΒΑΣΤΗΝΩ . . . . . . MHT and CEBACTHMHTPOΠAΦ. Sestini says (Lett.
di Contin., V., pp. 35, 36), that two of the first three came from
Galatia ; but he was led to attribute all the coins to Sebaste, the
modern Sivas, on seeing the last coin, which belongs to the Chaudoir
collection.* This attribution is certainly false : for the ancient name
of Sivas was Σεβάστεια not Σεβαστή, and it was not in Paphlagonia.
Either Sestini misread the last coin and all belong to the Galatian
Sebaste (Ankyra), or the Phrygian Sebaste, or else an otherwise
unknown Sebaste Paphlagoniae must have existed. I am indebted to

* This collection is now, I believe, in St. Petersburg: my authority is M. Waddington,
if I do not misrepresent hi

Mr. Wroth's ' Coins of Pontus and Bithynia,' and to his private letters, for much help on this and other points. But see p. 453.

P. 194 (F, 84). Timolaion is erroneously given as a city that struck coins by Mr. Head, ' Hist. Num.,' p. 435. The coin formerly attributed is, according to Mr. Wroth, ' Coinage of Pontus,' &c., p. xiii, a badly preserved coin of Akmonia.

P. 194 (F, 85). The era of Amisos is generally agreed to date B.C. 33, when the tyrant Straton was expelled and the city freed. But Strabo, p. 547, certainly says that the liberation took place in 30, during Augustus's eastern journey, and this contradiction led me to investigate the subject more minutely. With the help of information freely given by Mr. Head and Mr. Wroth, I reach the following conclusions :—When Amisos was set free, it adopted as its era the great victory of its liberator at Actium. The battle was fought on Sept. 2 in the year 31, and the current civil year at that date was reckoned as the year 1. The year of Amisos must have ended either at the autumn equinox or the winter solstice : the evidence is not absolutely certain as to which of these points was the new year, but is inconsistent with a spring or summer new year, and points to an autumn change as more probable. The following important dates occur on coins reported to me :—

Amisos	1	ends Sept. 22,	B.C.	31	Actium, Sept. 2, 31
	101	,,	,, A.D.	70	Galba (died Jan. 69) as $\theta\epsilon\dot{o}s\ \sigma\epsilon\beta\alpha\sigma\tau\dot{o}s$
	168	,,	,,	137	Sabina,
	169	,,	,,	138	L. Aelius Caesar, died Jan. 138
	248	,,	,,	217	Caracalla, died April 8, 217
	27[2]	,,	,,	241	Gordian III,, began to reign 239
	272	,,	,,	241	Tranquillina, became empress 241.

The coin of Galba was struck after his death, for he is styled $\theta\epsilon\dot{o}s$; and no inference can be drawn from the fact that he died in the year of Amisos 100. The date on the coin of Sabina is important : it shows that her death was not announced at Amisos till after the year 168 had been running some time, i.e. till after September 23, 136. The last date is also important. It is inferred by Schiller from the coins of Alexandria that Tranquillina was married to Gordian III. between Aug. 30, 241 and Aug. 29, 242. From the comparison of this coin of Amisos we may now argue that the marriage took place before Sept. 22, 241.

The principle that the ordinary civil year in which the era occurred was reckoned as 1 is important, and I shall therefore confirm it by another case. It is of course well known that the era of the province Asia (used, however, only in Phrygia and the eastern parts of Lydia, never in the western and more civilised parts of the province) is the reorganisation by Sulla, B.C. 84. But it has been proved conclusively that the year 1 of that era begins in 85 B.C. The ordinary civil year which was running, when the reorganisation was carried into effect, was reckoned 1. A Phrygian inscription is dated ροβ′ in the month Panemos in the consulship of Domitian XIV. and L. Minucius Rufus,* i.e. between Jan. and April of 88 A.D. Now Panemos is the ninth month of the year, therefore the Phrygian year must have begun during the summer. It may seem strange that the Phrygian year began in summer, and I have myself hitherto always supposed it to begin, like the year of the Aegean coast cities, and of Asia in general, at the autumn equinox; but the above result agrees exactly with M. Waddington's conclusion (on Le Bas 980) that the year 1 had begun before Aug. 31, 85 B.C.

As to the exact day when the Phrygian year began, only two possibilities seem open; it must have begun either at the summer solstice, or about July 1, when the Roman Proconsuls of Asia probably entered on office.† Now it is highly improbable that the first day of the Phrygian year would have been changed from the usual Asian date at the autumn equinox except for the sake of being accommodated to a Roman custom and a solar year. I therefore conclude that in Phrygia and Upper Lydia the solar year was in vogue, and began on July 1st. The inscription in question, then, is dated in March, 88 A.D. Many dates which have hitherto been explained on the supposition that the Phrygian era began in the latter part of 85 B.C. must be changed according to the following table.

First Phrygian month called Dios				is July
Second	"	"	" Apellaios	" August
Third	"	"	" Audunaios	" September
Fourth	"	"	" Peritios	" October
Fifth	"	"	" Dustros	" November
Sixth	"	"	" Xanthikos Artemisios	" December
Seventh	"	"	" Artemisios	" January
Eighth	"	"	" Daisios	" February
Ninth	"	"	" Panemos	" March
Tenth	"	"	" Loos	" April
Eleventh	"	"	" Gorpiaios	" May
Twelfth	"	"	" Hyperberetaios	" June

I shall take another example from the eras of Cibyra and of the province Pamphylia. M. Waddington (Le Bas, No. 1213) says that the year 1 of the Cibyratic era began at the autumn equinox of the year 25 (a pour point de départ l'automne de l'année 778). But the year 193 of Cibyra was running during the months of June, July, A.D. 218, for coins of Elagabalus, who was declared emperor on May 16, and of Macrinus, who died on June 8, in that year, both occur with the date 193. There-

* Klein gives, on uncertain grounds, the praenomen of this consul as Quintus. The inscription, 'Journ. Hell. Stud.,' 1883, p. 432, gives the correct form. New consuls came into office on April 15.

† I assume that there was an official date for the entrance of the new proconsul to office, and take approximately the date July 1.

fore the year 193 of Cibyra began Sept. 217, and ended Sept. 218; which proves that the year 1 of Cibyra began Sept. 24 and ended Sept. 25. From this I infer that some important event took place during that year which led the people to reckon the current year as the first of their new system.

According to my interpretation of an inscription of Palaiopolis in Pisidia, published ASP., D, 16, the year 150 of Cibyra corresponded to the year 102 of another era which was also employed there. This other era I suppose to be that of the formation of the new province Pamphylia-Lycia by Vespasian. Palaiopolis is divided only by the small river Lysis from the territory of the province Asia and conventus Cibyra, in which the era of Cibyra was commonly used; and its inhabitants therefore naturally employed both their own provincial era and the Cibyratic era. Now if the year 102 extend from Sept. 174 to Sept. 175 (which is 150 of Cibyra), the year 1 extends from Sept. 73 to Sept. 74. I therefore understand that, when a new governor arrived in spring or summer, A.D. 74, to govern the new province Lycia-Pamphylia, the inhabitants reckoned the year that was running when the new system began as the year 1.

P. 196 (F, 86). Mr. Wroth, ' Coinage of Pontus,' &c., p. 13, shows that the coinage of Dion or Dia is confined, so far as is known, to the age of Mithradates : the imperial coin of Augustus attributed to it in ' Hist. Num.,' p. 440, is a badly preserved coin of Sardis. This therefore proves that it is not likely to be the twelfth city meant by Pliny, which then must rather be a komopolis composed of the regiones Doris or Dablis and Tataion, in which there were curiales, implying a certain political constitution (Cod. Theod., XII., 1, 119).

P. 197 (F, 88). The account of the province Bithynia given by Mr. Hardy in his most useful and praiseworthy edition of Pliny's correspondence with Trajan, p. 49, is not quite correct. He makes the Sangarios the eastern boundary, and yet names in the province several cities far east of the Sangarios. The more usual statement, that the Billaios is the boundary, is hardly less inaccurate on the opposite side. The Billaios lies east of the strict boundary of Bithynia. Yet it is not an uncommon statement that the Billaios lies west of the Bithynian frontier, and that the Parthenios is nearer the true boundary ; and Prof. Kiepert, in his latest map, places the frontier line much further east even than the Parthenios. The proof given in the text from Strabo and Justinian of the true frontier seems to me conclusive. The very name Heracleia in Ponto is itself conclusive : there is no other sense for it, as used on imperial coins, than " in the province Pontus," though I do not deny that originally the city may have been distinguished from others of the same name as " Heracleia on the (Euxine) Sea." In the new province of Bithynia, formed not later than Diocletian, Heracleia was included, but not Krateia or Tion (Justinian, Novel. XXIX.). Moreover, the letter of Pliny to Trajan, 75, seems conclusive that Heracleia and Tion were both in Pontus, not in Bithynia.

Mr. Hardy also attributes to Pliny the list of the XII. civitates of Bithynia, which he gives. Pliny gives only the number, but not the names, mentioning only Juliopolis or Gordou Kome, and (perhaps) Daskylion. The list depends, not on the authority of Pliny, but on that of Marquardt, and is, as I have shown in the text, incorrect. Marquardt's error in naming Tium as one of the eleven cities of Pontus, and Tius as one of the twelve of Bithynia (in addition to Cius), has now become traditional, and is repeated by every person who speaks about the province. Tius and Tium are the same city, which belongs to Pontus. Mr. Hardy also speaks of Prusias or Hyppias: the name Hyppias (or rather Hypias) for the city does not, so far as I know, occur.

I mention these faults, not from any desire to pick faults in a most careful and meritorious book, but as an example of the numerous errors that I find in almost every paragraph of every writer touching on Asia Minor. If we must speak about Asia Minor, surely it is as well that there should be some trustworthy book to use as an authority, for it cannot be expected that every one shall verify from original authorities every statement about the country.

P. 203 (G, 10). Since this was written, further study has shown me that Koloneia in Constantine must mean Koloneia of Armenia. The blunder which this implies is much more serious than the one which I have attributed to him in the text, and shows astounding ignorance of geography, but no other interpretation seems possible. It is then necessary to beware of correcting a geographical error in Constantine. In Them. p. 14, he ought to have said that Salutaris extends from Akroenos to Amorion, but we must not actually alter his text. In Them., p. 19, he makes Rodentos and Podantos two places, whereas they are only a wrong and a right name of one place.

P. 217 (G, 38). While I think that the course of the military road from Dorylaion to the Halys was as I have described it in the text, I fully acknowledge that the proof is incomplete. The alternative route down the Tembris valley and up the Istanoz Su to Ankyra has much to recommend it : it was the Roman road, and it seems the more natural road. But the arguments that lead me to prefer the other route are, (1) the situation of Justinianopolis, whose obvious importance requires a situation on the road, (2) the situation of Kaborkion, which can hardly have been very far from the road, (3) the bridge Zompi, which seems to have been decidedly further south than the mouth of the Tembris. Doubt exists only on the section between Akkilaion-Krasos and Gorbeous-Akarbous ; but the rest is more nearly certain.

P. 219 (G, 23). Gezatorix is evidently a Gaulish chief, and bears a most interesting name, which connects the Gauls of Asia with those of the west. My friend, Mr. Neil, points out to me that Gezatorix is for Gaisato-rix, king of the Gaisati, or "Spearmen."

P. 232 (H, 20). Gelzer remarks that the elevation of Amorion to be a metropolis over a group of bishoprics is probably earlier than the sack of the city by the Arabs in 838. It was autokephalos in 787.

P. 236 (H, 25). Prof. W. Robertson Smith writes to me that this route "is to be found in more original form in Ibn-Khordādhbeh, p. 101, sq. (Transl., p. 74)" as—

Forest of 'Ammūria.

15 m. to the villages of Harrāb.
 2 „ „ Sāgharī, the river of 'Ammūria.
12 „ „ Al-Ilj (the Barbarian), or on another reading, Al-Fajj.
15 „ „ Falāmī (var. Calāmī) of the forest.
12 „ „ The Jews' Castle, Ḥiṣn-al-Yahūd.
18 „ „ Sandābari.
35 „ „ The meadow of the King's Asses in Daraulia (Dorylaion).
15 „ „ Ḥiṣn Gharūbulī (with several variants).
 3 „ „ Kanais-al-Malik (the King's Churches).
25 „ „ Al-Tolūl (the Hillocks).
15 „ „ Al-Akwār.
15 „ „ Malājina.
 5 „ „ The King's Stables.
30 „ „ Ḥiṣn-al-Ghabrā.
25 „ „ The Strait.

This more accurate account confirms the interpretation in the text. The Sangarios and Dorylaion are established. The distance—30 or 35—from Dorylaion to Santabaris points to the situation of the latter at Bardakchi.

Gharūbulī or Gharoboli is mentioned also in another place by Edrisi, as one of the eleven fortresses of the district Lamchik, the others being Nikia, el Jehoudi, Agradh, Libadhia (Dorylaion), and Nikomedia. The route here given shows that Gharoboli is probably the fortress called Kiz Kale, marked by Kiepert beside Inn Ongu (Inn Oghi). Al-Akwar or El-Agradh must be Vezir Khan, and Al-Tolūl or Múlawwen must be Bilejik. The King's Churches, the Basilika of Anna Comnena on the road alike to Kotiaion and to Dorylaion from Nikaia, must be Inn Ongu. El Jehoudi is clearly Ḥiṣn-al-Yahūd.

The other great divisions of Asia Minor, according to Edrisi, are Abhlakhonia, Malatia, El-Afa-chim, Batalous (including Alamin, Merdj-el-Chahm, Machkensin or Mechkenis, Barghouth, Amouria), Djarsioun (Housba = Sivas), Baklan (Ankira, Tamalo, Talbour, Tokhat, Kaisari), Arminiac (Konia, Khizlassa [elsewhere put in Baklan], Ladikie, Dirakio, Kaloumi, Belouti), Djaldia (Arsea or Erzeroum), Selefkia, Benadek (Adana, El-Massissa, Korra, Tibra, El-Adjouf, Dzoul'kila).

Colonel Stewart gave me the following estimates from Brussa,—

18 miles Gemlek, 48 Isnik (Nikaia), 64½ Lefke, 80½ Bilejik, 98¾ Yeni Sheher, 112 Aine Göl. Another route is from Isnik, 16½ Lefke, 26 Vezir Khan, 36½ Bilejik, 44½ Yeni Keui, 54½ Sugut, 80 Sugut Keui, 85½ Eski Sheher (Dorylaion), 123 Kutaya.

P. 245 (K, 7) Juliopolis was perexigua civitas in A.D. 112, as Pliny mentions to Trajan, Ep. 73. Ignatius is mentioned, in 869, sometimes as bishop of Juliopolis, sometimes as bishop of Basileion.

P. 246 (K, 10). Theodorus is said, in 'Dict. Christ. Biogr.', to have been bishop of Daras or Anastasiopolis. He was really bishop of Lagania : I know no authority for the statement about Daras, which is a city of Mesopotamia, never mentioned in the biography of S. Theodorus. The date of the birth of Theodorus is uncertain, but must have been about 540–50.

P. 247 (K, 11). Since the text has been printed Sir C. W. Wilson informs me that the road Caesareia-Terzili-Göne-Alaja, to which I have attributed so much importance here and on pp. 265 and 268, is actually a route of the first consequence. It is the araba route from Caesareia to the coast at Samsun. Goods carried on horseback can find a shorter route, but waggons from Samsun (Amisos) go by Marsovan (Phazemon), Tchorum, Alaja, to Caesareia. The distance from Marsovan by Kanli Bunar Pass, Doghanji (24 miles), and Sitlik Boghaz, to Tchorum is about 36 miles, and from Tchorum by Tekiye Hatab Dere and Babu Oglu (12 miles) to Alaja in Hussein Ova is about 27 miles. The point where this road crossed the Byzantine military road would be an important centre, and hence we understand why Basilika Therma was a bishopric.

P. 248 (K, 14). Kaloumne must be the same place that is called by Edrisi Kaloumi. Edrisi mentions as cities of the Arminiac district, Konia, Khizlassa, Ladikie, Dirakio, Kaloumi, Belouti. Of these Konia and Ladikie really belong to the Anatolic Theme, called Batalous by Edrisi. I have found some reference to Kaloumne in one of the Byzantine writers, but have lost the note on the point : perhaps this may meet the eye of some reader who can complete my account of the place.

The suggestion that Kaloumne (see p. 445) is Kotch Hisar, rests solely on the fact that Kaloumne was a place that became important only in very late time. Such places usually continue to be important in Turkish time. It was in Galatia, and its growing importance must be due to its situation on a road that acquired importance only in later time. That was the case with the direct road from Ankyra to Archelais, which was of no consequence while the route by Parnassos was in use, but which must rise to importance after that route fell into decay. Kotch Hisar could hardly be in Roman Galatia, according to the boundaries indicated by Ptolemy, but the Jerusalem Itinerary extends Galatia much further south than Ptolemy does. Kademna which is given in Phrygia Salutaris in Notitia I., is perhaps Kaloumne erroneously spelt and transferred to the wrong province.

P. 253 (K, 21). Ptolemy's enumeration of the cities of Pontus Galaticus and Polemoniacus (v. 6, § 9, 10) is on the whole so good as to be probably taken, in the main, from a Roman document. Pontus Galaticus was added to Galatia, B.C. 7, as is proved by the era of Amaseia, combined with Strabo, p. 561 ; but it was probably enlarged, in B.C. 2, by the addition of some territory on the south, including Sebastopolis-Heracleopolis, and in A.D. 38–9 by the addition of Komana and some territory on the east, taken probably after the death of Dyteutos. The districts which Ptolemy calls Pontus Polemoniacus and Cappadocicus were incorporated in the Province of Galatia in A.D. 63. That era appears on the coins of Neocaesareia and Zela, in Polemoniacus, and Kerasous and Trapezous in Cappadocicus. From the names we may conclude that the former was subject to the dynasty of Polemon, but not the latter.

The kingdoms of Pylaemenes and Deiotarus seem to have been incorporated in Galatia in B.C. 7, as is shown by the era of Neoclaudiopolis and Gangra, and to have constituted the district which was henceforth, under the name Paphlagonia, included in the province Galatia.

But Ptolemy's enumeration of the cities of Galatia (V. 4, § 6, 9) is not good ; in all probability he was deceived by the name Paphlagonia applied to a part of the province Galatia, and mentions in this Paphlagonia all the names which he could, from other authorities, include in Paphlagonia, and thus puts in the Roman province various cities that belong to the Pontic part of Paphlagonia, i.e. to the province Bithynia-Pontus. Also his Claudiopolis, § 9, seems to be identical with his Neoclaudiopolis, § 6.

P. 262–3 (L, 13). After the remarks in Addenda to p. 247, the idea suggests itself that the trade-route to Amisos passed not by Ladik and Ahmed Serai but by Marsovan (Phazemon): the former is only a horse-road, the latter is an araba-road.

Pp. 275–6 (N, 6) and p. 326 (P, 8). Compare also the following, from the Council of A.D. 680 (Acta, p. 646): Georgius Episcopus territorii Daranysensis (Δαρανάλεως) seu Analiblae magnae Armeniorum regionis. Comparing the Greek form Daranalis with Ptolemy's Karnalis of Chamanene and Karmala of Melitene, we may hazard the conjecture, confirming and completing the theory advanced in the text (p. 288–91), that in reality there are two places, Daranalis or Darnalis, near the borders of Armenia Minor, and Karmalis on the river Karmalas, which have been confused and misplaced by Ptolemy.

P. 285 (O, I.). Compare Parthey, p. 318, 129, Κολωνία ἡ νῦν Τάξαρα.

P. 305 (O, VII.). A comparison of the list of A.D. 692 with that of

Notitiæ, VII., VIII., I., makes it probable that Theodosiopolis of Armenia was the great fortress of Kamache or Ani.

P. 324 (P, 6). Gelzer has shown that Eukhaita was an arch-bishopric before 553 : he is disposed to think that it was elevated to that rank between 536 and 553. I still continue to think that its elevation had taken place before Hierocles. It became a metropolis between 886 and 959, as Gelzer shows, p. 540.

I may add two further arguments that the passage in Notitia III. about Eukhaita and Neai Patrai is corrupt, and that the four bishoprics probably are subject to Eukhaita. (1) Other Notitiæ show that Marmaritzana was subject to Neai Patrai, but Notitia III. adds it by error to the bishoprics subject to the preceding metropolis of Mitylene. (2) Notitia III. goes on to state that there are no bishoprics subject to Khonai; but I have shown in CB that a group of bishoprics round Khonai were in all probability subject to it.

I therefore think that Notitia III. ought to read, Τῷ Νέων Πατρῶν, ὁ Μαρμαριτζάνων. Τῷ Εὐχαίτων, ὁ Γαζάλων κ.τ.λ. Τῷ Ἀμάστριδος θρόνος ὑποκείμενος οὐκ ἔστιν. Τῷ Χωνῶν, ὁ Σανάου κ.τ.λ. Notitia X. gives this arrangement, except for Khonai.

P. 341 (Q, 15) and p. 368 (T, 22). The statement of Edrisi that Dzoul-kila, Adana, El-Massissa (i.e. Missis, Mansista, or Mopsouestia), Korra, Tibra, and El-Adjouf, were the chief fortresses of Benadek, quite confirms the opinion expressed in the note to p. 341. The fortresses in this list seem to be south of Tauros, and I cannot therefore place Dzoul-kila or Dsu-l-kala on the road from the Gates to Ankyra, where Sideropalos probably must have been (Theophan., p. 482). It is then necessary to give up the identification of Sideropalos with Dsu-l-kala, which rests only on the resemblance of name, always a very slippery and uncertain ground (p. 101 and p. 430). The difficulties all dis-appear if we identify Safssaf with Sideropalos, and Dsu-l-kala with Andrasos. The latter is a fortress on one of the Isaurian passes, the former a fortress of Cappadocia.

P. 341 (Q, 16). Gelzer, p. 543, comes from different reasons to the same conclusion as to the date when Herakleia-Kybistra was raised to the rank of an archbishopric.

P. 346 (Q, 28). The Pyrgos of Barbarossa's march must evidently have replaced Ilistra, the site of which is close to it. The possibility must be alluded to that this Pyrgos is meant by the bishopric Pyrgoi of Notitiæ III., X., XIII., and even by the Anydroi Pyrgoi of Theophanes. This view is not taken in the text, because these Notitiæ give Ilistra as a separate bishopric; but considering the loose way in which these registers were kept, this reason is not conclusive. The point must be left uncertain, but I incline to the view taken in the text on the ground of the epithet Anydroi, which points to the great waterless plains about Crbugh and Savatra

P. 348 (Q, 35). The reasoning here is too compressed to be clear. There was an imperial estate between Andabalis and Tyana: it was a great centre for horse-breeding, and in the fourth century the equi curules produced there are mentioned in the Jerusalem Itinerary, which calls the estate "Villa Pampali." This corrupt name has been emended to Palmati, and it has been supposed that the race-horses equi Palmatiani, derived their name from Palmatius (CB, § LIV), a lessee of the estate. The head of the monastery Pasa, which must be in the neighbourhood, had to provide horses for the post-service (Q, 33). This imperial estate must, as I argue, be identified with the imperial estate near Tyana, whose existence at a later date under the name Drizes I prove in the text. Then I infer from the Dragai of Ptolemy that the name existed already in the second century. The estate evidently comprised the splendid land about Bor, and extended past the springs of Xanxaris to the neighbourhood of Andabalis. There is every probability that the breeding of these horses belonged to the priests of Zeus Asmabaios or Asbamaios at an early time, and that the property and the trade was inherited from them by the Cappadocian kings and the Roman emperors. Prof. Sayce informs me that some of the clay tablets inscribed with cuneiform characters, which I purchased from a dealer in Kaisari, relate to the sale of horses. Independent reasons make it probable that these tablets come ultimately from Tyana.* The contradiction between the cold fountains of Philostratus, the salt fountains of Strabo, and the hot springs at Xanxaris, is doubtless to be explained by the existence of several fountains. The neighbourhood of Bor is exceedingly well watered, and I now regret that I did not explore the sources of the water which flows in abundance through the town. The name Τύανα ought to be in English Twana rather than Tyana: Twana was pronounced Dana by Xenophon.

P. 353 (R, 6). Those who desiderate any further proof of my identification of Loulon with Halala-Faustinopolis will find it in the signature of A.D. 879, Φίλιππος Λούλου. Loulon was therefore a bishopric, and, as is frequently the case in the Councils of the eighth and ninth centuries, the native name Loulon had taken the place of a Græco-Roman title.† The proof that this name was Faustinopolis is, I think, conclusive.

P. 368 (T, 24). The Latin list of the bishoprics of Isauria published by Gelzer, p. 565, adds some further evidence. This list gives Mosbda (i.e. Mousbanda) and Nefelia (i.e. Nephelis) which are found in no Notitia, while it omits Juliosebaste, Hierapolis and Lauzados. There can be little doubt that Nephelis is the native name of Juliosebaste: for

---

* But see p. 39, note ‡, to the contrary.

† I have elsewhere mentioned numerous examples of this, e.g. Prakana, Kardabounda, Nephelis, &c.

the position of the latter in Hierocles corresponds well to the position of
Nephelis in the Peripli (see Leake, pp. 199–200). Nephelis is mentioned
as a bishopric in 451, Sebastia (i.e. Juliosebaste) in 458; the identity of
the two suits all the facts known to me. The Latin list has nine
bishoprics, from Kalenderis to Yotapi (i.e. Iotape), in the same order as
Hierocles, substituting Nephelis for Juliosebaste.

This list gives as three separate bishoprics, Mousbada, Sbide,
and Sibilia (under the form Sevila). This proves that Sbide and
Sibilia (as is done in my text) must be distinguished as separate
bishoprics, though their names approximate in form. Notitia III.
also distinguishes ὁ Συβάλων and ὁ Συνήδων (i.e. Συβήδων) as separate
bishoprics. Gelzer's Latin list omits Hierapolis entirely, and in
all probability this proves that one of the three, Sibilia, Sbide, or
Mousbada, is identical with it. Sbide appears along with Hierapolis in
several lists, and must therefore be a different place from it. The
order of the Latin list, Claudiopolis, Diocaesareia, Oropi (i.e. Olbe),
Dalisandos, Sevila, when compared with Hierocles, makes it highly
probable that Sevila or Sibila is identical with Hierapolis. If this
identity is accepted, then the various arguments that have been
collected in the text about the people Koropisseis, about Sibila, and
about Hierapolis, coincide in establishing that that people, with their
chief city Sibila-Hierapolis, inhabited the northern part of Isauria
close to Lykaonia, on the road between Claudiopolis and Laranda.
Frederick Barbarossa passed though Sibilia when he marched along this
road.

This identification of Sibila as the native name of Hierapolis also
confirms the separation that I have made between Verinopolis-Psebila of
Lykaonia and Sibila of Isauria.

P. 376 (T, 46). The statement in the text is perhaps too brief and
obscure. The title applied to Carminius might also be applied to any
other governor of Lycia-Pamphylia, for a few towns, which belonged
according to the pre-Roman ethnic system to Isauria, were included,
probably from 74 A.D. onwards, in the province Lycia-Pamphylia.
These towns are Lyrbe, Kolobrassos, Kasai, Laerte, Kibyra, Korakesion,
and Syedra, which are all mentioned by Ptolemy as towns of Cilicia
Tracheia, but in the Roman Pamphylia. Beginning from some period in
the second or early third century, Cilicia Tracheia came to be designated
as Isauria, a name which by Strabo and Ptolemy is restricted to a small
district about Lystra and Isaura; hence the inscription says that
Carminius governed Lycia, Pamphylia, and Isauria, just as the legates
of Galatia are often said to govern Paphlagonia and Phrygia, though
they only ruled small parts of these countries.

P. 381 (T, 61). The apparent contradiction that Sebaste struck
imperial coins from Augustus onwards and autonomous coins between
38 and 72 would no doubt be resolved by a study of the coins, which is

not in my power. The city may have been at some period included in the Empire, then made autonomous, and then taken under the Empire again, but it can hardly be supposed to have been striking at the same time imperial and autonomous coins.

P. 385. Leo Diaconus, p. 52, however, correctly places Mopsouestia on the Pyramos. His geography is usually very accurate, though he does put Claudiopolis in Galatia, instead of Honorias: Κλανδιούπολις, τὸ εὐδαιμονέστατον χωρίον τῶν Γαλατῶν. This, however, is a pure error, arising from forgetfulness of the old historical divisions, which had lost all political reality since the institution of the Themes, though they were still kept up in the ecclesiastical arrangement. It is, of course, impossible in this passage to understand Neoclaudiopolis-Andrapa, which was included in the Roman Province Galatia, because there is no example of the use of the name Neoclaudiopolis in Byzantine times, and Andrapa could not be called εὐδαιμονέστατον Γαλατῶν.

P. 385. The statement in Parthey, p. 313, 29, Καστάβαλλα Κιλικίας ἡ νῦν Μάμιστα is certainly incorrect.

P. 386. Kabissos is also mentioned as a bishopric of Cilicia Secunda in the Latin Notitia published by Gelzer, 'Zft. f. protest. Theologie,' XII. p. 564. This Notitia gives Mopsouestia as autokephalos, as does also Nilus Doxapatrius, and adds nine bishoprics subject to Anazarbos, viz., the eight that are given in Notitia I. (reading Cambrisopolis = Καβισσόπολις) with the addition of Sysya. This last is obviously the modern Sis (see p. 385). Sis and Flavias are therefore mentioned as separate bishoprics in this Notitia, whereas I identify them. But the Latin writer, who copied out at Antioch a Greek Notitia (Gelzer, loc. cit., p. 568), the arrangement in which belonged to a much earlier date, knew that Sis was the seat of a bishop in his time, but did not know that it was given in his list under the name Flavias. He therefore on his own authority added Sisia at the end of the list.

P. 396 (V., 10). It may be inferred from Gelzer's articles (see Addenda to p. 89) that Mistheia was elevated to the rank of auto-kephalos about 810–820; and that Neapolis, Kotiaion, and Selge were recognised as autokephaloi about 820–38, about which time also Amorion became a metropolis.

P. 332 (Q, 3). A village of the territory of Lystra was named Kilistra (see my paper in 'Bull. Corr. Hell.,' 1883, p. 314). It retains the old name, 6 miles N.W. from Lystra, and contains a remarkable series of churches cut in the rock.

P. 347 (Q, 33). Pasa and Paspasa were probably alternative forms. So in Phrygia (C, 18) inscriptions have both Salouda and Salsalouda, and I have unnecessarily supposed that the latter was due to an error of the engraver: in Ephesos there was a tribe Benneis or Bembineis, Wood, Inscr. Temp., p. 4.

P. 368.   The Latin list published by Gelzer, of bishoprics subject to Seleuceia of Isauria, is so important and so difficult of access in the Jahrbuch that I add it here:—

13 Claudiopolis	5 Lamos	16 Germanicopolis
11 Diocaesareia	6 Antiocheia parva	— Mosbda
12 Oropi	7 Nefelia	— Domaeciopolis
15 Dalisandos	8 Ristria	21 Sbidi
14 Sevila	9 Selenunta	— Zinonopolis
2 Kelenderis	10 Yotapi	20 Andrasson
3 Anemori	18 Philadelphia parva	19 Miloy
4 Titopolis	17 Yrinopolis	22 Neapolis

I give this list in the original order, and prefix the numbers showing the place of each town in Hierocles : No. 23 Lauzados is omitted in the Latin list.   Three cities given in the Latin list are omitted by Hierocles.

P. 117.   Gambreion, placed by Franz on C. I. G., No. 3562, at Kinik between Pergamos and Germe, has been omitted.*

Pp. 193, 440.   Niese's papers on Strabo in Rhein. Mus. 1883, and Hermes, though they have taught me much since I .read them in April 1890, have not altered my opinion about the eleven civitates in the province Pontus as arranged by Pompey.

P. 247.   Mithridation in Pontus, given by Pompey to Brogitarus, when he made him king of the Trokmoi in B.C. 63 or 62, must be a city on the frontier of Galatia and Pontus, taken into the Roman province Galatia in B.C. 25.   It is, therefore, most probably a temporary name of Eukhaita (unless that town was part of Gazelonitis, as is very likely) or Karissa or Euagina.

P. 376.   Mommsen, differing from Marquardt, p. 387, considers that Cilicia was separated from Syria, and governed by a praetorian legate from as early as 58 A.D.   See Res G. D. Aug., p. 173.

P. 442.   In March 1890 I saw Kubitschek's article, "die sullanische Aera" in A. E. Mittheil. a. Oesterr., 1890.   His polemic against Cichorius in "Berlin. Sitzungsber.," 1889, p. 365, who places the era in 84, is conclusive.   Kubitschek makes it Sept. 23, 85.   I still prefer June 22 or July 1, 85.   I do not admit that an inscription of Apollonia can be taken in evidence of an era, which, as Mommsen observes, is confined to Phrygia and the eastern parts of Lydia.   Kubitschek doubts my copy of the Trajanopolis inscription.   I have verified it on the impression, and am permitted also to quote Prof. Th. Mommsen's opinion, after inspecting the impression.   My reading is correct.   The titles of the emperor show complete ignorance of the proper forms, and

* Pakaleia in C. I. G., 3568, must not be connected with Pankaleia (p. 231); M. Waddington (on Le Bas, 1011) corrects the text to Paraleia.

are consistent with any year of Hadrian's reign. The last lines
are :—

> ἐπιμεληθέντων [Σωσ]θ[έν]ους 'Αρτε[μι-
> δώρου τοῦ Μενίππου καὶ Φιλάνθου Σωσ-
> θένους. ἔτους σδ´. μη(νὸς) Δείου β´.

I have not seen Cichorius's paper.

At the last moment, through the kindness of Dr. Imhoof Blumer, I
am able to add the following notes from his "Griechische Münzen."
He rejects all coins of Dia in Bithynia, referring them to Diospolis-
Kabeira-Neocaesareia. He dates the era of Amaseia in 2 B.C., of
Komana Pontica in 35 A.D., of Gangra in an uncertain year, 4 B.C. at
latest. He accepts Sebaste of Paphlagonia as a city coining money, and
takes it as a name of Kytoros : I should rather, from the facts which he
quotes, take it as a title assumed by Amastris for a few years. His
explanation of Nikomedeia Dipontos can hardly be accepted. It means
that the territory of the city extended from sea to sea, i.e. from the gulf
of Astakos to the Euxine. The facts quoted by him about the name
Ketis or Kietis disprove the theory advanced by Svoronos, and disputed
on p. 455.

P. 253 (K, 21). The changes in Galatia Provincia, may be completed
as follows. The evidence is fragmentary and insufficient. Most of the
dates are got from coins, according to the corrections of Imhoof
Blumer.

B.C. 25. The kingdom of Amyntas formed into a province, including
the three Galatian tribes, Lykaonia as far as Lystra,
Isaura and Derbe,* the greater part of Pisidia, Milyas,
and Kabalis.

7–4. Paphlagonia, with Gangra and Andrapa, is added to the
province on the death of Deiotarus Philadelphus. The
exact year is uncertain.

6. Komama, and probably Augustus's other colonies, Olbasa,
Kremna, Parlais, Lystra, Antiocheia, founded.

3 or 2. Quirinius, governor of Syria, conquers the Homonades.
Apparently, they must have been attached to Galatia.
rather than to Syria-Cilicia. See Mommsen, Res Gest.
D. Aug., p. 177.

2. Sebastopolis and part of Kolopene added to the province on
the death of Ateporix ; also Amaseia and probably
Gazelonitis.

A.D. 35. Komana, and probably Ibora, Verisa, and even Siara, added
to the province on the death of Dyteutos. The districts
of Amaseia, Gazelonitis, Sebastopolis, and Komana, are

---

* Derbe was in B.C. 20 attached (Strab. p. 569) to the Eleventh Strategia of
Cappadocia : see pp. 337, 372.

summed up by Ptolemy under the name Pontus Galaticus.

P. 364 (T 7). At the last moment M. Waddington points out to me a piece of evidence which I had by an unpardonable and hardly conceivable oversight omitted* : Diocaesareia struck coins as Metropolis Kennaton (see 'Hist. Num.,' s.v.). To sum up the evidence about Diocaesareia-Prakana, it was—

1. In the Decapolis, i.e. on the Ermenek Su or lower Kalykadnos ;
2. In Kennatis, which struck coins along with Lalassis both under the dynast Polemon and as a Koinon, and must therefore be conterminous with it ;
3. Not far from Seleuceia (see p. 364) ;
4. On the road from Laranda to Seleuceia ;
5. A frontier city between the Turks of Konia and the Byzantines, at the time when the latter possessed Seleuceia and the road along the coast.
6. According to my interpretation of a coin, adjoining Olba ;
7. Mentioned along with Claudiopolis and Olba by Hierocles, in the valuable Latin list, p. 452, and in Notitia III. ;
8. Mentioned along with Claudiopolis and Hierapolis-Koropissos in Notitia I.

These arguments seem conclusive. The only doubt that remains is whether Leake's conjectural position of Claudiopolis at Mut is correct, in which case Diocaesareia should be placed on the road between it and Seleuceia, or whether Leake is wrong and Diocaesareia was at Mut. Mut seems to be the important and central city on the great road from Laranda to Seleuceia : now Claudiopolis is a Roman Colony, which would naturally be placed on such a road, and for this reason I feel bound to follow Leake. Diocaesareia, to judge from its coinage, was a more important city than Claudiopolis, of which no coins are known : Diocaesareia is implied in several references to be on the above-mentioned road, and the historical allusions show its importance in the twelfth century ; but Claudiopolis is hardly mentioned throughout history, and bishops of Claudiopolis are much less frequent at the Councils than those of Diocaesareia (unless Kardabounda be the native name of Claudiopolis). The arguments 5 to 8 however suggest that Diocaesareia was between Claudiopolis and Mut. It is evident that in any case Claudiopolis and Diocaesareia were neighbouring cities, and the example of the ancient Laodiceia ad Lycum and the modern Denizli (Thingozlu according to Mas Latrie, Trésor de Chron., p. 1800) show that the comparative importance of neighbouring cities may vary much between the latest Byzantine and the Turkish time.†

* It is given in my table of Isaurian cities.

† I can add in Sept. 1890 the confirmatory epigraphic evidence, discovered by us in July, that Claudiopolis was situated at Mut.

Now what was the line of road from Claudiopolis (Mut) to Seleuceia? Col. Stewart traversed this road, crossing the Kalykadnos south of Mut, and keeping the right side of the river. Frederick Barbarossa, who must have marched by way of Mut, traversed the mountains by Sibilia, reached and crossed the river of Selephica, i.e. the Kalykadnos, and then again traversed the mountains to Seleuceia, where he was drowned while a second time fording the river (see p. 346).

Diocaesareia, then, along with Kennatis, I have placed on the south side of the Kalykadnos, not far from Claudiopolis. This position shows that M. Waddington's restoration of the coin of Polemon (see p. 373) may still be correct, though that which I have proposed is also plausible.

P. 366 (T 15). M. Svoronos's paper in Ἐφημ. Ἀρχ. 1889, p. 67 (shown me by Mr. Head), proves the existence of a form ΚΙΗΤΩΝ in the legend on coins of Koropissos, as confirmed by an Athenian inscription. He therefore concludes that the Koropissos which struck coins is the city between Archelais and Savatra, and not a city of Isauria. He has not observed in the first place. Koropassos, not Koropissos, is given by Strabo, the sole authority who mentions it (except perhaps Ptolemy under the form Adopissos); secondly, that Koropassos was apparently a mere village, which it is hardly justifiable to turn into a metropolis of an otherwise unknown people; and thirdly, that at the Nicene Council Athenaeus Corpissitanus is mentioned among the bishops of Isauria, so that he is not correct in saying that Koropissos of Isauria is quite unknown. It also probably occurs in the Peutinger Table as Coriopio. I see no difficulty in taking Κιήτων and Κήτων as equivalent forms, reproducing in Greek letters an Isaurian name, which was pronounced with y following the Κ. A similar example of the spirant w introduced after Δ in Isaurian pronunciation is explained on p. 312, note, and p. 402. The spirant y is represented in Greek by Ι in the Pamphylian forms ΕΣΤΡΕΔΙΙΥΣ, ΣΕΛΥΜΙΙΥΣ, ΣΤΛΕΓΙΙΥΣ. See p. 453.

P. 373 (T 41), 417, 450. The proposed identification of Laerte and Iotapa (Smith's Dict., s.v. Iotapa) is impossible, for coins of both cities occur. But they seem necessarily to be very near each other, Laerte in Pamphylia provincia according to Ptolemy, while Iotapa is proved by its very name to have been in the kingdom of Antiochus and Iotapa.

P. 375, and p. 371. Lakanatis should perhaps be placed further west than Selentis. The evidence is unsatisfactory. The argument that it was south of the Ermenek Su (p. 371) depends on the assumption that the coins of Antiochus reading ΛΑΚΑΝΑΤΩΝ belong to the period 41–72, when Antiochus seems only to have had territory near the coast; but they may have been struck in 38 (see p. 375).

P. 380 (T 56). The passage of Cinnamus, p. 180, which is quoted on p. 382, T 63, may seem to be adverse to the situation assigned to

Lamos; but that passage is a serious difficulty in other respects, for it distinctly implies that the fortress of Lamos was in Cilicia. Possibly the word Cilicia is used by Cinnamus in the old and wider sense, including Cilicia Tracheia. The situation which I assign to Lamos, however, is merely a choice among difficulties, which I cannot clear up completely. Cinnamus and Strabo are distinctly adverse to me. Mr. Bent has kindly sent me a slight sketch of his splendid discoveries near the river Lamos; and between the mouth of the river and the site of Olba are several ruins which may belong to the city Lamos. For the present, however, the arguments in this difficult case are not so strong as to make me waver in my allegiance to the Byzantine documents.

P. 390 (V. 6). An additional argument for the site of Parlais so far to the west might be found in the inference drawn by Mommsen in his last edition of the Monumentum Ancyranum, p. 119, that Augustus founded no colonies in Lykaonia, but only in Pisidia. But in the first place Augustus must have interpreted the name Pisidia in a very wide sense; for he founded Lystra. In the second place the inference from his words and his omissions cannot be pressed, for he does not claim to have founded any colonies in Galatia, yet Germa (see p. 224) seems to be his foundation.

P. 423. M. Waddington informs me that on grounds of style, he is disposed to place Titakaza in Mysia.

I purchased a copy of Rittmeister von Diest's " Von Pergamon über den Dindymos zum Pontus " in London on May 5, 1890; and have to add some notes after a hasty glance over his most interesting and accurately written account of his journey. His paper is in many respects a model of what such a paper should be. In one point I am indebted to him for an important correction; but in all other places where he breaks a lance with me, I remain of opinion that my arguments are untouched and unshaken.

His descriptions of the country are clear, and his map is, in those parts where I have travelled, like a picture of what I saw. I have been struck with the same quality in Admiral Spratt's map of Pisidia, whereas in Kiepert's maps, drawn not from sight but from the reports of travellers, it is notably absent. In my book all attempt to describe the country has been precluded by consideration of space and time: and I see little prospect that I shall ever be allowed by other work to record great part of what I have learned about the country.

Von Diest pays great attention to the explanation of Turkish words, and we find in his work few errors. In a number of cases he gives me new information as to the meaning of names. My knowledge of Turkish has been entirely picked up by ear from the peasants, and it is exceedingly difficult to get from them any explanation of a name. I have always paid great attention to distinguishing Turkish from non-Turkish names; but the peasants can hardly be brought to understand what you want when you ask what is the meaning of the name of their village. A village is called Öküz Eyük; you ask the meaning; the invariable reply is "It is the name." If after five minutes of explanation and questioning you elicit at last that the name means "Ox-Mound," you are very lucky. Of the slighter errors that occur in Von Diest's paper, I give some examples: p. 10, Karaveli, personal name, should be Kara Veli, "Black Veli;" p. 5, Eri-göl should probably be Egri Göz, "Squint Eye," a very common name; ibid., Kotch means "Ram;" p. 15, Jaila (Yaila), "summer residence of nomadic or semi-nomadic tribes;" p. 17, Jaghschilar (Yaghjilar), "Hunters;" p. 19, Kösse, a word commonly misunderstood, is given correctly (or nearly so); p. 27, the account of Seibek (Zeibek) is thoroughly accurate for the first time in print, so far as I have seen; p. 28, Kara-Chiderli; Heuder (as I have spelt it) is, if I rightly understand my informant, the name of John Baptist; ibid., Harmanar should be Harmanlar.

On p. 11 (compare my p. 117) he describes the ruins at Bergas, where Dr. Schuchhardt places Perperine. The fullest description is given by Fabricius in Athen. Mittheil., 1886. No evidence for the name Perperiné is given except a general argument from the words of Strabo, p. 607. The passage of Galen, quoted in this book, p. 117 and p. 13, seems to have escaped the notice of all these writers. Galen expressly states that Perperine bordered on Pergamos.

Von Diest fixes Larissa at Burnudschuk (Burunjük), relying chiefly on Aristides's description of his journey from Smyrna to Kyme and Pergamos; he does not mention that I discussed the journey at length, and fixed Larissa accordingly, in 1881. He also discusses the situation of Neon Teichos; he rejects the situation at Yanik Keui (which I proposed in 1881), and places it between Boz Keui and Öküz Keui, where, however, he says that he has in vain looked for ruins. He concludes from this, not as he ought that his situation is wrong, but that all traces have disappeared. Let me quote Prof. Ernst Fabricius against him ('Theben,' p. 5): "menschliche Ansiedelungen pflegen die natürliche Beschaffenheit des Bodens in einer Weise umzugestalten, dass die Spuren auf Jahrtausende unvertilgbar bleiben." These words are indubitably true.

Not to spend a couple of pages on a point that I proved in 1881, I need only say that Von Diest's arguments do not seem to me to touch the point at issue. Neon Teichos and Larissa were rival cities competing for the command of the Hermas plain. Strabo's account of the foundation of Neon Teichos by Locrians before Kyme itself was founded, which Von Diest takes for real history, is a mere myth founded on the historical relation between Larissa and Neon Teichos.

Several cases have struck me in which Von Diest has not quite accurately represented my words. On p. 26 he says that "Ramsay, der zuletzt diese Gegend bereiste," states the sources of the Pythikos as being at Aigai. I was the first and not the latest visitor to Aigai, viz. in January, 1881. I went up from Ali Agha to it one day, and returned within forty-eight hours. The country was a blank on the maps, and, speaking in contrast to Myrina at the mouth, I loosely said that Aigai was "near the head of the" Pythikos. I am afraid that I have in many other cases used a similar expression, though I knew that the place of which I was speaking was miles below the actual source. The sketch map which I gave represented only what I had seen. No one had ever before put the Pythikos on a map, and I simply put it in as far as my eyes had seen it; and my sketch was printed, omitting part of what I placed on it (viz. the two rivulets surrounding Aigai mentioned in my text): as I did not see a proof of the map, it was out of my power to make any correction. This took place in 1881, and even in 1882 the map published by M. Pottier in the Bulletin makes the Pythikos rise far below Aigai and quite near the sea. Perhaps this is what Von Diest is thinking about.

On p. 32 Von Diest attributes to me the paper describing the Pythikos valley and the ruins of Usun Assarlyk (Uzun Hassanli is the correct name), the description of which is so vague that he complains that even an eye-witness cannot follow it. I did not write the paper; I have not explored the valley of the Pythikos; I have never seen the ruins at Uzun Hassanli.

On p. 48 he says that I have not visited the Murad Dagh (Mount Dindymos). That is not quite accurate. It is true that I did not make the same route as Von Diest describes; but I have been very near Bel Ova, and received detailed information about Bel Ova, Oisu, and the other places described by Von Diest. All the names which he gives are familiar to me. My opinion was that there was here no city, but only villages comprised within the bishopric of Appia. Von Diest's clear and admirable description only confirms my opinion; but still I fully acknowledge that of the two names which he suggests, Tiberiopolis may possibly belong to this neighbourhood. It is, however, highly improbable that a city with a coinage like Tiberiopolis should be situated in this remote and obscure district, where I doubt whether any trace of Græco-Roman civilisation existed until the third century. I still see no reason to alter any opinion expressed in C. B., part II., about this district, and regard Von Diest's work as a distinct confirmation of mine.

Von Diest argues on p. 41 against my opinion about Koula, and about the ancient village Koloe in Kara Tash district (see pp. 123 and 432). His arguments contain several inaccuracies. He considers it improbable "that the stone should have been carried ten miles across the mountains. Such statements of the Turks are always untrustworthy. The sixty-three Greek coins found in the neighbourhood attest that an ancient city existed at Koula; Koula, therefore, is Koloe." I have only to remark that I have known larger stones carried a longer distance; that there are no mountains between Kara Tash and Koula; that I do not depend in this instance on any statement of Turks; that I have proved the existence of an ancient city Satala near Koula, and of a Byzantine fortress Opsikion even nearer still; and that Koloe was a remote country village and not a city. I may also say that I have known Asia Minor more years than Von Diest months; that I have visited Koula three times, seen the stone on every visit, and investigated its history as carefully as I could. Von Diest spent one night in Koula, and saw no ancient remains except some coins purchased by a physician in the town; yet I know that numerous ancient remains exist in the town, brought chiefly from Satala, partly also from Tabala, Maeonia, and even greater distances. On the strength of this limited acquaintance with the town and its surroundings, Von Diest is not justified in waiving aside my assertion, that the stone in question was brought from Kara Tash by a Greek dealer in madder-root, with the words "derartige Angaben der Turken sind stets unzuverlässig." After ten years' experience I also have learned something about the worthlessness or value of such evidence; and I have also learned that some travellers will pick up trustworthy information and see numerous remains where others will find no remains, and be told only falsehoods.

Von Diest places Trajanopolis at Ushak on the authority of Kiepert. I have shown that Trajanopolis was situated at Giaour Euren, "Infidel Ruins," about six English miles east of Ushak. Von Diest gives this name incorrectly as Giauren. His transcription of Turkish names sometimes shows that he has not understood the peasants' pronunciation, which often slurs over a syllable (compare his Hadjischein for Hadji Hussein, on p. 47). Unfortunately, Von Diest did not explore the branch of the Senaros that flows from Tchedje Keui past Banaz to Islam Keui. I have a suspicion that Alia may be found beside Banaz. Banaz was formerly the seat of government, which recently has been changed to Islam Keui. See p. 138.

After reading Von Diest's remarks about the Tembris valley, I see nothing to alter in what I have said about Prepenissos, Kotiaion, and Dorylaion. On the few points in which he differs from me I remain unconvinced by his arguments, and it is not advisable to spend more time on them.

We now come to a point in which Von Diest (p. 58) enables me to correct a mistaken argument in the text of this book (p. 207 ff.). I had refused to accept Texier's identification of Mudurlu with Modrene; but according to Von Diest the official name is Mudurnu. I cannot refuse to identify Mudurnu with Modrene. I must follow the natural and simplest interpretation of the evidence, whatever difficulties be caused thereby. Mudurlu, then, is a remarkable and indisputable example, such as I have long sought, of popular etymology modifying a name to get a form with a meaning in Turkish. I have, therefore, to retract and apologise for my words in speaking of Kiepert's "error" in identifying Mudurlu with Modrene.

Next arises the question, does this affect the site of Mela, which was included under the same bishopric? I must answer in the negative. Justinianopolis-Mela seems to me to be placed on the Byzantine Military Road by the argument in Chapter G. But, if Ibora on the Iris and Pimolisa on the Halys were united under one bishop, I see no difficulty in assuming that Modrene and Mela, at a less distance from each other, were united under one bishop.

Another difficulty arises with regard to the river Gallos and the village Modra at its source. Von Diest accepts Perrot's view that Modra also was situated at Mudurlu. This I cannot accept. Strabo distinctly asserts that Modra was in Phrygia Epiktetos, or Phrygia towards the Hellespont (p. 543), and Mudurlu cannot possibly be in Phrygia.* Moreover the bishopric of Gallos was subject to the metropolitan of Nikomedeia, and I have tried to show what were the limits of Nikomedeian authority. The argument which I have advanced about the river Gallos from Strabo's statement as to its distance from Nikomedeia is also, I think, strong. Von Diest's argument on p. 58 is founded on a mistranslation. Strabo does not say that the Sangarios becomes navigable in consequence of the access of water from the river Gallos.

The change of position of Modrene relieves us of the difficulty with regard to the bounds of the Themes, as described on p. 211.

Justinian's bridge over the Sangarios (see p. 214) is said by Von Diest to be about 6 or 8 kilometres from the present bed of the river. It is built over the river Tchark Su (which flows out of the Sabandja Lake, and joins the Sangarios not very far from the sea), the Melas of Pachymeres, II., p. 331 (see p. 210). It has now no connection with the Sangarios, though the country between them is level, so that a former connection is quite possible. The bridge has eight arches, and is 435 metres long.

Von Diest's paper is full of information about the Kaikos valley. It remains for some one now to do the Kaystros and Maeander valleys.

P. 127 and p. 155. MM. Waddington and Imhoof Blumer assign all the coins to Germe on the Kaikos. The opinion expressed in the text was not founded on proper study, and for the present I of course defer to their opinion.

P. 342. Mr. Bent has justified my forecast completely; he has discovered Hieropolis (i.e. Kastabala), with inscriptions of Artemis Perasia, on the north side of the Pyramos, where it comes nearest Osmanie. Considering the remarkably diverse opinions of M. Th. Reinach and M. Imhoof Blumer, the confirmation is highly satisfactory.

* Perrot's work is not accessible to me in Aberdeen. Von Diest reports that Perrot considers Strabo guilty of an error. I prefer to follow Strabo.

INDEX OF ANCIENT AUTHORS QUOTED IN PART II.,

EXCEPTING NOTITIÆ, HIEROCLES, ACTA SANCTORUM, STRABO, PLINY THE ELDER, PTOLEMY.

NB.—Byzantine historians are quoted by pages of Bonn edition, unless otherwise mentioned.

The ordinary numerals refer to pages in this Volume: the **black** *numerals to pages or chapters of the authors cited.*

ACROPOLITA, GEORGIUS:
p. **13**, 154, 158; **20**, 189; **30**, 122, 123, 129, 130n., 159, 159n., 211; **31**, 157n, 157, 158; **37**, 157n.; **38**, 157; **50**, 162; **64**, 184; **73**, 162; **91**, 116n.; **110**, 116n.; **111**, 121n.; **173**, 191; **187**, 116n.; **192**, 183; **194**, 129, 130; **195**, 130n.

ALEXIUS COMNENUS:
Novella (Lib. ii. Nov. 4, Leunclav., Jus. Gr.–Rom., p. 130) 244n.

AMMIANUS MARCELLINUS:
xiv. 2, 13, 163; **25**, 363n., 373.
xxiii. 6, 347.
xxv. 3, 180; **10**, 196n., 241n.
xxvi. 8, 241n.

ANNA COMNENA:
Vol. i. **171**, 231; **305**, 188; **306**, 190; **315**, 163n., 209.
Vol. ii. **26**, 191; **75**, 185; **79**, 210; **89, 90**, 211; **113**, 420; **115**, 279n.; **120**, 384; **121**, 380n.; **126**, 385; **138**, 385, 386; **241**, 386; **252**, 108n., 114n., 118n.; **265**, 118n.; **268**, 114n.; **279**, 186, 208n.; **280**, 118n., 129, 158, 207; **281**, 157, 236; **284**, 213; **310**, 159; **312**, 185, 209; **314**, 155n.; **322**, 201n.; **324**, 198, 233; **325, 327**, 231; **329**, 140.

ANONYMORUM OPERA:
Tract. de haeresibus (ap. Coteler. Eccl. Gr. Mon., ii. p. 293), 137.
Vat. 60b., 368n.
See NICEPHORUS PHOCAS, GEOGRAPHI.

APPIAN:
Bell. Mithr., **105**, 336n.

ARISTIDES, AELIUS:
Hieroi Logoi, p. **458**, 157; **502**, 157; **503**, 155; **537**, 157.

ATHENAEUS:
ii. p. **43A**, 113, 135, 143n., 164, 431.
iii. 14, 381; p. **578**, 99.

ATTALIOTA, MICHAEL:
p. **104** ff. 292; **121, 122**, 290n., 292, 351: **123**, 272; **125**, 267; **135–138**, 385n.; **139**, 217n.; **144**, 187n.; **146**, 219, 267; **168**, 267; **174**, 356n.; **184**, 215, 216n.; **189**, 188; **224**, 111; **267**, 188n.; **268**, 184n., 187.

ALTERATIONS PROPOSED IN THE TEXT OF

INDEX OF PROPER NAMES.*

* See pp. 5 note, 12. Modern local names are not as a rule given.

GREEK PROPER NAMES.

SUGGESTIONS

IN SEPTEMBER, 1890, AFTER A JOURNEY IN ASIA MINOR.

Page 46. I have learned, in the certainly Roman road from Corycos to Olba, that several narrow old roadways, which I formerly took for early Turkish, are probably Roman.

139, § 36. Löbbecke (Zft. f. Num., 1890, 23) reads on another coin CIOXAPA-KEITΩN. Is this an error of engraver for [I]ΕPO? or is the error in IEPO? Both cannot, as Löbbecke assumes, be right.

271, 272. The Roman Road probably went by the Kuru Tchai pass.

336, note §. Zosta is not an ancient site. Derbe was situated at Gudelissin, two miles N.W.

358, § 3. The roads are Laranda-Philadelpheia (Maliya)-Dalisandos-Claudiopolis-Diocaesareia-Seleuceia, and Laranda-Coropissos-Olba-Corycos : but probably connections existed Coropissos-Claudiopolis and Olba-Seleuceia. Dalisandos is about five miles N.W. from Mut.

391, l. 39. The ruins are beside Kashakli, on the araba road to the coast.

408. Zorzila probably at Karadja Assar, Tityassos near Bademli in the district called Yeni Sheher. Buldur was in Sagalassian territory, till at length it took the place of Sagalassos as chief centre of population. On Map insert roads from Adada to Perga, to Prostanna and Apameia, to Zorzila, Tityassos and Antioch.

Table of Isauria. Two coins of Kestros belong to Mr. Lawson. A coin, which perhaps was struck by Claudiopolis, was bought by us at Laranda.

The terms "Asia Minor" and "Anatolia" are used rather loosely throughout this work as equivalent, denoting the whole peninsula west of Armenia and Mount Amanus.

N.B.—The reader is requested to complete or correct from the Addenda many statements in the text, using the Index of Proper Names. On the abbreviations CB and ASP, see p. 102 note.